FIGHTING
FOR THE
FATHERLAND

By the same author:

COLD WAR WARRIORS
The Story of the Duke of Edinburgh's Royal Regiment
(Berkshire and Wiltshire), 1959–1994

'FIRST REICH'
Inside the German Army during the War with France,
1870–1871

BATTLES IN FOCUS
Dien Bien Phu, 1954

WARS OF THE COLD WAR
Campaigns and Conflicts, 1945–1990

WAR SUMMITS
The Meetings that Shaped World War II
and the Post-war World

FIGHTING
FOR THE
FATHERLAND

The Story of the German Soldier
from 1648 to the Present Day

DAVID STONE

Foreword by Richard Holmes

CONWAY

A Conway Book

© David Stone 2006

First published in Great Britain in 2006 by Conway
An imprint of Anova Books Ltd
151 Freston Road
London W10 6TH
www.anovabooks.com

British Library Cataloguing in Publication Data:
A catalogue record for this book is available from
the British Library

ISBN 10: 1 84486 036 1
ISBN 13: 9 781844 860 364

Edited and designed by DAG Publications Ltd
Designed by David Gibbons
Edited by Michael Boxall
Cartography by Anthony A. Evans

Printed by Creative Print & Design, Ebbw Vale, Wales

Most of the illustrations and photographs used in this work
are from the author's private collection, and from the photo
library of Anova Books Company Ltd. (formerly Chrysalis
Books Group). The author also wishes to acknowledge the
use of additional images from the following sources: Bender
Publishing, California, USA (page 20, top right); Die
Bundeswehr, Germany (pages 16, 23 and 24); Charles
Woolley/Schiffer Publishing, Pennsylvania, USA (page 6,
bottom, and page 7); Deutsches Historisches Museum,
Berlin, Germany (page 9, bottom right); Squadron/Signal
Publications, Michigan, USA (page 19, top, and page 20, top
left); and the former (c.1900) Werner Company, Chicago,
USA (page 14, bottom). All page references refer to the three
sections of illustrations.

Contents

Foreword

by Professor Richard Holmes, CBE, TD

WHETHER YOU ADMIRE IT or despise it or, like so many of us, are caught between the two emotions, there is no denying either the scale of the German army's impact on history or the remarkable quality of its performance in triumph or adversity. Although we cannot properly speak of a German army until 1871 when the German Empire was proclaimed in the Hall of Mirrors at Versailles, as David Stone demonstrates, the military traditions of Brandenburg–Prussia ran well back into the seventeenth century, and under Frederick the Great the Prussian army made its distinctive mark on Europe. Indeed, in the intimate relationship between the rise of the Prussian army and that of the state it served, we can see metaphors for much of subsequent German history. As Sir Michael Howard wrote, the Prussian state 'was called into being to provide for the needs of the King of Prussia's army'.

Yet it was not the Prussian tradition alone that formed the German army, for there were distinctive elements in the amalgam from other parts of the new empire. Bavarians too made excellent soldiers, though there was often a tension between the light-hearted, often Roman Catholic, south and the more dour, generally Protestant, north. Among the many other states swept up into the German Empire no British reader should forget Hanover. For many years, kings of England were electors of Hanover too, and Hanoverian and British soldiers were brothers in arms on many a bloody field. The King's German Legion, largely recruited from among George III's Hanoverian subjects, was one of the most reliable elements of Wellington's peninsula army. In 1812 Sergeant Edward Costello of the 95th Rifles watched some of its cavalry escorting French prisoners, several wounded in a sharp battle at Garcia Hernandez, where German cavalry had broken three squares of French infantry. He observed that 'I never before saw such severe-looking sabre cuts as many of them has received ... The escort consisted chiefly of the Germans that had taken them prisoners, and it was pleasing to behold these gallant fellows, in the true spirit of glory, paying the greatest attention to the wants of the wounded.'

Prussia's military excellence sprang in part from the state's vulnerable position, with potentially hostile neighbours on three sides. She had no natural barrier between herself and an opponent, unlike Britain, and no distant steppe into which her armies could retreat, trading space for time, unlike Russia. The creation of an effective army began as an essential of national survival, although, as we shall see in these pages, it went on to become a key element of international expansion too. While we must be cautious in the way we link a soldier's origins to his martial qualities, it is clear that both social organization and regional background are important. As the examples of Highlanders and Gurkhas suggest, a harsh landscape often breeds hard men and good soldiers. Frederick the Great himself believed that his Pomeranians, in particular, naturally made fine soldiers, and 'would rout the devil out of hell'. One of his generals, watching in admiration as a regiment pressed home its attack at Prague in 1757, scorning to fire but using only the bayonet, observed: 'After all they were Pomeranians ... the best infantry in the world.' The minor nobility of Prussia, often without much in the way of wealth or land, but with an enduring commitment to the king's service, and a regard for the status that this brought them, formed the officer corps of the Prussian army, and after 1871 still provided a solid thread of brave, reliable leadership within the German army.

David Stone is right to emphasize the importance of the Austro–Prussian and Franco–Prussian wars. Although both were of relatively short duration, they did not simply bring about the unification of Germany, and establish the new state as a major player in European politics. The events of 1870–1 contributed to the outbreak of the First World War by leaving France beaten, as well as embittered by the loss of her provinces of Alsace and Lorraine. They ushered in a change in the relationship between the army and civilian society, a process of militarization that made the officer a god and the reserve officer a demigod, and the increase of military influence upon politics, which led one observer to ask, on the eve of the First World War: 'Who rules in Berlin? Bethmann [the Chancellor] or Moltke [the Chief of the General Staff]?' The armies of Prussia and her neighbours had played a key role in beating imperial France, and thus in establishing a united Germany, but the legacy of their victory was baneful.

The ingredients of German military excellence begin with Prussia's geostrategic position and the martial qualities of some of her population. The status of the army in civilian society was never wholly consistent, but for much of the eighteenth and nineteenth centuries it was high, and on the eve of war in 1914 it was very high indeed: this buttressed the army's own self-regard. The Germans took training very seriously, and were capable of devising ways of using it and recruitment to alleviate the effects of military defeat in the aftermath of Jena in 1806 and Versailles in 1919. They were better than most at devising doctrine and ensuring that it was properly understood, and they took military education seriously, even in the midst of major war. If there were times (like the gap between the death of Frederick the Great and the battle of Jena) when they rested on outworn laurels – and paid the penalty for doing so – they were often capable of ground-breaking innovation, or the swift adaptation of the ideas of others. In the nineteenth and early twentieth centuries they linked the products of burgeoning industry to the demands of the army and, though the process was not always perfect (witness the case of tank production in the Second World War), they produced generations of reliable, state of the art weapons and ancillary equipment: not for nothing is the German-designed 5-gallon can still widely known as the jerrican!

The product of this was an army which excelled at the tactical level: one analyst, looking at its achievement in the Second World War, suggested that it performed consistently higher than the British or the Americans, and that it did so whether it was attacking or defending, advancing or retreating, enjoyed numerical superiority or was itself outnumbered. In the wars of 1866 and 1870–1 this high level of tactical achievement was matched by strategic single-mindedness, thanks largely to the existence of two robust military and political pillars in the persons of Moltke and Bismarck. In the two great wars of the twentieth century, however, German failure was primarily strategic. In both of these conflicts Germany found herself opposed by Britain, France, Russia and the United States, a situation almost guaranteed to ensure that the army's tactical quality would eventually be ground to dust by the economic strength, maritime power, industrial resources and manpower reserves of her opponents. In one sense, the sheer quality of the German army induced its political leaders to call upon it to perform the impossible: its spectacular attempts to do so are the story of this book.

Richard Holmes
Cranfield University, 2006

9

Introduction
and Acknowledgements

EVER SINCE the mid- to late-seventeenth century, German (or Prussian) militarism has been an increasingly dominant influence in European history, and from the late nineteenth century it exerted a similar influence upon world history. From the wholesale devastation and slaughter that was visited upon what was euphemistically called 'the first German empire' – the Holy Roman Empire that had existed since the time of Charlemagne in AD 800 – during the Thirty Years War from 1618 to 1648 there emerged the seeds of what later germinated and blossomed into German nationalism: a movement indisputably inspired and led by the state of Prussia.

But the road towards Germany's destiny was not straightforward, and its often turbulent political evolution was mirrored by that of its army. Following the military successes achieved by Frederick William of Brandenburg 'The Great Elector', then Frederick III (later Frederick I of Prussia), and finally Frederick II – 'Frederick the Great' – between 1640 and 1786, the Prussian army was allowed to stagnate; so that over the next two decades, under the rule of Frederick William III, much of the advantage it had gained under his three predecessors was dissipated. But this period of temporary decline also saw the emergence of such great military thinkers, trainers and organizers as Clausewitz, Gneisenau and Scharnhorst: men who were destined to shape not only Germany's military future but also that of the wider international profession of arms for generations to come. Then, in the mid-nineteenth century, began a new 'golden age' of Prussian and German militarism, guided by the able hands of von Moltke, von Roon, Bismarck, and the future King William I of Prussia. Success followed success – first against Denmark in Schleswig-Holstein in 1864, then against Austria in 1866, and finally against France in 1870–1. By early 1871 the German army's victories had enabled the creation of the first truly German empire, the 'Second Reich', on 18 January of that year. But this remarkable achievement also set Germany on an ever more ambitious imperialistic road which in 1914 resulted in the catastrophe of the First World War. Germany's eventual defeat in 1918 (although very many of its soldiers did not accept it as such) subsequently led the nation and its armed forces directly into the political maelstrom of the Weimar Republic,

National Socialism, and the Third Reich, which culminated in what eventually proved to be an even greater catastrophe, the Second World War. This global conflict provided some of the most challenging and testing battlegrounds ever encountered by the German soldier. Finally it also resulted in his total defeat amid the debris of Germany's 'Götterdämmerung' in 1945.

Then, from the ruins of the Third Reich and the former Wehrmacht, a new German military force – the Bundeswehr – arose in what had become the Federal Republic of West Germany, while in the Soviet-occupied German Democratic Republic in the East a 'Nationale Volksarmee' was formed. The anti-militaristic culture of the post-1945 era set the agenda for the Bundeswehr, until the higher priorities of NATO and the immediacy of the Soviet and Warsaw Pact threat restored an appropriate degree of strategic pragmatism and war-fighting capability to the West German armed forces. In the meantime, on the other side of the Inner German Border, the Nationale Volksarmee evolved into what was probably the most competent of all the non-Soviet Warsaw Pact armies. Eventually, almost half a century later at the end of the Cold War, German reunification was achieved in 1990, when these two ideologically very different – but none the less still undeniably German – forces were joined together. Consequently, there is again today a single German army, a potent and militarily capable force with a potentially global role within the so-called 'new world order' of the twenty-first century. From this it follows that a new military culture – with very different social and wider political priorities and safeguards – today underwrites the post-Cold War Bundeswehr; while the German soldier has once again been required to adapt to an entirely new set of circumstances matched to the much changed security needs of a reunited and reinvigorated Germany.

Arguably, the deep imprint of the jackboot – which has for many come to symbolize German militarism, together with the spiked 'Pickelhaube' helmet and later the coal-scuttle-shaped 'Stahlhelm' – upon the path of history has far exceeded the historical impact of the armed forces of any other European nation. Certainly, German militarism has dominated European political and military thinking and events for the last two centuries, especially so after 1871. This is indeed remarkable, and suggests that the German fighting man must himself have been quite remarkable to have achieved and maintained such a formidable reputation. Whether admired or hated, envied or emulated, lauded or reviled, over time the German soldier's effect on world events has frequently been out of all proportion both to the size of the German armed forces and to that of the nation from which he comes.

✠✠✠✠✠✠✠✠✠✠✠✠

Inevitably, the armed forces of sovereign nations are conditioned and shaped by the history, the culture and the nature of the society from which they are drawn. Society's impact is particularly significant in the case of conscripted or impressed forces, although all-regular professional forces cannot escape the fact that their manpower is necessarily derived from the national population and so will broadly reflect its traits, its strengths and its weaknesses. Similarly, the experience and presentation of the more parochial history and events and the specific characteristics of an area's local culture all influence to varying degrees the perceptions, nature and performance of individuals and groups of fighting men drawn from the different geographical areas of a single nation. Further differences – both individual and corporate – also exist between those men recruited from the town or city and those whose background is predominantly that of the rural countryside. Consequently, the powerful blend of history – which generates tradition, heritage, patriotism and national pride – with culture and socio-economic background has long been a fundamental factor affecting the development, character, and effectiveness of a national fighting force and of those who serve within it. This was patently so in the seventeenth and eighteenth centuries, and as armies and the conflicts between clearly identifiable states became more regularized in the succeeding two centuries it became even more so.

But change is constant, and history is probably the greatest catalyst for such change, which might occasionally be both extensive and occur very rapidly indeed. While the flow of history generally involves a multi-stranded progression of activities, events, actions and reactions, in some cases a single event may be so significant and traumatic for a nation that it stands out as a defining moment in its life: determining – for better or worse – not only the future course of development of the nation affected but also, inevitably, that of its armed forces. Such happenings usually have the effect of changing irrevocably the course of a nation's history, or indeed that of a number of nations, and events such as these have shaped the development of the world since time began.

Necessarily, this story considers a number of the key clashes of arms that were defining moments in the evolution of what has, in more recent times, often been termed 'the German war machine', together with some of the significant political and organizational events affecting its development. This account, however, is first and foremost the story of the German army as an entity or institution and of its progress throughout the great conflicts of history, rather than the story of the conflicts themselves. Neither is this a history of Germany as such, albeit that the story of the

Prussian army, and subsequently that of the military forces of the united Germany, is central to the story of the creation of the German nation.

It follows, therefore, that this account is necessarily selective and this is particularly so where it deals with the Kaiser's army of 1914–1918 and that of the Third Reich during the Second World War. Countless works on these periods of history exist already; therefore, this account seeks to draw out the defining moments of these conflicts for the German army rather than to provide a blow-by-blow account of every campaign fought by it during these wars. Indeed, although much of the world is understandably more familiar with the story of the two world wars than with Germany's wars of unification in the previous century, it is certainly arguable that the German army which went to war in 1939 was in practice something of an aberration when compared to all of its forebears and with its modern successors; with the albeit much shorter Franco-Prussian War of 1870–1 actually being of much greater historical significance than the 1939–45 conflict in terms of its formative and cultural impact upon the wider history, heritage and traditions of the German army and German militarism.

Inevitably, a work that covers such a wide span of history will contain omissions, but what must certainly not be omitted are my expressions of sincere thanks to those who played a significant part in bringing this book to the point of publication. First, I am most grateful to Professor Richard Holmes – my occasional literary mentor since the mid-1990s – for consenting to provide such an informed and thoughtful foreword for the work. It is indeed comforting to know that such an esteemed military historian shares my own long-held views on the particular historical importance of the Franco-Prussian conflict of 1870–1, and (by implication) the way in which the historical significance of that war has for far too long been overlooked by many historians, notwithstanding Professor Michael Howard's seminal work on the subject in 1961. Next, I am once again indebted to Jeremy Whitehorn of Heartland Old Books, at Tiverton in Devon, for allowing me unrestricted access to his vast collection of rare, out-of-print and first editions of military, historical and political books and manuscripts. Much of the anecdotal and factual material for the work's chapters on the seventeenth century and on the Kaiser's army was discovered on his bookshelves.

Meanwhile, without the extensive assistance, research material and invaluable advice on the post-1945 and present-day Bundeswehr provided so readily by my friend and former professional colleague, Oberstleutnant Jorg-Peter Hellerling of the Bundeswehr and his son Peer, my original aspiration to move this account well beyond the end of the Third Reich and into the present day might well have remained little more than an aspiration. Peter's up-to-the-minute information and informed comments on many aspects of today's Bundeswehr were absolutely indispensable, and my debt of gratitude to him is all the greater as his assistance was provided while he was simultaneously filling a key staff appointment in a panzergrenadier division committed to NATO peacekeeping duties in Kosovo.

Next, I am once again extremely grateful both to my former military colleague Colonel Nigel Flower and to my wife Prue for wading through the all too many pages of unedited text, correcting and making the constructive suggestions that have enabled my ever-helpful publishers to turn my own typescript into what is, I hope, a readable, informative and thought-provoking account.

Concerning my sources, I am also indebted to those publishers and authors who have kindly permitted me to quote text or to use illustrations from their own works. However (as is so often the case when writing history), in a very few cases my attempts to contact some sources proved unsuccessful, despite all efforts having been made to do so. Nevertheless, the bibliography does indicate the last known publishing details of all of the references used or consulted – irrespective of whether this usage was extensive, supplementary or amplifying in nature, or was merely used to cross-check or confirm a specific fact.

Indeed, with such extensive sources of reference material and the support of such diligent proof-readers and advisers it is my belief that the reader will find much of which to approve in this work. If it should be found to contain any errors, significant omissions or factual misrepresentations the fault is of course mine alone.

Finally, I wish to pay personal tribute to the many members of the West German Bundeswehr and its post-1990 successor with and alongside whom I have so often been privileged to serve.[1] Over time, my countless conversations, discussions and professional association with these most professional of soldiers – with general officers and with ordinary soldiers, with regulars and with conscripts, on operations, in staff appointments, and off-duty – provided much of the inspiration for this work, together with a number of the insights that will be found within its pages. It is, therefore, my sincere hope that this text represents a fitting tribute to the modern German army, as well as being an appropriate and objective analysis of the principal elements of the illustrious heritage and often turbulent history upon which that remarkable fighting force is founded.

David Stone

PART ONE
Origins

I

Myths, Legends and History

THE ORIGINS of what eventually came to be characterized as 'German militarism' were firmly rooted in a particularly violent and turbulent period of history that occurred during the early part of the seventeenth century, and specifically the cataclysmic and often horrific events which afflicted virtually every part of Germany and its population between 1618 and 1648. While these events stood out as the catalyst which began and then enabled an almost unbroken process of development that would inexorably carry the German fighting man to his historic destiny, other influences also directly affected the ethos of tradition and culture in which he lived and fought. Several of these well pre-dated the seventeenth century, and prominent among them was the burgeoning number of historical facts, myths and legends that have underwritten a gradually growing German identity and awareness ever since AD 9: one of many defining moments in the story of the origins and development of the German warrior.

This was the year in which the Germanic tribes led by Arminius, the son of the chief of the Cherusci tribe – a young man who had formerly seen service as a Roman officer serving under Tiberius in AD 5–6 as well as having been a staff officer to Publius Quinctilius Varus from AD 7 – lured the Roman forces deep into the damp, dark ravines, hills and dense forests at the northern end of the Teutoburger Wald, to the north of what is today the city of Osnabrück. As the legions moved ever deeper into this forested wilderness, each day they became increasingly fragmented and spread out. Then at last Arminius struck, at Kalkriese near Wiehengebirge. There, while the Roman troops and their multitude of camp followers were assailed by a torrential rainstorm, their ability to manoeuvre hampered by flooded rivers and falling trees, the massed army of Germanic tribesmen surrounded and comprehensively annihilated the XVII, XVIII and XIX Legions. To achieve this remarkable victory – one of the key formative battles of European history, for it subsequently led directly to Augustus Caesar abandoning Roman control of all the territory between the Rhine and the Elbe – Arminius had united many of the disparate tribes in the areas which today comprise Westphalia and Hessen. Consequently, the Roman defeat at Kalkriese was one of the first occasions on which a form of national 'German fighting force' might truly be said to have appeared on the field of battle. Certainly it marked the point at which a discernible coalition of the Germanic tribes was formed: a coalition that would in due course play a major part in the final destruction of Rome and its once-mighty empire. For the future German state and the national consciousness of its people, the historical and cultural impact of Arminius' victory was particularly significant and long-lasting.[2]

Then, in later times, history became intertwined with legends – particularly those concerned with the mighty River Rhine, with its many castles and islands, torrents and whirlpools, jagged rocks and towering cliffs, and the succession of towns and villages along its length. Notable among these legends were the plentiful tales of bravery and chivalry – many with an underlying moral or religious aspect – and especially the stories of Beowulf, of Dietrich, of Lohengrin the Swan Knight of Kleve, of the Lorelei, of the Lay of Hildebrand, and the poem *Parsifal*. But undoubtedly the most famous legend was the world-renowned 'Song of the Nibelungen' – the *Nibelungenlied* – composed late in the twelfth century and which was possibly of Austrian or Tyrolese origin. This saga (as many others) was inspired by the Scandinavian and Germanic myths of ancient times, being broadly based upon the stories of the members of the court of Burgundy at Worms some six centuries earlier. By their deeds, by their obsession with honour, fidelity, loyalty, retribution and revenge, and with their almost superhuman skills as warriors, the Nibelungen – the warrior heroes of the tale – provided a rich if somewhat violent cultural heritage and foundation of folklore for the people of Germany, for whom the Nibelungen have regularly been portrayed as the very essence of all that is 'Germanic'.[3] Clearly the true importance of the Rhine legends in German culture is a subject in its own right.[4] But in the context of this work, the evocative deeds and images of Siegfried, Brunhilde, Kriemhilde, Gunther, Hagen, Attila and a score of other heroes and villains – male and female alike – show that they were patently warriors first and foremost; and amid the wholesale slaughter, the unquestioning love, the glorious triumphs and heart-wrenching tragedies of the Rhine legends lie something of the warrior culture, the fatalism, the romanticism and the intangible sense of destiny that influenced aspects of the development of the German fighting man well into the twentieth century, and which was occasionally exploited unashamedly to promote his love of country – his 'Heimat' – and his role as its defender.

Closely linked with perceptions of German militarism was the Teutonic Order of military and religious knights, which was originally established at Acre in 1190, during the Third Crusade. Indeed, the term 'teutonic' was sometimes used by non-Germans as a somewhat derogatory term for German militarism into the mid-twentieth century, although the military capability of the Teutonic Order had in fact been abandoned at the end of the Napoleonic Wars. Yet here again the members of an overtly military, religious and chivalrous order, who were originally known as the Hospitallers of Saint Mary of the German House in Jerusalem, provided another strand of the warrior heritage that would underscore the heritage and character of Germany. When the Teutonic Order returned from the Holy Land to the eastern part of Europe, it became actively involved in fighting the Slavs, and during the fourteenth and fifteenth centuries the Teutonic Knights successively exerted their dominance over the areas that became known as Pomerania, Prussia, the Baltic States and Germany; with the directing focus of the order established at Marienburg in Prussia. Significantly, the badge of the Teutonic Order was a black cross on a white background: the identifying national symbol that continues to be used by Germany's armed forces today. Also worthy of note is the fact that the power base of the Teutonic Order in Germany was originally established in Prussia (whose national colours adopted in later times were also black and white) and remained there until the religious element moved to Mergentheim in the sixteenth century, while the more secular part of the community remained in Prussia which was transformed into a principality by the Hohenzollern Grand Master of the Order. Prussia was eventually destined to play an absolutely key role in the development of the German fighting man, while the Hohenzollerns were destined to rule Brandenburg and Brandenburg–Prussia, then Prussia and finally Germany until 1918. Thus the Teutonic Order and its band of knights provided yet another important historical influence that subsequently shaped the heritage and nature of a wider Germany and the men who fought for it.[5]

Throughout much of the Middle Ages the Germanic way of warfare was governed by a feudal system in which the emperor or king reigned supreme, and exerted his authority and military power through the knights and nobles who owed their allegiance to him, and then through the mass of men-at-arms, serfs and vassals who in turn served the lords who owned both the land on which they lived and their absolute duty of service and obedience. During this period the disparate forces of the many German states generally followed the standard of the one-headed black eagle emblazoned upon the yellow flag of the empire. The soldier's weapons of war included a wide range of weapons – daggers, swords, battle-axes, two-handed swords, lances, clubs and maces. The militias and members of the bands raised for the local defence of the towns and cities relied mainly upon pikes and halberds, plus a multiplicity of knives and other weapons designed for close-quarter fighting. The crossbow was also used extensively in mainland Europe, whereas (almost uniquely) the longbow proliferated in England. Body armour was much in use to protect men and horses alike, the knights and the wealthy usually adopting full suits of armour, while the foot soldiers generally wore a helmet and varying extents of leg, arm and body protection depending upon what they could afford or (more usually) capture in battle. Shields of all shapes, types and sizes were used both by the mounted knights and by the dismounted men. Recognition of and between these armed groups was rudimentary and was customarily achieved by the use of banners, shield devices, the adoption of coloured sashes, and the wearing of similarly coloured coats. In due course, during the late twelfth century, the relative disorganization of the feudal system gave way to the development of permanently established armed forces and to a concept of mercenary soldiering in Germany.

This change and the increasing need for soldiers to master and exercise a range of specialist skills received added momentum with the invention of gunpowder and the widespread introduction of all sorts of cannon and firearms on the battlefield. By the close of the fourteenth century the German princes and the cities possessed large numbers of bombards, culverins, muskets and pistols.

In parallel with this military pragmatism, in October 1517 the radical teachings of a Wittenberg monk, Martin Luther, were in direct contravention of the teachings of Roman Catholicism. He was not prepared to accept that God's grace could be bought with earthly goods, and promoted his unshakeable belief that man could achieve God's mercy 'by faith ... and by the Holy Scriptures alone'. In early-sixteenth century Germany this was literally an earth-shattering concept which threatened the whole social and religious order of Europe and was to result in the Reformation. This precipitated the many religious conflicts which subsequently blighted central Europe. The heady mix of religious tumult, advances in military technology, and the final breakdown of the feudal system, ushered in the age of the professional soldier or mercenary, and in Germany these men were termed 'Landsknecht'.[6] A German account of the organization and equipment of the Landsknecht forces of the empire in the mid-sixteenth century indicated not only how far the business of war had moved on since the days of the feudal system, but also provided a very early insight into what might be regarded as a typically Germanic approach to the whole matter of war: a systematic and pragmatic approach that would be evident time and again in the future.

The chief of the Landsknechte [*sic*] bore the title of commanding general or commander-in chief, and as such was responsible only to the sovereign or 'pay-lord'. The general staff consisted of the war paymaster, the purser-general, the quartermaster-general, the surgeon-general, the army-herald, the provost-marshal, and the functionary who levied the war-tax. The Landsknechte were divided into regiments, brought together by enlistment and commanded by a colonel, who received a monthly pay of 400 guilders. The regimental staff was formed of the lieutenant-colonel, the quartermaster, the regimental chaplain, surgeon, regimental-provost, the sergeant, and a special corporal, who had to tend to the camp-followers and the camp-prostitutes. Each regiment had from ten to sixteen companies (Fähnlein) of 400 men, commanded by a captain. Subordinated to the captain were the lieutenant, the standard bearer, sergeant-major, chaplain, and corporal. In front of each squadron marched from twelve to fifteen musketeers, armed with a small double arquebus or musket. These carried on a strap, thrown over the left shoulder, twelve wooden caps, each containing a charge of powder, also a pouch with bullets and a box with priming powder. The musketeers were followed by the arquebusiers. Their chief weapon, the arquebus, was formerly provided with a match-lock, but now carried a wheel-lock, invented at Nuremburg in 1517. The arquebusiers and musketeers wore a short two-edged sword, also a light body-armour, and a morion or head-piece. They were followed by the 'pikemen', provided with cuirass, armlets, and greaves, plate-aprons and morions or casques, and armed with a short sword, two wheel-lock pistols, and heavy pike, or a two-handed broad-sword and halberd.[7]

The Landsknecht cavalry regiment numbered about 750 men with 1,000 horses. It was sub-divided into groups called 'guidons' or 'ensigns', each of 180 heavy cavalrymen and sixty light cavalrymen. The heavy cavalry soldiers were armed with a lance, a heavy sabre, a mace and two pistols. The light cavalry element had a carbine, a sabre and pistols. These cavalry units gave birth to what became known as the 'German Riders': lightly armoured men equipped with sabres and a large number of various short-barrelled hand-held firearms such as carbines and pistols. These German Riders perfected the tactic of riding in massed columns at best speed to within pistol range of the enemy, halting, quickly turning into line to face the foe, and firing a devastating volley. This first rank then split into two parts, each of which rode away around each flank, reloaded, and (if required) returned to form a new rear rank. In the meantime, the other ranks of their comrades were repeating the drill of firing and retiring, thereby keeping up a constant fire against the enemy, while all the time remaining mounted and thereby maintaining the ability to manoeuvre or redeploy if necessary.

The ready availability of gunpowder had of course transformed warfare, and in the sixteenth century the Landsknecht artillery was a key part of any armed force, whether deployed against another army or against the many fortified castles that had once proved impervious to physical attack but which were now so vulnerable to cannon fire. Most of the Landsknecht artillery was cast at Nuremburg or Augsburg, in which cities large quantities of gunpowder and all other sorts of firearms were also made.

> The artillery and the material for projectile warfare was under the direction of the master-general of the ordnance. His subordinates were a lieutenant, a paymaster, a master of the ordnance, and several gunners. The service of a single piece was under a master of the gun and artificers. The guns or carronades were either field-guns or siege-guns. The former were the falconet, falcon, and the culverin, which, served by eighteen men, threw a ball of forty pounds weight. The latter were called the great 'quartan-culverin', the songstress, the nightingale, the basilisk, and the 'sharfmetze', which threw an iron ball, weighing a hundred pounds. Besides these were howitzers, which hurled stone balls of two hundred pounds weight.[8]

These powerful new weapons not only forced extensive changes to the soldier's tactics but also led to radical changes in the design and construction of the fortifications he now sought to defend. Thus the new ways of military thinking and of waging war that swept across central Europe in the sixteenth century had by its end set the stage for a devastating conflict that would eventually end both the strategic primacy enjoyed by the empire and also the whole concept of the mercenary army. It would also prove to be a defining moment in the story of the German fighting man.

Indeed, for Germany (and by extension for many other states in the centuries that followed) the single tumultuous conflict that took place during the first half of the seventeenth century proved to be the catalyst for change which eventually gave birth to one of the most formidable military nations (and therefore military forces) that the world has seen since the days of the mighty Roman Empire. Thus it enabled the creation and development of what was in later times termed 'German militarism', with all that flowed therefrom. That defining moment in German history was the savage and seminal conflict which raged across central Europe – but primarily and most importantly within Germany and the Holy Roman Empire – from 1618 to 1648: the bitter and lengthy European conflict which was subsequently accorded the title 'the Thirty Years War'.

2

Conceived in Chaos

Germany and the Thirty Years War, 1618–1648

A RECOUNTING of the detailed course of the Thirty Years War lies well beyond the intended boundaries of this work. But the particular nature of the conflict and its impact upon the German states and the population of Germany are central to understanding the origins of the future development of German military power. The war began as a religious dispute in the Kingdom of Bohemia: one between the Protestant Estates that were then demanding their religious freedom, and the Habsburg leadership – with the latter determined to enforce the Roman Catholic Counter-Reformation. Religious argument deteriorated into violence in 1620 when Emperor Ferdinand II, the elected King of Bohemia, suppressed the Protestants. The subsequent war ignited by this persecution then developed into a succession of campaigns, sieges and battles which pitted the Roman Catholic dynasties of Habsburg and Wittelsbach against the Protestants, who by then enjoyed the substantial military support provided by King Gustavus Adolphus of Sweden until his death at the battle of Luetzen in 1632. Among a multitude of parallel agendas and power-plays, the rapidly widening conflict was also set against France's long-running struggle with the Habsburgs to achieve dominance throughout Europe. Despite the strength of its own Catholicism, France generally supported the Protestant forces (including those of the German princes who resented the Habsburgs' imperial authority over them). The French Cardinal Richelieu, and later Mazarin, however, ensured most astutely that virtually all the fighting was conducted well beyond French territory, in Germany.

By the war's end in 1648 the imperial power of the Habsburgs was broken, French domination of mainland Europe was largely undisputed, and a fairly ill-defined and disparate form of peace had been achieved at the expense of the devastation of much of Germany: where the pre-war population of seventeen million had been reduced to eight million during thirty years of conflict. For the people of Germany the Thirty Years War was an unprecedented and traumatizing disaster, and for the many German states and princedoms of the Holy Roman Empire that lay sandwiched between France in the west and Poland in the east, the nature and consequences of the war ultimately changed everything.

By the late 1630s, the barbarism and atrocities routinely perpetrated by the Imperial, Swedish and Bavarian armies and other combatants throughout the length and breadth of Germany had reached unprecedented levels. A principle of 'no quarter' was all too often in evidence, and was applied by the imperialist forces as a matter of deliberate policy whenever they were confronted by Swedish troops. While the generals still maintained a degree of control over the grand strategy of the war, its prosecution was by then almost entirely in the hands of the soldiers and diverse bands of armed men who roamed the giant battlefield which Germany had become during the two decades of conflict since 1618. But by then also, many of the military commanders and most of those they led had all but forgotten the lofty – if often misguided – ideals for which they or their predecessors had originally gone to war. By the beginning of its second decade the chaos and sheer dreadfulness of the war had already become very evident. Relating just a few of the all too numerous recorded trials and tribulations of the Thirty Years War serves both to illustrate and to reinforce this fact.

During the sack of Kempten the Imperialists had killed children *en masse* in the town cellars, where they had been trying to escape the carnage in the streets above. The soldiers threw women out of the upper storeys of the houses and even boiled one housewife alive in her own kitchen cauldron. The burgomaster was shot out of hand, seventy houses were deliberately fired, the homeless inhabitants – men, women and children – being driven into the river and slaughtered. In Landsberg, Swedish troops spread gunpowder over their prisoners and set fire to them. In Calw, Bavarian troops confined the citizens within the town; having positioned artillery to fire at the gates, they then set fire to the town, and as the people scrambled to escape the flames they were mown down by the Bavarian gunners.

The city of Magdeburg on the River Elbe achieved particular notoriety when, on 20 May 1631, the besieged city fell to imperial forces. The entry of the attackers was soon followed by a litany of unprecedented excesses as the soldiers – drunk both by their success and by their liberation of the remaining stocks of alcohol – set about venting their anger upon the civilian population and plundering the city. Suddenly, some hours after the end of any further resistance by the defenders, fires broke out in as many as twenty widely dispersed locations. The city was soon a raging furnace as flames swept through the wooden houses, fanned by a strong wind. Meanwhile, in the cellars of these buildings, many civilians and inebriated imperial soldiers alike were trapped and burnt to death. Magdeburg burned for three days, and for fourteen days thereafter a grim train of wagons transported the charred corpses to the River Elbe for disposal. All along the river banks for miles below the city, swollen bodies were washed up among the reed beds, where they were torn apart and devoured by great clouds of birds of prey that wheeled in the grey, smoke-stained skies above. Incredibly, despite the destruction of most of the city, three cellars full of wine casks had survived the inferno. These were subsequently discovered by the imperial troops who returned once the fires were finally extinguished, and the citizens' ordeal resumed as drunken, marauding and totally out of control soldiers once again roamed the streets of the devastated city. The population of Magdeburg had numbered about thirty thousand before the siege; by its end it had been reduced to some five thousand, mostly women – many of whom were subsequently forced to march away with the victorious Imperial army as servants of the soldiers.

Everywhere were told the stories of prisoners bound and left to die of starvation or exposure, of priests tethered under military wagons and forced to crawl beneath them until they dropped dead of exhaustion, of children kidnapped and held for ransom, and of the poor and wealthy civilians who were alike imprisoned, starved and tortured to reveal the whereabouts of their supposed hoards of wealth which the soldiers routinely assumed had been hidden.

Predictably, the constant movement of armies across Germany turned the indigenous rural population into one of refugees. Countless villages lay plundered and deserted, and the population of many towns had dropped to a tenth of their pre-war size. The scorched earth policy carried out by some commanders left towns such as Bayreuth, Calw, Creussen, Eichstätt and Fürth devastated, together with vast swathes of countryside dotted with the smoking embers of hundreds of once prosperous villages. All economic activity declined; only the rat population thrived and multiplied, further decimating the remnants of any crops that had survived thus far, and hastening the spread of disease. As this refugee population ebbed and flowed across Germany it found little or no succour, and thousands succumbed to hunger, exposure, exhaustion or the plague. The resources of the very few refugee camps that did exist were overwhelmed, as were those of the hospitals. The citizens of those towns which had thus far escaped destruction – among them Strasburg, Hanau, Haguenau and (to the south) Zürich – had neither the resources nor the desire to assist these incomers, who were therefore forced either to move on, or to lie down and die at the gates or on the town streets. Even for those living within the towns, the burgeoning rat population had widely become a staple source of food for the citizens left starving after one or other of the passing armies had relieved them of any remaining food supplies. Everywhere, large numbers of the civilian population of Germany were gradually starving to death.

At Calw a pastor observed a woman on a roadside reduced to gnawing the raw flesh of a dead horse in competition with a hungry dog and a flock of ravens. In Alsace the bodies of hanged criminals were quickly taken from the gallows, butchered and eaten. Here also goatskins, grass and acorns were routinely cooked and devoured. Meanwhile, the meat market at Worms offered cats, dogs and rats for sale, although even the first two of these doubtful delicacies were usually in short supply. Near Worms, a gypsy cauldron was found to contain half-cooked human hands and feet, and not far from Wertheim a quantity of human bones was discovered in a pit: all fresh, fleshless and sucked to the marrow. Throughout the Rhineland a watch was set to prevent grave robbers digging up the newly interred and selling their flesh; and at Zweibrücken a woman confessed to having eaten her own dead child.

In the areas close to the great refugee camps at Frankfurt, Coburg and Fulda, cannibalism was rife, and the living were constantly in fear of being murdered and eaten by the desperate refugees. Starvation was endemic throughout Germany, but was at its worst along the Rhine and into south-western Germany. And superimposed upon the hopelessly weakened populace were visitations of the plague: frequently exacerbated by the passage to and fro of the diverse armies which carried the dreaded disease far and wide. In Munich, a Spanish army briefly transiting the city left behind it a plague that killed ten thousand citizens during the following four months. Similarly, Swedish troops had left a trail of plague behind them at Stettin, at Spandau, in Durlach and Lorch, at Würzburg, and throughout the whole province of Württemberg.[9]

Scarce wonder then that towards the beginning of the final decade of this terrible war, the social, moral and even (given that the war had in large part originally been a religious conflict) the religious constraints, principles and behavioural norms of civilized society had all but ceased to exist; while instances of dissent, rebellion and the breakdown of any recognizable form of social structure or law and order ebbed and flowed across much of the wasteland that was now Germany.

It was not until 1648 and the Peace of Westphalia, negotiated and signed jointly by a Roman Catholic delegation sitting at Münster and a Protestant delegation based at Osnabrück, that the Thirty Years War finally came to an end. An uneasy peace descended upon a devastated Germany and upon those members of its population who had survived the thirty years of conflict, or had managed to escape elsewhere while it had raged and who now began to return to reclaim their shattered farms, villages, towns and cities.

Yet great danger still stalked the land, for much of Germany was dominated by several large armies and by a plethora of armed bands. Very many of these now-unemployed (mainly foreign) soldiers – suddenly denied the profitable lifestyle that they had enjoyed for three decades – soon turned to organized banditry to maintain a standard of living to which they had become all too accustomed. Even the regular soldiers were not beyond such lawlessness, and a number of properly constituted Swedish regiments based at Neumarkt, Langenarch, Überlingen, Schweinfurt, Meinau, Anhalt and Eger mutinied and seized their units' pay chests. Although many of the formed companies soon moved off to hire themselves out to other rulers in states such as Venice, Savoy, Spain, Transylvania, Russia and England, numbers still remained in Germany, determined to live off the country by their wits, reinforced by the considerable power of the weapons they still had very much to hand. This situation was a direct consequence of the deliberate use by the empire and others of armies of professional soldiers, such as the Landsknechts, during the previous century.

The statistics of destruction compiled from German sources – although undoubtedly exaggerated in some cases – were none the less breathtaking. During the war the Swedes alone were accused of destroying nearly two thousand castles, eighteen thousand villages and more than fifteen hundred towns. Bavaria claimed to have lost some eighty thousand families and nine hundred villages, Bohemia five-sixths of its villages and three-quarters of its population. In Württemberg the number of inhabitants was said to have fallen to a sixth, in Nassau to a fifth, in Henneberg to a third, in the wasted Palatinate to a fiftieth of its original size. The population of Colmar was halved, that of Wolfenbüttel had sunk to an eighth, of Magdeburg to a tenth, of Haguenau to a fifth, of Olmütz to less than a fifteenth. Minden, Hameln, Göttingen, Magdeburg, by their own account, stood in ruins ... the population of München numbered twenty-two thousand in 1620, seventeen thousand in 1650; Augsburg forty-eight thousand in 1620, twenty-one thousand in 1650. Chemnitz sank from nearly a thousand to under two hundred, Pirna from eight hundred and seventy-six to fifty-four. The population of Marburg, eleven times occupied [by various forces], dwindled by half and the municipal debt rose to seven times its original size; two hundred years later the burghers were still paying interest on loans raised by the war. The population of Berlin-Kölln decreased by a quarter, that of Neu Brandenburg by nearly a half. In the Altmark,

Salzwedel, Tangermunde and Gardelegen had lost a third of their people, Seehausen and Stendal more than half, Werben and Osterburg two-thirds. As many as two hundred ships had sailed yearly across the Sound from the ports of East Friesland in 1621; by the last decade of the war the average number in a year was ten.'[10]

The scale of the destruction wrought upon the rural countryside was almost impossible to quantify. But, whereas some urban centres actually managed to profit from the war through the promotion of related trade and commerce, the universally applied military concept of armies living off the land across which they operated meant that (with a very few exceptions) the rural economy and structure of Germany in 1650 was at best in ruins and in many areas non-existent. This situation was exacerbated as a multitude of princes, other nobles, landowners and officials now sought to restore their former dominance over an often resentful post-war peasant population.

The presence of foreign armies in Germany during thirty years of war had also reinforced a pre-war mistrust of non-German influences and this now fuelled a post-war resentment of the tide of international culture and fashion – particularly from France, which was by then virtually omnipotent in Europe – that now swept into Germany. Only in the north and west and in the urban areas was this trend generally received somewhat more positively, albeit grudgingly. In the meantime, this widened the gulf between the peasant population and its masters, and between the nobility and an increasingly disaffected middle class. The latter found itself powerless to prevent what it saw as the relegation of German culture and identity in favour of that of those foreign nations who had been in large measure directly responsible for Germany's parlous situation at the end of the war.

Of the Germanic nations, it was only in Austria that the Habsburg rulers generally embraced the new influences now sweeping across the Empire. This did nothing to endear Austria to the population of northern Germany, where Austria's post-war actions (including the cession of Alsace to France, albeit that this was forced upon Austria by Bavaria) were regarded as little less than a betrayal: a perception that was destined to grow and fester, and would eventually erupt into a short but defining conflict almost two hundred years later, in 1866.

Arguably, the war had actually provided an opportunity during its early years for the principal German states to come together and create a national identity and power base. The obvious leader of the day had been John George, the Elector of Saxony, but any move in that direction had been forestalled first of all by the fears and parochialism of Maximilian, Duke (and later Elector) of Bavaria, and subsequently by the martial ambitions of Gustavus Adolphus, the King of Sweden. So the moment – one of several such opportunities during the war – had passed by, and a truly German empire would not be achieved for another two hundred and thirty years, until 1871.

Perhaps, if Germany had possessed the wherewithal and the traditions of exploration and colonization displayed by its European near-neighbours of Spain, France, England, Portugal and the United Provinces – and if Germany had also enjoyed better access to maritime outlets – the country might well have been able to look beyond its borders to lift itself out of its post-war demise. But it had neither the attributes, nor the experience, nor the leadership necessary to pursue such a course, and in any case certain of the terms of the Peace of Westphalia actually had the effect of limiting any maritime ambitions by Germany in the future. Indeed, it would not be until the late nineteenth century that Imperial Germany would at last embark upon a major policy of expansion and colonization beyond Europe; by which stage the world of international politics was a very different place and Germany had certainly left it much too late to win an overseas empire. Consequently, Germany's largely self-imposed 'European perspective', established in large part in 1648, was destined subsequently to shape much of that country's foreign and defence policy right up to the post-Cold War era at the end of the twentieth century.

This then was the dismal legacy of the Thirty Years War for Germany: poverty, pestilence, plague, devastation, military domination, economic ruin, insecurity, instability, and a disrupted and dysfunctional society. In 1648 the fragmented country, which was by then generally known as Germany, also lacked any true sense of national identity, and its future looked bleak indeed. While Germany's economic and developmental situation at the start of the war in 1618 had been by no means healthy (and had in several respects contributed directly to the causes of the war), '... it is certain that never before, and possibly never since, in her history had there been so universal a sense of irretrievable disaster, so widespread a consciousness of the horror of the period which lay behind'.[11]

Returning, therefore, to the original proposition, a catastrophe on such a scale cannot be anything less than a defining moment in the history of any nation or group of peoples, and so it was for Germany in 1648. Subsequent events would show that the Thirty Years War not only laid the foundations of several of the more immediate disputes and conflicts that followed it, but it also sowed many of the seeds of disharmony, resentment

and mistrust that would become central to German perceptions and attitudes prior to and during the two World Wars almost three centuries later.
It also began to shape the nature of the individual German citizen and the
population of the country as a whole, while the shattered rural economy
and its traumatized population sought to revive itself, in order to re-estab-
lish the self-sustaining foundation upon which the disparate German
princedoms and states depended.

The restoration of the concept of the home, the Heimat, and its fundamental importance to the future cohesiveness of German society was very
evident to all members of the rural population in particular at this time –
landowners and peasants alike. But if Germany was to succeed it needed
two things that were certainly lacking in 1648: firm leadership and the
military strength to ensure that in the future other nations would not be
able to turn Germany into Europe's chosen battleground. To these two
might be added national unity, although this was probably implicit in the
achievement of the first two requirements. But by the end of the Thirty
Years War the German states were militarily impotent and a leadership
vacuum was all too evident. Clearly Germany's restoration and revival
would remain distant for some time to come.

The seeds of change, however, were already germinating in the north
German state of Brandenburg. There, on 1 December 1640, Frederick
William, the Elector (later 'the Great Elector') of Brandenburg became the
head of that state and commander-in-chief of its army. Frederick William
was an astute and tireless ruler, who was also politically very aware of the
way in which both Brandenburg and Saxony had first been isolated and
then neutralized during the war. But with the conflict at last at an end he
was now determined first of all to restore and then expand his state's
power and prestige, and he knew very well that a strong army was absolutely essential to this process. So it was that from the widespread devastation and chaos of the Thirty Years War there emerged a leader, a state,
and a state in embryo that would together shape the destiny and military
fortunes first of Brandenburg, then of Prussia and finally of a united
Germany during the subsequent three and a half centuries. And
throughout the turbulent succession of military victories and defeats, the
conquests and catastrophes that would be visited upon Germany from
1648 to the present day, at the very core of these conflicts and national
aspirations was always to be found the ordinary German fighting man,
fulfilling – whether willingly or otherwise, but almost invariably without
question – his sacred duty to his head of state, and his patriotic duty to his
Fatherland.

3

'For King and Fatherland'

Brandenburg and Prussia, 1640–1713

FREDERICK WILLIAM, The Great Elector, was born at Berlin-Kölln, close to the River Spree, on 16 February 1620. Twenty years later he succeeded his father, the physically and morally weak and unassertive George William, as ruler of Brandenburg. Frederick William's Hohenzollern predecessor had ruled from just after the start of the Thirty Years War and had proved to be an entirely inadequate leader for that period of unparalleled turmoil, during which devastation, depopulation and disease had ranged unchecked across his lands; but especially so in the Mark of Brandenburg. Frederick William, however, was a ruler in a very different mould. Indeed, the all too visible deprivations visited upon Brandenburg and to a lesser extent Pomerania and East Prussia during his father's rule now directly shaped his own approach to his destiny and that of the state he now ruled.

During the Thirty Years War the Elector of Brandenburg, George William, had provided an army of some 10,000 soldiers to combat the Swedish forces of Gustavus Adolphus. This was in no sense a national army of Brandenburg or of East Prussia (the two territories that would in due course join to form the state of 'Prussia'), consisting as it did of various groups and bands of troops whose predecessors had for many years been the independent companies of mercenaries who had traditionally garrisoned the castles and main urban areas of Brandenburg and East Prussia. Even the soldiers of the more modern army, who had ostensibly fought under the auspices of the Elector of Brandenburg between 1618 and 1648, owed their primary allegiance to nobody but themselves in practice, and secondly to their principal paymaster, the Austrian Holy Roman Emperor, to whom the Elector of Brandenburg in any case owed his own allegiance. And these men were more often than not led by foreign officers whose priorities were focused upon personal advancement – military or social – and upon acquiring personal wealth, rather than upon any wider consideration of the domestic needs or foreign policy of Brandenburg. Not surprisingly, these troops and their officers often proved unreliable, their disregard of orders, desertion and the pursuit of more parochial or personal conflicts being quite commonplace. When Frederick William became head of state and commander-in-chief of the army on 1

December 1640 – with some eight years of the Thirty Years War still to run – he had already realized clearly that the development of an effective, disciplined and large army was a fundamental prerequisite for restoring his shattered country, and by extension for achieving his wider social, economic and constitutional aspirations for the nation.

In order to fulfil his aims, Frederick William placed himself at the head of a nation-wide administrative system that was in practice centred upon and primarily supportive of the army's supply organization, the 'Kriegskommissariat'. The Great Elector's plan was entirely pragmatic, but was necessarily implemented at some cost, for in order to guarantee his absolute power and to gain the considerable financial support essential to take forward his aims and create an effective standing army, Frederick William entered into an important undertaking with the nobility of Brandenburg, East Prussia and the other lands he ruled. In 1653 he secured the unqualified support of the nobles – the Junkers – on the understanding that they would be the exclusive source of the officers for what would be Prussia's new army, while at the same time the peasants who populated their estates would revert to the status of serfs. While this somewhat unedifying arrangement was probably unavoidable if Prussia was ever to rise and become a powerful nation, it was nevertheless highly significant. Its particular importance lay in the fact that it established a precedent for the creation of a Prussian officer class founded on birth and privilege rather than on ability, and this seventeenth-century precedent subsequently (if somewhat anachronistically) variously inhibited, enabled and shaped the development of Prussia, of Germany, and of their armed forces during the next three centuries – certainly until 1918, but arguably until 1945. Indeed, the middle classes who populated the lands east of the River Elbe after the Thirty Years War were unable to oppose the restoration and extension of the power of the nobility in 1653, yet these were the very same citizens whose industry and intellect could have provided enormous benefits of skill and leadership for state and army alike.

In later years promotion and advancement on merit were increasingly introduced within the army; despite this, throughout the history of the Brandenburg-Prussian army, the military and social mores of the nobility that originally populated its officer class continued to dominate virtually every aspect of German military development, together with the life, fate and fortune of the German soldier. Subsequently, the absolute power and perpetuation of the ethos of this semi-closed society – an exclusive officer's club in all but name – frequently proved to be more of a liability than an asset to the professional development of the German army during the next three hundred years.

The standing army that Frederick William created during the forty-eight years of his rule finally comprised some thirty-six infantry battalions and forty squadrons of cavalry: eight of dragoons and thirty-two of cuirassiers, all supported by about 140 artillery pieces. The 30,000[12] men of the army (recruited from a total population of only about one and a half million) were disciplined, well trained and led by an officer corps that was generally self-sustaining, through a requirement for the sons of the Prussian nobility and those from the highest social and educated strata of Prussian society to attend courses of three years at a number of new military academies, before following in their fathers' footsteps in the service of the nation.

Notwithstanding the fact that Frederick William had already made some discernible progress in regularizing the dress of his troops, the adoption of readily identifiable uniforms was still at a relatively early stage, and the use of coloured sashes and badges was still widely used as the basis of unit identification. Although many of the iron helmets and more extravagant pieces of armour routinely seen during the Thirty Years War were finally abandoned in favour of more suitable clothes in which to conduct a more technologically advanced brand of warfare, some of these items perpetuated in use, especially in the cavalry where (for example) the cuirass remained in service for a further two hundred years. But in the main, the 'uniform' of the ordinary soldier owed more to civilian fashion and personal affluence than to martial splendour. For head-dress there was the ubiquitous wide-brimmed round hat that offered protection from sun, wind and rain. It was worn by pikemen, halberdiers, musketeers, and by many cavalrymen. In due course the musketeers adopted the practice of turning up one side of the hat so that its brim did not hinder the handling of the musket.[13]

As muskets and cannon were used ever more extensively by the armies, the need for coats of a uniform colour became increasingly necessary, so that the identity of bodies of men might be discerned at a distance on battlefields that were now largely obscured by the smoke of burning gunpowder. But during its formative years the regular army of Brandenburg generally still followed the practice of most other European armies by using badges, belts, sashes or armbands to distinguish its units. Only towards the very end of the seventeenth century, with the development of new textile manufacturing and dyeing techniques, did it become possible to produce large quantities of identical or near-identical uniforms. At that stage Brandenburg-Prussia adopted the familiar grey-blue – or 'Prussian blue' – for the uniform coats of most (but by no means all) of its army units.

While he was creating the new army, Frederick William was also expanding the civil service and the economy of Brandenburg-Prussia, always matching their development first and foremost to the needs of the army. Pragmatism and Brandenburg-Prussia's requirements dominated all his policies and actions. One such example of this occurred late in his reign in 1685, when he encouraged the exiled French Huguenots to settle in Brandenburg, at which time his Edict of Potsdam extended to them freedom of religion and a range of economic privileges and commercial opportunities. This was but a part of a comprehensive immigration policy designed to repopulate Brandenburg and East Prussia with the trades, skills and wider expertise that the emerging state of Prussia desperately needed during the years of regeneration after the Thirty Years War.

Nevertheless, all these reforms were set against a European backdrop in which political intriguing, minor clashes of arms and wider conflicts, and ever-changing balances of power continued apace. In June 1675 the newly constituted regular army of Brandenburg was engaged in a major battle against the forces of a Swedish expeditionary force commanded by Field Marshal Count Karl Gustav von Wrangel. The outcome of what became known as the battle of Fehrbellin was the first victory of Brandenburg's national army gained without recourse to foreign troops or the assistance of allies, and it marked the real beginning of Brandenburg's imminent trans-formation into the state of Prussia. Fehrbellin was also Brandenburg's prin-cipal clash of arms during Frederick William's time as Elector. As such, it serves to illustrate and validate the remarkable progress that he had already made in developing the nation's army and new-found international power.

The convoluted political circumstances of Brandenburg's committal to war in 1672 were typical of the age. Previously, Louis XIV of France had found his ambition to extend France's eastern borders to the Rhine balked by the Dutch – regarded by Louis as France's principal competitor in Europe – and in order to defeat them decisively and thereby ensure that the Netherlands would never again frustrate French territorial aspirations, Louis concluded treaties of alliance with England and Sweden. In Sweden's case, France agreed to pay regular subsidies in return for occasional military support against the Dutch. In April 1672 the French invaded the Nether-lands, and Frederick William – a former student at the University of Leyden, who had acquired and maintained a strong affinity with and admiration for the Dutch people – immediately set out to counter this aggression. But the French attacked Brandenburg's western territories in Westphalia and Kleve, diverting Frederick William's response and effectively (albeit temporarily) preventing his involvement in the war. As Louis' armies continued eastwards into the Palatinate, the Holy Roman Emperor, Leopold I, became alarmed by French expansionism and an imperial alliance was constructed to counter the threat. The army of Brandenburg was a major part of the impe- rial force thus formed and during the winter at the end of 1674 Frederick William marched the army towards the River Main, where his army was to join with the main imperial army the following spring.

Louis perceived the potential threat posed to his army, and now invoked the Franco–Swedish alliance, desiring Sweden to attack Brandenburg directly in a bid to force Frederick William to protect his home territory rather than join the imperial army. At this point the Swedes – albeit with little enthusiasm, despite the substantial sums that they had already received from France – deployed a sizeable force[14] commanded by Field Marshal Gustav Graf von Wrangel to Swedish-owned Eastern Pomerania. This territory, also known as Swedish Pomerania, was a recurring source of dispute between Sweden and Brandenburg-Prussia throughout much of Frederick William's time as Elector. Initially, the Swedes claimed that they were simply seeking supplies and winter quarters, but as winter gave way to spring they advanced into eastern and northern Brandenburg, plundering and destroying all in their path.

As spring turned to early summer the Swedish army turned west, and in early June began moving towards the Elbe, with the eventual aim of supporting Louis' forces on the Lower Rhine. But by then, news of the Swedish incursion and the serious peril to Brandenburg-Prussia had reached Frederick William, encamped on the River Main, and he had immediately ordered his army to return to deal with the Swedish threat. The Brandenburg army reached the city of Magdeburg on the River Elbe on 21 June 1675. The city of Brandenburg was about fifty miles to the north-east, with Berlin and Potsdam a further thirty-five miles beyond it to the east. Meanwhile, the Swedish force had spread out into an arc facing south and west, its left flank in the city of Brandenburg, its right secured upon the town of Havelburg some forty miles to the north. The River Havel ran east and south from the Elbe at Havelburg, via Rathenow (which had also been garrisoned by the Swedes) and on southwards to Brandenburg; the Swedish dispositions followed the line of the river, to the east of which was a vast area of lakes, marshes and minor rivers. This waterlogged ground was traversed by a very few good roads and causeways elevated above the marshland. Generally, road bridges over the waterways and rivers in this sparsely populated area

were to be found only at the towns, such as those at Nauen, Flatow and
Fehrbellin.

Ever mindful of the need to achieve surprise, on his arrival at Magdeburg Frederick William ordered the gates to be closed and the city to be
secured. For two days no one was allowed to leave it apart from his own
reconnaissance patrols, while his army rested after their long march and
prepared for battle. By 23 June these patrols had provided a fairly accurate
picture of the Swedish deployment and Frederick William decided to focus
his main attack against the garrison at Rathenow, with a view to splitting
the Swedish army. At the same time, secondary attacks would be launched
against the Swedish garrisons at Brandenburg and Havelburg.

On the night of 24 June, 7,000 Brandenburg troops marched out of
Magdeburg and headed north towards Rathenow. The force comprised
1,200 musketeers, 5,000 men of twelve cavalry regiments and a dragoon regiment of 600 men. To save time and to enable the musketeers to move at the
same speed as the cavalry, these infantrymen were transported by a convoy
of forty wagons: a real innovation for the period and one that was indicative
of the style of warfare that Prussia would demonstrate time and again in the
years to come. Although launched at relatively short notice, meticulous planning attended the impending attack against Rathenow. The expedition was
provided with the necessary supplies for a five-day campaign, together with
a number of small boats to enable the force to manoeuvre freely without
depending upon roads and bridges. By dawn on 25 June the Brandenburgers
were within three miles of their objective, but a torrential rainstorm, which
lasted most of the day, forced them to postpone their assault until that night.
As darkness closed in about Rathenow, Frederick William's soldiers struck.

There were two bridges over the Havel at Rathenow, and Field Marshal
Georg Derfflinger, one of Brandenburg's most competent military
commanders, accomplished the capture of the first bridge, which provided
the main access into the fortified town, by convincing the Swedish pickets
that his men were Swedish troops withdrawing before an advancing Brandenburg army. The gatehouse guard lowered the drawbridge, and were
quickly overcome by the Brandenburgers. In the meantime, a second
assault force commanded by Adjutant General Cannowski had used the
boats that had accompanied the expedition to transport 600 men with the
flow of the river into Rathenow from the south. There, they engaged in a
brief period of street fighting before the other bridge was taken, at which
stage the remainder of the out-thought and out-manoeuvred Swedish
garrison surrendered. The attack at Rathenow had been superbly executed,
and the secondary attacks at Brandenburg and Havelburg had also enjoyed

success, not least of which being the capture of some 200 cavalry horses. As a result of these actions across its entire front, the Swedish army had been split in two and was now forced to withdraw eastwards in order to consolidate. But behind them lay a large expanse of marshland, and von Wrangel was very aware that his troops would have to use the few roads and bridges that were available. The main withdrawal route would be via Nauen to Flatow and then northwards to Fehrbellin and the area beyond, where von Wrangel could reconstitute his divided command. By midday on 26 June, the entire Swedish force was moving eastwards, well on the way to Nauen. But Frederick William had already anticipated this and was determined to pursue the Swedes and bring them to battle once more.

The main body of the Swedes moved through Nauen on 27 June and continued north towards Flatow. They were aware that the Brandenburgers were in pursuit; indeed, Frederick William himself was leading the troops that were close on their heels. In order to be able to press the Swedes hard, Frederick William had left his infantry and much of his artillery behind, using his cavalry to maintain contact with the retreating soldiers. But while the Swedes were aware of their immediate pursuers, little did they know that a certain Colonel Joachim Henning had already outflanked them by leading a force of 100 cavalrymen and thirty dragoons directly through the marshland to Fehrbellin. Henning was one of the relatively few Brandenburg officers who, despite being of peasant stock, had risen through the ranks and achieved his promotions on sheer merit. But as well as being a competent soldier and commander, he had another very relevant attribute: an intimate knowledge of the inhospitable and waterlogged terrain between Rathenow and Fehrbellin. He got his force across the marshes to Fehrbellin and destroyed what Frederick William had correctly identified as its vital bridge before the Swedish troops arrived. Consequently, daylight on 28 June found the main Swedish force, which was at that stage under the command of Lieutenant General Waldemar von Wrangel (a relative of the Field Marshal), unable to cross the river. With little option, therefore, von Wrangel had drawn up his command facing south towards the pursuing Brandenburg army. The Swedes numbered some 16,000 men, with twelve squadrons of cavalry drawn up on each flank (each of these groups numbering 4,500 men) and in the centre 7,000 infantrymen were deployed in eight brigades and drawn up in two ranks, while thirty-eight artillery pieces were in support. When Frederick William arrived he had just 6,000 cavalry and twelve artillery pieces, but no infantry. Despite this he knew that he could not afford to let the Swedes escape, and so against all the odds and the advice of many of his generals he decided to attack.

The Brandenburg artillery was deployed into the protection of some sand dunes, from where it soon brought down a telling fire on to the Swedish right flank. After several salvoes Frederick William himself led a spirited cavalry charge against the Swedish right, but this brought the Brandenburgers dangerously close to the Swedish infantry and they sustained casualties from the Swedish artillery. One cannon ball passed close to Frederick William and killed his equerry Froben at his side. Nevertheless, the Brandenburg cavalry, ably directed and led by the Prince of Homburg, forced the Swedish cavalry back on the right, at which point von Wrangel ordered his infantry to counter-attack against the Brandenburg artillery. Thereafter, the focus of the battle was about this artillery, as the fighting ebbed and flowed until darkness fell. But by then the Swedes had managed to repair the bridge at Fehrbellin. Consequently, despite

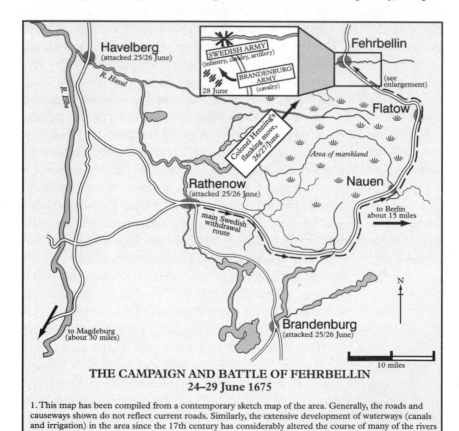

THE CAMPAIGN AND BATTLE OF FEHRBELLIN
24–29 June 1675

1. This map has been compiled from a contemporary sketch map of the area. Generally, the roads and causeways shown do not reflect current roads. Similarly, the extensive development of waterways (canals and irrigation) in the area since the 17th century has considerably altered the course of many of the rivers shown.
2. The general direction shown for Colonel Henning's flanking move on 26/27 June is indicative only.
3. The positions shown for the Swedish and the Brandenburg armies on 28 June are indicative only.

having sustained many casualties during the day, the remnants of von Wrangel's force were at last able to withdraw to the relative safety of the other side of the river. But once there, rather than attempting to consolidate with a view to resuming their strategic mission, the Swedish troops continued northwards out of Brandenburg.

Although the overall scale of Fehrbellin was less than that of many other battles, and at the tactical level the Swedes were able to mitigate the extent of their defeat by laying emphasis on the fact that they had eventually managed to retreat rather than suffer a total defeat on the battlefield, the importance of this clash in the story of the German soldier should not be underestimated. Brandenburg, by the force of arms of its own national army, unaided by any other, had conducted a considerable march from the Main to Magdeburg, planned and executed a series of co-ordinated attacks against a renowned military power, and had achieved complete surprise, out-thinking and out-manoeuvring a force almost three times greater than its own.

Finally, the Brandenburg army had ejected the Swedes from their territory, destroying forever the long-standing reputation of Swedish military might, and opened the way for Brandenburg-Prussia to carry the war into Swedish Pomerania – the original launch base for von Wrangel's ill-fated expedition – during the next two years. By the end of 1677 both Stralsund and Stettin were in Frederick William's hands. Internationally, Sweden's humiliation at the hands of Brandenburg encouraged both Denmark and the Dutch republic to take up arms against Sweden, although the Danish invasion was eventually repulsed by Charles XI of Sweden. In the meantime, Louis XIV did manage through diplomacy and negotiation – aided and abetted by the Emperor's signing a peace treaty with France in 1678, when he somewhat disloyally withdrew his earlier support for Brandenburg-Prussia – to secure the restoration of much of the territory of his Swedish ally which had been seized by Brandenburg in the years following Fehrbellin. But Frederick William retained some 40,000 square miles of the former Swedish land in Germany, an early indicator of the steady expansion and rise to prominence of Brandenburg-Prussia; an unstoppable process of which all Europe was now very well aware.

Despite Frederick William's temporary falling out with the Emperor, the Brandenburg-Prussian army soon found itself fighting alongside the imperial banners once more when, in the mid-1680s, the Great Elector sent a large contingent of 12,000 troops into Hungary to join the forces then attempting to push back the Muslim tide which had earlier swept into the Holy Roman Empire under the Turkish flag and laid siege to Vienna.

Ever since the end of the Thirty Years War the imperial Habsburg rulers had become ever more preoccupied by their Hungarian, Slavonic and Italian interests, and the consequent need to deal with the Turkish onslaught, rather than by those issues affecting the empire's German territories and subjects. In 1683 the Polish King John Sobieski had defeated the Turks at Vienna and relieved the city, but the war had continued as the Europeans sought to recapture Hungary and eject the Turks from that country.

While the earlier account of the reorganization of Brandenburg's army and its victory at Fehrbellin indicated the sea change that was taking place in the nature of soldiering in Brandenburg-Prussia, it does not fully convey the true nature of the warfare, or the perils and privations of the conflicts of the time that daily beset the Brandenburg soldier on campaign. Also, despite the dramatically improved provisioning arrangements within the army, it was still expected to live off the land, so the seventeenth-century army on campaign continued to be the scourge of the countryside. The first-hand accounts in the journal of Master Johann Dietz, Surgeon in the Army of the Great Elector and Barber to the Royal Court, are illuminating and enable a better understanding of the realities of the sort of warfare in which Frederick William's troops were involved.[15] Master Dietz accompanied the Brandenburg troops during their campaign against the Turks in Hungary in 1686, which concluded with their successful participation in the defeat of the Turkish army at the great fortress of Ofen[16] on the River Danube.

Master Dietz's account of the Brandenburg contingent's campaign into Hungary begins when he '… was accepted as army surgeon … by the artillery, under the command of Colonel Weiler, whose father, Major-General Weiler, was at the same time Commandant of the fortress of Spandau and had to order [i.e., procure] everything. The most blessed Elector Friedrich Wilhelm sent 12,000 men to the Turkish War in *anno* 1686, what with infantry, cavalry and artillery, without counting volunteers, baggage-trains, camp-followers, etc.' Dietz continues:

> We marched by way of Frankfurt and Krossen. So far the Elector accompanied us (for he was indeed a great lover of soldiers). His tent was pitched and a formal three days' encampment was held. The beer and water in the little town were quite exhausted, by the cattle and by so many men; so that there was no more to be had, and we had to bring it from a very long distance. At last the march was sounded and the camp broken up for departure.
>
> The beneficent Elector, like a loving and valiant hero, took leave of us all in front of the troops, with tears. Moreover, he said: 'Now march off, children, in

God's name! I shall not see all of you again!' And so indeed it fell out. Of twelve thousand men, not counting their wives, children, and servants, or independent persons, less than three thousand returned …

At first we marched some little way into Poland, whence the husbandmen had all run away; at most a dumb or blind person or some aged woman would be left in the village; all their livestock was hidden in great holes in the ground, lined with straw, or otherwise concealed; and some of these places, with a great plenty of stock in them, we discovered, killing and eating what we found. Already there was an appearance of dearth. Farther on, however, we found people in some of the villages, and a sorry state they were in … cow and calf, pig and dog, man and wife, lay all together; one could not sit upright for the reek in the living-room … of lice there was plenty … [and] the people lived like cattle. [However] going through Silesia, by way of Breslau, matters were better as we drew near to Troppau. I lodged for two days in a large village a mile from Breslau, at the house of a wealthy cattle-dealer, in billets which our quartermaster had procured for himself and me.

But now, to resume our march. We proceeded on our way, on horseback, over the Alps and by way of Jablunka, which is a fortified blockhouse [in this case, a specially constructed log fortification occupied by a battery of cannon], and here there is more than two miles of swamp, crossed by a causeway of logs, with swamp and forest on either hand, which makes very unsafe travelling.

Superstition and religion were never far from the minds of the soldiers of the time and the line between the two was often blurred. Such matters – with the attitudes and fears they produced – also sat comfortably alongside the old Germanic myths and legends. Despite being a relatively well-educated and God-fearing Protestant, Dietz made numerous references to such matters in his journal and on one such occasion he clearly believed that he had experienced a close encounter with the 'Rübezahl', a forest hobgoblin which allegedly worked its mischief in the rural countryside.

In the mountains nearby I heard a great deal about Rübezahl, and one fine night I came upon him. There is no question but that there is something in the legends; either an outcast forest goblin or the Devil making sport. For I heard with my own ears, when we were lying indoors one night on a bed of straw, how at midnight there was a terrifying bustling and clattering of horses and hounds, and of hunting, which passed the house several times over. The people told us that this was a nightly matter and no novelty to them. They told us also many things of the Rübezahl; how he annoyed and plagued people, and had the power of avenging himself on those that spoke of him disrespectfully, by means of thunderstorms, etc. So, in his neighbourhood, I behaved as though all this were true.

Dysentery, plague, food poisoning and numerous other malaises were ever-present, and Dietz himself fell ill near Trentino, where the army encamped and 'either went into billets or had to lie in the open fields'.

Although he recovered, having survived on a diet of 'raw apples … washed down with water' for the final forty miles of the march bound upon his horse, 'as we no longer had any wagons left', this sickness was widespread in the army, when 'Many of us ate grass during this illness, and never lived to see Hungary.' The army's situation improved somewhat as it passed through Kremnitz and Schemnitz, acquiring a few replacement wagons. But the enemy were now never far away, and at Gran Dietz noted that the troops 'crossed a bridge of boats amidst the thundering of the guns in the higher fort'; at Gran also 'we were once more able to obtain good wine and mead'. Ever deeper into Hungary the Brandenburgers marched, and Dietz noted that 'the once beautiful Hungary was a wilderness' with its deserted countryside and devastated villages '… it was full of wild dogs, which attacked men and cattle just as wolves do; more, they scratched up dead bodies from the battlefields and elsewhere'. The army passed by the destroyed towns of Waitzen and Neuhäusel, the latter of which had been in Turkish hands since 1663 but had fallen to the Christian forces on 19 August 1685 after a one-month siege. At last, after a short passage by boat down the Danube – during which they ran the gauntlet of cannon fire from Turkish shore batteries – the Brandenburgers finally arrived at Pesth, close to their objective, the fortified township of Ofen. There, they joined the other imperial and Bavarian forces already besieging Ofen. At Pesth, Dietz noted that another 'bridge of boats' had been constructed right across the Danube, being 'over a mile' long: testimony to the skill of the imperial army's engineers. Ofen itself was held by the Turks, together with (according to Dietz) 'many Frenchmen', and the effective handling of the Turkish artillery during the siege may well have been the fruit of French technical expertise.

The surgical arrangements at the siege of Ofen were never better than rudimentary. A steady succession of wounded were brought to Dietz 'on tent-poles' and, as he was based with the artillery, many of these men had been injured by cannon or mortar fire. Consequently their wounds were usually extensive and therefore fatal. Wounds sustained by the soldiers in the trenches tended to be from bullets or edged weapons. Indeed, the fighting about Ofen was desperate, as the Turks launched many spirited sorties against the besiegers. On one occasion, following a night-long rainstorm, the Brandenburg musketeers were unable to ignite or keep alight the slow-match of their matchlocks. Perceiving their advantage the Turks attacked, when '… two hundred [Brandenburg] men were cut down and beheaded. Among them was the valiant Lieutenant-Colonel Löschbrandt, and many another well-known officer. Moreover, they came charging over the palisades and trenches so far that they spiked some of our guns, but these were soon bored out again.'

Frederick William's soldiers gained a degree of notoriety with the Turks, who apparently 'feared the Brandenburgers as they feared the Devil'. One Brandenburg battery also attracted special attention from the Turkish guns following their setting up of two forges adjacent to the guns, which heated the shot so that 'the balls were rammed into the guns red-hot, and immediately shot into the city' where 'fires were incessantly breaking out, now here, now there, wherever the red-hot balls had fallen'. Apparently, only the Brandenburg gunners used this technique at Ofen, so that when the Turks went to pick up a cannon ball, it burned their hands; they used to say: 'That is a Brandenburger ball.'

As was usually the case during a siege, mortars were used at Ofen, where their high trajectory carried their bombs above and far into the fortifications. Dietz observed this particular fire both incoming and outgoing:

> At first I did not understand what was meant when the sentry called out 'Fire! Fire!' Everybody ran a little to one side and fell flat on the ground. I alone remained standing until I understood what was happening. For the bombs, when they fell, first made a hole in the ground and lay there, as long as the fuse was burning; it was after this that they did their work, hurling their outer portion with such violence about them, and to some extent upwards, with a terrible buzzing and whistling, so that all they struck was shattered in fragments. – It is a pleasure to watch them at night, when the firing commonly takes place. The bombs rise like rockets, often so high that one can no longer see the fuse burning; then suddenly they fall, with a shrieking and whistling, to their appointed place in the city or elsewhere, whence there often rose, after the explosion, a pitiful howling and shrieking.

On 15 July 1686 a mortar bomb scored a direct hit on the Turks' main magazine, which blew up and destroyed thirty yards of the city wall and killed 500 of the city's defenders. For half an hour a dense cloud of smoke and dust obscured everything. Dietz noted that this was the time for the imperial forces to seize the opportunity to storm the fortress, 'yet we lay there six weeks longer, losing many men and despoiling the people. It was merely that the General could not agree with the Duke of Lorraine, who was acting as commander-in-chief.' Such difficulties of command were virtually unavoidable with such campaigns conducted by alliance or coalition forces. The Turks – some 200,000 strong within and in the area about Ofen – worked day and night and soon repaired the great gap which had been created in their defences.

✠✠✠✠✠✠✠✠✠✠✠✠

Five more times the imperial troops launched assaults but each time they were repulsed. Certainly the Brandenburgers were invariably to the fore in these attacks, and Dietz noted '... that when others were most frequently repulsed in their storming-parties and assaults, the Brandenburger soldiers climbed up on the breaches in the walls, waved their hats and shouted: "Forward! Forward! Up again, brothers!" But such courage was the cause of many a valiant officer or soldier biting the dust.'

As the siege progressed Dietz observed that (in his opinion, in initiatives inspired by the Frenchmen in the city) the defenders employed '... all sorts of new preparations and stratagems of war, with brimstone, powder and stink-bags in particular; and the women hurled them by means of pitchforks under the feet of our storming parties, so that they were burned all over and, by fifties or hundreds, quite naked, black and charred, flung themselves into the Danube in their agony'. Mines were also used extensively by the Turks, often being exploded under the Brandenburgers after they had seized a section of the city and thought themselves secure, the huge explosion being the precursor to a counter-attack. During what proved to be the final weeks of the siege Dietz fell ill again, this time with dysentery, at a time when the imperial forces were already on short rations, having all but depleted the resources of the countryside for many miles around. Remarkably, he managed to acquire a quantity of pickled gherkins from a musketeer, and having devoured these, his fever notwithstanding, Dietz fell asleep for about eight hours. He awoke to find the fever broken and the dysentery purged!

The accommodation arrangements made for the troops on the march and in encampments when billets were not available were very much a matter for the individual soldier. Tents were available for more senior persons and for specialists such as Dietz, but for the majority of ordinary soldiers it was merely a matter of picking a dry patch of ground on which to sleep. Although Dietz often used a tent, on many occasions (when on the march) this was not available. In any event, he always '... had my bed of brambles and brushwood instead of straw, of which we had none [another indication of the worsening supply problem], made half an ell in height above the ground. This was a very good thing for me, since the greatest number of deaths [presumably as a consequence of the cold and wet] took place among those who lay flat on the ground. The mattress was of old sacks and the coverlet of canvas from old tents. – This too was an improvement, for we often had to lie under the open heavens, when my saddle was my pillow, and my horse used to graze in the night with one leg hobbled ... [Despite the improvised mattress] I often woke of a morning with half my body lying in the water, yet I slept soundly.'

The Brandenburgers' permanent campsites before Ofen were entirely surrounded by deep entrenchments designed to check the rush of any surprise attack by cavalry or infantry. But the camps themselves were often well within the range of some of the Turkish guns, so that 'the cannon balls often came rolling or bouncing through our camp, and one day one of us, thinking to stop the ball with his foot, had his boot carried away, and part of his leg with it'. Despite the risk, however, the enormous importance of religion to the Christian soldiers was exemplified by the fact that Divine Services continued to take place regularly, although 'the enemy used to fire his cannon into our assemblies, prayer-meetings and Sunday services, which were held with the greatest reverence under an outstretched canopy or awning before the drum, or a field table, when the Sacrament was administered, and general confession heard and absolution granted, so that tent and tent-poles (and once two horses, but no men) were shot to pieces'.

Despite the entrenchments surrounding the imperial camps and the use of wagons to provide a bulwark to protect the artillery, they still proved vulnerable to surprise attacks. Three days after the army (which then included Brandenburg, Swedish, Saxon, Walloon and Bavarian troops, and others) had moved its positions, the Turks noted that the Swedes had not quite completed their new defences. The Turks were quick to seize the opportunity when, as Dietz recorded:

> Early one morning, when it was scarce growing light, the whole Turkish army entered our camp through this gap. I heard first the roll-call and then the alarm sounded by the cavalry. I ran out of the tent, and lo! There came the whole Turkish army, like a swarm of bees ... uttering terrifying cries ... All whom they met were put to death. Before our troops could stand to arms and take their places many were caught unawares and slain.

But then five regiments – one of cuirassiers and four of infantry – of the Duke of Lorraine intervened; together with the artillery, which swept away the attackers still seeking to gain entry to the camp. The imperial troops now dealt with the six to eight thousand Turks trapped within, and the Bavarians, Walloons and Brandenburgers forced the survivors against and into the perimeter trenches where they were killed to a man by the pikemen. Only about 600 Turks escaped back into Ofen, most of whom had sustained wounds.

Seven days later a set-piece battle was fought, following a three-day stand-off while the armies faced each other across a deep ravine and engaged in desultory artillery fire. Eventually battle was joined, when the

Turkish right wing launched an attack against the Imperial army's left. Soon the whole army was engaged, and 'There was nothing to be seen or felt but the thunder and lightning and reek of the guns, screams and shouts, the rolling of the drums, the rattle of the alarm and the calling of bugles. [While] the guns, loaded with canister, played furiously upon the Turks and were dragged hither and thither as the enemy manoeuvred.' After a few hours the Turks – initially some 150,000 strong – began to withdraw, and were pursued for about a mile before the battle drew to a close. Meanwhile, the Bavarians had gained a lodgement within part of the city and were besieging the inner fortress with some 300 men. The Turks tried unsuccessfully to smoke the Bavarians out with huge fires of straw and brushwood. The siege was now drawing to its end, as it entered its eleventh week; the date was 2 September 1686 and, in an assault somewhat reminiscent of Frederick William's surprise attack at Rathenow eleven years before, the Germanic fighting men of Brandenburg and Bavaria were about to conclude the matter. Dietz maintained a detailed account of the final assault and of the chaos and slaughter that almost inevitably followed a protracted siege – especially one conducted against non-Christian forces! Even almost four decades after the end of the Thirty Years War, the business of warfare had lost none of its barbarism and it was within this environment of daily hardship and routine violence that the ordinary German fighting men of the time lived, fought and died. Dietz wrote of the final fall of Ofen:

> Certain bodies of picked men in every regiment and company, infantry as well as cavalry, and certain grenadiers, were told to provide themselves with powder and lead and also to lay in wine and brandy. From this I certainly concluded that stormy weather lay ahead of us ...
>
> It was just about that hour of broad noon when the Turks used to sleep or eat. They were wholly unaware that our [Brandenburg] men, in the greatest silence, without firing a single shot, were climbing over the breach. The same arrangements had been made on the part of the Bavarians ... Directly the first shot was fired the alarm was sounded, and it was all continual firing and bombing and casting of stones from the catapults, with musketry fire and clash of swords; even the Turkish women and children, and thereto the Jews, of whom there were many in the city, took arms and entered upon a desperate defence of the breach, so that corpses lay piled there to the height of a tall man. But to no avail, as they must have known. They might defend themselves and shout as they liked; the city was captured.
>
> Not even the child in the mother's body was spared. All who were encountered were put to death. As I then saw with my own eyes ... women were lying there still holding their discharged pistols, or sometimes a naked sabre. They were stripped naked and had been run through and through with pikes, the

womb especially; and their bodies were ripped open so that the yet unborn children fell out; which to me was the most lamentable thing. Naked children of one or two years of age were spitted and flung over the city walls! I was amazed by what was done and to see that mankind shows itself far crueller to its own than the beasts. The two commanders, one of whom was blind, were shot, and lay in the market-place before one of the mosques, surrounded by numbers of Turks, who had not carried arms, or offended in any way, but would be taken thence as prisoners. Those who were not slain in the fury of battle, or such of the Jews and Christians [the latter presumably the French military personnel assisting the Turks] as had concealed themselves, withdrew to the citadel, which held out two days longer, stoutly defended, until it capitulated, when they had to surrender themselves as prisoners of war.

Following the fall of the city, the Brandenburgers and the Bavarians led a vigorous pursuit of the Turks to 'beyond Essek'. But the end of the year was fast approaching, together with the onset of the harsh eastern European winter which would of necessity halt the campaigning season. Consequently, both sides finally broke contact, and the Turks continued their withdrawal to winter quarters in what Dietz noted as 'Greekish Weissenburg'. The successful end of the campaign also signalled the beginning of the Brandenburgers' long return march to Berlin. Remarkably, they had no horses left for the artillery, and so Hungarian oxen were purchased to draw the guns, which now included 'many Turkish guns and mortars, among others a Brandenburger piece which had long ago been given up for lost'. The army fell back to Komorn, a large triangular-shaped fortress that lay between two branches of the Danube. There it camped on an island close to the nearby small market town for three weeks while preparing for the journey home. While there, the first heavy snowfalls of the winter occurred. However, 'our little company [of Brandenburg artillerymen] was so rejoiced to think that it was going home, that in the morning, when the cheery artillery réveillé was sounded, we often used to dance in the snow before our tents – although we had neither food nor money – because the contending parties had, as far as we were concerned, concluded peace'.

Despite being the victors at Ofen, and notwithstanding Frederick William's organization of the Brandenburg army, the threat of starvation was ever-present for the fighting men on campaign, especially in an impoverished region such as rural Hungary, for '... the Hungarians gave us nothing, not even a drink of water, without money; for all they cared we might have died ... [and] here many of our men died and many suffered from starvation'. Isolated foraging parties ran the constant risk of being killed by the local populace, while those suspected of such attacks were summarily hanged by the roadside. Eventually the army reached Breslau, then Krossen, where the troops had to remain in quarantine for four weeks while

'... the Hungarian sickness was hung round our necks like a curse. And there was not a day but numbers of our soldiers died, so that our position was a pitiable one, for we were getting no pay. My own coats and shirts were in tatters. And although I had to tend the sick and physic them and make them sound again, I was so full of vermin that I got no rest of a night. On this account I had to creep stark naked into the hay at night, for only then could I get any rest. At last came orders that we were to march to Berlin. But even then we could not show ourselves by day, but had to lodge without the gates, at a place appointed. There we received some of our pay and our discharge. And then – off and away!'

Master Johann Dietz's manuscript continued with an account of the rest of his life, which later also included military service with the Danish army, but with his return to Berlin at the end of 1686 or early 1687 his direct involvement with the Brandenburg army ended. From his writings it may be deduced that Frederick William's new standing army was indeed one of the most effective European armies of its time, and certainly its exemplary operational performance and apparently sound morale and discipline in such extremes of privation, sickness and starvation are testimony to this. But the campaign to eject the Turks from Ofen also illustrated all too starkly just how far short even the new model army of Brandenburg still fell in terms of its logistical support and aspects of its command and control. It also showed the extent to which the ever-present threat of the plague and diverse other diseases were the constant companions of the German fighting man in an age when medical support and surgery still drew extensively upon myth, religion and superstition to effect the art of healing and the problematic process of recovery.

Despite the dramatic achievements of the Great Elector on behalf both of his country and of the house of Hohenzollern, Frederick William was hampered by a continuing and unavoidable reliance upon the financial support of imperial Austria, the Netherlands and England in order to pursue his political and military goals. He had also attracted (inevitably perhaps, but undoubtedly with some justification) a certain reputation for political unreliability among his allies and neighbours. But needs must, and Brandenburg, with a spread of poor and (in 1648) largely devastated territories that ranged from Kleve, Mark, Ravensburg, Geldres, Moers, Lingen and Tecklenburg in the west, to Pomerania and the electorate of Brandenburg in the centre, and to the east Prussian state of the former

Teutonic Knights in the east, was neither financially nor commercially self-sufficient. By the end of the Great Elector's reign the need for foreign funding and the undesirable impact of this need upon Prussia were the inevitable prices to be paid if Frederick William's formidable standing army was to continue as such. But, given these constraints, Frederick William had without question begun a process of military evolution that would thereafter prove unstoppable – despite the occasional and some-times significant setback – and his work, carried out with such dedication after 1640 right up to his death in 1688,[17] provided the foundation upon which would be built the remarkable German military state of the future, and the system and population of German fighting men that supported it.

On 9 May 1688, the Great Elector's third son succeeded him as Fred-erick III of Brandenburg (Frederick's two elder brothers had both pre-deceased him, one as an infant and one at the age of nineteen), but the new elector and ruler of Brandenburg was quite different from his father. On his accession, Frederick was indeed in an enviable position, having inher-ited not only a stable and increasingly powerful state, firmly founded upon the principles of absolutism, but also a state benefiting from a prosperous economy and from the security provided by its now formidable national army.

However, although he demonstrated a certain aptitude for diplomacy and for the intriguing that has characterized the art of politics since time immemorial, he also had a well-developed love of the visible trappings of power. Consequently, despite the not insignificant achievement of being awarded the kingship of the principality of Prussia (following a lengthy process of negotiation with the emperor and with the kings of Poland and Saxony, much assisted by the disbursement of a considerable amount of money to these influential men), his profligate management of the court and the self-serving avarice and incompetence of his many court favourites precipitated the state into debt, impoverished large numbers of the population, and squandered much of the work that had been carried out by his father.

Certainly Frederick III promoted the arts and sciences, together with industry and manufacturing – he founded the University of Halle/Saale in 1694 and the Berlin Society of the Sciences in 1700 – but the period of profligacy, excess, stagnation and the worsening lifestyle of most of his subjects over which he presided was not one of the more illustrious chap-ters in the story of Brandenburg and Prussia. Nevertheless, Frederick did make one notable contribution to the history of his country and to the status of the house of Hohenzollern when, on 18 January 1701, amid great pomp and ceremony in the Prussian capital of Königsberg, he crowned himself Frederick I and named himself 'King in Prussia'. Whatever his wider failings as a monarch, Frederick had transformed the Hohenzollerns into royalty, and had thus created a royal dynasty that was destined to rule Prussia and then Germany in an unbroken line until 1918. At the same time, the fighting men of Prussia now owed their allegiance and duty of service to a duly anointed king, a matter of considerable pride, importance and social consequence for the Prussian state's officers and soldiers alike.[18]

And with Frederick's death in Berlin on 25 February 1713, the new-found status of the Prussian army was about to be matched by a dramatic resurgence of its professional capability as Frederick William I became King of Prussia, a ruler who later became known universally as 'The Soldier King'.

4

Era of the Drill Sergeants

The Army of 'the Soldier King', 1713–1740

MANY HISTORIES of Germany have consistently accorded to
Frederick II, 'the Great', the principal credit for the creation of the
Prussian and German military machine. But, as we have already seen, the
foundations of this organization were in fact laid many years earlier.
Although Frederick undoubtedly deserves a great many of the accolades
heaped upon him, he could neither have completed the development of
the eighteenth-century Prussian army into the ultimate fighting force it
was to become, nor would he have been in a position to use it to such decisive effect to advance the interests of Prussia on the international stage,
without the work of his great grandfather the Great Elector and the subsequent work that was carried out so successfully by his father, Frederick
William I, 'the Soldier King', from 1713 to 1740.

Frederick William I of Prussia was a well-educated, focused and determined man with an exemplary sense of the duties and responsibilities of a
ruler; he was militarily and commercially aware, and so was already very
familiar with Prussia's needs and its parlous economic situation at the time
of the death of his father, Frederick I, on 25 February 1713. His many
detractors and critics tend to interpret his energetic pursuit of Prussian military advancement as obsessive militarism, and his character as that of a
violent, mercurial and frightening man. Nevertheless, his actions stand as a
record of his successes on behalf of the state he ruled, and it is on that record
set against the wider backdrop of the age in which he ruled that Frederick
William should be judged, rather than on his personal flaws and foibles.

He immediately set about reducing significantly all areas of public
expenditure, especially the amounts spent on the court. Rapidly – and in
the face of not a little opposition – the profligacy and excesses of the Prussian court were virtually eliminated. In parallel, however, he implemented
a sound range of measures designed to regenerate and rejuvenate the
economy throughout the Prussian lands. His economic policies were
underwritten by the consolidation of the state administration into a single
General Directorate in 1723, and by the centralization and efficient control
of the collection of the state purchase tax. His social awareness was illustrated by the establishment of a major state public hospital in 1727. Clearly
he was destined to achieve great things for Prussia, but, if his social and

economic actions redressed the ill-judged actions of his father and placed Prussia once more to the forefront of the German states, it was for his enlargement and training of the Prussian army that he will always be remembered. An eighteenth-century observation on his reign by Christian, Graf von Krockow, accurately summarized the nature of the Prussian ruler and his true place in the history of his nation:

> The Prussian revolution was the work of one man: Frederick William. It was his achievement, hour for hour, day for day, year for year, throughout his entire life, surrounded by incomprehension, lethargy and resistance wherever he looked ... He was the father of a modern state organization and of Prussian military might.[19]

Despite the generally favourable view taken of him by many German historians, he has also been characterized by many, both within and beyond Germany, as a mean, unpleasant and crude man, whose obsession with military discipline produced an exemplary army only at the expense of introducing a code of martial sanctions that was routinely brutal in its nature and its implementation. Certainly his treatment of the son who would eventually succeed him was harsh, and the young prince – an intelligent, well-read, cultured and confirmed Francophile, certainly very unlike his father – was frequently beaten, sworn at and generally despised by Frederick William. On one occasion the ruler is alleged to have attempted to strangle his son. On another, after young Frederick and a comrade, Katte, absconded from their regiment and tried to leave Prussia, the monarch imprisoned his son and ordered him to witness the execution of his friend Katte.

But, as with so much recorded as history, an objective and fair assessment of Frederick William's character undoubtedly lies somewhere between these two extremes. In any case, insofar as his contribution to the state and its army are concerned, it is undoubtedly more appropriate to judge him by his achievements as a ruler and commander-in-chief rather than merely as a man. Also, while probably not the preferred route to achieving the necessary self-sufficiency and inner strength necessary to rule a nation such as Prussia, the hardships and deprivations suffered by the young Frederick at the hands of his father contributed to the essential hardening and desensitizing of a man who would later direct and lead Prussia during the final forty-five years of the country's rise to military primacy in eighteenth-century Europe.

Clearly, Frederick William's role in the development of the army was crucial, and his formative influence upon the nature of the soldiers was critical. He also engendered among the aristocracy and well-to-do citizens the concept of 'being Prussian' and that to serve Prussia militarily was to achieve the highest ideal in life.

Yet the army still depended upon enlistment rather than conscription, and there were many exemptions from any sort of compulsory military service. Pragmatically and inevitably perhaps, from the outset these exemptions included the sons of noblemen and those of the wealthiest citizens. Later on, whole territories, towns, social classes, trade groups, corporations and certain individuals were exempted, despite Frederick William's declaration that 'all inhabitants of the state are born to bear arms'. But despite the many exemptions from compulsory military service, in principle every young man of average height was expected and thus required to adopt what soon came to be known as 'the king's coat' and to bear arms on behalf of Prussia, so that by the latter part of his reign the army numbered some 82,000, although about 26,000 were enlisted non-Prussians. Similarly, there was a clear expectation – often reinforced by the king's messengers if necessary – that most of the young men of the great houses of the Prussian nobility would enlist into the Prussian corps of cadets for training as officers and leaders of the rapidly expanding army. Certainly none were left in any doubt of the advantages of serving as a Prussian officer, and in due course even the reigning sovereigns of the principalities of Braunschweig and Anhalt willingly served as officers within the army of the King of Prussia. Indeed, in the officer corps of this army the great, the wealthy and the powerful served as military equals alongside many of those who had little to commend their social status other than a title, possessing little or nothing by way of wealth or property. As ever, the nature and effectiveness of the army were shaped by the officers who led it and by their soldiers, and Frederick William addressed both these aspects with determination.

Throughout much of eighteenth-century Europe the typical army officer was frequently attracted to a military career and was accepted for it on the basis of precedent, his social standing and his personal wealth, or indeed the simple need to earn a reasonable living by any means possible. The fact that he was an officer was more often than not of secondary importance to the wider social stratum into which he had been born and within which he lived. An officer who was not high-born would not necessarily attract any special prestige by virtue of being an officer. Indeed, in the southern German states of Bavaria, Württemberg, Baden and Hesse, the aristocracy generally pursued careers in the law or civil service rather than the army, the officers of those states' armies often being of low social standing in consequence. In some places – the bishopric of Mayence is but one example – the public perception of the army was such that an officer would not countenance wearing uniform except on duty, while the officer's acceptance in polite society depended on his being a gentleman by birth. This then was the norm throughout most of Europe, and its stark contrast with the Prussian military model is an indication of how revolutionary Frederick William's reform of the Prussian officer corps truly was.

In the best traditions of leading by example, right at the start of his reign Frederick William adopted a simple and practical form of military uniform to replace the extravagant French-style court dress of his father's reign. Habitually, he wore this uniform throughout most of his time as ruler – invariably from 1725 – and this was the origin of the later references to 'the king's coat': a description that would persist until the very end of the Hohenzollern monarchy. But apart from being quite revolutionary at the time, this was a very astute policy decision both within the nation and the army. At a stroke the king had physically underlined his position as the principal officer of the Prussian army, while elevating the standing of every other Prussian officer to the status of 'gentleman' by making him a professional comrade of the king himself. Directly contrary to the wider European practice, the officer's prestige flowed from being an officer, not from his social background. The success of the common bond forged between the king and his officers (any of whom were now accorded the right and privilege to address the monarch directly by 'immediate application'), and between the officers themselves through the unifying medium of the uniform, was central to Frederick William's reinvigoration and reorganization of the Prussian army. Indeed, in this army no special badges indicated an officer's rank, and even the generals could only be identified by a white ostrich feather worn on their hat and by the fact that they usually affected the uniform of their former regiment.

Even the lowliest officer was the social equal of a senior civilian war councillor, and if the same officer had already experienced combat he took precedence over all such senior administrators. Despite the radical nature of what was just as much a social as a military revolution, Frederick William's officers generally repaid their monarch well with reliability and loyalty, so that both the king and, later, his son routinely entrusted military officers with important administrative and diplomatic missions rather than using civilian officials. They also set officers to direct and control many aspects of the civilian administration. Quite simply, they both judged that these military men exhibited better self-discipline, loyalty, initiative and ability (together with the personal presence and authority necessary to achieve the desired result) than their civilian comparators, a shrewd judgement which was validated time and again during the next seven decades.

But what of the ordinary soldiers who served under these officers, the fighting men who would finally determine Prussia's defeat or victory on the battlefield?

The many exemptions from regular military service that were introduced progressively over the next half century meant that much of the Prussian army's manpower was found from the lower socio-economic orders of the time. These included the peasants, agricultural labourers and other unskilled workers, the lesser artisans, and all types of servants. A limited recruitment pool such as this always ran the risk that the main standing army might lack the mass of trained manpower to counter a major threat to the state or indeed to launch offensive operations at short notice. Nevertheless, by the latter part of his reign Frederick William had largely resolved this potential military weakness. He managed to create and maintain a viable standing army, with responsibility for the defence of the whole of the Prussian territories, and at the same time he managed both to compensate for the disappearance of the old and long discredited local militias and levies and for any possible need to call upon groups of foreign mercenaries to fight for the Prussian state.

He achieved this by transforming the broad principle that every able-bodied Prussian man (apart from the many formalized exemptions) was liable for military service into what became known as the 'canton system' of military service. The Canton Regulations were introduced in 1727, and by these Prussia was divided into districts (or cantons), each of which was linked to a specific regiment and from which men would be drawn and subsequently serve together. In theory, the military service liability was for life, and those men – the 'cantonists' – called into the army in peacetime served just two months with the regiment each year, and were then sent back to resume their civilian work for the remaining ten months, during which time of course they were neither supported nor paid by the state. The Canton Regulations, with the localization of recruitment and regimental ties, were in many ways a modernized extension of the old concept of the knights and nobles taking their own men-at-arms and retainers on campaign, these groups then coming together to make up a disparate but formed army. In any event, although this system would much later be shown to have a number of flaws, in Frederick William's time and in that of his successor it underwrote the whole security of the state and the viability of the army that defended it. It also established a number of principles and precedents that would be revived in other forms during the development of the army in the latter part of the following century.

In parallel with its recruitment and general reorganization, the army supply system was completely revamped. The separate regiments were provided with their own distinctive uniforms and equipment. All the infantrymen were provided with a firearm and bayonet, units of uhlans (lancers) and hussars were added to the cavalry, and the army's weapons were henceforth manufactured only in Prussia.

Thus was the army significantly enlarged, suitably officered, effectively equipped and given unprecedented prestige and standing in Prussia; but its professional reputation stemmed directly from its training and preparation for war, and to this vital matter Frederick William addressed himself assiduously, well justifying the epithet of 'the Soldier King'.

Drill and strict discipline were the foundation on which the army's training was based, and its parades, exercises and evolutions were soon the talk of Europe and the envy of many other states. In Berlin and nearby Potsdam the royal parks were transformed into parade grounds, and on these great open spaces the Prussian soldiers were drilled exhaustively in the manoeuvres they would use in war. Among them were to be seen the 'Potsdam Grenadiers' – every man more than six feet tall – and Frederick William's obsession with acquiring these giant soldiers for his army has often attracted more populist attention and implied criticism than have his wider military achievements.[20]

The king habitually supervised and inspected the training of his army as a whole and that of the Potsdam Grenadiers in particular, and any irregularity in the drill or dressing of his troops on the parade grounds of Berlin or Potsdam would invariably attract a blow of his cane. Irrespective of rank or station, fear of punishment was an unavoidable and necessary element in the regime Frederick William had created, and suicides were by no means unusual in the army. Not surprisingly, the occasional mutiny that did occur was always dealt with expeditiously, but usually by the execution of a likely ringleader rather than of any greater numbers of those involved, for soldiers (those of the Potsdam Grenadiers especially!) were assets much too valuable to be disposed of lightly.

The manual of arms was the military training bible of the officers and sergeants, and within its pages were to be found detailed descriptions of all the drills and formations required to present a file, a battalion, a regiment in such a way that these bodies of troops could inflict what was literally a moving wall of musket fire against their opponents. The handling of the artillery was also covered, together with that of the cavalry – although the latter occupied a somewhat lesser priority than the infantry and the artillery in the consciousness of Frederick William and his great companion and principal military adviser, Field Marshal the Prince Leopold of Anhalt-Dessau. In their view cavalry had been both inefficient and of little tactical consequence in the recent War of the Spanish Succession.

Indeed, 'the Old Dessauer' was instrumental in shaping the new Prussian army. He developed the concept of the infantry marching in time, with steps of a set length and with seventy-two such paces per minute (to match the rate at which the human heart beats). He invented and brought into general service the first metal ramrod for the infantry musket. Finally, he ensured that the standards of drill and discipline of the Prussian army were uncompromising. By the time of Frederick William's death at Potsdam on 31 May 1740, the Soldier King and the Old Dessauer had elevated the Prussian army – some 82,000[21] strong drawn from a population of a mere two and a half millions – to become the premier military force in Europe. This despite the fact that within eighteenth-century continental Europe Prussia ranked no more than tenth in overall size, thirteenth in size of population and only fourth in terms of the overall size of its army. Nevertheless, and rather remarkably perhaps, this finely honed military machine had yet to prove itself in major combat, and it was left to Frederick William's third son to complete this rite of passage for the Prussian army after he became the king of Prussia as Frederick II, in May 1740.

5

Masters of the Battlefield

The Army of Frederick the Great, 1740-1786

WHEN FREDERICK assumed power many in Prussia anticipated a
period that would contrast very directly with the militaristic regime
of his father. The young ruler was well known for his individuality,
curiosity, sound judgement and intellect, all leavened by an obsession with
literature and his appreciation of the arts, of culture and of virtually all
things French. Indeed, Frederick was a close friend of the writer and
philosopher Voltaire, and the official language of the Prussian court was
still French. A further example of his Francophile inclinations was his
founding of the Prussian Order of Merit – the famous *Pour le Mérite* – in
1740, which was a direct copy of the French award founded by Louis XV
of France.[22] On the other hand he was a somewhat introspective and
sometimes unfathomable man, to the extent that some of his subjects
described him as taciturn and unpredictable, an enigma even. This view
was given substance within the year when, contrary to the expectations of
many, Frederick set Prussia's army firmly on the road to war in a bid to
seize Silesia from Austria. Thus began four decades during which
Prussia, its ruler and its army were tested to the utmost in the crucible of
conflict, and from which all three would emerge much changed from their
circumstances of 1740. Frederick's wars and style of rule also triggered a
century of tension between Prussia and Austria and incurred the distrust
of several of the other great European powers, while also sowing some of
the seeds of the type of German nationalism that would recur time and
again during the next two centuries.

Undoubtedly, in his youth Frederick had entertained hopes of being
able to rule as a benevolent and enlightened despot at the head of a state
at peace with itself and with all other nations, promoting the humanitarian
ideals of justice and the well-being of his people. But by the time that he
gained power he was already aware that these aspirations were unrealistic
and that his destiny was to take Prussia forward on its journey towards
becoming a great power – which, ultimately, could only be achieved by
force of arms. Accordingly, he placed the army at the centre of his plans
for Prussia, just as his father had done. And, in another continuation of his
father's policies, he militarized the Prussian state in its entirety. Five-sixths
of the country's national expenditure was for the army, and even the so-

called civil service became yet another department controlled by and set firmly within the army.

His approach to the organization, manning, training and use of the army were very much his own, however, especially during the first half of his reign, before the constant attrition of his soldiers and the debilitating impact of years of warfare forced a return to some of the military training and disciplinary methods that were more reminiscent of his father's time. Also, as had his predecessors, Frederick was now relying to an even greater extent on the support of the Prussian nobility and great landowners – the Junkers – to provide the leadership not only of the burgeoning Prussian state, but much more importantly to fill the ranks of its officer corps. This reliance on the limited and ever more exclusive source of military expertise and leadership inevitably came at a price.

Frederick pursued a two-track approach to the development of the army. The Junkers were granted privileges and advantages and in return they gave him their support and loyalty, and sent very many of their sons as cadets to the officer training school. There, they received a military education which included the practicalities of discipline and soldiering and the concepts of patriotism and *esprit de corps*. Almost without exception these officers to be were Prussians. Frederick's insistence on maintaining the privileged position of the Prussian nobility at the core of the army is understandable. Very many of the ordinary soldiers in the rapidly expanding army were not Prussian, and (with memories of the foreign bands of the Thirty Years War still very much in mind) their motivation might well be suspect. Indeed, Frederick's concept for the training of the army was entirely pragmatic. He understood the potential limitations of the soldiers and of the weapons of the time and devised a system that took account of both. This was based primarily upon the three core functions of drill, manoeuvre and discipline. The very essence of everyday life and discipline in the army of Frederick the Great was encapsulated in an extract from notes on the 'New Regulations for Prussian Infantry', published in London in 1757:

> One of the essential Parts of the Prussian Service is that Regularity, which is so carefully attended to from the highest Officer down to the private Man: the Soldier being obliged to hold himself in continual Readiness to parade, is by that means kept constantly employed in preserving his Arms, Clothes, Accoutrements and Person, in proper Order.
>
> Recruits are not only taught to walk, stand, and exercise, but also to dress. In the Evening every Soldier must curl up his Hair in Papers, and in case he is not able to dress it properly himself against the Parade-time in the Morning,

he must have it done at the Captain's Quarters by the Friseur of the Company, where the non-commissioned Officers are to take care that the Men are powdered, brushed, and properly dressed, whenever they go upon Guard, or the Company is to be reviewed.

That there may be a Uniformity in the Appearance of the Hair, all the Men are to have it dressed in the same Manner. The Grenadiers are to wear Whiskers, which they are to tie up at Night, that they may lose no time in dressing them in the Morning. The whiskers are to be raised with black Wax, to keep them stiff and smooth.

All Soldiers and non-commissioned Officers, are to put on their Gaiters before they are dressed; and that there may be no Wrinkles in them, a false Calf is fixed, so as to fill up the Hollow between the inside of the Knee and the Calf of the Leg.

When a Soldier is to appear on the Parade, or to mount Guard, the Buttons of his Gaiters and every thing of Brass about him must be perfectly bright. Every Year in the Month of May the whole Army is new cloathed [sic] from Head to Foot, and the old Clothes the Soldiers are allowed to sell, the Facings and Collars being first cut off, that the Peasants may not appear in the Uniforms of Soldiers.

A Soldier who has been on Furlough, must, at his Return to the Company, bring with him a tanned Calf's-Skin (which are very cheap in Prussia) and three Ells of coarse Linen, and deliver them to the Captain at Arms, who deposits them in the Company's Store-Room, in order to be returned to the Soldier, when he shall want Shoes, Gaiters, or Pieces of Linen for mending the Lining of his Clothes.

All Arms, Halberds, and Espontons are well polished: And that the Arms may continue so, every Soldier has a thick piece of Buck-Skin in his Pouch, with which he is to rub the Barrel of his Piece very well as soon as he is relieved from his Post, as Sentry; or comes off Guard: By the frequent Repetition of this, the Polish becomes so lasting, as at length not to be spotted even by Rain; besides, the Arms are burnished by the regimental Gunsmith with sweet Oil, Emery, Starch-Powder, and the Steel-Polisher. The Stock of the Firelock is rubbed over with a brown Paste, and afterwards, very hard with Oil and Wax, which give it a Gloss.

The slings are varnished with red; the Paste both hardens the Stock and secures it from the Worm; and the red Varnish is also a good Preservative to the Leather.

The Pouches are of the thickest tanned Leather, and to be kept glossy, by being frequently rubbed with black Wax, that the Cartridge-Box may not contract any Damp, or the Rain penetrate into it. Every Soldier has sixty Cartridges in his Box, which are tied up close in a leather Bag; and on all Parties detached against the Enemy, are carefully examined.

The Cartridge-Boxes, Slings, Waistcoats, Hat-Laces, Stockings, Facings and Collars for every Company are coloured together, in the Quarters of the Captain at Arms, that there may be no Difference between them, which would sometimes be the case, especially in the Yellows.

A Comb, Brush, Looking-glass, Wax for the Shoes and Whiskers, a Piece of Buff-Leather, a wooden Polisher, a Screw-Driver, a Set of Gaiter Buttons, a

Hook for buttoning the Gaiters, and a Worm, are little Articles which no Soldier is to be without.[23]

Despite this apparent preoccupation with appearance, uniformity, and what were in some instances the artificialities involved in achieving and maintaining this appearance, it is noteworthy that practicality was also in evidence. Generally, Prussian soldiers wore a shorter coat than those of the other European armies, these being less cumbersome to march, manoeuvre and fight in. Similarly, the woollen breeches worn in winter were replaced by white linen breeches in the summer months, and the hot, heavy, oversized and generally extravagant head-dress so much favoured by the commanders of many armies were not to be seen in the Prussian army, where suitably small and lightweight grenadier caps and infantry hats were issued to the soldiers.

Without a doubt, Prussian discipline was hard and the punishments for wrongdoing or professional negligence were harsh. Nevertheless, there were numerous examples of Frederick's ability to relate to his soldiers, and of the affection with which they regarded their uncompromising taskmaster. In part, this reflected the deprivations and hardships borne universally by all but the wealthy and privileged in the eighteenth century. Measured against these vagaries of everyday life, those experienced in the army (where death was in any case accepted as a likely consequence of service) were often less unpleasant than those which afflicted much of the civilian population of the time. However, this affection also reflected Frederick's even-handed approach to justice and to his selfless vision for the Prussian state, both of which traits were obvious to his people and to his soldiers alike. He demanded everything from his army, but in return he rewarded them with esteem, professionalism and the prospect of military glory, and for the soldier of the 1740s and 1750s this was in many cases reward enough.

Pragmatically, Frederick determined that as a matter of principle his (possibly unreliable and sometimes foreign) soldiers should be more afraid of their (indisputably reliable and invariably Prussian) officers than of the enemy. Undoubtedly this oft-quoted maxim was exaggerated, as great numbers of Frederick's soldiers consistently demonstrated a genuine affection and respect for their commander-in-chief, a perception that has by and large stood the test of time and of critical analysis of his reign. In any event, Frederick well understood that the parade ground was in reality nothing less than a peacetime battlefield, and that perfection on the former led to success on the wartime equivalent of the latter. Consequently, drill

– literally the tactics of soldiering in the eighteenth century – quite rightly continued as the cornerstone of Prussian military training.

Soldiers were viewed not as individuals but merely as very small parts of manoeuvre units such as companies and battalions. But on his induction into the army the recruit was taught his various duties, how to handle his musket and bayonet, and the drill movements required of him individually or in groups of two or three men by a junior officer, and without fear of punishment at this stage. When deemed to have been fully trained in these basic skills, he took his place in the company and battalion and was then liable to incur the wrath of his superiors and to attract any of the wide range of harsh punishments that could result from (for example) offences such as idleness, inattention, coughing, sneezing, talking or moving unbidden on parade.

These perfect standards of discipline, awareness, steadiness in all situations, and an immediate, unthinking obedience to orders, were all absolutely essential if the Prussian military machine was to achieve and maintain its goals, and so any shortcomings – however minor – by soldiers or officers were simply not tolerated. By extension, any deficiencies attributable to a unit reflected upon every commander throughout the chain of command above it and, with Frederick as commander-in-chief taking a direct interest in every aspect of his army, the consequences of an individual's failure upon the whole unit could be both dire and virtually irretrievable. Small wonder then that when an English traveller, Dr John Moore, MD, observed the Prussian army undergoing training in Berlin in 1779, he noted that it was 'the best disciplined and the readiest for service at a minute's warning of any now in the world or perhaps that ever was in it'.[24]

The individual soldier armed with his notoriously inaccurate musket could hardly influence a battle directly. But when hundreds of muskets were deployed at the right place and time to produce literally a wall of fire (usually five rounds per minute, using the recently introduced paper cartridges and iron ramrods), their impact could be devastating; as was the use of the carefully controlled bayonet charge by the massed infantrymen to complete the enemy's defeat and precipitate a rout. Despite the advances in weapon and projectile technology, the bayonet remained both symbolically and practically at the core of the infantry's fighting doctrine, and for any army committed to the pre-eminence of the offence over defensive action this was both correct and inevitable.[25]

From all this it is clear that the concept of the 'thinking soldier' of more modern times would have been most inappropriate in the wars that Prussia's army chose to fight in the eighteenth century. Only the more senior commanders needed such flair and vision, while at the tactical level knowledge of the drill manual and absolute mastery of the equipment and weapons available were the keys to victory and personal advancement for the regimental officers and their men alike. For the officers, Frederick produced a textbook or manual of 'Military Instructions', which ranks alongside works such as Clausewitz's internationally acclaimed *On War* as one of the great publications of military literature. The wide availability of this manual throughout the army, while no doubt also produced as an aid to Frederick in crystallizing his many thoughts and ideas on the art of war, meant that every commander had the means readily at his disposal to get inside the mind of the most senior officer of the Prussian army, that of its commander-in-chief and monarch.

Having set in place the principles governing the army's training and tactical doctrine, Frederick and his advisers set about matching a Prussian regiment's speed of manoeuvre to the characteristics of its weapons, so that:

> A Prussian battalion is a moving battery ... the rapidity in loading is such that it can triple the fire of all other troops. This gives to the Prussians a superiority of three to one.[26]

At the same time he developed the concept of the point of main effort or 'oblique order of battle', by which the utmost effort would be made against one of the enemy's flanks while the remainder of the army maintained its positions and prevented reinforcement of that flank by the enemy. Once the defence was broken, a relatively small force could roll up the enemy by attacking along his defensive line rather than against his front and centre. Meanwhile, if the initial flank assault should fail, the bulk of the army remained largely intact to cover the subsequent withdrawal. Implicit in this concept was the assumption that the Prussians would always take the offensive, something that was only practicable with soldiers trained to the degree of instinctive obedience and discipline that Frederick's army had achieved. That said, it was an inescapable fact that Prussia's geo-strategic position and circumstances meant that neither defensive options nor readily defendable territory were available to the army.

Prussia could never sustain a strategic defeat, the consequences of which would surely be the speedy dismemberment of the Prussian state and its consignment to oblivion by the many enemies that surrounded it. Therefore, the success of his offensive theories notwithstanding, Frederick had simply understood and responded appropriately to the specific strategic imperatives affecting his country, rather than inventing some completely new form of warfare.[27] Thereafter, and in later times, the German high command's preoccupation with the need for offensive action and its many successes in carrying it through would be seen time and again.

So it was that the Germans learnt well in the course of Frederick's wars that an army's effective defence might prevent or modify an enemy victory, but that it could never achieve an overall victory without major offensive action, and that as such the defence is merely a period of preparation, consolidation or respite prior to taking offensive action. With all this very much in mind, only months after he had succeeded to the throne, Frederick at last launched the military machine that had been so assiduously nurtured by his father across the border into Austrian Silesia in late 1740 and into what soon became a major European war, the War of the Austrian Succession.

The political rationale for Frederick's decision to invade was both tenuous and somewhat suspect. He had recognized Maria Theresa's succession to the Imperial throne and in the course of doing so he offered Prussian support for an Austria that was in military decline. Directly linked to this offer of military support was Frederick's proposal that Prussia should occupy Silesia. This was a blatant ploy and not surprisingly Austria rejected any Prussian claim to Silesia. Consequently, Frederick's well-prepared regiments had marched south-east into Silesia, and on 11 April 1741 they inflicted a telling defeat on the Austrians at Mollwitz. That success, together with much diplomatic manoeuvring and intrigue, and a later victory at Hohenfriedberg in June 1745, enabled Frederick to retain Silesia and Glatz, thereby adding about 16,000 square miles of territory to his domain together with another one million people, thus increasing the manpower resources available to Prussia by almost a third. He also, despite his initial aggression, came to an accommodation with Austria. Finally, although he later became an exceptionally competent military commander in his own right, Frederick learnt many lessons during the first of his Silesian wars. Although nominally in command at Mollwitz, after making a number of ill-judged decisions he effectively passed command to Field Marshal von Schwerin. This acknowledgement of his own inexperience, the trust he placed in his subordinates and his readiness to delegate such important responsibilities were truly the marks of a great commander and ruler. At Mollwitz, his faith in von Schwerin was fully justified by the impressive victory that the Field Marshal delivered to his monarch that day.

The uneasy peace which followed lasted no more than a decade, and in 1756 Prussia became embroiled in a war against Austria, Saxony, Russia and France, and was supported by England. This new conflict developed into the Seven Years War and by its start the Prussian army of the late-1750s and the 1760s was well experienced not only in matters of drill, organization and supply, but also in the deadly business of destroying its enemies with considerable efficiency. But by 1756 Prussia's enemies had also observed and learned from the developments that had been taking place in the Prussian army. Accordingly, the results of many of the battles of the Seven Years War were frequently more indicative of the training and discipline of the soldiers engaged than of the tactical competence of their commanders. However, in matters of drill and discipline the Prussian army more or less managed to retain the edge that had been established by the Great Elector a hundred years earlier, which had then been honed to perfection by the Soldier King and Frederick the Great.

The organization of the Prussian army in 1760 is shown in detail with accompanying notes at Appendix 2.

This then was the thoroughly professional army – more than 200,000 strong – with which Prussia conducted the Seven Years War, a conflict which entirely validated its organization and training, and the tactical doctrine and drills that it applied on the battlefield. The war – a 'world war' in all but name – also confirmed Frederick as one of the great military commanders and strategists of the eighteenth century. Indeed, during his reign he had already attracted the title of 'Friedrich der Grosse' (the Great) both within and beyond Prussia, as well as the less formal nickname 'der Alte Fritz' (the Old Fritz), which was widely used as a term of affection by a Prussian populace (military and civilian alike) that viewed their ruler as stern and demanding but also as a just and caring father figure, a ruler who was speedily moving Prussia towards great power status. Quite early in the Seven Years War the army's capability and the efficacy of its commander's military doctrine were decisively demonstrated by two great victories, both won in 1757. The first of these was at Rossbach in November and the second the following month at Leuthen. Together, these great clashes of arms – which were directly linked to each other strategically – epitomized all of the martial qualities of the Prussian army, the professionalism of its senior commanders and regimental officers and the discipline and tenacity of their soldiers.

The two battles followed the coming together of France and Austria as allies in May 1756, which was preceded by Prussia allying itself with England in January (although England's global war with France meant that it could only provide funding support, not military manpower). Russia, Saxony and Sweden came in with France and Austria and by mid-1756 Prussia's population of four million was opposed by a coalition of nations with a total population in excess of seventy million. Not alarmed by this, in July Frederick deployed 37,000 men to safeguard his acquisitions in Silesia, 26,000 to defend against a Russian attack, and a further 11,000 men to guard against a Swedish incursion. But, perceiving Austria to be the principal threat and holding true to his doctrine of offensive action, in August 1756 he launched a pre-emptive attack into Saxony, occupying Dresden. After this came the blockading of Pirna and what was claimed as a Prussian victory at the battle of Lobositz on 1 October, although it is arguable whether either Prussia or Austria was in fact the clear victor. The next year saw the Prussians defeat a larger Austrian force and capture Prague on 6 May, albeit with heavy casualties, including the loss of Frederick's trusted adviser and commander, Field Marshal Schwerin – the hero of Mollwitz in 1741. Then at Prague, the more modern Austrian artillery devastated Frederick's infantry battalions. The carnage wrought by this artillery upon the iron-disciplined but necessarily close-packed columns of soldiers led to a rapid upgrading of Prussia's artillery equipment and its tactical employment – notably the development of highly mobile units of horse artillery. At Kolin, on 18 June, Austrian troops, who were by now increasingly wise to Prussian tactics, forced a premature deployment of Frederick's flanking move, and the Prussians again suffered horrific losses to the Austrian artillery. But although the army was suffering reverses and Prussia was absorbing attacks and raids on virtually all sides, Frederick continued to mount offensive operations and reconstituted his forces time and again to regain the strategic initiative just when the situation seemed irretrievable.

In 1757, the Austrians were threatening to overrun and regain Silesia, mounting ever more audacious raids into the Prussian heartland. The Russians were laying waste to parts of eastern Prussia and committing atrocities against the population that were in many cases reminiscent of the worst excesses of the Thirty Years War. A large Franco-Imperial army was on the point of coming together to attack into Thuringia from the southwest, and many international observers thought that Prussia's situation was at last beyond redemption, and Frederick's luck and good fortune in terminal decline. But then, in the early winter of 1757, the campaign of Rossbach and Leuthen took place.

The Battle of Rossbach, 5 November 1757

Arguably, Rossbach was the most decisive battle of the Seven Years War in Europe. Certainly Frederick's defeat of a much larger and predominantly French army, comprised of some 50,000 French and Imperial soldiers from

Austria, Württemberg and Franconia, together with small contingents from Switzerland and a number of other minor states, was sensational – not least because he achieved this success with a force of no more than about 22,000 men, but also because this battle was Prussia's first great victory against France, one of the first-rate Continental military powers of the day. This victory marked the true start of almost two hundred years of bitter enmity and a cycle of occasional but invariably devastating armed conflicts between France and Prussia, and later Germany.

At the outset of the war the empress Maria Theresa of Austria, her army now reorganized along the lines of the Prussian model during the period since its defeat in the first of the Silesian wars, was determined to recover the Silesian territory lost in 1745. She had acquired powerful allies, France and Russia, and from the north Sweden was also posing a direct threat to Prussia. The allies' strategy was, as ever, designed to capitalize on their significant numerical advantage, by splitting the Prussian army and forcing Frederick to fight on two fronts simultaneously: against an Austrian army to the east in Silesia and against a Franco-Imperial army to the south-west in Thuringia, thereby dissipating his numerically smaller force. True to the doctrine of mobility and the principle of the concentration of force, Frederick resolved to prioritize and defeat each threat separately, even if this decision unavoidably entailed the loss of some Prussian territory in the short term.

In September Frederick learned that the main Imperial army had joined with the French force and was moving towards him through lower Saxony. The combined Franco-Imperial army – now some 50,000 strong[28] – was under the overall command of the Prince of Sachsen-Hildburghausen, although the large French contingent was commanded by the Prince de Soubise. Although Hildburghausen was a competent general, his troops lacked training and discipline, while Soubise lacked ability and experience and commanded troops who were relatively well trained and equipped, but whose ill-discipline was exemplified by the trail of pillage and destruction they inflicted upon Saxony as they advanced to meet the Prussians. The orders that the Franco-Imperial commanders had received from Versailles and Vienna respectively seemed at first sight to be straightforward, but on closer examination the two commanders found that they in fact conflicted with each other. While Maria Theresa required nothing less than the complete removal of all Prussian forces from Saxony and the reduction of Frederick's strategically vital fortresses on the River Elbe, de Soubise had been instructed to allow the Imperial troops – primarily the Austrians – to conduct the main part of the campaign. Thus, this large but indifferently

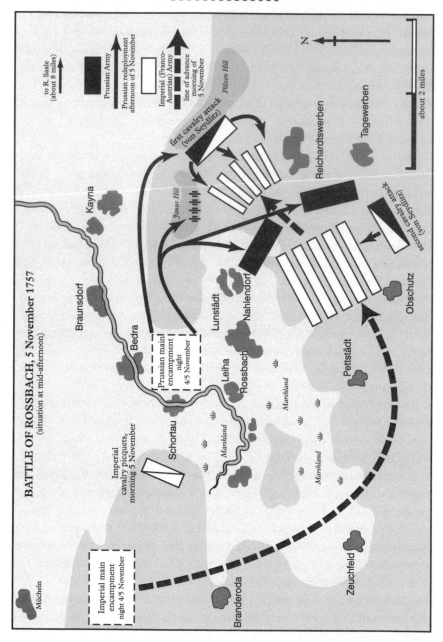

BATTLE OF ROSSBACH, 5 November 1757
(situation at mid-afternoon)

to R. Saale
(about 8 miles)

Prussian Army

Prussian redeployment
afternoon of 5 November

Imperial (Franco-
Austrian) Army

line of advance
morning of
5 November

N

about 2 miles

Pölzen Hill

first cavalry attack
(von Seydlitz)

second cavalry attack
(von Seydlitz)

Janus Hill

Reichardtswerben

Tagewerben

Kayna

Braunsdorf

Bedra

Lunstädt

Nahlendorf

Obschutz

Prussian main
encampment
night
4/5 November

Leiha

Rossbach

Pettstädt

Marshland

Schortau

Marshland

Marshland

Marshland

Imperial
cavalry picquets,
morning 5 November

Imperial main
encampment
night 4/5 November

Branderoda

Zeuchfeld

Mücheln

commanded and potentially unreliable army marched slowly onwards to its date with destiny.

In response Frederick's army marched southwards, at the most impressive rate of twelve miles each day, only to have the enemy halt and then appear to withdraw before he could bring them to battle. At this point, however, the army's mobility and ability to redeploy were tested to the utmost when news suddenly arrived that an Austrian general, Count Hadik, had occupied the Prussian capital, Berlin. He turned about and began to move back to deal with this incursion, but before he could do so he was advised that the Franco-Imperial army was once more on the move. This time Frederick was determined that his enemies would not escape the confrontation he sought.[29]

The morning of 4 November found the army once again in western Saxony, this time encamped within and to the north of the village of Rossbach, in an area of swampland some eight miles to the west of the River Saale. The ground rose away to the east, west and south of Rossbach, so that the village lay in a partially closed valley, which was open on its north side and from which a river flowed. Having received intelligence of Frederick's deployment, the Franco-Imperial commanders decided to use the high ground to the south of Rossbach to outflank the Prussians and cut them off from their lines of communication and supply across the Saale. Implicit in this decision, and certainly in von Hildburghausen's mind, was also the hope that Frederick could be outflanked and decisively defeated.

By first light on 5 November, with advanced detachments of Austrian and French troops already in place on the high ground to the west of and overlooking the small village of Schortau, which lay in the river valley immediately to the west of the main Prussian camp, the allied army set about implementing its plan. This entailed a seven-mile march up into the low hills beyond Zeuchfeld, then eastwards along the ridgeline past Pettstädt and Obschutz towards Tagewerben and Reichardtswerben, and on to the Janus and Pölzen hills around and well behind the Prussian left flank. As the drums and fifes struck up the marching tunes and the buglers and trumpeters sounded assembly, the Franco-Imperial commanders quickly realized that a prompt deployment was out of the question, as large numbers of the French soldiers were away from the allied camp, still engaged in the looting and pillaging which had already characterized the French contingent's behaviour throughout the earlier part of the campaign. By the time that a fair degree of order and organization had been restored it was already 11.30 a.m., at which time the five great columns of infantry soldiers, together with the artillery and the whole assemblage headed and flanked by squadrons of allied cavalry, set off on their sweeping march around Frederick's flank. Thus far the Prussians appeared either oblivious to or little interested in the large force that was moving along the ridgeline to the south of Rossbach. Meanwhile, in a medieval mansion in Rossbach, Frederick was enjoying a relaxed lunch with his senior commanders, as the Franco-Imperial army moved inexorably on.

Fortuitously, one of those commanders was the thirty-six-year-old cavalry Major General von Seydlitz, an outstandingly competent officer, an excellent horseman, and a charismatic leader, known as much for his uncompromising professionalism as for his calm temperament and relaxed demeanour. Habitually, he affected a clay pipe, which had become his trademark and was always with him, even on the battlefield. Looks can be deceptive, however. The demands on his cavalry made by von Seydlitz – especially the speed, vigour and aggression with which the charge was to be driven home, irrespective of terrain – had inevitably resulted in a number of deaths in training. But he led by personal example with little regard for his own safety, although the offensive actions of his cavalry units were characterized more by well-directed aggression and daring than by any ill-judged recklessness on the part of their commander.

While Frederick was apparently less concerned by the allied movement than was his cavalry general, von Seydlitz had ensured that this move was at least kept under constant observation. This was achieved by one Captain Gaudi who was posted high up in the attic roof of the mansion. From there Gaudi provided a steady flow of reports on the allied army's progress. Eventually, von Seydlitz judged that both the threat and the opportunity could be ignored no longer, and he ordered the Prussian cavalry ready to move. The artillery followed suit, and by 2.30 p.m. Frederick agreed that the situation indeed warranted action. The infantry quickly struck camp – the watching French reported that the whole drill took no more than two minutes – and immediately formed up in their regiments. They then set off towards the Janus Hill to the east, with a view to turning south later and intercepting the Franco-Imperial force on the high ground farther to the south. Sixteen heavy cannon and two howitzers accompanied the Prussians and in due course they took up positions on the Janus Hill itself.

The cavalry pickets that had been watching the Prussian encampment from the hills to the west of Schortau ever since first light quickly sent word to de Soubise and von Hildburghausen that the enemy was on the move and, as the columns of infantry were observed to have headed out of sight beyond the high ground to the east, the two commanders decided that Frederick was seeking to avoid combat by withdrawing his army to the Saale, there possibly to establish a defence on the river line. They sensed that they had at last gained a tactical advantage, and pressed their marching columns to move ever faster to cut off what they believed to be a Prussian withdrawal.

In the meantime, Frederick had given von Seydlitz overall command of all the Prussian cavalry – some thirty-eight squadrons in total – and this large group of horsemen had led the orderly if somewhat hasty Prussian counter-move into the low hills, finally moving into cover from view behind the Pölzen Hill. Then, as the Prussian artillery on Janus Hill began to engage the head of the advancing columns, the force of Prussian cavalrymen – almost six and a half thousand men – quickly formed into two long ranks facing south and west. The troopers looked expectantly to von Seydlitz for his next order.

A quick blessing by the pastor who routinely accompanied the troops, then both lines of cavalrymen urged their horses forward at the walk for not more than a hundred paces. A brief final check just below the brow of the hill, still out of sight of the Franco-Imperial troops, then von Seydlitz at last ordered the charge. The trumpets blew, the troopers screamed their battle cries, and the blades of several thousand swords were brought down from the carry and pointed straight ahead. The ground reverberated as the hooves of more than three thousand horses carried the first line of Prussian cuirassiers, dragoons, Garde du Corps, Gens d'armes and hussars to death or glory. At their head, with his personal bugler riding close behind, rode Major General von Seydlitz, the straw-yellow uniform of his former regiment readily discernible amid the predominantly blue uniforms of the dragoons and cuirassiers. Von Seydlitz's choice of the place and time for the attack were perfect, and the speed and momentum gained during the first charge slightly downhill produced a devastating shock effect against the French and Austrian troopers as the Prussian horsemen thundered straight into the advancing allied cavalry, driving deeply into and then right through their shattered ranks.

In a very few places a bitterly contested mêlée ensued, although most of the Franco-Imperial cavalry collapsed under the onslaught, only a couple of Austrian regiments managing to provide enough of a fighting response for the French reserve cavalry to attempt to forestall a total disaster. However, that force was then itself struck by the charge of the second half of von Seydlitz's cavalry. As all further resistance crumbled away, the surviving French and other Imperial cavalrymen withdrew to the south and west in an effort to save themselves. The temptation for the Prussian cavalrymen to pursue the demoralized enemy troopers must have been very great indeed, but their own discipline and training were again very evident when von Seydlitz halted his triumphant squadrons in the area of

Tagewerben, there to ready them for their next task. This was a drill that the Prussian cavalry had exercised exhaustively under Seydlitz's direction and by halting and rallying after a charge, without then withdrawing to consolidate, these cavalry squadrons were quickly ready for further offensive action or redeployment as appropriate. But first of all it was time for the Prussian infantrymen, now under Frederick's personal command, to enter the fray. By now Frederick had established his place of command by a large elm tree at the small village of Lunstädt, about a mile to the east of Rossbach, from where he was able to observe the outcome of Seydlitz's charge, the progress of the Prussian infantry manoeuvre, and the actions of the Franco-Imperial army.[30]

From their former camp the battalions of blue-coated soldiers had at first marched out of sight into the hills, but then they had turned southwards and now emerged into the view of the allies immediately to the west of Reichardtswerben, where they deployed into line between the site of von Seydlitz's charge and no more than a few hundred yards ahead of the advancing Franco-Imperial troops. The Prussian left flank battalions continued to extend the line so that it began to outflank the advancing column. Above the steady lines of blue the standards of the Prussian infantry regiments flapped and fluttered on the breeze. Most were emblazoned with the familiar segmented cross design in blue, black, green, grey, light-blue, purple, gold and red, with some – such as the white flag of the élite 6th Grenadier-Garde Regiment – of a single colour. Every standard bore the distinctive black eagle of Prussia at its centre, and virtually every standard also showed the results of its exposure to shot and shell, and to the ravages of sun, wind and rain on many campaigns and fields of battle.

The ranks of Prussian infantrymen stood facing west, bayonets fixed, muskets ready, and eager to give battle. The French, Austrian and other Imperial troops advanced, but as they came within a couple of hundred paces of the unbroken lines of Prussian infantrymen they wavered. Officers began to lose control as some soldiers halted and then began edging backwards. Some fired their muskets. Others simply turned and ran rather than face the forest of bayonets and the imminent storm of fire that awaited them. A few French regiments continued their advance, bayonets fixed, but they lacked the combat power or determination to carry the attack through, and as the left flank battalions of Prussians opened fire into the flank of the column these regiments also broke amid a shambles of death and destruction. The impact of the sudden and unexpected sight of the disciplined lines of Prussian soldiers had been such that, of Frederick's infantry regiments, only the seven battalions on the left flank had needed to fire at all before the Prussian infantry closed with their foes to complete their destruction with the bayonet. At that moment, von Seydlitz (notwithstanding that he had sustained a bullet wound in the arm) transformed the Franco-Imperial defeat into a rout by launching his reconstituted squadrons into another spirited charge against the retreating infantry, this time from the cavalry's concealed assembly area in Tagewerben. Although some units – such as two regiments of Swiss troops in the service of the French king, Louis XV – attempted to make a stand against the Prussian onslaught, the final outcome was not in doubt as the surviving French, Austrian and other Imperial troops took advantage of the onset of night to make good their escape westwards into the relative safety of the hills and forests of Thuringia. They left about 5,000[31] of their number lying dead or wounded on the battlefield. A further 5,000 who were taken prisoner included eight generals and 300 other officers. In contrast, Frederick's regiments suffered just 548 casualties at Rossbach. The Prussians also captured sixty-seven cannon, a considerable number of regimental standards or colours, and the bulk of the Franco-Imperial army's baggage train.

The clash of arms at Rossbach was a particularly significant event in the story of the German army and of those who served in its ranks. First and foremost it exemplified the success of Frederick's training methods, which had conferred upon the Prussian army a qualitative and morale advantage that was out of all proportion to its theoretical capability based upon numerical size alone. Next, it illustrated the efficacy of the offensive role of the cavalry when used *en masse*, but at the same time carefully controlled. Von Seydlitz had demonstrated the successful employment of cavalry to perfection, and was rewarded with promotion to the rank of lieutenant general and membership of the Order of the Black Eagle. Indeed, had von Seydlitz not prompted Frederick to order the Prussian redeployment at 2.30 that afternoon, it is conceivable that the outcome of the day might have been somewhat different. But while Frederick had been slow to react that day, one of the qualities of a great commander is the ability to select his subordinates well, to accept their advice, and then to trust and delegate responsibility to them without hesitation. So, while many quite rightly attribute the victory at Rossbach to von Seydlitz rather than to Frederick, it is also indisputable that, as commander-in-chief, it was Frederick's decision that enabled von Seydlitz to deliver the Prussian victory at Rossbach.

But there was also a less tangible but more enduring outcome of Rossbach, one that would continue to be an ever-present part of the backdrop to all of Prussia's and Germany's wars during the next two centuries. It was also one that went to the very heart of the ordinary German fighting man's perception of his enemies. In a text penned some time after the battle, that same Captain Gaudi who had provided the vital observation and intelligence reports to Frederick and von Seydlitz noted that:

> [There exists] the natural hate which the ordinary man in Germany, but especially the Magdeburgers, inhabitants of the Mark and the Pomeranians, feels in his heart for all who bear the name of Frenchman. It is a feeling which he imbibes with his mother's milk. Our troops were not content merely to do their duty and advance bravely against the enemy, for it must have struck everyone who observed their conduct that they were fighting out of real hatred. This was particularly noticeable from the behaviour of the cavalrymen as they hewed their way into the enemy infantry, and the officers found great difficulty in bringing the troopers to grant quarter.[32]

Although Frederick in his youth had been educated by a French governess and was still a consummate Francophile, favouring the culture, literature and language of France over that of his own nation, the views now held by large numbers of his subjects were inescapable. In many ways Rossbach simply exposed and reinforced the loathing that the individual German – soldier and civilian alike – held for France and which had originally been established during the Thirty Years War a century before. Such feelings were now reinforced time and again by the ill-disciplined, rapacious behaviour of French troops during each subsequent campaign that involved French troops on German territory, while the violence wrought by the Prussians at Rossbach upon the French troops in particular illustrates all too clearly the existence of attitudes that would shape the perceptions of the ordinary Prussian and German officer and soldier whenever Germany was threatened militarily by France in the future. Rossbach also threw into stark relief the extent to which the once formidable capability of the French army had declined by the second half of the eighteenth century. The destruction of the French at Rossbach further enhanced Frederick's reputation and that of the Prussian army. It also effectively removed the threat posed to Prussia by France for the remainder of the war, while at the same time enabling Frederick to concentrate the army against the Austrians to the east, in Silesia.

The Battle of Leuthen, 5 December 1757
Notwithstanding Frederick's victory at Rossbach, the strength of the coalition forces ranged against Prussia remained formidable, and during

the final weeks of November the Prussians suffered defeats by the Austrians at Schweidnitz and at Breslau (Wroclaw). These successes boosted Austrian confidence and, as Frederick had chosen not to follow the customary practice of eighteenth-century European armies and retire into winter quarters until the spring, early December 1757 found the Prussian army facing a huge Austrian army in the sparsely populated countryside of eastern Silesia. The marshy landscape was covered with a heavy blanket of snow, and much of the water-logged plain was frozen hard by the already bitterly cold temperatures common in the region at that time of year. Despite a significant numerical disadvantage and some of the recent reverses that had been suffered by the Prussians, Frederick was determined to bring the Austrians to battle and thus to settle the matter of Prussia's possession of Silesia once and for all.[33] To achieve this, the Prussians had marched more than 170 miles in just twelve days. As Frederick told his generals at their final meeting prior to the battle on 5 December, 'I shall attack, against all the rules of the art [of war], the army of Prince Charles [of Lorraine], nearly thrice as strong as our own, wher-ever I find it.'[34] Frederick had assessed that the coming battle would be a defining moment for Prussia and despite the obvious risks involved he already knew very well the ground on which it would be fought, having often manoeuvred the army over it prior to the war.

Significantly, he directed that all his troops should be informed of his decision to attack and the rationale for it. Although this instance is often quoted as a prime example of Frederick's style of command, it was certainly not the first such occasion on which his soldiers had similarly been made fully aware of the wider tactical plan, and even of the strategic situation. This readiness to trust his troops with information usually reserved exclusively for the more senior officers – whether imparted via those officers or by addressing his army directly, or even in conversation with individual soldiers – was another mark of Frederick's true qualities of leadership and his genius as a military commander. At this pre-battle conference Frederick also outlined his plan of attack. In a classic manoeuvre, he intended to deceive the Austrians with a feint against their right flank to draw away their reserves. If successful, this would be followed by a speedy redeployment southwards, with the main assault being launched against the Austrian left.

The predominantly Austrian army was commanded jointly by Prince Charles of Lorraine and Field Marshal Daun. It comprised some eighty-four infantry battalions and 144 squadrons of cavalry – a total of as many as 80,000 men – and 210 artillery pieces. Against this army the Prussians could field no more than forty-eight infantry battalions, 128 squadrons of cavalry, and 167 guns, of which seventy-one were large-calibre artillery pieces (removed from the fortress at Glogau (Glogow) and hauled to the battlefield by requisitioned farm horses). At Leuthen, of the 36,000 men available to the Prussians, 24,000 were infantry and 12,000 cavalry.[35]

On 4 December the Austrian commanders established their army on a frontage of some five and a half miles, from Nippern in the north, through Frobelwitz and Leuthen in the centre, to Sagschütz in the south. Leuthen itself was garrisoned in some strength. On the Austrian right, the marshland and bogs immediately to the south of Nippern provided a potential obstacle, while running south to north to the rear of the army the small river of Schweidnitz offered itself as either an obstacle to the offence or a barrier for the defence. However, of all these terrain factors and considerations, Frederick was already very well aware. The security of the left flank was enhanced by the construction and emplacement of a number of obstacles, including the spiked log *abatis* then commonly used to close the breaches in fortifications. The regiments were deployed in two lines, with the cavalry held in reserve at the rear. The Austrian commanders established their principal headquarters in a flour mill at Frobelwitz. Then, throughout that day, the Austrians adjusted and improved their formidable if somewhat extended defensive position. That night the soldiers were able to rest and prepare for the next day's battle.

In the meantime, the Prussians had advanced eastwards along the Breslau road. They had halted well short of Borne on the night of 4 December, where they too readied themselves for the coming battle. The soldiers struck camp before first light and, shortly after 5.00 a.m. on 5 December, four columns of Prussian troops advanced purposefully along and astride the snow-covered highway towards the small village of Borne. At dawn, a damp, cold and heavy mist masked from view both the Prussian advance and the Austrian positions that lay ahead. Frederick commanded the army's strong advance guard in person, and as these ten battalions and the sixty squadrons of cavalry screening them approached Borne they saw a solid line of cavalry pickets strung out across the road, and away to either side of it, with more horsemen just visible through the mist within the village. Although Frederick was unsure whether or not this force was part of the main position, he immediately launched a frontal and flanking attack from the line of march and was rewarded by the speedy capitulation of Borne, which included the capture of some 800 prisoners and the death of General Nostitz, the Austrian detachment commander. The village had been held by no more than five Austrian regiments, whose survivors now withdrew eastwards. At that point the winter sun at last appeared in a steel-grey sky, the morning mist dissipated, and the full extent of the Austrian lines, some two to three miles away, came fully into view. But while the Prussians could see the Austrian dispositions, Frederick's main force was still concealed from the Austrians' view by the ground that sloped down from Borne. Now Frederick moved to implement his plan of attack, and thereafter all went precisely as he had anticipated.

The feint attack, by the Prussian cavalry, went in on the Austrian right, and became in practice a pursuit of the survivors of the assault on Borne – who also conveyed a useful degree of panic to the troops at the main position when they regained its safety. In any event, the Austrian right flank commander, Count Lucchessi, was so convinced that his regiments were now the object of the main Prussian attack that Field Marshal Daun was persuaded to send the reserve cavalry and some squadrons from the left flank (where General Nadasti commanded) to strengthen the right. In reality, the extensive area of marshland south of Nippern would certainly have inhibited a successful turning of the Austrian right flank by the Prussians, as Frederick well knew. But with the premature redeployment of the Austrian reserve, the battle was developing exactly as the Prussian ruler had planned. Without halting, the four advancing columns of infantry and cavalry formed into two columns and turned right, still out of sight of the Austrians, to march southwards across their enemy's entire front. In the meantime, the much smaller Prussian force to the north maintained its pressure upon the Austrian right, though without seeking to breach the defensive line. The Prussian columns advanced with General Wedel's advance guard to the fore, with General Retzow's main force of infantry on the left, and General Ziethen's cavalry (forty-three squadrons) together with Prince Maurice of Dessau's infantry (six battalions) on the right.[36] A further twenty-five squadrons of cavalry commanded by Prince Eugene of Württemberg were held to the rear. Throughout the deployment, squadrons of hussars screened the move and provided its flank security.

Frederick's tactics of choice were well known by friend and foe alike by 1757. Nevertheless, Prince Charles and Field Marshal Daun had deployed their troops in anticipation of a frontal assault by the Prussians, and when the only significant battlefield activity was apparently that on the right flank, still with no sign of the Prussian main body, they thought that Frederick had assessed the Austrian position as being too strong, and had decided to avoid a confrontation that day. Then, at mid-morning, reports of large numbers of blue-coated soldiers moving in columns between Lobetnitz and Sagschütz suddenly began arriving at the

Austrian headquarters. Squadrons of extravagantly uniformed hussars moved ahead of and to the flanks of these columns. The Austrians had been outsmarted, and now General Nadasti desperately requested the return of his troops from the right flank, with all other available support.

The blow fell first upon Sagschütz, soon after midday. There, after General Wedel's advance guard at the head of the columns had become directly engaged with the Austrian defenders of the village, some six battalions supported by a battery of six guns stormed the small group of houses, huts and farm buildings. The Austrian position fell within an hour. General Nadasti launched a counter-attack against the leading forty-three squadrons of Prussian cavalry, but it was too late. General Ziethen's hussars dealt first with this attack and then regrouped to the rear of their accompanying infantry before proceeding to counter-charge and pursue the stream of Austrian soldiers who had survived both the cavalry attack

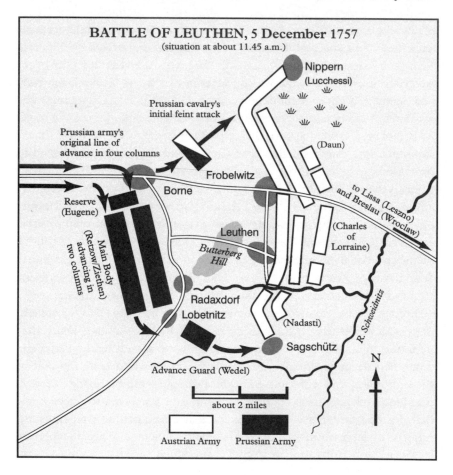

BATTLE OF LEUTHEN, 5 December 1757
(situation at about 11.45 a.m.)

Nippern
(Lucchessi)

Prussian cavalry's
initial feint attack

Prussian army's
original line of
advance in four columns

(Daun)

Frobelwitz

Borne

to Lissa (Leszno)
and Breslau (Wroclaw)

Reserve
(Eugene)

Leuthen

(Charles
of
Lorraine)

Butterberg
Hill

Main Body
(Retzow/Ziethen)
advancing in
two columns

Radaxdorf
Lobetnitz

(Nadasti)

R. Schweidnitz

Sagschütz

N

Advance Guard (Wedel)

about 2 miles

Austrian Army   Prussian Army

and that at Sagschütz as they scrambled northwards in search of safety. Frederick's main body of infantry and artillery followed Ziethen's cavalrymen, as the Austrian left began to collapse. It was now mid-afternoon.

The focus of the battle moved to Leuthen itself, where the garrison had been reinforced by troops hastily recalled from the right flank by Prince Charles. The village was literally crammed with soldiers and equipment, and virtually every Prussian shell (the case shot especially) that landed therein caused numerous casualties. Buildings collapsed and burned, charges of gunpowder exploded, hasty barricades were constructed, confusion reigned, and the dead and dying lay everywhere. The Austrians fought stubbornly and resisted all attempts to overcome them, until the Prussian guard battalions finally stormed the village. However, the price of this success was clear to see by the numbers of Prussian soldiers lying inert upon the snow-covered fields about Leuthen. The fight for this key village allowed Charles and Daun time to prepare their troops to meet the further advance they now knew was inevitable, and they had adjusted their line to face south and thus bar the way to Frederick with infantry and artillery. A co-ordinated attack by Retzov's infantry and Driesen's cavalry was beaten back by an Austrian battery sited on the high ground to the east of Leuthen. Frederick's response was to move his own artillery – including ten of his heavy guns – on the Butterberg Hill,[37] from which the Prussian counter-battery fire effectively neutralized the Austrian battery that was impeding the Prussian advance. As soon as this was suppressed, the Prussians resumed their assault northwards against what had been the original centre of the enemy army. This close co-ordination of infantry, artillery and cavalry by the Prussians was a particular feature of Leuthen, and would also emerge as a key aspect of German tactical doctrine in later times.

Dusk was fast approaching as the wintry sun dipped towards the horizon, and at about 4.00 p.m. the Austrian right flank commander, Lucchessi, prepared to launch a final counter-attack by his cavalry in an attempt to retrieve the day. But (much as Seydlitz had done a month earlier at Tagewerben on the battlefield of Rossbach), Driesen had held some forty squadrons of cavalry in reserve for just this eventuality and had used the buildings of Radaxdorf to conceal this force. When the Austrians were on the verge of attacking they were struck by the full force of forty squadrons of Prussian cavalry which debouched from behind the Butterberg and fell upon them – thirty frontally, five against the flank and five against the rear. Lucchessi was killed during the mêlée. At the same time the Prussian infantry attacked the remaining Austrian infantry and artillery from multiple directions. The rout was complete and the pursuit towards Breslau began, although as night fell Frederick halted his hussars at Lissa (Leszno), just a few miles east of Leuthen. By then the battle on 5 December had cost Frederick some 6,000 soldiers killed and wounded.[38]

Next day the Prussians consolidated and rested, and then spent three days dealing with individual stragglers or groups of Austrian soldiers that had remained in the area. Frederick spent the night of 5 December in Schloss Lissa, where the unexpected arrival of the Prussian ruler and his troops caused an understandable amount of consternation to the Austrian cavalry officers who were still in quarters there, blissfully unaware of their army's catastrophic defeat at Leuthen.[39] The Austrian casualties numbered in excess of 10,000, with a further 21,000 men taken prisoner, together with the loss of 116 guns, 4,000 carts and wagons and fifty-one regimental colours or standards. Two thousand more prisoners were taken on 9 December.[40] The future emperor of France, Napoleon I, later described Leuthen as 'a masterpiece of movements, manoeuvres, and resolution ... Alone, it is sufficient to immortalize Frederick and place him in the rank of the greatest generals.'

The strategic success achieved at Leuthen was confirmed by the capitulation of Breslau on 19 December, this important town having previously been captured by the Austrians from General Bevern just a month earlier, on 22 November.[41] At Breslau, the Prussians captured a further 17,000 men and eighty-one guns. The fall of Breslau also ultimately guaranteed Prussian possession of Silesia. But the Seven Years War continued for a further five years, during which Prussia suffered defeats at Hochkirch (where 37,000 Prussians opposed 90,000 Austrians) on 14 October 1758, and then in 1759 at Kunersdorf (with 26,000 men against 70,000 Russians) on 12 August, and at Maxen on 21 November. Also, Berlin was temporarily occupied by Russian forces in 1759. However, these reverses were offset by Prussian victories at Zorndorf (where the Prussians sustained 35 per cent casualties against the Russian losses of 53 per cent) on 25 August 1758, and then in 1760 against the Austrians at Liegnitz – where Frederick fielded just 30,000 men against 90,000 Austrian soldiers – on 15 August, and subsequently at Torgau (but with losses of 13,000 compared to 11,000 Austrian casualties) on 3 November.[42] At last, in 1762 Russia withdrew from the coalition against Prussia, which precipitated the end of the war, and at the Peace of Hubertusberg in February 1763 Prussia's retention of Silesia was confirmed and regularized. The following year, Catherine the Great of Russia concluded an eight-year alliance with Prussia. Finally, in 1772, in concert with Austria and Russia, Frederick agreed to a partition of Poland by which he gained West Prussia, which finally enabled East Prussia, Brandenburg and Pomerania to be connected, creating a single Prussian state in all but name.

During much of Frederick the Great's reign, Prussia was in a constant state of war, with the forces of formidable coalitions of the major European powers often threatening the kingdom on all sides. Several times during the course of the Seven Years War foreign armies entered Prussian territory and fought major battles thereon. As the war continued, the casualties sustained by the Prussian army meant that Frederick was increasingly constrained to employ non-Prussian troops, although the vital funding support he enjoyed from England meant that he was able to pay for such troops, together with the equipment needed by the army as a whole. But this dilution of the Prussian military element in the army ran contrary to the work carried out by Frederick's predecessors following their experience of mercenary bands during the Thirty Years War. Even the eventual and unavoidable adoption of a more formalized system of conscription in Prussian territory from 1772 (many would say that such a system already existed in all but name!) could not obviate the need for the army to take significant numbers of foreigners into its ranks in order to offset its losses in combat.

This also coloured Frederick's view of the quality and motivation of the army, as his best Prussian troops became casualties over time and were then necessarily replaced by less well-trained recruits and by what was all too often the poor-quality manpower provided by (for example) the independent or 'Free Towns', the minor German principalities, and from elsewhere within the rapidly decaying Holy Roman Empire. In turn, this led to a further hardening of the system of drill and discipline in order to turn this human raw material into effective soldiers as expeditiously as possible, so as to maintain a qualitative military superiority that would compensate for and negate the enemy's quantitative superiority. In parallel with this, some of his contemporaries noted that Frederick's own attitude to the ordinary soldiers had hardened and that he was perhaps less trusting of these men than had been the case in the early years of his rule. Perhaps the diametrically opposed views held by Frederick *vis-à-vis* the vast majority of his ordinary subjects on the wider merits of France also contributed to this perception.

In fact, Frederick had little need for concern. There is ample evidence that the ordinary soldiers, Prussian and non-Prussian alike, continued to revere Frederick as an outstanding military commander and a firm but just ruler – and as the charismatic father of a Prussian nation which had been forged in the fire and carnage of countless battles to emerge at last as the pre-eminent military power in continental Europe. The civilian population similarly revered a man who had dedicated himself to establishing for Prussia an efficient administration, a sound legal system, an enviable education system, a competitive economy and a burgeoning cultural environment. He had also settled and promoted the agricultural development of much of Prussia's eastern territory.

If his confidence in the motivation of his soldiers had waned during the years of conflict, Frederick's reliance upon the nobility who continued to be his principal source of officers had become much greater. Once again, as a steady succession of his trusted generals succumbed to death or wounds on the battlefield, Frederick sought to replace them with men whose loyalty and dedication he could (in his own mind) be absolutely certain were entirely above reproach because they came from the same noble stock as those who had served and fallen, and therefore the natural code of honour tied inextricably to their birthright meant that they could not be otherwise. Indeed, although he had, of necessity, employed increasing numbers of officers of non-noble birth during the Seven Years War, once that conflict ended he set about replacing them with officers from the noble houses not only of Prussia but also from other imperial and European countries. Although the Prussian officer's life was physically hard, demanding and no sinecure, it was a life of genuine status and privilege; so much so that on several occasions Frederick found it necessary to rein back (though with only limited success) the escalating power within the wider Prussian society of the officer class he had – both deliberately and of necessity – created and fostered.

Despite his enormous contribution to the development of Prussia and its army, Frederick was none the less a man of his time, and he therefore accepted the eighteenth century's preoccupation with noble birth and that the concept of 'honour' could only be properly understood and applied by those of noble birth or who had been ennobled. This particular feature of his control and management of the army would have a resonance and impact upon the nature of the German army – its officer corps in particular – long after his death.[43] Also of course the members of the Prussian nobility, who were generally French-speaking, were much more receptive to French culture than the non French-speaking commoners, and this had further strengthened the personal bond between Frederick and his noble-born officers.

Frederick the Great died wearing his blue soldier's coat and uniform, sitting in his favourite chair at the beautiful Sanssouci Palace in Potsdam, on 17 August 1786. By then he was a frail, bent and elderly man, although his intellect, awareness and mind were as keen as ever and his eyes remained bright and all-seeing right to the end. During his final years he had worked tirelessly in his extensive library, with the aim (some said) of leaving to posterity a literary rather than a military memory of his rule. Certainly this represented in many ways a return to the way in which he had, in his youth, hoped that his reign might be spent, and with time he had come to acknowledge quite openly that resort to armed conflict was in many ways the least imaginative way to resolve international disputes.

His legacy to Frederick William II, the son of his brother August William, was a well-established but war-weary state and the best disciplined force of fighting men on the Continent. By developing, refining, hardening in combat, and concluding what may quite correctly be termed the first phase of the development of German militarism, Frederick the Great had also bequeathed to the wider world a potentially more sinister military culture and an even more significant war machine in embryo. His death marked not only the end of Prussia's meteoric rise on the international stage, but also heralded a period of complacency and stagnation for the army – a period during which its fortunes would very far decline from the triumph and glory of Rossbach and Leuthen into ignominy and defeat at the hands of the charismatic new leader of the despised French nation, Napoleon Bonaparte.

6

Complacency, Stagnation and Defeat
1786–1806

FREDERICK THE GREAT'S legacy to his nephew was both impressive and daunting. The standing army of more than 200,000 men was probably the most professional army in Europe at the time, and it was already the model for several other major European states. Prussian drill, tactics, uniforms and discipline were all copied to varying degrees, and Frederick's writings on strategy, training and all matters military were assiduously studied and – as far as possible – emulated by others. Foremost among Prussia's military imitators were Russia and France, the latter having suffered significantly at the hands of the Prussian army in past conflicts. Frederick's legacy to Prussia was also one of national pride and self-esteem at a level unprecedented in the nation's history, and such unifying attributes were now especially timely, as the territories and populations of West Prussia and Silesia had been taken fully into the Prussian fold during his reign.

Despite all that had been achieved by Frederick personally and by his army, Prussia's recent military successes had bred increasing complacency within a state that had for too long been at war and which now looked forward to a period of security, peace and prosperity. The army's proven tactics and well-established procedures actually began to stifle innovative thought, while the core elements of Prussian militarism – drill, discipline and total obedience – continued to be regarded as infallible panaceas that would guarantee Prussian military success in the future. So it was that, although its size had continued to increase throughout the eighteenth century (reaching a peak of more than 250,000 men by 1797, although very many of these soldiers were from other German states), its professionalism and effectiveness steadily declined after 1786. This decline was set against a background of increasing political awareness and liberalism that characterized the final decades of the eighteenth century in much of Europe.

Frederick William II assumed the Prussian throne on 17 August 1786, at the start of what would prove to be an inauspicious reign, and one that reflected many of the less attractive mores of European society at the time. He had neither the energy nor the practical aptitude to maintain or adapt and modernize the state and the army. Although he did achieve a few military and administrative reforms, his moral weaknesses also left him vulnerable to the inflexible and reactionary attitudes of the Prussian nobility in whom the real control of the army firmly resided. Such genuine enthusiasm as he did display was reserved primarily for creative and artistic pursuits, notably music and architecture, together with a succession of mistresses and the advancement of his personal favourites at court. The king was also strongly attracted to spiritualism, which much influenced his approach to the business of politics and government, and diminished his ability to implement any really substantive progress or reforms in those areas. Given a leader who was so different from his predecessors, it is perhaps small wonder that Prussia's military and international decline accelerated rapidly during Frederick William's eleven-year reign.

He did attempt to modernize some aspects of the army and, more importantly, relate it to the wider needs and circumstances of the Prussian state. In recognition of the increasing need for tactical flexibility and the mobility of troops on the battlefield, an increased emphasis on the light infantry role was demonstrated by the conversion of a number of fusilier units to light infantry. Similarly, Field Marshal von Mollendorf was required to head a reform commission in 1788, charged with reviewing the existing system of army recruitment *vis-à-vis* the competing needs of the wider state economy. Tellingly, the commission's findings were not implemented – foremost among which had been the need for the state to unfetter itself from its reliance on foreign troops, by introducing a system of universal conscripted service throughout Prussia. Of course, this concept was by no means new, and the Saxon prince Marshal Saxe had advocated it during the first part of the eighteenth century; as had the Prussian writer Justus Möser in 1770, who emphasized the honour, pride and self-respect that the profession of arms inculcated in individuals and (by implication) in the nation as a whole. The seeds had been sown, nevertheless, and the concept of universal military service would emerge again less than fifty years later, but with a much more positive outcome on that occasion.

Accordingly, as the flames of revolution blazed across neighbouring France from 1789, the Prussian army remained essentially unchanged from the force that Frederick the Great had commanded during the Seven Years War. Consequently, as Frederick William and the other European monarchs debated their response to the threat posed to their own states by the principles of *Liberté, Egalité, Fraternité* now emanating from Paris, the Prussian army was still mainly officered by a nobility that drew its confidence and security from its memories of the historic victories of Frederick the Great. Meanwhile, the fighting men under their command were by and large still recruited from Prussia's rural peasantry, alongside whom there were still serving large numbers of non-Prussian foreign mercenaries; by 1792 50 per cent of the Prussian army was comprised of foreigners, including many Poles. Even very modest attempts to introduce a measure of equality into the army – such as junior officers abandoning their horses in order to march with the soldiers they commanded – were stonewalled by an officer corps that saw such revolutionary ideas as 'degrading' and a major attack upon their status of privilege and superiority.[44] It was inconceivable that France's revolutionary army – surely an 'army' in name only – would be any match for a 'real' army such as that fielded by Prussia, or indeed by any of the other Germanic states? But at Valmy on 20 September 1792, the true mettle of France's new revolutionary army was revealed at last, together with the true extent of the military decline of Prussia and that of its allies Austria and Saxony.

With a view to restoring the monarchy in France, and under no little pressure from numbers of French aristocrats and other royalist *émigrés* who had been forced to flee the country as the revolution gained pace, Prussia and Austria had signed the Treaty of Berlin on 7 February 1792. This coalition was designed to reimpose the absolute authority of the French monarchy by force of arms, and France declared war upon it on 20 April. Some of the early clashes were unremarkable and often resulted in the French troops fleeing the field in disarray. But then, on 19 July the Duke of Brunswick led an allied army of 42,000 Prussians, 29,000 Austrians and 6,000 Hessians across the Rhine, with a view to raising the French populace against the revolution and restoring Louis XVI to power. In fact, this Austro-Prussian invasion inflamed the Paris mob, which promptly stormed the Tuileries and imprisoned the king and the royal family in the Conciergerie gaol. In the meantime, the Duke of Brunswick's army advanced steadily towards Paris. *En route* they captured first Longwy and then Verdun, these battlefield successes subsequently prompting the murder of between 1,100 and 1,400 of the aristocrats, members of the Swiss Guard, and other political prisoners held by the revolutionary authorities in Paris! The army of (predominantly) Prussian and Austrian soldiers continued its march towards the capital, but then two French armies – Kellerman's Army of the Centre and Dumouriez's Army of the North – intercepted the invaders at the small village of Valmy, some thirty miles to the west of Verdun.

The clash (to call it a battle would be to overrate it) at Valmy began when, despite the opposing advice of the other French commanders, Dumouriez decided to deploy his army on the hills that encircled and overlooked the village, where he resolved to stand firm against the expected Prussian onslaught. The French at Valmy numbered about 36,000, while the total number of Prussians actually engaged was about 34,000, the latter supported by some fifty-eight guns. Far from being a 'revolutionary army', the French at Valmy had only two battalions of revo lutionary army volunteers, the remainder of the force comprised of regiments of the line of the old French army. In addition, the forty cannon supporting the French were part of the recently reorganized and updated French artillery, and this would prove to be decisive.

The morning of 20 September dawned damp and foggy, and the Duke of Brunswick, no doubt emboldened by his successes at Longwy and Verdun, had advanced directly towards the French positions without pause, in confident anticipation of yet another rapid French retreat in the face of the Prussian bayonets. But, as the fog lifted, Dumouriez's regiments still stood firm, and at midday a furious artillery duel began. The range was about 1,350 yards and over the next two hours each side fired about 20,000 rounds of shot and shell. At 2 p.m. the Prussians advanced, in the expectation that their artillery fire would have all but broken the French. However, the reverse happened when Kellerman's own artillery stopped the Prussians in their tracks. Subsequent Prussian attempts to launch a further attack were also thwarted by the French artillery and it is noteworthy that this was virtually the first occasion on which Prussian soldiers had come under sustained and accurate artillery fire since the days of Frederick the Great. The Duke of Brunswick had seen that (apart from two French regiments which had indeed broken under the Prussian cannonade) the French infantry were still standing firm and that their cavalry was ready for offensive action. Although the French had lost about 300 men and the Prussians only 185, he decided that his force could not advance further, and as rain deluged the scene, turning much of the battle-field into a quagmire, he ordered a withdrawal back to the frontier. The artillery ceased firing at 4 p.m., and as night began to fall the wet and now dispirited soldiers, many of them suffering severely from the effects of dysentery, began the long march back eastwards. Had Dumouriez launched an attack at that moment, he might well have destroyed the Prussian force, but he failed to exploit his advantage and instead moved his army north, in order to attack the Austrian Netherlands.[45]

Although more of a skirmish than a full-scale battle, the clash at Valmy none the less shattered the myth of Prussian military invincibility that had been achieved during the time of Frederick the Great and which had been so assiduously cultivated since then. It also tarnished the reputation of the

Duke of Brunswick, a general who had long been regarded as being the Austro-Prussian alliance's most proficient military commander. Subsequently, the received wisdom within the Prussian officer corps and government concerning the events at Valmy was that they had been occasioned by a failure of command rather than by any fundamental deficiencies of the Prussian army – a politically convenient but patently unfair, incorrect and simplistic conclusion. Finally, Valmy had even wider repercussions within France, for on the following day the French monarchy was abolished, France was proclaimed a republic, and the fate of Louis XVI, Marie-Antoinette, and many hundreds of aristocrats and other so-called enemies of the revolution, was sealed.

Valmy should have provided Prussia in particular with a timely wake-up call concerning its declining military capability, but its real impact was not accorded the wider significance it deserved. Meanwhile, the strategically indecisive holding campaign conducted against the French in the Rhine valley during 1793 (which was followed by a peace treaty between Prussia and France the following year), together with Berlin's preoccupation with suppressing resistance to its partition of Poland, served to mask and divert criticism of the events of 20 September 1792. Indeed, the Prussian army's campaign against resistance in Poland, while successful, was hardly glorious and involved significantly more men and *matériel* than should reasonably have been required for the task. This bitter and little-known campaign also resulted in the death through disease of no less than one-third of the troops fielded by Prussia. This was stark testimony to the deficiencies in the preventive health measures of the army sent to Poland, and by extension it was a telling indictment of the careless management of the army's most valuable asset – its soldiers – by the Prussian government and the high command.

On 16 November 1797, at the palace in Potsdam, Frederick William II died. His had been a short and in many ways regressive reign, certainly where the army was concerned. He was succeeded by his son, now Frederick William III, who would reign for some forty-three years. For the Prussian army, the new king's ascension heralded a period of great turbulence and change. It would also involve further catastrophic defeats before Prussia eventually emerged victorious. It would see the forces of stagnation and reaction pitted against those of enlightenment and reform. It would be a period of war, peace and revolution. But, most importantly, it was during these years that the foundations of what might be termed the 'golden age of Prussian militarism' were laid by a whole new generation of Prussian military thinkers and commanders.

✠✠✠✠✠✠✠✠✠✠✠✠✠

For the new French republic, Valmy had been but a beginning, and with Napoleon Bonaparte (who was proclaimed as the French emperor in 1804) at its head, the reinvigorated and reorganized armies of France moved from victory to victory. On 2 December 1805 Russia and Austria were soundly defeated at Austerlitz, some seventy miles to the north of Vienna, after which Napoleon sought to prevent any further German resistance by establishing the Confederation of the Rhine, with just thirty German states all now dominated by France. Austria was neutralized and Russian forces had withdrawn beyond the River Vistula. Prussia had dissociated itself from the Austro-Russian alliance that had preceded Austerlitz and so had fortuitously avoided involvement in what was one of Napoleon's greatest and most important victories. But it had been induced to give up some of its territory in the south and west, in return for which it was permitted to occupy Hanover (which in turn antagonized Great Britain and exacerbated Prussia's isolation). Meanwhile, some southern German states, such as Bavaria, were much more content than others to support and directly participate in furthering French military ambitions. The wider dilution of the German national identity and independence eventually rebounded upon France, as it provided the Germans with the very cause and reason to confront France that Napoleon had intended to pre-empt. Only its alliance with Saxony and the continued support it enjoyed from Russia meant that Prussia maintained much of its original identity, and less than a year after Austerlitz it at last put both this and the capability of the Prussian army to the test against the conqueror of Europe.

In the late summer of 1806 Frederick William decided that the extent of French domination had become intolerable, a situation aggravated by further difficulties over the issue of Hanover and the threat posed by the sizeable (some 160,000 men) French military presence on the Rhine, where most of the army had remained after the successful campaign of the *Grande Armée* in 1805. During August and September Prussian troops mobilized and moved slowly southwards. Prussia had already issued an ultimatum to France, pursuant to a withdrawal of its troops from German territory in the Rhine region and to securing Prussian control of Hanover, and throughout September and early October Frederick William and his government hoped and (naïvely) anticipated that the French would negotiate a compromise. Not surprisingly, Napoleon chose to fight, and on 14 October the French – by then about 186,000 strong – brought the Prussian armies to battle at Jena–Auerstadt. *En route*, several skirmishes between the two armies had already resulted in Prussian losses of more than 300 casualties, 500 prisoners and much weaponry and equipment, including a pontoon bridging train. In one such fight, at Saalfeld, the Prussians also lost Prince Louis Ferdinand of Prussia, one of their youngest and most proficient division commanders, who was killed while his division was securing the south-west approaches to the Prussian main concentration area.

Meanwhile, at the head of an army of about 200,000 men, Frederick William had advanced to meet the French during the days prior to the 14th. In reality, the unavoidable dispersal of numerous detachments of troops to secure various towns, forts and other locations meant that the Prussians had not many more than 120,000 soldiers available for offensive

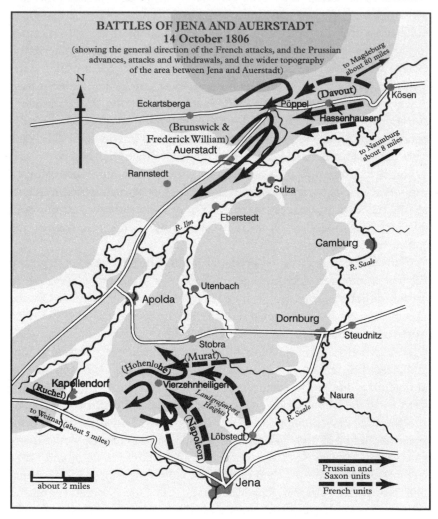

action. Of these, about 18,000 comprised the Saxon contingent, within which the soldiers' low morale and lack of enthusiasm for the campaign were daily becoming ever more evident. Frederick William's chief military advisers were the 82-year-old Field Marshal von Mollendorf, the Duke of Brunswick, and the 60-year-old Prince Frederick Louis von Hohenlohe. The conservative Brunswick's ideas of the most suitable strategy to employ were very different from those put forward by the much more competent von Hohenlohe, and Frederick William spent much time trying to ameliorate the disputes between his commanders. The Prussian military cabinet, comprising the administrative heads of all the arms and services and their supporting secretariats, accompanied the oversized and barely operational Prussian headquarters.

On 13 October the French reached Jena in the Thüringer Wald and identified what they believed (erroneously, because of dense fog) to be the entire Prussian army deployed on the heights to their north. In fact, the main Prussian force under the Duke of Brunswick was at Auerstadt,[46] about twenty miles away to the north. There also was Frederick William. In any event, the next morning Napoleon attacked what was in fact only the best part of two corps of the Prussian army and some Saxon units, commanded overall by von Hohenlohe and numbering some 30,000 men in all. Realizing that he had most of the French army attacking him, von Hohenlohe sent for General Rüchel's corps of between 15,000 and 20,000 men to assist him. They arrived too late and were then mishandled by their commander, who was killed that day. Thus the outcome of the battle was hardly in doubt. Despite the bravery of many of the individual Prussian soldiers and regimental officers, together with the good leadership displayed by many junior commanders, the Prussians were progressively overwhelmed. In some cases bravery and inflexibility were inseparable, such as at the strategically vital French-held village of Vierzehnheiligen, where an attacking force of many thousands of Prussian infantrymen stood in the open and doggedly exchanged fire with the well-protected French riflemen for some two hours, and were systematically decimated by the continuous storm of French counter-fire. The Prussians could not break into Vierzehnheiligen and the matter was finally decided by an irresistible charge of Marshal Murat's 15,000 heavy cavalrymen, which broke the Prussian line and precipitated a general retreat.

By noon, the arrival of yet more French troops meant that Napoleon had more than 80,000 men against the remnant of von Hohenlohe's 30,000, and the Prussian force had all but disintegrated. By 1 p.m. the French had begun a general advance. It was then that Rüchel's troops had arrived on the scene. Had they been deployed to cover the withdrawal of von Hohenlohe's force, this might have reduced the Prussian losses; but they were committed to attack the advancing French, and so were quickly turned and forced to join the retreat towards Weimar. Meanwhile, the French dragoons and cuirassiers pursued the fleeing Prussian and Saxon soldiers and cut them down mercilessly, offering no quarter and revelling in the opportunity to inflict a belated if savage revenge for the victories of Frederick the Great against France up to a century before, as well as redressing what France now viewed as the unjustified arrogance and military pretensions of its Germanic neighbour.

Although the battle of Jena is better known than that which took place at Auerstadt on the same day, the latter was in some ways the more important. There, as many as 60,000[47] Prussians under the command of the Duke of Brunswick were attacked by 28,750 French soldiers of Marshal Davout's corps, who were in the process of trying to outflank what they then believed was the main Prussian army at Jena. Once again, fog masked the situation at 7 a.m. when battle was joined at the village of Hassenhausen. Both sides tried to envelop the other and several major infantry assaults were launched by the Prussians. Four full-scale charges by the Prussian cavalry under General Gebhard Leberecht von Blücher, Prince of Wahlstadt, failed to break the French infantry squares. Despite their lesser numbers, the French held firm. Frederick William had his horse killed beneath him. Field Marshal von Mollendorf was unhorsed and later captured, and a number of other senior Prussian commanders were killed or wounded. At mid-morning, the Duke of Brunswick fell shot through the head and, with the high command disrupted (the chief of staff, von Scharnhorst, had already been dispatched to command the left flank, and Frederick William – nominally the Prussian commander-in-chief – lacked any useful military experience), the Prussian action soon dissolved into a number of separate, uncoordinated battles. Although the two Prussian reserve divisions remained uncommitted, the arrival of another French division at about 10.30 a.m. effectively halted further Prussian attacks. At this point the king, after consultation with his surviving military advisers, decided not to continue the fight. A notable dissenter from this course was von Blücher, who counselled that the two reserve divisions still provided a means to attack and win the day. However, the die was cast, and the Prussians began to disengage.

Although he finally took 3,000 prisoners and 115 artillery pieces at Auerstadt, Davout's corps was too exhausted to pursue the Prussians, who withdrew in reasonably good order despite their losses of 10,000 men killed or wounded. However, Frederick William and those of his senior commanders who were still left then unknowingly became the architects of their own rout, for instead of heading north they directed the army southwards to rejoin von Hohenlohe, entirely unaware of the disaster which had occurred at Jena. That night, the news reached the king and the direction of the army's retreat was changed twice more. Order and counter-order were swiftly and inevitably followed by disorder, as the chaotic retreat from Jena started to become intermingled with that from Auerstadt. By dawn on 15 October the Prussian field army had lost any remaining claim to be a cohesive fighting force. The two battles had cost the Prussians 25,000 men killed or wounded and a further 25,000 taken prisoner, plus more than 200 guns. Just three weeks after the French had crossed the border from France, Napoleon and his victorious troops entered Berlin.

Frederick William and his surviving Prussian units retreated to East Prussia and into Silesia. Some regiments and divisions still remained viable and moved in good order, their earlier defeat notwithstanding. One such was the division commanded by General von Blücher, which had in fact acquitted itself well at Jena–Auerstadt. In East Prussia a Russian army joined the Prussians, although in the short campaign that followed France was again triumphant. With Blücher's surrender at Ratekau, near Lübeck on the Baltic coast, a little more than three weeks after Jena, all further Prussian resistance west of the Rivers Oder and Neisse ceased. However, some forces fought on in East Prussia and Silesia, demonstrating that Prussian martial prowess had not been entirely crushed. In 1807, during the French siege of the Baltic port of Kolberg, one Count Augustus Wilhelm Neithardt von Gneisenau (then a major) distinguished himself as the garrison's commander, and Kolberg became a national symbol of Prussian resistance to Napoleon. So also did Second Lieutenant Ferdinand von Schill of the 2nd Regiment of Brandenburg Hussars, who preceded Gneisenau as the commander at Kolberg and who subsequently led a military uprising against the French in 1809.[48]

On 8 February 1807, at Preussiche-Eylau, one Gerhard Johann David von Scharnhorst was serving as chief of staff to the Prussian corps then operating in the bitter cold amid the winter snows of East Prussia. As such, he was largely responsible for the timely deployment of Prussian troops to avert what would otherwise have almost certainly been a Russian defeat at French hands. The names of Blücher, Scharnhorst and Gneisenau would soon move into prominence once again. But Prussia's strategic capability had been broken at Jena–Auerstadt, and by the summer of 1807 the campaign had drawn to its all too inevitable conclusion.

✠✠✠✠✠✠✠✠✠✠✠✠

On 25 July 1807 Prussia signed the Peace of Tilsit with France, by which it lost all of its possessions in Poland and all of its territory to the west of the River Elbe. In addition, Prussia was required to pay a prodigiously large financial indemnity to France. But perhaps the most humiliating blow for the Prussian military was Napoleon's order that the Prussian memorial to its great victory over France at Rossbach in 1757 be removed from the field in which it had stood for more than a century and taken to France. Later, Frederick the Great's sword, orders and decorations were removed from his coffin in the garrison church at Potsdam and sent to France.

For Prussia, Jena–Auerstadt and the events that followed during the next eight months were at the same time both disastrous and historic. The sheer extent of the Prussian defeats demonstrated beyond any possible doubt that the glory days and military methodology of Frederick the Great were indeed history and that the hard-won military reputation of former times was largely irrelevant in the new century. Indeed, Prussia's military decline and its ill-judged decision to confront Napoleon's armies in 1806 had led to two routs on such a scale that they effectively removed the country from the war against Napoleon from mid-1807 until 1813. But the exposure of this situation at last opened the way for some of the analysis and reforms that should have been implemented many years earlier, and as a matter of great urgency during the years after Valmy.

But as Frederick William's somewhat uncertain reign continued, other names were now emerging to gain prominence upon Prussia's military stage. Among these were several men who would eventually become well known internationally – for better or worse, depending upon the perspective of the country in question. Foremost were Blücher, Yorck, Clausewitz, Scharnhorst, Gneisenau, Grolman and Müffling, all of whose work would eventually enable their successors – von Roon, von Moltke and von Bismarck – to develop the army into a formidable and thoroughly modern war machine that would subsequently carry Prussia and the other Germanic states forward to achieve unification in 1871. Such historic goals are rarely achieved easily. The story of Prussia and its army during the first decade of Frederick William's rule had already proved the truth of this, not least because the new king himself was by no means amenable to change, and on matters military he acceded all too readily to the arguments of an officer corps that was still characterized by reactionary views and dominated by the Prussian nobility.

However, the events of 1806 and 1807 had provided a catalyst for change and made this inevitable. While it is a matter of record that Fred-

✠ ✠ ✠ ✠ ✠ ✠ ✠ ✠ ✠ ✠ ✠ ✠ ✠

erick William III would eventually accept, and agree to some important army reforms, it is also true that – despite his less than happy experience as a military commander – in most cases he did so with much reluctance. Such sanctions were generally the unavoidable consequences of Prussian military defeats, or were necessitated by wider international events which demanded an appropriate response from the Prussian king, rather than proactive initiatives by the monarch. Despite this, and although Frederick William himself was by no means a great king or military leader, he led Prussia through a period during which the nation and its army endured and experienced great military events, including the final defeat of Napoleon in 1815. Therefore, even though it was largely by default and by association rather than by the direct involvement of the king, the reign of Frederick William III has a particular significance in the wider story of the development of the Prussian army as it moved slowly but inexorably towards what would become its 'golden age'.

7

Renaissance, Revolution and Reform, 1807–1857

AFTER THE PEACE OF TILSIT, the subsequent development of the Prussian army followed two complementary but distinctly separate courses. First, there was its continual involvement in the international conflict with Napoleon, and later with the events that followed the eventual defeat of France. Secondly, however, there was wide-ranging and intense activity to study, review, reorganize and fundamentally reform the army. Although it attracted less visibility (while also engendering a fair amount of reactionary resistance) it was this forward-looking activity that eventually created the war-winning Prussian armies of 1864, 1866 and 1871, as well as having a considerable influence upon aspects of the German army during the first half of the twentieth century.

The disasters at Jena–Auerstadt had resonated deeply with Frederick William and, despite France's weakened position with its Peninsula campaign in Spain and Portugal and an Austrian invasion of Bavaria in 1809, the king refused to move against Napoleon again. Where Prussian resistance to the French did occur, it was generally limited to isolated and unauthorized ventures, such as that by Major von Schill in Brandenburg and at Stralsund. Without Prussian military support, the Austrians were duly defeated at Ratisbon and Wagram in the spring and summer of 1809. But Frederick William's enforced accommodation with Paris went even further when, in 1812, about 180,000 troops from a number of German states – notably Bavaria, Westphalia, Kleve-Berg and Saxony – made up a sizeable contingent of the 600,000-strong *Grande Armée* when Napoleon invaded Russia. Not surprisingly, this overt Germanic support for the traditional enemy, France, attracted much criticism within Prussia.

Matters came to a head when Napoleon's ill-fated venture failed, and the Prussian corps, which had been largely employed in operations along the Baltic coast, agreed a truce with the Russians at Riga which effectively gave the corps neutral status. The Prussian corps was by then commanded by General Yorck von Wartenburg, an experienced soldier who had commanded the rearguard during the retreat from Jena–Auerstadt. Von Yorck's decision is of particular interest for four reasons. First, it was prompted by his discussions with a Prussian officer who had entered Russian service in 1811 in protest against Prussia's military support for

France. This was a certain Colonel Karl Philip Gottlieb von Clausewitz, who was also instrumental in negotiating the truce and Convention of Tauroggen signed by Yorck on 30 December 1812. We shall hear more of von Clausewitz later. Secondly, the neutralization of the Prussian corps precipitated a surge of nationalism in Prussia, which at last forced Frederick William to renounce entirely any further support for France. He also moved the Prussian capital east to Breslau, the better to secure his government and the monarchy following this decision. Thirdly, while Yorck gained much popular support, his decision was condemned by some within the officer corps who viewed it as a violation of his officer's oath and therefore of his honour as a Prussian officer. The perceived conflict between the wider needs of the nation and the officer's oath of loyalty, together with the concept of an officer's military duty and honour, would variously continue to bedevil the Prussian and German army right through to 1945. Finally, Prussia's decoupling from the military ambitions of Napoleon resulted in East Prussia raising its own self-defence force or militia, while at the same time welcoming the Russian army into its territory, all without sanction by the Prussian government or king. This in turn paved the way for the implementation of the much-needed army reforms which would in due course formally establish such regional forces as the Landwehr and later the Landsturm. Accordingly, although he was still reluctant to take any measures that might diminish the power and authority of the monarchy, Frederick William continued to approve some army reforms, as well as developing what was now a formidable military alliance with Russia.

During 1814, with France still dominating the south German states through the Confederation of the Rhine, more than 50,000 volunteers from the many German states came to join the Prussian army in order to fight the French. In part this response had been prompted by Frederick William's famous appeal to German nationalism made in his proclamation *An Mein Volk*, issued on 16 March the previous year, but the original catalyst for all this was undoubtedly General von Yorck's historic decision made at Riga in December 1812.

With the Prussian military capability once more in the ascendant and Napoleon's fortunes declining, the campaign against France proceeded apace. Despite some reverses, by 26 August 1813 Prussia together with Russia, Austria and Sweden mustered almost half a million men for what developed into Prussia's 'War of Liberation'. The allies formed four separate armies and one Prussian corps was attached to each. The French army numbered about 450,000. The defining moment of the campaign of 1813 came at Leipzig, when Napoleon was soundly defeated by the allies on 16–19 October. His own Bavarian and Saxon allies had already deserted him. While the allied casualties amounted to some 54,000, the French lost about 100,000 men (including deserters) at Leipzig, and as many as 500,000 during the whole campaign. The French casualties and losses included fifty-four generals (six killed, twelve wounded, thirty-six captured), 325 guns, 900 ammunition wagons, 40,000 muskets and twenty-eight standards and eagles. Such losses were unsustainable and, with the British and their allies advancing into France from Spain and the Prussians and their allies marching into France from the south and south-east, Paris finally fell to a short but hard-fought combined assault by Blücher's Army of Silesia and the Austrian troops of Prince Karl von Schwarzenberg's Army of Bohemia on 31 March 1814. This was followed by Napoleon's abdication on 6 April. During the previous year, with Prussian military fortunes clearly in the ascendant once again, Frederick William III had instituted the Iron Cross as a new decoration awarded to soldiers of all ranks who had carried out acts of distinction during the Wars of Liberation 1813–14. The fame and martial symbolism of this particular award would endure for the next 130 years.[49]

The events of April 1814 did not quite mark the end of the Napoleonic Wars, however, for the erstwhile emperor escaped from his exile on the island of Elba and raised a new army to threaten Europe in 1815. For 100 days there was consternation across the Continent, when a newly raised French army marched into Belgium intent on destroying first the Prussians and then the Anglo-Dutch armies. But it was not to be. At Ligny on 16 June the Prussians, with an army of 117,000 men and about 300 guns under the redoubtable if somewhat conservative Field Marshal von Blücher, suffered significant casualties and were checked; but – contrary to Napoleon's estimation – the Prussian army was still a viable fighting force despite its mauling at Ligny. Similarly, a British force struck by the French at Quatre Bras fought a vigorous delaying action and sustained numbers of casualties before it was able to disengage and move north to join the rest of the allied army to form the main Anglo-Dutch position at Waterloo.

The legendary battle of Waterloo was fought on 18 June, when the hard-pressed Anglo-Dutch-Belgian army (which also included some other national contingents, including the Hanoverian 'King's German Legion'), commanded by the Duke of Wellington, held firm against the French onslaught all day. Then, with the French army still posing a significant threat to the allies, the Prussians appeared on the French right flank. Field Marshal von Blücher (who had already been wounded and nearly captured at Ligny) had promised Wellington that he would arrive to support him and, despite the reservations expressed by his chief of staff von Gneisenau, he had moved with all speed to join Wellington at Waterloo. The Prussian contribution to the battle was both essential and – far from being an inspired strategic afterthought or a mission to save the day for the Anglo-Dutch-Belgian allies – it was something that both Wellington and Blücher had always understood would be a crucial part of the allied design for battle at Waterloo.

In any event, despite the lengthy forced march that the weary soldiers had just carried out in order to avoid the force sent by Napoleon to prevent their involvement in the battle at Waterloo, the Prussian regiments immediately launched their attack deep into the French right. Their arrival was a complete surprise for Napoleon, and the battle was quickly transformed into a rout as the French army at last collapsed and began to retreat. By and large, the exhausted Anglo-Dutch units remained in place on the battlefield while the Prussian cavalry conducted a fragmented but none the less ruthless pursuit of the French. This action was all too reminiscent of the French pursuit of the retreating Prussians by the dragoons and cuirassiers at Jena nine years before. So it was that on 18 June 1815 the Prussian army finally completed the destruction of the last army led by Napoleon I. It had at last avenged the humiliation of Jena–Auerstadt, and it had ensured the subsequent capture and permanent confinement of Napoleon Bonaparte on St Helena.

At the end of the Napoleonic Wars the Congress of Vienna finally disposed of the former Holy Roman Empire (which had in reality already been effectively neutralized during the Napoleonic Wars) and established a German Confederation of thirty-five autonomous states and free cities. These were represented by a Diet of eleven members, who were appointed by the various state and town governments. The Diet sat at Frankfurt-am-Main and was presided over by Austria. Thus, in 1816 Prussia found itself to be one of the more influential states within the newly formed German Confederation or 'Bund'. Prussia was also one of the principal military contributors to the new federal army, together with the other two principal states involved, Austria and Bavaria. The remainder of the confederation's lesser states, principalities, duchies and free cities all contributed various levels of military support to the federal army and the Confederation had the theoretical capability to generate a total force of about 550,000 men if so required.

✠✠✠✠✠✠✠✠✠✠✠✠

During the remaining twenty-five years of Frederick William's reign the army was mainly concerned with internal security operations rather with any major wars. Despite the changes that were now taking place within the army, its authority and the power of its nine corps commanders were unprecedented. Always responsible directly to the king, from 1820 these generals were empowered to deal with civil disturbances and to impose martial law without reference to the civil police or governmental authorities. The Prussian army of 1830 included forty-four regiments of the guard, grenadiers and infantry and thirty-eight regiments of cavalry; the Landwehr could muster a further forty infantry regiments and thirty-two cavalry regiments.

In 1830 the army was deployed to suppress a wave of active dissent in Poland, and then was variously employed within Germany to restore order after revolutionary activities in France – specifically the July revolution in Paris – threatened to spill over into Germany. More parochially, the army was also required to deal with a number of dissenting and liberalizing political movements within the smaller German states. All this accorded well with Frederick William's long-held views on the right of the monarch to retain absolute power, and the army enabled him to maintain this position. The same views were also held by his successor, Frederick William IV, who succeeded his father on 7 June 1840.

His eighteen-year reign was notable for two events. The first was the wave of revolt that swept across Europe during the 'Year of Revolutions' in 1848. The ensuing violence threatened to engulf Germany, and the outcome of the revolution had particular significance for the Prussian army. The second event was Frederick William's own failing health, which led to his younger brother, William, becoming regent on 7 October 1858. Subsequently, he became king in his own right on Frederick William's death at the Sanssouci Palace in Potsdam on 2 January 1861. King William I of Prussia would later complete a process that had begun in the time of Frederick William the Great Elector more than two centuries earlier, when he would preside over the crucial developments that would enable the German army to become once again the premier army in continental Europe.

But that was for the future, and (despite reputedly being a liberal, with a consuming interest in the arts and their promotion and architecture in particular) Frederick William IV would do nothing that might diminish his 'divine right' to rule as an absolute monarch. His obsession with the undoubted divine rationale for his inherited position was so strong that when, as one of the consequences of the 1848 revolutions, an opportunity was presented for him to become emperor of a German empire that would exclude Austria, he refused the offer. He gave as his reason the fact that the offer had come from the Frankfurt National Assembly, not from God.

The revolutions of 1848 were as widely dispersed as Berlin, Paris, Milan, Prague, Budapest and Vienna. In Paris the revolutionaries called for a democratic state. In Italy, Hungary, Poland and Bohemia, the goal was independence from Austria and the Habsburg Empire, or at least equal statehood within it. In Germany the objectives were a liberal constitution and unity as a German nation. In March 1848 the revolution that had begun in Paris with the overthrow of the French king by republicans the previous month arrived first in the Rhineland and then in Berlin. A popular uprising broke out on 18 and 19 March, which resulted in extensive street fighting when the army was brought in to restore order. Then, after several weeks of indecision, Frederick William indicated that a constitution would be granted, and that Prussia would be merged into a greater Germany with himself as the focus of a German nationalist movement. However, this was too little, too late, as the liberal revolution gained momentum and swept through Prussia, Austria and the other German states. Prussian liberals were enraged by the use of the army to suppress the revolutionary movement, both within Prussia and in Poland, while many in the officer corps were dismayed by what they viewed as Frederick William's half-hearted action to crush these movements. Eventually, the army acted decisively in Prussia, when General von Wrangel declared martial law in Berlin in November 1848, and moved some 40,000 troops into the capital to enforce this measure. This action was balanced by the proclamation of a Prussian constitution on 5 December, but, most significantly, the army was not included in any of its provisions and thus maintained its direct allegiance to the king, whose own powers and authority were also unaffected by the new constitution. It was therefore a largely meaningless gesture.

However successful it might have been when quelling dissent and revolution, the Prussian regular army was shown to be deficient in a number of areas – notably organization, command and control – when a federal German army, 35,000 strong and commanded by the Prussian General von Prittwitz, took the field against Denmark in March 1849 for the first of two Schleswig-Holstein wars. The diplomatic issues involved were complex, but in essence both wars came about because of Denmark's claim – and Prussia's objection – to Danish control of the two duchies of Schleswig (which was part German- and part Danish-speaking) and Holstein (which was German-speaking). The federal army comprised a Prussian division, a

Saxon brigade, a Hanoverian brigade and three other composite federal formations, including 15,000 Schleswig-Holsteiners. Despite several German victories at the start of the war, the Danes finally defeated the federal forces near Fredericia and this quite unexpected defeat called seriously into question the quality of the German forces and the doubtful efficiency of their mobilization and conscription arrangements.

This first Schleswig-Holstein war was but a military diversion from the potentially much greater threat posed to Germany by the continued undercurrent of political unrest that was still evident in the spring of 1849. Despite the seemingly never-ending political discussions of the Diet at Frankfurt, protests and violence again broke out in May 1849, this time in Dresden, and a new wave of revolutionary fervour soon spread right across Germany. The various state armies were ordered to suppress this unrest, and by the late summer of that year the federal army had also been brought in to deal with the movement in Germany. The armies of Prussia and Austria had been extensively involved in wiping out the remaining pockets of resistance, and the bayonets of a number of Prussian detached contingents had stiffened the resolve of other local forces in a number of south German states. Given their head, the commanders of these Prussian units dealt decisively, and sometimes ruthlessly, with the insurgents. Everywhere, the barricades were stormed or simply disappeared as the army regained its control of the situation. In several of these clashes the regular troops found themselves opposed by Landwehr militiamen and so the seeds of a future distrust of such regional units were firmly planted in the minds of many Prussian officers and regular soldiers. Clearly, they thought, the Landwehr should be reorganized and brought back within the overall ambit of the Prussian high command.

It was after the revolt in Germany had been put down that Frederick William had been offered – but had rejected – the leadership of a new German empire that excluded Austria. While acceptance would have antagonized Austria, the king's refusal, and his subsequent signing of the Convention of Olmütz on 29 November 1849 (which rejected any form of German empire that did not include Austria), in fact antagonized Prussian reactionaries and German nationalists alike, and also exacerbated the wider hostility to Austria that had long existed in Prussia. The Convention of Olmütz was yet another unfortunate act at a late stage in what had already proved to be an inauspicious reign, one which petered out just eight years later when Frederick William suffered a serious stroke, enabling his brother to take power as regent. The ailing Frederick William IV died just over three years later.

Although the somewhat lacklustre reigns of Frederick William III and Frederick William IV can be characterized by misjudgements, missed opportunities and indecisiveness, they witnessed a period during which a number of army reforms were implemented successfully, and these coincided with a remarkable burgeoning of conceptual military thinking in Prussia. But virtually all the consequent progress and achievements were largely brought about despite rather than because of the head of state. To review the scope of these formative activities and to highlight in detail some of the men who proposed and carried them out between 1807 and 1857, it is first necessary to turn the clock back to the period that followed the Prussian defeats at Jena–Auerstadt.

General Gerhard Johann David von Scharnhorst

Born in 1715, he was the son of a Westphalian farmer. In 1733, he attended the small military school of Wilhelmstein, which had been established by Graf Wilhelm von Schaumburg-Lippe on an island in the middle of the artificially extended lake of Steinhuder Meer, to the west of Hanover. There he excelled in all aspects of the military art and his vocation was clear. He demonstrated a formidable mix of personal qualities that included intellect, energy, sensitivity, organizational skills and pragmatism. His subsequent military career began in 1788, as an artillery officer in Hanoverian service, rising to the rank of captain. His early campaign experience included participation in the Duke of York's campaign in Flanders 1793–4, when his ability and courage were duly noted. Despite this, his advancement was slow, probably because of his fairly nondescript social background, and in 1801 he decided to move to the Prussian army with a view to improving his prospects.

The move proved astute, and he was subsequently promoted lieutenant colonel – which meant that he was automatically ennobled – in the field artillery. Subsequently, he became principal military assistant to Frederick William III, and was later appointed to what became the Kriegsakademie in Berlin. There, he expanded the curriculum and ensured that the study of strategy and military doctrine became core subjects. By 1804 he had changed the former Officers' Military Institute into the Academy for Young Officers, which was in practice a Kriegsakademie or 'war school'. In Berlin, he also set up a society for the discussion of military doctrine and organization. Among his students in Berlin was Karl von Clausewitz. During the ill-fated Jena–Auerstadt campaign, Scharnhorst served as chief of staff to the Duke of Brunswick. At Auerstadt he was wounded, captured, and later exchanged in time to participate in the battle of

Preussiche-Eylau in 1807. In July of that year he was promoted major general and appointed Minister of War and chief of the general staff. At that stage he was also appointed to establish and head the Military Reorganization Commission, working with reformers such as Gneisenau, Boyen and Grolman, and with others who understood that the time for change was already well overdue.

The Commission was required to review all aspects of the policies affecting the army and its diverse affairs in peacetime, together with its preparation for and conduct of war. The Commission's military reformers were supported by two of its civilian members, Stein, the Prime Minister of Prussia, and Könen, who was the country's Auditor-General. But some members of the Commission were not comfortable with the concept of reform and saw no need of it. Frederick William avoided direct involvement in its deliberations or peripheral lobbying by arranging for the Commission's contact with the monarch to be directed exclusively via his adjutant, Karl von Lottum. Despite some of the Commission's successes falling short of its reforming aspirations, in terms of its longer-term impact upon the army and the nation, Scharnhorst's leadership and direction of this body was probably his greatest enduring contribution to the development of the Prussian and later the German army. Foremost in this was his promotion of the concept of universal military service, although in this particular area the results Scharnhorst sought would not finally be adopted during his time in military service.

The remit of the Military Reorganization Commission was subdivided into four broad policy areas, which together impinged upon all aspects of the Prussian army. Its deliberations, proposals and recommendations were developed over several years. They involved the recruitment, training and generation of forces, an analysis of the officer corps in light of the defeats of 1806, various aspects of admission to the officer corps and an officer's subsequent advancement therein, and, lastly, the Prussian army's disciplinary and legal code and its application.

A particularly vital matter was to ensure that Prussia could generate forces sufficient to deal with any future threats, especially any posed by France. Scharnhorst firmly believed that patriotism should be the soldier's principal motivation to serve. Indeed, he held that military service was a citizen's fundamental obligation to his country, and this implied a system of universal military service. At the same time, such a system needed to accommodate the wider economic and social needs of the country. This led the Commission to propose that the army be divided between the professional standing force and a militia. The latter would be required to provide their own uniforms, weapons and equipment; the standing army would comprise those who were unable or did not wish to fund their own military service. In addition to producing the manpower levels required, this solution obviated the need for the state to fund most of the militia's everyday needs. The proposal was not accepted. On the one hand, the forces of reaction saw (quite correctly) that universal service would end the primacy of the nobility and the traditional practice of filling the lower ranks with the lower socio-economic members of the population – mainly from the rural areas – with mercenaries employed if and as necessary. On the other, the French had noted the possible resurgence of Prussian military capability post-Jena–Auerstadt, and had limited the size of the Prussian army to just 42,000 men in the standing army, with no add-on militia. Napoleon ensured that this constraint was included in the terms of the 1808 Convention of Paris.

However, there had already been some progress in the affairs of Prussian military service, and in 1806 there had been a reduction in the extent of exemptions from military service, and the abolition of the enlistment of foreigners. It now fell to Scharnhorst and his colleagues to try and circumvent the Convention of Paris without directly breaking its provisions. By no means an easy task, they managed to do it while increasing the potential size and capability of the army to forty-four infantry battalions, seventy-six squadrons of cavalry and forty-five artillery companies.[50] The system that they adopted was known as the 'Krümper System'.

This involved combining the conscription and training system so that numbers of young men were called up and trained each year by the regular army cadre, but were then discharged in sufficient time so that the obligatory 42,000 manpower ceiling was not breached. To ensure that these trainees were not shown to exceed the ceiling on the army rolls, equivalent numbers of trained soldiers were sent on leave from each company, their places being taken temporarily by the trainees. In fact, the resultant reserve strength was less than had been anticipated (the total reserves available in 1813 numbered about 65,675, having been 53,523 in 1807).

Nevertheless, the idea of universal military service had at last moved beyond the realms of mere theory. In 1813, the Landwehr and the Landsturm (the latter more of a home guard than a militia) were established as a source of reserves which included all able-bodied men between the ages of eighteen and forty-five. Although much of the Landsturm of 1813–14 proved to be unruly, insubordinate and often politically volatile, and so was less successful than had been hoped, these important reforms did take effect in time for Prussia to play its vital part in the final defeat of

Napoleon. First of all, during the War of Liberation in 1813 and 1814, and then during the Waterloo campaign of 1815, when four Prussian army corps totalling 117,000 men with 300 guns took the field.

In the meantime, in parallel with the Commission's work on military reforms, extensive social changes were taking place in Prussia. Despite the inertia of the reactionary elements, there was none the less a new emphasis on advancement in government service through merit rather than by birth or patronage, together with an end to the system of serfdom that still blighted the rural countryside, and the introduction of a new national education system. These undercurrents of social change reinforced and informed the work of the Commission, as well as legitimizing many of its principles in the wider civilian context.

Another important matter that the Commission considered was the fall-out from the defeats of 1806. This involved a critical review of the actions and conduct of the entire officer corps, no mean achievement given the power which that body still wielded. Of the 142 general officers who had been serving in 1806, seventeen were dismissed (of whom some were punished and seven executed for their actions during the war),[51] eighty-six more were retired and just twenty-two remained in service. By 1812 only eight were still serving. Sweeping dismissals of incompetent but more junior officers, and the retirement of many of the older junior officers, took place throughout the army, and the removal of these men undoubtedly revitalized the force. At the same time, in 1808 the Commission announced three very radical proposals designed to break the nobility's stranglehold on the officer corps by basing its future membership upon ability and merit alone. It was proposed that anyone who had the appropriate education and personal qualities could be considered for a commission; examinations for promotion should include a wider intellectual assessment, not only military knowledge; and finally, the system of the advancement of senior officers based only upon their length of service should be abolished.

These measures did gain the force of law, but, inevitably perhaps given the far-reaching implications of the reforms, they were in various ways circumvented or much modified in their application. And the educational requirements effectively debarred many competent potential officers. A regiment's officers continued to select or veto its own potential intake. Officers' regimental courts of honour continued to be the principal means of setting the behavioural standard and of investigating and (if necessary) disciplining officers, and cadet schools usually required their candidates to be the sons of officers. So, in the short term, the impact of these reforms

odified to take full account of the Napoleonic Wars and Prussia's
s of 1806. In parallel with this work, von Scharnhorst introduced a
amme of 'staff rides', whereby the general staff officers studied
ial theatres of operation in detail, on the ground, analyzing the
, making map assessments, and preparing detailed deployment
ons for the army. Although this innovative form of officer training
temporarily after von Scharnhorst's departure, it was subse-
ly revived by General von Müffling, who served as chief of the
al staff through the 1820s.

e regulations of 1812 dispensed with the echeloning of battalions in
nd called for a mix of skirmishers, firing lines and battalions in
ns. Within an army corps the four brigades would fulfil the roles of
sion or deception, main attack force, and reserve, and the battalion
ations would be determined by their brigade's task. The balance
een skirmishers and close order columns would be revised as the
developed, with the battalion columns being the most efficient way
ncentrating the maximum force while also maintaining command
control. Meanwhile, the cavalry was now required to co-ordinate its
ns closely with those of the infantry and to act primarily in support
e latter, while the artillery was concentrated at the point of main
t, in support of the infantry assault. Many of the tactics routinely
loyed in the French army were adopted by the Prussians, as were
ral features of the French soldier's uniform and equipment, such as
shako, laced boots with breeches and gaiters, and coats with tails.
uably, the merits of the French army, and that of Napoleon as a mili-
commander, were over-emphasized by the Prussians in the post-1815
od, a perspective that was balanced by an almost obsessive Prussian
ke of most of the non-military aspects of France, its politics, its
ure, its international ambitions, and what was generally perceived to be
unwarranted arrogance of its people. Nevertheless, these were the
e French people who had conquered much of Europe before eventu-
succumbing first of all to the rigours of the Russian winter and then
he united onslaught of the armies of the other great European powers.
ver Prussia needed an example of the benefits that could accrue from
cing an entire nation under arms in order to achieve a common
rpose, revolutionary and Napoleonic France was surely such a one, and
hin the next few decades, events would show that the lesson had indeed
n noted in Prussia.

It was during the time of the Commission that the principle was estab-
hed by which the army's corps – each of which was largely autonomous

was somewhat limited, and the Commissic
commission, followed by promotion on merit
part. But a number of key principles had bee

The final subject that the Commission de
military law, discipline and punishment. The
that the old system of harsh punishments w
modern army and a positive disincentive t
better-qualified recruit to join in the first place
ment was abolished, together with other outd;
Desertion now resulted in a substantial pr
execution. The Prussian articles of war were re
of military law to civilians was reviewed. But th
virtual immunity from civil legal sanctions, anc
treatment of soldiers by their superiors was st
first important steps had been taken, however,
during the succeeding years.

There were also several other spin-offs from
Reorganization Commission. In 1809, a Ministr
together with a council of ministers. Frederick
about both of these, fearing a reduction of his ow
the army. Accordingly, the Ministry of War wa
department (headed by von Scharnhorst) and a
ment (headed by the conservative Karl Heinrich v
Thus the king avoided having to appoint a
powerful, Minister of War, or indeed any need to
and influence to von Scharnhorst alone. Fortunatel
colleague, Hermann von Boyen, became Minister
move forward much of the Commission's early v
regarding universal military service, organization o
service.

The tactical lessons of 1806 had also been co
Military Reorganization Commission, and on 17
instruction on the tactics for brigades. A Prussian t
alent of a division in many other armies, so this im
last provided clear tactical doctrine and direction f(
operational level of command. Then, in 1812, a
(comprising von Scharnhorst, von Clausewitz and
von Wartenburg) produced a new manual of mil
reality this document was a tactics training manual
the relevant experiences of warfare in the time of 1

now r
defeat
progr
poten
terrai
soluti
lapse
quen
gener
Th
line
colur
diver
form
betw
battl
of c
and
actic
of tl
effo
emp
seve
the
Arg
tary
peri
disl
cult
the
san
ally
to
If
pla
pu
wi
be

lis

now modified to take full account of the Napoleonic Wars and Prussia's defeats of 1806. In parallel with this work, von Scharnhorst introduced a programme of 'staff rides', whereby the general staff officers studied potential theatres of operation in detail, on the ground, analyzing the terrain, making map assessments, and preparing detailed deployment solutions for the army. Although this innovative form of officer training lapsed temporarily after von Scharnhorst's departure, it was subsequently revived by General von Müffling, who served as chief of the general staff through the 1820s.

The regulations of 1812 dispensed with the echeloning of battalions in line and called for a mix of skirmishers, firing lines and battalions in columns. Within an army corps the four brigades would fulfil the roles of diversion or deception, main attack force, and reserve, and the battalion formations would be determined by their brigade's task. The balance between skirmishers and close order columns would be revised as the battle developed, with the battalion columns being the most efficient way of concentrating the maximum force while also maintaining command and control. Meanwhile, the cavalry was now required to co-ordinate its actions closely with those of the infantry and to act primarily in support of the latter, while the artillery was concentrated at the point of main effort, in support of the infantry assault. Many of the tactics routinely employed in the French army were adopted by the Prussians, as were several features of the French soldier's uniform and equipment, such as the shako, laced boots with breeches and gaiters, and coats with tails. Arguably, the merits of the French army, and that of Napoleon as a military commander, were over-emphasized by the Prussians in the post-1815 period, a perspective that was balanced by an almost obsessive Prussian dislike of most of the non-military aspects of France, its politics, its culture, its international ambitions, and what was generally perceived to be the unwarranted arrogance of its people. Nevertheless, these were the same French people who had conquered much of Europe before eventually succumbing first of all to the rigours of the Russian winter and then to the united onslaught of the armies of the other great European powers. If ever Prussia needed an example of the benefits that could accrue from placing an entire nation under arms in order to achieve a common purpose, revolutionary and Napoleonic France was surely such a one, and within the next few decades, events would show that the lesson had indeed been noted in Prussia.

It was during the time of the Commission that the principle was established by which the army's corps – each of which was largely autonomous was somewhat limited, and the Commission's goals of admission to a commission, followed by promotion on merit alone, were achieved only in part. But a number of key principles had been established.

The final subject that the Commission dealt with directly was that of military law, discipline and punishment. The reformers were quite clear that the old system of harsh punishments was both inappropriate in a modern army and a positive disincentive to the better-educated and better-qualified recruit to join in the first place. In 1808, corporal punishment was abolished, together with other outdated physical punishments. Desertion now resulted in a substantial prison sentence rather than execution. The Prussian articles of war were redrawn and the application of military law to civilians was reviewed. But the army continued to enjoy virtual immunity from civil legal sanctions, and there is no doubt that ill-treatment of soldiers by their superiors was still fairly widespread. The first important steps had been taken, however, and would be built upon during the succeeding years.

There were also several other spin-offs from the work of the Military Reorganization Commission. In 1809, a Ministry of War was established, together with a council of ministers. Frederick William had reservations about both of these, fearing a reduction of his own power and control over the army. Accordingly, the Ministry of War was divided into a general department (headed by von Scharnhorst) and an administrative department (headed by the conservative Karl Heinrich von Wylich und Lottum). Thus the king avoided having to appoint a single, potentially very powerful, Minister of War, or indeed any need to give yet more authority and influence to von Scharnhorst alone. Fortunately, in 1814 his reforming colleague, Hermann von Boyen, became Minister of War and was able to move forward much of the Commission's early work and the proposals regarding universal military service, organization of reserves and terms of service.

The tactical lessons of 1806 had also been considered by the 1807 Military Reorganization Commission, and on 17 July 1809 it issued an instruction on the tactics for brigades. A Prussian brigade was the equivalent of a division in many other armies, so this important publication at last provided clear tactical doctrine and direction for commanders at the operational level of command. Then, in 1812, a separate commission (comprising von Scharnhorst, von Clausewitz and General Hans Yorck von Wartenburg) produced a new manual of military regulations. In reality this document was a tactics training manual, which incorporated the relevant experiences of warfare in the time of Frederick the Great, and comprised of infantry, cavalry, artillery and support services – were to be clearly identified with a specific area or region of Prussia. Its units were to be based there, it would recruit from there, and the towns and villages of that region would be host to the regiments and units that were now permanently garrisoned there. The military concept of 'regimental tribalism' has always been recognized as a fundamental strength of fighting units and, while it was by no means a new concept, its positive and deliberate application would prove to be a very real strength of the Prussian and German army in the years ahead.

In 1810 von Scharnhorst had fallen foul of a French decree which forbade non-Prussians from serving in the Prussian army, and he had therefore been obliged temporarily to leave Prussian service. But as Napoleon's fortunes and influence began to wane, he was recalled to the army in 1812 as von Blücher's chief of staff. While serving in that capacity, he was wounded at the battle of Lützen on 2 May 1813.[52] The wound was not serious, and he was dispatched to Prague to negotiate aspects of Austria's entry into the war against France. But the relatively inconsequential wound then became infected and he died of blood poisoning on 28 June 1813. He was replaced as Blücher's chief of staff by von Gneisenau.

Quite apart from the army's loss of sheer professional ability, von Scharnhorst's death was a tragedy for all those more liberal Prussian officers and officials who had a wider vision of the army's future, and who needed men such as he to implement their envisaged reforms. Of the many great Prussian military reformers, Scharnhorst was probably the greatest, and many of the proposals that he was unable to implement during his lifetime were subsequently revived by his successors and carried through in later years.

General Karl von Clausewitz

He was born in 1780 and embarked upon his military career in the Prussian army in 1792, at the age of just twelve. Subsequently, he fought during the French Revolutionary Wars in the Vosges region and in the Rhineland. In 1801 he attended the embryo Kriegsakademie in Berlin, where he encountered and was much influenced by the superintendent and principal instructor, von Scharnhorst. Von Clausewitz was at Auerstadt in 1806 and commanded part of the rearguard during the subsequent retreat. Captured and sent to France, he spent seven months as a prisoner, during which time he acquired an abiding hatred of the French and their military aspirations. Once returned to Prussia, he became involved with von Scharnhorst and the reform movement, but when Frederick William III concluded his alliance with France in 1812 von Clausewitz joined some thirty or so other officers who resigned their Prussian commissions and offered their services to the Russian tsar. Later, he was directly involved with General von Yorck in negotiating the neutrality of the Prussian contingent serving with Napoleon's *Grande Armée*, and with the Convention of Tauroggen. As was the case with von Yorck, Clausewitz attracted some criticism and accusations of treason from reactionary members of the officer corps when he became involved with the development of irregular forces to fight the French. This was an activity not sanctioned by the Prussian king and therefore (some argued) contrary to his duty to his monarch. But in April 1814 he was reinstated as a Prussian officer and served as chief of staff to General Thielmann's 3rd Corps during the Waterloo campaign. Most appropriately, in 1818 he was appointed superintendent of the Allgemeine Kriegsschule in Berlin, where he continued his conceptual and historical writing on all aspects of war. When the Prussian army embarked on its mission of 'Army of Observation' during the unrest in Poland during 1831, he attended the campaign as the chief of staff to the Prussian commander, Field Marshal von Gneisenau, but he contracted cholera and died some months later.

The untimely loss of yet another great Prussian military thinker and reformer was a blow not only for Prussia but also for military professionals world-wide. However, Clausewitz had committed much of his thinking to notes, and was in the process of writing and refining his seminal work *Vom Kriege* – 'On War' – when he died. A year later, in 1832, his widow edited and published the first edition of the complete manuscript in several volumes. The final volume appeared in 1834, though in a somewhat disjointed form because Clausewitz had only completed the refinement and editing of the first part of his *magnum opus* at the time of his death. Although *Vom Kriege* did not achieve immediate recognition either within the army or in the wider country, the military thinkers of the day increasingly came to understand its importance, and within three decades the new men of power and influence in the Prussian army – notably General Helmuth von Moltke, who became chief of the Great General Staff in 1857 – ensured that *Vom Kriege* became required reading throughout the army. In broad terms, von Clausewitz's text provided the Prussian army (and in due course many others) with a full exposition of his thoughts, theories and principles on and for armed conflict at every level. His work set out a valid conceptual basis for considering the nature, effects and imperatives of war in its widest sense, with all of these set against the military lessons, experiences and examples of history. It also addressed the inter-relationship between war and politics, and the influence of the human element and sheer chance upon these as well as upon the conduct of war itself.

Field Marshal Augustus Wilhelm Neithardt von Gneisenau

Born in 1760, he was the son of a lieutenant in the Austrian artillery, who had served during the Seven Years War. After spending two years at the university in Erfurt he completed a short period of service in an Austrian hussar regiment before joining the army of Ansbach-Bayreuth, with which he went to participate in the British campaign in North America. He also adopted the 'von Gneisenau' title from that of an Austrian noble family to which his family was distantly related. 1786 saw him in Prussian service as a captain, and until 1806 he completed a succession of tours of duty in various Prussian garrisons, achieving the rank of major. He served at Jena–Auerstadt and then became famous as the commander of the besieged garrison at Kolberg in 1807, when he was promoted lieutenant colonel and awarded the *Pour le Mérite* decoration. Later, he was promoted major general, by which time his ability had come to the attention of von Scharnhorst who chose him to serve as a member of the Military Reorganization Commission in 1807. He was probably von Scharnhorst's greatest supporter and confidant.

In 1813 he was appointed chief of staff to von Blücher. He fought at Leipzig, and was ennobled thereafter. As chief of staff during the Waterloo campaign he assumed temporary command of the Prussian army when Blücher was unhorsed and nearly captured at Ligny on 16 June 1815. He ordered the army's withdrawal to Wavre and thus enabled it to rally in time for Blücher to resume command and order its move to join Wellington at Waterloo, this despite von Gneisenau's increasing caution and distrust of non-Prussian allies after 1814, which had caused him to counsel Blücher against what he regarded as a risky course of action. Fortuitously, on that occasion Blücher did not follow his chief of staff's advice, despite the exemplary professional relationship that the two men enjoyed.

As an informed and liberal thinker, von Gneisenau was yet another frustrated casualty of Frederick William III's failure to carry through the necessary political and military reforms, and in 1816 he resigned his commission. He returned to military service in 1818 when he was appointed governor of Berlin. On the tenth anniversary of Waterloo he was promoted Field Marshal, and in 1831 he was appointed commander of the Prussian Army of Observation during the Polish revolt against Russian rule. Then, at Posen on 21 August 1831, he succumbed to the epidemic of cholera then sweeping across Europe. His chief of staff had died in the same way earlier that year.

Quite apart from his major contribution to the process of reform, von Gneisenau in many ways typified the liberal Prussian officer. He was professional, courageous, pragmatic, open-minded and a very talented staff officer, with special abilities in the areas of organization and administration. As such his particular talents had perfectly complemented those of Blücher during the years he served as the latter's chief of staff.

General Hermann von Boyen and General von Grolman

Although perhaps less well known beyond Germany than are von Scharnhorst, von Gneisenau and von Clausewitz, von Boyen was instrumental in carrying on the work of these men and in some cases realizing their aspirations in later years. He served as Prussian Minister of War from 1814 to 1819 and from 1841 to 1847 and so was well placed to do this. But much of his time was occupied with combating the anti-reformers in the government and the army, who continued to enjoy the tacit support of Frederick William III. As Prussian Minister of War from 1814 he was at last able to take forward von Scharnhorst's original concept of universal service. He did so with the Army Law of 3 September 1814. By this, at twenty years of age the army's recruits were required to complete three years of regular service, followed by two with the reserves, and then transfer to the first section or class of the Landwehr for seven years. This was followed by a further seven years with the second section from age thirty-three. Finally, at about age forty, individuals were transferred to the Landsturm (which also included all men aged from seventeen to forty-nine who were exempted regular army or Landwehr service). The soldier's initial selection for service was by lot, with complementary arrangements made for substitution and for certain exemptions.

Following von Scharnhorst's original idea for the militia, those men who could afford to support themselves while in military service served only one year with the regular army before transferring to the Landwehr, most of them subsequently gaining commissions. But neither the officers nor the militia-style soldiers of the Landwehr were particularly well regarded by the professional army, who viewed the Landwehr both as a threat to the status and authority of the regular army (which had almost 30,000 men fewer than the Landwehr) and – more importantly – as a potential source of political dissent, revolution or armed insurrection in the future. In 1830, the general staff proposed a modification of these terms of service, so that the length of regular army service was reduced to two years, and that with the Landwehr was increased by one year. This reflected the fact that by now more young men were becoming available for training than the system could train or absorb. Despite some concerns over the professional performance of the recruits who would undergo just two years of regular service, this measure meant that Prussia's trained military reserves would eventually be increased by about 50 per cent, and the proposal was approved by the king in 1833 and implemented forthwith.

Another important contribution made by Boyen was the appointment of his fellow reformer, Grolman, as head of the ministry's second department (in effect, chief of the general staff), which meant that the general staff organization which supported the high command was extensively reformed and reorganized from 1816. Based on the three main strategic threats to Prussia, he organized the staff with a separate division to study and develop operational contingency plans for each of these three geographical regions. Then, true to the principles expounded by Clausewitz, Grolman set up a fourth division of the general staff to study the events and lessons of military history. A fifth division provided officers from the Great General Staff in Berlin for service with the headquarters of the army's corps and divisions. Meanwhile, all staff officers were required to carry out regular periods of duty at regimental level so that they maintained an awareness of the practicalities of their profession at that level of command. Grolman's innovative approach to staff training took forward the ideas of the Military Reorganization Commission by improving the in-service education of the officer corps, its technical awareness in particular. In 1818 Grolman appointed von Clausewitz as director of the Allgemeine Kriegsschule in Berlin, but this appointment did not have the impact upon the curriculum that Grolman had hoped. This was because of the resignation of both Grolman and Boyen in 1819 in protest against the Carlsbad Decrees announced that August, which had been followed by the placing of the Landwehr under the direct command of the army.[53] The departure of Boyen and Grolman seriously undercut von Clausewitz's high-level support. Despite the by now all too familiar opposition he had encountered, Grolman had nevertheless managed to implement his changes to the general staff, as well as advancing the technical and strategic infrastructure support for the Prussian army in matters such as the country's road network, the development of a military telegraphic communications system, and the pre-positioning of strategic combat supplies (notably ammunition) in depots sited to match the general staff's contingency plans.

Following the death of Frederick William III and the accession of Frederick William IV in 1840, Boyen was reappointed as Minister of War in

1841. This enabled him to implement several reforms, mostly technological. Foremost among these was his gaining official approval for the introduction of the breech-loading Dreyse needle-gun throughout the Prussian army, although this process was not finally completed until the early 1860s. Boyen was also able to address successfully some of the humanitarian aspects of soldiering. These resulted in improvements to the conditions of service, pay, rations, and the military disciplinary code. Despite his allegedly liberal sentiments, however, Frederick William IV maintained his predecessor's inflexible position on wider reforms and anything that might diminish the royal prerogative or its control of the army. Consequently, in 1847 Boyen resigned his appointment for the second and final time. He died the following year, during the Year of Revolutions in Europe.

Three Chiefs of the General Staff: General von Müffling, Major General von Krauseneck and General von Reyher

Finally, between 1820 and 1857, three successive chiefs of the general staff further contributed to the development of what was at long last re-emerging as a most professional and, in many ways, a much reformed Prussian army. The first of these, General von Müffling, is possibly less deserving of the title 'reformer' than many others and, as a politically very conservative and reactionary officer, he would probably have refuted the accolade most forcefully. Nevertheless, while he rejected absolutely Scharnhorst's concept of universal service and the populist or liberal role of the Landwehr, he was instrumental in advancing the professional competence of the general staff. As chief of the general staff during the decade to 1829, he reinstituted the staff rides introduced originally by von Scharnhorst. From these was developed the routine use of maps and terrain sketches to plan operations and in 1824 the first manual for conducting the Kriegsspiel or 'war game' was issued and taken into general use throughout the army during the next fifteen or so years. The Kriegsspiel allowed commanders to carry out their analyses and decision-making, supported by their staffs using maps rather than with troops and other resources needing to be present on the ground. The decisions made, the procedures adopted, and probable outcomes of all these, could be reviewed and discussed in great detail at the end of the Kriegsspiel. Use of the war game was not confined only to the officers and in due course it was adopted for non-commissioned officer training as well. Today, the modern equivalents of the staff ride and the Kriegsspiel are still to be found in the training programme of virtually every professional army, usually based on a combination of map analysis and walking the ground, but routinely on the use also of high-technology imagery and computer-assisted decision-making.

Von Müffling reorganized the general staff divisions, allocating them functional rather than geographical focuses. He also initiated a detailed study of the 1813–15 campaigns, and directed the first production of a general staff manual, which dealt with virtually every aspect of the duties, procedures and activities of the general staff and its individual officers.

Major General von Krauseneck succeeded von Müffling in 1829 and, having worked previously with von Scharnhorst, he not only consolidated von Müffling's work but over the next nineteen years he also built on the progress that had been made by Grolman, so that the army took full account of the important technological advances that were emerging in the fields of communications and mobility during the first part of the nine-teenth century.

Finally, in 1848 the very able and militarily enlightened officer General von Reyher succeeded von Krauseneck. He continued the work of his predecessors as far as possible but (just as his predecessors had been) he was often frustrated by the reactionary opposition that still impeded progress, while yet again the opposition of Frederick William IV to liber-alism and reform in the army often proved to be an insurmountable obstacle. Despite the temporary strengthening of the reactionaries following the unrest and bloodshed of the revolution of 1848 and 1849, von Reyher still achieved much to enhance the army's professionalism and capability. Then fate once again took a hand. In October 1857 von Reyher died, and before a successor could be named by Frederick William, who was himself already in ill-health, the Prussian monarch suffered a stroke so debilitating that his younger brother, William, was appointed first as the king's deputy, then as regent. One of the new regent's first actions was to appoint his own choice of chief of the general staff. William appointed General Helmuth von Moltke to the post in 1857, a position that he would occupy for the next three decades – thirty years that would prove to be in very many ways the heyday or 'golden age' of the Prussian army, and indeed of the wider concept of German militarism.

PART TWO

The Golden Age

8

Dress Rehearsals
The Wars of 1864 and 1866

A S HAD BEEN SO with all of its predecessors, the army that went to war against France in 1870 was a product of its heritage and recent history and the form it finally achieved in the second half of the nineteenth century exemplified what could reasonably be regarded as being the 'golden age' of German militarism. This was especially and specifically the result of the work, since the late 1850s, of four Prussians. They were the commander-in-chief of the army, King William I, who succeeded to the Prussian throne in 1861 (but who, it will be recalled, had in reality ruled Prussia from 1858 as regent in place of his brother, Frederick William IV); Albrecht von Roon, Minister of War from 1859; Helmuth von Moltke, chief of the general staff from 1858; and finally Otto von Bismarck, the Minister-President of Prussia since 1862. That all of these men had come to positions of power and prominence at roughly the same time, all with broadly similar national and strategic aspirations, was both fortuitous and significant, firstly for Prussia and later for the whole of Germany. So also was their general concurrence on how these aspirations could be achieved, and in particular on the vital need to create and maintain a large, well-trained and professional military organization in Prussia, and subsequently in Germany. They all came to their respective appointments with an awareness of what had become, by the mid-nineteenth century, a number of serious weaknesses in Prussia's military organization and capability despite the several reforms that had been carried out during the previous few decades.

The defeat of Napoleon in 1815 and the removal of the threat of a Europe dominated by France had increased the Prussian territory and had already demonstrated that the military decline which had occurred after the death of Frederick the Great was by no means irreversible, and that the old martial spirit and potential were still very much present. But the protracted period of peace in Europe after 1815 had increasingly allowed political complacency and military stagnation to set in, so that the original reforms proposed and developed by Scharnhorst and Gneisenau, many of which had been completed by about 1830, remained in place with little significant change or improvement for almost the next three decades. Furthermore, despite the wider social changes in the country as a whole, the officer corps continued to be almost exclusively the preserve of the Prussian nobility. Finally, notwithstanding the important policy changes and organizational reforms that had been achieved, there had been a continuing reluctance of the government throughout the years following the Napoleonic wars to fund many of the more practical manpower and equipment needs of the military. Despite the various reforms that had been implemented during the reigns of Frederick William III and Frederick William IV the evidence of their impact was in many cases organizational and cost-constrained rather than substantive and innovative or inspirational and operational.

Then, in 1858 Prince William of Prussia assumed the position of regent, and so became both the executive ruler of Prussia and the commander-in-chief of its armed forces. This event, together with the coming to power of von Roon, von Moltke and von Bismarck all at about the same time, subsequently proved to be one of the defining moments of both German and European history. It signalled the beginning of the next and arguably the most significant resurgence of Prussian militarism. Within just thirteen years this would first of all make Prussia the undisputed leader of a united Germany. It would then enable the creation of a new German empire. Finally, it would lay the foundations for the achievement by the end of the century of German military primacy within Europe. This strategic situation would then continue (despite some set-backs due to internal economic and political difficulties after 1900) until the latter part of the First World War.

Von Roon had clearly identified the weaknesses in the army which had manifested themselves during the years that followed the Congress of Vienna of 1816. Throughout that time it had relied for its manpower intakes upon the old 1814 conscription law which, as time passed, had proved progressively less able to generate the necessary size and quality of forces at a time of crisis that had originally been intended by von Scharnhorst and von Gneisenau. The failings in the system were particularly evident during the partial mobilization of the first section of the Landwehr in response to events in France, Belgium and Poland, and within Germany itself, during the 'Year of Revolutions' in 1848. On that occasion many of the Landwehr units called to the colours proved less than professional when they were (often belatedly) formed up for duty. The 1814 law also failed to take account of the now much increased size of the Prussian population, and consequently of the considerable numbers of able-bodied men potentially available for military service but who were not called forward, because of administrative and organizational shortfalls in the existing system of conscription. Meanwhile, the size, quality and command arrangements of the Prussian regular army on campaign had also shown themselves to be less than satisfactory during the first Schleswig-Holstein war in 1849.

All this was no doubt still well to the fore in the mind of Prince William, himself a professional soldier, when he became regent in 1858. Soon thereafter he directed General von Roon to carry out a review of the current applicability of the 1814 mobilization and conscription laws and of the effectiveness of the Landwehr. Von Roon was to report the outcome of this study to him personally by memorandum. Not surprisingly, the resultant review was highly critical of the existing Prussian armed forces, but at the same time proposed a number of radical reforms that would resolve the existing deficiencies and at the same time enable a complete updating of the entire Prussian military system.

The key proposals of von Roon's plan concerned the role and organization of the Landwehr. This element of the army would no longer be required to provide formed Landwehr units to take the field alongside the regular units. Rather, it should henceforth provide both a second-line reserve of reinforcements and a pool of reserve divisions. These new 'Landwehr divisions' and the units within them would in fact be based on a core of key personnel and cadres from the regular army. This meant that the individual qualities of the young regular soldier and those of the older, but usually more experienced, veteran would complement each other within Prussian regiments and units. The British war correspondent Archibald Forbes, when commenting upon the relationship between the Landwehr soldier and his regular counterpart some years later, observed that:

> The war strength of a [Prussian] regiment is just double its peace strength, and the increment consists of the reserve. The medalled men of [the war against Austria in] 1866, and of the Schleswig-Holstein campaigns, called up from reserve, are welded into the same ranks with the young soldiers who are serving their first period of three years. Bayonet for bayonet, the old and the young soldiers balance each other, and the amalgamation is perfect between dash and steadiness – between whatever recklessness there may be in the bravery of youth, and the staid valour of maturer years.[54]

In von Roon's plan, the Landsturm would in future include all able-bodied men, virtually without exception, who were liable for military service but who had not for whatever reason undergone full-time regular service in the army or navy. All these measures were intended to provide depth to the regular army's reserves of trained manpower, and they were underwritten by an updated conscription law based on universal military service. Von Roon calculated that this would enable Prussia to field a trained army of about 500,000 men on mobilization. His proposals called for a conscript's service to start on 1 January of the year in which he completed his twentieth year, and to last for seven years from the date of joining. Only three of these years were to be served with the colours (except in the cavalry, where the term was to be for four years), the remainder being spent with the regular army reserve. After seven years, at the age of twenty-seven, the fully trained soldier would be transferred to the Landwehr for a further five years.

Predictably, Prince William welcomed and supported von Roon's proposals enthusiastically, but they attracted strong opposition from the Prussian Assembly both on constitutional and budgetary grounds, and strongly expressed liberal opinions and opposition were voiced by a number of the members. These objections were even supported by the then Minister of War, von Bonin, and this might well have proved a significant obstacle to making any progress with the much-needed reforms.

Fortuitously, however, in 1859 France and Austria went to war, which triggered a Prussian mobilization. The failings in the system, much magnified since 1849, were now clear for all to see and this enabled William to replace von Bonin by von Roon as Minister of War. Despite this move, von Roon's recommendations continued to be opposed by liberals within the Assembly, which flatly refused to sanction any of the necessary military expenditure and a virtual impasse persisted for three years, until 1862. This was the year after that in which William had finally succeeded to the Prussian throne as King William I. At that point von Bismarck, who was by then Prussia's new Minister-President, took a decisive hand in the affair. He ruled that, irrespective of the views of the Assembly it was the duty of the crown to take any and all such action that the monarch deemed necessary for the welfare of the state and the effective conduct of all its business. That was the end of the matter and thereafter the implementation of von Roon's recommendations moved forward apace.

A year later, in 1863, the Prussian Assembly was dissolved. In any event, the need of legal approval by that legislative body had by now become somewhat academic, as the ever-pragmatic government had arbitrarily implemented a number of the army reforms since 1858, without having referred them to the Assembly. The long-running issue was finally resolved in 1867 when a retrospective bill was passed to legalize the earlier reorganization of the army and the new arrangements that had already been made for its conscription and terms of service.

The reorganization delivered a rapid and dramatic expansion of the Prussian army. It was carried out during the years 1860 to 1865 and laid the foundations of the Prussian military organization that finally went to war against France in 1870. This expansion involved a number of fundamental changes that went right to the heart of the Prussian regimental system and organization.

First, each regular infantry regiment was required to form the cadre element of a Landwehr regiment. These new 'combined regiments' initially bore the same numerical designations as those of the parent regiments from which their cadre element had been drawn, and so were very clearly a part of those regiments from the outset. By the end of 1860 these regiments, suitably stiffened by the regular cadres, were in fact accorded their own regimental numbers and identities. Thus thirty-six new regiments, including four guard regiments, were added to the Prussian army's order of battle. Next, the other existing reserve units were enhanced by the addition of third battalions to the guard reserve and line infantry reserve regiments, the latter of which were then redesignated as 'fusilier' regiments.

The number of Prussian cavalry units was increased by the simple expedient of all squadrons that were at that time detached from their parent units being reorganized and redesignated as new dragoon or lancer ('uhlan')[55] regiments. By this means ten new cavalry regiments were formed in relatively short order. Finally, the Prussian artillery was brigaded from 1864, each brigade comprising two artillery regiments. One of these was made up of field and horse artillery batteries and the other one was designated as garrison (or in other words 'heavy') artillery.

As the introduction of von Roon's plans moved ever closer to full implementation, Bismarck was actively seeking a suitable war in which to validate the effectiveness of the newly organized army. He also needed to assess its future potential as the tool by which he would advance his foreign policy objectives and ultimately achieve German unification. An opportunity to test the war machine came in 1864, when the old dispute between Prussia and Denmark over Schleswig-Holstein resurfaced some fifteen years after the ignominious defeat of the German federal forces at the hands of the Danes at the end of the first Schleswig-Holstein war. From this new conflict the opportunity would also emerge a couple of years later for Prussia finally to displace its former ally Austria from its traditional and long-standing position at the head of the German states.

The Second Schleswig-Holstein War, 1864

On this occasion, the issue involved a problem over the Danish succession. It centred on the fact that Frederick VII of Denmark (who was also the Duke of Schleswig and of Holstein) had no male heir, and so his chosen successor (Prince Christian) could not, Bismarck argued, legally continue to rule over the two duchies. Bismarck supported the claim of Prince Frederick of Augustenburg to the succession and enlisted Austria's military support for Prussia's candidate. The war that ensued was relatively short. The Austro-Prussian forces were commanded by the Prussian Field Marshal von Wrangel (who, as a general, had successfully subdued the Danes in 1848) and the Austrian General Gablenz. Their army began the war on 2 February 1864 with a bombardment of Missunde. The strategically important Danish strongholds of Düppel and Alsen fell by the end of June, and King Christian concluded an armistice on 20 July. Although a speedy Austro-Prussian victory had been achieved, and despite the considerable progress which had already been made with the reform of the Prussian army, there was nevertheless a consensus among many of the foreign observers of the war that the soldiers of the Austrian contingent had actually performed somewhat better than their Prussian brothers-in-arms. This independent criticism was levelled particularly at von Wrangel and the Prussian high command rather than at the regimental commanders and the actions carried out at the tactical level, but it clearly provided much food for thought both for von Roon and for Bismarck. But it did indicate the need of much more work by von Moltke, who was by now chief of the general staff, before the Prussian war machine could again be committed to war justifiably confident of its ability to deliver victory.

The political and territorial outcome of the second Schleswig-Holstein conflict was settled on 30 October by the Treaty of Vienna, which was subsequently amended by a convention at Gastein in 1865. The main political outcome was that Schleswig was henceforth to be governed by Prussia, and Holstein by Austria. This apparently equitable situation in practice sowed the seeds of the political opportunity Bismarck needed to subdue Austria militarily, and it led to war between Prussia and Austria in 1866.

The Austro-Prussian War, 1866

The confrontation between Austria and Prussia occurred when Prussia cited its displeasure over the manner of Austria's government of Holstein. In addition, the former dispute over which duke should rightfully govern the two duchies remained unresolved and had been a continuing source of friction. The situation was made more difficult by Prussia having withdrawn its support for its original candidate, Frederick, who then promptly sought – and received – the support of Austria. Meanwhile, Prussian troops had forcibly ejected the Austrian forces from Holstein. The German Confederation assembled at Vienna where, on 14 June, Austria demanded that the federal army be mobilized to move against Prussia. This event effectively signalled the end of the old German Confederation and of the Bund. War was declared next day.

The Prussian order of battle for the war against Austria merits some study, as many of its operational commanders were destined to play key roles in the much greater conflict that would take place four years later. Indeed, several of the names that appeared in 1866 were destined to re-appear in the German army's senior officer lists time and again over the next eight decades as their successors maintained the military traditions established by their forebears in the nineteenth century. During the war against Austria, the experience gained by these men in what was a limited, but none the less modern, war was invaluable, and to the credit of von Moltke and King William they subsequently left in place or advanced many of those who had commanded the armies, corps and divisions against the Austrians, thereby allowing them carry forward their experi-ence into the next war.

The Prussian army that took the field against Austria in 1866 comprised the 1st and 2nd Armies, the Army of the Elbe, and the three strategic reserve corps, the whole being commanded by King William, with General von Moltke as the chief of staff. The detailed composition, order of battle, principal commanders and command arrangements of the Prussian army in June 1866 are shown at Appendix 3.

In anticipation of the coming conflict, the Prussians had begun moving their corps to concentration areas close to the frontier from 16 May, and during the next three weeks they positioned 197,000 men, 55,000 horses, 864 guns and 3,500 wagons in dispersed locations, from which they would be able to come together as a single force within five days. Initially, the Prussian mobilization was complicated by a lack of reliable intelligence about Austrian intentions, and a need to split the army in readiness to deal with several threats simultaneously. But by mid-June it became clear that the Austrians intended to adopt a defensive strategy and so the strategic initiative passed to the Prussians. Indeed, the reallocation of the 1st Corps to the 2nd Army on about 11 June reflected the receipt of new intelligence that the Austrian mobilization was incomplete and that Saxony was not to be defended, thus releasing the 1st Corps to reinforce what would shortly become the Prussian offensive's point of main effort.

Although not all of the forces available to Prussia were directly employed against the Austrians, the Prussian army had at its disposal in June 1866 some 335,000 fully trained and mobilized troops. Against this Austria and its south German allies were in theory able to mobilize forces in greater numerical strength. But many of these troops were of lesser quality in terms of motivation, training and organization, or were equipped with weapons inferior to those of the Prussians. The 390,000 men under Austrian command as at 15 June 1866 comprised:

Austrian Army of the North:	247,000
Saxony:	24,000
Bavaria:	52,000
Württemberg:	16,000
Baden:	11,000
Hanover:	18,000
The Hesses:	22,000

The Austrian-led federal army fielded about 1,000 guns.

The war that ensued following Emperor Franz Josef of Austria's declaration of war on 15 June lasted just seven weeks, during which Prussia comprehensively demonstrated its military superiority over Austria and its allies of Saxony and Hanover. Prussia had learnt well from the war in 1864 and the effects of von Roon's reforms were now plain to see. At the outset, Prussia was able to deploy nine guard regiments and seventy-two line infantry regiments. These regiments comprised a total of two hundred and fifty-four battalions. All the regular infantry were armed with the bolt-operated breech-loading Dreyse needle-gun, which had been introduced into Prussian service progressively from the late 1840s. The rate of fire and accuracy of this 'state of the art' rifle proved decisive on the battlefields of 1866, where it easily outclassed the muzzle-loading weapons with which the Austrians were still equipped. The Prussian soldiers were able to fire up to six (and sometimes more) shots for every one fired by their Austrian opponents.[56]

There were eight guard cavalry regiments, eight regiments of cuirassiers, eight of dragoons, twelve of hussars and twelve of uhlans. Thus the Prussian cavalry arm comprised no less than two hundred squadrons. In support, there were nine of the newly established two-regiment artillery brigades, with a total of 864 guns. Most of the artillery weapons had only been introduced into service in the early 1860s, and were predominantly the steel, breech-loading guns manufactured by Krupps of Essen. All of these were the most modern artillery pieces in military service anywhere

European Warfare and the Thirty Years War

The European wars of the fifteenth, sixteenth and early seventeenth centuries were largely fought by well-armed bands of professional soldiers or mercenaries called landsknechts (right) whose loyalty was regularly governed by material self-interest rather than by patriotism or other higher ideals. Nevertheless, the landsknechts provided a foundation of military expertise from which many aspects of the professionalism of the later German armies were subsequently developed. During the Thirty Years War, from 1618 to 1648, most of Germany's countryside and many of its towns and cities were devastated. The civilian population succumbed to starvation, plague and the other ravages of war. Many people were forced to act as 'beasts of burden' in order to survive (below). The devastating war was a timely if traumatic catalyst that led subsequently to the creation of a national army for Brandenburg–Prussia.

Reformers and Innovators of the Nineteenth Century

General von Scharnhorst

General von Gneisenau

General von Boyen

General von Clausewitz

Architects of the Second Reich and its War Machine

Count Otto von Bismarck

King (later Kaiser) William I

Field Marshal Count Helmuth von Moltke

Field Marshal Count Albrecht von Roon

Above: The culmination of the so-called 'Death Ride' of General von Bredow's 12th Cavalry Brigade at Mars-la-Tour–Vionville, 16 August 1870, during the Franco-Prussian War. (From an illustration by E. Hünten)

Below: Interrogation at the village of Ste-Marie-aux-Chênes of a French courier caught trying to carry dispatches into the besieged city of Metz, September 1870. The seated Prussian officers are (left to right) a hussar, a dragoon, a staff officer and a lancer (uhlan), while Prussian infantrymen and hussars look on. (From a painting by A. de Neuville)

Above: Field Marshal Count Alfred von Schlieffen, the originator of the Schlieffen Plan. This strategic concept was designed to enable Germany to conduct a successful war on two fronts, and thereby to achieve the defeat of both France and Russia if and when required.

Above: Imperial Germany's warlords in 1914. Standing, left to right: von Bülow, von Mackensen, von Moltke, Crown Prince William of Prussia, von François, von Ludendorff, von Falkenhayn, von Einem, von Beseler, von Bethmann-Hollweg, von Heeringen. Seated, left to right: Crown Prince Rupert of Bavaria, Duke Albrecht of Württemberg, Kaiser William II, von Kluck, von Emmich, von Haeseler, von Hindenburg, von Tirpitz.

The First World War: a new sort of warfare

Above: Entrenched infantry and Maxim machine-gun positions on the Eastern Front in early 1915. Note the cloth covers fitted to the spiked pickelhaube helmets; the identifying number of the regiment was usually painted on the front of these.

Left: Prussian infantrymen on the Western Front, *c.*1916. Their front-line trench is well constructed, with additional side dugouts and shelters. The various items of captured equipment – a helmet and a Chasseur bugle horn – are probably indicative of a recent clash with French troops.

Right: As the war in the West dragged on, assault troops became the élite units of trench warfare. Often fighting hand-to-hand with grenades, knives and clubs as well as pistols, rifles and bayonets, the assault troops exemplified German military professionalism and the offensive spirit of the soldier of the time. This assault trooper, shown in early 1917, is in fact a cavalry trooper whose unit has been re-designated as an infantry assault unit.

Below: A machine-gun Type 08/15 with its crew, *c.*1917. The combination of machine guns, artillery and field defences such as barbed wire quickly rendered the tactics of the pre-1914 era obsolete and precipitated the development of new tactics, training methods and equipment (such as the tank).

Above: General Wilhelm Groener, first chief of staff of the post-1918 Reichswehr, who managed the successful return of the army to Germany in 1918. However, he was then responsible for fostering the concept of the army's betrayal by the civilian government and treachery on the home front, in a deliberate bid by the high command to preserve the nature and cohesion of the army as the country moved inexorably towards political turmoil and revolution.

Above: The warrior betrayed? A disabled First World War veteran and holder of the Iron Cross First Class forced to beg for charity on a Berlin street, post-1918.

Left: The Kapp-Lüttwitz Putsch, Pariserplatz, Berlin, March 1920. The right-wing political allegiance of these troops (almost certainly members of the Erhardt Brigade) is indicated by the swastikas (used as an Aryan and right-wing symbol in Germany since about 1910) emblazoned on the truck side and on their helmets.

at the time, and all fired shells that were detonated by percussion fuses rather than by the older system of pre-set time fuses.

The first action took place on 26 June, at Hühnerwasser in Northern Bohemia, where the Army of the Elbe easily overcame an Austrian force. The same day, the 1st Army defeated some fifteen Austrian battalions at Pódol and opened the way for a general Prussian advance into Bohemia, towards Königgrätz (or Sadowa as it was known locally). Thereafter a succession of minor battles took place, mainly in Bohemia. These included Tratenau, Nachod and Oswiecim (in Galicia) on 27 June, Münchengrätz, Soor (or Burkersdorf) and Skalitz on 28 June, followed by Gitschin and Schweinschaedel on 29 June. Although the Prussians were successful in most of these engagements – one notable exception being the serious but temporary reverse they suffered at Hanover's hands at Langensalza on 27 June[57] – the Austrian and Saxon soldiers generally fought well, and on several occasions they inflicted significant losses on the Prussians.

On 3 July the Prussians finally brought the full weight of their three armies to bear upon the main Austrian army at Königgrätz (as the battle was known to the Prussians) in Bohemia. There, some 221,000 Prussians with 191 infantry battalions, 184 cavalry squadrons, and 130 artillery batteries defeated about 206,000[58] Austrian and Saxon troops, comprising 202 infantry battalions and 158 cavalry squadrons, supported by about 700 guns. Despite the overall Prussian numerical superiority, until the arrival of the Prussian Crown Prince's 2nd Army in the late afternoon, the Austrian commander Field Marshal Ludwig, Ritter von Benedek, was actually enjoying a significant advantage. Although Benedek had his full force available throughout the day, and the Prussian 2nd Army – 115,000 strong – had been hampered by distance and heavy rain as it moved up to strike the Austrian flank, Benedek failed to exploit this situation. Nevertheless, the 2nd Army's difficulties did contribute to the fact that part of the Austrian army subsequently escaped the field and was then able to fight on for almost three more weeks.

The battle raged from 8.00 a.m. until 4.30 p.m., when the Austrian and Saxon forces finally collapsed and retreated in some disorder across the River Elbe. The defeat was comprehensive and the Prussians did not pursue them. The Austrians and the Saxon corps lost 4,861 men killed, 13,920 wounded and 25,419 missing – 44,200 in all (of which 1,450 were Saxons). They also lost 160 guns to the Prussians, whose own losses amounted to 1,830 killed, 6,688 wounded and 276 missing – just 8,794 men in total. Although the war continued until the final engagement, on 22 July at Blumenau, a village lying about three miles north-east of the

junction of the Rivers March and Danube, Königgrätz was the decisive
battle and all that occurred thereafter was little more than the harrying by
the Prussian 2nd Army of the retreating Austrians. In the meantime, the
remainder of the victorious Prussian forces encamped outside Vienna and
Pressburg. An armistice was arranged on 22 July, a preliminary peace
treaty was signed at Nikolsburg on 26 July, and this was ratified at Prague
on 30 August. Although the main action of the conflict had taken place in
Bohemia, other minor clashes had occurred between the Prussians and
Austria's south German allies in the west, but here also the Prussians had
triumphed.

Commenting upon the comparative tactics used by the Prussians and
the Austrians during the campaign, Lieutenant Bürde,[59] a Prussian reserve
officer, observed that:

> In the campaign of 1859 the French infantry, though armed with an inferior
> rifle [but not for much longer], usually charged the Austrians with the bayonet
> and drove them in after a short fight. This had the result that after the war the
> bayonet charge, with little or no previous fire action, was preached as the best
> form for attack. The Prussians, however, had soon recognized the non-validity
> of this mode of attack, and though not dispensing with a bayonet charge, stress
> was laid upon careful preparation by fire.

These remarks highlight the difference between the Austrian approach
to warfare – one still largely reminiscent of the former Napoleonic era –
and the way in which the Prussians were already exploiting their superior
technology and more modern training methods to good effect. Bürde also
noted that 'the Prussians had imparted a considerable amount of mobility
to their infantry, and had carefully taught them to use folds of the ground,
ravines, etc., for small flanking movements by companies and even
sections'. Meanwhile, the Austrians generally manoeuvred their infantry in
the old way, in massed battalions in close order, with little or no regard to
any available cover. Time and again Bürde observed that 'When Austrians
and Prussians met, the former usually attempted a bayonet charge with
bravery, but the effective fire of the Prussians soon brought their advance
to a stand still.'

Bürde also offered the opinion that the Austrian artillery was better
handled than that of the Prussians, coming into action more speedily and
with its firepower better co-ordinated. Certainly the Prussian artillery did
not always fully exploit tactically its undoubted technological superiority
and this was a matter that was addressed expeditiously after the war. The
Prussian cavalry – as ever rather slower to adapt to the new ways of

warfare than its infantry counterpart – also came in for some criticism
and, according to Bürde, 'For purposes of observation and reconnoitring
the Prussian cavalry was very badly handled in this war.' This was probably a valid statement, given the somewhat haphazard flow of intelligence
to the Prussian high command immediately prior to and during the war.
Despite its considerable effectiveness as a fighting arm, the failings of the
Prussian cavalry when required to carry out the more esoteric missions of
surveillance and reconnaissance continued and would again be all too
evident during the next and much greater conflict just four years later.

Its defeat at Königgrätz marked the end of Austria's leadership of the
Bund, which was then formally dissolved, together with the federal
German army, at Augsburg on 24 August 1866. The Peace of Prague
concluded the Austro–Prussian confrontation, and the Treaty of Berlin
provided a measure of independence for the south German states – but
only to the extent that Bismarck had always intended. Meanwhile, Prussia
had annexed Hanover, Hesse-Kassel, Nassau, Frankfurt-am-Main and

THE STATES OF THE NORTH
GERMAN CONFEDERATION
IN 1870

Schleswig-Holstein. These north German states added 4,200,000 people to the population of Prussia and its territories, with obvious implications for the future size of the army.

On 15 December 1866 Prussia convened a conference in Berlin, attended by the deputies of all the north German states (all those to the north of the River Main). This conference agreed the constitution for a new North German Confederation, headed *de facto* by Prussia, which assumed the federal presidency.

At last Bismarck's plans were about to come to fruition. German unification was all but achieved. Austria had been displaced from its historical position of primacy within Germany, and the Prussian army had demonstrated its formidable capability in the series of victories that culminated with Königgrätz. All that remained was to incorporate the military forces of the newly acquired states into an army of the North German Confederation, and to ensure that any remaining lessons from the conflicts against Denmark and Austria had been well and truly learned.

Prussia now had at its disposal a thoroughly modern war machine – in truth, one that was now German rather than Prussian in character and in all but name – and that war machine was almost ready to embark upon what would prove to be the most important military venture that it had yet undertaken in its two-hundred-year history. This new venture was nothing less than the military defeat of Prussia's arch-enemy France, together with the humiliation of a French emperor whose dynastic name was all too familiar to the Prussians, for in 1870 the Second French Empire was ruled by Napoleon III.

9

Anatomy of a Modern War Machine
1866–1870

THE DEFEAT OF AUSTRIA and the establishment of the North German Confederation gave the Prussian leadership a little less than four years in which to finalize their military plans and reorganizations. The annexed states provided a large influx of new forces, and their incorporation into the new North German Confederation's army also involved further extensive changes for the existing Prussian army. But von Moltke and the Prussian general staff would soon prove that they were well up to the task.

Organization: the Sinews of War

The events of 1866 resulted in three new army corps being placed at Prussia's disposal. The former armies of the newly incorporated north German states were generally reorganized and reformed, so that they adopted the same establishment and organization as the equivalent Prussian units. A modified form of the concept which had previously been applied successfully to the Landwehr was used once again, and large numbers of Prussian officers and non-commissioned officers were assigned to the regiments found by the newly annexed states. In some instances complete companies of Prussian soldiers were posted to provide the core of the new regiments. This cross-posting process was not one-way only, however; a number of officers of the former armies of Hanover, Kassel and Nassau were also posted to existing Prussian units.

This army expansion produced twenty-four new infantry regiments, which were designated as regiments numbered '73' to '96' in the Prussian order of battle. The regiments numbered '1' to '72' were the existing Prussian regiments. The Prussian army's system of numbering its units had generally grouped them regionally, and the numbers of certain regiments and units also indicated their seniority or precedence in the army's order of battle. In addition, many units had supplementary numbers, titles and sub-titles that related to their specific histories, royal connections or other affiliations and previous service, or which indicated their regional and recruiting links. Where practicable, this convention was carried forward into the wider army organization that emerged after 1866. Two such examples of regional affiliations indicated by a secondary or supplementary title were the '29th Infantry Regiment (Rhenish No 3)' and the '16th Regiment of Dragoons (Hanoverian No 2)'.

Although the new regiments received their territorially linked names in line with the Prussian system in 1867, they were generally not stationed in their parent recruiting districts until some years later. This was almost certainly a deliberate policy designed to forestall any resurgence of militant nationalism in the former non-Prussian states at that time.

The reorganization of the cavalry from October 1866 followed a similar and by now familiar pattern, with Prussian squadrons taken from existing regiments providing the core of the new regiments. No fewer than seventeen new regiments of hussars, uhlans, and dragoons were formed in 1866, and three more regiments of dragoons were added in the following year. As with the infantry, they were allocated numbers within the Prussian order of battle that placed them in order of seniority or precedence after the existing Prussian cavalry units. Finally, in 1867, all the Prussian cavalry regiments were required to form fifth 'depot and reception squadrons', which were intended further to improve the North German Confederation's mobilization process.

Three new artillery regiments were created, using the same method of reorganization, redesignation and cross-posting. Each of these regiments comprised three field artillery units, each of four batteries (two heavy, two light) and one unit of horse artillery, consisting of a further three batteries.

Within the North German Confederation only Saxony was permitted to retain a national military identity and to administer and direct its armed forces through the Saxon Ministry of War. This was due to the significant size of the forces it contributed to the Confederation. Consequently, Saxony formed the 12th (Royal Saxon) Corps, which (in 1870) was commanded by the Crown Prince of Saxony. The Saxon reorganization to reflect the Prussian establishment took place in 1867, from which it produced eight infantry regiments (each of three battalions) and four cavalry regiments, with two each of uhlans and hussars.

Although much of the reorganization centred upon the north German states, the defeat of Austria and the intentionally generous handling of that country's erstwhile south German allies by Bismarck had allowed the kingdom of Bavaria, together with the smaller states of Württemberg, Baden and Hesse-Darmstadt, to be allied secretly with Prussia prior to what was by now the imminent war against France.

The Bavarian army, although it was militarily less modern than its north German counterpart, was a very significant addition to the Prussian-led forces. Its infantry arm included one regiment of the guard and fifteen line infantry regiments. In 1866 each Bavarian infantry regiment comprised six companies. The Bavarian cavalry included three regiments of cuirassiers, six regiments of light cavalry and three uhlan regiments. There were four regiments of artillery and one regiment of engineers. In 1868 the Bavarian army reorganized on the Prussian model, when the infantry battalions reduced from six to four companies and the soldiers of one cuirassier and one uhlan regiment were reallocated so that the remaining cavalry regiments would match the Prussian five-squadron organization. The Bavarian artillery and engineer support units were partially reorganized on to the Prussian establishment, and by 1870 the artillery was able to field more than 200 rifled breech-loading guns.

The standard rifle used throughout the Bavarian army was the Podewil. This was a breech-loader which had been converted from a muzzle-loader. To its cost, Bavaria did not adopt the Dreyse needle-gun, and when it went to war in 1870 only four Bavarian infantry battalions had been equipped with its own new weapon of choice, the improved Werder rifle. While most of the armies of the other German states had adopted the familiar dark-blue jacket, grey trousers and spiked 'Pickelhaube' helmet then worn by the Prussian army, Bavaria's soldiers retained the distinctive light-blue uniform they had worn for the previous 150 years.

Of the other south German states, Württemberg contributed fifteen infantry battalions and ten cavalry squadrons, Baden thirteen battalions and twelve cavalry squadrons. Unlike Bavaria, these two states had readily embraced the Prussian military organization and procedures, so that by 1870 Prussian artillery and the Dreyse needle-gun had been fully adopted by their soldiers. Finally, the remaining south German state, Hesse-Darmstadt, under a bilateral agreement with Prussia, formed the 25th (Hessian) Division of the North German Army and so for all practical purposes it was regarded thereafter as being fully integrated into the new federal army.

Manpower: the Soldiers

Apart from the various national (state) exceptions already noted, the soldiers were generally dressed and equipped in accordance with the Prussian model. On campaign the soldier carried about sixty-four pounds of equipment (compared to the fifty-five pounds carried by the British soldier of 1870). This was the basic combat load, but it could be increased to as much as one hundred pounds in full campaign marching order.

The German soldier's equipment, as Archibald Forbes (a 'special correspondent' during the Franco-Prussian War for the London *Morning*

Advertiser and the *Daily News*)[60] noted, included his 'needle-gun, heavy knapsack, eighty rounds of ammunition, huge greatcoat, camp kettle, sword [bayonet], ... spade [or other entrenching tool], water-bottle [which was of a particularly effective design, comprising a flat-shaped glass flask, covered with thick, stiff leather, and fitted with a screw stopper], haversack, and lots of odds and ends dangling about them, with perhaps a loaf, like a curling stone, under the arm'.[61] The infantryman's basic equipment was supported on a waist belt and two bracing straps, all of black leather, with ammunition pouches mounted on the left and right front sides of the belt. The 'heavy knapsack' was made of natural hide, and about its top and sides the greatcoat or a blanket could be secured. Where the knapsack was not carried, the blanket or greatcoat was often rolled up into a long sausage shape, which could then be secured over the soldier's left shoulder and across his body. Although significantly less ostentatious and colourful than the uniforms of the French army of the day, the German army's many regiments, branches, services and regional groupings all displayed their identity and origins with pride through a multiplicity of uniform differences, insignia and embellishments.[62]

The German soldier of 1870 was generally fatalistic and pragmatic, but nevertheless a God-fearing man. Religion featured prominently in the life of every regiment, divine services being held before and after battle and to mark all the principal religious festivals if the operational situation permitted. The first phrase of the inscription 'MIT GOTT FUR KOENIG UND VATERLAND' borne on the scroll of the Prussian Pickelhaube helmet plate was by no means mere symbolism.[63] The observance and celebration of Christmas and the New Year attracted particular importance throughout the army, the rituals and celebrations often verging on a benign form of mysticism or superstition. While the Germans of Bavaria and the southern states were predominantly Roman Catholic, those from Prussia and the other north German states were overwhelmingly Protestant, where the legacy and influence of Martin Luther's sixteenth-century teachings remained strong. However, far from the situation that had existed during the Thirty Years War, and which had indeed triggered that conflict, any occasional friction between the soldiers of the northern and southern state contingents was now merely symptomatic of professional or national pride rather of any deep-seated religious differences.

Irrespective of his social background and whether he came from the town or from the countryside, the German soldier's principal material pleasures were beer – usually of the light or lager variety, although darker and stronger beers were often favoured by the south German soldiers – and tobacco. The latter was always in plentiful supply in the German army and it was either smoked or taken as snuff by all ranks; appropriate quantities were invariably to be found in the uniform pouches or pockets of the majority of the soldiers. Indeed, most soldiers possessed pipes that were often both ornate and much cherished items, usually being of at least one-ounce capacity. It was also quite usual for the German cavalry in particular – officers and troopers alike – to charge into battle with cigars firmly clenched between their teeth!

Manpower: the Officers

Although the more senior commanders and the general staff officers who supported them could undoubtedly claim much of the credit for the German successes at the operational and strategic level, at the tactical level of command success or failure was almost exclusively in the hands of the regimental officers. These junior and field-grade officers had paid a consistently high personal price in casualties sustained during the wars with Denmark and Austria, and many would shortly be called upon to make the supreme sacrifice during the war with France. As was so with their soldiers, the regimental officers came from all levels of German society, class and relative wealth. But all were professionally competent and had been extremely well trained to a common high standard in the art of war. Irrespective of their social background, they still enjoyed a privileged position in German society, especially after the victories against Denmark and Austria. All of them belonged to what was in effect an exclusive club – their regiment   and acceptance into the regiment of their choice was still subject to the approval and agreement of those who would subsequently be a potential candidate's brother officers.

Typical of the career pattern of the German officer of the 1860s and 1870s was that of a company commander of the 4th (East Prussian) Infantry Regiment, some details of which were recorded by Archibald Forbes following his conversation with him during the siege of Metz in 1870:

> He came to the regiment from the gymnasium [grammar or high school], in the capacity of avantageur. An avantageur is neither more nor less than a private soldier who aspires to a commission. On joining he had to pass an examination to demonstrate his general scholarship. For twelve months he served in the ranks, rising meanwhile to the non-commissioned rank of Vice-feldwebel, and then he went for a year to the military school. On leaving this, he had to pass an examination on everything relating to the art military, and

then he came back to the regiment as a Degenfähnrich, that is to say as the wearer of a sword without commissioned rank for six months longer. The officers of the regiment then voted him eligible for a commission, and expressed their readiness, by the same vote, to accept him as a comrade and credit to the service; this step being an indispensable prelude to a commission. Whereupon the King was graciously pleased to sign his commission as a second lieutenant, a rank which he had contentedly held for six years, and may hold still, for aught I know to the contrary. He wore the medals for 1866 [the Austrian campaign]; he had commanded the company for the last two years, because his seniors had been killed off; he was looking forward with hope to be a premier lieutenant in the course of another year, and a captain in perhaps ten more. His pay in wartime was about eleven pounds, ten shillings a month, in peace he had not much more than about half as much. And he was a thoroughly contented, even-minded, German gentleman, proud of the service, proud that he bore a commission in it, very hungry for the Iron Cross, fond of fun, and fonder still of work and fighting.[64]

Indeed, the financial constraints on a German officer's lifestyle in peacetime were quite significant as 'the basic pay for a major-general was the 1870 British equivalent of £37 a month, although substantial subsidiary allowances were added to this; that of a first lieutenant was about £6 a month. No officer could marry without leave and a subaltern officer had to show that his fiancée had a private income of £125 a year; the fiancée of a second-class captain had to have £75 a year. Above that rank no private fortune was required.'[65] This career profile and the personal circumstances and wider social constraints affecting his everyday life were typical of those of the many hundreds of officers who, although very competent regimental officers, would never be selected to join the élite ranks of the general staff and therefore were almost certainly debarred from achieving the highest ranks. For these men, however, the honour and duty of serving their fatherland – and the personal prestige they derived from doing so – were enough.

Images of a War Machine

As with most armies of the time, the uniform rules and regulations for the German Army of 1870 were extensive and complex, but also included many anachronisms, and sometimes matters of detail were ignored at the whim of a particular commander. In the main, however, the German infantry that marched west in July 1870 wore the familiar dark-blue woollen jacket piped scarlet, and with scarlet collar. The jacket worn by the Prussian, Hessian and Saxon units was single-breasted, that of the Württemberg regiments was double-breasted. The collar of all regiments of the Prussian guard was embellished with two distinctive bars of white lace, although some other élite units also bore this distinguishing insignia, in white or yellow. Almost without exception the infantrymen wore dark-grey woollen trousers piped in scarlet, which were worn tucked into dark-brown or black, calf-length leather boots.

The Pickelhaube helmet, which soon became what was probably the most enduring symbol of German militarism for more than half a century, was in almost universal use.[66] It was made of black, cloth-lined leather and had a small drooped peak at the front and a neck guard at the rear. A metal spike (infantry) or ball (artillery) was mounted centrally on its top.[67] Generally, the helmet front was emblazoned with a large Prussian-style spread-eagle. Both Saxony and Hesse used their own distinctive insignia (in the latter case a lion emblem) on the front of their soldiers' Pickel-haube. The metal insignia and other helmet fittings were usually of brass. Exceptionally, at the outset of the war in 1870 the infantry regiments of Württemberg still wore a dark-blue kepi, piped scarlet and bearing a cockade in the colours of Württemberg on the front. But that state also adopted the Pickelhaube during the following year.

The corps to which a unit belonged was indicated by its shoulder-strap colour and by coloured embellishments on the cuffs. At battalion and company level an infantryman's parent unit or sub-unit was readily iden-tifiable by the colour combination used for the several parts of the deco-rative side-arm knot (Troddel) that was attached to his bayonet frog.

As was also the case in many other armies of the day, the title 'guard' indicated an implied or actual level of training, discipline, commitment and allegiance to the state and the sovereign which (arguably) exceeded that to be found in the line infantry regiments. So it was also in the Prussian Guard Corps, which was recruited from throughout the Kingdom of Prussia and was normally based in the prestigious garrisons in Berlin, at Spandau and Potsdam. The Guard Corps displayed several dress distinctions that immediately identified them as élite troops. Their Pickelhaube bore the familiar spread-eagle helmet plate, but of a slightly modified design, with a silver-star badge super-imposed upon it. Their blue woollen jacket was the same as those issued to the rest of the infantry, apart from the two bars of white lace on the collar and cuffs. Finally, unlike the numerical regimental identification system used by the rest of the German infantry, in the Guard Corps the colour of a guardsman's jacket shoulder-straps indicated his parent regiment. Most of the Guard Corps was uniformed thus, the only significant exceptions being the two guard rifle battalions, the Garde-Schützen and the Garde-Jäger, both of which wore a green instead of a blue tunic, and a black shako emblazoned with a large version of the silver-star guards' badge rather than the Pickelhaube with its spread-eagle insignia.

A notable exception to the German uniform norms was the dress of the Bavarian infantry. Their jackets and trousers were of light-blue material, piped scarlet, and with the collar and cuffs of the facing colour of the regiment. The Bavarian infantryman also wore a black leather helmet emblazoned on the front with the cipher of their monarch King Ludwig II (a large scrolled letter 'L' beneath a crown) instead of the Prussian-style spread-eagle. Also, instead of the familiar Prussian spike or ball, the Bavarian helmet was fitted with a distinctive black crest of bearskin, which ran from the base of the helmet at the rear to its top. Forbes, ever the most critical of military observers, was not particularly impressed by the Bavarian uniform, and he noted that:

> The light blue of the Bavarian uniform does not wear well in point of looks – it gets soiled in no time and then even the officers look seedy. The helmet, too, is a creation of intensest [*sic*] ugliness. It has no split crow [i.e., the Prussian-style spread-eagle] in gold on the front, but the letter 'L' for the King's initial, and it is surmounted by a ridgy tuft of upstanding bear's-skin ... But the Bavarian soldiers, [in] spite of an ugly uniform, were fine fellows, and right serviceable-looking soldiers.[68]

The only other significant exceptions to the general rules for the German infantry uniforms were to be found in certain of the line Jäger regiments. Here (as with the Garde-Schützen and Garde-Jäger regiments), a black glazed shako was worn by these light infantry sharpshooters instead of the Pickelhaube, and a dark-green jacket with a red collar, cuffs and shoulder-straps in place of the dark-blue tunic worn by the line infantrymen.

Greater variations of uniform were to be found within the cavalry, with its various regiments of dragoons, cuirassiers, hussars and lancers. The dragoons, whose traditional role was as mounted infantry, were equipped with a jacket similar to those of the infantry, but usually of light-blue rather than dark-blue, and with piping, collar, shoulder-straps and cuffs of the appropriate regimental colour. The dragoons' trousers were dark-blue, and their leather-reinforced overalls were dark-grey, piped scarlet. Their helmet was of black leather and very similar to those provided for the infantry, but with additional metal embellishments. In order to carry out their operational role, the trooper in a dragoon regiment was armed with a cavalry carbine and a light cavalry-pattern sabre.

The senior cavalry regiments of the German army were the cuirassiers. They were the heavy cavalry, whose bold employment as shock troops at the right moment could often turn or decide the outcome of a battle decisively. The jacket and trousers of the German cuirassiers were all white (apart from those of the Bavarian cuirassiers, who wore an all light-blue uniform), with coloured embellishments to indicate the regiment. The cuirassier helmet used on campaign was made of white metal with yellow metal (usually brass) features and fittings. The helmet worn by virtually all German cuirassiers featured the usual spike, as well as an extended metal neck protector that came down low at the back. But the Bavarian cuirassier's helmet featured the familiar black bearskin crest in place of the spike. On active service all cuirassiers wore a protective breast and back-plate (the 'cuirass') of black or gunmetal-coloured iron. The helmet and cuirass of the guard cuirassier regiments were of yellow metal. When over-alls, which were reinforced with leather, were worn they were usually dark-grey with scarlet piping. The cuirassiers' thigh-length riding boots were of black leather. Their principal weapon was a heavy, straight-bladed sword, which was supplemented by a pistol or a cavalry carbine.

The hussar uniforms, as with those worn by the hussars of other European nations, were both ornate and colourful. The regiment was identified by the colour of the tunic which was embellished with rows of corded and looped lace across the chest and on the cuffs and back. Certain regiments, including the guard hussars, wore the traditional hussar 'pelisse' (hussar jacket) slung across the left shoulder and secured at the neck by a cord or chain. Their riding-trousers were usually dark-blue. As with the hussars of most other nations, the German hussars wore a black or very dark-brown busby of sealskin, embellished with regimental insignia on the front and with a cloth bag on the top, overhanging on the left side. The busby bag was red for most (but not all) hussar regiments. These regiments included the 1st and 2nd Life (or 'Bodyguard') Hussar ('Leibhusaren') Regiments, and the 17th (Brunswick) Hussar Regiment, all of which wore the famous 'death's head' (or 'Totenkopf') cap badge. As a light cavalryman, the hussar's standard weapons were the light cavalry sabre and the carbine.

Among the best-known German cavalry units of the day were the uhlans, or lancers. They routinely guarded and patrolled the frontiers and so were literally the nation's first line of defence. In addition to operating in the traditional light cavalry role, they were also expected to provide early intelligence of enemy activity. These cavalrymen were equipped with lances of oak or ash, ten feet five inches long, tipped with a four-sided steel point that was almost thirteen inches long. The lance bore a two-colour pennant which showed the regional affiliation of the regiment. These were white over black for Prussia, black and red for Württemberg, white over green for Saxony and white and light-blue for Bavaria. In addition to the lance the uhlan trooper was armed with a lightweight sabre and a cavalry carbine. The non-commissioned officers and others, such as trumpeters, who were not equipped with the lance, were armed with the same pattern of sabre as that provided for the dragoons. The uhlan jacket was dark-blue (apart from that worn by the Bavarians, who wore dark-green, and the Saxons, light-blue) and double-breasted, with a plastron buttoned across the chest. It was piped in the regimental facing colour and the cuffs, collar and turnbacks were usually of the same facing colour. All uhlan regiments wore the 'czapska', the unique and most distinctive black leather lancer helmet. The original design of this head-dress was Polish. It was emblazoned with the Prussian eagle in metal on the front, being surmounted by a four-sided, fluted central crest with a flat top, which bore the national cockade on its left side. The uhlans, much assisted by the aggressive image conveyed by the lances they carried, struck considerable fear into their enemies and well suited them for employment as shock troops and for pursuit operations during the war. Indeed, the later successes of the uhlans against the French in 1870 and 1871 were such that in 1889 Emperor William II of Germany directed that all units of the German cavalry were to be equipped with this weapon, the shaft of which was by then made of rolled steel rather than of wood.

The third combat arm was the artillery. This included both the field artillery, with their teams of horses, guns and limbers, and the foot or garrison artillery units. These gun crews were uniformed much as the infantry, with dark-blue jacket and grey trousers, but with the ball – symbolizing a cannon-ball – in place of the spike on their Pickelhaube. The field artillery jacket had black cuffs and collar, with red piping and scarlet shoulder-straps, while the foot (that is the 'heavy' or 'siege') artillery were identifiable by their white shoulder-straps. Saxon artillery units wore a dark-green jacket with scarlet cuffs, shoulder-straps, collar and piping.

This then was the general organization and appearance of the combat arms of the war machine that had emerged in Germany by July 1870. But such infantry, cavalry and artillery combat power can only truly realize its full potential in war if it is complemented effectively by the necessary supporting arms and services. In the German army this support fell to the 'pioneers' (the engineers) and to the 'military train', as well as to an extensive range of other troops and specialist units with all sorts of complementary support, administrative and supply functions.

Supporting, Administrative and Supply Services

The army engineer units were trained in mobility and counter-mobility work, such as the repair and construction of roads, bridges and railroads or the demolition of these, together with the construction and repair of fortifications, field defences, obstacles, gun emplacements, trench systems and the laying of landmines. They also maintained, repaired and constructed the telegraph lines which complemented the army's visual signalling systems. The telegraph had assumed ever-increasing importance in the Prussian army since the invention of the passage of information electronically and of the Morse code in 1844. The engineer troops also included the specialist railway engineer regiments (readily identifiable as élite units by the yellow letter 'E' for 'Eisenbahn' (railway) that was displayed together with their battalion number on the scarlet shoulder-straps of their jacket, and by the guards-style white lace bars worn on their cuffs and collar). These units maintained the particular skills necessary to construct and operate the railway systems that were so essential to the general staff's mobilization plans. Engineer units could also carry out obstacle crossings, such as those over rivers using pontoon bridges, a capability essential to the successful conduct of offensive operations and for maintaining the momentum of an advance.[69]

In war, various aspects of the engineer role overlapped that of the military train, or supply troops. These troops comprised units and sections dealing with general administration, accounting and commissariat, pay and finance (including that involved with the administration of occupied areas), the provision of food, forage and ammunition, and with the establishment and actual operation of field post offices. There were also the medical (or 'sanitary') service, the veterinary officers, and a host of other administrative units and individual officers and soldiers fulfilling an almost infinite range of specialist roles and supporting functions. All of these personnel were generally uniformed in the ubiquitous dark-blue jacket and grey trousers, with either the Pickelhaube or the dark-blue general service forage cap (the 'Feldmütze') worn as head-dress, but with insignia, piping and other embellishments to indicate their particular branch or service. These officers and soldiers were equipped with side arms, carbines, rifles and other specialist equipment appropriate to their specific operational roles.

Once deployed in support of an operation, the military train usually divided into two echelons or 'baggage trains'. One of these would be located about ten miles to the rear of the supported formation and cater for its short-term needs, the other would be much farther to the rear, having with it all that the formation required for a sustained period of combat. Attached to the military train on mobilization there might be (for example) an engineer pontoon bridging train, detachments of field telegraph troops, and a number of field hospitals of the medical service.

The War Machine in Perspective

The theoretical or 'paper' peacetime establishment of the army necessarily differed from its planned war establishment. Not surprisingly, these establishments were also at variance with the actual number of troops and resources that Germany eventually fielded against France in 1870. Indeed, such broad personnel and resource statistics are often less important to an objective analysis of military capability than are the numbers of complete manoeuvre formations and units available for deployment. Nevertheless, both for completeness and as an indication of the precise calculations of men and resources that had been carried out by the Prussian general staff, it is instructive to summarize the peacetime and war establishments of the army, as well as the number and composition of manoeuvre units that the Germans were actually able to launch against France. The planned or established strengths and organization of the army of the North German Confederation in 1870 are shown at Tables 1 and 2 of Appendix 4. But the German army that took the field against France also included the armies of Bavaria, Württemberg and Baden. This meant that Prussia and its allies of the North German Confederation and southern Germany were potentially able to dispose of well over one and a half million men, although of course not all of these were committed operationally during what would prove to be a relatively short war. The details of these forces are shown in Tables 3 and 4 of Appendix 4.

Self-evidently, the German army of 1870 was a huge, diverse, and very complex organization. In some respects it was almost a 'multinational' force, although having a common language. It had the capacity to wreak wholesale destruction and violence upon an adversary on a scale previously unprecedented in European warfare. So how was this remarkable military force to be mobilized, moved, directed, deployed and commanded effectively? The German system of command and control has, ever since 1871, been credited with being the single most important factor that enabled and then ensured the army's success against the French, and the unique organization that achieved this outcome was the German general staff, which in 1870 was still headed by General (later Count) Helmuth von Moltke.

Command and Control: the German General Staff

In 1870 von Moltke was in his seventieth year. He, above all others, was responsible for the introduction, development, training and refinement of the general staff system of command and control. His own professional staff credentials were impeccable and he had consistently demonstrated his outstanding ability during the campaign fought over Schleswig-Holstein in 1864 and that against Austria in 1866. However, he has been described as 'a remote and dedicated professional' and this was perhaps indicative of the fact that his particular abilities as a staff officer were not always entirely mirrored by his wider powers of leadership and his occasional inability to control some of his senior subordinate commanders in the field.

The general staff concept had of course originated in Prussia and was now carried forward vigorously into the much-expanded army. Although staff systems in their earliest forms could be traced back to the Prussian army of the early eighteenth century, von Moltke had perfected the general staff model in 1857. The members of the general staff were quite simply the most competent and intellectually astute officers of the army, and appointment to the general staff was a highly competitive, selective and continuing process. The general staff dealt with all matters concerned with 'the movement, quartering, engagement and mobilizing of the troops, and to warfare in general'. This last area of responsibility in effect provided a right and duty to be involved in all aspects of the conduct of operations. Despite this wide remit, the actual number of general staff officers was relatively small. There were just 200 in 1870, which rose to a figure approaching 250 by the end of the war with France.

Officers who had completed three years' service and who were recommended to do so applied to take an entrance examination that would admit them to the Kriegsakademie. There they completed a course of three years, which also included periods of service with units of the field army to ensure that their theoretical training and studies were always balanced by practical experience. Rigorous assessment of the students continued throughout the course. This first step culminated in a suitably testing examination that determined the immediate future employment of the officer. This might be either as an instructor at a military school, or as an adjutant (dealing with all aspects of the routine staff work and management of the army), or as a general staff officer. Of an annual Kriegsakademie intake of about 400 officers, only 120 usually reached the final examination point, and of these only the top ten or twelve officers were taken annually for general staff employment.

These few outstanding officers next completed between two and three years attached to the Great General Staff in Berlin, where the training, education, assessment and selection process continued. Finally, those officers who successfully completed this time under the direct supervision of the chief of the general staff were assigned permanently to the general staff, although any decline in their performance could always result in a rapid return to regimental duty. They were subsequently employed in general staff appointments at all levels of command down to division, and progressed in rank and responsibility within the general staff system. Theirs was a process of continuous personal professional development, which blended service with troops, staff work, travel, and all forms of intellectual development to prepare them for the most important appointments and ultimately, if appropriate, for high command. Throughout their service these officers enjoyed a deservedly privileged position, and when serving as the chief of staff of a formation they would invariably assume command of that division, corps or army in the absence of its commanding general. Their presence in every major headquarters, installation and organization also guaranteed the chief of the general staff a first-hand view of the activities and performance of every part of the army, together with the ability to influence these very directly. This then was the remarkable corporate military brain which now directed the German army in its entirety, a brain that had prepared it particularly well during the previous decade for its greatest challenge yet, the conquest and humiliation of France.

IO

Clash of Eagles
The War with France, 1870–1871

OF THE MANY GREAT CONFLICTS that have ebbed and flowed across Europe over the centuries, the Franco-Prussian War (or perhaps more accurately the 'Franco-German War') enabled the unification of Germany and the birth of the German empire. It therefore merits a very special place in the history of both Europe and of the world. Furthermore, although of relatively short duration, this clash of arms between France and Germany subsequently paved the way for the two most destructive conflicts that the world has yet endured: the First and Second World Wars. Although it only involved these two great Continental powers, Germany's victory and an unfortunate and unforeseen succession of post-1871 events in that country set it on a potentially disastrous and ill-judged course that over time acquired an awful inevitability. Indeed, while virtually every war begets its successors to some extent, the direct causal linkage between 1870–1 and 1914 is irrefutable; as is the connection between the outcome of the First World War in 1918 and the rise of National Socialism in Germany, and therefore the Second World War that it spawned in 1939. The Franco-Prussian War also marked the point at which the influence of the German army became both a prominent and a dominant power within the German state, rather than simply the means by which the German state gained and maintained its international power, prestige and influence. For those who served in the army, the second half of the nineteenth century was most assuredly the 'golden age of German militarism'; it was also the period during which a supremely confident German war machine embarked – albeit naïvely and unwittingly – upon what would eventually prove to be its road to perdition.

The causes of the Franco-Prussian War were complex and various, but stemmed primarily from a Franco–German dispute over the succession to the Spanish throne, fuelled by an obsessive desire by many of the French people to humiliate Prussia: a desire that was actively supported by several senior French ministers and diplomats. All this actually fitted in very well with Minister-President Count Otto von Bismarck's plans for the unification and pre-eminence of Prussia and Germany in Europe: for which the neutralization of France as a military and imperial competitor was a prerequisite.

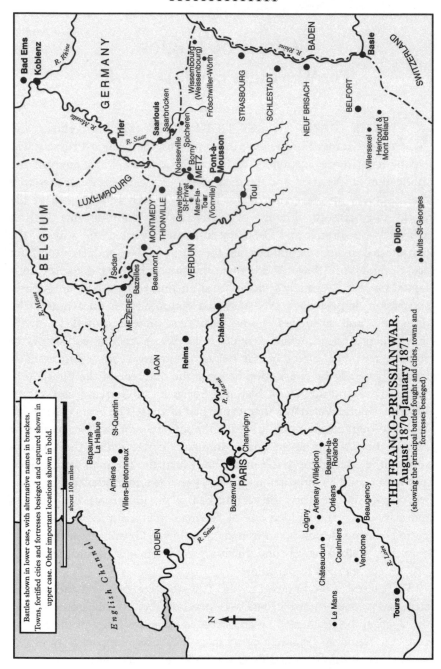

THE FRANCO-PRUSSIAN WAR,
August 1870–January 1871
(showing the principal battles fought and cities, towns and
fortresses besieged)

Battles shown in lower case, with alternative names in brackets.
Towns, fortified cities and fortresses besieged and captured shown in
upper case. Other important locations shown in bold.

about 100 miles

Although France had declared war on Prussia on 19 July 1870 – a situation that had been most astutely contrived by Bismarck with the leaking of the so-called 'Ems telegram' to the German press in mid-July – the first fighting did not take place until mid-morning on Tuesday, 2 August, when the 2nd French Corps, with a strength in excess of 60,000 men, advanced to seize the small town of Saarbrücken with its strategically important bridges over the River Saar.

The six months of warfare that followed fall very broadly into four distinct but overlapping parts. First, a number of battles were fought at or close to the Franco–German frontier. In addition to the small-scale but significant fight at Saarbrücken on 2 August and the battle at Wissembourg on 4 August, these included the clashes at Spicheren (6 August), and Fröschwiller-Wörth (6 August). At Wissembourg and Fröschwiller-Wörth the Bavarian troops fought courageously and successfully alongside their north German comrades and thus demonstrated the truly 'German' nature of the army from the outset. Next came the major set-piece clashes at Mars-la-Tour (16 August) and Gravelotte–St-Privat (18 August). In these great blood-lettings the Germans, although emerging victorious, suffered considerable losses and learned hard lessons. These two great battles also laid the foundations for Napoleon III's final defeat at Sedan (1 September) and for the subsequent fall of the strategically vital fortress city of Metz (27 October). The third phase was really a campaign within a campaign, and was the lengthy siege of Paris, which lasted from 19 September 1870 to 28 January 1871. The last phase of the war featured the campaign waged against the Germans by the armies of the newly established French Third Republic, after the collapse of the French Second Empire at Sedan. This was fought during one of Europe's worst winters and involved extensive guerrilla warfare and several major battles. The fighting was particularly bitter, with extreme hardships endured by all the combatants, and with numerous atrocities committed – by the French in particular – but which prompted the inevitable German reprisals.

By the end of six months' fighting, on 23 January 1871, at least 150,000 French soldiers had been killed, and about the same number wounded. The Prussians and their allies had sustained losses of some 28,208 dead and 88,488 wounded.[70]

Clearly, a full account of the war is beyond the scope of this work,[71] although its pivotal role in the development of the German army and the story of those who served in it certainly demands analysis and selective amplification. Accordingly, a number of specific events or types of action are dealt with in some detail. Among these are the outbreak of the war and the first 'clash of eagles' at Saarbrücken, the two key offensive battles at Mars-la-Tour and at Gravelotte–St-Privat, the three major sieges of Strasbourg, Metz and Paris, and finally certain aspects of the campaign conducted against the forces of the French Third Republic, which provided an early and telling insight into the nature of warfare yet to come. Of necessity, this unavoidable selectivity is to the exclusion of many other important events and battles, for example the major battle at Sedan on 1 and 2 September 1870. But apart from the importance of its political outcome, in that it was at that encircled fortress town that Napoleon III and his empire finally suffered defeat, the battle at Sedan does not move the story of the German army forward significantly; other than to confirm the skill and strategic planning of von Moltke and the general staff, and the absolute dominance of the German artillery. Similarly, the protracted siege of Paris from September 1870 to late January 1871 is mentioned only in passing, and more particularly where an aspect of that siege directly affected the German army's tactics, procedures or campaign lifestyle.

In each of the cases that have been selected, the focus is primarily on the tactical rather than strategic level of command (other than where it impinges directly upon the activities of von Moltke and the general staff), and it also deals with the type and changing nature of the fighting in which the ordinary German soldiers were engaged. Lastly, because of its great impact upon the future of Germany and of Europe, the principal features of the German military victory are also considered as a whole – not least because they subsequently affected the German army very directly during the almost five decades from 1871 until the outbreak of the First World War.

Saarbrücken, 2 August 1870

The battle of Saarbrücken is often dismissed as a minor incident, of little consequence to the war as a whole. Although small-scale with relatively few casualties, its outcome was to influence very directly the course of much of that which followed. It was at Saarbrücken that the French saw what they perceived – erroneously as it turned out – to be a vindication of their intended grand strategy of decisive offensive action followed by a speedy invasion of Prussia, and the conduct of the fight fuelled French complacency in their assessment of the German military capability.

As is so often the case in war, the first clash between the soldiers marching with the French army's eagles and those under the black eagles of Prussia came about almost by default when, on 30 July, in response to pressure of French public opinion on Napoleon and the army to take offensive action, the French commander Marshal Bazaine was ordered to cross the Saar and occupy the small but militarily important frontier town of Saarbrücken. General Frossard was the overall commander of a French attacking force with high morale and which was confident of achieving a resounding victory.

Saarbrücken lay right on the border, astride the main rail and road routes between Metz in France and Kaiserslautern in Germany. The town straddled the Saar and, in 1870, there were three bridges in the town, including a strategically important railway bridge. The section of the town to the north, on the right or east bank of the Saar, was called St Johann, that to the south of the river was Saarbrücken (or 'Saarbrück') proper. The town, lying as it did in the Saar valley, was overlooked on all sides by a range of wooded knolls. To the west of the river, towards the town of Forbach some five miles distant, the main road rose steeply to a long, high ridge and plateau which entirely dominated that part of the valley in general and the town in particular. From there the ground rolled away gently into the French heartland to the west.

Ever since the declaration of war, the French had manned a chain of frontier posts, tented camps and permanent blockhouses in some strength running all along the ridgeline adjacent to Saarbrücken and well beyond the town of Sarreguemines to the south. In the Saarbrücken area, many of the German pickets were from the 40th Regiment of Fusiliers (Hohen-zollern) and from the locally based lancers of the 7th Regiment of Uhlans (Rhenish), who manned positions in the valley and on the various stretches of high ground adjacent to the frontier on the Prussian side. These German advanced and supporting positions were deployed on both banks of the Saar, as well as within and on the outskirts of Saarbrücken. In anticipation of the coming conflict the German soldiers had partially blocked the town's bridges across the river with barrels filled with stones. More of these obstacles were placed near by, ready to be rolled into place to block the thoroughfare if necessary.

On the morning of the French assault, Saarbrücken lay within the tactical area of responsibility of the 8th German Corps, commanded by General von Goeben. It was defended by twelve companies of the 40th Regiment of Fusiliers and of the 69th Regiment of Infantry (Rhenish No. 7), a force that numbered not more than 3,000 men. These infantry companies were organized into four battalions, supported by a battery of horse artillery and four squadrons of cavalry, which added about 600 more men. The nearest significant supporting force was based at the village of Lebach, some fifteen miles to the north. The German defenders of the town were nominally commanded by a Colonel von Pestal,[72] who had been the local commander at Saarbrücken since the declaration of war in mid-July, but overall control of the German frontier outposts in the area was in the hands of one Count von Gneisenau.[73] His own orders, and consequently those issued to his subordinates, required the German forces to avoid any commitment to a pitched battle at this early stage of the war, and to withdraw to the area of Lebach if pressed hard. Indeed, on 2 August, the German mobilization and movement of troops to concentration areas close to the frontier had still not been completed.

By chance, the war correspondent Archibald Forbes had for some days been staying at Saarbrücken, and on 2 August he was uniquely well placed to witness the first real battle of the Franco-Prussian War.[74] The French main axis of advance was to the north-east, generally astride the road via Forbach to Saarbrücken, and just after 10 a.m. between six and seven thousand French troops flooded down the three roads leading to the town, their supporting artillery already emplaced on the plateau and high ground overlooking the river. Lines of skirmishers advanced towards Saarbrücken; cavalry galloped left and right to secure the flanks, while to the rear massed battalions of line infantry prepared for the assault.

Shortly thereafter the French riflemen opened fire along their entire frontage; together with their artillery sited on the plateau overlooking the town. At this stage the fusiliers of the 40th Regiment began a hasty retreat towards the town, all the time lashed by a hail of shot and shell. They withdrew through the south-west suburbs of Saarbrücken, across the bridge, and into St Johann, where they established a new position on the edge of the town, near the railway station and astride the main road to Lebach. By then considerable numbers of French shells were falling on to the town and its environs, and as he hurried back with the fusiliers Forbes observed one of the first German casualties of the war, when:

As I stopped to take breath, a fusilier on the edge of the bank was shot through the back and came crashing down the shrubs on to the road at my feet. His back was broken, I think; anyhow he could not move the upper part of his body, but he took a grateful pull at the flask which I held to his lips ... Just as I turned the corner which brought me in sight of the Uhlans [who had been taking cover at a cutting and bend in the road leading to the road bridge in the town] a shell burst in the centre of a knot of fusiliers who were hurrying down the road. Had the party been in the shell itself, it could not have been more effectually shattered. A sergeant and five men were struck down by this one shell – how many of these were killed I did not stop to look … The town was naturally in a state of intense excitement, but the people in the houses lining the street that leads to the height stuck to their homes like rabbits to their burrows, even when the shells were crashing into the houses and sweeping down the thoroughfare.[75]

The clash at Saarbrücken was also notable as the first occasion on which the Germans encountered the French 'secret weapon', the mitrailleuse – an early form of machine-gun. At Saarbrücken, Forbes also came under fire from this potentially devastating weapon.[76] He later wrote that:

> We here heard for the first time the mitrailleuses at work. The bullets spattered very close together [on the bridge and] along the narrow track. The report was very curious and distinctive. It … gave one a lively sensation of his coat being torn down the back … one may form some conception of the report of the mitrailleuse by listening to a police rattle. It is unquestionable that the mitrailleuse fire swept the [Saar] bridge thoroughly; nothing could live where its hail fell.[77]

The fight had lasted for about an hour, when the Germans withdrew the last of their advanced outposts from the left bank of the river. Once the town and its bridges came under sustained French artillery fire, von Gneisenau withdrew his troops; first to the area of the railway station and subsequently to a new defensive position between Saarbrücken and Lebach. This left the town unoccupied by the Germans, although it was kept under observation by patrols of uhlans. So it was that by mid-afternoon the battle, such as it was, had more or less come to an end. During the evening, the French moved part of their forces into Saarbrücken, but neglected to do so in strength or to pursue the withdrawing Germans. Inexplicably, neither did they cross the Saar and occupy St Johann nor did they destroy the Saar bridges, railway lines or telegraph system. The French may well have neglected to destroy these communications systems in anticipation of using them to support their own future advance eastwards. But leaving the telegraph system intact certainly worked to their disadvantage, as this ensured that the German headquarters at Mainz continued to receive timely intelligence reports of the situation on the Saar throughout the battle, and also on the subsequent French activities once it had ended. During this fight, the French casualties amounted to eighty-six killed or wounded; the Germans sustained eighty-three casualties.

The battle had left the French Army of the Rhine over-extended and unsuitably deployed to deal with the subsequent moves by the German 1st Army about Saarlouis to the north and by the German 3rd Army at Wissembourg to the south-east. But, most importantly, it also represented a badly missed opportunity by the French to exploit their tactical success and disrupt the German forces during the critical final stage of their deployment, when (despite the subsequent claims of some German commanders to the contrary) there was no doubt that their troops had been caught off-balance. Certainly, on 2 August, the German armies were not yet ready to begin their own offensive, nor would they have been able to conduct an effective defensive battle beyond the Saar against a determined French army. Indeed, the nearest significant German reserves were still at Neunkirchen, some sixteen miles to the east of Saarbrücken. In theory, therefore, as the French cautiously consolidated their positions in the town during the night of Tuesday 2 August, the road to the Rhine lay wide open.

True to form, von Moltke and the German general staff quickly identified the potential threat and within forty-eight hours they had taken all necessary action to rectify it. Simultaneously, the last few strands of the German preparations for their invasion of France finally came together.

In the meantime, on cobbled streets and along the wide boulevards of Paris, and in the capital's fashionable coffee houses, cafés and salons, ecstatic crowds and groups of citizens celebrated the French army's victory at Saarbrücken, and the capture of what they believed was but the first of many such German towns that would soon be in French hands. They also believed without question an entirely false report that the Prussian Crown Prince had been captured during the battle. The French capital's church bells rang out and the French press hailed the successful invasion of the territory of the hated enemy: Prussia. These entirely unjustified celebrations all served to reinforce and add credibility to grossly exaggerated reports of the reduction of Saarbrücken to rubble, together with the destruction of a complete German corps. The widespread euphoria within France also allowed Napoleon III to maintain for a little longer a misplaced belief that he could still persuade the south German states to join France in a crusade against Prussia, and even bring Austria into the conflict as a French ally.

Just two days later, on Thursday, 4 August, the French emperor was finally disabused of any such fanciful beliefs. On that morning, 50,000 men of the German 3rd Army burst over the border at Wissembourg (or 'Weissenburg' as it was known to the Germans), where the somewhat under-strength 2nd French Division, commanded by General Abel Douay, was quickly overwhelmed and comprehensively defeated. The meticulously prepared war machine had assumed the offensive, as German infantry and cavalry formations swept across the frontier and onwards into France. Never again during the Franco-Prussian War were German soldiers required to fight on German soil.

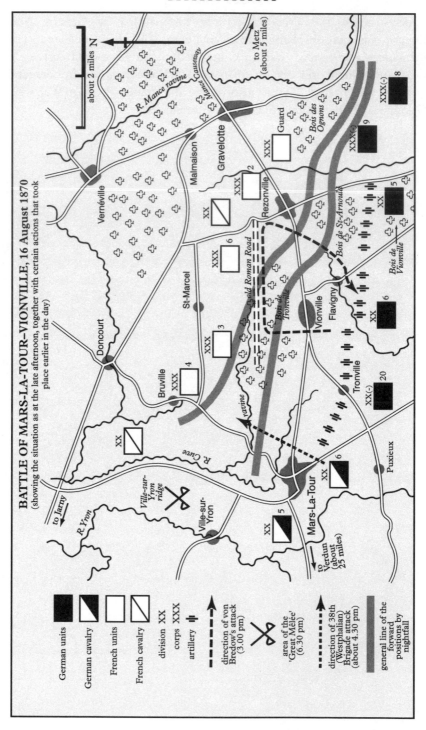

BATTLE OF MARS-LA-TOUR–VIONVILLE, 16 August 1870
(showing the situation as at the late afternoon, together with certain actions that took place earlier in the day)

about 2 miles N

to Metz
(about 5 miles)

R. Mance ravine

Manœ Causeway

8

XXX(-)

Bois des Ognons

9

XXX(-)

Guard

XXX

2

XXX

Rezonville

Malmaison

Gravelotte

Bois de St-Arnould

5

XX

Bois de Vionville

Vernéville

XX

6

XXX

St-Marcel

Vionville

Flavigny

6

XX

Gold Roman Road

Bois de Tronville

3

XXX

ravine

Doncourt

4

XXX

Bruville

Tronville

20

XX(-)

R. Cnce

Puxieux

XX

6

XX

Mars-La-Tour

to Jarny

R.Yron

Ville-sur-Yron ridge

Ville-sur-Yron

5

XX

to Verdun (about 25 miles)

German units

German cavalry

French units

French cavalry

division XX
corps XXX
artillery

direction of von Bredow's attack (3.00 pm)

area of the 'Great Mêlée' (6.30 pm)

direction of 38th (Westphalian) Brigade attack (about 4.30 pm)

general line of the forward positions by nightfall

11

Prelude to an Inferno
Mars-la-Tour, 1870

THE BATTLE OF MARS-LA-TOUR, or 'Vionville' as it was generally termed in most of the subsequent German accounts of the conflict, was the first of two great battles that would determine the military outcome of Germany's war against the armies of the Second French Empire of Napoleon III. The second, Gravelotte–St-Privat, which followed almost immediately, was in many respects a resumption of the former.

By mid-August, 1870, the French had entirely lost the initiative they had very temporarily enjoyed at Saarbrücken. The outcome of the frontier battles had also precipitated near-panic and a number of political changes in Paris, so that Napoleon's strategic plan now called for Marshal Bazaine's army to fall back from Metz via Verdun to Châlons-sur-Marne, there to join the corps commanded by Marshal MacMahon and Marshal Failly, so that their united forces would ensure the safety of the capital. Very belatedly, Bazaine received the executive orders to do this late on 13 August, by which time von Moltke's armies were already moving to cut off and ensnare the unfortunately titled French Army of the Rhine within or immediately to the west of Metz. While some parts of Bazaine's army were on the move on Sunday, 14 August, by the morning of Tuesday the 16th the German 1st and 2nd Armies were already moving generally west and north, to cut off the line of Bazaine's retreat towards Verdun.

In practice, the French commanders had failed to appreciate, and therefore to exploit, an incorrect assessment by Prince Frederick Charles. Commanding the seven corps of the German 2nd Army, the Prince was convinced that the bulk of the French Army of the Rhine had already left Metz and was well on the road west to Verdun. Although the course of the developing battle soon indicated Prince Frederick Charles's error all too clearly, the morning of 16 August found more than half (four corps) of the 2nd Army still advancing west rather than north-west: in a direction contrary to von Moltke's intention that this army should advance northwards at that time. The Prince's incorrect assessment resulted in the battle of Mars-la-Tour–Vionville becoming, for much of the day, a contest between a single army corps – Lieutenant

General von Alvensleben's 3rd German Corps, which was comprised almost exclusively of Brandenburg infantry and cavalry regiments – and three French corps.

At the end of what David Ascoli aptly called 'a day of battle'[78] in his epic work on Mars-la-Tour, it was yet again the sheer determination and courage of the German regimental officers and soldiers, despite appalling casualties, and the quantity and superior quality of their artillery, that determined the outcome of the day. Although the brunt of the positional fighting fell as usual upon the infantry of both sides, Mars-la-Tour–Vionville was also notable for the three great cavalry actions that took place during the battle. Frederick the Great's legacy to the Prussian cavalry which was used to such good effect at Rossbach and Leuthen was well in evidence at Mars-la-Tour, and Forbes later recounted that 'It was the sight of the war to have seen those cavalry charges on the day of Vionville.'[79] These spectacular and violent clashes between dragoons, cuirassiers, hussars, German uhlans and French *lanciers* and *chasseurs* were arguably the last use of massed cavalry on such a scale in a European war.

During the night of 15 August, some probing of the French positions by the ubiquitous uhlans and other German cavalry reconnaissance patrols had been carried out. A few minor skirmishes had also taken place. By 5 a.m., the Germans had identified Bazaine's left flank as lying along the general line of the villages of Flavigny, Vionville and Rezonville.

The first significant contact between the two forces occurred soon after 9 a.m., when the twenty-four guns of General Rheinbaben's 5th Cavalry Division (then under the command of the 10th German Corps) opened fire on the encamped cavalrymen of General Forton's division in and around Vionville. The artillery action began at the direct insistence and instigation of the Chief of Staff of the 10th German Corps, Colonel Caprivi, who achieved political prominence in 1890 when he succeeded Count Otto von Bismarck as Chancellor of the German empire. His personal certainty of the tactical situation, influence and authority (notwithstanding the presence of several more senior officers) in initiating the battle on 16 August demonstrated the ability and status of the German general staff officer within the field army. The German artillery fire was observed to have been immediately effective:

> The surprise was complete. As the first shells burst among the French tents and horse-lines, Murat's dragoons and de Grammont's cuirassiers – names

resonant of former glories [of the First French Empire] – broke and fled, sweeping away in their confusion the civilian baggage train which cluttered the main road behind them. It was not until the panic-stricken mob reached a safer haven beyond Rezonville that a measure of order was restored.[80]

The artillery fire alerted the soldiers of the 2nd, 3rd and 6th French Corps to the fact that the advance elements of the main German force had arrived in the area to the south of the Rezonville–Mars-la-Tour road. At the same time, it was becoming clearer by the minute to Lieutenant General von Alvensleben that his 3rd Corps was indeed confronted by what was in fact the best part of three French corps. But, in line with his army commander's original assessment, von Alvensleben was still inclined to believe that his troops had encountered a strong French rearguard, and that the majority of the Army of the Rhine was already well to the west *en route* to Verdun. Accordingly he pushed forward General Stülpnagel's 5th Division, determined to cut off the French force with which he was now in contact. The French responded to this threat from the south, and pushed the more northerly elements of the 3rd German Corps back towards the main body, which was by now arriving on the high ground to the south of the village of Rezonville. The uncharacteristically resolute French response, carried out mainly by General Frossard's 2nd French Corps, should at this stage have confirmed to the Germans that the tactical situation was not quite that which they had assumed.

The 5th German Division suffered such heavy casualties during this early contact that it was unable to advance any further. Its hard-won positions were tenuously held, and were maintained only with the everincreasing artillery support from the area south-west of Flavigny. But it had effectively neutralized the 2nd French Corps on the left flank of the Army of the Rhine, and that corps failed to exert any further significant influence on the course of the battle.

Meanwhile, by about 10 a.m. it was at last clear to von Alvensleben that his single corps was opposed by the entire Army of the Rhine. He sent this intelligence to Prince Frederick Charles, who was then still with the 2nd Army's headquarters at Pont-à-Mousson, on the Moselle, some ten or twelve miles away. He also directed the 6th German Division, commanded by General Buddenbrock, at that time advancing north-west towards Mars-la-Tour, to turn eastwards and seize Vionville. That accomplished, 6th Division was then to take the village of Flavigny.

To that end, the Duke of Mecklenberg-Schwerin had advanced the 6th Cavalry Division and was already forcing the French outposts to give up their positions within the Bois de Vionville when General Buddenbrock reached the plateau that overlooked Flavigny at about 11 a.m. His artillery quickly came into action on the brow of a hill at Tronville, and his infantry prepared to attack. Soon afterwards, General von Alvensleben ordered the assault to begin and the lines of German infantry advanced on Flavigny and Vionville.

Flavigny was strongly held by the French, and was the scene of particularly vicious hand-to-hand fighting; as also was the contest for Vionville, although the garrison there comprised no more than a single battalion supported by three batteries of 4-pounder guns. Inevitably the Germans overcame the French troops and soon both villages were in their hands. The fields were strewn with the dead and seriously wounded of both sides, but Buddenbrock's success might yet prove to be short-lived. Fortuitously, however, the reserve artillery of the 3rd Corps, some fifteen batteries, rode hell for leather up from the Gorze ravine, and deployed to the south-east and south-west of Flavigny; from where it could support the 6th Division and also begin bombarding the French troops moving through Rezonville. Throughout the day additional batteries arrived on the scene, so that by its end the Germans had a total of 210 guns so sited that they were able to engage the French more or less unconstrained. These guns were positioned in a broad arc on the high ground between Mars-la-Tour and the Bois de St Arnould.

Towards midday the Brandenburg infantrymen of the 35th and 64th Regiments, together with the 52nd Regiment (from the 5th German Division) consolidated the German hold on the groups of farms, barns and houses that comprised the villages of Vionville and Flavigny, but any further advance was effectively barred by the firmly entrenched infantry of the several French corps in positions to their north and east.

At this stage, fearful of yet another attack by the 6th Division, the French attacked the Brandenburgers with a spectacular but ill-advised cavalry charge by the cuirassiers and lancers of the Imperial Guard. This action demonstrated yet again the deadly effectiveness of the German infantry's breech-loading Dreyse needle-guns against unsupported cavalry. In short order, the two French cavalry regiments were decimated, and the German hussars of General Redern's 13th Cavalry Brigade completed their destruction.

Despite this local success, the 3rd German Corps was still stalled along its two-division front, and continued to take casualties which further reduced its overall strength. Deployed to its north and east by then were the whole of the 2nd and 6th French Corps, the Imperial Guard and

General Forton's division of cavalry, plus significant elements of the 3rd French Corps. In terms of military logic, therefore, von Alvensleben's position was virtually untenable. Had Marshal Bazaine realized this and launched a major attack, the French could almost certainly have achieved a decisive success, despite the impressive weight of the German artillery support.

As the morning drew on, however, the potentially crucial moment of French advantage eventually passed. In the meantime, the 3rd German Corps continued to fight a desperate battle: to conceal its true strength and avoid a military defeat, but also to gain time and to hold the Army of the Rhine as close to Metz as possible.

Von Alvensleben was very aware of the critical need to gain time for the remainder of the German 2nd Army to arrive if von Moltke's grand plan to trap and neutralize Bazaine's army was to succeed; at about midday this led directly to his decision to order a major cavalry charge against Marshal Canrobert's 6th French Corps to the north of Rezonville. The attack was to be carried out by General von Bredow's 12th Cavalry Brigade of the 5th Cavalry Division. What transpired was an action that subsequently became widely characterised as 'von Bredow's death ride'. Any implied criticism is unjust, because this costly tactical move was well calculated to achieve a more important operational goal. General von Bredow received his orders at about 2 p.m. and spent about thirty minutes reconnoitring the ground, planning the attack, and arranging the security of his flanks.

A German account captured much of the essence of the action as the 12th Cavalry Brigade's armoured cuirassiers with their heavy cavalry swords, followed by their more lightly equipped uhlan comrades-in-arms, their black-and-white lance pennants fluttering below the wickedly sharp steel tips of their weapons, formed into two lines of battle and prepared for action:

> In the first [ranks] were three squadrons of the [7th] Magdeburg Regiment of Cuirassiers, led by Count von Schmettow, on the left wing along the border of the woods; and in the second were three squadrons of the Altmärkische Regiment of Uhlans No. 16, led by Major von Dollen, on the right wing, one hundred paces to the rear; the gallant Bredow with his staff keeping about in line with the cuirassiers.[81] With loud hurrahs the six squadrons started on a trot, wheeling about to the left in the valley. Traversing the slope they deployed to the right. After having reached the plateau, they rode at breakneck speed against the batteries of Tixier and those of the 6th [French] Corps, and against the division of Lafont de Villiers. They received on the left the Chassepot fire of Tixier's infantry and

that of the 9th Regiment; in front they had to face fire and shrapnel. Of the first battery only two pieces had time to [begin to] limber up, but before this happened the cuirassiers fell upon them like a hurricane. Ahead of all was Schmettow, with Lieutenant Craignish of Campbell at his side, and a non-commissioned officer. Schmettow unhorsed the French major, while Campbell and the sergeant put another officer hors de combat. In the battery everything was laid low; the 'wild hunt' dashed against the infantry of Lonnay's brigade, formed in two columns, on the side of which was a battery. The cuirassiers rode down the front column, breaking through their fire; the uhlans closing up, the battery was captured and everything that did not take flight was cut to pieces. The second line of the French was now attacked. Here, after an advance of three thousand paces, the small body of horse was surrounded on all sides, first by the division Forton and [then by] the division Valabrègue breaking forth from an opening in the woods. Two squadrons of the [10th] French cuirassiers fell upon the rear of Schmettow's riders, the 7th [French] Cuirassiers fell upon their flanks, the brigade Murat of the dragoons threw themselves in front, followed by Valabrègue's chasseurs and hussars, 3,100 horse against 800 of the six squadrons ... The exhausted riders now had to cut their way back. After rally had been sounded, General von Bredow retreated a short distance to the valley of Rezonville, then wheeled about to the right. Schmettow's aide-de-camp fell from his horse wounded, one trumpeter was shot down, Captain von Heister was unhorsed after receiving thirteen wounds. Campbell tried to wrest a standard from the French cuirassiers and was rescued only by the most heroic efforts of his men. Count von Kalckreuth received fifteen wounds, Major von Dollen was unhorsed and taken prisoner, while Captain Mayer of the cuirassiers was killed. The brigade, however, forced its way back through the batteries previously ridden down, and through the columns of infantry which followed them up and fired several volleys into them. Unpursued by the enemy, however, they arrived beyond Vionville. The wounded and unhorsed riders, and those detained by the exhaustion of their horses, had to surrender. Schmettow ordered the first trumpeter whom he met to sound the regimental signal. The trumpet was found to be pierced by a bullet, and its sound was like that of a dirge, penetrating to the very marrow of the bones. Of the eleven platoons of cuirassiers only three could be mustered, consisting of seven officers and seventy men, and six officers and eighty men of the uhlans. Later it was ascertained that the cuirassiers had lost seven officers, 189 men and 209 horses, the uhlans lost nine officers, 174 men and 200 horses; of the total force of 800 men, 363 were left dead or wounded, officers included. The sacrifice of the gallant band of heroes had, however, not been made in vain, a breathing spell having been accorded to the almost exhausted Brandenburg infantry.[82]

Von Bredow's charge severely reduced the strength of the German brigade, but (quite apart from having been in the best traditions of the shock use of cavalry) it had unquestionably achieved its principal mission. The 6th French Corps was unable to take any further offensive action that day, other than a brief sortie by some of its units during the final stages of the battle. Meanwhile, the desperately needed time had been bought for the 3rd German Corps. Ammunition, for the artillery in particular, was replenished and some of the many casualties were at last able to be removed and treated. Also, where the tactical situation allowed, some much-needed drinking-water was brought up to the infantry soldiers who had by then been manning the forward lines under the blazing sun for several hours. But most importantly, the time won at such cost by von Bredow's troopers allowed the approaching 10th German Corps, commanded by General Voigts-Rhetz, to move ever closer to the sound of the guns and to assist its comrades of the somewhat beleaguered 3rd Corps.

But French reinforcements were also moving forward, and, in the area of Bruville and Tronville to the north of the Germans' exposed left flank, they launched an attack with three divisions against the Bois de Tronville.

Within and along the edge of the woods a little to the north of Tronville were the remaining soldiers of the 20th and 24th (Brandenburg) Regiments, together with just four newly arrived infantry battalions of the 37th Brigade from the 10th German Corps. The outcome of the subsequent clash between some 30,000 Frenchmen and about 4,000 Germans was inevitable. During an hour of very hard fighting, the 37th Brigade's units sustained more than 1,200 casualties. Those of the 20th and 24th Regiments – which had already suffered extensively during the early part of the battle – were equally crippling. Not surprisingly, the Germans were forced to withdraw to the village of Tronville itself, with the exception of a couple of companies of Brandenburg infantry who resolutely continued to hold their positions in the woods. This withdrawal left von Alvensleben's left flank seriously threatened, but the threat proved transitory because, at about 3.30 p.m., the leading brigades of the 19th and 20th German Divisions of General Voigts-Rhetz's 10th German Corps at last began to arrive in some strength at Tronville and at Mars-la-Tour.

Voigts-Rhetz noted the deteriorating German situation on the left flank. He also judged that the French troops who had just expelled the German infantry from the Bois de Tronville were now over-extended and therefore susceptible to an immediate counter-attack. Accordingly, he gambled upon the committal of his leading brigade without carrying out an effective reconnaissance or a proper assessment of the relative strength of the opposing French forces. The sweating, thirsty, dust-covered Westphalian infantrymen of the 19th German Division's 38th Brigade, already weary from their long forced march under a blazing sun, were almost immediately ordered to attack towards Bruville. The outcome of this precipitate attack by about 4,700 Germans against about 20,000 Frenchmen was fairly predictable:

> [Soon after four o'clock][83] the brigade advanced steadily, after having passed the burning village of Mars-la-Tour under a storm of shell [fire] and the fire of the mitrailleuses, which calamitously reduced its ranks. The rear division thronged between the front one; after a run of from one hundred to one hundred and fifty paces the troops dropped on the ground, [then] jumping up and rushing forward till they reached the edge of a ravine, fifty feet deep and separating them from the enemy.[84] They ran down, traversed the ravine, and scaled the opposite banks, where they were met in mass by [General] Grenier's battalions, and on the left flanks by those of [General] Cissey. The five battalions could not withstand the murderous fire of two [French] divisions. All mounted officers were laid low and the wounded and killed lay in heaps on the ground.[85]

The attack stalled in the ravine, and after about ten minutes a spirited French counter-attack broke the German line; the survivors bolted up the slope and back on to the road to Mars-la-Tour. The Westphalians' casualties included no fewer than seventy-two officers killed and 2,542 men killed or wounded,[86] but once again the French failed to exploit their advantage by taking the offensive. General Voigts-Rhetz took immediate pre-emptive action to retrieve the deteriorating situation. This resulted in the second significant German cavalry charge of the day as five squadrons, totalling about 600 horsemen, of the two Guard Dragoon Regiments of the 3rd Brigade of the Guard Cavalry were committed to the battle. At about 5 p.m. Generals von Brandenburg and von Rheinbaben received orders to charge the same French troops who less than an hour before had repulsed and all but destroyed the 38th Brigade. Once again, though at considerable cost, the German cavalrymen achieved their mission.

Although the German cavalry brigade suffered considerable losses, its attack restored somewhat the disastrous situation resulting from the earlier assault by the 38th Brigade of the 19th German Division towards Bruville. It also removed any further inclination on the part of the infantry regiments of the 4th French Corps to press their advance against Mars-la-Tour. And so events moved inexorably towards the final great cavalry encounter of the battle.

The 'great mêlée' (as it was later termed in many accounts of the battle) came about when the French commander of the 4th Corps, General

Ladmirault, and the German commander of the 10th Corps, General Voigts-Rhetz, both decided at virtually the same time to use the massed cavalry each had at his disposal to outflank and roll up the left and right flanks of their opponents. The orders were issued, and not long before 7 p.m., the sun by now low in the sky, more than 5,000 German and French horsemen – more than forty-nine German cavalry squadrons and three French cavalry divisions – began to move.

There now [about 6.45 p.m.] appeared on the open ridge of Ville-sur-Yron a large force of French cavalry. Ladmirault led forth the Chasseurs d'Afrique of Du [Barail's] division, the cavalry division Legrand and the brigade Garde de France upon the plateau stretching towards the Yron creek. He wheeled about to the left and then advanced to the right in four compact masses overlapping each other, the brigade of [Montaigu's] hussars forming the van. On the German side the cavalry forces drawn up between Tronville and Puxieux started to give battle: in front were the 13th (Schleswig-Holstein) Dragoons under Major von Trotha, followed by the fourth squadron of the [2nd] Dragoon Guards. They drew somewhat to the right and wheeled about half to the left towards [Montaigu's] brigade of hussars. In the rear Barby's brigade appeared, wheeling to the left about Mars-la-Tour, followed by the 4th Westphalian Cuirassiers, the 13th Hanoverian Uhlans, and the 19th Oldenburg Dragoons; in the second rear column were the 2nd Hanoverian Dragoons and the 10th Magdeburg Hussars.[87] ... As the 3,000 German horsemen, after having reached the heights north of Mars-la-Tour, sighted the enemy, they broke forth in triumphal cheers: "There they are, there they are!" they cried. The Schleswig-Holstein Dragoons, waiting majestically for the charge of [Montaigu's] brigade of hussars, delivered fire and dashed upon the enemy, sabre in hand, with deafening cheers. A terrible conflict ensued, the small horses of the French being run over by the heavy German steeds. The French succeeded in breaking through, only to be received and cut to pieces by the Magdeburg Hussars. General [Montaigu] was [severely wounded and] taken prisoner. The squadrons separated; wheeling about, the dragoons also took part in the attack. General Legrand now rushed forward with the French dragoons; the first squadron of the Oldenburg Dragoons fell upon them, most of them being unhorsed, as only sixty riders kept their saddles. But the [shock of the French attack] was checked; a furious hand-to-hand encounter took place. General Legrand's riders were cut to pieces by the Oldenburgers;[88] the Hanoverian Dragoons also closing up, the Germans were victorious. On from the extreme left swept the 13th Uhlans and fell on the flank of the [French] Empress's Dragoons, the fifth squadron of the [2nd] Dragoon Guards moving against them from another quarter. Colonel von Schack, the leader of the Hanoverian Uhlans, rode deep into the ranks of the enemy, where he fell, his body not being recovered for some time. The bulk of the Chasseurs d'Afrique rushed upon the Hanoverian Uhlans, but at this moment the Westphalian Cuirassiers broke into the chasseurs in a wedge-shaped mass, the Hanoverian Dragoons also attacked them on flank and rear. The earth trembled under the stamping of the 6,000 [*sic*] horse, man fought against man with long sword, sabre, carbine and revolver. Not long did the furious mêlée last; the enemy's horsemen extricating themselves, first one by one, then in squads, and soon the whole mass escaped, disappearing like a huge cloud of dust in a northerly direction, pursued by the German riders to the woods of Bruville. The trumpets sounded the rally, the field was cleared of the enemy. The regiments drew up and returned to Mars-la-Tour, later on to Puxieux. The Schleswig-Holstein Dragoons covered the retreat, followed at a considerable distance by Clérembault's French troopers.[89]

By about 7 p.m. the two sides had drawn apart with neither the clear victor, the whole mêlée having lasted for not much more than twenty minutes. Not since that afternoon in August 1870 have the cavalry regiments of two great European armies come together and engaged in mortal combat on such a scale as they did during the great mêlée in the early evening on the day of the battle of Mars-la-Tour. Apart from some sporadic skirmishes, the great cavalry battle signalled the end of the fighting on the western part of the battlefield and about the village of Mars-la-Tour.

However, the long day of combat was still not quite done. As the shadows lengthened across the shell-torn woods, ruined and burning villages and scarred fields, German reinforcements, including elements of the 9th German Corps, were arriving in some strength to the south of Rezonville, on the German right flank. Earlier, at about 3.30, Prince Frederick Charles had at last arrived on the battlefield from Pont-à-Mousson. Although he was far too late to have influenced the actions of von Alvensleben and Voigts-Rhetz, he was determined to inflict a final blow upon what he had by now realized was indeed the whole of the French Army of the Rhine. With darkness fast approaching, he identified a last chance to complete the containment of the French by denying them any access to the roads to the west. To do that it was necessary to take the key village of Rezonville.

Yet again – despite their direct involvement in the battle throughout most of the day – the Brandenburg infantrymen of the 6th Division were ordered to attack, together with some of their fellow Brandenburgers from the 5th Division's 10th Brigade. They advanced from Vionville and Flavigny soon after 7 p.m., and initially made good progress. But when they were a little less than 1,000 yards from the buildings on the outskirts of Rezonville the attack was halted by a storm of artillery, mitrailleuse and Chassepot fire. Consequently, the German infantrymen had no option but to withdraw back to Vionville and Flavigny as night fell over the battlefield. Remarkably, despite the failure of the infantry attack and the onset of night, Prince Frederick Charles persisted with his desire to inflict a final blow on the French centre and so ordered what turned out to be the final action of the battle. This task fell to the two cavalry brigades of the 6th German Cavalry Division, the 14th and the 15th, the soldiers of which came mainly from Brandenburg and Schleswig-Holstein. Although it was by now nearly 9 p.m. and quite dark, the brigades charged directly at the French centre: at the very least an extremely risky venture for cavalry at night. Nevertheless, having achieved complete surprise, the German cuirassiers, uhlans and hussars quickly overran the French pickets and outposts deployed before Rezonville, inflicting a number of casualties and causing confusion beyond all normal expectations.

But once the horsemen reached the edge of the village the pendulum again swung against them as they were subjected to massed, accurate Chassepot fire from French infantrymen in the barns and houses. Among the 700 casualties they sustained was the commander of the 14th Brigade. The survivors of the 6th Cavalry Division retired into the darkness, which to some extent covered what was by then their considerable disorder.

Although neither the Brandenburg infantry regiments' night attack nor that by the 6th Cavalry Division could in any tactical sense be considered successes, in the wider scheme of events these final aggressive and entirely unexpected forays against Rezonville did confirm Marshal Bazaine's assessment of the situation. There was really no doubt in his mind that he could no longer reach Verdun and Châlons with the Army of the Rhine. Accordingly, he now decided that his only option was to conduct a defensive battle on the plain before Metz: a course of action that in fact matched very well von Moltke's own plans for dealing with the French Army of the Rhine.

By nine o'clock that evening an uneasy silence had settled over the battlefield. The soldiers bivouacked more or less in the positions in which they had ended the day's fighting, while the scarred landscape, ruined villages and devastated woodland now became primarily the preserve of the Krankenträger (the stretcher-bearers) of the ambulance staff, of groups of nuns such as the medically trained Sisters of Mercy, and of the two armies' surgeons. Indeed, the numbers of casualties sustained by both sides were substantial. Ascoli's analysis stated that the Germans had lost 15,788 men: of whom 4,421 were killed, 10,402 wounded and 965 missing. The Germans also lost 1,300 horses, mainly during the three great cavalry engagements. The French suffered 1,367 killed, 10,120 wounded and 5,472 missing: a total of 16,959. Although the overall totals are broadly comparable, the real significance of these figures was that the German losses – including a much higher number of fatalities – had been incurred almost entirely by just two corps and their supporting arms. The French casualties were incurred by no fewer than three deployed corps, two cavalry divisions and elements of two other corps. Proportionally, therefore, the German losses were especially significant.

The German 3rd Corps sustained particularly high losses; overall a total of 310 officers and 6,641 men. The 52nd (Brandenburg) Infantry Regiment lost eighteen officers and 345 men killed and thirty-two officers and 1,202 men wounded. The 3rd (Westphalian) Infantry Regiment No. 16 lost forty-nine officers and 1,736 men killed or wounded. The 24th (Brandenburg) Infantry Regiment lost forty-seven officers and 1,099 men killed or wounded. The 11th Grenadier Regiment (of the 9th German Corps, elements of which joined the battle in the late afternoon) lost forty-one officers and 1,119 men killed or wounded.

Nevertheless, inasmuch as the withdrawal of the French Army of the Rhine had been very effectively halted, Mars-la-Tour was a German success and (with a few exceptions) a vindication of the training and martial acumen of the German army and its commanders. A brief summary of the relative strengths of the two armies engaged during the battle on 16 August reveals the true extent of von Alvensleben's enforced but none the less successful operational subterfuge:

It is impossible to state exactly the numbers present on the field – probably 125,000 French to 77,000 Germans. The latter brought up two complete Corps, the 3rd and the 10th, two divisions of cavalry, the 5th and 6th – these sustained the shock and bore the chief loss – a brigade of the 8th Corps, the 11th Regiment from the 9th, and four Hessian regiments of that Corps under Prince Louis, the husband of the British Princess Alice. They also had, in action or reserve, 246 guns. The French mustered the Imperial Guard, the 2nd Corps, three divisions and one regiment of the 6th Corps, three divisions of the 3rd, and two of the 4th Corps, five divisions of cavalry, and 390 guns; so that on the 16th [of August], they were, at all times, numerically superior in every arm. When Alvensleben came into action a little after ten o'clock with the 3rd Corps and two divisions of cavalry – perhaps 33,000 men – they had in their front the 2nd and 6th Corps, the Guard, and the Reserve Cavalry – not less than 72,000, the guns on the French side being always superior in number. The 3rd [French] Corps, less one division, was at ten o'clock only three miles from the field; these and half the 4th Corps arrived in the afternoon, adding more than 55,000 men to the total, while the Germans could only bring up the 10th, and parts of the 8th and 9th, fewer than 40,000, some of them marching into line late in the evening.[90]

Clearly, the fact that the Army of the Rhine had retired towards Metz at the end of the fighting and that it had been forced further to delay (in fact, to abandon) its planned move towards Verdun was unequivocal evidence of the important German success at Mars-la-Tour–Vionville; notwithstanding the several miscalculations and costly reverses that the Germans had suffered during the battle.

As ever, the day had finally been won for the Germans by a mixture of the tactical flair of some commanders, blended with the training standards, discipline and bravery of the individual German soldiers; all of which was certainly underwritten by the power of the German artillery, but also profited from a very large amount of luck! It had been won despite the dogged determination and often ferocious fighting ability of the ordinary French soldiers, where their usually brave, but nevertheless irresolute and often unprofessional, senior officers had been a major contributory factor to the German success. Despite the potentially disastrous handicap imposed upon them from the outset of the battle, the professional competence of Generals von Alvensleben[91] and Voigts-Rhetz finally allowed them to overcome the imbalance of numbers that they faced throughout much of the day. Finally, the superior organization and resource management of the German war machine provided the firm military foundation upon which the success of 16 August was based.

The combat about Mars-la-Tour–Vionville precipitated and shaped the next great battle of the war, Gravelotte–St-Privat. Indeed, neither Mars-la-Tour nor Gravelotte–St-Privat can be considered in isolation, as the latter was really an extension of the former, although on a much greater scale. While von Moltke had certainly not sought the battle of 16 August, it had nevertheless achieved more than he could reasonably have dared to hope for. By the morning of Wednesday 17 August, despite a reduced reconnaissance capability (due principally to the severe casualties suffered by the German cavalry the previous day), he knew for certain that the entire French Army of the Rhine was now effectively contained within or somewhere just to the west of Metz and that it could now be prevented from joining with the embryo Army of Châlons. He knew that there was considerable confusion in the French army's immediate rear area, with a partial breakdown of its supply lines into and within Metz and with its lines of communication to the west now severed. Finally, he knew that his plan for the destruction of Marshal Bazaine's Army of the Rhine was now on the verge of coming to fruition, as the corps, divisions and regiments of the German First and Second Armies hurried to complete their replenishment, reorganization and redeployment for the coming battle of Gravelotte–St-Privat.

12

The Inferno

Gravelotte–St-Privat and Sedan, 1870

THE GERMAN COMMANDER-IN-CHIEF, the King of Prussia, accompanied by von Moltke and the staff, visited the earlier battlefield at 6 a.m. on the Wednesday. It had been an unusually chilly night, but as the sun rose into a clear blue sky another very hot, dry day was in prospect. The royal party met Prince Frederick Charles near Flavigny and together surveyed the French dispositions to the north between Bruville and Rezonville. They discussed plans for the next day's action, although the confused nature of the French activity they had observed and the paucity of information from the German cavalry patrols gave no clear indication of Marshal Bazaine's future intentions. At 2 p.m. the initial orders for the coming battle were issued in writing by von Moltke to the principal commanders at the hamlet of Flavigny. These stated that: 'The 2nd Army will, early in the morning at 5 o'clock, commence operations and advance in echelon between Ville-sur-Yron and Rezonville. The 8th Army Corps will co-operate in this movement with the 2nd Army on its right. The 7th Army Corps will at first have the duty of covering the movement of 2nd Army against any demonstrations on the part of the enemy from the side of Metz. The King's further orders will depend on the action taken by the enemy. Communications for his Majesty will next find him on the height south of Flavigny.'[92] The King and his retinue returned to the main headquarters at Pont-à-Mousson.

The die was cast, and the two German armies, a total of some 230,000 men with more than 726 guns, were directed to march directly north-east soon after sunrise on 18 August, with a view to intercepting a French army that the Germans anticipated would already be *en route* for Verdun. Consequently, the formations adopted for the move were designed to facilitate a speedy advance rather than immediate readiness for battle. Certainly the Germans – still virtually blinded by lack of information from their cavalry patrols – did not expect to encounter a major French defensive position to the west of Metz.

In fact, on that Thursday morning any move to the north-west from Metz was very far from Marshal Bazaine's mind. Following their precipitate withdrawal towards Metz on the night of 16 August, the

✠✠✠✠✠✠✠✠✠✠✠✠

French had in fact occupied a strong defensive line, almost nine miles long, based on the range of low hills to the west of Metz. To the north, the French right flank was well secured by the substantial stone buildings of the village of St-Privat, and further south, the village of Amanvillers offered the French soldiers a strong position with excellent

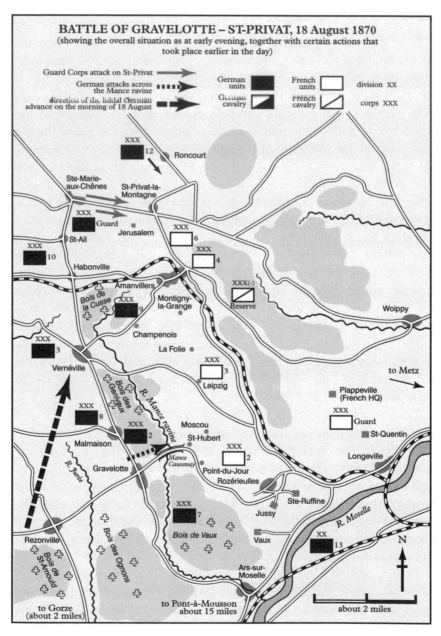

BATTLE OF GRAVELOTTE – ST-PRIVAT, 18 August 1870
(showing the overall situation as at early evening, together with certain actions that took place earlier in the day)

fields of fire to the south and west. Even farther to the south the French commanders had utilized the increasingly wooded and broken ground to establish equally sound positions based on a succession of ravines, gravel pits and close country.

Scattered throughout the French positions were several buildings and large farms. The latter were of the local style, with substantial perimeter walls and solidly built barns, outbuildings and farmhouses, all of which could be made into mini-fortresses in relatively short order. Notable among these newly created strongpoints were the farms at Jerusalem, Montigny-la-Grange, Leipzig, Moscou, St-Hubert and Point-du-Jour. From much of the high ground occupied by the Army of the Rhine, the rolling countryside towards the battlefield of 16 August could be clearly observed and, in many cases, dominated very effectively by artillery, Chassepot and mitrailleuse fire. These positions also enjoyed the additional advantage of being not more than one mile from the outer ring of the fortresses that protected Metz. Indeed, Marshal Bazaine had established his own headquarters in the formidable fort at Plappeville, well to the south of the French line and close to the main road routes back into Metz via the village of Woippy. The French defensive line of entrenchments, rifle-pits, strongpoints and fortifications were manned by about 126,000 men, supported by 520 guns, and should have been virtually impregnable. But a litany of poor staff work, lacklustre command and control, and a deficiency of entrenching-tools, combined to deny the French once again the advantage that they might otherwise have enjoyed.

On the early morning of Thursday, 18 August, Prince Frederick Charles's corps commanders came together to receive their final orders for the 2nd Army's role in the forthcoming battle. Frederick Charles's final words to his commanders at that meeting reiterated von Moltke's own orders to the German army shortly prior to the war: 'Your duty is to march forward, find the enemy, prevent his escape, and fight him wherever you find him.'

Gravelotte–St-Privat, 18 August 1870

Shortly before 9 a.m., observers at the French centre saw (to their undoubted amazement) the entire right flank of the German 2nd Army marching obliquely across its front. This manoeuvre was conducted in massed division-size blocks of men, with the corps artillery occupying the intervening spaces. The huge force advanced on an overall frontage of about eight miles, and its formation and form of movement apparently took no account of having to deal with a possible attack against its exposed flank. But Bazaine took no action to exploit this situation and by 10 a.m. the Germans had at last identified the presence of the French encampments and positions to their east; the moment of French tactical advantage had once again passed. However, Prince Frederick Charles decided that these were no more than the French rearguard, whereas it was in fact the French centre, comprised of most of two corps and some elements of a third. In any event, based upon his incorrect assessment, he directed the 2nd Army to wheel to the east, in order to engage the French.

At about the same time General von Moltke, who by now had received the initial reports from 2nd Army concerning their sightings of the French positions, amended his own assessment of the situation. He now believed that the French line extended no further north than Amanvillers, that village being on the French extreme right flank. Consequently, he ordered 2nd Army (less the 9th Corps which was to continue north-east to Vernéville) to continue its advance eastwards to envelop and roll up the French army from its right flank, while 1st Army would attack directly east from Gravelotte against the French left.

Now, with the battle gaining pace, the staff activity was becoming ever more frenetic, and the German supreme headquarters at Flavigny began to reveal some important practical shortcomings. A huge and virtually set-piece battle was about to be fought, on a frontage of more than eight miles with an overall depth of up to about three miles, over ground that encompassed a complete mix of all kinds of terrain types, including several small urban areas, and was to be fought with many of what were then the most modern weapons available. Yet tactical command, control and decision-making were still largely dependent on the ability of commanders physically to see the progress of the fighting for themselves, and their communication and information systems still relied almost entirely upon mounted messengers.

So, despite the modernity of much of its war machine, the German high command at Gravelotte–St-Privat was still constrained to operate in the field in much the same way as Wellington had at Waterloo more than half a century earlier, although there the area of the main combat had been relatively small and most of the ground had been visible to the principal commanders throughout the battle. Also, the accuracy, range and power of the weapons used at Waterloo in 1815 were much less advanced than those available in 1870. As these problems were much greater for an attacking force than for one that was in a static defensive position, it is not surprising that events on the ground soon began to outpace the ability of the German high command to control them as directly and effectively as von Moltke would undoubtedly have wished.

The advance units of the 25th (Hessian) Division of General von Manstein's 9th German Corps, which included a battery of artillery, reached their assigned objective at Vernéville and, having established itself on the rising ground to the east of the village, the single battery opened fire on the French positions around Amanvillers. It was now a quarter of an hour before noon. Just before this, however, Prince Frederick Charles had received reports of French activity in the village of St-Privat, farther to the north, and he realized that the French line probably extended well beyond the limit suggested by his earlier assessment.

When he had ordered his artillery at Vernéville to open fire on the French encampment, von Manstein was largely unaware of the significant French presence in St-Privat. But in light of this discovery it was clear that the 2nd Army now needed to move farther north so as to outflank the French line, so Frederick Charles sent orders to General von Manstein to delay his imminent attack. But the new orders arrived too late. So it was that the single battery of Hessian artillery fired the first shots of the battle of Gravelotte–St-Privat a little before midday on Thursday 18 August. The artillerymen in particular, and subsequently the rest of the 25th (Hessian) Division and much of the 9th German Corps, were no doubt surprised by the violence and efficacy of the response by the 'French rearguard', which in reality included most of the 4th and some of the 6th French Corps artillery. The French gunners soon began to engage the recently arrived German batteries from their prepared positions, in many cases at ranges of less than 1,000 yards. French mitrailleuses and some infantry also entered the fray.

The Hessian battery of six guns which had opened the engagement was speedily reinforced, first by most of the divisional artillery and then by batteries from the corps artillery, so that a total of fifty-four guns were soon deployed on the hillside to the north-east of Vernéville. But their hastily occupied position was badly exposed to French fire from the front, the flanks and even (on the left) from the rear. Consequently, the 9th Corps artillery paid a high price for the decision to engage the enemy camp at Amanvillers.

Meanwhile, having heard the increasing barrage of the artillery duel to the north, King William and von Moltke had moved the main German headquarters forward from Flavigny to the area of Rezonville shortly after noon.

✠✠✠✠✠✠✠✠✠✠✠✠✠

Although fighting raged along the full extent of the French line at varying levels of intensity throughout the afternoon, the principal action of the battle now centred upon two almost discrete areas. In the south (German 1st Army) was the Mance ravine to the east of Gravelotte, and the high ground towards Metz which lay beyond. Meanwhile, to the north (German 2nd Army) there was the small walled village of St-Privat.

The 1st Army's battle just to the east of Gravelotte began shortly after midday, when the increasing sound of artillery fire to the north clearly indicated that the 2nd Army was in contact with the French, and the elderly commander of the 1st Army, General von Steinmetz, decided that it was propitious to order an attack by General von Goeben's 8th Corps,[93] with the aim of capturing the tactically important farm complex of St-Hubert on the high ground beyond the Mance ravine. This farm was defended by a single infantry battalion.

By 1 p.m. a total of 150 guns had been deployed to each side of Gravelotte, ready to support the forthcoming attack. But the range to the French positions was too great for the guns to engage them effectively, so they were directed to take up new positions along the western side of the Mance ravine. As this brought them within range of the French riflemen just across the ravine, the two divisions (15th and 16th) of the 8th Corps were first ordered to attack across the obstacle in order to prepare and secure the way for the German artillery to move forward. Shortly before 2.30 p.m., the 8th Corps, with three brigades (29th, 30th and 31st) in the initial assault, advanced astride the road from Gravelotte and started down the wooded slopes into the ravine and to the stream that ran through it.

At first the soldiers made good progress, despite the increasingly thick scrub and woodland, which combined with the gradient and a number of gravel-pits to break up their assault formation as they scrambled down to the bottom; and although groups began to lose contact with their commanders and individuals with their comrades, they soon reached the stream. But as the infantrymen waded through the water and clambered out of it on the eastern side, a storm of Chassepot fire and bursting artillery shells lashed their ranks.

The thick undergrowth afforded some concealment as they struggled up the far bank, still under heavy fire, but it also served further to fragment the brigades as they moved up to the edge of the trees and to the gravel-pits below their objective of the St-Hubert farm and the nearby Point-du-Jour. Consequently, the 8th Corps' attack soon ground to a halt in the face of the continuous storm of French fire.

One of the regiments with the 29th Brigade of the 16th Division was the 33rd Regiment of Fusiliers (East Prussia),[94] and the desperate situation below the Point-du-Jour provided one fusilier with an opportunity to gain the Iron Cross:

> An under-officer and a fusilier patrolled towards the Point-du-Jour; the terrible fire from the trenches compelled them very soon to seek cover in the roadside ditch; but the fusilier, who was well supplied with cartridges, left his comrade, and crept across the open field a few hundred paces nearer the enemy, and found shelter behind a little knoll. From here he fired upon the team of an ammunition cart, which had just arrived, and from which cartridges were being issued. His shots drove the cart away; and the French fired several volleys against the concealed marksman. His helmet and tunic were riddled, but he did not creep back again until his pouch was empty and his rifle too foul[ed] for further use.[95]

While the German infantry were bearing the brunt of the French fire, the 1st Army's artillery was able to move forward as planned, so that by 3 p.m. some 150 guns were able to engage St-Hubert from positions on the west edge of the Mance ravine. The farm complex was quickly reduced to an inferno of blazing timbers and rubble, and within half an hour the few survivors of the small garrison of the strongpoint had withdrawn the short distance to the main line of French entrenchments. This at last enabled the German infantry to rush forward and occupy the battered and burning buildings, although they could make no further advance as they were once again subjected to a steady hail of fire from the farm at Moscou to the north and from the Point-du-Jour to the south.

Despite this, von Steinmetz interpreted the capture of St-Hubert as the beginning of a collapse of the French positions on the surrounding heights. Accordingly, he launched a further attack across the Mance ravine, this time with the aim of capturing the Point-du-Jour. The attack was to be conducted by the 25th and 28th Brigades of General von Zastrow's 7th Corps, with the 27th Brigade held in reserve. This new attack began at about 4 p.m.

> The French seemed to catch at the significance of the movement instantaneously as it was begun: their infantry, rushing to the left through the poplar trees on the chaussée, formed across the southern plateau, so as to flank as well as front the Germans when they should come staggering up on to this new battlefield. More batteries were dashed hurriedly into position and got into fire. Those previously there swung their trails round to the north somewhat, and their muzzles thus looked the way the German brigades were toiling upwards. High up as were the French, the depth of the ravine

afforded the Germans miserably little cover from their fire. For the French gunners could see almost into its bed; and although the inverse rise could not be reached by a direct fire, they yet let fall upon it a plunging fire which, from the steepness of the slope, was much more destructive than plunging fires for the most part are. The loss must have been terrible in those ranks while they were struggling on to the debouchment [sic]. At length the edge of the wood and the lip of the ravine were gained. You could see groups and isolated men straggling out into the open and falling into formation in that momentary confusion which always attends such a reorganization. Just then cannon, mitrailleuse, infantry fire, as if by signal, burst into one fell combination of outpour ... There were efforts to make head[way] against it ... detached rushes of rash men who were not to be convinced of the impossible till overtaken by arguments which crushed conviction in, while they crushed motion and life out. It was piteous to watch the efforts ... I watched those soldiers struggling grimly for foothold on the edge of that deadly plateau. They would not give it up. Even as one attempt was beaten back and crushed down, there were men pushing staunchly on to make another. It seemed such a little way, such a very little way up to the poplar trees there and to victory ... I do not know whether an order came that the brigades should give up the useless persistence in courting annihilation, or whether they drew back in realization of the insanity of such persistence. They did abandon it, and shrunk back off the plateau, lying down on the inverse bank of the ravine, screened from the enemy's direct fire, but exposed to the plunging fire, and raked by French infantry detachments that had pushed forward to the brink of the ravine, further northward, opposite St-Hubert.[96]

Incredibly, soon after 4 p.m. – notwithstanding the continued French rifle and artillery fire, the rapidly mounting casualties, the total confusion in and at the sides of the Mance ravine, and the fact that no more forward movement had been achieved on the eastern side of the ravine – von Steinmetz decided that the 7th Corps attack had been sufficiently successful to justify the committal of the 1st Cavalry Division to seize the high ground and establish gun positions there; the cavalry and supporting horse artillery, together with the 7th Corps artillery, were directed to advance along what was by now the severely choked road and causeway.

Indeed, the causeway was the only viable route by which horses and guns could have crossed the obstacle in normal circumstances, but now the road was a scene of almost indescribable chaos. Many hundreds of the unwounded survivors of the earlier attacks were hopelessly intermingled with those of the subsequent assault. Yet more hundreds of dead and wounded lay in the ravine and the adjacent gravel-pits. Debris, dead horses and dead or wounded soldiers littered the causeway and its approach road. Units, many of them by now leaderless, were jumbled together. Weapons could not be brought to bear, and survival

rather than offensive action was the priority for very many of the
shocked and exhausted soldiers. Still the French fired on the ravine and
into the midst of all this rode the 1st Cavalry Division and the accompanying horse artillery.

> We saw them wheel off into the road and clatter down the Gravelotte slope at
> a trot. Behind them, at a swinging canter to overtake the guns, dashed a noble
> regiment of Uhlans [the 4th Regiment of Uhlans]. How gallantly the
> horsemen rode on their way to death! Artillery and cavalry disappeared into
> the ravine ... The French infantry fire spurted out of the rifle-pits on the
> further brink; several batteries of mitrailleuses, in regularly constructed
> emplacements, took to grinding sedulously their cursed output; the cannon
> further back on the Point-du-Jour made practice over the heads of the
> mitrailleuse men and the sharpshooters, down into the bosom of the gorge.
> The German artillerymen did, as it appeared, get [two batteries] into action,
> with the muzzles of their pieces sticking up into the air, but guns were
> dismounted, and [due to the casualties they sustained] the gun detachments
> had to be reinforced over and over again, from the reserves in the rear by
> Gravelotte. As for the Uhlans, the morrow furnished a chart of their doings –
> a chart on which the courses were traced in by dead men and horses. They
> had striven to charge up the inverse slope of the chaussée on to the plateau of
> St-Hubert, and they had failed. Men and horses, not many, – it must have
> been a mad forlorn hope of reckless men, - lay on the roadway in the gutters,
> just on the brink of the plateau; there were none further, but very many all the
> way behind.[97]

In fact, the 4th Regiment of Uhlans was the only cavalry regiment to
reach the plateau beyond the ravine. Some of them did manage to deploy
on the hill to the right of the road, but the casualties that they then suffered
(almost half their number) soon forced their withdrawal down into the
ravine. Thus the 1st Army's action on the right flank was more or less
halted by late on that Thursday afternoon, while von Moltke's long-held
reservations about von Steinmetz as an army commander were shown to
have been all too valid.

But at about 4.30 p.m. von Steinmetz sought King William's permission
to commit his reserve brigades, the 27th from the 7th Corps and the 32nd
from the 8th Corps, to the attack against the Point-du-Jour. The fanciful
rationale offered by von Steinmetz for what was in fact the reinforcement
of his earlier failure was the fiction that the French troops on the heights
were about to collapse, and that the presence of the elements of three
German regiments in the St-Hubert farm complex indicated that the 1st
Army had already achieved a firm foothold on the plateau.

There were indeed forty-three companies of Prussian infantry in the
general area of St-Hubert and the hillside below the farm, but they were

now a very disparate force – one that was much depleted by casualties, unable to move forward, and which was in reality no more than the residue of some seven different regiments. Although von Moltke was by now at the village of Malmaison, which was relatively close to the scene of the 1st Army's battle, and so was probably aware of the true situation in the Mance ravine, he did not contest von Steinmetz's request. In light of von Moltke's lack of opposition to the 1st Army commander's proposal, the king acquiesced and the next phase of the desperate battle for the Point-du-Jour was set to begin at 6 p.m. During the next hour the infantrymen of the two reserve brigades prepared to advance along the road from Gravelotte and then on down into the horror of the Mance ravine.

Not surprisingly, this attack suffered much the same fate as those that had preceded it. Although the German infantry did manage to work their way up to the crest of the eastern side, they were met by a hurricane of bullets and shellfire as they broke cover at the edge of the wood at the top. Men fell dead or wounded all about and the survivors quickly sought refuge at the bottom of the ravine, being enthusiastically pursued for part of the way by a swarm of French skirmishers. The panic this caused was contagious. At about 6.30 p.m. hundreds of distraught German soldiers cascaded down the eastern slope, on to the flat bottom of the ravine, across the Mance, and then fled in total disorder back up the western slope and onwards along the road to Gravelotte. The scale of this chaos was further magnified by loose teams of artillery horses and diverse groups of cavalry that also competed with the infantrymen for space on the narrow road back to Gravelotte. Their flight took them past and through the staff of the German headquarters, now at Malmaison, and onwards towards Rezonville, where the retreat was finally halted. Even King William and his staff became directly involved in stemming – by using the flat of their swords – the flood of terrified soldiers! French shells fell amid the panicked troops all the while.

The final act in the sorry tale of 1st Army's attempts to seize the ground to the east of the Mance ravine followed soon afterwards. The 2nd Corps, commanded by General Fransecky, normally belonged to the 2nd Army, but had been placed under the command of the 1st Army earlier during the day. At about 7 p.m. with darkness falling fast, the 3rd Division of the 2nd Corps arrived at Gravelotte and – virtually without pause – marched on down the road and into the notorious ravine. Their progress from Gravelotte to the edge of the ravine was illuminated by the 'redder-forked tongues of fire which were bursting out of the [château and] burning farm-buildings of Malmaison, where the wounded Frenchmen were being roasted alive, in miserable helplessness' due to the French artillery having shelled the field hospital there, mistakenly believing it to be a German headquarters.[98]

The column of soldiers divided at the causeway and deployed left and right before beginning the ascent of the eastern slope. The whole way their progress was impeded by the casualties and detritus of the earlier attacks. True to form, they were met at the top of the slope by the usual blizzard of fire, and sustained more than 1,300 casualties in a matter of minutes. But the horror of the situation was further compounded by the attacking Germans of the 3rd Division mistaking for French infantrymen the German survivors of the earlier, partly successful assault on the farm at St-Hubert. For an hour, in darkness and confusion, Germans fired on Germans, until the surviving soldiers at St-Hubert finally abandoned their hard-won positions in and about the ruined farm buildings and retreated down the hillside.

At this stage General Fransecky at last ascertained what had happened, and ordered the 3rd Division to withdraw to the bottom of the ravine, covered by the 4th Division of his 2nd German Corps, which then occupied the line just vacated by the retreating survivors of the 7th and 8th Corps. At long last a great silence fell over the Mance ravine, punctuated only by the sound of an occasional explosion, the detonation of an isolated artillery shell or the crackle of a quick flurry of rifle fire. By 10 p.m. all firing had ceased and the silence was absolute, save for the cries of the hundreds of wounded soldiers still lying within and about the dark wooded depths of the Mance ravine.

Had Bazaine decided to press the undoubted advantage that the French had achieved against the 1st Army on the German right flank, the final outcome of the battle might well have been very different. General von Steinmetz's 1st Army had sustained 4,300 casualties at the hands of General Frossard's 2nd French Corps, which had itself lost a mere 621 men during the battles about St-Hubert, the Point-du-Jour and the Mance ravine.

The Mance ravine was not the only site of bitter fighting that afternoon. While the soldiers of the 1st Army had been consigned to the chaos there throughout much of the day, their comrades of the 2nd Army had been drawn into another inferno of shot and shell; this time on the open plain to the west and south-west of the strongly fortified villages of Ste-Marie-aux-Chênes and St-Privat-la-Montagne, at the northern end of the French line.

The course of the afternoon's events on the German left flank had their origins in Prince Frederick Charles's earlier incorrect assessment that the French right was based on the village of Amanvillers rather than St-Privat. Subsequently, the additional march northwards to compensate for this error had imposed an unfortunate delay on the deployment of the 2nd Army. This was further compounded by an earlier problem that had occurred at first light, when the 12th (Royal Saxon) Corps had found itself competing with the Guard Corps for movement routes through Mars-la-Tour.[99] The delays resulting from this uncharacteristic error of staff work by the German headquarters had subsequently resulted in General von Manstein's 9th Corps being placed in some peril during the first few hours of its battle against the French centre about Amanvillers.

It also meant that the 2nd Army's crucial attack on Ste-Marie-aux-Chênes (which was defended by some 1,500 infantrymen plus a single battery of artillery) did not begin until 3 p.m., when the 47th Brigade of the 24th (Royal Saxon) Infantry Division and the 1st Guards Division, supported by the concentrated fire of more than seventy guns, swept towards the village from the north-west and south respectively. Consequently, it was not until just after 3.30 that the village was secured, though at the cost of a considerable number of casualties and with the French garrison having withdrawn in good order and with its guns to join the garrison at St-Privat. An attempt by the Saxon soldiers to follow up their success by an immediate attack on St-Privat was comprehensively defeated by the French riflemen entrenched on the slope between the two villages, and so the Germans had, for the time being, to settle for consolidating their occupation of Ste-Marie-aux-Chênes.

In the meantime the remainder of the 12th (Royal Saxon) Corps had continued its wide flanking march to the north-east while the balance of the Guard Corps had successively turned eastwards by brigades. By late afternoon the 1st Guards Brigade was at Ste-Marie-aux-Chênes, the 2nd and 3rd Guards Brigades were in the area of St-Ail, and 4th Guards Brigade was at Habonville. More than 100 German guns had been positioned south of Ste-Marie-aux-Chênes and were engaging, with limited success, the area of St-Privat and the farm of Jerusalem a little to the south-west of the village. All of the Guards brigades faced towards their ultimate objective, the fortified village of St-Privat-la-Montagne. The village was little more than a mile away and, shimmering in the August afternoon heat, its grey stone walls and church spire were clearly visible on the skyline at the top of the open and gently rising slope that lay before the lines of guardsmen. At 4.30 Prince Frederick Charles ordered the commander of the Guard Corps, Prince Augustus of Württemberg, for the attack on St-Privat.

The ranks of Prussian guardsmen stood in half-battalion groups under the beat of the sun. Earlier on, it had not been anticipated by the German high command that these men would be required to engage in combat on 18 August, but rather that this would be only a day of marching and manoeuvre followed, probably, by their committal to battle on Friday the 19th. Consequently, the guardsmen were weary, thirsty, covered in dust, and were still equipped with their full marching order – about 100 pounds of equipment per man, including knapsacks, rolled greatcoats, weapons and full loads of ammunition. Although they would soon need the ammunition, the other equipment would shortly prove to be an unwelcome encumbrance. At 4.30 a lull descended over the north end of the battlefield, and a little over half an hour later the four separate brigades of guardsmen began what developed into a series of simultaneous and sequential attacks in their bid to capture the village of St-Privat.

At a little after five, the battle having been renewed, General von Manstein[100] ordered the 3rd Brigade of the Guards [1st and 3rd Guard Grenadier Regiments and the Garde-Schützen Battalion] to the attack [with the task of preventing General Cissey's division from intervening in the forthcoming battle for St-Privat.] Advancing [from the Bois de la Cusse] in well-formed columns and in the best of order, the battalions were received with a terrible shower of bullets, which thinned their ranks in a frightful manner. The smallest ridges, affording some shelter, were used to good advantage; after every halt there was another advance. Up to seven o'clock in the evening, the brave soldiers had pushed themselves forward to within eight hundred paces of Amanvillers, located to the south of St-Privat, which place they could not take from sheer exhaustion ...

[In the meantime,] at half-past five o'clock the commander of the 2nd Division of the Guards led the 4th Brigade [from just south of St-Ail] in person in the assault upon the advanced outwork Jerusalem, part of the village of St-Privat stretching towards Amanvillers. The enemy was found lying there protected by hedges and rifle-pits, but beyond the reach of the needle-gun. The rapid firing chassepots made big gaps in the columns of the brigade as it advanced in regular fighting order. Without the slightest cover, the brave battalions, having by this time lost almost all their officers, now pushed ahead; but only the edge of the position [still some 800 yards from the objective] could be taken by the 4th Brigade, which, however, drove the enemy back to Jerusalem ...

It was found impossible to reach the first line of the enemy in spite of the fact that the remains of the brigade held the captured territory. Half an hour later, when the 4th Brigade had done its task, the 1st [Brigade] of the Guards, under General von Kessel, made an attack on St-Privat [from the direction of] Ste-Marie-aux-Chênes ... The same spectacle seen on the south side was seen also here. The route of the battalions was marked by heaps of dead and wounded, and in a short time all the commanders were hors-de-combat. The right wing, nevertheless, advanced up to within nine hundred paces, and the left to within six hundred paces of the enemy. The fighting of the decimated Germans grew less and less.[101]

Shortly after a quarter past six o'clock it was the turn of the 2nd Guards Brigade. Picking their way through and around the casualties sustained by the 1st and 4th Brigades, the 2nd Brigade advanced from Ste-Marie-aux-Chênes astride the minor road that ran to St-Privat. The earlier experience of the other brigades was soon repeated when they were stopped in their tracks by a veritable storm of Chassepot bullets. They were still about 1,000 yards short of their objective. The guardsmen found what little cover they could in folds in the open ground and behind the bodies of their fallen comrades. They had been halted roughly in line with the point at which the 1st and 4th Brigades' survivors lay, so that the remnants of the three brigades formed a more or less cohesive firing line. Remarkably, this line of riflemen continued to edge forward in small groups and as individuals until, by about 6.30, they were some 600 yards from the bullet-scarred, loop-holed walls of St-Privat. At this point, all further forward movement being impossible, Prince Frederick Charles took stock of a situation that was at best a stalemate and at worst might yet threaten the outcome of the battle.

Indeed, by now the German situation at St-Privat, and the continuing débâcle of the 1st Army at the Mance ravine, did not augur well for a German victory at Gravelotte–St-Privat, and the German headquarters staff began to plan accordingly.

Now the commander of the 2nd Army finally took the action that he should have taken at the start of the Guard Corps' initial attack towards St-Privat some one and a half hours earlier. Having seen the attack by the 2nd Guards Brigade falter and come to a halt, Prince Frederick Charles directed all the artillery at his disposal to concentrate its fire against the fortifications of St-Privat and Jerusalem.

Having received his orders from Frederick Charles, General von Pape, the commander of the 1st Guards Division, ordered four batteries of artillery to be placed in position one thousand paces from the village, together with the entire Guard Corps artillery and the guns of the 10th and 12th Corps: 208 guns in total. This massive weight of artillery fire soon reduced much of St-Privat to rubble, with virtually the entire village in flames. The French rifle fire reduced significantly, although it was still sufficiently lethal to prevent the prostrate lines of guardsmen from standing up and advancing; however, von Pape did move the 2nd Guard Grenadier Regiment forward to join the line, together with the 4th Regiment of Guards as a reserve for the left-hand brigade. But it finally fell to the Saxon troops to break the impasse.

The Saxon Corps now advanced on the village, their move carefully coordinated with the fire of seven batteries of artillery. Together with parts of the units of the Guard Corps, fifteen battalions of Saxon infantrymen of the 45th and 47th Brigades encircled the north and west sides of St-Privat. As eighty-four guns of the Saxon Corps' own artillery maintained their bombardment of the village, von Pape moved forward the Guard Fusilier Regiment from Ste-Marie-aux-Chênes, where it had been held in reserve.

By 7.30 p.m., all was at last set for the Germans to resume their full-scale attack on St-Privat. In an action subsequently immortalized in a painting by the contemporary French artist Alphonse de Neuville:

> The drums beat the general assault; the troops advanced with flying colours up to the village and scaled the walls that surrounded the town and yards; the houses were then stormed one by one. The 3rd Battalion of the Body-guards and the 9th Company of the 4th Regiment assaulted the church, the 3rd Company of the 4th Regiment of the Guards bore down on the ceme tery, the Fusiliers of the 1st Regiment of the Guards advanced upon the farmsteads lying south of Jerusalem, and the Franz Regiment took Jerusalem proper.[102]

The sun was setting as the guardsmen and the Saxon infantry stormed into the village to engage in a period of furious and bloody hand-to-hand fighting that finally delivered the ruined and burning village of St-Privat to them. By the time that St-Privat finally fell to the German onslaught, its French garrison had sustained 50 per cent casualties.

Although the capture of St-Privat is generally credited to the Prussian Guard Corps, it could not have been achieved without the critical involvement of the 12th (Royal Saxon) Corps. The role of this corps was absolutely crucial, and their success gave von Moltke an opportunity to turn the French right flank. The very long flanking march they had been required to carry out via Ste-Marie-aux-Chênes meant that the Saxons had not been able to come fully into action until 3 p.m. however, their impact when they did enter the battle is clear testimony to the professionalism displayed by its commander, Prince George, the Crown Prince of Saxony, and to the fighting qualities of the Saxon soldiers. There was a certain irony in the fact that just four years earlier Saxony had been staunch allies of Austria during its 1866 war against Prussia, when its troops had been locked in battle with many of the very same Prussian troops for whom they had just performed such valuable service.

While the German infantrymen broke through the perimeter defences of St-Privat and began the exhausting task of clearing the French out of every house, barn and farm, General von Manstein's 9th Corps, which had remained generally static for most of the day since its initial artillery engagement just before midday, advanced and successfully stormed the village of Amanvillers. The tide of battle had at last begun to turn in the Germans' favour with the collapse of the French right flank.

Not surprisingly, it was with a measure of disbelief, and undoubtedly with considerable relief, that the staff of the German headquarters at Malmaison received the reports that St-Privat had finally been taken, that the French right flank had been turned, and that Bazaine's Army of the Rhine had retired into the security of the ring of fortresses surrounding Metz. Even without the revelation at dawn on 19 August that the French had also vacated the area of the Point-du-Jour, it had been clear to the Germans by about 10.30 the previous evening that the 1st and 2nd Armies had indeed finally won the day, although at a terrible cost.

By contrast the French losses were comparatively light; 7,853 officers and men of the Army of the Rhine dead or wounded, of whom 1,144 were dead or had sustained what would prove to be fatal wounds. A further 4,419 men had been taken prisoner. These totals need to be set against an estimated total of between 120,000 and 150, 000 men who were actually engaged in the fighting. Indeed, the total strength of the Army of the Rhine once it was confined within Metz was in the order of 173,000 men, including the town's garrison. The losses suffered by the victors, however, were as sobering as they were revealing. Of a total strength of 203,402 officers and men engaged in the battle, 20,159 lay dead or wounded, 5,237 of whom were dead or died later from wounds received. A further 493 men were missing.

Even more salutary was the breakdown of the casualties sustained during the frontal attacks mounted by the Guard Corps against the village of St-Privat. There, after just over thirty minutes in action, 2,440 guardsmen lay dead, 5,511 were wounded and 179 were missing. The Garde-Schützen Battalion had lost nineteen officers (plus one surgeon) and 431 men; the 1st Regiment of Foot-Guards thirty-six officers and 1,056 men; the 2nd Regiment of Foot-Guards thirty-nine officers and 1,076 men; the 3rd Regiment of Foot-Guards thirty-six officers and 1,060 men; the 4th Regiment of Foot-Guards twenty-nine officers and 902 men;

the 1st Guard Grenadier Regiment (Emperor Alexander of Russia) twenty-seven officers and 820 men; the 2nd Guard Grenadier Regiment (Emperor Franz) thirty-eight officers and 1,020 men; the 3rd Guard Grenadier Regiment (Queen Elizabeth) twenty-one officers and 433 men; and, finally, the 4th Guard Grenadier Regiment (Queen Augusta) twenty-seven officers and 902 men. For its overall size, the Garde-Schützen Battalion's losses were especially devastating, 451 casualties being sustained during the attack by 3rd Guards Brigade towards Amanvillers, shortly before 5 p.m. But the battalion's total losses during the day amounted to no fewer than 700 officers and men and, at its end, with every officer either dead or wounded, command of the battalion was left in the hands of an officer cadet. Given that the wartime strength of a battalion was about 1,000 all ranks, and that of a regiment about 3,200, the casualties incurred by the separate regiments of the élite Guard Corps indicate the truly devastating effect that the battle of Gravelotte–St-Privat had upon the overall combat effectiveness of that élite element of the German war machine.

If proof were needed both of the power of the weapons of the modern era and of the changed nature of the wars in which they were now to be employed, the dead and wounded of Gravelotte–St-Privat and of Mars-la-Tour–Vionville provided an abundance of such evidence. Statistically, more Germans had been killed or wounded by the Chassepot than by any other weapon. Not unexpectedly, more French soldiers had fallen to the shellfire of the breech-loading Krupps artillery than to any other German weapon system. Directly linked to this, the vital importance of properly prepared defensive positions – and hence what was now the indispensable role of the entrenching-tool in modern warfare – was well highlighted by these battles.

The lessons of 16 and 18 August had been learned too late for the dead still lying in the Mance ravine, on the fields about St-Privat, or in one of the many hastily dug communal graves that soon dotted the battlefield. But soon after the second of the two great battles that had been fought to the west of Metz, various orders emerged from the German high command which indicated that some of the lessons of the first two weeks of the campaign had indeed been noted.

First, the technological superiority of the French Chassepot could not be gainsaid, and the Germans knew that the frontal attacks employed in former times simply invited huge numbers of casualties and risked defeat. Consequently, the traditional infantry tactic for a direct assault – a procedure virtually unchanged from that described in the Prussian Army Regulations of 1812 – whereby a battalion column would follow up close behind the forward firing-line or skirmishers, was abandoned forthwith. At the end of August the high command directed that in future, 'In the attack the artillery will commence with a well-directed fire, and in the very rare case where the frontal attack over open ground becomes necessary, company columns and half-battalion columns, as laid down in the Field Exercises and practised on the drill-ground, must be resorted to.'[103] As commander-in-chief, William himself put his signature to this directive.

The Germans also recognized the value of capturing Chassepots for their own use and, in mid-September during the forthcoming siege of Metz, Prince Charles Frederick encouraged his soldiers to acquire these weapons:

> Patrols must be on the constant look out for opportunities of irritating the hostile outposts, and, especially at night or during foggy weather, to harass them by minor attacks and by taking prisoners. I shall give Iron Crosses to those who distinguish themselves in such enterprises. The long-ranging rifles of the enemy (the Chassepots), which should be seized at every opportunity, may be advantageously used by good marksmen.'[104]

Of the several major battles of the Franco-Prussian War, Mars-la-Tour and Gravelotte–St-Privat exemplify the positive and the negative aspects of the German army of the day. The two separate days of intense combat had seen a veritable inferno of fire, primarily by the French Chassepots and the German Krupps artillery, but the motivation and determination of the German soldiers were often quite remarkable. Many of these men who had been exposed to the new horrors of this modern war were reservists, but they generally remained steady under fire and finally achieved their objectives.[105]

Here was proof positive that by 1870 the army had produced a level of discipline, training, self-confidence, national pride and confidence in its military leaders that generally transcended the often-appalling combat situations in which it found itself that August. In the light of this, it is perhaps unremarkable that even the ill-judged committal of the Guard Corps at St-Privat and the negligent committal of the 1st Army at the Mance ravine did not give rise to overt criticism of commanders such as General von Steinmetz and Prince Augustus of Württemberg by their soldiers. Undoubtedly the truism that soldiers will forgive a commander almost anything, provided that he delivers the final victory to them, applied during the days and weeks following the battle at Gravelotte–St-Privat.[106]

Without a doubt the battles of 16 and 18 August were the turning-point of the war and made an eventual German victory inevitable. While the neutralization of the Army of the Rhine by its withdrawal into Metz was the most significant and most visible outcome of the fighting, these two battles also precipitated far-reaching political events and a new strategic agenda. In France, these resulted ultimately in the fall of the Napoleonic dynasty, the end of the French Second Empire, and the military defeat of the French nation. For the Germans, von Moltke could now be confident that the army could achieve all that he had planned. At the same time, Bismarck saw that his much wider political aims for German unification were both achievable and moving ever closer to their fruition. Their sovereign also believed that the victory at Gravelotte–St-Privat was the defining moment of the campaign. Surely, William thought, with the Army of the Rhine effectively confined within the ring of fortresses about Metz, the time had come for France to accept defeat before more lives were lost, before more French territory fell under German control, and before more French towns and cities were laid waste by the powerful German artillery?

But King William was all too soon disabused of this not unreasonable but somewhat over-optimistic view, as news began to reach the German headquarters of the formation at Châlons-sur-Marne, to the south of Reims, of a new French Army under the command of Marshal MacMahon. By 21 August the French Army of Châlons numbered more than 130,000 men, although many of these were of fairly mixed quality and had undergone only limited training. But this army was equipped with 423 guns and so represented a powerful new threat to German success.

Von Moltke had wisely anticipated the emergence of just such a threat, as indeed he had also appreciated that Paris itself might not give way to the Germans without a fight. Accordingly, as early as Friday, 19 August, he had already begun to implement his plan for the next phase of the campaign, and the activities of the German armies during the next two weeks exemplified their consummate professionalism as von Moltke and the German war machine relentlessly carried the campaign against the imperial French forces through to its inevitable conclusion.

At the outset, von Moltke had not envisaged laying siege to Metz. He had always hoped to bring the French Army to battle on the plains of eastern France, or even before the gates of Paris, in order to defeat it decisively. But the German forces now had to deal simultaneously with the new threat posed by the Army of Châlons, while keeping the Army of the Rhine contained in Metz, and finally they had to maintain and conclude successfully the siege of Strasbourg. In addition, there was always the possibility that Paris would eventually need to be taken by force of arms. With all these requirements and considerations in mind, over the next twenty-four hours the three German armies were extensively reconfigured.

In the course of this reorganization of the three German armies on 19 August, General von Steinmetz's ill-judged and impetuous actions in command of the 1st Army on 18 August (he had also been similarly insubordinate at the battle of Spicheren on 6 August, although with less disastrous consequences) were at last dealt with when the entire 1st Army was subordinated to Prince Frederick Charles, whose 2nd Army now had the mission of besieging Metz.[107]

In the meantime, the German forces prepared for what they anticipated – incorrectly as it turned out – would be the last great battle that would set the seal on the final and comprehensive defeat of France. Battle with the French Army of Châlons was eventually joined on 1 September, when the army of Marshal MacMahon was trapped at the fortress town of Sedan, close to the French-Belgian border. MacMahon had been marching to relieve Bazaine at Metz, but a junction of the two forces was never realistically achievable or even strategically sensible.

The Battle of Sedan, 1–2 September, 1870

At Sedan, two armies numbering some 224,000 Germans surrounded an already demoralized and weary French force of about half the German strength. The French emperor, Napoleon III, was there with the army. Despite the numerical imbalance, the battle was notable for the bravery and desperate fighting of the French against all the odds. It was also notable for the ferocity of the attacking Bavarian infantrymen in the nearby town of Bazeilles, which gave rise to claims and counter-claims that French civilians had fired on the Bavarians, which had led the German troops to execute numbers of these allegedly unofficial combatants. Despite some heroic French counter-attacks and sorties, and some glorious but generally suicidal cavalry charges, the outcome was never in doubt. By the evening of 1 September a grand total of 683 German artillery guns were positioned in the hills about the battered town, into which most of the French had by now withdrawn. Indeed, despite a number of infantry clashes, Sedan was a victory for the German artillery and, having rained their shells upon the French both within and beyond Sedan during 1 September, the massed firepower that was now ranged upon the town made the French surrender inevitable. The next morning the Army of Châlons surrendered, Napoleon III became a prisoner of the Germans, and the French Second Empire was no more. The former Army of the Rhine, which was then still besieged in Metz, negotiated a surrender on 26 October, the fortress city formally capitulating on the 29th.

The statistics of victory and defeat at Sedan were impressive. The Germans had sustained 8,924 casualties, whereas the French lost 3,220 killed, 14,811 wounded and 21,000 captured in the field. But the total number of prisoners resulting from the capitulation was 83,000, with a further 3,000 disarmed in Belgium. Only a few hundred French soldiers avoided capture and escaped back into France, towards Mézières in particular. In addition, French losses to the Germans included one eagle, two flags, 419 field guns and mitrailleuses, 139 heavy artillery guns, at least 66,000 rifles and muskets, plus large numbers of wagons and horses, together with substantial quantities of ammunition, provisions and all manner of military supplies.

On 3 September the Germans established a temporary prison camp within the loop of the Meuse, the Iges peninsula, to the north-west of Sedan. With no food (the Germans were themselves temporarily short that day), little drinking-water and limited shelter against persistent rain, the tens of thousands of defeated soldiers confined there soon termed the place '*le Camp de Misère*'. Emile Zola described in graphic detail the privations allegedly suffered by these men in his novel *La Débâcle*, although his account may be somewhat exaggerated. Nevertheless, conditions for the more than 70,000 men confined by the Meuse undoubtedly deteriorated as the days passed and the focus of German activity moved away from Sedan, their resources being needed elsewhere. The number of prisoners held on the Iges peninsula did reduce progressively from 5 September, as successive groups of 2,000 were sent daily to captivity in Germany, where they stayed until their release in March 1871.

Despite the existence of various dispersed pockets of French troops in numerous garrisons in the western provinces of France, the German soldiers might have been forgiven for assuming that their decisive victory at Sedan meant the end of the war. Two imperial French armies had been soundly defeated and the French Emperor was a prisoner. Surely all that remained to be done was to stage a victory parade and then a triumphant return home to Germany? But, just as the Second French Empire died in Paris, on 4 September a provisional Government of National Defence was formed and the Third French Republic rose like a phoenix from the ashes of the imperial débâcle. The emergence of this new enemy heralded a new campaign and in many ways a quite different sort of warfare, thus presenting a whole range of new and generally unsought challenges for all the officers and men in the German army.

13

Total War

Unification and the Defeat of France, 1871

NO MATTER HOW ILLOGICAL or perverse it might have seemed to be when viewed from Berlin, the government of the newly proclaimed French Third Republic was determined to maintain the territorial integrity of France, and this inevitably meant a continuation of the war. Just as so much of the momentum that took the Second French Empire into the war had originated in Paris, so the principal driving force for this policy came from the politicians and people of the capital. Some of the key political figures that now emerged included Jules Favre, the Minister of Foreign Affairs, Léon Gambetta, the Minister of the Interior (who soon became the Minister of War also), and General Louis Jules Trochu, formerly the Military Governor of Paris, who now assumed the position of President of the Council, and so in effect became the new head of the government. All three of these men – Gambetta in particular – were fully committed to what they declared was to be a 'guerra à outrance' (war to the bitter end), one that would involve the entire French nation in the conflict and the business of ejecting the German invaders. At the beginning of the war, King William I had proclaimed that Germany's quarrel was not with the French people but with their ruler. But with Napoleon now in captivity the whole situation had changed significantly and the speedy total victory that the German high command had both planned for and (not unreasonably) anticipated could not now be achieved.

So it was that, as the disconsolate and defeated soldiers of the former Army of Châlons marched into captivity and the German sieges of the isolated French forces in Strasbourg, Metz and elsewhere drew towards their inevitable conclusion, von Moltke issued his orders for the conduct of the next phase. Central to these was an acceptance that Paris would have to be taken by force of arms, an operation that would undoubtedly be a lengthy and bloody affair.

With all this clearly in mind, and despite the fact that the battle at Sedan had concluded just three days earlier, by 5 September the main German headquarters was already being established well to the south-west in Reims, as the German armies redeployed and cast their eyes towards what they now knew would be their final objective. For the elated and justifiably confident soldiers of the Army of the Meuse, the erstwhile victors of the frontier battles, of Mars-la-Tour, of Gravelotte–St-Privat and of Sedan, their new battle cry as they marched south and west was '… Nach Paris!' However, the forthcoming great siege of Paris would be but a part of the six-month winter campaign that now lay ahead of them. Although the soldiers did not then know it, the German army was also about to embark on what would prove to be an increasingly bitter campaign: one that would pit its soldiers against the forces of the new Third Republic, and therefore against the whole of the French nation, its soldiers – both regular and irregular – and many of its civilians alike. At the same time, the more or less general support for the German cause elsewhere in central Europe and in Britain, which had held steady throughout the campaign to Sedan, began to waver as the war was transformed from one waged against a politically and morally flawed French empire into one that was now to be waged against the ordinary people of France.

Clearly a full account of either the siege of Paris, which lasted from 20 September 1870 to 28 January 1871, or of the outcome of the lesser but none the less important sieges – such as those of Metz and Strasbourg – or of the numerous and often quite significant battles that took place during the *guerre à outrance*, is necessarily beyond the intended scope of this work. Nevertheless, the events of the next few months provide many illuminating vignettes and images of the German soldier on campaign, as well as illustrating the changing nature of the fighting, and the changing demands placed upon him.

The Sieges: Metz, Strasbourg and Paris

At the time of Sedan, von Moltke had no intention of launching an assault on Paris, and determined that the city should fall to a siege. With some 150,000 German soldiers available and uncommitted after Sedan, even with the sieges of Metz and Strasbourg still in progress (with 200,000 Germans surrounding Metz and 40,000 at Strasbourg), von Moltke was still confident of his ability to invest Paris. So it was, on Tuesday, 20 September, that soldiers of the German Army of the Meuse on the right or north-easterly banks of the Rivers Seine and Marne linked up with their comrades of the 3rd Army, who were on the left or south-westerly banks of the two great rivers which flowed through and around Paris. Meanwhile, beyond the besieging infantry's entrenchments, and in the countryside all about Paris, the troopers of the German cavalry divisions ranged far and wide. Thus was the French capital encircled and the great siege began.

But the success of this, as of any other siege, depended not only on the troops now in place about the city. It also needed the additional heavy artillery batteries that would conduct any future bombardment of the city. The besiegers also required the daily replenishment of many tons of ammunition, provisions, engineer stores and other resources, which would involve constant movement in and out of the lines. But by 20 September the German lines of communication were far more extended than had been the case throughout August and early September, and these vital routes had become increasingly vulnerable to direct attack or sabotage. Indeed, the troops originally held in northern Germany to counter any French sea landing on the coast had recently been formed into a 13th German Corps, commanded by the Grand Duke of Mecklenberg-Schwerin, which had been moved forward specifically to protect the lines of communication.

The two main railway lines between Germany and the Paris area assumed an even greater strategic importance as the days passed. One of these ran through Metz, Sedan and Reims, the other passed through Lunéville, Nancy, Bar-le-Duc and Châlons-sur-Marne; as the siege progressed the constant disruption of these vital supply lines by the many irregular or *franc-tireur* units in what was now the German rear increased rapidly. To compound the Germans' problems, many of the isolated forts on or adjacent to these rail and road routes were still occupied by French troops and these provided bases from which the irregular forces could launch their raids; and served too as rallying points and symbols of continuing French resistance. Of the several fortresses and fortified towns in which the French army still held out, the most important were the fortress city of Metz and the fortified town of Strasbourg.

The force besieging Strasbourg was based mainly on units from the Grand Duchy of Baden, plus two Prussian Landwehr divisions deployed from home defence duties on the German North Sea coast. It was commanded by General von Werder, who was determined to bring the siege to a rapid conclusion and was well aware that the superiority of the German artillery provided him with the means to do so. Accordingly, it began with an artillery bombardment on 14 August which caused much panic among the populace. The French garrison was about 17,000 strong, and commanded by General Uhrich. The city had few underground shelters for the protection of the civilians or of the garrison, or to safeguard its *matériel*. On that day Strasbourg had sufficient food stocks for sixty days, and the wherewithal for baking bread sufficient for 180 days.

As the siege progressed, General Uhrich resolutely refused a succession of requests from General von Werder for the surrender of the town. But as more and more of the public buildings and civilian dwellings were reduced to rubble by the German artillery, the municipal authorities tried to persuade him to surrender. In the meantime, from 29 August the Germans gradually worked their way forward until they had positioned their batteries so that the fire of nearly 100 heavy siege guns and mortars was concentrated on the breaching point for an assault. By 17 September a hole had been made in the town's main defensive wall and much of the area adjacent to the breach lay in ruins. Eventually, on Tuesday, 27 September, with a full-scale assault clearly imminent, Uhrich asked for terms of surrender, which were courteously offered and honourably accepted.

Viewed in the context of the German war machine's wider operations, the siege of Strasbourg illustrates quite convincingly the superlative technical and organizational qualities of the German army's engineers, pioneers and artillery. The siege featured elements both of the old and of the new approach to warfare. The traditional meticulous preparation of parallel lines of trenches and siege batteries, in strict accordance with the then doctrine for conducting a siege, contrasted quite starkly with the early and indiscriminate shelling of civilian non-combatant targets to bring about a quick capitulation; by the time they surrendered the garrison troops of Strasbourg had become thoroughly demoralized and ill-disciplined.

The siege of Metz was quite different. This formidable fortress city, surrounded by a ring of forts, was defended not only by its normal complement of garrison troops but also by the Army of the Rhine, which had taken refuge there following the battle of Gravelotte–St-Privat. The city had large quantities of ammunition and other supplies, and the forts were well provided with artillery and mortars. But they were entirely surrounded by Prince Frederick Charles's 2nd Army, and the population had been greatly increased by the influx of more than 170,000 additional soldiers; food was in short supply and was reducing rapidly with every day that passed.

One of the regiments that found itself in the lines about Metz after its participation in the fighting at Gravelotte was the 33rd (East Prussian) Regiment of Fusiliers. A contemporary account describes how:

> Both sides set up observation posts. The 33rd had one near Jussy. With a telescope the subaltern posted there could distinctly see the French regiments in bivouac ... The blockade was to some extent a time of enforced inactivity. Occasionally men on patrol or sentry duty were wounded, but there was little to break the monotony ... In early September the life of the besieging army was not too bad when the glorious harvest weather, the comfort of cantonments, and the

regular and good rations made the investment far more pleasant, and the monotony of the life less burdensome. There was time, too, to repair our hardly-used clothes and weapons. Life in the camps became almost as regular as in garrison; drill and the usual parades etc. helped to maintain the good behaviour and discipline of the troops. Unhappily, the health of many of the men had been much shaken, partly by the great strain put upon them at the beginning of the war, and partly by the recent bad weather. Two battalion commanders had been struck down, one by dysentery and the other by typhus ... By the middle of the month a 'live-and-let-live' policy had grown up among the troops and the French could even dare to dig up potatoes between the outposts ... By the beginning of October there was a good deal of disease. The sick report for the 2nd included 511 officers and men. By this time the regiment was concentrated at Sorbey. A beacon was set up on the heights of Haute Beux, with an officer and six men in charge. As soon as the beacon was observed in flames the alarm was to be sounded in the cantonments. In order to avoid false alarm arising from errors in observation, stakes with cross-bars pointing in the direction of the beacon were set up in the cantonments. The weather [finally] broke early in October and by the middle of the month the roads were quagmires, and the trenches and communications knee-deep in water.

Later, on 14 October the 33rd Regiment moved into a new position. There, it occupied what was apparently a much more active sector of the line.

An observation post was established at the Merci-le-Haut château. This post was one of danger, for the gunners in Fort St-Quentin persistently tried to frighten the officers on duty out of the place with shells; the projectiles, however, soon ceased to alarm, for they very seldom burst ... Three infantry picquets remained day and night in the trenches; one in front of the Laquenexy copse; a second south of Merci-le-Haut, near the Strasbourg road; a third behind a signal house on the Saarbrücken railroad. A Jäger post was thrown forward by day into the avenue which led from Merci to the Strasbourg road. One battalion formed the outposts, two companies in the Laquenexy copse; the others in the wood north-west of Jury. The latter was prepared for defence. A deep trench was dug, and the salients were entangled [usually with chevaux-de-frise]. Detached posts, under non-commissioned officers, were posted at the salients. Gun emplacements were constructed between two little walls, and here a section of artillery took post. A company was stationed as escort in a shed close at hand. Jury was strongly fortified, and a deep communication [trench] led to the Jury wood ... The enemy was very close at hand. He had already made several attempts against the position ... In order to give the picquets the power of firing at long range, they were armed with captured chassepots.[108]

By late September, many of the troops manning the German forward positions had been armed with Chassepots in place of their needle-guns, which enabled them to trade fire with the French riflemen on equal terms.

In the 2nd Battalion of the 4th (East Prussian) Infantry Regiment, seventy-five Chassepots were in regular use, and were transferred from Feldwache to Feldwache, and soldier to soldier as the daily changes of guard were carried out.[109] Certainly the German infantrymen much preferred the Chassepot, of which very considerable quantities were available after Sedan.

In addition to the Chassepots, some of the forward positions during the siege of Paris were apparently armed with a newly developed weapon specifically designed to counter the long-range sniper fire carried out by the French. The 'Wallbüchse' as it was called operated on the same principle as the needle-gun, but the balls it fired were made of iron, and the calibre was about three times greater. These balls could be fired at targets more than 2,500 yards away, and their weight and power could penetrate the fascines that protected artillery batteries. Indeed, the gun's recoil was so strong that it was fitted with a spring in the stock to mitigate it. Not surprisingly, the Wallbüchse was a cumbersome weapon whose operation required two men, one to aim it and one to operate the breech; references to its existence and use in action are few.

While he was attached to the 2nd Army at Metz, specifically to the 4th (East Prussian) Infantry Regiment, a unit within the 2nd Division of the 1st Corps based about the village of Flanville, Archibald Forbes was able to observe at first-hand the everyday life of a Prussian infantry regiment during the siege. On his arrival Forbes was welcomed by the 4th Regiment's commanding officer and assigned accommodation in a château with 'the officers of No. 6 Company [who] assigned me six feet by four of straw in the corner of the drawing-room, in which there was not a scrap of furniture but a grand piano, on which a sequence of voluntaries, sometimes accompanied by singing, sometimes by dancing, seemed constantly going on.'[110] Shortly afterwards, he was conducted around the German outposts by the company commander, Lieutenant Werth, and recorded his own impressions of the German defensive lines and positions.

> To the front there lay, first, the foreposts, then the Feldwachen, and lastly the single sentries ... The first line occupied a section of continuous entrenchment which ran right round Metz. All the villages were roughly fortified by barricades, chevaux-de-frise, etc; holes had been broken through all the houses for firing, and, indeed, every village formed a very respectable, if rough and ready fortress. The foreposts lay either in single houses, also well fortified by entrenchments and barricades, or in the field behind earthworks of no considerable magnitude. The Feldwachen chiefly occupied woods or the gardens of châteaux. A Feldwache which may be taken as typical, I noticed in the village of

Lauvallière ... Here lay two companies, arms piled close at hand, and ready for a sortie from the enemy at a moment's warning ... All the front was pitted over with the craters of shells. The men of one of the regiments were erecting quite a permanent barrack of wood, the sides covered with earth, behind an isolated brewery a little way in the rear of Lauvallière ... We went forward to the edge of a wood near Mey, accompanied by two Prussian patrols, and got a warning to go back in the shape of a sharp fusillade from a garden in the environs of Mey.

With the onset of night, the Germans modified their deployment in order to forestall any sortie or surprise attack that might be mounted by the garrison in Metz. 'At night the Feldwache always went forward to the post occupied during the day by the farthest outlying sentry. Here it broke right and left into small picquets, leaving a strong nucleus in the centre. The front, at a distance of 200 or 300 yards, was continually traversed by cavalry patrols, who often rode right in among the sleeping Frenchmen, whose system of night vigilance was not brilliant. Then there would be a pistol shot and a round of wild chassepot firing in the dark.'[111]

True to its tradition of professionalism, and despite the close proximity of the enemy, the German army continued to train assiduously while besieging Metz. Drill was a feature of the daily routine, when a whole range of tactics were practised up to and including battalion-level. Also, a constant trickle of new recruits was arriving at the field armies, and these all required further training to prepare them for their role in the regiment.

After coffee, drill begins. The young soldiers are at the goose-step in the flower-garden; the older hands practising skirmishing by companies in the neighbouring vineyards. At nine comes appel – a kind of parade without arms, at which the clothes and accoutrements of the men are carefully inspected. The [unit] appel only takes place occasionally, but the under officers have a minor appel every day, at each of which in turn there is an inspection of a separate article. Now it is arms, now boots, now cloaks – the under officer is responsible for the condition of his Schaft or squad, and he takes care he shall not incur a reprimand through any want of vigilance.[112]

In anticipation of a long siege, the officers and soldiers of the 4th Regiment made themselves as comfortable as possible in the various farms and buildings that lay in and about Flanville, itself a very small village adjacent to two large châteaux. There, with any cover at a premium, the soldiers occupied every house, loft, passageway and shed. In the meantime, the officers appropriated parts of the two châteaux for their use. One was occupied by a company of soldiers as well as a number of officers, and on the lawn outside were stacked the troops' needle-guns, ready for immediate use. As a further indication of the extent to which the war was now

impinging upon the lives of the civilian population of France, Forbes
noted that 'The flower-beds had been trodden down almost beyond the
power of recognition. A Corporalschaft occupied the conservatory, and
the flower-garden was a drill ground. The château had been pelted by the
French in the battle of the 1st of September – it was still within the range
of their guns – and the roof had been shattered by shells. We occupied the
drawing-room, in which were two great mirrors reaching to the roof. The
one over the mantelpiece had been penetrated by a bullet exactly in the
centre, and fantastically starred in all directions.'[113] Throughout the war,
the German armies of occupation also enjoyed to the full the local wines
that they found in the cellars of very many French houses and châteaux.
Consequently, and despite the unavoidable privations of life in the field,
the German officers and soldiers conducting the sieges in France managed
to develop what was certainly a quite acceptable routine and standard of
living in the field.

> After appel [came] the officers' breakfast. The feeding is homely, and eaten in
> a homely fashion … Breakfast over, comes an interval of visiting, gossiping,
> and beer drinking, for we have our own marketender [canteen facility] on the
> lawn, and Saarbrück is only forty miles away. Some write, some read, others
> sleep; it is astonishing how much sleep it takes to tire some people. The men
> employ themselves in tailoring, in seeing to the rations, in conducting the
> cooking of the dinner, and in smoking in the bright sunshine. Dinner is a rather
> discursive meal; you imagine you have finished it when you have eaten of the
> rice, the soup, and the mincemeat in your particular room, but going the round
> you find another mess devoting their attention to plums and schinken [ham],
> and you join in of course. Then you go a little farther, and find the inmates of
> another room topping off with chocolate or coffee and a petit verre.

With the day's work done, card playing, dancing, playing music, reading
books and singing were the main forms of off-duty entertainment for all
ranks, although the more lively activities usually centred upon the officers'
mess. Also of course – as has been so for soldiers on campaign since time
immemorial – there was the interminable writing and reading of letters to
and from home. The German army's Feldpost provided a most efficient
postal system, by which, in addition to letters, all manner of items passed
to and from the soldiers in the field, including clothing, hams, drink,
tobacco, and so on. The high command well recognized the importance of
the Feldpost for the morale of its troops.

Another matter that had a bearing upon the army's morale was the
importance of religion. Divine Service was both an essential and a routine
feature of military life, whether in barracks or on campaign. On Thursday

6 October, a typical regimental church service was conducted in the field
at Retonfay during the siege of Metz when :

> The division chaplain officiated, and the brigadier-general was present with his
> staff. It was a fine sight to see the six battalions, numbering as many thousand
> men, drawn up in a hollow square, with the clergyman and the regimental band
> in the centre. The service commenced with a hymn, in which all the troops
> joined with fervour. Then the minister preached a kind of informal sermon. He
> selected no Scripture text, his text was the duty of a Christian soldier in war
> time … he spoke of the friends at home longing for tidings from the front and
> yet half afraid to hear them lest they should learn that the loved one had fallen
> in battle … It was remarkable what an effect the chaplain's words had in stim-
> ulating correspondence when the service was over. Round each Feldwebel
> there was quite a little crowd eager to obtain the 'Correspondence Karte' [field
> postcard] on which the troops mostly wrote their brief epistles, and the post
> corporal had enough to do to carry the great bag with which he [later] went
> over to the Feldpost in Flanville.[114]

Wherever practicable, the officers and soldiers tried to maintain a
degree of normality in their daily routine, particularly in matters of hospi-
tality and entertainment. In peacetime, it had been normal for the officers
of Prussian regiments while stationed in Germany to hold a 'camp fire' or
similar informal social gathering each week 'to which the married officers
bring their good ladies, and whither also the "beauty and fashion" of the
garrison town are invited.' In the evening of the same day as the church
service, the officers and men of the 4th (East Prussian) Infantry Regiment observed this military tradition at Retonfay, when they gathered
within a specially constructed and suitably decorated 'woodland glade' by
a small river just outside the village. All the officers wore their best
uniform and jugs and bottles of beer served by the officers' servants
circulated freely among them, and also found their way to the many
soldiers who had gathered to watch the festivities. At nightfall a bonfire
was lit, and all ranks enjoyed the entertainment provided by the regimental band, which also accompanied the enthusiastic singing of regimental, patriotic and nostalgic songs of the Fatherland. The event was set
throughout against the sound of the steady firing of the German and
French artillery.[115]

The last sortie of any consequence launched from Metz came the very
next day, on a damp autumn morning shrouded by the heavy mists that
rose from the Moselle. It failed, and as if to set the seal on the French
predicament, the generally good weather ended abruptly, and gave way to
forty-eight hours of incessant rain.

The worsening weather affected the besiegers, many of whom were living in emplacements and bunkers rather than in buildings. Bronchitis and diarrhoea became commonplace; cases of typhus soon assumed almost epidemic proportions. However, the German medical services were among the most efficient of the day, and most of the sick were quickly evacuated by wagons to the railheads and then by rail to receive treatment and convalesce in Germany. The carriages of the German military hospital trains had entrances at each end and were fitted with triple tiers of bunk beds down each side. One carriage was used exclusively as a treatment and medical or surgical support facility and (in a contemporary description) as a 'laboratory'. Another coach provided accommodation for the medical attendants. A third carriage was a kitchen, serving patients and medical staff alike. Once into Germany, hospital trains also attracted substantial donations of food and other items at many of the towns and cities through which they passed and halted *en route*, the local civil administrators having been notified in advance of their arrival.[116]

Dwindling supplies of food in Metz, deteriorating French military and civilian morale, the failure of Bazaine's sorties from the city, and a series of attempted mass desertions – all of which attempts were rebuffed by the Germans in order further to compound the food situation – combined with the worsening weather to hasten the fall of Metz. All the while the German artillery was clearly visible, ranged about the city in considerable numbers. Allied to this, the widening war in the French provinces meant that the commander of the German 2nd Army was not inclined to negotiate anything less than the capitulation of the fortress city.

The end finally came on a wet and gloomy Saturday, 29 October. When the city capitulated, three marshals of France, forty-seven general officers and 6,000 regimental officers were among 173,000 men who became prisoners-of-war. Together with the men of the garrison, fifty-three eagles, standards and other colours were taken. Finally, 541 field guns of all types, 800 siege guns, 100 mitrailleuses, and 300,000 rifles fell into German hands. Virtually all of these weapons were still entirely serviceable. From 30 October, drafts – each of some 3,000 prisoners – were dispatched by rail to Germany.[117]

Although the French Second Empire had in reality been defeated at Sedan, the capitulation of Metz was in fact the final action in the war between Germany and the former imperial French armies, and the Berlin government at once determined that Metz was henceforth to be an integral and permanent feature of Germany's western frontier defences. The principal German commanders received their due rewards from King

William I, when General von Moltke became Count von Moltke, and the Prussian Crown Prince and Prince Frederick Charles were made field marshals. Victory celebrations would be premature because the war against the Third Republic was continuing unabated, and in Paris the new French government was giving every indication of its intention to resist the besieging German armies come what might.

When the ring of steel finally closed about Paris, the French garrison numbered about 400,000 men. First, there were more than 106,000 regular soldiers, sailors and marines. Admittedly, many of the soldiers were of doubtful quality, but the sailors and marines were disciplined and well trained. At the outset of the war the Garde Nationale had been some 24,000 strong, but the military governor of Paris, General Trochu, had rapidly increased this number to 90,000 by mid-September, and then added to its strength so that it eventually totalled almost 340,000 men. Finally, there was a colourful if disparate array of *francs-tireurs* and privately raised units within the Paris garrison. Although they were often badly disciplined and poorly trained, these volunteer units added several thousand more men to the overall manpower available for the defence of the French capital.

Two German armies had arrived at Paris on Saturday, 17 September: the Crown Prince of Saxony's Army of the Meuse and the Crown Prince of Prussia's 3rd Army. The Army of the Meuse was responsible for the northern side of the city while the 3rd Army invested the southern side. Three days later, on the morning of 20 September, these two armies completed the encirclement of the capital, which was then cut off by road, rail and river from access to the outside world. Thereafter, for the government and population in Paris, balloons and pigeons were the only means of communication beyond the city walls and past the German besiegers. And so what history later called the 'Great Siege of Paris' began.

The sheer magnitude and diversity of the tasks now facing the army were enormous. The German line ran for almost fifty miles; the telegraph lines connecting the headquarters of the three armies had a length of nearly sixty miles. By 21 October, the besieging army numbered 202,030 foot-soldiers, 33,734 horses and 898 cannon. As soon as these troops had deployed, they constructed a double tier of fortifications, and all the villages, châteaux and public parks within range of the guns of the Paris forts were made suitable for defence by infantry. All the streets were provided with *abatis* by felling trees and placing them in a line with their branches pointed towards the enemy. More and more artillery redoubts were built and equipped with heavy and with light batteries. Large areas were inundated by damming and redirecting waterways, lakes and rivers. To the south of Paris, the Bavarians prepared three investing lines. The batteries posted on this side were about 2,500 yards from the city's fortifications; those on the north side were stationed at a distance of 4,000 yards. Every position was equipped with a telegraph system. A comprehensive chain of outposts, all provided with telescopes, was established and linked to a light-signal system. To assist the speedy movement of reserves, a trestle-bridge was constructed over the Marne, and six pontoon bridges over the Seine, and three ferry sites were established.

Inevitably, the absence of an early assault, and the clear indication that one was not forthcoming in the foreseeable future, led to a series of limited sorties by the garrison. These were politically motivated rather than tactically necessary, and their overall failure, despite some limited successes, actually did more harm than good to the morale of those within the city. From the outset there was a considerable amount of low-level contact between the outposts and sentries of both sides, an activity closely regulated but positively encouraged by the German high command, which understood the value of the intelligence it produced. As the siege drew on, German food became an ever more powerful trading commodity and was freely exchanged for information about conditions in the city, the garrison, its plans and defences. Even in those instances where some success was achieved, this tended to induce excessive optimism on the part of the French leadership and the citizens they sought to defend. As early as 30 September a sortie by 20,000 men against the German 3rd Army positions to the south ended in disaster. An attack against the 2nd Bavarian Corps on 13 October had resulted in some gains and the capture by the French of some 200 prisoners, though at the cost of about 400 casualties to each side. But this was something of a hollow victory, as there was no question of consolidating their success and so the French were obliged to withdraw into the city at the end of their excursion. Nevertheless, this operation did inspire the garrison to make urgent plans for a much more significant sortie; one that would permit the breakout of a much larger force – possibly as many as 40,000 strong – with a view to its subsequent link-up with one of the French armies then operating in the provinces. To achieve this, the leaders in Paris needed to communicate with those who controlled the French forces beyond the city, and the Germans had already discovered and destroyed the telegraph cable that had been laid along the bed of the Seine.

With the telegraph link to the outside world gone, the French initially relied upon homing pigeons carrying micro-photographic messages.

However, although 303 birds were dispatched and fifty-nine arrived in Paris, each of the many birds that were downed by German fire, sparrow-hawks and other predators, or succumbed to storms, the bitter cold, or to any other misadventure *en route* were potentially an important source of intelligence information to the Germans. Accordingly, although the pigeons provided a useful service, the French adopted the manned coal-gas balloon as a more secure means of transporting messages and people out of the capital.

The first manned flight from the city was on Friday 23 September, when a balloon safely completed a three-hour journey of sixty-five miles, having passed over the German lines at a height of about 10,000 feet. At the start of the siege there were only seven balloons in Paris, but soon after this successful manned flight, the regular use of balloons to carry messages, personnel and pigeons was formalized. A contract was placed for their commercial production and on 26 September a routine postal service began, with outward-bound balloon flights up to three times each week.[118]

The German high command's attempted solution to the balloon problem was twofold. First, they tried to shoot them down, but in this they were largely unsuccessful. Next, but more successfully, they dispatched cavalry patrols to follow the balloons, in the hope of capturing the passengers and other contents of the basket when they eventually landed. Indeed, the Germans declared that the occupants of these balloons would be treated as spies, and could therefore face summary execution if captured. Throughout the siege, patrols of frustrated and weary hussars and uhlans could regularly be seen galloping madly across the French fields, all too often balked by hedgerows, ditches and rivers, while trying to keep up with the large gas-filled cotton globes that drifted silently through the clouds above them. Later, the Germans supplemented the cavalrymen's efforts with a system of observers, who used the telegraph system to report the presence and direction of these flights. This allowed them to alert in advance the troops in the probable landfall area.

The Paris garrison launched several sorties in strength against the German forces surrounding the city, and some of these forays subsequently developed into battles in their own right. The more notable of these engagements included that at Le Bourget on 30 October, when the 3rd and 4th Prussian Guard Regiments fought a desperately violent house-to-house battle to recapture the village following its occupation during a successful French sortie on the 27th. The bitter nature of this fighting was exemplified by an incident that occurred shortly after the death in action of one of the popular regimental commanders, Colonel Zaluskovski, when:

> In a room at the top of the stairs stood a French officer, who shot down with his revolver the first soldier who entered, and then, throwing his weapon on the floor, appealed for quarter to an officer who was among the first to enter. The officer would have granted it, but for once the bonds of discipline were burst. The men had heard the cry of 'Pardon'; they saw their comrade lying dead before them, and the fury of angry revenge was stronger within them than the voice of their officer could control ...[119]

Le Bourget finally fell to the guardsmen, but the 1st Battalion of the 3rd (Queen Elizabeth) Regiment of Grenadier Guards alone lost eight of its officers killed and twelve wounded. Almost 20 per cent of the regiment's fatal casualties were officers. Overall, the Prussians lost almost 500 men at Le Bourget. But the French were decisively defeated and ejected from the village, as well as leaving 1,200 prisoners in German hands, and the French did not reoccupy Le Bourget again at any time during the remaining months of the siege.

Devastated by the loss of Le Bourget, the next major action was the so-called 'Great Sortie', in which the Württemberg and Saxon troops were extensively involved. After several postponements, changes of plan and much political interference, the attack was planned to begin with a diversionary attack on 29 November, followed by the main action the next day, and was to be directed towards the villages of Villiers and Champigny, to the south-east of Paris. The diversionary attack duly went ahead on 29 October as originally planned and cost the French 1,000 dead and wounded and 300 men taken prisoner, all to little purpose as by now the Germans were well aware of the French intentions. Initially, the main attack on 30 November crossed the Marne successfully and gained some ground, capturing Champigny and Brie. But beyond lay the next objectives, the villages of Coeuilly and Villiers-sur-Marne. They were held by the men of the Württemberg Division and had been developed into formidable strongholds during the five weeks that they had occupied them. Despite a heavy bombardment by the French field artillery, and several attempts to outflank the villages, the French could not move the defenders. The attackers' casualties increased steadily and the battle rolled back and forth until, at dawn on 2 December, the Crown Prince of Saxony ordered a counter-attack by the 2nd German Corps. This pushed the French back towards Champigny and Paris, but the counter-attack eventually slowed and halted in the face of the intense Chassepot fire, now combined with that of the artillery batteries of the Paris forts as the advancing Germans came within their range. Both sides established new positions where they were. That night the temperature continued to fall and the pools of rainwater of the previous week froze into sheets of ice. The Germans were well prepared for this, but the French troops, who had been equipped only for a rapid advance to break out and join up with the French Army of the Loire, had no blankets, no tents, and had not had an opportunity to prepare hot food for three days and nights. Two days later, on the morning of 4 October, the exhausted and frozen soldiers abandoned their line and withdrew into Paris.

During the Great Sortie the Württemberg division lost 40 officers and 1,500 rank and file killed, wounded and missing, while the Saxon Corps lost 76 officers and 2,000 rank and file. Among the officers of the 2nd (Württemberg) Jäger Battalion who fell at Champigny on 2 December was First Lieutenant Knight, an Englishman. He had joined the Württemberg army in 1857, and when the war broke out was on a visit to England. He hastened back to his regiment and had served throughout the campaign to 2 December unscathed, until he was shot dead by a Chassepot that day. Knight was apparently a very popular officer in his regiment and he was subsequently buried in Pontault, a village close to where he fell at Champigny.

Further sorties were planned and executed by the garrison on 21 and 22 December, but on 17 December, with a growing disparity between the views of von Moltke and the high command and those held by Bismarck on the best way to resolve the impasse at Paris – specifically, by starvation or by bombardment, the decision was finally taken that a limited bombardment of the forts on the south side of Paris should begin as soon as a ten-day reserve of ammunition – 500 shells for each gun – was in place at the main ammunition storage and distribution point. For some time Bismarck had advocated a bombardment of the city, to bring about an early end to the war, and thereby achieve his ultimate goal of German unification.

Indeed, the longer the war went on, the more the political disquiet in Berlin was fuelled by the constant demands of the general staff for additional men and resources from Germany to maintain the war effort. The result of this was that von Moltke was blamed both by von Bismarck and von Roon for allowing the siege to run on, thereby forcing the Fatherland, at no little cost, to provide the wherewithal to sustain it. Predictably, this led to accusations of military profligacy and ineptness in the use of those resources already in place.

The war had also become increasingly bitter as the campaign conducted by the irregular units of *francs-tireurs* against the German lines of communication and against the German armies operating in the French provinces gained momentum. The irregular and independent nature of the *francs-tireurs* was further emphasized as increasing numbers of revolutionaries, republicans and adventurers flocked into France to join these colourful and often extravagantly uniformed units. The rise of this form of guerrilla warfare provided an unwelcome indication of the sort of combat that would recur in the future, and of the sometimes extreme counter-measures taken to redress it.

Much political rhetoric was used to inflame or inspire the *francs-tireurs*. The republican leadership urged them to 'Carry out *coups de main* and *pointes*, capture convoys, cut roads and railways, destroy bridges ... These troops must wage real partisan war, and for that they will need vigour, dash, intelligence and above all a great deal of cunning,' and to 'harass the enemy's detachments without pause or relaxation ... disturb him day and night, always and everywhere'. The exhortations of François Steenackers, the Director of Posts and Telegraphs, were reminiscent of the worst days of the first French revolution. He proposed that the irregular units should '... harass the enemy and hang from trees all the enemies they can take, well and truly by the neck, after having mutilated them'. He also suggested that the war should be taken to the German homeland by recruiting between 20,000 and 30,000 Kabyle tribesmen from France's colonies in North Africa, subsequently 'throwing them into Germany with leave to burn, pillage and rape all they find on the way... In short I suggest the type of war which the Spaniards waged against us under the First Empire and the Mexicans under the Second.' Predictably, the German commanders usually responded to this type of activity with severe reprisals against the *francs-tireurs* and those who supported them.

When caught, French irregular snipers were usually hanged or shot. Where the general source of the shots was identified – but not that of the sharpshooter, the building, farm or village was often burned down, and those suspected of assisting or concealing *francs-tireurs* could expect summary execution. On one occasion, during a meeting between the two statesmen, Bismarck declared to the French Minister of Foreign Affairs, Jules Favre, that the large number of snipers operating against the German supply convoys and columns of men moving between Sedan and Paris '... are not soldiers: we are treating them as murderers'. Typically, when a small cavalry detachment based at Ablis, near Epernon, was surrounded by *francs-tireurs* and only just escaped from them, the German troops returned later in strength and burned down the whole village. In some areas, such as the Vosges mountains, especially during the first four months of the war, the *francs-tireurs* posed a particular threat, and von Moltke had to direct the redeployment of a large force from the troops besieging Strasbourg to deal with them and clear them from Alsace.

Mr G. T. Robinson, the Special Correspondent of the *Manchester Guardian*, who was with the French forces in Metz during the siege, noted a 'Prussian proclamation denouncing the *francs-tireurs* as "traitors" and condemning them to instant execution' which, in his view, led to a French determination '... to act with corresponding severity, and the war became one of bitter reprisals, and, as far as possible, of extermination'. He observed that 'There can be no question that the Prussians did themselves a great injury with neutral nations by this injudicious and indefensible act of power.'

A report in the Berlin-published *Börsen Courier* also illustrated the severe sanctions taken by the Germans against these irregular fighters. In an item date-lined 'Versailles, November 20th' the publication reported that among the wounded and prisoners taken in a certain action about that date there were a number of *francs-tireurs*, who were brought to Versailles, where the main German headquarters then was. The newspaper account went on to relate that 'Short work was made of them: they were placed in a row, and one after another got a bullet through his head. A general order for the whole army has been published forbidding most expressly to bring them in as prisoners, and ordering to shoot them down [after trial] by drum-head court-martial wherever they show themselves.' The extract went on to state that 'Many were summarily strung up.'[120] But such actions were perhaps to be expected, as von Moltke had clearly defined the relative status of the *francs-tireurs* at the start of the war, when he had declared that they were not legitimate belligerents and so, when captured, were summarily to be shot. Many other accounts of *francs-tireurs* excesses, summary executions and reprisals abounded in the newspapers of the time. As Archibald Forbes recorded following a French sortie against Colombey on 28 September during the siege of Metz: 'A captain of the 44th Regiment was killed under circumstances which were a disgrace to civilized warfare. When his detachment was in retreat he fell wounded severely, but not mortally. His men placed him in shelter, and then left him as they fell back. When they recovered the village, they found the corpse of their captain mangled barbarously – his fingers cut off for the sake of the rings he wore, and his throat cut from ear to ear. I found the Germans justly incensed at this atrocity.'[121]

Gradually, the level of *franc-tireur* activity reduced, as the preventative and retaliatory action of the Germans became more effective and much of the local population began to doubt the long-term value of this campaign. In some areas the local civil authorities actively condemned what were viewed as acts of terrorism, but by then the hitherto clear line between soldier and civilian, between combatant and non-combatant, had become obscured, which had in turn changed both sides' perceptions of the way in which the war should be fought.

Meanwhile, internationally, and in Europe in particular, support for the German cause began to waver, as skilled French orators visited the governments and legislative assemblies of the neutral countries to put their case. They represented the view that the war had become one of ruthless attrition by the German invaders against the ordinary people of France, a proposition reinforced by the activities of the *francs-tireurs* and by the German action taken against them. Undoubtedly time was beginning to conspire against the Germans and to mitigate their successes of August and September the previous year. In mid-December the growing concern of the high command about this bad publicity finally tipped the balance of the argument about the advisability of bombarding Paris in favour of commencing this action as soon as practicable. But before the decision was implemented, the German soldiers still had time to celebrate Christmas as traditionally as their icy and often snow-bound positions about the French capital allowed.

Certainly their less than ideal circumstances did not prevent the officers and soldiers of the 2nd Battalion of the 103rd Infantry Regiment (Saxon No. 4) marking the occasion appropriately, despite the fact that they occupied an encampment that lay within 1,000 yards of the French outposts.

The kitchen was a part of the hut partitioned off, and we had the battalion cook there – a resplendent being in a white cap and apron. Before dinner he entered in state and lit the candles on the Christmas tree, a goodly sprout, from every bough of which dangled cakes and comfits. The cloth – we had a cloth, never mind about its colour – was laid, the plates and wine were warmed, and we drew around the social board. [The Christmas dinner comprised:] Soup – Liebig's extract. Fish – sardines, caviare [*sic*]. Entrées – goose sausage, ham sausage, a variety of undistinguishable sausage. Pièces de résistance – boiled beef and macaroni, roast mutton, and potato-salad. Divertissements – Schinken, compot [*sic*] of pears, ditto of apples, preserved sauerkraut. Cheese, fresh butter, fruit, nuts, biscuits, tarts etc. The potables were as follows:- One barrel of beer ... very good red wine, champagne iced – a little too much in fact. The caterer had stuck the bottles outside on his first arrival, and it seemed as if the wine had frozen in a solid mass. When it came to be poured out it would not run. [However, just as a hatchet was about to be used to smash the bottles and so liberate the frozen wine, it was found, through the judicious use of a skewer, that the ice was] only about half an inch thick, and that below there lay a limpid pint of liquid champagne. We pricked all the bottles with the skewer, and got on beautifully ... After dinner there were but two toasts. One was 'The King of Saxony'; the other 'Frau Majorin von Schönberg' [who had provided, via the Feldpost to her officer husband, the barrel of beer that had just been drunk]. Both were drunk with enthusiasm; the latter – in her beer – with positive effusion. Then we got to song-singing ... Instrumental accompaniments were forbidden on account of the proximity of the enemy, but the choruses were loud enough to raise the dead, let alone the Frenchmen...[122]

All too soon after these celebrations had concluded, on 27 December some seventy-six heavy guns opened a steady fire on Paris. As the bombardment continued, the winter weather grew worse. An ample covering of snow lay all over the area and the Seine was frozen solid over most of its length. Dense, freezing fog appeared on many of the mornings after Christmas and contributed to the general discomfort and uneasiness of the outposts of both sides, as well as hampering observation of the artillery fire. The bitterly cold weather prompted a surge in bronchial and rheumatic ailments among the troops, though the incidence of dysentery and typhus reduced. In recognition of the prevailing conditions, the Germans adapted their routine activities accordingly. The traditional pattern of two hours on sentry duty and four hours off was replaced by one hour on and two hours off. As with soldiers of most armies, the German soldiers had learned to go off to sleep at a moment's notice, so that this reduction of the unbroken period for rest did not affect them adversely, while at the same time the shortening of the duty period was much to their benefit.

Although many of the troops were in relatively well-found positions in the villages and outlying farms about Paris, their living conditions were by no means ideal, particularly as the weather steadily deteriorated. On 4 January 1871, Oberleutnant Ralph Freiherr von Kreusser of the 1st Bavarian Infantry Regiment wrote to his English mother about his regiment's newly occupied positions in a deserted French village and of how 'the 2nd Prussian Corps, which we have relieved, in its wild pleasure about leaving it, has smashed every window in the village, quite forgetting of course that other troops had the same right and claims to warmth as they. – As the village is quite forsaken by its inhabitants, our only food consists in ½lb of tough mutton, 1½lb of bread and very dirty water.' He went on to write, 'Luckily we can get our post regularly, so please send me immediately (in several packets as they won't take too large ones at the Post Office) the following list: every week, 1 lb of sugar; one pot of condensed milk; one packet of candles (as we sit in utter darkness till you send us some); one box of wax[ed] matches, not only to light the candles when they come, but also the fire; one bottle of either arrack or rum to mix with water for dinner and to prepare grog for the evening. Occasionally, tea, French mustard, cheese or ham or tongue, [and] a pencil, but never any sort of sausage or chocolate, as these things do not agree with our present fare… do pray send me these things as soon as possible for my appetite in this cold weather cannot be satisfied by ½lb of bad mutton.'[123] Whatever the failings of the Bavarian commissariat might have been, the Feldpost was clearly operating as effectively as ever.

Despite the continuing programme of military training, together with the regular turns of sentry duty, patrols and so on, the long winter evenings left the soldiers with much time to themselves. Inevitably, therefore, the consumption of alcohol and the incidence of drunkenness increased in some of the German units in the lines about Paris. During the first part of the war, throughout the campaign on the Saar, up to the fall of Sedan and at Metz, the soldiers' standards of discipline and behaviour had generally been exemplary. But by January 1871 many of the regular soldiers of the regiments who had marched west in early August were either wounded or dead and had been replaced by others, many of whom had considerably less service and training than those they replaced; and some of whom were undoubtedly not so fully committed as their predecessors. This was less of a problem for the German armies actively engaged in the French provinces, but for the static forces besieging Paris the effects of inactivity and boredom presented a daily challenge for the commanders at all levels. On those occasions when a cask or two of beer – the German soldier's drink of choice – did become available, their contents were usually consumed within an hour of their being offered for sale. But a general shortage of beer was offset by the relatively easy availability of cheap rum, schnapps and arrack, which had wholly predictable results and provided another very practical reason for the German high command to seek an early end to the siege.

Despite such relative aberrations, however, the army generally remained true to its traditions of discipline and professionalism, both of which were underwritten by the strong Christian beliefs and religious faith of most officers and soldiers. On the evening of New Year's Day, Archibald Forbes attended a church service for the 24th (Saxon) Division held in the old church at Chelles, 'a fine old church … with massive stone pillars, old Norman arches, much stained glass, carved oaken work, and Popish decoration generally'. Attendance at the service was voluntary.

The 24th Division's chaplain preached what Forbes described as 'something between a sermon, an address and a prayer' from the altar steps, within the body of the congregation rather than from the pulpit. The chaplain was clearly something of an orator, who addressed many of the themes that were foremost in the minds of soldiers in wartime. But he also displayed a degree of political awareness that would undoubtedly have found favour with von Bismarck had he been present, as he warmed to his unashamedly nationalistic theme of sacrifice, honour and duty, saying, '... yet we know our brothers died in a good cause. They fell "für König und Vaterland", and surely they are "mit Gott". And the war, sad and solemn episode in our history as it is in one sense, has had yet another glorious result. It has made our Fatherland not a name, but a reality. Already one race, one people, we are now one nation – Saxon, Prussian, Mecklenberger, Badener, Bavarian, we are all now children of the great German Empire.'[124]

Such occasions reinforced the almost tangible significance of the inscription 'MIT GOTT FUR KOENIG UND VATERLAND' on the Prussian helmet-plate scroll. The susceptibility of the German soldier to passionate oratory, and the appeal of the concepts of 'the Fatherland' and 'one race, one people, one nation', together with the implied mysticism of the warrior's death in battle, were all in evidence at the church service at Chelles on Sunday 1 January 1871. Arguably, this susceptibility was – and still is – a fundamental feature of the Germanic character and military psyche; a characteristic that has, throughout the history of Germany and its army, proved to be a very great national strength, but one which also played a significant part in setting Germany on the road to disaster in the next century.

As the New Year began, so the bombardment continued, and at 7 a.m. on 19 January, the Paris garrison launched its final sortie – some 60,000 strong – towards the German positions on the Montretout–Buzenval ridge. The French infantry poured across the open fields and began to work their way up the lower slopes of the ridge. The red-trousered regulars and blue-trousered Gardes Nationales pressed forward side by side, seeking out those who had besieged and humiliated them during the previous four months.

But, as the slopes that fronted the main German positions grew steeper, the slippery and often liquid mud that covered them began to slow the advance. German shells tore great gaps in the ranks, and gradually the initial enthusiasm and resolve of the French infantrymen weakened. As the leading units of the attackers neared the German trenches – where row upon row of the spike-helmeted, grey-greatcoated Prussian infantry waited, their rifles

ready – the comprehensive array of barriers, *abatis* and a host of other obstacles slowed the attack even more. These constructions broke and fragmented
the cohesion of the column formation that was so essential to maintain effective control of the non-regular troops. The woods that covered the higher
slopes of the ridge further disrupted the columns, and from their defensive
positions the Prussian infantry poured their concentrated rifle fire on to the
exposed French soldiers below them. The momentum of the attack faltered,
stalled and finally died. In various groups of individuals, units and part-
units, the soldiers sought cover and could advance no further, despite the
exhortations and personal gallantry of many of their officers.

The arrival of an additional French column made no difference to the
outcome of the battle. As the German fire continued unabated the morale
of the Gardes Nationales disintegrated, and the evening darkness cast a
shadow over the battlefield. As night fell the shattered French regiments
disengaged and finally withdrew into Paris. The battle of Buzenval cost the
French 4,000 men killed and wounded; the German losses amounted to a
mere 700.

The particular importance of this final failure of French arms at Paris
was its impact upon the already low morale of those within the city, both
military and civilian. After 19 January it was at last clear to all except the
most dedicated and extreme republicans that unless the city capitulated
the immediate future promised only starvation, bitter cold with little or
no fuel, and an unceasing hail of German shells.[125] At the same time,
news of the French defeats at Le Mans on 12 January and at St-Quentin
on 19 January reached Paris. A short period of political turbulence in
the city was soon followed by significant negotiations to end the siege,
while the German artillery continued its bombardment. Then, on the
stroke of midnight on 27 January, the German batteries ceased fire. The
following day a general armistice commenced, when the Paris garrison
surrendered its 602 field-guns, 177,000 rifles, 1,200 ammunition
wagons and 1,362 siege-guns. The garrison, some 7,456 officers and
241,686 men, were declared prisoners-of-war and all the regular troops
of the line were ordered to lay down their arms, only 12,000 men and
the National Guard being permitted to retain them for the preservation
of public order.

In the meantime, in the midst of the siege and bombardment, Bismarck
finally achieved his ultimate goals: German unity and the creation of a
new German empire. At Versailles, on 18 January, a glittering ceremony
was conducted in the Galerie des Glaces at the Royal Headquarters.
Despite the intrigues, personality clashes, hidden agendas, and political

and diplomatic conflicts with which the German coalition and much of its leadership had become beset as the war had dragged on after Sedan, on that day King William I of Prussia was proclaimed Kaiser of a unified Germany and head of the Second Reich by the many princes of the German states who had gathered there.

Throughout the siege of Paris, and indeed ever since Sedan, the German armies in the French provinces had been battling the forces of the Third Republic, and despite their ill-trained and often *ad hoc* nature the French achieved some early successes, particularly against the forces of the south German states. At Châteaudun, on 18 October, a strong force of the irregular *franc-tireurs* fought well, and although they finally lost the day they showed that they could be effective soldiers when well led. Then, on 9 November at Coulmiers, the 1st Bavarian Corps was defeated by the 15th and 16th Corps of the French Army of the Loire, a setback for the Germans that allowed the French to reoccupy Orléans and sounded a timely wake-up call for the German high command. Thereafter, the 1st Bavarian Corps was regrouped with two Prussian divisions, under the overall command of the Grand Duke of Mecklenberg-Schwerin.

On 24 November, the French Army of the North carried out a surprise attack against the German 1st Army at Villers-Bretonneux, achieving some initial success before being forced to withdraw to Arras and Lille. But at Beaune-la-Rolande, the 18th and 20th Corps of the Army of the Loire were defeated by just two brigades of General Voigts-Rhetz's 10th (Hanoverian) Corps. Although the Bavarians suffered yet another reverse at Villépion on 1 December, this time at the hands of General Chanzy's 16th Corps, the very next day the battle of Loigny resulted in the defeat of much of the 15th, 16th and 17th Corps by the force commanded by the Grand Duke of Mecklenberg-Schwerin. This enabled the reoccupation of Orléans by the Germans and – much assisted by the onset of appalling conditions of low temperatures, snow and ice – prompted a rapid decline in the morale of the French army. Chanzy suffered a further reverse at Beaugency on 8 December, and at Nuits on 18 December the Baden Division under General von Glümer won a close-fought battle against the Gardes Nationales of General Crémer. In the last battle of 1870, the French Army of the North achieved a hard-fought draw against General Manteuffel's 1st and 8th Corps on 23 December, at La Hallue. The same forces fought a further indecisive action at Bapaume on 2–3 January, 1871.

Despite their occasional successes, the French forces could not sustain the conflict indefinitely. Between 6 and 12 January the Army of the Loire crumbled away during fighting about Le Mans, with 25,000 casualties and many thousands more deserters. The French Army of the East, commanded by General Bourbaki, fought an uncertain action at Villersexel on 9 January, followed by others about Belfort between 15 and 17 January, which ended in a defeat at the hands of General von Werder's 14th Corps. During the last days of January, the remaining troops of the Army of the East withdrew into the mountains of the Jura, closely pursued by a newly constituted German Army of the South under General Manteuffel. On 1 February, having suffered extremes of winter weather in the mountain passes, the surviving French troops of Bourbaki's army withdrew into Switzerland, where they were interned. At St-Quentin on 19 January – on the same day that the last sortie was launched from Paris at Buzenval – General Faidherbe's Army of the North finally succumbed to General von Goeben's 1st Army in the last major clash of the war. On 26 January the peace treaty was signed, and on 1 March the victorious German troops at last entered Paris.

The War in Retrospect

Notwithstanding its few reverses and command and control difficulties, the German victory against France had been a remarkable feat of arms. Despite the fact that France actually had (in theory) more men, greater industrial capacity and more funding available than Germany in July 1870, it was never able to translate these potentially decisive advantages into battlefield success. This reflected a level of ineptitude and disorganization that was then endemic in both the French government and the French army. In a couple of areas the French did possess a significant tactical or technological advantage. These were the Chassepot and the mitrailleuse; but here again the French army failed to exploit these potentially battle-winning advantages, and all too often the French failures of command meant that the soldiers armed with these weapons were all too often misdirected or wrongly deployed. On the other hand, the effectiveness of the Chassepot was certainly not lost on the Germans and in 1888 a much improved magazine-loading bolt-action rifle was introduced throughout the army to replace the Dreyse needle-gun.

The real key to the German army's success, however, was not one of technology (although the superiority of the German artillery had been a major contributor to von Moltke's victory); rather it had been one of organization and planning, and at the heart of this was the army's campaign planning, which included that for its logistic support, and for its initial mobilization. Even the fundamental matter of campaign maps exemplified the difference between the French and the German approach to modern warfare. From the outset, the French government and high command had assumed that the war would be fought exclusively on German soil. Accordingly, the French high command had not issued any maps of France to its army. Such administrative failings typified France's overall lack of preparedness for the war, and were nothing less than a blatant betrayal of its soldiers; one that the Germans were subsequently able to exploit to such good effect. The officers of the German general staff meanwhile had developed their comprehensive plans for the forthcoming campaign against France over almost two years, using detailed maps of eastern France – so detailed in fact that the Prussian-drawn maps of France were actually much more accurate than those available in France itself. The German maps not only included the smallest roads and byways but also the precise number of inhabitants of every town and village.

So it was also with the somewhat more complicated matter of mobilization. Although all that was necessary for the German regular units was for them to move to the frontier (and here the German organization and use of the railways was once again the key to the success of this operation), the mobilization of the large numbers of reservists needed to boost the size of the army for war was a much more complex affair.

The German mobilization began with the call to arms sent from a district headquarters in each major city to the numerous local authorities in the lesser towns, villages and rural parishes. Once received locally, these call-up notices were issued to named individuals, who then mustered and moved off as a group to the district or regional headquarters. There they received their new uniforms and equipment, leaving their civilian clothing on a designated peg ready for collection at the end of the campaign. The reservists also received details of the location of their parent regiment, and a ticket for the train that would transport them there. During this mobilization phase all rail traffic in Germany was subordinated to the direction of the general staff. As a result of these arrangements, in July 1870 the mobilization, transportation and assembly of three German armies in areas near the border of France – a total of more than 384,000 men – was accomplished in just eighteen days, with the means to move a further three corps by rail to reinforce those armies within three weeks.

Across the border in France the mobilization situation was very different. This was due primarily to the French army's lack of a regionally based system of recall for service. Consequently, thousands of individual reservists had to traverse France from their normal places of work, first to their regimental depots, and then yet again in order finally to join the units to which they had been assigned. Once at their destination – sometimes after up to two weeks' travelling – they then found more often than not that their unit had already deployed. Many soldiers simply never found their own units. Similar problems affected the French logistics and supply system. Also, whereas the German mobilization plan generally required all units to be complete before their final deployment to the frontier, those of the French mobilized and moved off both under-strength and piecemeal. Little thought had been given to this mass movement of men and *matériel* on the French railway network which, unlike that in Germany, had to compete with the routine civilian and commercial rail traffic.

Indeed, while the general staff's plans had always included the use of the almost 7,400 miles of state roads that existed in 1848 to move its forces within Prussia and to its borders, and to that end had actively supported a co-ordinated programme of civil and military road construction, undoubt-edly the most important mobility asset of the Franco-Prussian War was the railway. The earliest recorded working railway line in Germany had run between Fürth and Nuremberg. At its inauguration in 1835 it had comprised a small steam engine drawing just two enclosed and one open passenger coaches. However, the general staff had immediately seized upon the military potential of this technology to facilitate a rapid mobi-lization and strategic deployment of the army, and studied this new means of transport exhaustively. By 1848 Prussia had almost 1,500 miles of rail-road in routine use and the staff had already incorporated this asset into their contingency plans.

The railway was the key to Germany's mobilization and was therefore a vital element in the strategic plan as well as essential to the effective support of the army's follow-on operations. The Germans used the railway system for the redeployment, reinforcement and resupply of the army; and even for some of the railway-mounted mobile gun batteries used against Paris. The railway was also essential to the support of the army's sieges, for the movement of the tons of artillery ammunition and engineer stores demanded by modern siege warfare. Finally, use of the railway enabled the evacuation of casualties and the early removal of prisoners from the combat area, so relieving the German field armies of the administrative responsibility for them; and at the end of the war, the railway of course also facilitated the relatively speedy return of the troops to Germany once they were released from their duties in France.

Surprisingly perhaps, the war with France produced relatively little in the way of significant tactical innovations. Throughout the conflict the overall pattern of many of the main battles was remarkably similar. Wher-ever the German infantry came within Chassepot range, they usually suffered heavy casualties, but they were then able to compensate for this by having superlative arrangements for manoeuvring, and for generating and committing reserves. This meant that – irrespective of the fact that they were often outnumbered overall – the Germans invariably managed to produce superior numbers and concentrate the maximum force at precisely the point at which it was actually needed. Also, as soon as an important French position or troop concentration was identified, the full weight of the modern German artillery was brought to bear upon it, the guns usually far out-ranging, out-shooting and out-shelling any that the French could use to counter them.

Throughout the war, the deciding factor both in large-scale and in more minor engagements had so often been the overwhelming firepower of the Krupps breech-loading steel guns, firing their percussion-detonated shells. Also, during the protracted sieges, such as those of Strasbourg, Metz and Paris, the heavy siege guns reduced many of the French fortresses and towns to rubble, while simultaneously crushing the morale of their garrisons and civilian populations, together with their desire to resist further.

On the other hand, many of the tactics used by the French had continued to be reminiscent of those used during the campaigns of Napoleon I, with excessive reliance upon *élan* and the bayonet or cavalry charge, and their great weakness was the fact that they had not been adapted to take account of the power of modern weaponry. The poor training of many French units meant that close-order formations and actions were the only workable means of maintaining command and control, but then the German artillery made short work of the formations and units that adopted such tactics. Lastly, while the ordinary French soldiers (including many of those from the French North African colonies) time and again proved their resilience and bravery, they were often led by officers who – although they were generally just as brave – were in many cases unprofessional; and the higher up the French chain of command one looked, the less effective the staff work, the leadership and the organization of the French army became.

While the French army generally continued to use the same tactics throughout the conflict, the Germans showed commendable flexibility when they changed from advancing their regiments and battalions in close order and adopted much more widely spaced tactical formations, especially after the heavy losses sustained at Gravelotte–St-Privat. Many of the more traditional German cavalry units took a little longer to adapt their way of doing business, but soon they too saw a dramatic reduction in the number of casualties sustained. Similarly, the effectiveness of the cavalry for reconnaissance improved over time.

The true measure of the army's success, however, was in fact political rather than military. Had France not been defeated and its military power neutralized, it would not have been possible to achieve German unification or the creation of the new German empire; for France would assuredly have seen such a development as a clear and present danger to its own position in Europe, and it would therefore sooner or later have been obliged to confront a united Germany with what might well have been better prepared forces and at a time and place of Paris's choosing. In any event, there can be little doubt that the carefully developed German war machine was the single most important factor that had enabled all that had come to pass. Accordingly, although the fall of Paris and the final defeat of the remaining French republican forces had yet to be achieved at the time that the Second Reich was created, the German army had already fulfilled all that its principal mission had required; and thus it had justified all the attention that had been lavished upon it by William, von Roon, von Moltke and von Bismarck during the previous two decades. On that historic January day in 1871, Count Otto von Bismarck was truly at the pinnacle of his personal power and achievements, and the German army had also well and truly fulfilled its own historic destiny.[126]

For the German emperor, his ministers and generals, the final triumph of German arms was the strategic culmination of the whole series of wars and campaigns that had begun a decade earlier. Meanwhile, within the wider historical perspective it was also nothing less than the culmination of a process of Prussian military and political development that spanned more than two centuries. Although much remained to be settled formally, active hostilities between the armies of France and Germany had finally come to an end. The German army had done all that had been asked of it, and it could at last return in triumph to the Fatherland with its honour and reputation secure and its prestige – nationally and internationally – never higher.

14

An Imperial Hubris
1871–1914

O N 17 MARCH, 1871, the Kaiser returned to a city that was no longer merely the old principal town of Brandenburg, and later the foremost city of Prussia. The new status which had now been conferred upon Berlin was that of the German imperial capital. Archibald Forbes was present to record the preparations for and the atmosphere surrounding William I's triumphant arrival in Berlin on that cold afternoon in mid-March.

It froze hard in Berlin during the night preceding March the 17th, the day of the Emperor's home-coming; and morning brought bright sun and cloudless sky. It brought also a universal ebullition of bunting. A crowd had collected in the morning under the statue of the Great Fritz [King Frederick II (the Great) of Prussia] opposite the Imperial Schloss. The crowd was drawn by a banner which floated from the pedestal, having a long poem stamped on the black and white linen. 'Hail Kaiser Wilhelm, hail to thee and to the brave German host thou leadest back from victory, ghost-like from afar. Like the clash of distant bells sounds the glad cheering of the conquerors. Old Fritz looks down with proud glance upon his descendants, approving greatly their valour.' ... All the forenoon the preparations in the way of decorations and for the illuminations steadily went on ... At one o'clock came guard-mounting. On this important day the guard was formed by the 2nd Guard and the Kaiser Franz Regiments, and consisted wholly of soldiers who had come back from the war ... Long before four o'clock every street was crowded, the throng being specially dense by the station, where the great people had begun to arrive to await the Royal arrival. The Princess Frederick Charles, Queen Elizabeth and the Baden family were among the earliest arrivals. A great cheer rang out as Count Bismarck, bluff and smiling, drove up with his wife in an open carriage. In the reserved portion of the platform all were in uniform or court dresses... [On the pillars] on either side of the royal passage were blazoned the words Metz and Strasburg, while over the statues of Victory behind were Sedan and Paris. [A little after twenty minutes after four o'clock] the train, bedizened with flags, rolled into the siding. Three carriages passed a flight of steps, and the fourth came into sight; there rose a mighty cheer, and at the window stood the Emperor Wilhelm, framed as in a picture.

The Emperor almost at once passed to his carriage, and drove off unescorted at a trot, followed by carriages containing the Royal Family and the other personages, along the Tiergarten, through the Brandenburg gate, and down Unter den Linden to the palace, amidst immense cheering. As he passed under the arch the Imperial flag was run up on the palace ... [Later, in response to the clamouring crowds,] he had to appear again on the balcony, helmet in hand and the Empress on his arm. His last appearance was at the window of the corner room where he [had] showed himself on the declaration of the war, and here he listened to the 'Wacht am Rhein', sung by the crowd. The Imperial Crown Prince had also to come repeatedly to an open window of his palace, accompanied by his wife and their children; the eldest boy, dressed in full Uhlan uniform, especially delighting the people.[127]

Then, some five days later, Forbes witnessed one of the first large-scale arrivals of German soldiers back in Berlin:

On the morning of the 22nd March, the Emperor's birthday, Berlin received her first regular consignment of home-coming warriors, in the shape of the 1st Battalion of the 2nd Guard Landwehr Regiment. The battalion had gone out over 1,000 strong; I do not care to estimate how far beneath that number it mustered as it marched down the [Unter den] Linden on the bright March morning … In its shortened column of fours it strode along behind the band of the 3rd Guard Regiment, who played their comrades in. Nearly all the men had bound green wreaths round their helmets. Some had stuck nosegays in the muzzle of their needle-guns; others carried chaplets [wreaths of flowers] on their bayonets.

After their Kaiser had had a look at them, and they had marched past the palace, the battalion broke into companies, each company taking a different direction to a halting point. I accompanied the 2nd Company through the Friedrich Strasse to the top of the Jäger Strasse. While it was in the [Unter den] Linden rigorous discipline was the order of the day. But it relaxed somewhat in the Friedrich Strasse, and the people got among their martial fellow-citizens.[128]

As the company marched on, wives, sons, daughters and family friends became more and more intermingled with the troops. Eventually it was impossible to maintain the formation, and the company halted at the top of Jäger Strasse. There, the regiment's lieutenant colonel rode up and bade his soldiers an emotional farewell. Finally, the company's captain strode out from the pavement and drew his command about him.

Orders as to disposal of arms and accoutrements, rendezvous for pay, etc., were the matters with which he had first to deal; then his voice changed, as, after a little pause, he addressed his command as 'comrades'. 'We have been together, men,' said he, 'through the campaign. I marched you out of Berlin, and now I march you back again. Not all indeed that went out with us have come back with us. God willed it that some should have fallen in the war, but they died for King and Fatherland. You have done your duty, men, as good Prussians, and so now adieu!' 'Adieu!' came back from every throat in answer, and with the response the company was disbanded.[129]

Although many civilians in Prussia and the other German states had begun to view the protracted conflict in France with increasing concern, as it had demanded ever more manpower and resources throughout the previous autumn and winter – and as the toll of casualties mounted, with a steady stream of wounded and disabled coming home – such doubts and uncertainties were speedily dispelled with the triumphant return of the soldiers that March, and any residual disapproval of the war was quickly forgotten; possibly a little too quickly. Undeniably, the German success had been stunning and had generally been achieved in the best traditions of the Prussian military ethos and code of conduct – apart from the punitive action taken against the French irregulars during the winter campaign. The creation of the new empire was a landmark in history, but it also placed Germany at a crossroads in respect of its future development, and this was particularly so for the war machine that had enabled this new empire to emerge.

Indeed, in the years that followed the defeat and humiliation of France, the imperial German army gradually became a victim of its own success as it sought to consolidate what was already its virtually unassailable position within Germany, and to enhance its formidable capability to support Germany's growing imperial ambitions. For the army and the German nation alike, the post-war period would prove to be an unsettling and unsatisfactory period of history, a period of contrasts during which the glittering military successes of 1870–1, if not actually squandered, were certainly not built upon as effectively as they perhaps deserved to be. But all that would occur over time, and in 1871 it was time for the high command to take stock of more recent events and to draw from them the lessons of the war. It might well be argued that the victory against France in 1871 was the true zenith of the German army's achievements in history, for despite its often remarkable successes on the battlefields of 1914–18 and 1939–45, its later conflicts were never underwritten by such a worthy national aspiration as the unification of Germany. Furthermore, the political agendas that would affect the nation and its army from 1933 were positively malign, and these eventually severely tarnished the wider reputation of what was, by 1940, undoubtedly the most professional and combat-effective army in Europe.

For the German army the period from the end of the Franco-Prussian War until the outbreak of the First World War in 1914 was characterized by four dominating influences or factors. First, there was the continued consolidation and enhancement of the already significant power, status and influence of the army – especially that of the officer corps – both within Germany and beyond. Next, there was Germany's new status as an imperial power, which would in turn generate colonial and global aspirations that later brought the army into direct competition with the navy for funding and resources. Thirdly, while the almost fifty years pre-1914 were largely a time of peace for Germany, it was during this period that the spectre of France and Russia as the new empire's potential enemies was raised and developed to such an extent that very detailed plans for dealing with these perceived threats occupied the German government and (more particularly) the general staff very directly. Eventually, the prospect of a war against one or both nations achieved such a level of acceptance in the German military consciousness that this outcome became virtually inevitable.

Finally, just as had been so for the previous two and a half centuries, the character of the Prussian leadership of the empire affected the development and nature of the army during the five decades prior to the great conflict which finally broke out in 1914. In fact, no less than three Prussian (or German) Kaisers were destined to direct and influence the course of imperial German history after 1871 and until 1918. In 1888 the well-educated, liberally inclined and cultured, but militarily astute, Frederick III died of throat cancer after just ninety-nine days on the throne. This particularly cruel turn of fate denied Germany what might well have been a real opportunity to reconcile and moderate the great international and internal

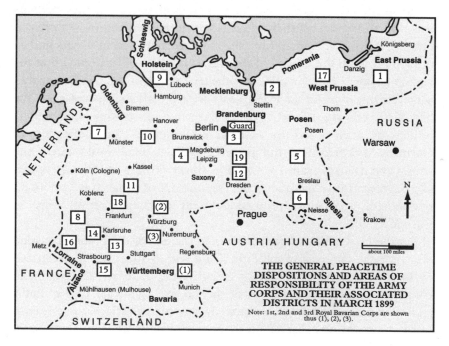

THE GENERAL PEACETIME
DISPOSITIONS AND AREAS OF
RESPONSIBILITY OF THE ARMY
CORPS AND THEIR ASSOCIATED
DISTRICTS IN MARCH 1899
Note: 1st, 2nd and 3rd Royal Bavarian Corps are shown
thus (1), (2), (3).

Above: Frederick William of Brandenburg, the Great Elector, at Fehrbellin, 28 June 1675.

Above: Frederick William I of Prussia, the 'Soldier King'.

Right: One of Prussia's renowned 'Potsdam Grenadiers', Grenadier James Kirkland, pictured in 1714.

Left: Frederick the Great, pictured in a characteristically martial setting at the head of his army. The Prussian monarch is immediately identifiable by his blue 'soldier's coat' with its single decoration, and by the cane he invariably carried.

Opposite page, top left: Frederick II, justifiably titled 'the Great' (despite the fact that he committed Prussia to an almost uninterrupted succession of wars during his reign from 1740 to 1786).

Left: General von Seydlitz, an exceptionally competent cavalry commander, whose foresight, initiative and offensive spirit ensured achievement of the decisive Prussian victory at Rossbach, 5 November 1757.

Right: General von Ziethen, Frederick II's remarkable cavalry commander who played a pivotal part in a number of Prussia's military victories, especially those at Torgau and at Leuthen.

Below: Leuthen, 5 December 1757, arguably Frederick's greatest strategic victory.

Above: On 18 June 1815, the timely arrival at Waterloo of the Prussians, commanded by Marshal Blücher (inset), secured the Duke of Wellington's final victory over Napoleon Bonaparte. Blücher's ability had previously been demonstrated at Auerstadt and Jena in 1806, and by his successes against the French during the Wars of Liberation, 1813–14.

Above: The Prussian defeat of the Austrians at Königgrätz on 3 July 1866, during the Austro-Prussian War, was a defining moment in European history. It displaced Austria as the leader of the German Bund and eventually paved the way for the creation of the Prussian-led Second Reich in January 1871.

Above: The Prussian Guard storms into the cemetery of St-Privat towards the end of the battle of Gravelotte–St-Privat on 18 August 1870, during the Franco-Prussian War (from an original painting by A. de Neuville). This hard-won victory enabled the neutralization of the French Army of the Rhine in Metz, and the end of the Second French Empire at Sedan just two weeks later.

Below: Immediately prior to the French collapse at Sedan, Prussia's Bavarian allies were involved in fierce hand-to-hand fighting in Bazeilles on 1 September 1870.

Above: With their widespread introduction in the nineteenth century, railways played a key role in all German strategic and mobilization planning. Here, the troops of one of the army's élite Railway Regiments maintains and constructs railway tracks in the 1880s.

Below: The late-nineteenth century saw military garrisons stationed in the new empire's far-flung colonies and overseas territories. One of the largest of these was in German East Africa, where the colonial troops illustrated are (left to right) a paymaster, a hospital attendant, a surgeon, a lieutenant, a field grade officer (full dress), a lieutenant, a corporal (with a native prisoner), native (Askari) infantrymen, a sergeant, a Sudanese trumpeter, an artificer and a senior sergeant (full dress).

Above: In 1914 virtually all the Imperial German Army adopted the new 'feldgrau' uniform, although a slightly greener shade of uniform was taken into use by the Jäger and 'Rifle' (Schützen) units (shown at the left of the illustration).

Below: The contrasting nature of warfare at the beginning and the end of the war is exemplified in these two German illustrations. Left, an attack by the 3rd Infantry Regiment ('Prinz Karl von Bayern') at Gorlice-Zarnow on 2 May 1915; right, Infantry Regiment 'Graf Barfuss' (4th Westphalian) No. 17 at Mörchingen in the Champagne area during the spring offensive of 1918.

The Modern Bundeswehr

Throughout the post-1945 Cold War years, armoured warfare continued to dominate much of the military thinking on conventional warfare. One of the best tanks of the time was the West German Leopard; an early version of the Leopard 2 in the mid-1980s is shown here. The appearance of the German soldier also changed over time, the field-grey combat uniform and US-style steel helmet (as worn by the soldier on the right) being replaced by a camouflage-pattern combat uniform and a non-metallic helmet in the mid-1990s. The infantry lieutenant (bottom) pictured in 2001 is wearing the new-style Kevlar helmet, camouflage uniform and body armour; he is armed with an Uzi MP2 submachine-gun and carries a tactical radio, binoculars and a fighting knife. (photos: Bundeswehr)

influences, ambitions and frictions that gradually transformed the victory and triumph of 1871 into an imperial hubris. The thirty-year reign of William II, Frederick's eldest son, would prove to be an imperialistic and militaristic regime which certainly favoured the army, but which at the same time encouraged and reinforced its self-aggrandizement, and consequently led to its further decoupling from the governmental control of the wider state it existed to serve.

During the years that followed the victory of 1871 the German army was reorganized and re-equipped to take full account of its recent experiences in France, the proven advantages of regionalization, the regimental system and the need to keep inessential changes to a minimum. The post-1871 organization also brought the forces of all of the German states, including the major contingents of Bavaria, Saxony and Württemberg within the formal order of battle of the imperial German army, so that from 1871 all these forces, together with those of Prussia, were formed into a single army, which was entirely at the disposal of its commander-in-chief, the Kaiser, both in peacetime and in time of war. Despite this centralized control by Berlin, the imperial army was funded by all the states of the North German Confederation, to which all the formerly independent German states now belonged.

The Kaiser had almost total control over this formidable force, and was entitled to inspect any part of it at will. There were only two exceptions. First, there was a diplomatic provision that, before he visited non-Prussian troops, he was obliged to inform the head of state of the contingent concerned of his intentions. Secondly, although every German soldier was bound to obey the emperor as his commander-in-chief, the Bavarian troops were only bound by this provision in time of war. Apart from these more general arrangements, the actual extent of the military dependence or otherwise of the various German states on Prussia depended very much on their bilateral agreements and conventions already concluded separately with Berlin.

Although strategic direction and major policy decisions continued to be controlled centrally, and were the everyday work of the all-powerful general staff, the command and training system in peacetime afforded a large measure of decentralization to the army corps distributed throughout Germany. The commander of each corps enjoyed a great deal of independence within a broad remit, which included responsibility for his corps' overall efficiency and preparedness for war, its recruiting and training. The corps areas equated to military districts in peacetime, and the locations and subordinations of the various units within each military district generally reflected their initial wartime subordination, as well as facilitating the speedy passage of call-up notices and instructions for the district's reservists in time of war or crisis. In 1898 there were twenty of these army corps in all, of which fifteen (including the Guard Corps) were composed almost entirely of Prussian troops and were administered by the Prussian War Ministry. The remaining five corps were the 1st and 2nd (Royal Bavarian) Corps, the 12th Corps (Royal Saxon No. 1), the 13th (Royal Württemberg) Corps and the 19th Corps (Royal Saxon No. 2). By the mid-1890s the peace establishment of the army was about 23,000 officers and 557,440 non-commissioned officers and men. Including all non combatants, the peacetime army included 585,490 soldiers and 97,850 horses.

On mobilization the army was divided into the field army, with four or five army corps combining to form separate field armies, and the home garrison army, which remained in Germany to defend the homeland and to maintain law and order. It was also required to continue recruiting and provide replacements for field army casualties. Once the army was formally mobilized, about 1,400,000 men would be able to take the field, and a further 960,000 within four weeks. In a situation of extreme crisis Germany could muster as many as seven million men by calling out every reservist, the Landsturm, and men who would not have completed their military training at that time. Thus the legacy of the war machine of von Bismarck and von Moltke during the 1870–1 conflict was a much-enhanced German army, designed to defend and carry forward the military needs of the German Empire into the new century. The organization and developing strength of the German imperial army between 1880 and 1900, and its peacetime deployment within Germany in 1900 are shown in Appendix 5.

These organizational refinements and a progressive increase in the army's strength were but a part of the legacy of 1871. Technology had played a significant part in the progress and outcome of the recent war, and some matters needed urgent action to redress German weaknesses in that area. Among these, the most pressing was undoubtedly the need to replace the standard rifle, and in 1888 a new magazine-loading bolt-action rifle – the Mauser – was introduced throughout the army to replace the trusty but now badly outdated Dreyse needle-gun.

The first version of the new Mauser rifle was a simple bolt- action weapon, but then, in 1884, a tubular magazine was added (located within the stock). Finally, in 1888, the version designated as the Mauser Box Magazine Repeating Rifle (or the Rifle Type '88) was adopted and issued.

The rifle's new box magazine held five rounds (calibre 0.310in) which were loaded from a metal clip, the cartridges containing smokeless powder. The Mauser had an effective range of up to 4,336 yards, although accurate fire at ranges up to 2,000 yards was the best achievable for all practical purposes.[130] A trained soldier could fire between ten and fifteen aimed shots each minute, and as many as thirty rounds per minute at the rapid rate. Subsequent improvements and modifications to this rifle were made, and by 1914 the new Type '98 was the standard rifle issued throughout the army, although considerable numbers of the Type '88 were still in use at the outbreak of the First World War.

The other weapon which had understandably attracted much interest during the war was the mitrailleuse. Although the true potential of these early machine-guns had not been realized by the French army in 1870 and 1871, their future significance was abundantly clear to the German general staff, and the later development of the renowned Maxim machine-gun, with its subsequent adoption by a number of armies, owed much to the reputation that the mitrailleuse had earned during the war. Extensive trials of the Maxim took place during the 1890s, and it was adopted in 1899, manufactured under licence. It was taken into official service in 1908 as the Maschinengewehr Modell 1908 (MG 08). In parallel with its widespread introduction – about 3,500 by 1914 – dedicated machine-gun units were also established to provide close fire support to the infantry. In 1913 there were 219 machine-gun companies, each with six guns plus one spare. In addition, each of the army's cavalry divisions were allocated an independent machine-gun battalion. There were also various other specialist and independent machine-gun units, and these increased significantly in number after 1914. Over the course of the next war, the ratio of MGs per combat infantrymen would increase from 1 per 500 in 1914 to 1 per 20 by 1918.

During the war, both sides had used a number of innovative means of communication and enhanced mobility with varying degrees of success. The French balloon flights from Paris had been largely successful and subsequently led to the development of manned, tethered observation balloons by the German army, so that specialist balloon detachments soon appeared in the German order of battle after the war. Here also the airship service with its Zeppelins had its origins.

Following their successful use of telegraph communications during the conflict, the German telegraph units were updated and expanded post-war. In the meantime, the railway system remained at the very heart of German strategic and operational planning.

If Frederick III had not died just ninety days after his father in 1888, and if Bismarck had not been forced by the new Kaiser William II to resign in 1890, the course of German history would undoubtedly have been somewhat different. Frederick's demise meant that William came to power prematurely and at a crucial time for his country. Indeed, had Frederick lived to complete his reign, William might never have succeeded him. Although intellectually astute, and artistic and creative by nature, the new Kaiser was variously described by a number of German commentators as arrogant, poor of judgement, unpredictable and an attention seeker. His frequently ostentatious behaviour, together with his often bombastic and insensitive public speeches fuelled suspicion and mistrust of the new Kaiser within the wider international and diplomatic community. Such traits inevitably made him vulnerable to flattery and to the wiles of his advisers, many of whom were pursuing their own political or parochial agendas. Foremost among these were the army – mainly in the guise of the general staff – and navy lobbyists who were advocating the expansion of the army and the uprating and expansion of the navy, which measures William endorsed enthusiastically. He was convinced that the threats posed to the empire necessitated the army enhancements, and that the need for the new empire to expand and acquire overseas colonies required Germany to have a world-class navy, one that was even capable of matching the British Royal Navy. Such ill-judged policies very soon brought William into conflict with his principal diplomatic adviser and elder statesman, Count Otto von Bismarck.

Despite Bismarck's readiness to commit Germany to war against France in 1870, Germany's situation was now much changed. Such bellicose or militaristic views were anathema to the German Minister-President, and ever since 1871 he had counselled diplomacy as the best way in which to secure the empire. Despite its prestigious position in Germany, the army did not grow significantly in size while Bismarck retained his power and William I was still Kaiser. Indeed, Bismarck saw positive advantages in creating a web of alliances and international rivalries among Germany's neighbours that would serve to divert or diminish any concerted military threat to the new empire, rather than relying upon the army alone to guarantee the security of the state. To that end he had tried to form an alliance with Russia and Austro-Hungary to counter possible aggression by France. This was unsuccessful, however, and in fact resulted in a Franco-Russian alliance, as Russia perceived that a strong German-Austrian-Hungarian grouping would pose a threat to its own territory. Indeed, as the years passed, Bismarck's diplomatic policies and initiatives were continually thwarted by the officers of the general staff, whose members openly advocated launching a pre-emptive war against France and Russia. It will be recalled that as early as 1870 and 1871 Bismarck's views on aspects of the war against France had been at variance with those of von Moltke and some of the general staff, but then of course the great goal of German unification had allowed such differences to be sublimated for the greater good of the nation.

In any event, within two years of his accession, William had so alienated Bismarck by the rejection of his counsel and by his unconstrained support for the general staff that the principal architect of the German nation had little option but to resign. He did so with understandable ill-grace, but in the certain knowledge that he had already well and truly achieved his great ambitions for German unification, together with Prussian primacy within the new empire; though the new regime's policies now risked squandering his earlier successes. Bismarck's departure in March 1890 marked the real beginning of Germany's march to 1914, and of two decades of largely unconstrained but sometimes ill-directed militarism based upon an army that – whilst professionally sound overall – had also begun to display certain flaws and weaknesses. These were variously occasioned by arrogance, reaction, stagnation, and by the simple fact that, apart from the Boxer campaign in China in 1900–1 and that conducted against the Hereros in South West Africa between 1904 and 1907, the German army fought no significant war between 1871 and 1914.

From its adoption in 1894, at the heart of the army's strategic planning was the Schlieffen Plan. This was designed to enable Germany to fight and win a war conducted on two fronts – against France and Russia. Although not adopted until 1894, the general staff planning for a war of this nature had been in progress ever since 1871, having been directed at first by von Moltke, who had initially planned for overwhelming force to be deployed against France, with a holding action against Russia pending its subsequent defeat. Later, he changed the plan to take account of new border defences then being constructed by France, together with a revised estimate of Russia's ability to mobilize, which indicated that it could do so more speedily than had originally been assessed. Consequently, the plan was amended: Russia would be defeated first, and then France. In 1888 von Moltke retired, having been succeeded as chief of the general staff by General Alfred von Waldersee, who left his predecessor's strategic plans largely unaltered. But in 1891 von Waldersee was himself succeeded by General Alfred von Schlieffen, who was destined to serve as chief of the general staff until 1906.

Von Schlieffen was the archetypal German general staff officer – dedicated, intellectually astute, professionally most competent, and above all else a pragmatist and an innovator. But he also exemplified the extent to which the general staff had become decoupled from the political realities of the late-nineteenth-century international scene, and this divergence of military and diplomatic activity and thinking meant that the plan was always founded upon a number of false assumptions. In short order he reassessed von Moltke's old plan and came to the conclusion that France posed the greater threat, and must therefore be defeated as quickly as possible. So von Schlieffen's plan called for more than 90 per cent of the army to be launched against France, using surprise, mobility and envelopment to defeat it in short order. The army would then turn its attention to the eastern front and the defeat of Russia. Over the next fifteen years von Schlieffen and the general staff further refined the plan, although the basic concept remained largely unaltered. A fundamental prerequisite was for Germany to have a sufficiently large army to carry it out, and thus the Schlieffen Plan was a key pillar of the general staff's argument for ever increasing manpower and resources. In 1906, General von Moltke ('the Younger') succeeded von Schlieffen. He reviewed the plan, and made a number of significant changes, all of which were in place by the time of its implementation in 1914.

The flaws in the modified Schlieffen Plan would become clear within weeks of the outbreak of the First World War, and although von Moltke subsequently felt constrained to resign in consequence of the responsibility he felt for having amended it, it is probably true to say that the original plan was overly optimistic both in its assessment of the strength of the French border defensive positions and of the ability of a German general staff, untried in the realities of modern warfare, to control armies on the huge scale that the empire deployed in 1914.

But irrespective of the debate over the validity of the plan itself, as with any such military contingency plan, the success of von Schlieffen's plan depended upon several additional but interdependent factors. These included an appropriate operational doctrine to support the strategic mission, operational readiness and training. Given that the plan was based almost entirely upon an offensive strategy, a very high level of readiness and of training standards maintained on a day-to-day basis were absolutely essential to its success; although this inevitably placed a significant burden upon what was in practice a peacetime army necessarily kept in a state of permanent readiness for war.

The army's operational doctrine was, as always, developed and directed by the general staff, and the process begun in earnest by von

Moltke in the mid-nineteenth century continued largely unchanged. By 1914 the total number of general staff officers was 625, an increase of only 375 since 1871, despite the significant changes and successive expansions that had taken place in the army since then. The Kriegsakademie continued its pivotal role of ensuring a common approach and consistency of military thought by those favoured officers selected for membership of the general staff. Despite this implied inflexibility, however, it was during the five decades after the Franco-Prussian War that the important concept of what became known as 'Auftragstaktik' was developed by the general staff and then disseminated throughout the army.

In simple terms, this doctrine of mission-orientated command required a commander to tell a subordinate what he had to do, without telling him how to do it. At the same time, a commander would make his subordinates fully aware of his own mission, so that, in the event of the operational situation changing, the overall mission could still be achieved successfully without recourse to issuing further specific orders. The adoption of a doctrine of this sort was virtually inevitable, given Germany's post-1871 strategic imperatives. However, the concept of Auftragstaktik subsequently retains its place at the heart of German military doctrine to the present day, being most effectively applied during the Second World War and during the later years of the Cold War period.[131]

In purely practical terms, it was essential for the effective conduct of offensive operations, but at the same time the flexibility and tactical responsibility it conferred upon junior commanders engendered the initiative, aggression and fighting spirit that were so often the hallmarks of the German army's combat commanders during both world wars. Despite this, the army's continued obsession with its traditional deployment drills – especially at the tactical level – still attracted accusations of inflexibility and stagnation from some contemporary commentators, as did the repetitious nature and intensity of an annual training cycle conducted against the background of a period of almost fifty years of peace for Germany in Europe.

Operational readiness was achieved through a combination of general staff or higher headquarters inspections and exercise alerts and training. Wherever a unit was based, it was always liable to an unannounced inspection or exercise alert. This was especially so for the so-called 'frontier corps' in East Prussia and on the border with France. On a number of occasions the Kaiser chose to carry out these tests of readiness in person.

During our last year in Trier we had been warned to prepare for a visit from our War Lord, the Emperor himself. He was at the time testing the efficiency of his hosts by paying surprise visits and, as is usual in such cases, there was little surprise about them when they did occur. The mis-en-scène, as it were, was as follows. His Majesty would leave Berlin surreptitiously, as it was supposed, destination unknown, of course. He would order his train to be stopped in the dead of night at some garrison town he proposed to favour, and with his trumpeter sounding the alarm, he would note the time taken by the troops to turn out in all panoply of war. The result was a demonstration of complete preparedness which was highly gratifying to all concerned.[132]

But the foundation of the army's capability was, as ever, its training. The annual cycle was based on the need to train a newly conscripted soldier from the basic stage to being able to participate proficiently in major manoeuvres twelve months later. On 1 October each year the new draft arrived and then began six months of basic training within their companies, so that in the spring of the following year the companies would come together for battalion field training.

Within the infantry, the battalion was regarded as the most basic manoeuvre unit, and these units repeatedly practised the drill of moving into an attack from the column of march (Aufmarsch – literally, 'marching into deployment'), deploying into attack formation (Entfaltung – or 'unfolding') and then into assault formation (Entwicklung – or 'development'). The assault formation comprised the assault troops, support elements and a reserve. Usually a battalion comprised four infantry companies with a fifth (machine-gun) company added by 1914, and each company had three platoons. Two of the infantry companies would advance from the flanks to act as skirmishers, while some 150 yards to their rear the other two companies formed the final assault element and a reserve. These manoeuvres were carried out on all sorts of terrain, and included practising the ability to return speedily from the extended attack final formation to the original column of route if the tactical situation changed. Such evolutions were usually carried out in double-time. In the meantime, the artillery's mission was to support the attack. The cavalry's role was primarily one of reconnaissance, although they did still train to exploit a breakthrough by the infantry, for pursuit, and for shock action. The widespread availability of carbines throughout the cavalry since the latter part of the nineteenth century also indicated an increasing use of these troops as mounted infantry.

Once the battalion training was complete, regimental and divisional manoeuvres took place during the summer, culminating in a more formal training period conducted at corps-level in the late summer and known as the 'Kaisermanöver'. Whole areas of Germany (often in regions adjacent to Germany's western or eastern frontiers) would be occupied by up to four army corps during these military extravaganzas, when farms, entire villages and provincial towns would play host to the numerous headquarters, regiments, battalions and companies of soldiers often for a number of weeks during September. William II always observed and took an active part in these somewhat contrived set-piece manoeuvres, which none the less provided a powerful demonstration of German military might to the foreign observers who were usually invited to attend them.

> The manoeuvres are ushered-in by the so-called 'Emperor's parade or review', which his majesty orders in the case of each army corps detailed to take part in them. The scheme calls for methodized railway transportation, and a concentration of the different army corps in the direction of the territory designed for the manoeuvres is effected. War-marches towards the landing point of the two armies opposing each other are instrumental in assembling the army for these manoeuvres. The assembling and advance of the army are covered by cavalry divisions, each from two to three brigades (or from twenty to thirty squadrons) strong, and under the leadership of specially selected commanders.[133]

These large-scale manoeuvres were often used as an opportunity to test the ability and suitability of officers for advancement, by temporarily placing such officers in command appointments one level above those which they normally occupied.

The Kaiser involved himself very directly in these events, and '[with the cavalry] often deciding the fate of the day by momentous charges [these] are often led by the Emperor personally, who also assumes command of the army, changing sides between the two parties often even on the same day'.[134] Clearly the Kaiser (in this case William II in about 1900) continued both to favour and to enjoy the more traditional role of the cavalry, as well as ensuring that his manoeuvre command would invariably be that which won the day!

With the end of the Kaisermanöver the training year also ended. Those soldiers who had fulfilled their regular army training obligation came to the end of their regular service (but not of their reserve liability), while in the regiments and the battalions preparations were already in train to receive the next year's conscripts. Thus was the Schlieffen Plan underwritten by a comprehensive system of constant readiness, a superlative and relentless training regime, and an operational doctrine that would support both the command and control and the offensive tactics necessary to achieve the mission.

But by 1900 a potential ground war was not the only strategic matter under consideration in Germany, as the new imperial German navy had emerged as a competitor for the nation's resources. Until the late 1880s the mission of the German navy had been primarily coastal defence and the protection of merchant shipping. Then, in 1897, Alfred von Tirpitz became secretary of state for the navy, determined to capitalize upon Germany's steel industry and expertise in the manufacture of artillery to create an oceanic navy that would both support the new empire's colonial aspirations and also persuade Britain into making colonial concessions. William supported von Tirpitz and the navy lobby, and so a major programme of shipbuilding was soon under way. However, Germany at the start of the twentieth century could not hope realistically to match the Royal Navy either in its expertise or in warship tonnage. Imperial Germany's frenzy of warship construction simply antagonized the British government and prompted Britain to begin its own programme of ship-building in order to maintain its maritime lead. This belated bid to achieve a German global maritime capability also meant that much-needed funding for the army – which was as ever seeking the additional manpower and resources essential to carry out the Schlieffen Plan – was in some cases diverted to naval projects, while at the same time such inter-service competition and the inevitable rivalry this engendered meant that no single cohesive land and maritime strategy was developed in time for the outbreak of the war in 1914.

Of course, most of those senior army officers who were now involved in this strategic planning and in the associated lobbying and single-service agendas were products of the officer corps system and the general staff selection and training process. However, thirty years after the end of the Franco-Prussian War, relatively few serving officers had faced the challenge of combat, while the forces of reaction, the continuing stranglehold of the nobility upon the officer corps, and the insidious influences prevalent in peacetime soldiering had converged to work to the positive detriment of some parts of the army; particularly when they impacted upon issues such as class prejudices, attitudes to the status of the officer, matters of discipline, and the management and welfare of the army's soldiers.

Accordingly, over time the prolonged period of relative peace that followed Germany's victory in 1871, together with the new pressures imposed by the country's new imperial status, produced a number of less than commendable traits within the army – this was especially so in parts of the officer corps and by extension within some of the more illustrious and traditional regiments. The lack of a war to fight led to the army turning ever in upon itself, and this introversion and introspection led in turn to the energies of some members of the Offiziers-kaste being directed towards preserving the primacy of the officer's place in German society, and of maintaining the officer corps as a profession that was almost exclusively that of the German aristocracy – certainly within all but the least fashionable regiments and the supporting and technical units. From this situation developed an honour code that, for many officers, placed the preservation of the good name of the army and the regiment above all other legal, practical and commonsense considerations. By the early twentieth century, young officers, who as sons of the nobility had in many cases been dispatched to military academies as early as eight years old and who had known little other than the military and regimental family environment (but who had never experienced the challenges of the warfare that always underlay their career path) accepted as the norm standards of behaviour which were antiquated, boorish, arrogant and snobbishly class-conscious.

At the close of the nineteenth century a few authors – but notably a Lieutenant Bilse and Count von Baudissin (the latter writing under the pen name of 'Baron von Schlicht', who was already an established writer of a number of humorous and other less serious works) – published what might be termed 'critical military novels', which were in fact *exposés* of everyday life in some parts of the German army of the day. Lieutenant Bilse wrote *Aus einer kleinen Garnison* (published in English as 'Life in a Garrison Town'), while von Baudissin's book was titled 'Life in a German Crack Regiment'.[135] Both works were originally published in German, but English-language editions soon followed. At the time these books caused a great sensation, as until then any public criticism of the army (and of its officers in particular) had been considered thoroughly unpatriotic, and the fact that both these books had been written by serving officers was at the same time unprecedented and quite scandalous. Nevertheless, in Germany some 40,000 copies of von Baudissin's book were sold before its circulation was banned by the local authorities, while by 1914 the English language edition had been reprinted no less than four times! For their literary *exposés*, both officers were formally disciplined, but by then the veneer of professional perfection which had for too long persisted after 1871 had been stripped from some important parts of the German army as an institution.

In practice, Lieutenant Bilse's book was of somewhat lesser significance than von Baudissin's as he chose to set it in a German cavalry regiment, whereas he was in fact a member of a battalion of the military train based at Saarbrücken. Although (as was grudgingly admitted at his court-martial!) the book accurately recorded the sorry state of discipline and the lack of professionalism in his own battalion of the military train, it was certainly not credible as an account of life in a 'typical' German cavalry regiment. Indeed, a British officer who was then serving with a German hussar regiment observed that, as the military train was very often a refuge for those officers who had been expelled from other regiments, 'perhaps Lieutenant Bilse's comrades consisted of an undue number of undesirables'.[136] Nevertheless, the book was read widely in Germany and elsewhere. Accordingly, it undoubtedly harmed the long-standing image of the army while at the same time indicating that perhaps all was not as well as it should be within the famous German war machine.

If the authorities could argue that Bilse's book lacked a degree of credibility due to the author's lack of first-hand experience of his chosen subject unit and the social strata depicted therein, the book published by Count von Baudissin could not be so criticized, and was therefore of much greater significance. In 'Life in a German Crack Regiment' the army establishment was for the first time confronted with a work written not by a junior middle-class officer such as Lieutenant Bilse, but with a book written by a member of the aristocracy, an officer who had himself served with just such an élite guard regiment as the fictional 'Franz Ferdinand Leopold' guard infantry regiment featured in his book. Although it was purportedly a work of fiction, 'Life in a German Crack Regiment' none the less provided a telling insight into the decayed nature of some parts of the army by the turn of the century, and especially so of the quite unjustified, outdated and positively detrimental influence of the nobility within the officer corps. By relating a number of incidents that he had undoubtedly experienced or witnessed himself, von Baudissin laid bare the class system, the associated prejudices and the more unedifying lifestyle trends which were by then rampant within the officer corps.

Foremost among these were the deep financial indebtedness of many officers, due very often to their gambling (an activity officially banned, but widely condoned), and an inflated social lifestyle that was reminiscent of the worst excesses of the eighteenth century. Closely allied to this was a general acceptance of drunkenness as the norm for many middle-grade and junior officers – both frequently and often on a grand scale. And there was an immutable belief within the officer corps that a German officer of any rank was invariably superior to all other members of German society, its laws, its behavioural conventions and its social niceties; a perpetuating belief that was energetically impressed upon the members of the civilian population whenever necessary!

Not surprisingly, such perverse and narrow attitudes fed through to the officer's professional life, and von Baudissin described a pervasive obsession with maintaining a veneer of military perfection within a working environment in which any misdemeanour or failing by an officer or by one of his subordinates could result in the summary dismissal of any officer deemed directly or indirectly responsible. Such summary dismissal almost invariably meant loss of income and loss of pension. But it also meant the loss of the vitally important entitlement to wear an officer's uniform, together with the social status that entitlement conferred.[137] This ultimate sanction was exemplified by the case of Captain Hoenig – a disabled veteran of the Franco-Prussian War who had subsequently dared to publish a critical analysis of the general staff. Being both crippled and half blind he had quite sensibly declined the subsequent invitation from one of the members of the general staff to fight a duel. A court of honour was convened to deal with what was certainly construed as Hoenig's betrayal of the army and the officer corps, but generally regarded as little less than treason in fact. This court included officers who had served alongside Hoenig during 1870–1, but nevertheless it stripped him of the right to wear his officer's uniform, and by so doing it had, in the eyes of a society so fixated with this privilege, also stripped him of his own honour.[138]

Wherever it did exist, this culture of blame and cover-up meant, for example, that officially regularized punishments were often abandoned in favour of unofficial disciplinary sanctions that would not need to be recorded on unit punishment sheets – always viewed as a tangible indication of an ill-disciplined unit – which in turn resulted in non-commissioned officers meting out physical beatings as punishments while the officers turned a blind eye, thus creating a culture of command through fear rather than respect, in which the bully thrived. Indeed, the accuracy of the culture described by von Baudissin in his book was more than validated by a number of factual reports in the 1880s and 1890s which recorded instances of physical abuse, bullying and intimidation at all levels and in all sorts of military establishments: from academies to recruit training units, and within a range of active regiments and other units. More often than not, inadequately supervised or poorly selected non-commissioned officers were to be found at the heart of the problem.[139]

As with any peacetime army, the fear of censure was endemic, and this led to great efforts being made to mask anything which might reflect ill upon the unit or its officers – from the lowliest ensign to the regimental commander. In von Baudissin's critical view, the army was ruled by a never-ending succession of inspections and appraisals, with every level of command fearful of any error or potential scandal that might occur at a subordinate level of command. By including in his work a lengthy discourse between a prematurely retired major and his son, a young and profligate lieutenant, von Baudissin provided a revealing insight into the core views and attitudes of the military aristocracy of the time, and this particular part of the book contained much of its special impact, where it set out quite clearly the ills of the German army of the day and some of the remedies necessary to redress them.

It would be entirely wrong to suggest that works such as those of Bilse and von Baudissin described a situation which obtained throughout the whole of the army by 1900. But there can be little doubt that they did highlight a gradually worsening situation in some units – a situation that clearly needed to be rectified. Accordingly, this book and some of the others that followed it were probably timely. In the meantime, in his telling criticism of the system, Count von Baudissin highlighted a state of affairs that not only threatened the integrity, professionalism and wider perception of the German army, but which all too accurately reflected the nation's early-twentieth-century imperial hubris, within which the army had by now become inextricably ensnared.

There were counters to such criticisms, however. The observations of Granville Baker, a young English officer serving with a Prussian hussar regiment at the turn of the century, continued to provide an informed and somewhat less negative insight into aspects of everyday life in the German army of the day. Soon after his arrival in the regiment he wrote on the process by which an officer was selected and trained.

There were two ways leading to an active commission. One was by way of a military college, or 'Kadetten-Korps', of which there was one for Prussia, near Berlin, another at Dresden for the Saxon Corps, and a third at München for the Bavarians. Prussia had besides these a number of preparatory institutions whence emerged on holidays, quaint little persons of serious deportment, dressed in the dark blue infantry uniform. These 'Kadetten-Korps' gave a sufficiently good education, leaving out Greek from the curriculum in favour of French and English which languages, however, generally vanished into oblivion after a few years soldiering. The Cadet education had this advantage, that youngsters acquired some of that sense of responsibility which is the chief result of our own [British] public school system. They rose in time to a position analogous to that of prefect, on strictly military lines of course. A further advantage of this avenue to a commission was that a cadet joined his regiment with the rank of a non-com. The other way to a commission led through the high schools, and this was the more popular among parents as it kept youngsters under constant home influence. These were generally the better educated, but they joined up as privates; physically, cadets were the hardier. On both lines of approach the first step taken when the lad was about to pass his final examination was the choice of a regiment. This was governed by the factors that influence parents and offspring in other countries under similar circumstances. Supposing then that a martial-minded youth decided to become a 9th Hussar, it was necessary to find out first, whether that regiment would take him. If his family were of suitable social standing and able to afford the gratification of having a hussar among them, the youngster would be invited to [the officers'] mess to be looked at. If he were found suitable on first acquaintance, he would join up as soon as a vacancy occurred and placed under the instruction of a senior subaltern who acted as dry nurse to him. He would live out of barracks and was expected to take most of his meals at mess, a somewhat trying discipline this, as he would have to spring to attention whenever an officer entered the room or addressed him – but it was wholesome. His work was that of any ordinary trooper, but he would be promoted to non-com within a year if he had not already, as a cadet, joined with that rank, and then he would be sent to a 'Kriegsschule', this was an establishment where young ensigns, as they were generally called, were put through a course similar to that given at Sandhurst and Woolwich. At the end of this period the youngster returned to his regiment, the officers of which then had to decide whether they considered him suitable as a comrade. Certificates and testimonials from the 'Kriegsschule' carried some weight, the opinion of the officers yet more, and if all agreed in favour of a candidate, a document to that effect was signed first by the junior subaltern and so on up to the C.O. It seldom happened that a candidate was turned down at the last moment, and when it did happen, the ruling of the regimental officers was rarely overridden by higher authority.[140]

The daily routine in all of the cadet schools was generally much the same and followed a predictable pattern; a cadet's typical weekday programme might include:

Time (Approx.)	Event	Remarks
0600	Reveille	
0700	Breakfast	Usually comprised of no more than black bread and coffee.
0800–1030	Classroom instruction	Standard academic and military-related subjects, including foreign languages, mathematics and history.
1030–1100	Break	A maximum thirty minutes, but often less.
1100–1400	Drill	Primarily ceremonial and as an adjunct to discipline and fostering instant obedience, rather than tactical; with short breaks as appropriate.

Time (Approx.)	Event	Remarks
1400	Lunch	While by no means substantial, this was usually the main meal of the day.
1500–1800	Physical training activities	Typically swimming, gymnastics, fencing and dancing. Dancing was viewed as an essential part of an officer's social training, and of much greater importance than sport. Where appropriate, other skill-at-arms activities might be included here.
1830–1930	Evening lecture(s) or study	Also preparation of uniform and equipment for the following day's activities.
2000	Evening meal	A light meal of bread and cheese, accompanied twice a week by a weak lager beer.
By 2200	Lights out	

The standards within these military colleges varied, both within those of a given German state – Prussia, Bavaria and so on – and between those of the various states. The supervisory and disciplinary regime in the cadet schools was certainly strict, and the process of physical hardening sometimes severe, although the extent of bullying, abuse and homosexual perversion therein has undoubtedly been much exaggerated by various critics of the German military state; as also were some of the more lurid tales of womanizing and wholesale drunkenness on the part of cadets. Nevertheless, the cadets undoubtedly viewed the army officers they one day aspired to be as role models, and wherever amorality, arrogance and class prejudice was exhibited by a member of the officer corps many cadets would not unnaturally emulate and adopt these traits themselves.[141]

Symptomatic perhaps of the changing nature and personal values of a peacetime army (albeit one that still bore the words 'MIT GOTT...' on its Pickelhaube and shako plates) was a reduced – although still important – emphasis upon the role of the church in its military life.

You seldom met a padre; he appeared not to fit exactly into the social box, or perhaps he did not want to do so. You might meet one at some big dinner, where he would open the proceedings with a lengthy grace in classical German which you heard nowhere but in the pulpit or on the stage, and then he would settle down to the business of the evening, eating. There was no elaborate church parade on which we turned out in our best [uniforms] and looked lovely, except on New Year's Day, and as we had generally been seeing the old year out, the next morning's programme was carried out without enthusiasm. On All Saints' Day again, we did no work, but dressed in our best, went to the [Trier military] cemetery and listened to orations which gave obvious satisfaction to the deliverers thereof. Otherwise church-going was a modest affair: a small party of men looking bored rather than devout, would march off to the garrison church under command of a non-com to join compulsory devotees from the infantry regiments. It appeared that there was not sufficient room in the garrison church for a full-bodied effort by the whole regiment [the 2nd Rhenish Hussar Regiment, No. 9], and when once in a while the hussars were given a larger amount of accommodation than usual, the occasion was graced by the presence of a subaltern. And even then we did not put on all our glory; we left our plumes behind.[142]

These observations made by a cavalry officer in about 1899 contrast quite markedly with those recorded by Archibald Forbes less than thirty years earlier, during the Franco-Prussian War. But, it is freely acknowledged that religion and the role of the church within the military have historically always been less prominent in peacetime than during times of crisis and armed conflict.

Traditionally, disputes between officers were settled either by fighting a duel or by the adjudication of a court of honour. Ever since the mid-nineteenth century courts of honour had dominated all matters pertaining to an officer's conduct and day-to-day life, and they had become a cornerstone of the arrangements for the self-regulation of the officer corps, and thus of its continued control by the nobility.

> Duelling amongst officers was of very rare occurrence, in a good regiment it would not happen at all. Any affair that arose had to be tried by a court of honour consisting of regimental officers and if it decided that you should fight, you did or left the army. Pistols were the only permissible weapons, and if you damaged your opponent you were generally relegated on open arrest to a fortress where you had considerable liberty but no occupation. In a strict military caste such as the Corps of Officers of the old German Army, everything possible was done to avoid an open scandal. If anything very outrageous occurred the offender's case was judged in secret and he was offered the alternative of suicide or flight from civil procedure. There was a story about a young officer who got into a horrible mess. The C.O. dramatically offered him choice of a revolver or a sum of money to get away with. The culprit took both – and went, it was said, to his native country the United States of America.[143]

Certainly the officers were disciplined very differently from those whom they commanded. At some stage during his attachment, the young British hussar officer became involved with the army's formal disciplinary and court-martial process, when he noted that:

> When the squadron commander was confronted by a case that called for severer treatment, there was no impressive display of visitors, under escort, to call upon the C.O. [as would be so in a British regiment]. It was the adjutant

who took the matter in hand as a kind of court of inquiry at which a subaltern assisted, generally in silence. The case, by this time voluminously recorded, would according to its gravity go before either a regimental or what would correspond to a district or general court-martial in the British Army. As long as the matter remained in the regiment the chances of fair treatment were pretty certain. But if the case had to go further, there intervened a separate judicial institution, the military lawyer. These men were real lawyers, not soldiers playing at it, and were the best-hated men in the army. They wore uniform, bore a sufficiently sonorous title, and assumed a martial air.

The lawyer first held an inquisition at which a subaltern assisted. The procedure consisted of examining accused and witnesses, and taking down their statements. On one occasion when I was assisting at the preliminary inquiry into an alleged offence committed by a Uhlan, the martial lawyer simply ordered his clerk to re-write the accusation as if it were a confession by the accused. 'But', remarked the Uhlan, 'I never said I did it, and I never did it either.' 'You must have done it,' retorted the lawyer, 'it is down here in black and white.' ... [these lawyers, literally 'military legal auditors' were to be found within the staff of every corps headquarters, and as a result of their inquiry into a case they would advise whether or not it should go for court-martial.]

A court-martial consisted of members of the rank of the accused and upwards, in the case of a trooper there would be three privates, three non-coms and so on, the principle being that the accused should be freely tried by his comrades of all ranks [and therefore no private soldiers would be present if the accused was a non-commissioned officer]. The members of the lowest rank gave their verdict first, and it was wonderful how they arrived at the opinion of the officers attending the court, without any apparent collusion. Anyway, all the members, as a rule, arrived at the same conclusion and it was not invariably the same as that of the lawyer [who had both presided over and conducted the court-martial proceedings].[144]

Throughout its history, the composition and nature of the officer corps had bedevilled the army's development. This was probably never more so than in the late-nineteenth century, when socialist undercurrents in Europe and the enormous increase in the country's population – some twenty-four million between 1871 and 1910 – and industrialized working class raised real fears of a workers' revolution in the minds of many officers. Such fears reinforced reactionary views and made the nobility ever more determined to maintain control of the officer corps. Certainly increasing numbers of the middle classes were becoming officers, especially in the technical and support units, although in many cases these men were ennobled as much because they were officers as because of their professional performance. This was one means by which military power remained in the hands of the nobility. But another acceptable route to a commission and the status that this conferred was as a reserve officer, and many middle-class officers followed this course, one that was infinitely more acceptable to the wider officer corps than had been what they regarded as the liberal and politically unreliable Landwehr officer of old.

Reserve officer commissions were gained following a voluntary one-year period – Einjährig-Freiwillige – of acceptable full-time service, two acceptable periods of annual training with the reserves, and success at a military examination. The aspiring reserve officer also had to undertake to clothe, feed and equip himself during his service. While still a somewhat lesser being than the regular officer, the reserve officer was none the less accorded all the status that his uniform demanded, and very many members of the middle class aspired to become a member of the Reserveoffizierskorps. Indeed, membership of the corps was often a prerequisite for advancement in many walks of civilian life, especially government service. Although their education, application and enthusiasm for military service meant that a considerable number of these reserve officers proved to be extremely proficient, many still held views every bit as reactionary as those of their more aristocratic comrades in arms, being just as fearful as the nobility of losing all that they had achieved to the very same industrialized socialist society which allegedly posed such a threat to their values and way of life. Exclusivity was ever-present, and the officer corps generally chose to sustain a continued shortfall in its manning wherever the only available alternative was the acceptance of a socially inferior or politically suspect officer candidate. The downside of this lack of officers in some cases resulted in an over-reliance upon the non-commissioned ranks, who were then required to assume additional responsibilities but without the supervision of an officer, and to this situation many of the reported instances of bullying and the ill-treatment of soldiers during the period can probably be attributed. In addition to the Einjährig-Freiwillige programme for the Reserveoffizierskorps, the army also offered two-, three- and four-year volunteer programmes for young men who had reached the age of seventeen and who wished to make the army their full-time career, or who for other reasons might wish to complete their service obligation at an earlier age; from these were found very many of the non-commissioned officers.

By 1900 the army was dealing with a continuous turnover of soldiers fulfilling their obligatory liability to military service. Having reached the age of seventeen, these young men first completed between two and three years with the Landsturm from the start of their eighteenth year, followed by two years with the regular (or 'standing') army from the end of their twentieth year to the age of twenty-two, and then five years with the reserves. By 1914 the pay of a regular soldier was about 1½d (equivalent to a little more than 3p) a day. The periods of regular (or 'colour') and reserve service were followed by five years' service with the 'first level' of the Landwehr and then service with the 'second level' of the Landwehr until 31 March of their thirty-ninth year. For cavalry troopers and horse artillerymen the regular and reserve commitments increased to three and four years respectively, but with these additional years being compensated by a reduction in their Landwehr liability to three years of 'first level' Landwehr service, before moving to the 'second level'. Finally, the citizen soldier served in the Landsturm until his service liability ended at age forty-five: a total of up to twenty-eight years in uniform as a regular and as a reservist. During his time as a reservist, the soldier would usually be recalled each September to attend for two weeks' refresher or update training with the reserves, although he could be required to complete two such training periods annually.

The quality of the ordinary soldiers remained generally high, the majority still coming from the rural rather than the urban areas, despite the fact that by the early years of the twentieth century almost 60 per cent of the population inhabited the towns and cities. However, those men conscripted from the rural areas were usually fitter than their urban counterparts, and brought with them the natural skills of the countryman (including a knowledge of the horses upon which the army still depended for most of its logistic and artillery support). It could be argued that the introduction of technologically much more sophisticated weapons and equipment – the machine-gun, telegraphic communications, surveillance balloons, the Zeppelin, the first military aircraft, improved artillery and engineer techniques and equipment, and steadily increasing amounts of motor transport (some 4,000 motor vehicles, including steam-engine prime movers, by 1914) – should have produced a commensurate increase in the number of soldiers recruited from the industrialized areas.

But few if any of these men experienced any form of active service or actual combat during their regular or reserve service. Some individual officers of the regular army served with the forces of other nations on loan or as training advisers, and as such might have been involved in those nations' conflicts. German officers were strongly represented as trainers and staff officers in the Turkish and Bulgarian armies. But only two conflicts – one international and one colonial – occurred during the period to disturb what was otherwise the peacetime existence of the German army from 1871 to 1914. The first of these was Germany's involvement in the Boxer rebellion in China in 1900 and 1901.

This was launched by a Chinese anti-foreign secret society called the 'Fists of Righteous Harmony' – hence the name 'Boxers'. The movement enjoyed the covert support of Tsu-hsi, the dowager empress. The Boxers emerged as an armed force in 1898 and carried out a number of attacks on foreign property and on the railway system. In May 1900, two British missionaries were murdered in Beijing; the European powers demanded the suppression of the Boxers, and when the Chinese authorities took no action they resolved to send an international military force to achieve this. The force, 2,000 strong, began its advance from Taku to Beijing on 10 June. In the meantime, the situation in Beijing had deteriorated rapidly, with the murder of a Japanese diplomat on 11 June and of the German minister, Baron von Ketteler, on 20 June. On the same day all the international legations came under attack. The Boxers were now openly supported by Chinese regular troops, whose involvement checked the expeditionary force just thirty miles from Beijing. It fell back on Tientsin, where the legations had also been under attack until they were relieved by the expeditionary force on 13–14 July. But by now another more substantial force of about 20,000 men, comprised of contingents from eight major powers (including a relatively small German contingent of 200), had been assembled. At this stage it was believed that the legations had fallen, but when news arrived that they were still holding out this force immediately set off for Beijing, defeating three separate Chinese and Boxer armies *en route*. On 14 August it entered the city and indeed found that, against all expectations, the legations had survived the siege. Originally, it was intended that the force commander would be General Alfred von Waldersee (the former chief of the general staff 1888 to 1891, who had been succeeded by von Schlieffen), but he had not arrived in China in time to assume command before the hurried advance on Beijing. He arrived in September, just in time to engage the Boxers in the area of Beijing, at Tientsin and Patachow, and in other parts of Northern China. He also oversaw the capture and destruction of the Boxer stronghold of Pao Ting Fu, the demolition of the Chinese Taku forts, and the bringing to justice and severe punishment of the Boxers, together with the imposition of punitive sanctions upon China. At the capture of Pao Ting Fu, the newly arrived German East Asia Brigade led the assault on the town, which was subsequently plundered by the allied troops and put to the torch. The German troops already stationed in China and those who were subsequently deployed to the campaign between the first Boxer riots in November 1899 and the signing of the peace protocol on 7 September 1901 included:[145]

- 3rd Seebataillon (1,126 men)
- One battery of Marine horse artillery (111 men)

- One Kommando Detachment (part infantry; part mounted) (800 men)
- Sailors from the German East Asia Naval Squadron (serving as infantry)
- The German East Asia Brigade (from 21 September 1900), comprised of:
  - Two infantry regiments (each of two battalions of 812 men)
  - One Uhlan regiment (600 men)
  - One field artillery regiment (three gun batteries; one howitzer battery)
  - One pioneer battalion (including telegraph and railroad companies)
  - Support troops (medical, train, ammunition handling, supply and other services)

After the campaign ended, most of the allies reduced their military presence in China significantly – typically to a single infantry regiment at most, with a small complement of supporting artillery and cavalry. But the Germans continued to maintain a force of some strength in the country and, although the Boxer uprising was undoubtedly of much greater significance in Chinese history than in that of Germany, the rebellion did produce one rather unedifying consequence for the victorious German contingent. It also illustrated that imperialism is rarely far from hubris. Following the murder of the German minister in Beijing on 20 June, the Kaiser, true to form, had made a somewhat ill-judged speech in which he exhorted the troops of the German contingent in China to wreak revenge upon the Boxers. The soldiers were to 'Make for yourselves reputations like the Huns of Attila. Spare none!' Ever obedient to the Kaiser's direction, they did just that, killing ruthlessly, plundering extensively, and earning from their allies a less than favourable reputation for their arrogant behaviour. Indeed, the origin of the widespread and – by implication – derogatory use of 'Hun' to describe German troops during the First World War is most frequently attributed directly to William II's inflammatory direction to the German troops sent to suppress the Boxers in 1900.

By the early twentieth century, the principal territories of Germany's colonial empire in Africa were South-West Africa, East Africa, Togoland and the Cameroons, and the army's second notable conflict of the period took place in its protectorate of German South-West Africa. This was the protracted campaign launched to suppress a revolt by the Hereros between 1904 and 1907. There, the authoritarian colonial regime of the Germans led to a general tribal uprising in which the Hereros were prominent, being well armed with firearms and deploying both cavalry and infantry against the German imperial forces in a series of bitterly fought and often quite extensive engagements. Although the rebellion was finally put down successfully, here also the very robust punitive action by the German forces (which included locally enlisted troops) routinely attracted accusations of the use of excess force, and that in a number of instances the German forces had waged a campaign of genocide against the Hereros.[146]

Understandably, the period of almost fifty years from 1870 to 1914 produced many changes for the German army – not least the fact that an army which had won its last major battles clad predominantly in blue (and in some cases red or even white!) uniforms with gold and silver embellishments, now (from 1910) took the field clothed in the ubiquitous feldgrau (field grey) uniform with which the German soldier would be identified for the next three decades. Only in the Jäger zu Pferde, the machine-gun units, and certain of the Jäger and Schutzen battalions was a greener shade of uniform – grüngrau – adopted. Although the Pickelhaube and shako existed still, they had also acquired a drab feldgrau cover by 1914, for use on active service and manoeuvres. This period of imperial awakening with its sometimes uneasy adjustment to its new-found status had, at the same time, been a time of contrasts, of lost opportunities, of stagnation and of anomalies just as much as one of progress, of innovation, of professional excellence and of martial success. As such it cannot easily be assessed or categorized as a whole. But by then, events well beyond German control were taking place elsewhere.

As the expansion of the French and Russian armies continued apace, a developing pre-1914 crisis in the Balkans steadily deepened. At the same time, Germany's relations with Great Britain had declined noticeably. There, the Conservative party had actively exploited public outrage and anti-German feeling during the general election of 1911 over what was perceived to be the growing German maritime threat to British commercial and imperial interests. Concurrently, in France a festering resentment over German possession of Alsace and Lorraine was growing ever stronger. In the Balkans, Austria and Germany both viewed Russia as a threat to their traditional influence within the area, while adjacent Turkey was hostile both to Britain and to Russia, but had for some years been fostering its links with Germany. Turkey's military connections with Germany were particularly close.

Consequently, in less than fifty years Germany had moved from its enviable position as the dominant continental power in Europe in 1871 to a situation in 1913 in which the government was in a political and funding crisis. In vain it had sought to sustain its naval programme in competition with the British Royal Navy, and at the same time to implement in full a major programme of army expansion and enhancements in readiness to deal both with France and with Russia, and to support its friends and allies – notably Austria – in the Balkans if so required. During the first half of 1914, the instability then building across much of Europe was pervasive and almost tangible; it was now only a matter of time before the always fragile peace of that continent would once again be shattered.

On a fine, warm summer day, Sunday, 28 June 1914, the Austrian Archduke Franz-Ferdinand and his wife were visiting Sarajevo, Bosnia. The archduke and his duchess had had a trying morning – while travelling to the town hall for an official reception following a review of troops on the Filipovitch parade ground, a bomb had been thrown at their car. Remarkably, although considerably shaken, they were both unhurt, and the would-be assassin had already been arrested. But he had an accomplice, and less than half an hour after the arrest of Cabrinovic for the failed bomb attack, Gavrilo Princip, another Serb, shot dead the archduke and the duchess as they were being driven close to the River Miljacka in eastern Sarajevo. Events moved rapidly thereafter, with Austria and Serbia soon declaring war on each other. This triggered the tightly interwoven system of international alliances between the greater and the lesser powers. On 1 August Germany mobilized and the Schlieffen Plan was implemented at the same time Germany sought to pre-empt a hostile move by France by moving German troops into neutral Belgium. This hostile act precipitated the British and Russian declarations of war against Germany and the First World War had begun.

Few among the seemingly endless field-grey columns of troops who so enthusiastically marched, rode or entrained for the frontiers and their war deployment positions that warm and sunny August could have had any premonition of the trials and tribulations that lay ahead of them, their nation and their empire, or that this new conflict would subsequently change many aspects of their redoubtable army for ever. Indeed, few if any of these soldiers would have entertained even for a moment the thought that, far from achieving great military glory and the final victory, they were in fact marching towards the proverbial abyss. Such was the final legacy of 1871, but – more particularly – it was ultimately a consequence of Germany's imperial hubris.

PART THREE

Into the Abyss

15

A War on Two Fronts, 1914

'WE HAD SEEN the generations before us grow old in security, and it seemed a wonderful dream to be permitted to fight as soldiers for our country's greatness, ready to give all we had. We felt ourselves grow to meet the responsibility that suddenly rested all its weight on our shoulders, and the past woke in us to make each a part of one terrific force. The word Fatherland like an old magic formula transformed us from the bottom, and loosing all ties of party and sect made us of one heart and mind. All of military age, to a man, thronged to the colours, eager to show by deeds that they were ready for the task their times laid upon them and that their country might rely upon them.'[147]

This text by Ernst Jünger perfectly encapsulated the spirit of euphoria, a heady blend of patriotism and duty – together with a less idealistic sense of an impending great adventure not to be missed, which surged through the German nation in 1914. Everywhere the young men of a country which had not experienced a major conflict since 1871 rushed to join the fight for their Fatherland, and the army that would carry that fight to their country's enemies. Of the army's first great Aufmarsch to war Jünger wrote:

> We set out in a rain of flowers to seek the death of heroes. The war was our dream of greatness, power and glory. It was a man's work, a duel in fields whose flowers would be stained with blood. There was no lovelier death in the world… anything rather than stay at home, anything to make one with the rest.[148]

Self-evidently, a full account of the part played by the German army on the battlefield from 1914 to 1918 is well beyond the intended scope of this work. But an account of the development of the army – not least the contrast between its organization and circumstances at the beginning of the war and at its end – during those four years is clearly relevant, together with a view of the changing attitudes of its soldiers as the war progressed. Implicit in this is an analysis of certain specific engagements or campaigns which were defining moments in the German army's war, and which therefore shaped the fate and fortunes of its soldiers. Similarly, some members of the high command, prominent amongst them Hindenburg and Ludendorff, deserve more than a mere passing reference, for they

were as always the architects both of the army's successes and of its failures and as such cannot be displaced from any account of its actions. But
while the broad framework of organization, high command, strategy and
tactics provides the essential background against which the story of
1914–18 must be set, the greater significance of those years was undoubtedly the sea change in attitudes and perceptions that it wrought within
Germany. Few historians would dispute the enormous impact of the First
World War on the political and social fabric of the German nation and its
army, an impact that eventually forced open the lid of a veritable Pandora's
Box – a box which contained the political ideology of National Socialism.

When Ernst Jünger and his fervently patriotic and enthusiastic
comrades-in-arms joined the great mobilization and Aufmarsch of 1914
and entrained to join their assigned units at or *en route* to concentration
areas adjacent to Germany's borders, in accordance with von Moltke's
modified Schlieffen Plan, they were part of a huge war machine that had
been extensively expanded and diversified technologically since 1871. But
the army still exhibited many of the social mores of a much earlier age,
together with the institutional flaws that had perpetuated during the
previous decades of peace. Nevertheless, the army that sallied forth in
August 1914 was a formidable fighting force, with a regular strength of
some 840,000 men, which rose to 3,840,000 within six days of mobilization. It was also almost certainly the best trained, best equipped and best
prepared European army of the day. Furthermore, in August 1914 it was
probably the best motivated army to be fielded by any of the great powers
for the impending conflict. The organization of the German imperial army
that went to war in 1914 is summarized at Appendix 6.

Although the organization of the combat formations soon changed to suit
specific situations and needs, the typical army corps of 1914 was comprised
of two divisions, each of two infantry brigades. Each brigade had two
infantry regiments, each of three battalions. There were five companies per
battalion, including a machine-gun company. The corps artillery support
usually included a field artillery brigade of two regiments, each of two battalions. These battalions had three or four batteries each, with six guns per
battery, although this was reduced to four by early 1915. There was also a
heavy (or 'foot') artillery regiment of two battalions, although as the war
developed these tended to be deployed geographically and remain in place
thereafter rather than being a fixed part of an individual corps and moving
with it. The corps cavalry element was usually two or three brigades, each
brigade comprised of two regiments. The cavalry regiments had up to four
squadrons, plus a machine-gun squadron and a depot squadron. Finally, a

Jäger or 'rifle' battalion usually completed the standard allocation of combat arms within the army corps at the outset of the war.

As usual, the army was supported by an extensive organization of engineer and pioneer units (some 150 pioneer companies in 1914), military train, medical and veterinary services (quite apart from the cavalry's continued use of horses, the army still relied predominantly upon horses to draw its field artillery and supply wagons), an air service (both dirigibles and aircraft), communications and railway units. Just as had been the case in 1870, the whole of this now even more complex war machine was directed by the high command through the auspices, co-ordination and direct involvement of the general staff.

The operations of the German army in 1914 were directed by two particular documents. Its strategic deployment and operational activities were of course based on the requirements of the Schlieffen Plan. But during the decades that followed the war of 1870–1, the general staff had also developed the *Kriegsbrauch im Landkriege* – literally 'rules for conduct of land warfare', but usually termed 'Field Service Regulations' in an English-language edition published in 1915 – which drew upon, updated and amplified many of the principles and philosophical thoughts that had been articulated by Clausewitz, Scharnhorst and Gneisenau in earlier times. The *Kriegsbrauch* was produced as a general staff publication and was issued widely throughout the officer corps. The manual provides a remarkably clear insight into the German army's approach to modern war and the way in which it expected its soldiers to conduct themselves on operations. As such it also explains some of the actions during the war that were later condemned by Germany's enemies as extreme or contrary to the laws of war. Interestingly, in several cases the contents of the *Kriegsbrauch* have greater resonance with certain of the army's actions during the 1939–45 conflict than with those during 1914–18.

At the outset the *Kriegsbrauch* established quite clearly that, provided they were necessary to achieve the objective, any and all actions, activities and methods of warfare were legitimate. The following text appears among some of the more significant pronouncements and requirements, advising:

● Caution against excessive concern with humanitarian issues, including certain of the principles espoused by the Geneva, Hague and Brussels conventions, especially those dealing with the civilian population of an occupied country. It was recognized that by its very nature modern war could not be limited to the combat conducted between military forces and that such warfare would inevitably involve action to achieve by any and all available means the destruction of 'the total intellectual and material resources' of an enemy state.

● Prisoners-of-war were to be treated as such – humanely and not criminal-ized – although they could be required to work if necessary. However, prag-matically perhaps, it was recognized that 'Prisoners should be killed only in the case of extreme necessity' although 'only the duty of self-preservation and the security of one's own state can justify it.' It is the frankness of this statement that is particularly striking, rather than its content, as the record of history shows that virtually no army can claim with any degree of certainty or credi-bility never to have killed numbers of its prisoners taken in war at some time or times during its existence.[149]

● The bombardment of areas that were not by definition 'fortifications' was acceptable in pursuit of the military objective. While churches, schools, libraries and buildings of particular cultural significance should not be bombarded if possible, their exemption from destruction could only be assured where their non-military use was certain.

● While the seizing and use of any strategic resources from an occupied country was acceptable, the looting of private property and of cultural collec-tions such as those found in museums and libraries was not condoned.

● With its experiences of fighting the French North African troops in 1870–1 very much in mind, the use of non-European troops – specifically non-Chris-tians or uncivilized natives – to fight in a European war was roundly condemned, and by implication such troops were placed beyond any expecta-tion of protection or treatment in accordance with the generally accepted arti-cles of war.

● Similarly, following its experiences of the campaign against the *francs-tireurs* in 1871, the German view of the illegitimacy of such irregular forces persisted in 1914. Despite their mastery of so many facets of warfare, the Germans never successfully conducted a guerrilla campaign or armed resistance of the sort carried out by the people of so many of the countries occupied by the German army at various times. It can only be concluded that this form of warfare was anathema to German military thinking and to its military code of honour. The Hague Conventions of 1899 and 1907 were included in the *Kriegsbrauch* as an appendix, but the main text made it quite clear that the general staff did not recognize the right of civilians to resist invasion, thereby indicating that such action was beyond the laws of armed conflict and (by implication) that any reprisals taken by the army in response to such action would be inevitable and legitimate.

● In similar vein, all forms of subterfuge, faithlessness and fraud, such as misuse of the Red Cross flag, breaking the terms of a parole or armistice, using surrender as a lure to kill the enemy, were condemned, together with incendiarism and robbery. Interestingly, the 'murder of the enemy's leaders' was also condemned, while the use of enemy and neutral uniforms, flags and identifying symbols was acceptable, although contrary to the Hague Convention on these matters.

✠✠✠✠✠✠✠✠✠✠✠✠✠

These then were some of the guiding principles that had already been firmly inculcated in the German officers and soldiers when they embarked upon their great adventure in 1914. But if the principles set out in the *Kriegsbrauch* directed their general prosecution of the war, their strategic direction remained firmly rooted in the Schlieffen Plan.

In summary, the plan in its 1914 form still called for the main offensive effort to be launched against the French, with a view to inflicting a telling defeat and forcing them out of the war within six weeks. The whole emphasis would then move to the eastern front in order to crush the Russian forces which, it had been anticipated, would by then still not be fully mobilized. In its original form, the plan had called for nine-tenths of the army to be engaged against France, the main effort being a right hook through the Netherlands, thereby avoiding the substantial line of French fortifications on the border. This would be followed by the destruction of the French army through a major attack into its northern flank and rear areas. But von Moltke had subsequently amended the plan, so that the eastern front had been strengthened by six divisions at the expense of a reduction of the western front's crucial right wing. The left wing of the western front was also strengthened at the expense of the right. The original plan had been unequivocal in its emphasis upon the defeat of France first of all, and the need therefore to place an overwhelming force on the German right in the west, while accepting a significant strategic risk in the east with the holding operation against the Russians. Now, however, the plan had become more of a compromise. The west was still the area of main effort, but with Germany's limited forces there spread more thinly, while those in the east remained weak when compared to the large numbers of Russian troops who could ultimately be deployed. The Schlieffen Plan in its various iterations had provoked much critical debate both prior to 1914 and afterwards, particularly von Moltke's amendments, but four particular flaws transcended any consideration of the redeployment of a few divisions.

First, for its success to be guaranteed the plan had always relied on the German army being much larger than that which was actually available – even as early as 1905 it had called for ninety-four divisions, whereas in fact only sixty were available. Manpower increases of 300,000 had been sought in 1912 and 1913, but only 136,000 had been authorized. So the plan was founded upon a false assumption from the outset, and as such was at best a high risk and at worst militarily unachievable.

Secondly, despite its initial success, the time needed to accomplish the great right hook had been grossly underestimated; apparently little thought had been given to the difficulties attending the speedy advance of huge numbers of men and horses, confronting a multitude of water obstacles, demolished bridges, destroyed railways, and roads blocked by columns of refugees – and opposition. To maintain its schedule, General Alexander von Kluck's 1st Army on the German right was required to advance an average of more than fourteen miles each day for three weeks, which would have been no mean achievement in peacetime. Despite the skills and intellect of the general staff, the optimism regarding some of the more fundamental aspects of the Schlieffen Plan was reminiscent of the situation in 1870. In similar vein, more than four decades after the débâcle of 1870–1, the French had at last realized the strategic importance of the railway and were able to move their operational reserves rapidly by rail to counter the German advance on horse and foot.

Next, the general staff had undoubtedly underestimated the difficulties involved in a single headquarters maintaining command, control and logistic support of large and dispersed mobile forces operating on two widely separated fronts. Perhaps the peace, and the sterility and predictability of the set-piece Kaisermanöver of the pre-war years had led to some potentially fatal false assumptions being made? At present, while

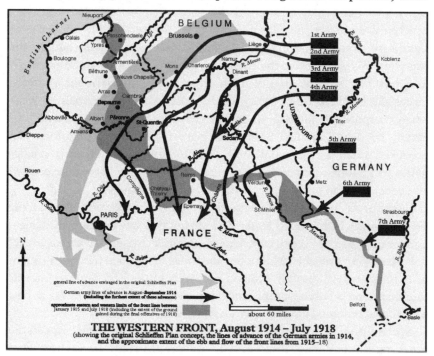

THE WESTERN FRONT, August 1914 – July 1918
(showing the original Schlieffen Plan concept, the lines of advance of the German armies in 1914, and the approximate extent of the ebb and flow of the front lines from 1915–18)

Auftragstaktik certainly meant that commanders would continue to operate energetically with little or no day-to-day direction, it also meant that the high command's communication with these commanders was often intermittent. As a result, the co-ordination of their actions or their re-direction as the campaign proceeded became increasingly difficult.

Finally, the political isolation of the general staff from many of the realities of the constantly changing international scene meant that from the outset the Schlieffen Plan was exclusively a military plan, with the implicit assumption that international considerations were of secondary or no importance. One consequence of this was the general staff's underestimation of the level of resistance that would be encountered by the Germans during their invasion of neutral Belgium. In the event, the Belgians' robust if short-lived resistance to the invaders had much wider international consequences, as the violation of Belgian neutrality was a key part of the rationale for Britain's early entry into the war. Meanwhile, the widely circulated reports of the killing of Belgian and French civil-ians (5,521 and 896 respectively) by the Germans during the 1914 campaign provided a welcome gift to the anti-German propagandists. One such incident occurred in Dinant on 23 August, where some 200 civilians were shot for having, allegedly, fired upon the Saxon troops. In all, some 674 civilians were killed by the Saxons in Dinant during their occupation of the town, these killings having been ordered by their corps commander. Despite its severity, it was an order that certainly accorded with the provisions of the *Kriegsbrauch*, although, as Dinant is immedi-ately adjacent to the Meuse, it is more than likely that the hostile fire which had provoked these reprisals originated from French sharp-shooters on the far bank of the river rather than from Belgian *tireurs* in Dinant.[150]

Despite the plan's inherent flaws and the unanticipated delays that these produced, the early progress made by the Germans in August 1914 seemed to augur well for success. It is in any case a timeless military truism that 'no plan survives contact with the enemy'. As 350,000 troops moved into Lorraine, another 400,000 marched into the heavily wooded hills and valleys of the Ardennes. Meanwhile, three armies – some 750,000 men in all – had been launched into Luxembourg and Belgium on their way to envelop the French left flank and roll up the French army from the north and from its rear. Just as the German high command had anticipated, the main counter-action was made against the German forces in Lorraine and the Ardennes, where the French were first stopped and then forced to withdraw behind their frontier. Brussels fell on 20 August, after which the main German attack fell upon the French forces deployed to defend the Franco-Belgian frontier. After a short attempt to hold on the Sambre, the French, outnumbered by about two to one, were forced to withdraw.

On 21 August the two corps of the British Expeditionary Force (BEF), almost 100,000 men, arrived at Mons, where they came into contact with forward cavalry units of von Kluck's 1st Army twenty-four hours later. Shortly after this the BEF was attacked by three German corps and had sustained 4,352 casualties by nightfall on 23 August, so that next day the British had no option but to begin their own fighting withdrawal westwards. Everywhere the Franco-British forces were retreating, and by 29 August the French alone had sustained 40,000 dead and 260,000 casualties overall.

Although the French and British were retreating, the strength of the resistance facing the German armies confounded the general staff's expectations, and by the end of August the critical timetable called for by the Schlieffen Plan was slipping day by day. Suffering increasing numbers of casualties (some 265,000 by 6 September) and delays, while lacking the necessary strength to continue its advance westwards, the 1st Army swung south and then south-east instead of proceeding west to envelop Paris. This made the German right flank vulnerable to attack, and precipitated a French counter-stroke by the newly constituted French 6th Army, launched from the Paris area. Realistically, the 1st Army had reached its limit of exploitation, and in the face of continued French attacks it began to withdraw north-eastwards on 5 September.

By this time the French had appreciated that the German point of main effort was indeed from the north, and so substantial forces urgently recalled from Lorraine struck General Karl von Bülow's 2nd Army on the Marne on 6 September. The battle raged during the days that followed. Then, as the BEF advanced to plug the gap between the two German armies created by von Kluck's withdrawal and to strike his newly exposed left flank, von Bülow was forced to withdraw in light of the threat now posed to his own formerly secure right flank. By 10 September the ebb and flow of the crucial battle of the Marne had all but ended, as the German armies halted their withdrawal and entrenched themselves along the line of the high ground beyond and overlooking the River Aisne. The Marne was a defining moment of the war, as it halted the German advance, frustrated the plans of the general staff, and effectively shaped the battle-lines drawn in the west that were to endure with little change for the next four years.

From 17 September both sides tried to outflank the other from the north, the conflict – and therefore the defensive lines – moving ever closer to the North Sea coast. Despite the best efforts of both sides, including a number of German offensives, the Anglo-French forces could not be dislodged. By Christmas 1914 an almost unbroken line of trenches, wire, strongpoints and a multiplicity of other fortifications ran from the coast of Flanders in the north, all the way down to the Franco-Swiss border in the south. Despite the decades of reconnaissance, analysis, assessment and updating, the strategic aims and intentions of the Schlieffen Plan had not been achieved, and from its failure there had instead emerged a most sophisticated defensive monstrosity that soon became known to all as the 'Western Front'. For the German army, the price of the failure of the plan had been nearly 900,000 casualties, together with the prospect of now having to fight a protracted war on two fronts.

But if Germany had not been favoured with the essential victory over France within six weeks that it had needed in August 1914, on the eastern front the army would eventually enjoy somewhat better fortunes against the Russians. But this campaign was already proceeding in ways that had certainly not been anticipated by the general staff, and here also the Germans experienced some early reverses.

Although they had expected that Russia would be slow to mobilize, it defied the general staff estimates by coming into action quite quickly against the forces in East Prussia, where the German 8th Army, about 200,000 strong and commanded by General von Prittwitz, had been deployed to secure the eastern frontier. While their overall professionalism and readiness to conduct offensive operations was of a much lesser order than that of the German soldiers, the Russians quickly responded to a French request to launch an offensive on the eastern front by moving two armies into East Prussia in mid-August; on the 17th the 3rd Corps of the Russian General Rennenkampf's 1st Army struck the German 1st Corps at Stallupönen. Altogether, the Russians fielded some 250 battalions against a German strength of about 144, but the German artillery was significantly stronger in terms of number of guns to battalions and of the amount of heavy artillery available to the 8th Army. Also, the Russian command and control arrangements were archaic. Compasses were available but few maps were issued – even at formation headquarters – and many junior officers could not read maps anyway. Insufficient telephone cable meant that operational messages were sent by radio, but often in clear because signallers either had no codes or else the recipients were incapable of decoding them. Little mechanical transport was available, and despite the updating action taken after Russia's humiliating defeat by Japan in 1904, many aspects of the army's support services were still primitive. Finally, neither the Russian commander-in-chief, General Jilinsky, nor his two army commanders, General Rennenkampf (1st Army) and General Samsonov (2nd Army) – who disliked each other – were of more than average competence as commanders. But then neither was the German 8th Army commander, as General von Prittwitz would demonstrate all too soon.

In response to the Russian attack, von Prittwitz ordered the 1st Corps, commanded by General Hermann von François, to withdraw his corps to Gumbinnen in the face of the Russian attack. Von François refused to do this but instead attacked the Russians, taking some 3,000 prisoners before at last being forced to fall back to Gumbinnen with the loss of seven guns. Meanwhile, General von Mackensen's 17th Corps and General Otto von Below's 1st Reserve Corps moved to reinforce von François, arriving at Gumbinnen at about midday on 20 August. Gumbinnen was then the scene of the next major clash, where von François had that morning attacked the Russian flank and taken a further 5,000 prisoners. However, as von Mackensen's corps – arriving at Gumbinnen ahead of von Below's corps – was committed to the battle, a local Russian advantage in artillery first halted the German advance, then broke the newly arrived corps. There followed the rare sight of an entire German corps rendered non-effective, with one division actually breaking and fleeing the battlefield. Many of its soldiers retreated as far as fifteen miles before their flight was finally halted. Although they had lost about 19,000 men, Gumbinnen was a victory for the Russian 1st Army, but it was one achieved in relative isolation, as General Jilinsky lacked both the aptitude and the essential command and control facilities to co-ordinate the actions of his two armies successfully and thus exploit Rennenkampf's success. But of much greater significance for the German army were the changes that the defeat at Gumbinnen brought about in the high command of the 8th Army, as these changes would later affect the future direction and eventual outcome of Germany's war very significantly.

In the belief that his rival's success at Gumbinnen heralded an imminent German collapse, and determined to gain his own victory, General Samsonov's 2nd Army pressed forward to the south of the Masurian lakes. These sizeable lakes now effectively divided the two Russian armies from each other and therefore 2nd Army could no longer be supported by 1st Army, but von Prittwitz reckoned that the Russian advance was so strong that the whole of 8th Army should now withdraw west of the Vistula. This intention was completely unacceptable to von Moltke and the general staff, and it was decided to replace von Prittwitz. The officer selected by von Moltke to take over command of 8th Army was General Paul von Beneckendorff und Hindenburg, while his chief of staff would be one General Erich von Ludendorff, an officer who had already gained a formidable reputation on the Western Front during the siege of Liège, where he had been deputy chief of staff of 2nd Army. Together with the Kaiser, few if any other figures shaped international perceptions of German militarism and of the archetypal Prussian officer to the extent of von Hindenburg and von Ludendorff, both in 1914–18 and during the post-war decade that followed.

Paul von Hindenburg was born in 1847 and, having gained a commission in the Prussian Guard, he served as a junior officer during the wars against Denmark, Austria and France in the period to 1871. Consistently regarded as a very capable, pragmatic and strong leader, he rose to command an army corps and then retired from active service in 1911. He had achieved this senior command position despite his well-known preference for service with troops rather than in staff appointments – a preference that rarely resulted in rapid advancement in any peacetime army. However, it earned him the respect and trust of those he commanded, and it would soon do so again. During his service his name had been taken under consideration as a possible contender for the post of chief of the general staff or for that of Prussian Minister of War. However, this was not to be, and when he retired as a corps commander his last experience of active service during a major conflict had been as a junior infantry officer in 1871. But then in late-August 1914 von Hindenburg was recalled to serve his country once again, this time as the commander of Germany's 8th Army in East Prussia, an area with which he was already very familiar.

Still wearing his old 1911-era uniform, von Hindenburg was met by his new chief of staff at the main railway station in Hanover on 23 August, from where they would travel together to the headquarters of 8th Army. General Erich von Ludendorff was a very different man from von Hindenburg, but the personalities of the two generals complemented each other very well. Born in 1865, and in due course commissioned into the infantry, von Ludendorff had no direct experience of combat or of a major conflict prior to 1914, but unlike von Hindenburg he readily accepted that a career on the general staff was the route to speedy professional advancement, and having achieved that he quickly demonstrated his aptitude, intellect and professional abilities. Despite his undoubted professional competence, he had also acquired a reputation as an ambitious, mercurial, violent and abrasive officer who carried these less positive traits into his approach to the organization and conduct of warfare. His vision of modern conflict was one of war waged to the utmost extent of the resources of the nation, with little thought for matters of morality or principle if these should prejudice the army's operations. From 1904 to 1913 von Ludendorff had worked in the operations and mobilization department of the general staff, rising within it to head that department from 1908 until 1913. In that capacity he had been very directly involved in the several measures proposed to increase the size of the army in the pre-war years, and had suffered the frustration of seeing the increases essential to the success of the Schlieffen Plan refused by the government in 1912 and 1913. Indeed, he had also been an important contributor to von Moltke's operational review and modification of various aspects of the plan, having worked closely with him in the years prior to the outbreak of war. So it was, at Hanover Hauptbahnhof on 23 August 1914, that the leadership duo which would just a year later assume overall command of the German army and war effort for the remainder of the war was formed. The two officers' onward journey to 8th Army headquarters at Marienburg on the Vistula took them north and east from Hanover, and they arrived there later that day. *En route* they developed their own strategy to deal with the Russians, and on 25 August von Hindenburg signed the operation order that committed 8th Army to what would become known as the battle of Tannenberg, a defining moment not only of the fighting on the eastern front but also of the wider war.

In fact, the operations staff at headquarters 8th Army had already produced a design for battle that virtually mirrored that which von Hindenburg and von Ludendorff devised on 23–4 August. There, the chief of operations, Major General Grünert, and (more particularly) his deputy, Lieutenant Colonel Max Hoffman, had also assessed that the disjointed command and control between the two Russian armies, together with the very different operational approaches of Rennenkampf and Samsonov, offered a real opportunity to isolate and destroy them separately. This could be achieved by employing the classic German tactic of conducting a holding action against one army while concentrating and employing the maximum force against the other. Furthermore, the almost non-existent co-ordination between the two Russian armies was exacerbated by the physical barrier of the Masurian lakes.

Given Samsonov's over-optimism and recklessness – even now he was pushing his 2nd Army onwards at best speed in order to attack the German right, with his already exhausted infantry regiments marching up to twelve miles a day – and Rennenkampf's caution, Samsonov clearly posed the greater threat. A captured Russian map showing 1st Army's operational plan and the steady flow of intelligence gleaned from German intercepts of Russian radio traffic (all sent in clear) tended to confirm this assessment. But, if the Germans had miscalculated and Rennenkampf did break through the predominantly cavalry force of just one division (which had necessarily been deployed on a frontage that exceeded twenty miles in order to hold the northern flank), 8th Army risked an overwhelming attack into its rear area while its main combat units were still dealing with Samsonov to the south. In any event, the meeting of minds between the new commander and his chief of staff and the in-place operations staff of 8th Army meant that the army's new offensive could be launched in fairly short order.[151] As ever, the railway would play a crucial part in moving major elements of the German corps speedily and largely undetected to concentrate against the Russian 2nd Army to the south.

Although the German 1st Corps was still detraining to the west of Tannenberg on 25 August, following its move south-west from Gumbinnen, Ludendorff was concerned by the threat posed by Rennenkampf and so ordered General von François to attack Samsonov's 2nd Army forthwith. This order was given despite the fact that none of 1st Corps' heavy artillery was yet available and neither 1st Reserve Corps nor 17th Corps would be able to support the attack, as both corps were still moving south by road to join the battle against Samsonov. General von François at first refused to launch such an ill-judged venture, but was then visited by von Hindenburg, von Ludendorff and Hoffman and, if the order were indeed to be confirmed, he agreed to do so on the understanding that the action would necessarily be carried out by the infantry alone! Hoffman, who was undoubtedly more in tune with the Russian deployment and activities than von Ludendorff, supported von François' decision, but did not declare this to the new chief of staff. Fortuitously, just then intelligence was received to the effect that Rennenkampf's progress was sufficiently slow that his army would not threaten 8th Army's rear, while at the same time Samsonov had ordered a pursuit of what he had assessed to be a demoralized and routed German 20th Corps, commanded by General von Scholtz. Accordingly, the original assessment of the Russian intentions made by Hoffman and Grünert was validated and von François was not required to carry out his premature attack – which also meant that Samsonov became even more deeply committed into the German trap.

The battle was finally joined when Samsonov's 2nd Army launched its own attack at dawn on 27 August, advancing north-west on a general line from Allenstein to Osterode. Thereupon, the two corps commanded by

✠✠✠✠✠✠✠✠✠✠✠✠

von Below (1st Reserve Corps) and von Mackensen (17th Corps), which were deployed well to the north of Tannenberg and to the north-east of Allenstein, fell upon the Russian right. By that evening the Russian advance had been halted, with many casualties, but Samsonov was by no means nonplussed by this unexpected turn of events, and still anticipated the imminent arrival of 1st Army from the north.

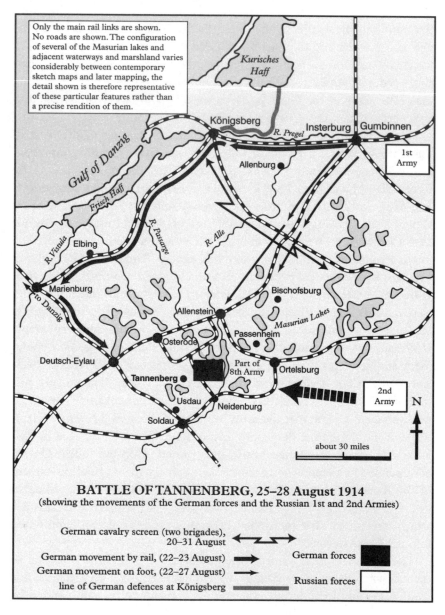

Only the main rail links are shown. No roads are shown. The configuration of several of the Masurian lakes and adjacent waterways and marshland varies considerably between contemporary sketch maps and later mapping, the detail shown is therefore representative of these particular features rather than a precise rendition of them.

BATTLE OF TANNENBERG, 25–28 August 1914
(showing the movements of the German forces and the Russian 1st and 2nd Armies)

German cavalry screen (two brigades), 20–31 August	
German movement by rail, (22–23 August)	German forces
German movement on foot, (22–27 August)	
line of German defences at Königsberg	Russian forces

✠✠✠✠✠✠✠✠✠✠✠✠✠

Early on the morning of 27 August General von François' 1st Corps –
now with its heavy artillery fully available – began a seven-hour bombardment of the Russian left, accompanied by attacks which virtually annihilated the Russian corps on the army's left wing. Meanwhile, Samsonov
threw five more divisions into the battle, but failed to break through the
German corps that had by then almost encircled him. By nightfall on the
27th the Russian army group commander, Jilinsky, was at last becoming
fully aware of the disaster unfolding with his 2nd Army and ordered
Rennenkampf to hasten his attack from the north.

On 28 August the fighting continued, and the German encirclement of
2nd Army was completed when von François once again disobeyed an
order from Ludendorff, this time to assist 20th Corps. In fact von Scholtz
did not need that assistance and, by driving instead upon Neidenburg, von
François' 1st Corps effectively cut off the potential escape route for the
Russians to the south. Although the remnant of the ensnared 2nd Army
fought on bravely and enjoyed some local successes, one of which was the
temporary recapture of Neidenburg, the end was not in doubt. Late on the
night of 29 August Samsonov walked alone into the dense fir woods,
unholstered his pistol, and shot himself. The last units of his decimated
army dug in and continued fighting until the morning of 31 August when,
the last of their ammunition gone and no hope of resupply or relief, they
finally surrendered. In the rout of 2nd Army 50,000 Russians had been
killed or wounded, with 92,000 prisoners taken by 31 August – the 'day of
harvesting' as von Hindenburg termed it – together with some 500 guns.
Tellingly, of the haul of prisoners taken, no fewer than 60,000 were directly
attributable to the actions of General von François, who yet again modified von Ludendorff's orders for his 1st Corps at the end of the main
battle and thereby ensured that the remaining Russian troops could not
infiltrate away to the south and east. Although his intuitive command of
the 1st Corps had been most effective, in the best traditions of the concept
of Auftragstaktik, and a key contributor to the German victory against 2nd
Army, von François had not endeared himself to von Ludendorff during
the battle of Tannenberg. Consequently, despite his clear ability and suitability for advancement, General Hermann von François remained a corps
commander throughout the war.

Meanwhile, now that he was aware of Samsonov's fate, Rennenkampf
withdrew his army, only to be pursued by the German forces which had
now been reinforced by an additional two corps from the Western Front.
During the battle of the Masurian lakes, which was fought between 7 and
14 September, von Hindenburg's army finally crippled Rennenkampf's

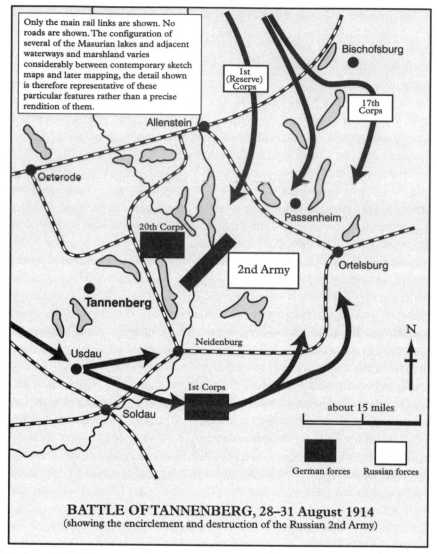

Only the main rail links are shown. No roads are shown. The configuration of several of the Masurian lakes and adjacent waterways and marshland varies considerably between contemporary sketch maps and later mapping, the detail shown is therefore representative of these particular features rather than a precise rendition of them.

Bischofsburg

1st (Reserve) Corps

17th Corps

Allenstein

Osterode

Passenheim

20th Corps

2nd Army

Ortelsburg

Tannenberg

Neidenburg

N

Usdau

1st Corps

about 15 miles

Soldau

German forces   Russian forces

BATTLE OF TANNENBERG, 28–31 August 1914
(showing the encirclement and destruction of the Russian 2nd Army)

force, which lost more than 125,000 men, including 30,000 as prisoners, together with 200 guns. But the defeat of the Russian 1st Army was not as decisive as that of 2nd Army had been, because Rennenkampf managed to disengage and withdraw part of his command successfully – often marching his men more than twenty miles a day on congested roads in blistering heat. Nevertheless, this follow-on battle had signalled the real end of the battle of Tannenberg which, if the Germans had lost it, would have dramatically altered the course and duration of the First World War, and the whole course of European history – notably that of Tsarist Russia.

✠✠✠✠✠✠✠✠✠✠✠✠

Tannenberg assured the future prominence and fortunes of von Hindenburg and von Ludendorff alike. The former continued as commander-in-chief for the eastern front throughout 1915, gaining credit for several further successes. By the end of that year his was a household name both in Germany and internationally, and when General Erich von Falkenhayn was relieved of his post as chief of the general staff in August 1916, von Hindenburg assumed that appointment and thus became, by default, the supreme warlord of Germany throughout the remaining years of the war. Von Ludendorff continued as von Hindenburg's principal adviser, so that from August 1916 he exerted a significant influence upon almost every aspect of an army that was by now engaged in a modern, industrialized war of attrition. He addressed the army's doctrine, tactics, technology and organization with great energy, together with the key policies and practicalities which affected the means of industrial production necessary to support the army. Whereas von Hindenburg was always the military and national figurehead of those years, he lacked the sheer ability of his subordinate. Von Ludendorff's was the intellect and the brain that drove the nature and spirit of the army and, arguably, that of the German nation in arms from 1916 to 1918, while von Hindenburg's great skill was to recognize his subordinate's considerable, if sometimes erratic, attributes and his own limitations. This enabled von Hindenburg to direct, support and focus the activities of von Ludendorff, while at the same time not deluding himself about his own abilities. The enormous breadth of the power and responsibilities that these two men assumed from 1916 turned them into the first real warlords of modern warfare – an historic process which had begun in August 1914 with the campaign to secure East Prussia, fought about the Masurian lakes and at Tannenberg.

But if Germany had cause to celebrate its victories on the eastern front in the late summer and autumn of 1914, on the Western Front its soldiers were facing a very different situation. There, the north–south system of trenches, which by now had been carved across much of the northern continent, was fast assuming a permanence that was very far removed from the concept of manoeuvre warfare for which the general staff had originally planned. As the first snows of the European winter fell upon the field-grey-clad soldiers in their emplacements, both they and the high command at last began to realize that they were now irrevocably committed to a potentially lengthy and wholly new sort of warfare on the Western Front – one that would be dominated by defence rather than offence, and by technology and logistics rather than by the sheer courage of ordinary men.

16

Stalemate in the West

Trench Warfare, 1915–1918

A S THE WINTER SNOWFALLS of December 1914 and January 1915 began to melt, much of the vast network of trenches that already existed became waterlogged; seas of mud, punctuated by deep tracts of dark water filling old shell-holes. Many of the earthworks soon became minor waterways, as great quantities of revetting, duckboards and sandbags were put in place to shore up or improve the trenches. Everywhere, miles of dense and rapidly rusting concentrations of barbed wire stretched across in front of the trenches in no man's land. The Schlieffen Plan had run its course in the west, and now the lines that both sides would occupy with only minor changes until 1918 were set. Although the German army had inflicted a telling defeat on the Russians the previous year, and in the west now held an important part of eastern France including a number of strategically important industrial areas, it was faced with the war on two fronts that the general staff had always sought to avoid. Furthermore, its long-standing commitment to offensive manoeuvre warfare was no longer practicable. At the outset of 1915 General Erich von Falkenhayn, chief of the general staff from 1914 until he was succeeded by von Hindenburg in 1916, had little choice but to order the army to adopt a defensive posture in the west, while seeking a victory in the east that would permit those divisions facing the Russians to redeploy to the Western Front. As ever, the railway network that supported the army permitted the relatively easy and speedy movement of troops and reserves between the two fronts and along their lengths.

Elsewhere, between 1914 and 1918 German colonial forces were also committed against the British, French and others in the Far East, the south Pacific and in East Africa. While these inter-colony campaigns were of limited strategic significance, they benefited Germany by tying down large numbers of troops of the opposing nations. Of these campaigns, that of Colonel Paul von Lettow-Vorbeck, the German military commander in German East Africa, was especially noteworthy. There, this exceptionally talented officer conducted a successful and arguably very un-German style of guerrilla campaign against the British and British imperial forces and their Belgian and Portuguese allies for four years, causing tens of thousands of these troops and large quantities of much-needed war resources to be diverted from the European battlefronts in order for them to be deployed against his 11,000 Schutztruppen, the majority of whom were native troops – the askaris. In 1917 he removed his force from German East Africa into neighbouring Portuguese East Africa and continued his vigorous campaign from there. When the armistice was declared in 1918 he remained undefeated, and subsequently 'put himself at the disposal' of the senior British officer in the area, rather than surrendering. Despite his steady succession of minor victories against vastly superior numbers, von Lettow-Vorbeck's campaign was but a side-show compared to the clash of titans that ensued on the Western Front and against Russia in the east from the beginning of 1915. The four years of unrelenting trench warfare which followed would change the nature of the German army for ever.

For the Germans, the war fought on the Western Front from 1915 to 1918 generally fell within a succession of three overlapping phases. First, the traditional campaign conducted throughout 1915 in accordance with the Schlieffen Plan, whose tenets came to grief when stalemates frustrated every attempt to achieve strategic advantage. The hundreds of miles of trenches which the opposing armies occupied by early 1916 exemplified this state of affairs. Then, by mid 1916, came an acceptance that the desired tactical doctrine was no longer viable, and the war became one of attrition into 1917.

Finally, by the end of 1917 technological advances – notably the development of the tank – enabled the resumption of a form of manoeuvring. But the Franco-British lead in tank development, and the arrival on the Western Front of American forces in ever greater numbers during the last twelve months of the war, meant that Germany was unable to regain the strategic initiative, despite the early success of its great offensive in 1918. Despite these changes of operational emphasis, throughout the years of the ebb and flow of battle on the Western Front the German soldier's very existence, daily routine and whole way of life were determined by the needs and nature of the trench warfare in which he had become totally engaged.

The German trench systems of 1915, 1916 and into 1917 became increasingly more sophisticated as time and the lack of any significant advances or withdrawals afforded the soldiers an almost infinite amount of time to improve the environment in which they lived, fought, and in many cases died. The emplacements were routinely dug to depths of ten or twelve metres, with rooms for resting, sleeping, eating, field kitchens, and for all manner of storage (which often included substantial quantities of ammunition and explosives). They were excavated deep underground and were all served by a network of trenches and tunnels giving ready access to the front line earthworks, as well as a multiplicity of exits, escape routes, and ventilation shafts. Many of these dugouts were set so far underground that even the heaviest shells could not affect them. The disadvantage of this, however, was the time that it might take to gain the surface in case of an alarm, where as many as forty steps might provide the principal means of access and exit for a relatively unsophisticated dugout, while the way into and out of some others was described as the equivalent of 'the stairs of a four-storeyed house'.

Most of these underground caverns had electric lighting, and telephone cables linked them with other parts of the line, while an abundance of time, monotony and the static nature of the conflict produced master-pieces of creativity as the soldiers constantly improved their living arrangements. Individual sleeping bays, wood-panelled walls, shelves, basic furniture, pictures in colour from the popular publication *Jugend*, doors and curtains were but a few of the more basic refinements that proliferated in the earthworks just behind the forward lines. Extensive revetting, concreting, floor-boards, duck-boards, ladders, and stairways all added to the security and comfort of the thousands of men for whom this had become home. The need to move easily and quickly from position to position was also one of the highest priorities. Nevertheless, with fifty metres of wire laid in front of the German trenches, with wooden knife-rests laced with barbed wire across every approach route, with forward outposts, with machine-guns covering every vulnerable area, and with hundreds of sentries constantly on alert, Ernst Jünger described the early war years as 'splendid days when, as a young officer, 'one could venture to sleep in pyjamas, and the automatic that lay to hand beside the ash-tray was only used when it was desired to break the monotony by going on patrol'. In the early years, 'one could traverse one's whole front like a mole without once coming to the surface'.[152]

As the months passed, both sides became technologically more innova-tive, and more aggressive and daring in their patrolling activities, while the risks inherent in occupying such well-made dugouts deep under the ground became increasingly evident as many of the obstacles in no man's land became more and more fragmented with little chance of repair or replacement. Although in theory no man's land separated the two armies, both lines of trenches were frequently linked by communications trenches, saps and other excavations that had been dug in earlier times, or which were left over from a time when the lines might have moved a few hundred metres east or west, with all such earthworks once entirely within the area controlled by the other side. Virtually any of these trenches provided possible routes by which attackers could infiltrate into the enemy's trench system. As the tactics of trench warfare changed and the technology of death and destruction advanced, so the grenades of the trench raiders, the clouds of poison gas, and the burning phosphorous of artillery shells and bombs all took an ever greater toll of troops who, while apparently well protected and secure in their underground fortresses, were at the same time unable to gain the surface in time to repel a surprise attack or trench raid, or to escape the noxious effects of the gas or the fire. Accordingly, the German high command directed that the forward trenches and their associated dugouts were to be no deeper underground than two metres, thus accepting greater casualties from artillery and mortar bombardment while reducing the risks of a surprise attack. Therefore, the forward trenches had so-called 'Siegfried shelters' dug into their sides, these being semi-circular holes extending some three metres into the side of the trench, with the curved corrugated iron roof supporting not more than two metres of overhead protection. These two-man shelters provided the front line troops – generally the infantry, together with the many cavalrymen who had increasingly been required to forego their horses – some measure of protection from artillery bombardment, but virtually none from a direct hit, and little if any from a shell-burst nearby .

Slightly forward of the main trench or built into its side were observation, sentry and sniper positions, often protected by steel plates with loopholes. Their use was largely abandoned during the first year of the war, their isolation and vulnerability outweighing their ability to provide early warning of an attack. Even when they were subsequently established much closer to the main trench line, these crucially important positions were invariably exposed and more often than not lacked any overhead cover, other than a sheet of canvas, or possibly a few pieces of wood.

Indeed, although the onset of a post-winter thaw or heavy rain usually affected the forward positions considerably worse than those occupying the depth positions, inundations of the trench systems were always thoroughly demoralizing, as carefully constructed and otherwise apparently sound earthworks were undermined, collapsed and dissolved into mud, bits of timber and lumps of chalk or stone, while all the time the seemingly unstoppable rivers of mud flowed freely along walkways and into dugouts, stores and sleeping-bays. This flooding ofen disinterred the many corpses buried after earlier battles, or revealed the mouldering remains of soldiers long since posted as missing in action. Meanwhile, the countless shell-holes that pock-marked the battlefield rapidly filled with water, several often joining together to form great expanses of filthy, muddy water – every one a potential death trap.

By late 1917 the advent of the tank dramatically reduced the dominance of the machine-gun, and introduced a degree of fluidity and uncertainty on the battlefield. At the same time it transformed the troglodyte (if relatively comfortable) existence that had been enjoyed in the preceding years by very many of those troops not directly in contact with the enemy. Now, such a lifestyle became an unacceptable luxury, in spite of the ever-present threat posed by artillery and mortar bombardment to the German soldiers who were now constrained to occupy the much less substantial forward trench systems constructed in late 1917 and 1918.

Apart from changes resulting from enemy action or occasioned by the preparation for some major offensive, the cycle of activity for a German unit – whether a company, a battalion or a regiment – on the Western Front fell broadly into three parts, with the troops rotating through front-line duties, reserve, and rest out of the line. Individuals would also be granted periods of leave in Germany, or possibly following a period of hospital treatment if they had been wounded, and would usually return to the same unit at the end of their time away. By mid-1918, some months after the last great German offensive of the war, the typical operational rotation for the soldiers of the 74th (Hanover) Infantry Regiment, then in positions to the south of Arras and one or two miles to the east of Hébuterne (which was occupied by the British), was six days in the forward line, two in reserve in the main support line, followed by four days in a rest area behind the lines.

In such forward positions in a relatively inactive sector the day would usually begin with a stand-to at dawn, the time when the night routine changed to that for the day as well as being the most likely time for an enemy attack. During the last hour of darkness, a breakfast of coffee, bread and some sort of meat paste would be brought up from a field kitchen sited some distance behind the lines and then taken forward in containers to the individual companies and platoons. Some desultory artillery and mortar exchanges might follow the onset of daylight, when both sides would register new targets and engage existing ones on an opportunity basis. Firing between the front line troops would probably be limited to opportunity sniping and machine-gunning of any suitable targets, while significant amounts of artillery fire falling directly upon the front line positions might be the precursor to an attack or possibly diversionary fire, or a bombardment designed to cover a patrol still seeking to regain its own lines after a raid during the previous night. The forward trenches were also vulnerable to a particular type of new weapon that had been developed as a direct response to the needs of trench warfare. This was the rifle grenade, a 'cast-iron cylinder through the centre of which was bored a rifled hole… the grenade fixed on the rifle-muzzle and projected by the force of the rifle shot', devised to overcome the problem of dropping explosives directly into forward trenches that were sometimes as little as thirty yards distant, but still too far away for a hand-grenade to be thrown into them. Fired almost vertically, the only warning of the arrival of these grenades or 'bombs' was a whistling sound as they dropped down to explode with often devastating effect.

Within an infantry battalion, during and shortly after stand-to, the company commanders would visit all their positions, accompanied by their officers and NCOs who had been on duty the previous night and whose written reports would already have been submitted prior to stand-to. These reports provided the basis of the company commanders' own morning reports, which would be dispatched to battalion headquarters by runner later in the morning. As a company commander reached each platoon position, the platoon commander would join him for his inspection.

Earlier, during the alert, all the soldiers would be fully dressed with helmets, weapons and equipment ready, and gas masks worn or to hand. Once the alert period ended, the majority of the soldiers might be resting in their Siegfried shelters, or cleaning their rifles (never all of them at the same time), or washing and shaving in an upturned helmet full of water, or mending clothing or equipment. They might also be digging to extend or improve their positions, or constructing some new obstacle to block a newly-identified infiltration route into the position. By 1918, the routine and very necessary use of gas masks meant that soldiers needed to be clean shaven. Consequently, the beards proudly affected by many of the soldiers in 1914 and 1915 had long since disappeared. If the threat of enemy action was high, or if the company had mounted a patrol the previous night, most of the men would have been on duty throughout the hours of darkness, often having had as little as two hours sleep between last and first light. Some would already have started their hours of duty as sentries, manning the observation positions at the parapet.

During the day, a constant stream of visitors usually appeared in the lines. Apart from routine visits by more senior regimental or formation commanders, or even by some exalted government minister or general (the 'top hats and leather helmets' as the soldiers called them) there might be general staff officers involved in planning a future operation or dealing with matters concerned with logistics, command and control. Artillery officers might also visit the forward positions to observe the fall of shot and register their guns. Undoubtedly there would also be many more mundane but none the less important visits, such as those when 'a junior medical officer pays a visit of inspection to the latrines; the gas-officer tests the masks, mouth-pieces and tubing'[153]and so on. In such ways the days in the trenches passed, generally unrelieved by the terror or excitement of any direct enemy action.

By late afternoon, with all his tasks completed and if not on some special company duty or posted as a sentry or observer, the officer and soldier alike might find a couple of hours in which to enjoy a pipe of tobacco, to read or write a letter, or indeed to catch up on the newspapers that were regularly delivered right up to the front line; alternatively, a couple of his comrades might huddle together into a Siegfried shelter for a game of cards. However, for most of the time the soldiers would be required to stay dispersed and at their allotted positions in the trench, or in the shelter immediately adjacent to that position. In the quieter sectors, a popular pastime was hunting and killing the ubiquitous rats – an activity that had almost acquired the status of a sport by the end the war!

Depending upon the operational situation, all the troops' meals were usually cooked centrally behind the lines and then carried forward in containers, the main meal usually arriving at or soon after last light. The standard fare usually included bread, potatoes, vegetables and meat, together with coffee (which had almost entirely become 'coffee-substitute' by 1918) and the ever-present meat paste intended to be eaten cold with bread during the day. The entitled amounts and methods of preparation of these rations varied considerably during the war, although irrespective of the quality of their rations the soldiers' constant complaint was that 'it does not fill us up'.

From time to time, limited quantities of wine, brandy and beer also found their way into the trenches; but despite the stresses of trench warfare drunkenness was apparently not a problem for the German army in the forward areas, and alcohol was in any case much more readily available in the rest areas and towns behind the lines. Indeed, a much greater threat to military discipline was evidently posed by a (probably) wood-based spirit called 'Ober-Ost' which was liberally prescribed to the troops for the treatment of influenza in the winter of 1917–18, a few glasses of which had 'a complete narcotic' effect. This was so much so that while Ernst Jünger's company was out of the line at

Ablainzeville, one of his comrades, Dohmeyer, 'Last night... riddled warrant-officer K.'s long boots (they share a dugout)... with revolver shots, in the belief apparently that he was rat-hunting.'[154] The winter of 1917–18 saw the beginning of the great European influenza epidemic, one that was destined to kill so many who had survived the war itself but who then became victims of its diseased aftermath. By mid-1918 increasing numbers of German soldiers were already succumbing to the epidemic and being removed from the front.

As night fell, in preparation for a stand-to at last light, the soldiers would once again put on their helmets, strap their greatcoats on to their packs, and take up their allotted positions along the trench line with their rifles, grenades, gas masks and other equipment immediately to hand. Thus day turned to night, signalling the hours of greatest peril, which would last until the grey light of dawn once more broke over the battlefront.

The routine while in reserve followed a similar pattern, but usually with a much-reduced requirement for sentries, with meals often being able to be delivered during daylight or indeed cooked close by, and in some cases with bunkers, blockhouses or fortified buildings available to be occupied rather than trenches. Although they might endure fewer vagaries than those in the front line, however, the troops in reserve were much more likely to be involved in all manner of work parties, or would be required to conduct night reconnaissance patrols, or trench raids to take prisoners. They were also at least as likely to attract the attention of the enemy artillery as their comrades in the forward positions, as the German reserve units and concentration areas were always categorized as priority targets. Finally, these reserve troops also had to be prepared to carry out counter attacks at short notice.

Whether in the forward trenches or the reserve lines, another hazard of such static warfare was the mine. Although by no means an innovation, the practice of tunnelling beneath the enemy trenches, filling the excavation with high explosive and then detonating it immediately before an assault or to destroy a particular fortification or emplacement, achieved new heights of expertise in the years after the front lines became more or less fixed. A German pioneer described life in the Lens area as being 'literally day and night on a volcano', where the whole region underground was already honeycombed with the shafts of coal mines – the plans of all of which were well used by the French. The subterranean work went on day and night, illuminated only by the glow of carbide lamps and torches, with German pioneers often able to hear the 'faint hammering, digging and picking' that betrayed the presence of the French pioneers working often only a few feet away from them. Sometimes one side's diggers would break through into the other's workings, when a brief and often savage fight for survival with pistols, digging tools, knives, bayonets and grenades ensued. In the early part of the war, before the German hand-grenades had pull-out fuses, the pioneers learnt 'always to have a cigar alight' so that they could instantly light the fuse of the improvised bombs they carried underground with them, made of 'tin boxes with a handle, filled with explosive, old nails, and scrap iron... heavy and unwieldy, but effective'.[155]

Where the pioneers judged that a French mining party was close by or about to break into their workings they would cover the noise of the dynamite charge being moved forward and emplaced by continuing to work with picks and shovels until the last minute. Then, as all work ceased and the pioneers ran back along the tunnel, the short fuse was lit and the last man ran back to safety. The charges used were usually very powerful, and all too often caused casualties to members of the party that had laid it, or the collapse of neighbouring galleries. Where one of these mine explosions destroyed a length of the trenches above it 'there was nothing for it but for both sides to storm the still warm crater while timber and debris descended from the sky'. While the soldiers above fought their war with rifles, machine-guns, and artillery, a parallel but very different sort of war was being waged by their comrades from the pioneer units in the very bowels of the earth beneath.

During 1916, the German army lost 434,000 men between 21 February and 18 December during its attempt to destroy the French army at Verdun, and a further 500,000 while countering the Franco-British attack at the Somme in July. Although the French lost more than 500,000 at Verdun and the British and French together sustained another 600,000 casualties on the Somme, the front-line positions remained largely unchanged, and the strategy of attrition directed by the chief of the general staff, von Falkenhayn, was discredited. On 29 August, von Hindenburg replaced von Falkenhayn and von Ludendorff was appointed quartermaster general. Meanwhile, during the blood baths of 1915 and 1916, a new form of offensive warfare had emerged from within the German army, together with the birth of the new organization to carry it out. Based upon the raiding parties of 1914 and 1915, the Germans had developed the assault detachments, or 'Stosstruppen', with the mission of taking the fight right into the enemy trenches. This concept and the later organization, employment, training and equipment of these units were in large measure pioneered and promoted by a Captain Ulrich Rohr. Quite apart from their impact upon the battlefield, these specially trained units exemplified the German army's offensive ethos and also established a pragmatic approach to the business of war that would once again be reflected in certain élite units of the future German military forces. Indeed, the members of what had became 'storm battalions' – Sturmbataillone – by 1918 were undoubtedly the élite units of the German army on the Western Front.

Originally, the army's raiding parties were not specialists. As the unacceptable cost of mounting frontal attacks became ever more evident, these small parties – each usually of no more than three men – would gain access to the enemy trench system and then roll it up by working their way along it, dealing out death and destruction in all directions. The raids were usually carried out at night or first light (crossing no man's land in daylight was rarely feasible), or in conjunction with a more general attack. Typically, one of the raiders would have an armoured shield (possibly one removed from a machine-gun) and a well-sharpened entrenching-tool. The second would be the grenadier, carrying two or more haversacks full of grenades; all with fuses modified from the usual five and a half seconds delay to just two or three seconds. The third man was armed with a trench knife or bayonet. All would probably carry pistols and one or more rifles might be carried (slung across the back), although their primary weapons were the grenades, or 'bombs', and their varied array of cold steel. A Very pistol to provide immediate illumination or for signalling might also be carried, together with the wire-cutters essential to deal with wire obstacles and to cut communication cables. In 1914 and 1915 the cloth-covered Pickelhaube helmet was usually worn, but with its distinctive spike or ball often removed. Then, from 1916, the newly issued steel helmet (Stahlhelm) was invariably used and was generally acknowledged to be the best-designed protective helmet of the war. Nevertheless, several very senior officers chose to wear the more traditional Pickelhaube throughout and after the conflict, conscious no doubt of its imperial heritage and martial symbolism.

The Stosstruppen were used extensively at Verdun, where they proved their considerable value. In due course they were allocated their own light artillery support in the form of an 'infantry gun battery'. This supporting unit was initially equipped with a 3.7cm gun, then later a 7.62cm weapon was introduced, which fired a 13lb high-explosive shell with an instantaneous fuse. These batteries of six guns were served by two officers and sixty or seventy other ranks, with one such battery per divisional sector. Meanwhile, by late 1916 most divisions had formed their own Sturmkompagnie, each of one officer and 120 men. Depending upon the operational situation, the three platoons of the company were often sub-allocated to regiments of the division. When not required for operations these personnel often trained the recruits and replacements destined for the battlefront. By 1918 most of the German armies on the Western Front had their own Sturmbataillone, each comprised of four assault companies, an infantry gun battery, a light mortar detachment, a flame-thrower detachment, a machine-gun company and a headquarters company. In total, some five independent storm companies and twelve storm battalions (including two Bavarian battalions) were deployed, with one storm battalion serving on the eastern front.

The uniforms, equipment and weapons adopted by the assault battalions were much modified to take account of their special role, with practicality, silent movement, camouflage and the immediate availability of firepower (including explosives) being their over-riding considerations. These men – the 'grenadiers' of the Stosstruppen – were truly the ultimate warriors in the era of trench warfare.[156] Indeed, several of the practical measures and equipment modifications developed and then adopted by the Stosstruppen were subsequently implemented or well in-train across the whole army by the end of 1916. These changes included the issue of a simpler and more functional field uniform, including the adoption of the steel helmet and, in some cases, the use of laced boots and puttees rather than the jackboot. The soldier's basic equipment was also modified where necessary to satisfy local operational conditions, or to meet the needs of some specialist role.

However, the period of time a unit spent in a rest area some distance behind the lines was usually far removed from the everyday front-line threats posed to life and limb by artillery bombardment, by the sniper's bullet, or by the dangers inherent in mounting or countering a trench raid. There, some distance behind the lines, the accommodation – while often still within the range of the heaviest artillery weapons and subject to an occasional air attack – would often be sited above ground, and might well be based within or close to a fortified village or town, or upon a complex of well-established bunkers or concrete emplacements. Near the ruined village of Achiet, in July 1918, Ernst Jünger's company was billeted in a mix of blockhouses and dugouts set into the side of a deep cutting. There, the soldiers shared the area with the anchorage for a captive observation balloon and with a tank repair unit, which indicated that they were still quite close to the forward area. During the early part of the war the army used these 'rest' periods for intensive top-up training, but in due course commanders judged that this was counter-productive – 'The men know how to use their arms. They use them every day in the line.'

Accordingly, although time out of the line usually included some sort of formal drill parade, an opportunity for a senior officer to address the soldiers or for Iron Crosses to be awarded, most of this precious time was usually filled by a host of more relaxing or recreational activities – football, bathing, card playing, reading, writing letters, attending divine service or possibly educational lectures, eating the food cooked by a field kitchen on-site, which might include freshly baked bread and the German army's ever-popular staple of pea and ham soup, sleeping, horse riding, hunting and shooting game (or the ever-present rats!). For many soldiers the simple pleasure of being able to enjoy walking upright in the fresh air in daylight, across green fields and in woods largely unaffected by the more obvious ravages of the war, with a relatively low chance of incurring injury or sudden death at enemy hands, was rest and relaxation enough.

In the late afternoon or evening the availability and consumption of copious amounts of beer and Schnapps from the canteen was also a most important morale booster in the rest area, where a regimental band might also perform. This was usually followed by the singing of the German army's traditional marches and patriotic folk songs, which would later give way to the more risqué soldier's refrains of the day, as the beer and Schnapps continued to flow. All too soon the unit's few days in the rest area would be over, when it would be time to return to the front line once again, but in such circumstances, the close comradeship forged in the front line between the officers and the soldiers inevitably blurred some of the traditional boundaries imposed by rank, with very many of these officers members of the Reserveoffizierskorps and Einjährigen rather than regular officers by the end of the war.[157]

By 1917 the 'front fighter' had emerged as the archetypal German soldier of the period, 'with his steel helmet, bedraggled uniform, burning eyes and drawn face ... imperturbable, toughened by the daily horror surrounding him, apathetic, resourceful, independent to the verge of insubordination; the man to whom war had become daily, bloody, hard work stripped of all the gay trappings that formerly used to conceal its worst horrors and of all its pseudo-heroics.'[158] Thus the trench warfare on the Western Front gave birth to some of the characteristics and attitudes of the German army that would emerge some two decades later, and altered forever many of the long-established prejudices of the previous half century, despite the considerable efforts of many traditionalists and reactionaries within the high command to maintain intact the ethos and integrity of the officer corps of former times.

As the months passed, the German army which had taken the field in 1914 had evolved into a very formidable modern fighting machine. By 1917 the four-regiment divisional organization had been reduced to three, and battalion strengths were also reduced in order to create new divisions. A host of specialist combat and support units had been formed to deal with particular aspects of this new warfare, and the size and capability of the artillery had increased significantly. Machine-gun units had also proliferated, including those designed for mountain warfare operations, for anti-aircraft defence, for operating with cavalry and cyclist units, and as light machine-gun sections and automatic rifle (Musketen) battalions, these last being deployed in depth as a reserve, with the specific mission of countering an enemy breakthrough. Surprisingly, perhaps, the army high command failed fully to appreciate the importance of the tank before its more general use by the British from late 1916, although their premature use in relatively ineffectual penny-packets much earlier that year may well have belied their real potential in the eyes of the German general staff. In any event, the German army first adopted the expedient of using suitably converted tanks captured from the Allies. Then in May 1917 a German-designed tank was first demonstrated, with production models later being manufactured and subsequently deployed with the field army.

Many changes were precipitated by the rapid advances in military technology as the army sought new weapons and tactical solutions with which it might break the deadlock on the Western Front, and many aspects of field engineering in particular had become a growth industry. In addition to their existing functions, the pioneers – now organized within the Corps of Engineers, the Fortress Construction Officers, and the Pioneer Corps – took on responsibility for flame throwers, trench mortars, mining, poison-gas apparatus, pontoon and other bridging, and operating searchlights. The responsibility for telegraph communications was taken on by a newly created Signal Corps from January 1917. At about the same time all ground transportation units – railway troops, the movements organization, and the mechanical transport units – came under the command of the Quartermaster-General's Department. The five airship battalions which had existed in 1914 were established as the Luftstreitkräfte (the Air Service) in 1916, as a separate branch of the army, while the static observation balloon units and aircraft support were deployed to army sectors as the operational situation required. Meanwhile, the use of Graf von Zeppelin's airships for the strategic bombing of London, together with the unrestricted use of U-boats, ushered in a whole new form of warfare whose impact was felt far beyond the armies in the field.

Despite the progress of mechanization, the army's continued reliance on horse-drawn field artillery and transport, and (although to a much lesser extent than in 1914) a mounted cavalry capability, meant that the veterinary services had expanded in size and importance throughout the war. The Veterinary Service Corps was commanded by a director-general of veterinary services, who had three general officers working directly for him, with one for each of the army's main operational theatres. Finally, the Medical Service Corps had also grown rapidly in size, expertise and complexity in response to the need to deal with the huge numbers of casualties sustained as the war progressed. A comprehensive organization of regimental aid posts, field ambulance units, motorized ambulance columns, ambulance trains, and military hospitals within the operational theatres and in Germany itself was supported by a chain of depots, stores units and a large part of the German home medical industry. Although the military doctors and surgeons were generally officers, they were supported by large numbers of enlisted-rank medical service troops (Sanitätsmannschaften), hospital orderlies and stretcher-bearers. The latter were categorized as non-combatants, and wore a Red Cross band on the upper left arm. The army at the beginning of 1918 was in many ways quite different from that which had gone to war in 1914.

Of course all these changes were initially triggered by the evolving war and by the responses directed by the high command and the general staff, and from 29 August 1916 this meant in practice by von Hindenburg and von Ludendorff. With the failure of von Falkenhayn's offensive at Verdun and his subsequent dismissal,[159] the strategy of attrition and annihilation applied in 1915 and into 1916 was at last seen to be inappropriate, and Germany looked to the new chief of staff and quartermaster-general to deliver the decisive victory it so urgently needed. Mindful of the increasing social and industrial unrest and of the weakening support for the war, the control of raw materials, production, financial policy and institutions, industrial labour, and even matters of foreign policy were progressively subjugated to military control with the overriding aim of supporting the war effort. On 13 July 1917 the Chancellor, Theobald von Bethmann Hollweg, was forced to resign when von Hindenburg and von Ludendorff telephoned their resignations to Berlin, stating that they could no longer work with him. Of course both men knew that the Kaiser neither would nor could accept their resignations, and this was no more than a ploy to remove a Chancellor who was prepared to consider not only a negotiated end to the war but also to advocate the implementation of democratic reforms within Germany, both of which positions were anathema to Germany's two premier warlords.

So, as the Kaiser's popularity, power and status waned, and the authority of the civilian government diminished even further, the army and the whole state of Germany both came ever more under the direct control of von Hindenburg and von Ludendorff. Both had entirely discarded any thoughts of a negotiated end to the war, and so Germany was now committed to a return to the indefinite war of attrition. As a consequence of this, on 1 February 1917, the high command authorized (against government ministerial advice) a new campaign of unrestricted submarine warfare, which was designed to break the naval blockade of Germany and also to prevent food and other resources reaching Britain. This momentous and arguably ill-judged decision quickly brought the United States into the war alongside Britain, France and their allies on 6 April, 1917. Although the American military commander, General John J. Pershing, did not arrive in France until 14 June, the commander of the US naval forces in European waters, Rear Admiral W. S. Sims, reached Britain on 9 April, thereby indicating quite clearly the strategic priority that the United States attached to countering the submarine threat.

For the army, the war of attrition meant that it had to be able to hold ground, regain ground, and also maintain its offensive spirit and flexibility. In December 1916, the high command published a much-revised operational doctrine in *The Principles of Command in the Defensive Battle in Positional Warfare*. This publication was aimed primarily at the Western Front, and divided the battle area into an outpost zone, a battle or fighting zone (within which it was planned that the main line would be held or regained), and a rear or depth zone. Implicit in this network of inter-linked fortifications and trenches were the creation of defensive deployments in considerable depth, the ability of fast-moving reserves and counter-attack forces to deal speedily with an enemy attack, and for the battle zone to be incapable of direct observation by enemy artillery spotters. By emphasizing the aggressive form of this defence, the army sought to mitigate the potentially negative and debilitating effects of trench warfare upon the soldiers who inhabited this subterranean existence for weeks and months on end. This proactive approach to the situation of unsought but unavoidable defence which had existed ever since the end of 1914 was exemplified by the development of specialist assault units such as the Stosstruppen.

But if the situation in the west had reached a virtual stalemate, elsewhere the war was progressing more satisfactorily for the Germans, and von Ludendorff was all too aware that only a major victory on the eastern front could release the divisions that were so essential to achieving a similar result in the west. In December 1916 an army comprised of

German, Austrian and Bulgarian troops defeated a Romanian force and occupied Romania. This further weakened the position of an already destabilized and war-weary Russia, and in February 1917 the first move in the impending revolution was evidenced by the fall of the Tsar's government and its replacement by a much more liberal body, albeit one that still favoured the Allies and which was still committed to continuing the war. But by now the Bolsheviks were also gaining in strength and influence. The Germans saw that Russia was on the verge of chaos, and that now was the moment to prompt its final capitulation. Accordingly, a safe conduct was provided to enable Lenin and his followers to move from exile across German-held territory and on to Russian soil in April 1917, with a view to their establishing a new regime in Russia – one that would agree to conclude an armistice with Germany.

Somewhat bizarrely, von Hindenburg and von Ludendorff were both wholeheartedly in favour of this arrangement, despite the innate fear of civil unrest and revolution that was ever-present within the German officer corps. Perhaps the wider international implications of the ascendancy of Bolshevism were under-estimated in Germany, although it was more the case that by 1917 the high command had become so mesmerized by the need to break the stalemate on the Western Front that almost anything which might achieve that end was acceptable. Certainly the support accorded to Lenin by Berlin was just as much a military-led decision as that which had been taken on unrestricted submarine warfare just a few months earlier, with both of these decisions ultimately having far-reaching and thoroughly undesirable strategic consequences both for Germany and for its army.

Having successfully fomented their revolution during the months following Lenin's return, in November 1917 the Bolsheviks finally usurped the Kerensky government in Moscow. The already shaky Russian army began to implode, an armistice was asked for, and on 22 December the Brest-Litovsk conference convened to discuss terms. The German terms were relatively severe, but after much discussion an agreement was finally achieved in March 1918, largely prompted by a resumption of the German offensive in the east in mid-February. However, the armistice and neutralization of the Russian military threat had already permitted the transfer of a number of German divisions to the Western Front by early 1918, although about twenty divisions remained in western Russia as occupation forces and with a view to the later expansion of German territory eastwards and into the Caucasus – aspirations that would be resurrected once again some two decades later.

At the beginning of 1918, von Hindenburg and von Ludendorff might well have looked forward to the new year with a fair degree of satisfaction and some well-founded confidence. Russia and Romania were effectively out of the war, Italy was much-weakened following its defeat at Caporetto in October 1917, two major Franco-British offensives had failed in 1917 and (although undoubtedly of some short-term concern) the use *en masse* of 378 tanks by the British at Cambrai on 20 November 1917 had certainly not been as decisive as many Allied military pundits claimed both then and later.[160] Also, the Allies had been weakened in the west by the diversion of forces elsewhere, not only to shore up Italy and to reinforce the continuing campaigns in various far-flung colonial territories, but also to pursue a forlorn-hope campaign in Russia. In the meantime, the German army had been able to reinforce the Western Front; it had more or less perfected and adopted its doctrine for the offensive defence, and it had complemented the December 1916 general staff publication *The Principles of Command in the Defensive Battle in Positional Warfare* with *The Attack in Positional Warfare* in 1918. In parallel, the German state and its industrial capability had by now been mobilized in their entirety to support the military campaign.

With a general staff assessment that the slow build-up of American troops on the Western Front meant that they could not pose a significant threat before mid-1918 at the earliest (only one US division was in France in December 1917, but the general staff estimated that as many as eighteen could be in France by midsummer 1918), the German high command set the spring of 1918 as the time at which they would launch a great new offensive designed finally to break the Franco-British front in the west. There, the French army was already experiencing mutinies[161] and the British capability had been much reduced by the huge losses they had sustained at Ypres between July and November 1917. In early 1918 many French divisions numbered no more than 6,000 men, and the French high command was unable to replace more than about one-third of their monthly losses, whereas the German high command estimated that by March that year its own army on the Western Front could generate as many as 200,000 more men than the total strength of the Franco-British forces deployed on that front. The Allies would be forced to sue for peace before the United States had the opportunity to become actively engaged on the Western Front, and elsewhere Germany's territorial ambitions in the east and overseas could be consolidated with impunity. Thus the concept of the Ludendorff spring offensive was born, then developed and planned by the general staff during the closing months of 1917 and the first three months of the following year.

✠✠✠✠✠✠✠✠✠✠✠✠✠

The first devastating blow would fall upon the southern part of the British line and strike towards Amiens. Next, the focus would move to the British-held Ypres salient to the north. Subsequently, the German armies would launch a major attack against the French forces, striking towards Compiègne, Château-Thierry and Epernay and the Marne. The strategic objective of Ludendorff's great offensive was to force the Franco-British leaders to sue for peace by inflicting a decisive and irretrievable series of defeats upon their armies on the Western Front before they could be reinforced by American troops.

By mid-March 1918 almost two hundred German divisions stood ready to inflict that final crushing blow against the Allies on the Western Front – a blow that it was generally anticipated would at last enable Germany to achieve its historic destiny, and the German army to reap the ultimate victory which its soldiers had hardly doubted, even for a moment, that they so richly deserved.

17

The Warrior Betrayed

The Last Offensive and the Armistice, 1918

A T 0505 ON THE STILL DARK and cold morning of 21 March 1918, the preliminary phase of the main barrage began.[162] The opening action of the Kaiserschlacht – the imperial battle – (known to the British as the Second Battle of the Somme) involved more than 4,000 field guns, 2,600 heavy artillery guns and 3,500 trench mortars, the bombardment planned to last for five hours. The German soldiers of the assault battalions crammed into the forward trench lines 'gasped at the colossal wall of flame over the English lines'[163] as thousands of high-explosive and poisonous-gas shells fell on to the British positions along the Somme. An anonymous German soldier described the noise and destruction as 'like the end of the world'. The bombardment gained in intensity, and at 0825 the heavy mortars – firing 2cwt bombs – joined in. Even in the German lines the noise was indescribable. The thousands of machine-guns that had by then added their storm of fire to the boiling sea of flames, explosions and smoke which were all that could be seen of the British lines were hardly noticeable. The extensive use of poisonous gas closely integrated with high-explosives was vital to the success of the barrage plan.[164]

Earlier, the troops had been moving forward to their assault positions ever since the evening of 17 March. Every aspect of the offensive had been analyzed and planned in minute detail by the general staff. The assault units had moved under cover of darkness, their march times precisely timed and laid down by the general staff, although some of them had been unable to avoid the attentions of the enemy artillery as they were guided into the various lines of trenches from which they would be launched on the great offensive that would win the war. The roads and tracks to the front had been a solid mass of men, artillery, horse-drawn transport and other vehicles for many days (or more accurately nights) prior to the offensive. Despite this impressive array of combat power, and although there were no fewer than 192 German divisions on the Western Front by March 1918, only fifty-six had fully achieved the levels of assault capability envisaged by the general staff in their key publication on *The Attack in Positional Warfare*.

At 0910, specially selected patrols scrambled over the edge of the trenches and crawled into positions in no man's land, ready to overwhelm any surviving resistance in the British forward trenches within minutes of the bombardment lifting. The noise was still mind-numbing, as pulses of air pressure and shock waves continued to batter the assault troops. 0937, time for a final drink, a last pull on a pipe or cigar, then, as a thousand watches showed 0940, the great mass of infantry surged forward to annihilate their enemy.

The British wire had virtually ceased to exist; their front line of trenches had been so pulverized that it had virtually disappeared. Nevertheless, from positions in the British second line a steady rate of machine-gun and rifle fire took its toll of the attackers. In the sector where Ernst Jünger's company of the 73rd Hanover Infantry were in the van, doggedly held British positions dug into the sides of the substantial railway embankment between Ecoust and Croisilles, maintained a brisk and accurate fire against the field-grey waves. Eventually, however, the German infantry managed to gain the side of the embankment and grenaded the defenders out of their strongpoints. Simultaneously, troops using the tactics of the Stosstruppen worked their way systematically along the British trench lines, killing and destroying all in their path. While fleeing from their former positions at the embankment, large numbers of British 'Tommies' were downed by the rifle fire of the German soldiers who had now fought their way on to its top. Despite the efficacy of the opening bombardment, the surprise which had undoubtedly been achieved, the debilitating effects of the poison gas, and the flight *en masse* of the soldiers from the forward positions, here and there isolated British machine-gun posts still took a steady toll of the attackers, as did the counter-fire of the British artillery. But although the German casualties mounted, the advance continued and the breakthrough was achieved.

As the morning drew on, Jünger estimated that his men were at least two to three miles into the British lines, with other German units moving forward each side of his own, and 'as far as the eye could see' behind them there were the follow-on units 'advancing in open order, ranks and columns'.[165] The attackers were unstoppable as they advanced into open countryside and to the rising ground beyond the Somme. At this point the attack faltered as the infantry outran their artillery support and began to sustain casualties from their own guns firing at maximum range. The first day of the great offensive drew to its close, as the assault units secured their new-won positions for the night. In the first twenty-four hours the Germans had won some 140 square miles of territory, at the cost of about 39,000 casualties.

But here the German soldiers – now with a little time to take stock of the positions they occupied – found things that were at the same time both morale-boosting and demoralizing. Men who for too long had had to make do with very bland, monotonous and often meagre rations based primarily on 'bread, watery soup and thin nondescript jam' found in the hastily vacated British dugouts a veritable Aladdin's cave of luxuries such as pipe tobacco, cigarettes, whisky, new clothing, 'a whole crate of eggs' and 'stacks of canned meat, tins of delicious English jam, and bottles of Camp Coffee, tomatoes and onions'.[166] Welcome though these finds were, they were also indicative of the failure of the German navy's strategy of starving Britain through submarine warfare, as well as of the significantly better supply arrangements enjoyed by the Franco-British armies. The victorious attackers also found large quantities of brand-new equipment, guns and much ammunition. Desultory fighting continued throughout the night, increasing in tempo as dawn approached, when the German artillery resumed its bombardment, but once again dropping some rounds short upon its own forward troops and causing a most unwelcome flurry of casualties.

In the sector where the 73rd Hanover Infantry were attacking (by now they had been combined with the 76th, due to the considerable casualties both regiments had sustained during the first day), the second day of the offensive yielded less success, as its momentum slowed in the face of what had developed into a fairly well-managed British withdrawal. Much of the day was spent engaged in bitter fighting against a Scottish highland regiment. Then, just as night fell with a cool breeze indicating a cold night to come, a German assault team managed to outflank the highlanders and the attack resumed with a new vigour. As the highlanders sought to regain their next line of defence they found that they were balked by their own wire, and thus exposed they fell in droves before the hail of German machine-gun fire.

By the end of 22 March large parts of the British 5th Army (upon which the full weight of the Kaiserschlacht had fallen) were disintegrating and falling back to the old Somme battlefields and the Germans were through the lines which had earlier been occupied by the British reserve formations. On 24 March Bapaume fell as the Germans drove towards Amiens, the capture of which would effectively split the French and British forces. As their situation deteriorated with each passing hour, the British high command started looking towards the Channel ports, while the French looked to the security of Paris. However, at that stage Marshal Foch (actively supported by the British commander, Haig) assumed overall direction of the battle from the over-pessimistic Marshal Pétain, and Foch resolved both to halt the Allied withdrawal and stop the German advance east of Amiens.

Consequently, although the Germans did advance farther and despite their having broken through the forward defensive lines on a front forty miles wide, this considerable achievement was still not in sufficient depth to provide the strategic breakout necessary to split the Franco-British armies. So it was that von Ludendorff's great offensive continued ever more slowly, and by 28 March it had all but ground to a halt in the vicinity of Albert. There the uncontrolled looting of British food and equipment depots by large numbers of undisciplined and often drunken German soldiers reached unprecedented depths. In the meantime, numbers of British reinforcements were now arriving from England, and a new French army some six divisions strong was moving to support the British and close any gap between the Franco-British armies. By 4 April many of the attacking German divisions were exhausted, large numbers of the irreplaceable Stosstruppen were dead, and von Ludendorff's great offensive had finally run its course.

So it was that the significant casualties sustained, the inability of the artillery to move fast enough to support the advancing infantry, a lack of mechanical transport to support the logistics chain, and an underestimation of the French ability and determination to aid the British upon whom the full weight of the first assault had fallen, all combined to thwart the German plans. Indeed, had none of these factors militated against von Ludendorff, the relatively small number of divisions that had been trained and readied for assault missions by early 1918 meant that the army's ability to exploit its success was in any case relatively limited. Next, the large quantities of food and other items that had long since become unavailable in Germany, but which were now found in abundance in the captured British military depots gave rise to widespread looting, and even resulted in a breakdown of the German army's legendary discipline in a number of units. Despite the carefully laid plans of the general staff, various aspects of the army's logistics and supply system were on the verge of collapse by early 1918. Similarly, the supply of many goods and services in Germany itself was also in dire straits.[167]

Finally, strategic success had always depended upon bringing about an early and total collapse of the Franco-British armies in the face of the offensive of 21 March. Had von Ludendorff concentrated the army on a narrower front, and then single-mindedly maintained that concentrated offensive action rather than becoming distracted by successes elsewhere and subsequently dissipating its strength, it might yet have broken the Franco-British alliance within the first few days – much in the manner foreseen by von Schlieffen in his original plan. However, when this first great offensive in the end produced little more than a fairly well-managed British withdrawal followed by effective Franco-British counter-action, von Hindenburg and von Ludendorff had irretrievably lost their army's greatest gamble since August 1914, and Germany had lost the war.

Despite the failure of the Kaiserschlacht, the army launched four more such ventures against the British and against the French between April and July 1918. But the forces available for these ventures decreased in scale with each successive offensive, as their reserves were all but exhausted. Nevertheless, the army continued to inflict significant casualties upon the Franco-British armies, who were by now receiving support from the US troops who had recently, if somewhat belatedly, arrived on the Western Front.[168] Although the force-level pendulum was swinging inexorably against the Germans, the conflict continued, with the German forces still winning numerous local engagements and also seizing substantial tracts of territory. But by mid-July the army had neither achieved its strategic objective nor was it able to take any further significant offensive action. The final offensive was launched in the area of Reims on 15 July, achieving very limited gains before it came to a halt, having resulted in large numbers of German casualties. Indeed, the army had suffered more than half a million casualties between March and mid-July, and the drastically reduced manpower and resources of many units had by then largely constrained them to doing little more than holding the territory or positions which they occupied. Nevertheless, for very many thousands of ordinary German officers and soldiers, the succession of lesser military successes between March and July together with the large numbers of Allied prisoners taken and territory gained – all of which was set against their continuing confidence in the ability of von Hindenburg to deliver the final victory to Germany – had certainly not prepared them for the devastating events that were about to befall them.

On 18 July a Franco-US offensive was launched towards Soissons. Then, on 8 August (the day on which it finally became plain that Germany could no longer forestall the inevitable), a British offensive on the Somme drove seven miles into the German lines along a front of fifteen miles. Here, the use of tanks *en masse* proved decisive. Large numbers of prisoners were taken, six German divisions simply fell apart in the face of the onslaught, and there were widespread reports of acts of indiscipline both at the front and in the rear areas.

Although the front stabilized once again, the army was now locked into a permanent situation of defence and gradual withdrawal, but still the German high command refused to acknowledge the situation, or the real

significance of the remorseless build-up of US forces in the west. For three
months von Ludendorff prevaricated, still hopeful of an outcome
favourable to Germany. Then, at the end of September, Germany's ally
Bulgaria capitulated, followed by Turkey and Austria at the end of
October. In Germany, industrial and political unrest were increasing
almost daily. Bolshevik elements were also attempting to foment revolution, following their success in Russia. At last the Kaiser, von Hindenburg
and von Ludendorff were forced to accept the reality of their country's
precarious situation.

In October the Kaiser directed the new Chancellor, Prince Max von
Baden, to negotiate an armistice with US President Woodrow Wilson, but
he indicated that he could not negotiate with Germany's military or
dynastic leadership. Thus the United States, despite being late-comers to
the conflict, determined the fate both of von Ludendorff and of the Kaiser.
Initially, frustrated by the President's response, von Ludendorff had determined to resume the active war, and issued a directive to the army to fight
on, but on 28 October he acknowledged the hopelessness of his position
and resigned, to be replaced by General Wilhelm Groener.[169] On 8
November Groener informed the Kaiser – who had by then sought refuge
at the headquarters of the army high command – that the army no longer
had any confidence in his leadership. Mutinies had broken out in the navy
at Kiel, Hamburg and Bremen, a revolution was in progress in Munich
and a Soviet republic had been proclaimed in Bavaria. On 9 November the
Kaiser's abdication was announced by the Chancellor, who also resigned.
The latter was succeeded by the socialist Chancellor, Friedrich Ebert. Von
Hindenburg was appointed supreme commander of the German forces
and Groener became, in effect, chief of the general staff. All over
Germany, the old order was disintegrating as the hard-won legacy of 1871
was being progressively, but haphazardly, dismantled.

For the army (and for the high command in particular) the overriding priorities were to maintain the honour of the officer corps,
together with the integrity of the army and its ability to maintain law
and order in a country threatened internally by the spread of Bolshevism. Already, various soldiers' and workers' councils modelled on the
Russian soviets were emerging to direct local government affairs and to
usurp the traditional chain of command of the army. The army also
needed to preserve its ability to defend Germany against the threats
(notably that from Poland) which were now perceived to exist on its
eastern frontiers. Accordingly, what would later prove to be an historic
policy decision was taken. Henceforth, the army would be portrayed

positively as a force that remained undefeated on the battlefield, an army that, in Groener's own words, had been betrayed by 'the poison [which] comes from home'. Thus the German military and its officers would be preserved and protected against all blame and criticism by the myth that its failure to win the war was directly and entirely attributable to the failure and mismanagement of the conflict by the German civil government. This was a perception which had already been considerably reinforced by the abdication of the last of the German Kaisers on 9 November and by the elevation of von Hindenburg and Groener to become the supreme power and authority in the land. The same day, a German socialist republic was proclaimed, although this merely served to accelerate the in-fighting and power struggles between the main socialist and communist groups. Two days later, the armistice was declared on 11 November and the First World War ended. The German army was given just thirty-one days in which to remove its troops from France, Belgium, Luxembourg and the Rhineland.

As the political events and general turmoil in Germany moved ever faster, Ebert, as Chancellor of the new provisional government, was much relieved when Groener offered to arrange the orderly return of the army from the east and from the Western Front to Germany, together with its guaranteed support for the government thereafter. The *quid pro quo* for this arrangement was government support for the army and against the revolutionary left, notably the Bolsheviks. Ironically, Ebert had earlier acquiesced to socialist calls for the establishing of soldiers' committees with the power to elect commanders, together with proposals to form a people's militia to replace the old army. But with revolution sweeping the country, the army was the only force now capable of restoring law and order and of maintaining the new republican government in power.

Shortly after the armistice was declared more than three million German soldiers withdrew from their positions west of the Rhine and returned to the Fatherland. They did so in exemplary fashion. Nevertheless, virtually every officer and soldier who did so was still convinced that the army remained undefeated and had been cheated of its rightful victory by treachery at home and betrayal by a civilian government which had begun to negotiate the armistice while the soldiers were still embattled at the front. A further one million troops returned to Germany from the eastern front. Army high command, the Oberheeresleitung (OHL), moved back to Kassel, and though it tried hard to maintain its cohesion, once back in Germany the army virtually disintegrated. Consequently, by the end of 1918 the force that had marched to war so optimistically in August

1914, and which had then fought on with such determination during four years of war, no longer existed.[170]

These soldiers who had endured so much but who had finally gained so little simply deserted in their many tens of thousands and went home. The vast majority – soldiers and officers alike – felt immensely frustrated, ill-used and bitterly angry that their Herculean efforts and sacrifices had apparently all been for naught. An uncertain future lay ahead of them and their country in late 1918 and (with their bitterness being actively promoted and fuelled by the high command and some senior members of the republican government) these much aggrieved former fighting men now considered themselves to be the very epitome of warriors betrayed. This was an emotive image that resonated all too easily with the German warrior culture and the myths and legends of the ancient folklore of the Rhine legends, of their Heimat and the Fatherland. And, as had been so violently demonstrated by those warriors of old, the warrior betrayed is potentially a volatile, suggestible and dangerous man, for such a betrayal can all too easily beget the desire for revenge and retribution.

18

The Road to Perdition
1919–1935

THE STORY OF THE ARMY in the fateful years from 1919 to 1935 was one of almost constant change occasioned by Germany's political turmoil in the post-1918 period, with so much of that which transpired during those turbulent years being precipitated by the terms of the post-war peace treaty, which were announced to the German delegation at Versailles on 7 May 1919. The punitive and in many ways humiliating requirements exacted by the Allied powers in 1919 became known at a moment when the shaky government of the German republic was managing to return a measure of control to the country through its ruthless suppression of the various revolutionary movements (but primarily the communists) by the semi-mercenary units of the blatantly right-wing 'Freikorps'. Indeed, from 6 February 1919 the government had been based in the small Thuringian town of Weimar, as the security situation in Berlin was judged too volatile for the government to remain there.

Strictly speaking, the Freikorps could not by definition be construed as the German army, and as such they do not merit detailed consideration in the story of that army. But for some years these paramilitary units were the only military forces authorized or tolerated by a government that otherwise lacked the means to maintain order and counter revolution. Also, it is incontrovertible that the Freikorps membership was in large measure made up of the disillusioned and angry officers and soldiers – the warriors betrayed – who had marched home from the east and west in November 1918 only to find the Fatherland for which they had fought riven by revolution and political turmoil, with rampant inflation, unemployment and economic decay contrasting starkly with the fortunes that had been accrued by the war profiteers. Meanwhile, the fighting force in which they had so recently found comradeship, patriotism and military success was now discarded, and dissipating with every day that passed. Accordingly, the Freikorps cannot be entirely excluded from the story of the German army, because its units not only played an historic part in shaping post-1918 Germany, they also provided a bridge between the armies of the Kaisers and the development of the new Reichswehr (or, in the case of the army specifically, the 'Reichsheer', although the more general term 'Reichswehr' has been used throughout for clarity) in the period leading up to the Second World War. While much of the complex politics of the time is beyond the scope of this work, the political violence that spawned the Freikorps and thus established or maintained the right-wing character of the German army is fundamental to understanding the nature of the army that would emerge by 1939, and to comprehending what would otherwise be incomprehensible – the rise of National Socialism and the iron control it would exert over that army from August 1934 with the institution of the oath of allegiance to the Führer.

Despite the orderly return of the army in November 1918, its subsequent disintegration meant that it was unable to carry out the internal security role that Groener and Ebert had foreseen. Throughout Germany various levels of revolutionary activity were seen, as left confronted right and radicals confronted moderates. In Berlin a so-called 'Council of People's Delegates', one of whom was Ebert, had speedily filled the void left by the old imperial government and this was the forerunner of the republican administration that would follow. But in late 1918 this body was far from democratic, its decisions being shaped primarily by the ever-present mobs of armed revolutionary guards in the streets. On 9 November 1918, just as the Kaiser was leaving for exile in the Netherlands and a new German republic was being proclaimed by Philipp Scheidemann at the Reichstag, the communist Karl Liebknecht of the Spartacus League was proclaiming a 'free socialist republic' from the balcony of his headquarters in Berlin's former imperial palace. Among Liebknecht's many supporters were large numbers of armed sailors, following the widespread mutinies in the German fleet at Kiel and other north German ports. Public order continued to break down and an attempt made by the army on Christmas Eve to clear the palace of the Spartacists was singularly unsuccessful, underlining the ever-increasing unreliability of such military forces. Clearly a new force was urgently required to act either in place of or alongside the army if the republic were to be saved and government authority restored.

Accordingly, the government authorized the general staff to raise new units (or 'Freikorps') specifically for the purpose of suppressing revolution and disorder at home and to defend the frontiers in the east in Silesia and along the Baltic littoral. These Freikorps were funded by the war ministry and many were based upon the now fragmented former regiments of the old army, often comprising all-arms groups of infantry, cavalry, artillery, and mine-thrower troops. Many Freikorps units were led by young captains, lieutenants and NCOs, and although their ranks were predominantly filled by former soldiers, they also included students, political activists and adventurers. Although remembered primarily for their suppression of left-wing organizations in Germany, the Freikorps also engaged successfully in full-scale military operations against Soviet forces in the Baltic area. Without exception, the Freikorps members held what were often very extreme right-wing views and had a fervent desire both to crush all leftist revolutions and to forestall any Polish encroachment – and by implication, Soviet influence – into Silesia and eastern Germany. Despite their nominal employment by the government and the operational direction of their units by the army high command, virtually every member of the Freikorps held a deep distrust of senior military officers and a 'fanatical hatred of the provisional government'.[171] The legacy of the betrayal of 1918 and the army's 'stab in the back' ran deep, and would continue to do so. In a number of cases, Freikorps units were established by individual military officers who then recruited their former comrades-in-arms into the unit, the latter owing their primary allegiance to the commander and comrades with whom they had shared the bonding experience of war rather than to a remote high command and a mistrusted government.

Although it had already engaged with the communists and other groups on a small scale at the end of 1918, by early 1919 the Freikorps was ready to take concerted action. In January it moved against Liebknecht's Spartacists in Berlin, just as the revolutionaries called for a mass demonstration and a general strike. There, the Freikorps action exemplified its operations throughout Germany, where field guns, machine-guns, flame-throwers and mortars were all employed by the Freikorps and by the troops operating alongside them. A week of bitterly contested street-fighting ensued. During this period Liebknecht and his associate Rosa Luxemburg were captured by the Freikorps on 15 January and taken for interrogation to the headquarters of the Guards Cavalry Division, then at the Eden Hotel on the Kurfürstendamm. There, a Hauptmann Waldemar Pabst directed that both were to be taken to the Moabit prison, but that they were to be shot *en route* 'while attempting to escape'. Liebknecht and Luxemburg were duly killed as ordered, and in later times they would be acknowledged as the first martyrs and heroes of the German communist party. The Freikorps captured almost 400 Spartacists in Berlin; then, during the course of further operations to annihilate the communist revolution in the city, as many as 1,200 Spartacists were killed by the Freikorps troopers by about mid-March.

Elsewhere, the Freikorps struck against the revolutionary forces in Bremen, Halle and the towns of Westphalia in February, in Brunswick and

✠✠✠✠✠✠✠✠✠✠✠✠✠

Magdeburg during April, and then (with some additional army assistance) against Munich and the so-called 'Soviet Republic of Bavaria'. On 6 and 7 April a force of Prussian, Bavarian and other south German Freikorps and other military units some 30,000 strong dispersed a force of between 50,000 and 60,000 revolutionary 'Red Guards', which had assembled to the north-west of the city at Dachau. Finally, the flames of revolution were extinguished in Saxony in early May.

Order had been restored, but the methods employed had almost invariably involved extreme violence and summary executions, and had laid a firm foundation of right-wing authority based primarily upon the military force of arms rather than the democratic process. Despite this, the Freikorps had already achieved considerable legitimacy on 6 March when the Weimar government accorded it the status of a 'provisional Reichswehr'. The organization's terms of service involved a period of voluntary military service for six or nine years, a provision for enlisted ranks to be commissioned on merit, the election of 'soldiers' councils', a much revised training regime, and the right of all soldiers to vote. In parallel, the army high command (which had moved from Kassel to the Pomeranian town of Kolberg in February, the better to direct operations on the eastern frontier with Poland) was already developing its plans for a reconstituted Reichswehr that would defend the new republic in the years ahead. This work was led by Groener and was taken forward rapidly by a small group of general staff officers early in 1919. These included Schleicher, Hammerstein, Willisen, Bock and Wetzell. They planned for the Freikorps to be transformed into a new German army with a peacetime strength of 300,000, to be in place by 1920.

Then, with Germany just beginning to emerge from the post-war nightmare of socialist revolution and the possibility of its becoming a communist state, the Allied powers at Versailles promulgated the draft conditions to be imposed upon Germany by the impending peace treaty. The terms were announced to the German delegation at Versailles on 7 May 1919. In retrospect it can be seen that some of the terms set were undoubtedly excessive and ill-advised. It is hardly surprising, therefore, that for the Germans in 1919 the Treaty of Versailles was anathema. Its terms were unacceptably punitive, unreasonable, humiliating, intolerable and dishonourable – even requiring Germany to admit its 'war guilt' and to submit its military leaders to trial for war crimes. For the officers and soldiers of the Freikorps and the regular army especially, the betrayals of 1918 were compounded by the treaty. The treaty effectively sought to emasculate an army (as well as disbanding the air force and neutralizing the navy) which was only just beginning to regain some of the power and status that it had enjoyed in former times and would, if fully implemented, leave Germany defenceless. Included in those parts of the treaty which dealt specifically with Germany's armed forces were the following requirements:

● The army was to comprise no more than 100,000 long-term volunteers, including no more than 4,000 officers. This army would be organized into two army groups (one based at Berlin, the other at Kassel) with a total of seven infantry divisions (twenty-one regiments) and three cavalry divisions (eighteen regiments) and an operational role that was to be limited to home defence and border security.

● The general staff was to be abolished. A 'military office' or Truppenamt was to be established to oversee day-to-day administrative matters (although this soon evolved into an organization that was in practice the general staff in all but name).

● All forms of planning and preparation for mobilization were forbidden.

● All military schools (apart from one arms school maintained for each arm), the Kriegsakademie, and all the officer training academies were to be abolished.

● The army was to be allowed no heavy weapons, or weapons that gave it an offensive capability. These included tanks, heavy artillery of all calibres, and combat aircraft. The navy was to be reduced to a coastal defence force.

● Henceforth, the principal or strongest arm was to be the cavalry (the arm that had, after 1914, been shown to be the least relevant and least effective in a modern war).

● The authorized scales of all small-arms (rifles, pistols, light machine-guns) were to be set at the bare minimum essential to provide a viable military capability.

The wider geo-strategic provisions of Versailles were no less Draconian. Here, the treaty denied Germany its secure borders, removed its colonial possessions, and permitted the detested Poles to acquire large areas of territory at Germany's expense.

● Germany was to lose all its overseas colonies, together with Alsace-Lorraine and certain other frontier territory to Belgium and France.

● The State of Poland (always a most emotive subject for Germans) was to gain large tracts of German territory in the east, including Danzig, now categorized as a Freistadt or 'free city'.

● A plebiscite would determine whether Silesia should in future be under German or Polish sovereignty.

● France was to assume responsibility for the 'protection' of the Saar coal-mining region for at least fifteen years, in compensation for the destruction of the French coal-mining industry.

● The Allied powers would occupy parts of the Rhineland for at least fifteen years as a guarantee of German compliance with the treaty requirements. To the east of the occupied zone, a demilitarized zone some thirty miles wide was to be established along its entire length.

● An Allied Control Commission was to be established to oversee German compliance with all the provisions of the Treaty of Versailles.

At a stroke, in their understandable but ill-judged desire to exact such telling retribution upon Germany, the Allied powers had created throughout the Fatherland a unifying sense of outrage in all sections of the population – military and non-military alike – that would later be successfully exploited to such devastating effect by Adolf Hitler and the National Socialist party's propagandists. Faced with no practicable alternatives, the government accepted the treaty and duly signed it on 28 June. True to his immutable principle of supporting the integrity of the army in all circumstances and of perpetuating the well-established myth of the 'stab in the back', von Hindenburg rejected the treaty entirely and had already resigned on 24 June, leaving Groener to become the military scapegoat for the emasculation of the German army. Indeed, when the terms drafted at Versailles were publicized they provoked calls by a number of generals for a military revolt, and for the establishment of a new German state in the east which would defy the Allied powers and the Poles alike. Meanwhile, on the eastern frontier the soldiers of several units demonstrated and called for a new war against Poland.

To his considerable credit given the mood of the time, Groener, ever the pragmatist, rejected all such suggestions and so maintained national stability while attracting to himself the censure of very many of his military colleagues.[172] Meanwhile, Ebert and the Weimar government shouldered the even greater share of political blame for accepting and signing the Treaty of Versailles. By so doing they further weakened their ability to govern, and the tenuous control they had over the military forces of what had by now become the 'Weimar Republic'. Faced with the inevitability of having to downsize the army, Groener proposed to the government's representative at the army high command, Gustav Noske, that a 'Preparatory Commission for a Peace Army' be established, headed by Major

General Hans von Seeckt. The commission met for the first time on 5 July 1919 and quickly set about the formidable task of developing the new German army within the constraints imposed at Versailles.

For the army the next two decades were dominated by three inter-related activities or events. First, there was the so-called 'Kapp-Lüttwitz putsch' in March 1920. This attempted military coup was born directly out of the dissent over the terms of the treaty, and, despite its failure in Berlin, the putsch had significant implications for the longer-term future of the army. In the meantime, the success of the putsch in Bavaria had enormous political importance for Germany as a whole. Next came von Seeckt's re-organization and development of the Reichswehr. Groener and his planning group had originally been the principal architects of this activity, but post-Versailles it fell to von Seeckt to create the new army in spite of the severe external constraints that had been placed upon it. Finally, there was the rise to political power of the 'Nationalsozialistische Deutsche Arbeiter-partei' (NSDAP) – the Nazis – and the way in which they finally gained total control of the Reichswehr. Together, these matters contributed directly to the creation and nature of the German army that would once again take the field in 1939.

Of itself, the Kapp putsch achieved little, and it certainly failed in its main aim of overthrowing the government. It was launched by a right-wing extremist group founded in July 1919 by von Ludendorff and Wolf-gang Kapp, the latter a rural official from East Prussia and a founding member of the Vaterlandspartei – literally, in this context, the 'patriotic party'. The group became the Nationale Vereinigung (National Association) in October 1919 and this organization of officers, politicians and other right-wing activists was their power-base. It actively promoted the 'stab in the back' propaganda line and the denial of Germany's guilt, while laying the blame for Germany's defeat directly upon the left, the revolutionary movements, and the Weimar government. In doing so it was acting entirely in accord with von Hindenburg's pronouncements on the German defeat of 1918.

Among the more prominent members of the group was General von Lüttwitz, the commander of all troops east of the Elbe and in Saxony, Thuringia and Hanover. In the autumn of 1919, the first reductions of the regular army in accordance with Versailles were announced. Subsequently, on 6 March 1920 the government ordered the reduction of the Reichswehr to 200,000 men by 15 May. Included in this was the disbandment of the Erhardt Marine Brigade, then quartered at Döberitz near Berlin. At the same time, fearing a military coup, on 10 and 11 March the government issued orders for Lieutenant Commander Erhardt, commander of the Marine Brigade, and General von Lüttwitz to be relieved of their posts. But before this could happen von Lüttwitz called on Ebert to halt all further disbandments, together with the resignation of the government and for new elections to the Reichstag. Not surprisingly Ebert refused, and dismissed von Lüttwitz from his post.

On the evening of 12 March the Erhardt Brigade marched on Berlin, and at seven o'clock the next morning von Lüttwitz led the brigade to occupy the government administrative district of Berlin. Elsewhere in Germany, including in Bavaria, other right-wing and Freikorps groups moved to support the putsch. The government decamped first to Dresden (where it found that the local army commander was sympathetic to the conspiracy!) and then on to Stuttgart. In Berlin, Kapp was proclaimed Chancellor. The head of the army, General Reinhardt, was replaced by General von Wrisberg, and other cabinet ministers were named. General von Seeckt, who was by now head of the Truppenamt, the thinly veiled and innocuous name for what was in reality the general staff, 'went on leave'. During the previous night, when the defence minister Gustav Noske had contemplated military action to forestall the coup, von Seeckt had demurred with the observation that 'There can surely be no idea of letting Reichswehr fight against Reichswehr. Do you, Minister of War, intend to let troops meet each other in battle about the Brandenburger Tor who a year and a half ago were fighting shoulder to shoulder against the enemy?'[173]

Despite its initial success, the putsch collapsed within just three days. Although support for it had been widespread, it had been fragmented and lacked both depth and sustainability. The trades unions had reacted by calling a general strike, which was extensively supported by workers throughout Germany. The civil service had refused to carry out Kapp's orders and directives. A number of officers at the defence ministry (among them von Lüttwitz's son-in law) had refused to obey orders. At the same time (and most importantly) large numbers of the Reichswehr had refused to support the putsch conspirators, especially in western and southern Germany, other than in Bavaria. On 18 March von Lüttwitz, Kapp and most of the main conspirators fled to Sweden. Von Seeckt conveniently returned from leave and arranged for the orderly withdrawal of the Erhardt Brigade to its barracks at Döberitz, where it was disarmed and disbanded.

Remarkably, and to the disgust of the trades unions, striking workers and middle-class democrats alike, no punitive action was taken against those who had supported or taken part in the putsch. This triggered

outbreaks of violence in Saxony, Thuringia and the Ruhr, where workers'
self-defence units and the communist members of a 'Red Army' battled
ferociously with regular troops and the Freikorps for several weeks.
Although this new upsurge of revolutionary violence was ruthlessly
suppressed and the government was soon able to return to Berlin, it is
noteworthy that whereas the army had declined to deal with the right-wing
putsch, it had once again set about the suppression of the left-wing movements with considerable enthusiasm and efficiency, thus fulfilling the role
that Groener and Ebert had originally foreseen for it in their agreement of
November 1918. The events of 12 to 18 March, and the precedents set on
the night of 12 March, not only resulted in Noske's resignation (he was
replaced by Otto Gessler) but also saw von Seeckt elevated to head of the
army command (Chef der Heeresleitung) and chief of staff. The power
and independence that this position conferred upon him now enabled him
to take forward the building of the new army during the six years that he
held this appointment, to 1926.

The position of the army itself had been clarified by the outfall from the
putsch, as it had proved its ability both to support the government and to
restore order within the state, whilst also demonstrating that it would not
tolerate political direction that did not match its perceptions of duty,
honour and the army's core role. In other words, it would not entertain any
orders or instructions that were predominantly democratic or socialistic in
nature. While von Seeckt would insist that he had ensured the apolitical
nature of the new Reichswehr, its corporate nature was therefore at best
traditional and at worst blatantly right-wing. As such, it would eventually
find an accommodation with the NSDAP by no means unpalatable. In the
meantime, from 1920 the officer corps would once again regard themselves and the army as an élite, pivotal and (in their view) independent
power to influence the conduct of Germany's domestic affairs. On the
other hand, after the putsch the democratic and political left would thereafter view the Reichswehr with great misgivings and profound mistrust.

Finally, the more immediate effects of the abortive putsch had been
much greater in Bavaria, where the move to the right had been even more
noticeable. There, the local Reichswehr commanders had forced the resignation of the social democrat state government, and its replacement by a
hard-line right-wing government with the declared aim of making Bavaria
a 'focus of order' for the whole of Germany. Small wonder then that
Bavaria – the great cities of Munich and Nuremberg in particular – became
a veritable Mecca for German right-wing extremism, and that in due
course Bavaria became the ideological home or Heimat of the NSDAP.

Among the famous names of German military leaders and commanders of the twentieth century – von Hindenburg, von Ludendorff, and later Guderian, Rommel, von Manstein, Model, Peiper and many more – the name of Major General Hans von Seeckt is perhaps somewhat less familiar outside Germany other than to historians. There are two reasons for this. First, his particular contribution to the development of the German army was organizational rather than on the battlefield. Secondly, he died in 1936 and so was uninvolved in the events from 1939 that once again impelled Germany to prominence on the international stage. Nevertheless, by his actions during the time of the Weimar administration up to 1926, von Seeckt was the man who created the Reichswehr war machine and revived the offensive capability (the constraints of Versailles notwithstanding) that became the professional foundation and organizational core of the dramatically expanded Wehrmacht with which Germany went to war in 1939. Therefore, von Seeckt's contribution to the story of the German army was most significant, for ultimately it enabled Adolf Hitler to proceed with his attempt to realize his political ambitions by force of arms. Inevitably perhaps, given the focal role he played in the story of the German army prior to the 1930s, there were both detractors and supporters of his policies and achievements.

Hans von Seeckt was both a typical and an atypical Prussian officer. On the one hand he came from a traditional Prussian military family and enjoyed a distinguished military career at regimental level (with the Kaiser Alexander Guard Grenadier Regiment) and as a member of the Prussian general staff. Born in 1866, he was too young to see service in the wars of unification, but travelled widely in Europe and overseas, thereby broadening his military experience. As chief of staff of the 3rd Army Corps from 1913, he planned the successful German breakthrough at Soissons in January 1915, and subsequently served with considerable distinction in senior staff appointments during the German campaigns in Galicia and Serbia, and later in staff and advisory posts with the Austrian and Turkish armies. In the immediate post-war period he was military expert to the peace delegation, acting chief of the general staff, and then served as head of the 'Preparatory Commission for the Peace Army'. Undoubtedly he was a traditionalist and held many reactionary views, foremost among which was the role of the German army as a non-political but nation-shaping force and an institution that was absolutely vital to the existence and nature of the German state. In broad terms, his vision was for the republic to have a modern version of the imperial army that had (in his view and that of the majority of the officer corps) served Germany so well from 1870 to 1918.

However, unlike many of his more closely focused professional contemporaries, he appreciated art, humanity and many of the intangibles of life, and
was described by one commentator as 'A man of the world in the best sense
of the term, adroit, self-possessed, skilful in the handling of men and affairs,
with a great appreciation of the beautiful in every form, music, art, women,
nature – he himself in later years said that vanity, sense of beauty, and the
cavalier's instinct were the three outstanding traits in his character.'[174] A
man of few words, his inscrutability earned him the nickname of the
'Sphinx', while his reputation as an organizer, innovator and diplomat
enabled him to exert great influence upon the politicians and ministers with
whom he worked and whose environment he understood all too well. This
despite his personal dislike of politicians and of a republican political
system which forever threatened the stability and good order of the state
during the Weimar era. Such views led him to direct that 'political activity
of every kind will be energetically kept out of the army. Political strife within
the Reichswehr is incompatible with the spirit of comradeship and discipline and can only harm military training'.[175]

Indeed, the active depoliticizing of the army in the years following the
Kapp putsch and the traumas inflicted upon Germany by the left–right
influences which had blossomed immediately after the war (and which
continued to do so to varying degrees throughout the Weimar years) was
a major objective of his reforms. Participation in political meetings and
organizations was forbidden and even the constitutional right of the
soldiers to vote was suspended. But this deliberate decoupling of the army
from the political process and awareness meant that it was also distanced
from any real comprehension of the malign political influences that would
emerge in Germany a few years later, and this was arguably one of the
factors which moved the Reichswehr significantly farther along the road to
perdition on which it had already set out.

This then was the man faced with the daunting task of creating an effective post-1920 German army against a continuing background of political
unrest, while at the same time not contravening (or at least not being seen
to contravene) the potentially crippling terms of the Treaty of Versailles.
General von Seeckt's reforms can conveniently be categorized as conceptual, organizational and educational – the last of which included training
in all its many forms. Predictably, all these reforms overlapped, were inter-
dependent, and were implemented progressively over a number of years.

His overriding aim was to move the army into a state of political
neutrality and away from the peccadilloes which had flowed from the indi-
vidualism inherent in the Freikorps units and which was exhibited by

From Old Order to New Order

Above: From the turmoil of 1918, Versailles, Weimar, economic collapse and revolution (with incidents such as the communist Spartacist revolt of 1919, shown here being suppressed by the Freikorps or government troops), the Nazi movement eventually emerged to create what would prove to be a very different sort of Fatherland.

Right: Exemplifying and contrasting the 'Old Order' and the 'New Order' in Germany is the attendance of Hitler and von Hindenburg at an event at the Tannenberg memorial in 1933.

Right: Meanwhile, in the military forces of the 'New Order' this contrast is highlighted by a picture of Waffen-SS Panzer General Josef 'Sepp' Dietrich (left), a founder member of the Nazi Party and a close associate of Hitler, discussing operations in early 1944 with Field Marshal Gerd von Runstedt, who was the very epitome of the traditional Prussian officer.

Panzer Leaders of the Third Reich

Above: Among the Third Reich's many noteworthy panzer commanders were (left to right) Ewald von Kleist, Hasso von Manteuffel and Hermann Hoth. These men routinely commanded sizeable, and often complex, all-arms battle-groups and formations with considerable success.

Below: infantry and armour advance in Russia during autumn 1942. Had Germany's war resources and its highest-level strategic direction matched more closely the remarkable abilities of many of the army's operational commanders, the outcome of the Second World War might well have been somewhat different.

Above: The vast expanse of the Russian steppe allowed armoured operations to be conducted on a grand scale. Here panzergrenadiers and a PzKpfw III tank of the 'Grossdeutschland' Division launch an attack in southern Russia (probably in the Don River–Voronezh area) during the summer of 1942.

Below: Panzer commanders such as Erwin Rommel, Erich von Manstein and Heinz Guderian (shown left to right) also used the innovative tactics that emphasized and applied to particularly good effect the close co-operation between armour, infantry, artillery and (especially during the early years of the war) close air-support.

Fighting Men of the Third Reich

Above left: A Feldwebel (warrant officer) of Panzergrenadier Division 'Grossdeutschland', southern Ukraine, summer 1942. He carries a Schmeisser MP 40 submachine-gun, a regulation dispatch or map case, MP 40 magazine pouches, and a torch with colour-changeable lenses.

Above right: A young Waffen-SS trooper wearing an early version of the Waffen-SS spring or autumn-pattern camouflage jacket or smock. He carries a Kar 98K rifle. Note the distinctive SS runes on the collar of his grey field jacket (worn underneath), which has been folded out over the collarless top of the camouflage jacket.

Left: A group of motorized infantry advances on foot through a Belgian town in May 1940. The soldiers are wearing the regulation uniform with which the army went to war in 1939–40. Their weapons include MP 40s, Kar 98K rifles and bayonets, and hand-grenades.

Above: Panzergrenadiers of Waffen-SS Regiment 'Germania' pictured in France during May 1940. Their weapons and equipment include a Luger '08 pistol, the ubiquitous Mauser Kar 98K rifle, and a lightweight 'Dreifuss' tripod for use with the MG 34 in the air defence role. Note the SS runes helmet insignia and the Waffen-SS sleeve eagle – two of the special insignia items that distinguished the Waffen-SS uniform from that worn by the army.

Above right: A machine-gunner and an Unteroffizier move through a field of maize in the Caucasus, late summer 1942. Their weapons include an MG 34 and (just visible) an MP 40. The MG 34 was the most widely used German machine-gun of the war.

Right: An MG-42 machine-gunner of the 2nd Company, 1st Battalion, SS-Panzergrenadier Regiment No. 1 close to Poteau, some twenty kilometres from St-Vith in the Belgian Ardennes. The picture was taken on or shortly after 18 December 1944, just a few days after the start of operation 'Wacht am Rhein'. This photograph conveys what is in many ways an archetypal image of the German fighting man at that stage of the war.

Cold War Warriors: the German Democratic Republic of East Germany (GDR)

Above: Infantrymen of the Nationale Volksarmee (NVA) on manoeuvres in the late 1970s. The troops are equipped with AK 47 assault rifles and are wearing the NVA summer combat uniform.

Below: A contingent of the élite Felix Dzierzynski Regiment on parade at Karl-Marx-Allee, East Berlin, on 7 October 1989. Just over a month later the Berlin Wall was opened, the Cold War came to an end, and the now-irrelevant GDR and its NVA were consigned to history.

Cold War Warriors: the Federal Republic of West Germany (FRG)

Opposite page top: An HS-30 armoured personnel carrier of the Bundeswehr on manoeuvres in the 1960s. It is armed with a 20mm cannon. The panzergrenadiers carried in the back compartment dismount over the top, through the large hatches. The soldiers are armed with G3 Heckler & Koch 7.62mm assault rifles and a fully dismountable MG 42/59 7.62mm Rheinmetall machine-gun (developed from the old MG42).

Opposite page bottom: Some Bundeswehr army uniforms in 1987, showing (from left to right) a Gefreiter of mountain troops, an Unteroffizier of panzer troops, a Stabsunteroffizier of infantry troops and an artillery major in 'No. 1 Dress' or walking-out uniform. (illustration: Bundeswehr)

The Bundeswehr Today

Notwithstanding the end of the Cold War, flexibility, fire-power and mobility remain at the core of the Bundeswehr's force development and strategic doctrine. During the first decade of the twenty-first century an effective airmobile capability (top) has assumed ever greater importance as the Bundeswehr continues to develop an appropriate operational strategy for today's asymmetric security threats. Meanwhile, proven and progressively developed equipment such as the Marder armoured infantry fighting vehicle (centre) and the Gepard mobile air defence system (bottom), together with the Bundeswehr's fleet of Leopard tanks, and an impressive arsenal of self-propelled artillery, engineer and armoured reconnaissance assets, typify its pragmatic and historically proven approach to war-fighting, and to maintaining Germany's defences against the full spectrum of threats that the country might face today and in the future. (photos: Bundeswehr)

many of their often charismatic and colourful but politically dangerous commanders. The army was to remain firmly connected to the 'old army' and its traditions, so that a clear thread of historical continuity and heritage could be readily identified within the Reichswehr. To that end, companies, batteries and squadrons of the Reichswehr adopted the names and heritage of the former regiments of the Kaiser's army and were known as 'tradition carriers' or Traditionsträger. For the wider German public, these links were publicized and emphasized through a wide range of commercial publications, such as the very popular and well-produced cigarette-card collections and albums of the cigarette manufacturers Haus Neuerburg of Köln am Rhein.[176]

Similarly, the protests of many liberals notwithstanding, von Seeckt maintained the Feldgrau uniform and Stahlhelm of the war period, which had become synonymous with the image of German militarism both at home and abroad. Following its introduction on the Verdun battlefield in February 1916, the German 'coal-scuttle' steel helmet had supplanted the Pickelhaube as the single uniform item which most typified the German soldier, and as such its retention was a matter of considerable importance to the army's many veterans. This was demonstrated by the post-war creation of the Stahlhelm organization for army veterans, which then flourished during the 1920s and 1930s before its absorption into the NSDAP paramilitary SA and SS organizations during 1933 and 1934.

General von Seeckt's reforms also sought to strengthen the ties between the nation and the army by reviving the system of geographical linking and the Landesmannschaften concept. Necessarily, this linking was now based upon the territory and populated areas of the Weimar republic rather than the greater Germany of the pre-1914 period. From this process the separate identities of the Bavarian, Prussian, Saxon and Württemberg units that had perpetuated ever since 1871 (despite the existence of a German general staff and unified command arrangements) largely disappeared, so that the Reichswehr was at last presented as the first truly national German army. With the transfer of executive power to the Minister of War in 1923 the local military to civilian interface blurred still further when the seven district commanders (all of whom were general officers) were given control of economic and day-to-day affairs in their areas. These included matters such as the provision of foodstuffs, labour conditions, prices, currency regulations, relief for the unemployed and (as clear evidence of the continuing Prussian influence) the 'limitation of luxury'. From 1923, the human face (or perhaps the new form of 'state socialism') of the Reichswehr was actively promoted and widely publicized through military band concerts staged in aid of charities, and by its provision of gifts for the poor of the various military districts. In these ways the army exhibited many of the traits seen in the former Prussian army prior to the mid-nine-teenth century, and von Seeckt's hand in this was very evident.

In regard to organization, von Seeckt had two matters to consider. First, he was bound to create an army within the terms of the treaty – or to circumvent those terms by various means. Secondly, given that the constrained army organization would inevitably be much smaller than that which Germany needed, the Reichswehr had to be developed as the professional cadre of a considerably greater national force in embryo, rather than as a complete army. His overall objective was to provide a small, well-trained professional army that was capable of conducting high-tempo offensive operations and achieving decisive results in short order. But behind and in support of this army there would be a large militia force capable of conducting defensive and security operations. In order to create a viable offensive capability it would also be necessary to achieve an appropriate mobile capability and, with Versailles having banned offensive weaponry, tanks, combat aircraft and heavy artillery, this presented von Seeckt and his colleagues with a considerable challenge.[177]

As ever, at the heart of the process of developing the new army was the officer corps. Of the 16,000 officers serving in the provisional Reichswehr when the Versailles terms were announced, only 4,000 were now permitted to serve in the new Reichswehr. Consequently, only the best and most experienced officers were retained, many of them having already demonstrated their abilities on the staff and (in the case of numbers of the more junior and middle-grade officers) in combat during the war. To maintain the strength of the officer corps, no more than 200 new ensigns were required annually. Consequently, there was neither concern about lack of numbers nor about the quality of those who were selected to command the Reichswehr soldiers, who were now twelve-year volunteers rather than the three-year conscripts of former times. These ordinary NCOs and soldiers were very different from their predecessors, and of 96,000 men serving in the Reichswehr in 1930, 9 per cent had completed secondary education, 1 per cent had matriculated and 3 per cent had been Einjährigen. Their overall educational, intellectual and practical abilities reflected the fact that the Reichswehr required no more than 8,000 volunteers each year, and that they could be selected from a population of sixty million.

These men of the new Reichswehr enjoyed a much better lifestyle than had their predecessors, von Seeckt's reforms having resulted in an updated and improved pay structure, which included the banding of the private soldier's pay in three separate grades based on his experience and qualifications. In parallel came new or extensively refurbished barracks, which provided more space for the individual soldier, better recreational facilities and a much better living environment overall. A review and relaxation of army regulations resulted in the ending of the long-standing late-night curfew rules for senior soldiers, and significant changes were made to the military code of discipline. Henceforth, the onus not to offend was placed upon the individual soldier's sense of duty and honour and the threat of dismissal from the army, rather than the fear of any traditional punishment. Lastly, in contrast to the importance of religion in day-to-day military life in the old Imperial army and its Prussian predecessors, church parades were finally abolished in the Reichswehr. Despite this, and somewhat anachronistically perhaps, the old 'GOTT MIT UNS' embossed text perpetuated on the soldier's belt plate until 1945. Arguably, this gradually diminishing emphasis on the spiritual perspective (and therefore by implication upon the moral perspective) contributed to the desensitizing of the professional officers and soldiers of the new Reichswehr in their future approach to the business of war.

To be sure, with the army still viewed as a somewhat less than prestigious career by much of post-1918 German society, those men who did seek a commission were following a vocation of service and duty to the Fatherland, rather than hoping to gain any of the social advantages and kudos of the officer corps which had been characterized by the officer's extravagant and often profligate lifestyle in the old Imperial army. Indeed, the Reichswehr officer was now expected to live on his army pay, which was increased appropriately in the course of von Seeckt's reforms. Such attitudes entirely reflected the ethos of the new Reichswehr, in which the deliberate inter-personal barriers which had been so assiduously maintained between officers and soldiers in the Imperial army were now modified, an officer's duty of care now being cited as being just as important as his ability as a tactical leader. The memory of the unprecedented breakdowns in discipline witnessed during the Kaiserschlacht of 1918 still haunted the German high command, and had indicated the urgent need to bring the officer–soldier relationship fully into the modern military age. Implicit in this was the need to recruit a quite different type of officer into the new Reichswehr.

The intellectual and educational standards of the officer corps were reinforced by the mandatory pre-selection requirement for an applicant to have matriculated. This initial hurdle was followed by a further four years of training before the young ensign's commission could be confirmed. Failure at any stage could result in his subsequent rejection. More advanced military training courses followed, with regular rigorous testing and assessment at all stages. Even though the officer had by then been commissioned, any subsequent decline in his performance, or a judgement that he lacked the ability to progress further, could still result in the termination of his commissioned service. Such was the nature of a highly selective meritocracy in which every officer was required and trained to command or to operate at least one level above their actual rank and appointment, and frequently at two or even three levels above. This concept was characterized as the 'leadership-based army' or Führerheer concept.

One of the results of this might well have been a dramatic increase in the number of officers commissioned from the ranks, with so many ordinary soldiers having demonstrated their ability and courage during the war. But while the way to a commission was regularized and eased for the well-educated soldier, with success in three examinations being the principal qualification providing access to the selection system for all officers, the officer corps of the late-1920s still came overwhelmingly from the traditional military families and officer class. Indeed, Versailles provided a still very traditional and Prussian-influenced high command with the opportunity to discharge large numbers of officers who had risen from the ranks during the war, many of whom had served with competence and distinction. Consequently, whereas in 1913 only 25 per cent of regular officers came from military families and from the well-established Offizierskaste, in 1929 no fewer than 67 per cent did so.

An analysis of the social status of the fathers of the Reichswehr officers serving in 1930 showed that 95 per cent were or had been of sufficient social standing for their sons to have been eligible candidates for a commission based upon the pre-1914 criteria. The social status of the balance (small farmers, artisans, minor officials and other workers) would have debarred their sons from gaining a commission prior to 1914. Similarly, of 195 ensigns commissioned in 1929, 164 had entered through the normal officer-selection system, while only thirty-one had been commissioned from the ranks.[178] Thus, although change was undoubtedly the order of the day throughout the Reichswehr, certain long-established traditions still influenced a great deal of army policy. This was especially so where the officer corps and the selection of its officer candidates were concerned, and would continue to be so until the Nazis gained overall power in 1933.

In this way the key principles affecting the new Reichswehr were determined and developed, together with the new arrangements for personnel, their terms of service and their selection that were necessary to generate forces up to the levels permitted by Versailles. In order to carry out its role the Reichswehr also had to be properly equipped and trained, and in spite of the considerable obstacles posed by Versailles, both its equipment and its training were focused upon the need to achieve an effective mobile offensive capability.

The volunteer soldiers now available were of a very high intellectual and educational quality, which (together with the ordinary soldier's twelve-year engagement) permitted a speedy progression from basic to more advanced training. At unit level individual training had evolved over the years up to 1926, and was by then divided into six categories. These were based on ability and experience, with separate training programmes for recruits, for older soldiers of limited ability, for NCO candidates, and for leaders at squad, platoon and company level. In 1930 this system was formally adopted throughout the Reichswehr. In 1927 a three-year army training cycle had already been introduced. This required non-specialist combat units to concentrate in succession upon the rifle, the machine-gun, and other technologies (such as gas warfare, support weapons, communications) in successive years, while at the same time maintaining their normal core training activities. Although drill remained an important element of recruit training it was drastically reduced for trained soldiers, as was gymnastics; sport and extended periods of practical field training now filled the time instead.[179]

Since Versailles had forbidden any mobilization planning, von Seeckt gradually transformed the Prussian and German high command's long-standing preoccupation with immediate readiness into a new emphasis on raising the professional standards of the individual officer and soldier to unprecedented levels. To that end, the use of individual initiative was increasingly promoted in the best traditions of Auftragstaktik, but at much lower levels of command. Training for small-unit offensive operations was conducted extensively, unashamedly building on the successful experiences of the former Stosstruppen. At higher levels, in recognition of the fact that Germany would almost certainly be confronted by superior enemy numbers in a future war, the mobile defence, fighting withdrawal, concentration of forces, and the delivery of the decisive counter-stroke were all studied and regularly exercised. Von Seeckt and others had resolved that never again would the German army become embroiled in the kind of static warfare it had experienced on the Western Front from 1914 to 1918.

The demise of the military academies consequent upon Versailles was largely circumvented by the theoretical and more intellectual training that had formerly been carried out by those institutions now being conducted within the separate divisions of the Reichswehr. This included staff training, written exercises, command and control exercises and other headquarters exercises with and without troops, and all manner of war games. At the same time, the Truppenamt continued to act as a general staff in all but name, under the direction of Major General Otto Hasse. It also had within it a small air planning staff for Germany's non-existent (in theory) combat air force. All field exercises were made as realistic as possible, with live-firing a common feature of these, including the frequent use of overhead fire support from machine-guns and from other light support weapons where these were available. In 1921, von Seeckt published a much-revised and updated edition of army field service regulations. This publication was entitled the *Command of Combined Arms Combat* and it encapsulated his vision for the Reichswehr's offensive capability in the future.

The army managed to exceed the laid-down manpower ceiling in various ways. These included the placing of significant numbers of officers and soldiers who would in other circumstances have served in the Reichswehr into the paramilitary Landespolizei. Other would-be Reichswehr soldiers – among them many members of the Stahlhelm organization – also served with the Grenzschutz-Ost in Silesia, where continued friction with the Poles resulted frequently in violent clashes. The creation of several other paramilitary bodies enabled military skills to be acquired and trained reserves to be developed covertly, outside the much more visible Reichswehr organization. Similarly, ordinary motor vehicles were used on exercises to represent tanks, and a number of cavalry units were allocated technical, specialist and support roles that in fact bore little resemblance to the traditional role of that arm. However, without the chance both to develop and exercise the tanks, aircraft and other heavy weapons that had been banned by Versailles, and to practise the troops who would use them, the aspirations set out for the Reichswehr in that new handbook could never realistically be achieved. But then, in 1922, the solution to this seemingly insurmountable problem came from a most unlikely source.

By 1922, Germany had already found friends overseas who were prepared to ignore the Versailles treaty and assist the country to regain its military capability. In Santander, Spain, the shipyards built new submarines for the German navy and provided suitable training facilities. In Sweden, the great armaments firm of Bofors collaborated with Krupps of Essen to develop and test new artillery weapons for the German army. But the country that was most directly responsible for developing the Reichswehr was, somewhat ironically, Soviet Russia. By a secret military agreement signed in 1922 in parallel with the Rapallo agreement concluded between Moscow and Berlin, Germany agreed to train the Red Army and to pay an annual amount to the Soviets, in return for which Soviet territory was put at the disposal of the Reichswehr for the development of, and training with, those weapons prohibited by Versailles. Soon Krupps and Junkers were working secretly in special Soviet factories to develop artillery and aircraft to support the Reichswehr, while complete units of artillery and armoured troops and groups of combat pilots were effectively concealed in Russia, living and training within various Red Army establishments, training areas and flying-schools. Between 1925 and 1933 some 130 army pilots and eighty observers were trained at Lipetsk; in 1925 a school of armoured warfare was established at Kazan, with the first German-manufactured tanks deployed there in 1928. The tactics of what would later become the 'panzer' arm were initially tested by reroling the seven innocently named transport battalions – Kraftfahrabteilungen – of the Reichswehr.

In Germany, during the 1920s and early 1930s, the army regularly used agricultural tractors and cars mocked-up to simulate tanks, to practise tactical handling of mechanized units. At higher levels of command, senior German officers often travelled secretly to Russia to see the various projects then in progress, as well as to observe Red Army manoeuvres.

Given the fundamental divergence of ideology between Bolshevist Russia and republican Germany, the Rapallo agreement was in many ways an unholy alliance indeed. However, von Seeckt's determination to secure this arrangement was entirely pragmatic, as both countries needed that which only the other could provide. At the same time, both Soviet Russia and Germany regarded the main western allies of 1914–18 – France, Britain and the United States – as unfriendly and potentially hostile powers. These perceptions were based on Versailles in Germany's case and on the counter-revolutionary intervention actions that had been taken by the allies from 1917 in the case of Russia.

So it was that between 1920 and 1926 General Hans von Seeckt was instrumental in reviving, developing and maintaining the new German military capability which the Versailles treaty had specifically sought to prevent. He achieved this against a background of continuing internal political unrest which often gave way to violence, and despite the vehement dislike of the Weimar republic by the army. In practice, von Seeckt by and large held the same view, despite his own position within the republic's governing body as military chief of staff, but he was prepared to sublimate his own views on the matter for the greater good of the army.

✠✠✠✠✠✠✠✠✠✠✠✠

The most dangerous year for von Seeckt's plans was 1923, when Franco-Belgian troops moved into the Ruhr on 11 January and occupied the area after Germany defaulted on its reparation payments. The government feared that this would provoke uprisings in the Rhineland, Bavaria and Silesia – with these actively inspired by France and Poland. These fears were shown to be justified when the communists and the right-wing organizations did indeed seek once again to overthrow the republic, and the secession of Bavaria seemed imminent. In Bavaria the army commander, General Otto von Lossow, refused to acknowledge von Seeckt's authority and declared his support for a right-wing take-over of power.

The Reichswehr was unable to act against the Franco-Belgian incursion and lacked the authority to deal decisively with the escalating internal unrest. Then, on 8 November, the so-called 'Beer Hall Putsch' took place in Munich when the Nazis, headed by Adolf Hitler, attempted to take power in Bavaria prior to marching on Berlin.[180] Although the police dealt effectively with the putsch, communist uprisings in Thuringia and Saxony and a worsening conflict with the Poles in Silesia resulted in Friedrich Ebert's government declaring a state of emergency. At last von Seeckt was able to act. Von Lossow was dismissed, the army in Bavaria was returned to national control, and the various communist insurrections were vigorously suppressed, together with the Polish-inspired unrest and incursions into Silesia. Von Seeckt and the army district commanders now enjoyed considerable power. But, with the situation restored and the army having once again proved its ability to maintain order and defend the republic (more so when operating against the left-wing movements and the Poles than against the right-wing organizations, with whose aims and policies many army officers still sympathized) von Seeckt returned the governing authority to Ebert in 1924, at which stage the state of emergency and the army primacy for internal security were ended.

From 1925 much political manoeuvring took place as von Hindenburg dominated army and government alike (and was viewed by many almost as a new Kaiser). The Minister of War from 1928 was Wilhelm Groener, and the Reichswehr was headed by General Wilhelm Heye following von Seeckt's resignation in 1926.[181] From 1932, General Kurt von Schleicher, a man close to and favoured by both von Hindenburg and Groener, exerted great influence upon a succession of Chancellors, being appointed Chancellor himself in December 1932, but then being forced to resign on 28 January the following year. Always a manipulative, politically ambitious, professionally competent and self-serving man, von Schleicher was a reactionary who had actively courted Hitler and the

Nazis from 1930, although he had done so primarily as a means of achieving his goals for Germany and the army rather than from any belief in the merits of the Nazi cause. Later, he tried unsuccessfully to use the Reichswehr and the trades unions together to contain the rapidly growing popularity and power of Adolf Hitler and the NSDAP. Consequently, his always dangerous involvement with the National Socialists placed him at the very centre of much of the political chaos which ensued from 1930 and this would eventually provoke his own death at the hands of the Nazis. This chaos included the demise of Minister of War Groener following his unsuccessful attempt to ban the NSDAP Sturmabteilung (the 'storm detachments', or 'SA'), and the fall of Chancellor Brüning with the appointment of Franz von Papen in his place, at which time von Schleicher became minister for the Reichswehr. Then, in July 1932, von Papen was forced to call an election. As a result the Nazis became the largest single party represented in the Reichstag. Hitler refused to accept a coalition government and von Hindenburg refused to appoint him Chancellor. A further election in November 1932 did not alter the situation materially and this led to von Schleicher's appointment as chancellor by von Hindenburg. His time in office lasted just over a month, as a coalition government was finally formed early in 1933, with Hitler as Chancellor and von Papen as his deputy.

This was a defining moment for Germany and its army. General Werner von Blomberg had earlier replaced von Schliecher as minister for the Reichswehr. In October 1933 General Ludwig Beck was appointed head of the Truppenamt, and in February 1934 Lieutenant General Werner von Fritsch became Chef der Heeresleitung. All of these generals now occupied key posts and all were Nazi sympathizers. Meanwhile, Hitler and the NSDAP moved to consolidate their political position and power within and over all of the principal civilian institutions of Germany. These included the police, the judiciary, the state civil services and the local administrative bodies. Neither did the army escape the attention of the Nazi political message. There, Hitler's patriotic orations and declared policies of rearming Germany, reintroducing military conscription, dispensing with the constraints imposed by Versailles, saving the state from the evils of communism,[182] and restoring Germany to its former greatness, found considerable favour throughout much of the Reichswehr. Many members of the officer corps viewed his statement that the new German state – a 'third Reich' no less – would be founded jointly upon the Nazi Party and the Reichswehr as reassuring, positively enthusing and thoroughly motivating after the uncertain and turbulent years of Weimar. Surely a few constraints on civil liberties and the new anti-Semitic laws that were now being introduced so speedily throughout Germany were of little consequence if the army was once again destined to become a real power both in Germany and in the wider world?

On 15 March 1933 instructions were issued to introduce the new Reichskokarde insignia and for the adoption of the eagle and swastika (Hakenkreuz) helmet decal, which incorporated the traditional German eagle with the NSDAP symbol. From 17 February 1934 the black-white-red shield helmet decal was also taken into use. Finally, instructions for the wearing of the spread-eagle and swastika national emblem were issued on 30 October 1935, although the national insignia had already been widely taken into use from early 1934.[183] So it was that by the end of 1935 the Nazi emblem was everywhere accepted and seen to be in everyday use as an integral part of the badge of the Reichswehr and of the German nation. In fact, this was a masterpiece of political presentation by the Nazis, one that visually reinforced the inseparable nature of the NSDAP from the nation in which it now held power.

The Nazis' swift progress into power was remarkable and in many ways ran contrary to the culture and nature of the German people. However, when considered within the totality of 1914–18, the shame of Versailles, the unpopularity of Weimar, the fear of Bolshevism, a perceived Polish threat and the (ostensibly) apolitical or isolationist development of the Reichswehr by von Seeckt, the rise of the NSDAP was perhaps less of an aberration than it might at first seem to be. The political process had been so weakened in the post-1918 years that, while the German people yearned for stability and a strong, capable, democratic and (within reason) liberal government, the Reichswehr was probably the only institution of the time that could have delivered this through whole-hearted support for the government and direct involvement in the political process. But the army's often half-hearted support for Weimar and the active opposition of many officers to the republican government created a political vacuum that opened the way for the NSDAP to fill it with alacrity.

Nevertheless, the Nazis might still have failed to achieve political power and the Weimar republic might yet have survived if other equally important factors had not militated against this. This was because the political events, turmoil, violence, and uncertainty of 1930 to 1934 had also been conducted against the wider background of escalating economic turbulence which had been triggered by the collapse of the Wall Street Stock Exchange in October 1929. The impact of the Crash was severe throughout Europe, but in Germany it proved devastating. By the summer of 1931 the awful extent of the economic disaster was evident throughout Germany. Confidence in German business had collapsed and foreign investment had fallen away. The country's once-booming manufacturing industry had swiftly disintegrated as German trade and overseas commercial markets stagnated and then crumbled. This in turn produced mass unemployment. Banks foreclosed, there was rampant inflation and the nation's financial system was in chaos. Inevitably, the blend of financial chaos, unemployment, dashed hopes, lost savings, ruined lives, anger and frustration had boiled over to precipitate regular outbreaks of violent street-fighting between political extremist groups, although by the early 1930s the only such groups of any consequence were the communists and the Nazis. This was the volatile, violent, polarized political environment in which Nazism thrived and of these two diametrically opposed groups the Nazis – much assisted on the streets of Germany by the paramilitary support provided by the brown-shirted troopers of the SA – finally emerged triumphant in 1933. They had done so with the tacit approval and passive support of very many members of the Reichswehr.

This support was reinforced by Hitler's rejection of a proposal made by Ernst Röhm (the commander of the Sturmabteilung) in February 1934 that the SA should provide the foundation for the creation of a new German army, a proposal that was understandably an anathema to the army. He also advocated the continuance of the National Socialist revolution, something that now ran contrary to Hitler's own agenda. Indeed, Röhm's timing was particularly ill-judged, as it coincided with a power-play by Himmler and Göring to supplant the SA with the Schutzstaffel (or 'SS'), the Nazi Party's own élite paramilitary self-protection and security force.

On 30 June 1934 the Nazi 'blood purge' – Die Nacht der langen Messer (or 'Night of the Long Knives') – was launched by scores of SS murder squads. During the few days that the 'blood purge' lasted, at least seventy-seven leading Nazis were arrested and summarily executed, together with at least another 100 others; the overall figure for those killed – SA men, political figures, civil servants, military officers – was almost certainly much higher. Despite his well-known contempt for the SA, the recently retired General von Schleicher and his wife were among those murdered, being shot down by six SS gunmen at their home in Neubabelsberg, Berlin, in front of their 14-year-old stepdaughter. Bizarrely, Hitler and his closest associates were personally involved in the blood bath despite the fact that numbers of those killed had variously been their friends, colleagues and comrades-in-arms in the old army, the Freikorps and the NSDAP for many years. Meanwhile, the Reichswehr provided some of the weapons and other facilities to the SS for their murderous operations, justifying this support with the argument that the SA's military aspirations had directly threatened the army, while at the same time Röhm's revolutionary political aspirations had also threatened the stability of the state.

The events of 30 June 1934 and the few days that followed would prove to be particularly significant for Germany and the army alike, for as well as consolidating Hitler's power and establishing the Nazis' political course for the next decade, the 'blood purge' also eliminated the SA and replaced it with the much more effective and ideologically focused SS. This organization later spawned the Waffen-SS – the 'armed SS' – which would fight alongside the German army on many of the battlefields in the west and in the east after 1939. So 1934 therefore marks the point at which any consideration of the German army cannot reasonably be dissociated entirely from a parallel, though subordinate, consideration of the Waffen-SS (as opposed to the Allgemeine-SS, the 'general SS').

Following the death of von Hindenburg on 2 August 1934, Hitler assumed the title of Führer instead of president and so took to himself absolute power throughout Germany. The Reichswehr, which for so long had abrogated its political responsibilities and denied its involvement in German politics during the formative years of the republic, now came fully within the Nazi purview. No longer were the soldiers required to swear their allegiance to the Reich, to its constitution and lawful institutions, and obedience to the president of the republic and their superior officers, as they had under the Weimar regime. Neither were they any longer to swear allegiance to 'the people of Germany and the Fatherland', in accordance with the modified and simplified oath introduced by Hitler in December 1933 soon after he gained power. On 2 August 1934 yet another version of the oath was promulgated. In this latest version every officer and soldier was required to 'swear by God this sacred oath that I shall render unconditional obedience to Adolf Hitler, the Führer of the German Reich, supreme commander of the armed forces, and that I shall at all times be prepared, as a brave soldier, to give my life for this oath'.

On 21 May 1935 the Reichswehr was renamed the Wehrmacht, within which every officer, soldier, sailor and airman now owed his duty, honour and loyalty not merely to the German state – the Fatherland – but to the man who had successfully contrived to present the very essence of the German state embodied in his own person as 'der Führer', Adolf Hitler.

19

Rearmament, Regeneration and Matters of Conscience, 1935–1939

THE TWO AND A HALF YEARS that preceded the formal creation of the Wehrmacht had witnessed an unprecedented period of military activity, in order that Germany's reinvigorated and regenerated armed forces might in due course achieve the overall military capability to support the grand designs and expansionist policies expounded by the Nazis and their charismatic leader. Fundamental to this was the urgent need to develop an army that could dissuade and if necessary counter any moves by the Allied Powers to prevent German rearmament and its inevitable contravention of the provisions of the Treaty of Versailles. The process had begun as soon as the Nazis came to power in January 1933, and continued apace until it was more or less complete by the end of 1938. By then the German army numbered no fewer than two million men, with intakes of 500,000 conscripted recruits joining for training each year.

These impressive manpower numbers masked capability shortfalls in several important areas, notably the development of an effective armoured force large enough to ensure the success of the Nazis' strategic aims. Furthermore, throughout the army's expansion from 1933 to 1939, it experienced considerable difficulties with officer and NCO recruitment and training, the burgeoning numbers of battalions, regiments, divisions and corps outstripping the availability of men qualified to train and command them. The numerous expediencies to which the army resorted while resolving its manning difficulties created a German army whose nature was very different from that of its Weimar and Reichswehr predecessor, and which was unrecognizable from the army of the imperial era prior to 1918.

The army was always able to obtain the necessary numbers of soldiers to fill its lowest ranks both through conscription (from 1935) and from the numbers of young men seeking a better lifestyle, career and quality of life than many of them could have aspired to in civilian life as labourers or unskilled workers. The in-barracks living conditions of the army of the mid-1930s were better than those in many other European armies.

The great care devoted to the improvement of the relationship between the officer and his men in the Reichswehr has been taken over into the new army, and the material welfare of the men greatly improved in every respect. Gone are the old cheerless barracks with their dreary red brick walls. The new quarters, which have risen during the last years [i.e., since 1933], are cheery, pleasant buildings, whitewashed and gaily painted with military scenes and the portraits of famous soldiers. Reading-rooms, furnished in the style of a wood-panelled country inn, are established and the light and airy living quarters, with their running hot and cold water, are far beyond what most of the soldiers are accustomed to at home, particularly in the case of special arms, such as the air force or the tank units. The food is excellent and much superior, both in quality and quantity, even to that of highly paid workers in the heavy industries. Great care is taken to see that the food is properly cooked and as much variety introduced into the menu as possible.[184]

Indeed, the officers received the same quality and quantity of food as those they commanded, and when on leave the food allowance paid was the same for officers and soldiers.

Also, from 1933, the Hitler Youth organization conditioned virtually all German boys most effectively for a future life of service to the Nazi state through military or other similarly institutionalized service, where a contemporary commentator noted that the army 'appears more like an exciting adventure' when contrasted with 'the harsh treatment of youngsters in the labour camps'.[185]

The politically inspired process of German rearmament between 1933 and 1939 was at the same time ambitious, innovative, speedy, pervasive and (despite some setbacks) generally successful. While it clearly supported the wider policies and foreign policy aspirations of Hitler and the NSDAP, it also exemplified the ability of the German military to develop and implement during a relatively short period of time a rearmament plan that impacted upon virtually every part of the German nation – the theoretical constraints of Versailles notwithstanding. The rate of the army's expansion was quite remarkable and the major milestones and achievements in this complex process are summarized, together with amplifying observations, at Appendix 7.

In parallel with the rapidly increasing size of the army, the Nazi Party's own paramilitary security force, the Schutzstaffel (or SS), had grown significantly since its original formation in 1923 as the SS-Stabswache in Berlin (which became the SS-Leibstandarte 'Adolf Hitler' in March 1933) and in 1925 as the SS-Verfügungstruppe (SS-VT) and the SS-Totenkopfverbände (SS-TV). Originally, the SS-VT was little more than a militarized security force for the Nazi Party, being recruited exclusively from Nazi Party members with Aryan blood and as such it was by no means as well trained or capable as its army comparator. Meanwhile, the

SS-TV was formed originally as a source of guards for the Nazi concentration camps, and to provide a politically reliable internal security force for Germany in time of war. Within the Nazi organization the SS finally achieved primacy over the SA following the violent part it had played in the suppression of its SA rivals in the Blood Purge of 30 June 1934.

By 1936 an SS-VT Inspectorate had been established to oversee the administration and development of what had become, by late 1939, the 'armed' or Waffen-SS headed by Reichsführer-SS (RF-SS) Heinrich Himmler.[186] Although patently not part of the German army, the military story of the Waffen-SS increasingly overlapped that of the army from 1939, with Waffen-SS units regularly fighting alongside or under the command of army formations. Similarly, at various stages of the coming war, army formations inevitably found themselves commanded by Waffen-SS headquarters. Although the Waffen-SS was understandably much more politicized than the army, its military organizations and general regulations were largely based upon those of the army, modified where necessary.

With the establishment of the SS-VT Inspectorate in 1936, the terms of service for the Waffen-SS were formalized and required its officers to serve for twenty-five years, its NCOs (sergeants and above) for twelve years, and other ranks for four years. Prior to the formal establishment of the Waffen-SS in 1940, units of the SS-VT's first three numbered motorized infantry regiments (the 1st 'Deutschland', 2nd 'Germania' and 3rd 'Der Führer') and the SS-Leibstandarte 'Adolf Hitler' (the 'LAH') participated in the German occupation of the Sudetenland and Austria, and the campaign in Czechoslovakia. Each regiment comprised three battalions, each of four companies with three platoons of four sections. The regiments had their own artillery, engineer, reconnaissance, air defence and communications support. In general, the performance of these units during the early campaigns up to and including the invasion of Poland fell well short of that of the army. But after the Polish campaign the Waffen-SS underwent extensive reorganization and retraining and thereafter it increasingly came to be regarded – somewhat grudgingly by many within the army who resented its existence and its competing calls upon Germany's always scarce military resources – as an élite military force. Despite this, its enviable fighting reputation on the battlefield would frequently be marred by the atrocities perpetrated by certain of its units. Consequently, although other parts of the German armed forces were by no means blameless in this particular matter, at the end of the war in 1945 the SS as a whole became 'the alibi of the German nation', with responsibility for virtually all the war crimes of the Third Reich period devolving directly upon that organization. Indeed, just as the Imperial German army had in former times come to be a form of state within the state, so the SS organization taken as a whole – including both the Waffen-SS and the Allgemeine-SS – evolved rapidly after 1934 into a far more dangerous and insidious form of self-contained and militarized Nazi state at the very heart of the Third Reich. Further consideration of the wider political impact and history of the Waffen-SS is beyond the scope of this work, although some aspects of the operational activities of some of its units during the war are briefly touched upon later.

For the Waffen-SS and the army alike, the majority of their manpower was to be found in the infantry arm. Although a number of forward thinkers had already appreciated that the only way for the army to return to a war of manoeuvre would be for it to develop the new panzer arm significantly, the infantry was still regarded by most as being the premier war-winning arm within the army. In 1938, the infantry division usually included three regiments with integral engineer and artillery support. A typical infantry regiment comprised:

● Three battalions, each of three infantry companies (all with their integral machine-guns and trench mortars), with the necessary battalion headquarters staff and communications specialists.

● Each of the three battalions also had a support or heavy weapons company. These included two groups of four heavy machine-guns mounted on horse-drawn carriages which could be used either in the ground role or for air defence. In addition, these support companies were equipped with a number of heavy trench mortars.

● Each regiment also had a howitzer company of horse-drawn light (3in) and heavy (6in) howitzers, an anti-tank company (four platoons, each of three anti-tank guns on motorized tractors), a signals platoon, a field engineer platoon, and a logistic support organization within a headquarters company.

● Finally, a troop of cavalry was assigned to each regiment for mounted reconnaissance. By 1938 the cavalry had virtually disappeared as a separate arm, its remaining units sub-allocated to operate with the light armour of the light divisions and for reconnaissance in support of the corps and divisions. In 1938, the only independent mounted cavalry formation still in existence was a single brigade based in East Prussia.

The essential and quite extensive use of horses within the many non-motorized infantry divisions is noteworthy. Despite the progressive mech-anization of the Wehrmacht and the continued need of a sizeable armoured capability, both these matters supported enthusiastically by Hitler, this unsatisfactory situation persisted in most theatres of operation throughout the war and would finally be a contributory factor in Germany's military defeat. Had Hitler delayed implementation of his strategic plans until the modernization and mechanization of the army had been completed, its ability to wage and to sustain (or possibly even to obviate) the sort of protracted war upon which it was shortly to embark would have been improved very significantly.

As had been the case when Prussia went to war almost a century before – first against Austria and then against France – the German artillery guns were once again able to provide most powerful and accurate support for the infantry and panzer divisions. But now a deliberate emphasis had been placed upon howitzers rather than field guns. This was the better to be able to use the howitzer's high trajectory fire to engage targets sited behind cover on reverse slopes, and to conceal the howitzer from enemy view and fire, while not impairing its firepower. The artillery also benefited from observation, sound-ranging and flash-spotting techniques, and anti-aircraft gunnery which had been tried, tested and refined during the Spanish Civil War. Despite the new technology incorporated in its weapons, the German artillery of 1938 was still generally dependent on horses to draw all but its heaviest guns and those which directly supported motorized infantry and panzer divisions.

But what of the panzer divisions which had by late 1938 become one of the most important arms in light of the new sort of conflict that was about to commence? Although very wide variations in equipment availability meant that the actual organization of the panzer regiment in 1938–9 was by no means standardized, the typical regiment of the time usually comprised two or three battalions. Each battalion then had two or three companies, each with three platoons of up to five tanks per platoon. Additional tanks were also found in the regimental, battalion and company headquarters. In addition to the regimental headquarters staff, each panzer regiment was supported by various combat engineer, signals, and logistic support units. Doctrinally, the panzers had become the 'weapon of opportunism' and as such they would be used to achieve a breakthrough, to exploit success, to paralyze the enemy by thrusting deeply into his rear areas, or to provide a highly mobile and powerful reserve force. Despite their combat potential, the panzers were still not regarded as the weapon that would bring about an enemy's final defeat; rather, they were the weapon that would enable the other arms to bring about that defeat.

Foremost among those officers championing the potential of the panzer arm were Heinz Wilhelm Guderian and Otto Lutz. As a junior staff officer Guderian had been involved with the early development of the panzer arm from the former transport battalions, together with the experiments and training conducted at Kazan in Russia from 1925. He had also studied the doctrine for the use of armour in other countries. Then, in the 1930s, while working directly for General der Panzertruppen Otto Lutz, Guderian was able to provide many of the tactical concepts and ideas which Lutz then translated into workable organizations and doctrine. In due course, the name of Colonel-General Guderian would be known far beyond Germany, as an expert in the theory of armoured warfare and with very extensive experience of the successful command of armoured formations in war.

The operational concepts spearheaded by the German panzer forces were eventually characterized by a journalist in 1939 after the Polish campaign, when rapid manoeuvre, all-arms co-operation, concentration of overwhelming firepower, abandonment of flank security for speed, envelopment and the final annihilation of the enemy forces were most aptly described by the single word 'Blitzkrieg', or 'lightning war'. In Blitzkrieg operations the panzers, supported by mechanized infantry, self-propelled or mobile artillery, combat engineers and close air support would cut through the enemy defence lines – ignoring, bypassing or avoiding areas where resistance was strong – to attack headquarters, communications and other vital support functions in depth, thereby rendering the enemy's front-line units ineffective. At the strategic and operational levels it was envisaged that this form of offensive action would comprise seven distinct but complementary and inter-dependent phases, in all but one of which the continued availability and liberal use of air power in close support of the ground operations was an inviolable prerequisite for success:

● The preparatory disruption of the enemy's rear areas and command, control and fixed communication facilities by fifth columnists, saboteurs and infiltrated small groups of special troops. This would neutralize his overall military capability and prejudice his mobilization plans, as well as creating fear and uncertainty and lowering his morale. Such operations were regarded as long-term, being conducted over the ten to twelve months prior to overt offensive action.

● The destruction of the enemy's air power on the ground, by a surprise bombing attack in overwhelming strength. The enemy air force would always pose the single greatest threat to the ground forces of an attacker constrained to move in the open.

● The interdiction of enemy troop movement and command facilities by bombers and fighter ground-attack aircraft. This prevented the movement of reserves and logistic resupply to counter the attack and sustain the defence.

● The neutralization (by preventing their redeployment or movement out of protected cover) or destruction of enemy units and formations by air attack, usually by dive-bombers.

● Infiltration and exploitation of gaps in the defence lines by light armoured and motorized all-arms forces to carry out reconnaissance in depth, identify undefended routes and exploit opportunities as appropriate. These operations signalled the start of the envelopment of the enemy forces.

● The armoured assault by the panzer units and their supporting arms, to achieve deep penetrations, seize key objectives, and to shock, overrun and destroy enemy forces as appropriate, but bypassing major urban areas and well defended strongpoints. These operations continued and reinforced the envelopment of the enemy forces, and thus enabled their subsequent annihilation by the armoured panzer units and the follow-on ground forces.

● The follow-up assault by non-motorized infantry divisions and their supporting arms, to destroy the enemy in detail, establish secure rear areas including the suppression of any irregular resistance forces, impose military administration upon occupied areas, and deal in detail with any locations by-passed earlier by the mobile forces. Finally, these forces would link up with the panzer formations to complete the operation or campaign.

In its updated form, this imaginative and bold concept epitomized the sort of war of manoeuvre that had eluded the Imperial army on the Western Front after 1914. It also accorded with the principles of Auftragstaktik which had been at the very core of German military thinking during the final decades of the Imperial army.

At first there was a good deal of scepticism (and a fair amount of subjective traditionalism and inter-arm and inter-service rivalry) about the efficacy of the Blitzkrieg concept. But this would be largely dissipated after the success of the campaigns of 1939 and 1940. In any case, the prospect of the army avoiding a rerun of the stagnation and attrition of 1915–18 was a powerful argument in favour of the panzer arm and its innovative form of warfare, quite apart from the fact that Hitler also supported the concept enthusiastically and so ensured its continued funding. The Führer saw quite correctly that it was the means by which he could achieve his strategic and expansionist goals within the political timeframe he had set for this. It also conveyed a powerful image of modern military might, innovation and offensive spirit that sat very well with the wider perceptions that the Nazis were then promoting through their propaganda both in Germany and internationally.

Quite apart from the relatively small size of the panzer formations as a proportion of the overall army, the quality of their tanks at the start of the war was very different from that at its end. In 1936 there were some 3,000 of the Panzerkampfwagen model 1 (Pz.Kpfw.1) in service. These two-man light tanks were armed with two machine-guns and had been used effectively during the Spanish Civil War. But by 1935 it was clear that they were much less capable than their Soviet and French equivalents and production ceased in March of that year, although the Pz.Kpfw.1 chassis continued in use as a command vehicle, weapons carrier, ambulance and similar. The Pz.Kpfw.2, 3 and 4 followed in 1935 and 1936, with a 20mm gun replacing the machine-guns as the main armament in the Pz.Kpfw.2. After the German occupation of Czechoslovakia in early 1939, 469 Czech T-38 tanks were seized and taken into use in the panzer units, and the Czech tank-production lines were also taken over by the Germans. These Czech light tanks had a four-man crew and mounted a 37mm gun and a machine-gun. They would soon provide valuable service to the German panzer divisions during the first part of the war, as well as making good much of the existing shortfall in German tank numbers at that time, prior to the arrival of the new German tanks in the panzer units.

At the outbreak of the war, the Pz.Kpfw.2 was the most numerous type of tank in service with the panzer units, although the newer but (in 1939) less numerous Pz.Kpfw.4 then just rolling off the production lines was a more capable and better-armed tank. By the time that the five-man crewed Pz.Kpfw.4 came fully into service in late 1939 (with just over 200 then available in panzer units) these tanks mounted a 75mm cannon and two machine-guns, with much improved mobility and armour protection compared to their predecessors. Somewhat remarkably perhaps, in light of the strategic importance of the arm, they were still under-gunned and under-armoured when set against their likely opposition. But their relatively light weight (about twenty tons, depending on the model) meant that they were both fast and manoeuvrable. It was not until 1942 that events on the battlefields of the Eastern Front would finally precipitate the production of the Pz.Kpfw.5 'Panther' tank – overall one of the best tanks deployed by any nation during the war.[187] Although the types of tanks used within the various panzer units varied considerably, the typical all-arms armoured division of 1939 generally had between 250 and 350 tanks at its disposal, together with more than 500 machine-guns, almost 100 anti-tank guns, about fifty howitzers and some 150 mortars.

While the new army was developing and expanding, changes were also afoot at its highest levels of command. Here also, politics dominated the restructuring of the high command as Hitler progressively tightened his direct control over the armed forces. As this process moved ahead the dilemma faced by many officers was plain. The large number of officers who had regarded the rise of the Nazis as a useful means by which to restore the prestige, power and influence of the old army now came to appreciate that they had finally lost control of the catalyst for change which they had supported either through their positive actions or (more usually) by their passivity during the 1930s.

Despite this, the army's renewed energy, high morale and the often electrifying excitement engendered by all that the Nazis were doing was both infectious and hard – indeed, unpatriotic – to gainsay. A revitalized Fatherland was rapidly emerging from the catastrophe and humiliation of Versailles, and from the doldrums, economic collapse and internal unrest of Weimar, to claim once again its rightful place among the premier nations of the world. And of course, this demanded an army that was second to none, for that which could not be achieved by negotiation or through peaceful coercion might well have to be achieved by what was now viewed as the entirely justifiable use of armed force. Had not that great Prussian military theorist von Clausewitz advocated war as a legitimate continuation of policy by other means? In the thoroughly militarized, politicized and energized National Socialist Third Reich such thoughts were at the same time seductive and all too easily rationalized, justified and accepted, by those in uniform and by those in civilian employment alike. Surely this was the Fatherland's destiny of which the Führer had so often spoken?

In late 1937 several senior officers spoke openly against Hitler's expansionist intentions, fearful in particular of a new war against France and Great Britain. Ever since 1935 others had criticized the speed of the rearmament process, correctly recognizing that in many cases quantity was being achieved at the expense of quality. Notable among these officers were Colonel-General Ludwig Beck, chief of the general staff, Colonel General Werner von Fritsch, commander-in-chief of the army, and Field Marshal Werner von Blomberg, the war minister. In January 1938 accusations of immorality were made against Blomberg's new wife and of alleged homosexuality by Fritsch. Blomberg was a widower, and his position as a field marshal had perhaps demanded a little more circumspection in his choice of a new bride than had been the case when he married his secretary Eva Gruhn on 12 January 1938. Certainly, Gruhn had enjoyed a somewhat colourful life and this was brought to Hitler's attention via the Berlin chief of police and then enthusiastically by Göring. Von Blomberg was accused of bringing the officer corps into disrepute and his position became untenable.

In the case of von Fritsch, a confirmed bachelor, the charge that he had committed a homosexual offence with one 'Bavarian Joe' (who was in modern parlance a 'rent boy') near Potsdam railway station in November 1934 had been originated by Himmler through the Gestapo and it was entirely false. Although an officers' court of honour subsequently exonerated von Fritsch absolutely, the damage had already been done.

Both von Blomberg and von Fritsch were forced to resign and on 4 February 1938 their retirements were announced officially.[188] This enabled Hitler to create an armed forces high command (Oberkommando der Wehrmacht, or 'OKW') at Zossen-Wünsdorf to the south of Berlin, with him at its head and with Major General (later Field Marshal) Wilhelm Keitel as its executive head and Colonel (later General) Alfred Jodl as the OKW head of operations. Both these men were totally committed to serve the Führer and to the use of the armed forces to further the expansionist ambitions of the National Socialist cause. Meanwhile, General Walther von Brauchitsch succeeded von Fritsch as commander-in-chief of the army, and the reserve army (Ersatzheer) was to be commanded by General Friedrich Fromm. During the post-January 1938 purge of those officers who were perceived to be less than supportive of Hitler's plans, some sixteen generals were relieved of their commands and a further forty-four senior commanders were transferred to other duties.[189] Everywhere, officers known to be loyal to Hitler were appointed to replace these men, and while some of the new appointees were professionally competent many were politically reliable rather than militarily capable.

Despite remaining in post, Beck became increasingly isolated, especially after Hitler's creation of OKW, and eventually resigned on 18 August 1938. He was replaced as chief of the general staff at the Oberkommando der Heeres (OKH) by General Franz Halder. Although he was another opponent of Hitler's policies, Halder (as did many other army officers) subsequently set his misgivings aside in order to carry out what was now widely regarded as a German officer's immutable duty to the nation and to the Führer to whom he had sworn his loyalty. After all, had not the Rhineland been enthusiastically returned to German control in 1936? Had not the crowds in Vienna greeted the jack-booted German troops rapturously in 1938? And had not the Sudetenland been returned to Germany the same year, followed by the occupation of the remainder of Czechoslovakia by spring of 1939? Surely this succession of triumphs indicated that Germany's destiny was indeed indivisible from that of the Führer and National Socialism?

The Munich agreement of 29 September 1938 had undoubtedly reinforced Hitler's stature as an accomplished international leader, and this had been further enhanced by his successful conclusion of the non-aggression pact with the Soviet Union on 23 August 1939.[190] Even if certain of the politically motivated actions of the SS against resistance groups, saboteurs, political activists, gypsies and Jews in the newly occupied territories were sometimes distasteful to army officers, these matters were generally considered to be none of the army's business and were inconsequential when set against the much wider future of the newly declared Third Reich and the crucial role that the army and its officers would have and then enjoy in that future. So it was, with some four and a half million men under arms, with any threat posed by the Soviet Union effectively neutralized, with internal security matters in the hands of the SS, with German industry and the economy on a war footing in all but name, and with a compliant high command in place, the stage was once again set for war in Europe.

Against such emotive and heady considerations, the observations of the German historian Dr Herbert Rosinski made in late 1938 are particularly noteworthy:

> Ludendorff in his vision of the 'totally mobilized' nation [had] still thought its leader would be the 'Super general' conducting it upon sober military considerations. [However] under the new form of 'extended strategy' it is obvious that the direction of the whole must lie in the hands of the political leader [i.e., Adolf Hitler], and it is very doubtful whether considerations of a purely military character will be allowed to play in his counsels a role corresponding to their real importance. In the 'Leader-General' of the Third Reich the German army may well find the prophet who sends it to Armageddon'.[191]

On the night of 31 August 1939, in the OKH rear headquarters at Zossen, in the OKH forward headquarters, and in the army command posts and command vehicles concealed in the villages and woods of East Prussia and along Germany's eastern border, the officers' maps all bore the title 'Polen'. At dawn the next day two German army groups with a total of more than 2,500 tanks and one and a half million soldiers, supported by almost 10,000 artillery pieces and the overwhelming close air support of the Luftwaffe's Stuka dive-bombers and other combat aircraft, crossed the border into Poland. The armoured units quickly lanced

through the border defences and roared on towards its capital, Warsaw.
Behind the panzer and motorized units came the infantry divisions.

Hitler had launched his ultimate gamble; the Blitzkrieg concept would
at last be tested in the deadly fires of war, and a defining moment in
German and world history had arrived. Just two decades after the end of
the Kaiser's war in 1918 – the 'Great War' or 'the war to end all wars' –
German soldiers were again on the march. Europe was once more the
focus of armed conflict on a grand scale, and the Second World War had
begun.

20

Unleashing the Blitzkrieg
1939–1940

SELF-EVIDENTLY, a full account of the Third Reich's military operations during the Second World War cannot be included in a history of this sort. Indeed, an almost infinite number of more general publications, together with a vast range of detailed academic and specialist works on virtually every aspect of this subject set at every level of command exist currently, with new titles being added almost weekly. Quite apart from all practical considerations, any attempt to cover comprehensively the years of conflict from 1939 to 1945 would almost certainly unbalance this wider history of the German army. It would do so by accentuating what was in many respects an historical and military aberration which, through force of circumstances, effectively broke the traditional mould of German military development during the period from 1935 to 1945, but more specifically during the years of warfare that began in 1939. Apart from its length and scale, the historical impact of the Second World War upon the story of the German army was, arguably and albeit in entirely different ways, no more or less than that of (for example) the wars of Frederick the Great, the wars of unification in the nineteenth century, or the First World War.

Accordingly, instead of attempting to embark upon a full but necessarily very broad and possibly unhelpful account of the army's war, aspects of two rather more specific campaigns that exemplified its operational and military thinking are considered in a little more detail. The second of these is the invasion of Russia in 1941 (the 'Great Patriotic War' as the Soviets termed it). Despite the huge Anglo-US contribution to the war in the west and in the Mediterranean theatre, the Eastern Front cannot reasonably be regarded as anything less than the main focus of German ground operations after June 1941, and therefore it was the campaign which more than any other ultimately determined the fate of the Third Reich and its army.

But first and foremost it is the offensive campaigns and armoured battles of 1939 and 1940 – the 'Angriffsschlacht' – that deserve particular consideration, for these stunning early successes substantially reinforced Hitler's position in Germany, both politically and as the military head of the nation's armed forces. And it was these understandable and enthusiastically

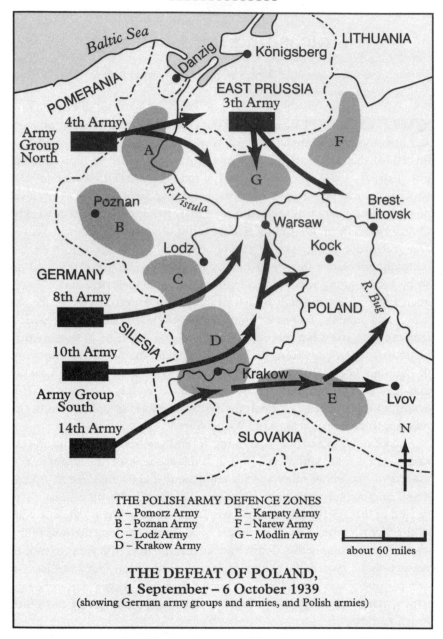

THE POLISH ARMY DEFENCE ZONES
A – Pomorz Army   E – Karpaty Army
B – Poznan Army   F – Narew Army
C – Lodz Army   G – Modlin Army
D – Krakow Army

about 60 miles

THE DEFEAT OF POLAND,
1 September – 6 October 1939
(showing German army groups and armies, and Polish armies)

supportive if misplaced judgements by his people and by his army's officers and soldiers alike that would subsequently result in the cataclysmic fate
which eventually engulfed the Third Reich, together with its rearmed and
regenerated army, just five years later.

The Defeat of Poland, September 1939

At dawn on 1 September 1939 the mailed fist of the panzer spearhead swept into Poland. The four light divisions, seven panzer divisions and four motorized divisions cut through the thinly spread Polish defence forces despite the fact that these same forces comprised some thirty infantry divisions and eleven cavalry brigades. In 1939 Poland had the fifth largest armed forces in the world, its army with one million men, 475 tanks and 2,800 artillery pieces, now manning well-established fixed fortifications and sheltered by several major river obstacles. Behind the German armoured divisions came forty infantry divisions and one cavalry brigade. The 4th and 3rd Armies of Army Group North struck from Pomerania and East Prussia, while the 8th, 10th and 14th Armies of Army Group South surged north-east from Slovakia and Silesia towards Warsaw and eastwards towards Lvov.

The 19th Army Corps, now commanded by General Heinz Guderian, was in the van of 4th Army's assault against the heavily fortified zone to the south of Danzig. There, the tanks were echeloned in waves, attacking on a frontage no greater than 5,000 yards, while the Stuka dive-bombers and the artillery maintained their bombardment of the Polish positions ahead of and to the flanks of the panzer units. The motorized infantry moved behind the tanks, ready to deal with any well-defended anti-tank positions, or with any strongpoints that could not be bypassed. During these early engagements Guderian directed the corps from his own command tank at the forefront of the action, frequently coming under direct Polish fire and on one occasion that of his own artillery! Although the panzer forces were at first inexperienced in the sheer speed of this new type of combat and suffered significant losses to the Polish anti-tank gunners, they learnt fast. By 5 September the Danzig Corridor was in German hands, Polish resistance was crumbling, and 4th and 3rd Armies had linked up in East Prussia. Everywhere the panzers were rolling along routes and through close terrain that the Poles had thought impassable by armoured forces.

Meanwhile, the armoured divisions of the three armies of Army Group South, commanded by General Gerd von Runstedt and his chief of staff General Erich von Manstein, thrust rapidly past Lodz and on towards Warsaw, past Krakow and on towards the River Vistula, and to Lvov and the River Bug. In every area the Polish defences were breaking down, huge numbers of shocked troops were surrendering as their defences collapsed in the face of the sheer speed, concentrated force and overwhelming fire-power of the German invaders. With its initial objectives achieved, 3rd

Army advanced on Warsaw while Guderian's 19th Corps of 4th Army now struck south towards Brest-Litovsk to the east of the River Bug, in the depths of Polish territory.

Only to the west of Warsaw were the Poles able to launch a counter-stroke. There, on 9 September, the Poznan Army, supported by the residue of the Pomorz Army to its north, struck 8th Army's flank guard. This attack came just as the Germans were primarily focused on the capture of Warsaw, where 4th Panzer Division had that same day already experienced the limitations of using armour in built-up areas, losing fifty-seven of 120 tanks engaged during three hours of fighting. At the same time, 10th Army had outrun its supply lines and was short of fuel. At first the Poles achieved some success against the German infantry divisions, but the speedy redeployment of 1st and 4th Panzer Divisions from the Vistula and Warsaw, together with forces from the north-west, enveloped and routed the Poznan Army in short order. By the evening of 15 September the Polish counter-stroke had been effectively neutralized, the scene of the action devastated by air attack, artillery fire and the attacking panzer divisions. The previous day Guderian's two panzer and one motorized infantry divisions had completed the encirclement of the strategically important communications hub of Brest-Litovsk. That city capitulated on 17 September, Warsaw fell on 27 September and the last Polish resistance ended at Kock on 6 October. By then both France and Great Britain had declared war on Germany on 3 September, France had failed to make good a promise to support Poland with an attack into western Germany on 17 September, and Soviet troops had unexpectedly occupied much of eastern Poland. Generally, the validity of the Blitzkrieg concept had been proved, although some important lessons had also been learnt by the army, and it was now time to take stock of the four-week campaign before the Wehrmacht turned its attention to its old aspirations and newly declared enemies beyond Germany's western and northern borders.

For the wider world, the reasons for the German success were not immediately evident; consequently the Wehrmacht's victory served to reinforce a growing international perception of German military invincibility and the view within Germany that Hitler's judgement and strategic ability were indeed infallible. But in the army it was acknowledged that the new form of fighting that it had brought to the battlefield carried with it its own difficulties which, though certainly not insurmountable, should now be addressed with the utmost dispatch.

At the higher levels it had soon become clear that many officers of the high command, geographically well separated from the fighting army groups, had not fully appreciated the speed with which the armoured formations now moved and the technical support and resources they needed to maintain their momentum. Neither had the inevitably frequent disconnection between the well-armoured tanks and their supporting but largely unprotected motorized infantry been resolved. Any physical separation of the infantry from the panzers could at best slow down the advance and at worst leave either of these arms isolated and vulnerable to enemy action. These difficulties would be resolved over time by an acceptance of even less direction and direct control of the panzer forces by the high command once they were launched into battle, together with the development and rapid promotion of a new breed of officers to command these units and formations. Men such as Guderian, von Manstein, von Manteuffel, Rommel and others would exploit the concept of Aufstragstaktik to the utmost in the battles ahead. Also, for the all-arms combat groups and divisions, the already high standards of training and co-operation were further improved. Meanwhile, the logistics issue – above all else the provision of fuel – would certainly improve as organizational, equipment and technological changes were made. But logistic difficulties would almost always constrain the panzer forces from fulfilling their true potential in the coming campaigns as they outran their resupply arrangements time and again.

Air-to-ground co-operation and support had worked well, but could be improved further, especially the close support of engaged ground formations. The tanks themselves had generally performed well, with no more than 25 per cent out of action with mechanical problems at any one time. Most of the 217 tanks destroyed by enemy action were the lighter tanks that had been successfully engaged by anti-tank guns. Few significant tank-versus-tank actions had taken place. Indeed, the light armoured divisions had revealed several serious shortcomings in action, where the lightness of their vehicles' armour, an insufficiency of tanks, and a lack of supporting motorized infantry all resulted in casualties and in a failure to realize their full potential. The invasion of Poland confirmed that the best mix of divisions in a panzer corps was two panzer divisions and one motorized infantry division, all with integral supporting arms and panzer and infantry sub-groupings. Not surprisingly, the non-motorized infantry divisions – moving on foot and with horse-drawn artillery and other transport – were unable to move or work at the tempo of the panzer divisions and this was also reflected in the literally pedestrian and unimaginative style of command displayed by many of them.

But perhaps the greatest lesson of Poland was that the army would need considerably more armoured divisions than it had, if it was to succeed. But in 1939 it was already much too late to generate such forces in the required strength now that the army was committed. To meet operational requirements they should have been ready, fully manned and equipped, prior to the commencement of hostilities. Despite the subsequent significant increases that were implemented (including the transformation of the original four light armoured divisions into the 6th, 7th, 8th and 9th Panzer Divisions) and the concentration of armoured forces for specific campaigns and operations to produce local armoured superiority, the continued lack of these divisions in large numbers during the next few years would always limit that which the army could realistically hope to achieve. Indeed, in the rush in later years to create, belatedly, more of the panzer divisions which had so well suited Hitler's war aims in 1939 and 1940, quantity was eventually accomplished only at the expense of quality.

Finally, although horses would of necessity continue to be widely used by the Germans for support and transportation throughout the war, the Polish campaign demonstrated all too clearly that the use of mounted cavalry for offensive action in general war was no longer a serious option. The rapid and bloody demise of the Polish cavalry units, which were so valiantly but also so wastefully launched in hopeless attacks to counter the advancing panzer formations, graphically illustrated the contrast between the old-style or traditional European armies and the devastatingly modern German war machine which had roared into Poland at the beginning of September 1939, and then annihilated the once-proud Polish army during just four weeks of fighting.

Next, on 9 April 1940, the Germans exercised their newly formed airborne (or air-landed) infantry and parachute battalions during their successful attacks on Denmark and Norway. These operations were planned and ordered by OKW in response to Hitler's concerns that Anglo-French support for the Finns (then under Soviet attack) would prejudice Germany's supplies of Swedish iron ore. Although the parachute units were officially a part of the Luftwaffe, these troops were in every other respect soldiers rather than airmen, and their use decisively complemented the attacks carried out by the conventional army formations. Tanks, but not panzer divisions, took part in the ground assaults and, apart from some continued resistance at Narvik, both countries were overwhelmed by the air and ground assaults. They finally fell under German control within four weeks. So it was that by May 1940 the Wehrmacht's high command was well prepared to include a parachute assault capability in its future operational plans, and specifically those for what was by now the imminent invasion of Germany's historical enemy,

France. The army now comprised 153 divisions (including ten panzer and six motorized infantry), of which no fewer than 136 were available for operations in the west, with the balance of eight divisions in Norway and Denmark, three in Germany and nine in eastern Germany, Poland and Czechoslovakia. In addition, three Waffen-SS divisions were available for operations alongside those of the army.

The Defeat of France, May 1940

Hitler had originally intended to attack France via Belgium as soon as the Polish campaign had concluded, with a view to subduing France, safeguarding the future security of the Ruhr, seizing control of the Channel coast and then establishing the forward air bases necessary to commence a bombing campaign against Britain. The planned offensive was codenamed 'Fall Gelb' (or 'Case Yellow'). But bad weather throughout the winter period forced a delay until the spring of 1940, by which time German operations in Scandinavia had been carried out. During the intervening months Hitler had increased his personal control of the army by the progressive marginalization of the chief of the general staff, General Franz Halder, and the army's commander-in-chief, General Walther von Brauchitsch, both of whom had expressed their reservations about an attack against France. The command and control vacuum created at OKH by their reducing influence was compensated for by the increased power enjoyed by Generals Keitel and Jodl at OKW. By early 1940, the direction of German strategic operations was firmly in the hands of Hitler and his generals at OKW. This situation was entirely different from that which had existed in the army since the mid-nineteenth century and until 1918, when its operational direction had been firmly in the hands of the general staff.

Originally, it had been planned by the OKH that three army groups – the predominantly armoured Army Group B in the north (with four armies, including nine panzer and four motorized divisions) and Army Group A (two armies) in the centre – would strike into France through Belgium and the Ardennes respectively, while Army Group C secured the southern border area and flank and then remained in reserve. But by May 1940 the whole emphasis had changed from the fairly conservative OKH plan to one that envisaged the main thrust not in the north but in the centre, through the Ardennes and towards Sedan. The earlier success of the panzers in Poland, moving across terrain that had been assessed as unsuitable for tanks, the historical significance of Sedan for Germany and France alike ever since 1870, together with the daring nature of the revised plan all combined to make it attractive to Hitler. Despite much resistance from the high command to changing the plan, a number of the officers who had fought in Poland had promoted the new approach robustly, and foremost among these were von Manstein and Guderian. But finally an element of fate intervened in the debate, when the unfortunate loss of a copy of the original OKH plan to the Belgians (and therefore by extension to France and Britain) in an air crash significantly undermined the continued OKH support for what was in many respects no more than a suitably modified version of the old Schlieffen Plan. This was what the French and British had always expected the Germans to do, based upon their own analysis of the ground, the perceived defensive strength of the French Maginot Line, and their own misconception of the correct use of armour on a modern battlefield and therefore of the type of war that the German army was now about to wage against them.

The much modified Fall Gelb plan still called for a diversionary attack against the Netherlands, Belgium and Luxembourg in line with the original plan, and this part of the offensive would initially be spearheaded by two panzer corps and supported by airborne and infantry units. It was designed to convince the Anglo-French forces that the long-anticipated

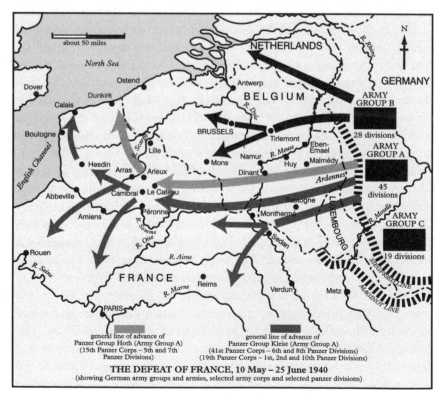

general line of advance of
Panzer Group Hoth (Army Group A)
(15th Panzer Corps – 5th and 7th
Panzer Divisions)

general line of advance of
Panzer Group Kleist (Army Group A)
(41st Panzer Corps – 6th and 8th Panzer Divisions)
(19th Panzer Corps – 1st, 2nd and 10th Panzer Divisions)

THE DEFEAT OF FRANCE, 10 May – 25 June 1940
(showing German army groups and armies, selected army corps and selected panzer divisions)

hook through Belgium and then south-west to seize Paris was indeed still
the German intention, and it was expected to provoke an Anglo-French
counter-move into Belgium, thus extending their lines of communication
and support.

In reality the main attack would now emanate from the midst of the
heavily forested (theoretically impassable for tanks) Ardennes, with some
forty-five divisions, of which ten were panzer divisions. The principal blow
would fall upon Sedan, where the breakthrough and consequent disloca-
tion of the Anglo-French forces would be achieved. Thereafter the panzer
divisions would not race for Paris, but would seize crossings over the River
Meuse, outflank the Maginot Line, cut through the Anglo-French armies
and separate them, and then strike west and north-west to trap the British
and the residue of their Belgian and French allies against the Channel
coast to complete their destruction. The ground attacks were to be
preceded by a number of daring *coup de main* operations by parachute
troops.

At the outset of the offensive the opposing forces were fairly evenly
matched in quantitative terms, although qualitatively the Germans
possessed a significant edge. The Dutch and Belgian armies comprised
no more than eight and eighteen divisions respectively, plus various
reserve forces. Meanwhile, the British Expeditionary Force (BEF) had
nine divisions under its command in northern France, with another division grouped with the French 2nd Army Group in the south. But the
main strength of the Allies lay in the three French army groups. These
were: 1st Army Group with twenty-two divisions, including two light
armoured and three motorized; 2nd Army Group with thirty-six divisions
(including its one British division); 3rd Army Group with fourteen divisions, and 7th Army with seven divisions, including one light armoured
and two motorized. The French reserves comprised twenty-two divisions,
three of which were armoured.

Within these army groups the French had about 3,000 modern, well-
armed and well-armoured tanks, with 1,292 of these grouped into light
and heavy tank divisions. The British had 210 light and 100 heavy tanks,
but all of them were allocated to support the infantry.[192] The relative
paucity of French anti-tank guns – no more than about 8,000 in May 1940
– fell far short of the numbers needed to counter the armoured threat that
was even now massing just across the frontier.

On the German side, Army Group B in the north had twenty-eight
divisions (including three panzer and two motorized) to carry out its
deception mission. The southern Army Group C had nineteen divisions

✠✠✠✠✠✠✠✠✠✠✠✠

for its security tasks in the south opposite the Maginot Line defences, while in the centre General von Runstedt's Army Group A had no fewer than forty-five divisions (including seven panzer and three motorized). The divisions of Army Group A were further sub-allocated within 4th, 12th and 16th Armies. But of particular significance was the panzer spearhead, grouped into Panzer Group Hoth (two panzer divisions, one of which was commanded by Rommel) and Panzer Group Kleist (five panzer divisions), for these were the formations that would bring about the defeat of France and the forthcoming offensive was therefore very much centred upon their actions. Within Panzer Group Kleist were the 41st and 19th Panzer Corps, commanded by General Reinhardt and General Guderian respectively. The German armoured forces deployed no more than 627 Pz.Kpfw.3 and Pz.Kpfw.4, 1,679 Pz.Kpfw.1 and Pz.Kpfw.2, and 381 of the Czech T-38 tanks seized in 1939, which produced a total of 2,687 tanks in all.

Crucially, by May 1940 Germany possessed more than 3,000 combat aircraft, including 400 of the Stuka dive-bombers that were so vital for the support of the panzer formations, while the French had about 1,200 aircraft, but no dive-bombers. Fighter strengths were about 800 French and British of various types, as opposed to 1,000 German fighters (virtually all of which enjoyed a technological superiority). Finally, France had just 150 medium and heavy bombers compared to Germany's 1,470. To counter the air threat, France had fewer than 3,000 anti-aircraft guns, the Germans had 9,300. Although the German field artillery with some 7,700 guns had many fewer than the 11,000 of the French, the latter's almost total reliance on horse-drawn guns meant that France was ill-prepared to conduct or counter motorized and armoured mobile operations.[193]

The attack against the Low Countries began on the night of 10 May. Within four days the Netherlands had collapsed and as anticipated the Allies moved troops into Belgium, engaging Army Group B along the River Dyle. On the morning of 13 May the first tank battles took place between Huy and Tirlemont, where 16th Panzer Corps supported by the ever-present Stukas infiltrated the French armoured screen. By 5.45 p.m. the Germans had forced a general withdrawal, which continued during the following two days. This action was still no more than a continuation of the wider deception, and in the face of more resolute opposition from 1st French Army, 16th Panzer Corps soon extricated itself from this battle prior to joining that which was then developing farther south.

In the meantime, the main blow had already smashed into France from the woods and defiles of the Ardennes as 15th Panzer Corps struck at

Dinant, 41st at Montherme, and 19th at Sedan. On a frontage of no more than fifty miles, the three panzer corps had raced to secure the crossings over the River Meuse and by the night of 12 May they were on the east bank of the Meuse and preparing to cross next morning. Despite heavy resistance, by mid-afternoon on 13 May all three corps had secured infantry bridgeheads on the far bank, and the engineers had begun to construct the ferries and bridges for the tanks to cross. By midnight the 15th and 19th Corps had these in place, using them to reinforce their bridgeheads with armour as quickly as possible.

The French failed to exploit the temporary vulnerability of the bridgeheads (especially that of 41st Corps) and as the panzers prepared to break out to the west and north, General Corap, commanding the French 9th Army, ordered a general withdrawal on the night of 14 May. By the following evening, elements of 1st and 7th Panzer Divisions – the former from Guderian's 19th Panzer Corps and the latter from Hoth's 15th Panzer Corps – were respectively fifteen and twenty-six miles west of the Meuse. The opposition was collapsing wherever the German tanks appeared, troops were surrendering in huge numbers, and French morale had been shattered as the impact of the Blitzkrieg struck fear into the consciousness of the French commanders and their soldiers alike.

The panzers rolled on, protected and supported by the virtually unchallenged air power of the Luftwaffe. But then, with total victory well within the grasp of their enthusiastic black-uniformed commanders, the panzer units became victims of their own success as the high command – specifically Hitler and von Runstedt – began to fear for the vulnerability of the divisions which had advanced so far ahead of the rest of the invading ground forces. Certainly they were irreplaceable and so the army could not afford to lose them, but with the French and British defence crumbling it was worthwhile allowing the advance to continue, and the only real question now was whether to strike at Paris or for the Channel. Caution prevailed and a halt was ordered to enable the non-panzer formations to catch up. Despite this, Guderian did persuade his panzer group commander, Kleist, to allow him a further twenty-four hours of activity, during which he advanced more than forty miles to the River Oise. Rommel also pushed his 7th Panzer Division on another fifty miles, reaching Le Cateau by the morning of 17 May. At that point a complete halt was ordered, although the clear evidence of the escalating French collapse (apart from a few local counter-attacks, which were soon dealt with) and of the retreat of the BEF westwards, together with the residue of Belgian and French forces in northern France, did allow the advance to resume later.

✶✶✶✶✶✶✶✶✶✶✶✶

By the mid-morning of 20 May the three leading panzer corps were on a line from Arleux, close to the River Scarpe, running generally south to Péronne on the River Somme. That evening the tank crewmen of 2nd Panzer Division had their first view of the Channel from their positions in Abbeville, the 1st Panzer Division was well established in Amiens, and the two panzer divisions of the 41st Corps – 6th and 8th – were in positions centred upon Le Boisle and Hesdin respectively. Meanwhile, in 15th Panzer Corps, the 7th Panzer Division had reached Arras, with 5th Panzer Division in the Cambrai area. Apparently, the way now lay wide open for the panzer corps to seize the Channel ports from Dunkirk to Boulogne and so envelop all the remaining undefeated Allied troops in northern France. But then the Germans suffered their first significant reverse, when the motorized infantry of Rommel's 25th Panzer Regiment – 7th Division's spearhead – was surprised by a group of seventy British heavy tanks near Arras, just when the German tanks were moving well ahead of their supporting infantry.

The British tanks wrought havoc among the unprotected infantry. Only when they were engaged by the divisional artillery and by a number of 88mm anti-aircraft guns (used most effectively in the anti-tank role) did the slaughter of the panzergrenadiers abate. Even the speedy return of the regiment's tanks made little difference, for they were then met by a storm of fire from a number of well-concealed British anti-tank guns, which destroyed twenty tanks in short order. Eventually 5th Panzer Division, urgently summoned from Cambrai, arrived on the scene, but by then the battle was more or less over. This short, sharp and tactically insignificant engagement had much wider implications at the operational and strategic levels of command, for the losses suffered served to confirm the high command's fears about over-extending the lines of advance, and underlined the vulnerabilities inherent in these divisions as they were then structured and equipped. But it had also shown those who witnessed the battle the enormous potential of the 88mm anti-aircraft gun as an anti-armour weapon, which Rommel would later employ most effectively during his campaign in North Africa.

In any event, the high command – fearful of losing its most important war-winning fighting formations – now ordered a halt to the helter-skelter advance of the first three weeks of May 1940. A general consolidation was to take place, with flanks and lines of communication properly secured, while the remaining ground forces caught up. Meanwhile, the panzer corps prepared to conduct deliberate assaults to take Boulogne and Calais, rather than making any attempt to engage directly the daily growing Allied salient about Dunkirk. The Luftwaffe would deal with this residual rump of the Allied armies in northern France.

Air attack alone could not overwhelm the Dunkirk salient, and, although Calais fell on 26 May, thus releasing 19th Panzer Corps for operations against the salient, it was by now defended strongly and in depth, and would require a major operation to overcome it. But, before this attack could be mounted, between 26 May and 4 June a mixed fleet of British, French and Belgian naval vessels, together with a disparate armada of privately owned craft of every type, had embarked 338,226 soldiers (of whom 198,315 were British and 139,911 were Allied, but predominantly French) from the Dunkirk beaches and conveyed them to safety in England. On 28 May the panzer divisions were withdrawn from their posi tions close to the Channel coast to prepare themselves for the task of defeating the remaining French forces to the south. So it was that the opportunity for the panzers to annihilate the Anglo-French forces at Dunkirk had been denied them by their own high command, a decision which underlined and had been precipitated in large part by the overall lack of panzer forces then available to the army.

During June the panzers struck south and west, supported by the bulk of the Fall Gelb non-motorized follow-on forces, which by now were well established on French territory. Although some stiff French resistance was encountered, with often spirited attacks by a number of French armoured units, such action was generally isolated and unsustainable. Certainly the heart had gone from the French army and both its high command and its government lacked the resolve to fight on. From 10 June the government was actively seeking ways in which to end the conflict. On 13 June Paris became an open city and was entered by the Germans next day. Guderian's panzers reached the Swiss frontier on 16 June, enveloping a huge number of French units between his corps and the French border. Cherbourg fell to Rommel's division on 19 June, where 1st British Armoured Division had belatedly and ill-advisedly been deployed to fight alongside the French defenders. Lyon fell on 20 June, and by 25 June the German line ran across southern France from Angoulême in the west, north of Limoges, through Clermont-Ferrand and St-Etienne, and then along the south side of the River Rhône to the Swiss frontier close to Geneva. The newly installed French president, Marshal Pétain, had already ordered an end to further resistance on 17 June, and by 25 June the battle for France had ended. The Germans controlled the Low Countries and all of northern France and a compliant French government had assumed power in the as yet unoccupied south of the country. The army's victory was complete, and what was universally seen as Hitler's strategic brilliance was acclaimed throughout Germany. Elsewhere, all this was viewed with considerable trepidation in Great Britain and the United States, as well as in the Soviet Union and the newly occupied countries of Scandinavia and Europe.

The Aftermath

The events of 1939 and 1940 established the potency of the panzer arm and provided the valuable lessons on which its future doctrine and German tank design were based. The first three priorities were to up-gun and up-armour the tanks and to provide armoured infantry with troop carriers that could move in close support of the panzers. In parallel, there was a pressing need to increase the size of the panzer arm. The viability of the panzer concept was in doubt no longer, and its occasional setbacks merely indicated those measures necessary to ensure that any existing vulnerabilities were quickly resolved.

Indeed, the remarkable ability of the armoured formations to operate in the close country of the Ardennes had also been well noted and was capitalized upon once again a little over four years later, in December 1944. By then the Allied invasion of D-Day on 6 June had taken place (when a lack of panzer forces had once again caused the high command to hesitate in making its decision to commit those panzer reserves that were available) and the Anglo-US forces were already firmly established on the European mainland. Then, out of the misty, snow-laden woods and valleys of the Ardennes in winter, Hitler and von Runstedt launched Operation 'Wacht am Rhein' against the ill-prepared US forces deployed in that area. This offensive was a daring but always risky bid to split the Anglo-US armies, to secure the Meuse and seize Antwerp, and thereby to gain time for the development and mass production of Germany's potentially devastating new V-weapons. The offensive was spearheaded by the armoured might of 6th SS-Panzer-Armee, commanded by SS-Oberst-Gruppenführer und Panzer-Generaloberst der Waffen-SS Joseph 'Sepp' Dietrich, a long-time friend and loyal supporter of Hitler ever since the early days of the Nazi Party.

What became known to the allies as the 'Battle of the Bulge' at first caused widespread panic among the almost totally surprised US formations which bore the brunt of the initial assault, notably the unfortunate US 28th Infantry Division. The consequent disarray and withdrawals at first threatened the entire Allied situation in the west. On 20 December no fewer than 9,000 US soldiers, mainly of the 422nd and 423rd Regiments of 106th Infantry Division on the Schnee Eifel, surrendered to the grenadiers of 18th Volks-Grenadier Division, in what was the worst American reverse in the NW Europe campaign. But, despite numerous other tactical successes, the continuing lack of resources and (by that stage of the war) of reserves to sustain the offensive's early achievements meant that the great assault eventually lost momentum and ground to a halt. Also, in December 1944 one of the other fundamental lessons of the Blitzkriegs of 1939 and 1940 could not be applied, as the Germans initially lacked the vital air support needed to sustain such operations while the weather was closed in. Then, once the mist and cloud finally lifted, they were immediately forced to relinquish any thoughts of air superiority in the face of the overwhelming Allied air power that was quickly launched against them.

The Ardennes offensive of December 1944 also gained particular notoriety for the so-called 'Malmédy Massacre' of 17 December, when up to eighty-six US prisoners were killed by Waffen-SS soldiers of Kampfgruppe Peiper (part of the 1st SS-Panzer-Division Leibstandarte Adolf Hitler) in a field at Baugnez crossroads, just over two miles to the southeast of Malmédy. The true facts of the incident were certainly very unclear in December 1944, and were probably considerably misrepresented at the war crimes trials conducted by the US military authorities at Dachau after the war, a number of aspects of the affair remaining matters of dispute to this day. Nevertheless, shortly after the discovery of the killings in December 1944 it was publicized very widely by the US army. While this provided the Allies with a major propaganda tool, it also led to a number of somewhat extreme retaliatory orders being promulgated by the Americans. One such order, issued on 21 December by the headquarters of 328th Regiment of the US 26th Infantry Division, stated that, 'No SS troops or paratroopers will be taken prisoner but will be shot on sight.'[194] In practice, such orders (together with the arguably ill-judged Allied announcement by US President Franklin D. Roosevelt at Casablanca on 24 January 1943 that nothing less than 'the unconditional surrender of Germany, Italy and Japan' would be acceptable to the Allies) served to strengthen the resolve of all German soldiers to fight on, as they had nothing to gain by surrendering in such circumstances. At the same time, such statements and policies by the Allies provided the Third Reich's propaganda minister Joseph Goebbels with a significant psychological weapon with which to strengthen the fortitude of the wider German population.[195]

Meanwhile, returning to the military situation in 1940, the precipitate entry of Italy into the war on 10 June, with the later need for Germany to go to the aid of its militarily colourful but professionally much less competent Axis ally, very soon involved Rommel's newly created Deutsche Afrika Korps fighting in the generally ideal tank terrain of North Africa. There, the old problems of overlong lines of communication, a lack of resources and a British general named Montgomery eventually brought an otherwise well-executed German campaign (in which the panzer units played a key role) of almost two years' duration to an abrupt end at El Alamein in October 1942. But, although El Alamein was the battle characterized by the British Prime Minister Winston Churchill as 'the end of the beginning' of the war against the Third Reich, viewed in hindsight it was in truth a crucial decision taken by Hitler himself in mid-1941 which actually sealed the fate of the so-called 'Thousand-Year Reich' and made its somewhat earlier demise inevitable.

On the morning of 22 June 1941 more than four million Axis soldiers (of whom at least three million were German), 3,360 tanks and seven thousand artillery pieces, with the support of two thousand aircraft, stormed across the German-Soviet border and struck deep into Russia as Hitler launched the Wehrmacht on Operation 'Barbarossa'. This was his bid to seize the Soviet oilfields and win 'Lebensraum' for German expansion in the east, but also to extinguish the Bolshevik communist ideology that was anathema to the National Socialists, while also taking the opportunity to eliminate those whom the Nazis had decided were the ethnically 'sub-human' Russians and Jews of eastern Europe.

Accordingly, while many soldiers might not have appreciated it on that morning in June 1941, the army's military role had at last become virtually indivisible from the political goals of the Nazi government and of the Führer to whom they had, since August 1934, been bound by their sacred soldier's oath to serve without question. While the Waffen-SS divisions that rolled into the Soviet Union alongside their Wehrmacht comrades-in-arms might well have exemplified the Nazi military ideal and political commitment, the army could not realistically distance itself from what had been widely presented by the Nazi leadership as Germany's crusade against Bolshevism, with all the potential consequences which that implied.[196]

Militarily, therefore, the German army had been committed to achieve a feat which not even the first Napoleon had been able to accomplish – the defeat of Russia. Despite its immense combat power and its understandable self-confidence following the campaigns of 1939 and 1940, together with its professional competence and its early successes against the Red Army, it would be in the vastness of Russia and in the frozen grip of its savagely unforgiving winters that the Third Reich's army would be forced to discover the foundations of its eventual Armageddon.

21

'Barbarossa' to 'Zitadelle'

The Eastern Front, 1941–1943

VIEWED IN HINDSIGHT, Hitler's obsession with the evils of Bolshevism, and his closely-related decision to attack his erstwhile Soviet ally, were a monumental error of judgement and a classic example of underestimating one's enemy. But, by early 1941, the perverted political ideology of the time had well and truly subsumed the legacy of common-sense and military pragmatism which had served Germany so well in the past. It had transformed an attack on the Soviet Union into a crusade in which the forces of National Socialism would finally and inevitably annihi-late the evils of its ideological arch-enemy, communism, enabling Germany to assume at last its rightful place at the head of the civilized nations of the world. Linked to this was Hitler's perception that by the end of June 1940 Great Britain (whose empire the Führer much admired) had for all prac-tical purposes already been defeated militarily, and that it was therefore only a matter of time until London sued for peace and joined the great Anglo-German crusade against the menace of Bolshevism. However, the eventual strategic decision to attack the Soviet Union was also surrounded by a complex web of political and diplomatic suspicion, intriguing and misunderstanding on the part of both Hitler and Stalin.

Hitler had accepted that Stalin was on the verge of supporting Great Britain against Germany, and used this mistaken belief to justify his even-tual decision. In fact, Churchill had already proposed this course of action to Stalin secretly, but the Soviet ruler had ignored the British communica-tions (believing that it was a trap set up by Churchill) and then dutifully informed his ally Hitler about them – thereby fuelling Hitler's own suspi-cions! Nevertheless, these suspicions were also reinforced by Stalin's reluc-tance to join with Germany in the war against Britain when this had been proposed to the Soviet leadership in November 1940; despite Hitler's offer to Stalin of a significant part of the British Empire's overseas territories once Britain had been defeated.

In practice, although the ever-pragmatic Soviet leader had no thoughts of embarking upon a war against Germany at that stage, he had neverthe-less anticipated that such a conflict would probably take place not less than two years hence. He suspected that Hitler's failure to launch an invasion of England in 1940 was indicative of a secret Anglo-German accommodation

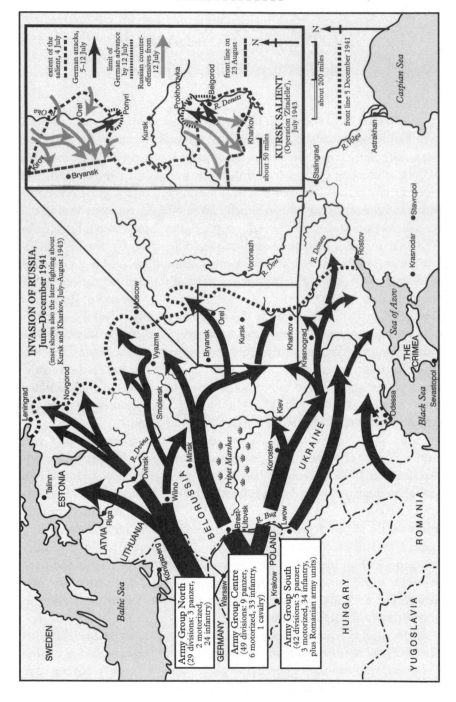

KURSK SALIENT
(Operation 'Zitadelle'),
July 1943

- - - - extent of the salient, 4 July
▶▶▶▶ German attacks, 5–12 July
- - - - limit of German advance by 12 July
▶ Russian counter-offensives from 12 July
- - - - front line on 23 August

about 50 miles

INVASION OF RUSSIA,
June–December 1941
(inset shows also the later fighting about
Kursk and Kharkov, July–August 1943)

▬▬▬▬ front line 5 December 1941

about 200 miles

Army Group North
(29 divisions: 3 panzer,
2 motorized,
24 infantry)

Army Group Centre
(49 divisions: 9 panzer,
6 motorized, 33 infantry,
1 cavalry)

Army Group South
(42 divisions: 5 panzer,
3 motorized, 34 infantry,
plus Romanian army units)

346

against the Soviet Union, and that acceptance of Hitler's invitation to declare war against Britain would in fact provide an excuse for that to happen – a view given added validity by Rudolf Hess's bizarre and ill-fated flight to Scotland in May 1941.[197] In any event, Stalin remained absolutely convinced and secure in the belief that Germany could not attack Russia in the short-term, and certainly not while Britain remained undefeated. He reasoned that an attack on Russia would involve Germany in a war on two fronts, which ran directly contrary to all military logic in light of Germany's limited resources and ability to fight such a widespread and potentially lengthy war of attrition. Consequently, for some time after the start of the German onslaught and despite all the evidence to the contrary, Stalin remained in a state of denial that Hitler had in fact reneged on the German-Soviet non-aggression pact, while also confounding all the realities of military commonsense and strategic logic.

At the same time, Hitler's belief that the Soviet state was fundamentally so flawed (36,671 of its best military personnel already executed, exiled or dismissed during Stalin's widespread purges of the officer corps since 1937) that the mere fact of a German offensive would result in its rapid demise was soon shown to be far from accurate, despite the considerable disquiet that Stalin's repressive totalitarian regime had provoked among significant sections of the population in western and southern Russia. Indeed, had Hitler understood that the Russian soldier's love of his motherland and readiness to obey his leaders without question (perhaps more from fear and a sense of duty to his country rather than a consequence of communist ideology or respect for the leadership) were akin to the German soldier's love of his Heimat and to his obligation of duty (embodied in and maintained by the soldier's oath), Operation 'Barbarossa' might have been undertaken in a very different form, and almost certainly not in mid-1941. Given the extent of pre-war German-Soviet military co-operation, especially during the early stages of Germany's rearmament during the 1930s, it was quite remarkable that the German military intelligence organization had so misunderstood or misrepresented the true nature of its erstwhile ally. Clearly, the widely held view in both the high command and throughout much of the army that the great new offensive in the east would simply develop as another short-term Blitzkrieg, similar to those of 1939 and 1940 but on a much greater scale, was hopelessly incorrect, and the German army was destined to pay a catastrophic price for this historic miscalculation by its Führer and his increasingly politicized and compliant high command at OKW. By the end of the war in May 1945, no fewer than 80 per cent of the army's total casualties from 1939 to 1945 would have been sustained during its four years' campaign against the Red Army on the Eastern Front, and the Wehrmacht as a whole would have incurred a staggering 1,015,000 fatal casualties on the Eastern Front between June 1941 and May 1945.

As the months passed, the soldiers who had marched, ridden and driven into the Soviet Union, all along the border from East Prussia, occupied Poland and down to Hungary and Romania in June 1941, had embarked upon a campaign that was very different from anything they had previously experienced. Although the army at first achieved a succession of victories, with spectacular advances, the annihilation of much of the Red Army in the west, and with many thousands of prisoners taken, by the end of the summer of 1941 its lines of communication and resupply were unprecedented in length. Russian resistance was stiffening and the army was also facing the imminent onset of the Russian winter, for which the Wehrmacht was ill-prepared as the high command had never expected it to have to endure such a winter in the field. At the same time, with German industrial mobilization never having achieved the scale necessary to sustain a war of attrition, the Wehrmacht was beginning to suffer critical shortages of the spares, fuel and other resources so essential to sustain a modern European army which relied upon these items to maintain its offensive capability: a capability exemplified by the panzer and motorized divisions, of which the army still had far too few.

In addition to the everyday military practicalities of war, the moral nature of the army's campaign also changed in Russia as it became directly implicated in the operations carried out by the Einsatzgruppen and Einsatzkommandos, the SS units and special police units that followed up the main advance and secured the rear areas, exterminating any partisans, Jews, gypsies, political commissars and many others categorized as 'Untermenschen' or designated as enemies of the Third Reich. Any pretence that the army had been able to remain separate from the politics of the time was illusory by mid-1941, when orders issued by senior army commanders included such statements as 'The annihilation of those same Jews who support Bolshevism and its organization for murder, the partisans, is a measure of self-preservation' (General Hermann Hoth, 4th Panzer Army), and 'the Jewish-Bolshevik system must be rooted out once and for all' (General Erich von Manstein). The chief of the general staff, General Franz Halder, had already acknowledged the inevitability of the army having to carry out collective reprisals against the Russian civilians and that the coming campaign would be a 'war of extermination', while numerous other documents clearly indicated that the coming campaign would entirely disregard the needs and any rights of the Russian civilian or soldier, being generally a punitive combat conducted to eliminate a dangerous political ideology and against a lesser race deserving of nothing less than annihilation. An opponent of the Hitler regime, the former ambassador, Ulrich von Hassell, encapsulated the practical consequences of the many such orders and policy directives issued to and within the army prior to Operation 'Barbarossa' when he noted that 'the army must [now] assume the onus of the murders and burnings which up to now have been confined to the SS'.[198]

As dawn broke following a short but hot and sultry night on 22 June 1941, thousands of guns were unmasked and began their bombardment of the Soviet border defences, while overhead waves of the Luftwaffe's ground-attack aircraft screamed eastwards to strike positions and head-quarters in depth, and to destroy the Soviet air force on the ground. Meanwhile, thousands more tank, armoured infantry carrier, truck and motorcycle engines started up, radio silence was broken, and the huge troop concentrations at last moved from their concealed hide areas east-wards to the border and into Russia. An enthusiastic and supremely self-confident German army finally entered the abyss which had been so thoroughly prepared for it by its Führer and by the expansionist, often extreme and generally populist politics of National Socialism ever since 1933. Meanwhile, just under six months later, on 7 December, the Japanese attack on Pearl Harbor would bring the United States into the war alongside Great Britain and the Soviet Union and prompt Germany to declare war against the United States, with the result that the great military power which Hitler had turned into an enemy in the east would thereafter be balanced by an even greater hostile military power on Germany's western flank.

Initially, the impressive progress made during 'Barbarossa' during its first three or four months no doubt served to allay any German reserva-tions about its advisability. At the outset, the army – four million men, 600,000 vehicles, 3,360 tanks, 7,184 artillery guns, most of the Wehrmacht's 600,000 horses and some two thousand aircraft – advanced on a front that was almost one thousand miles long and ran from the Baltic in the north to the Black Sea in the south.[199] In the north, Army Group North (commanded by Field Marshal Ritter von Leeb), with three panzer divisions, two motorized divisions and twenty-four infantry divisions, attacked from East Prussia, through Latvia, Lithuania and Estonia, capturing Riga on 1 July, before joining with Finnish forces about Leningrad and besieging the city from 19 August. Meanwhile, Field

✠✠✠✠✠✠✠✠✠✠✠✠

Marshal Fedor von Bock's Army Group Centre, with nine panzer divisions, six motorized divisions, thirty-three infantry divisions and one cavalry division struck eastwards from occupied Poland to capture Smolensk on 15 July. By 29 June two panzer groups had also cut off some 300,000 soldiers at Minsk. Finally, Army Group South, under the command of Field Marshal Gerd von Runstedt, with five panzer divisions, three motorized divisions and thirty-four infantry divisions, as well as a number of units from Germany's Romanian ally, advanced into the south-west of the Soviet Union, into Bessarabia, and towards Odessa and Kharkov, which fell on 24 October.

By 25 November the panzers were less than twenty miles from Moscow. They could and should have been there very much earlier, had they not been diverted by Hitler to carry out other tasks between mid-July and early October. As early as mid-July, evidence of the discord between Hitler, OKW, OKH and some of the formation commanders in the field was emerging, as the campaign threatened to run on longer than had been envisaged, but with no longer-term strategic objectives yet set for it. In mid-September the first snows of the winter fell in the north; in mid-October heavy rain and sleet made vehicle movement virtually impossible, and only the plummeting temperatures in mid-November at last froze the ground and enabled the advance to continue, although the bitter cold brought with it many other problems.

By late November the German offensive gradually ground to a halt along a generally north–south line that ran so close to one of its major objectives, the Soviet capital, that the German soldiers could see the onion-dome towers of the Kremlin from their forward positions. But by then the Wehrmacht's campaign had reached its high-watermark. In early December the Red Army – by now reinforced by the arrival of more than thirty divisions of Mongolian troops from Siberia – launched its first major counter-offensive to save Moscow, a series of concerted attacks by some 500,000 troops on a frontage of 600 miles from Leningrad to Kursk, which forced parts of Army Group Centre to withdraw into defensive positions established as much as 200 miles to the west of their front line of a few days before.

The reverses sustained in December exacerbated the ill-feeling and distrust that existed between the OKW, the OKH and various commanders, and Hitler seized the opportunity to dismiss many of the OKH senior staff officers, together with a number of the field commanders in Russia, including such well-known and competent officers as von Runstedt, von Leeb, and Guderian. At the same time Hitler removed General von Brauchitsch as commander-in-chief of the army and assumed the appointment himself, a move that effectively gave Hitler direct operational control of the army's campaign in Russia. This was followed by a further centralization at OKW rather than OKH of several of the army's other powers and responsibilities – including its right to select and promote its own officers – so that by 1942 the army had finally lost the authority to control its own destiny, both administratively and operationally. In Russia it had also lost about 900,000 casualties, more than 2,300 armoured vehicles, and 50 per cent of its original complement of horses by the spring of 1942. Meanwhile, although the army in the east had gained no fewer than twenty-nine new divisions since the previous June, this had generally been at the expense of not replacing the casualties sustained by the original divisions, so that the impressive number of divisions shown on the army's order of battle was mitigated by the fact that most of them were seriously below their established strength. Nevertheless, despite ever more shortages and the hardships suffered during the recent winter, the soldiers' morale generally remained high as they prepared to carry out Hitler's orders for a new summer offensive. Instead of resuming the assault to capture Moscow, this new attack – Operation 'Blue' – was to be carried out by Army Group South in the Ukraine and taken on into the Caucasus with its strategically vital oil fields.

On 28 June, 1942, while the northern and central army groups maintained a defensive posture, sixty-eight German divisions supported by fifty Italian, Romanian and Hungarian formations struck towards Voronezh on the River Don. After a week of heavy fighting Voronezh fell on 5 July, while concurrent attacks cleared the Crimea and the Kerch Peninsula and captured Sevastopol. At this stage, on 9 July, Army Group South was split into Army Groups A and B. The former had the mission of securing the Donets Basin north of Rostov before moving south into the Caucasus and advancing to a line from Baku to Batumi, thereby gaining control of the oilfields, while Army Group B advanced to capture the city and military-industrial complex on the River Volga at Stalingrad. The offensive progressed well at first, with Army Group B making rapid progress. But then, on 16 July, Hitler ordered 4th Panzer Army to redeploy to assist Army Group A, just as Army Group B was approaching Stalingrad. Then, realizing that the city might provide a base from which Army Group A could be threatened, Hitler countermanded his earlier order and returned 4th Panzer Army to Army Group B. This succession of 'order, counter-order, and disorder' meant that neither the oil fields nor Stalingrad had been accorded the higher priority. Consequently neither army group had sufficient combat power to achieve its objectives, so that the offensive gradually lost its momentum.

The Battle of Stalingrad, 7 September 1942 to 2 February 1943

The capture of Stavropol on 5 August and Krasnodar on 9 August marked the limit of Army Group A's progress. Meanwhile, well to the north-east in the western suburbs of the great city of Stalingrad, the infantrymen of 6th Army, commanded by General Friedrich Paulus, who had been fighting on the city's outskirts ever since 7 August, began to encounter growing resistance as they fought their way into the city on 23 and 24 August. This assault would subsequently prove to be the precursor to one of the defining battles of the war and the five-month-long battle of Stalingrad had begun. On the same day, 24 August, Hitler replaced the increasingly pessimistic General Halder as chief of the general staff by General Kurt Zeitzler, a man acquiescent to Hitler's wishes and who has been described by one historian as 'an obedient optimist'.[200] By late 1942 Hitler had surrounded himself with such officers, and this situation was already having fatal consequences for the thousands of German soldiers loyally fighting for the Fatherland on the front line of the Eastern Front.

The security of the 6th Army's flanks was the responsibility of the disparate Italian, Hungarian and Romanian units, and with Paulus's army already deeply enmeshed in fighting the battle for Stalingrad street-by-street and house-by-house, a major counter-stroke by the Red Army on 19 November cut through the Romanian units, surrounding the 250,000 men of the 6th Army, two Romanian divisions and part of 4th Panzer Army within the city. By 22 November these forces were effectively cut off from the rest of the German army and were only able to receive resupply by air, something that the Luftwaffe patently lacked the capability to achieve despite Göring's assurances to the contrary. Nevertheless, Hitler ordered 6th Army to stand and fight until or unless relieved. Elsewhere, with Stalingrad surrounded on 19 November, Army Group A had now become vulnerable and in late December the more than a quarter of a million German troops then in the Caucasus were withdrawn northwards and away from the immediate threat facing them.

In the meantime, a few divisions formed as 'Army Group Don' with about 230 tanks and commanded by General Erich von Manstein were grouped together to relieve Stalingrad. Despite their unavoidably slow advance against the combined rigours of a second Russian winter and in the face of growing Soviet resistance, this force did manage to come within thirty miles of 6th Army's defensive perimeter by mid-December. But a deteriorating situation on Army Group Don's flanks due to the collapse of the Italian 8th Army, together with Paulus's refusal to attempt a breakout to link up with the relieving force, soon compelled von Manstein to withdraw his army group, and by the end of December the distance between the beleaguered 6th Army and the nearest units of the main German force exceeded a hundred miles.

By January 1943 the 6th Army was facing annihilation as the Soviet attackers – constantly reinforced by fresh troops ferried across the River Volga – began to consolidate their positions within the city, gaining ever more ground day-by-day. Eventually the Soviet capture of the airfield removed the army's last link with the outside world and increasing numbers of individual German troops began to surrender, despite the summary fate that befell these prisoners-of-war in very many cases. On 26 January, the two main parts of the attacking Soviet forces came together at the centre of Stalingrad, thereby shattering the cohesion of what was left of the German defence.

The final act in the drama came on 31 January, when Hitler announced that General Paulus had been promoted field marshal; no German field marshal had ever been taken alive in battle. But Paulus and his army had endured enough. On the same day he attempted to negotiate suitable terms of surrender and on 2 February the last of the 91,000 German and Axis soldiers still more or less alive at Stalingrad were taken into Soviet captivity. The prisoners included one field marshal and twenty-two generals. Of these prisoners-of-war, almost 50 per cent were dead by the spring of 1943. Many were summarily shot by their captors, even more succumbed to disease, starvation and the bitter cold. In all, more than 200,000 men were killed or captured during the battles for Stalingrad, and of those captured fewer than 5,000 eventually returned to Germany following their release from Soviet prison camps some ten years later.

Remarkably perhaps, 6th Army's capitulation at Stalingrad destroyed neither the Wehrmacht's offensive capability nor its will to fight (both of which would once again be clearly in evidence just five months later during the great armoured battle of Kursk), but it was a major catastrophe for the army, both psychologically and in more tangible terms, with so many men and so much equipment lost in vain. Certainly it was the defining moment of the war on the Eastern Front, and provided an indication of the likely outcome of the wider war for Germany. Not surprisingly, such indications went unheeded by Hitler and his generally acquiescent high command.

✠✠✠✠✠✠✠✠✠✠✠✠

Operation 'Zitadelle': the Battle of Kursk, July 1943

The battle of Kursk had its roots in the wider fallout from the demise of the 6th Army at Stalingrad and the earlier withdrawal of Army Group A in late November 1942, together with the mounting scale and daring of the Soviet attacks. On 8 February 1943 one of these attacks succeeded in recapturing Kursk and striking on west towards Kharkov. This move created a salient which extended well into the German-held territory and so provided an opportunity to cut off and destroy much of the Soviet force. To that end the 2nd SS-Panzer-Korps, commanded by SS-Ober-gruppenführer und General der Waffen-SS Paul Hausser, was ordered by Hitler to hold Kharkov, prior to a German counter-attack. But after a week of bitter fighting within the largely ruined city, the Waffen-SS troopers were finally forced to abandon Kharkov to the Red Army on 15 February. This withdrawal in turn over-extended the Soviet line and on 19 February, at Krasnograd, Hausser's corps and part of 4th Panzer Army launched a surprise armoured attack which resulted in more than 23,000 Soviet casualties and about 9,000 captured. This forced the Russians to withdraw in some disarray. By late March, as winter turned to spring and the iron-hard frozen ground gradually turned to mud, Kharkov was again in German hands, as was Orel to the north, while well over a million Soviet troops were now deployed within what had become the 160-miles-wide Kursk salient. Once again Hitler decided that an opportunity existed to strike into the salient, isolating and then destroying the mass of units therein. What eventually followed, though not until July, culminated in the largest tank battle in the history of warfare to that date, but it also signalled that the ability of the army's panzer units to conduct their Blitzkrieg-style operations with impunity had finally come to an end.

The delay in launching what was designated Operation 'Zitadelle' (Citadel) was occasioned by the need to complete other operations in the Kharkov area beforehand, by the constraints that the spring thaw imposed on armoured movement and, finally, by the need to muster sufficient quantities of armour – principally tanks and assault guns – to carry out the operation. Although the three months' delay to July was probably unavoid-able, it is arguable that this fatally prejudiced the operation from the outset, not least because the Soviets were forewarned of the German plan – probably by the Western Allies utilizing the 'take' of intelligence from their Enigma code intercepts, but with the source having been represented to Moscow as a highly placed spy in the OKH (as the Russians were still officially unaware that the British had captured an Enigma machine and broken its code system). Early indications of the German intentions were later followed up with the precise date that the operation was scheduled to begin, 5 July 1943.

In any event, the 1,300,000 Red Army soldiers within the salient used the three months to turn the salient into a veritable fortress of anti-tank obstacles, ditches and gun emplacements, minefields and well-prepared infantry strongpoints, the whole network of defensive positions up to 120 miles deep and supported by no fewer than 20,220 guns, 3,600 tanks and 2,400 aircraft; with a sizeable armoured counter-strike force held in reserve to the east of the salient. Surprisingly, quite apart from continuing to believe that the security of the forthcoming operation had not been compromised, the Germans were also largely unaware of the true extent of the Soviet defensive preparations within the Kursk salient. The Soviet battle-plan at Kursk was masterminded by Marshal Georgii K. Zhukov and was carried out by his subordinate commanders Rokossovsky, Vatutin and Koniev; all of whom would later inflict a terrible retribution upon Germany and the Wehrmacht during the last eighteen months of the war.

In the south, the German formation deployed for the 'Zitadelle' offensive was 4th Panzer Army – reinforced following the loss of a large part of the original 4th Army during the fighting at Stalingrad in January. In July 1943 this extensively reconstituted army had six panzer divisions, five panzergrenadier divisions and eleven non-armoured divisions. The army had about 1,300 tanks, plus many self-propelled assault guns and other armoured vehicles. The northern German force was 9th Army, with six panzer divisions, one panzergrenadier division, about 800 tanks and other armoured vehicles, and fourteen non-armoured divisions. By 1943, in addition to the earlier Pz.Kpfw.4, the German tank fleet now included numbers of the new Pz.Kpfw.5 'Panther' tank with its well-sloped armour and 75mm main armament, and the formidable Pz.Kpfw.6 'Tiger' tank, which mounted a powerful 88mm gun. This weapon was also mounted on the heavily armoured 'Elefant' (originally titled 'Ferdinand') self-propelled assault guns, which by 1943 were included in the panzer and panzergrenadier division's armoured vehicle inventory. Ninety of these were committed to 'Zitadelle'. With no fewer than 2,200 tanks and about 1,000 assault guns in these two armies, this meant that about 70 per cent of the German armoured capability on the Eastern Front had been committed to the battle. About 1,800 aircraft supported the two armies, which was some 65 per cent of the German air capability on the Eastern Front. In all, the two armies totalled about 900,000 men.[201]

At about 0200 on 5 July, with the offensive due to commence at 0500, the Russian artillery fired a massive bombardment against the German armour and troop concentrations, indicating all too clearly that this would be no surprise attack. The German units had already been subjected to frequent harassing attacks by partisans as they moved into their positions for the operation. Despite such disconcerting occurrences, the spearheads of 9th Army and 4th Panzer Army surged across their start-lines to the north and the south at 0500 hours in accordance with the plan to reach Kursk and so cut off the Russian troops within the salient. Both forces quickly found themselves embroiled in a morass of anti-armour defences supported by a huge weight of fire from hundreds of tanks, anti-tank guns and other artillery. By the close of 5 July parts of 4th Panzer Army had advanced no more than eight miles, the rest having achieved even less. In the north, 9th Army only achieved four miles of penetration. Everywhere the offensive stalled, with rapidly mounting casualties to men and armoured vehicles. Although the Luftwaffe's Stukas provided close air support at the outset, this was insufficient to unlock the planned Blitzkrieg by the panzers; in any case, the Russian Ilyushin Il-2 'Sturmovik' ground-attack aircraft were all the time inflicting their own punishment upon the exposed German armour. The assault quickly degenerated into a battle of attrition, with separate deliberate attacks being required to overcome every strongpoint, line of defence and fortified village; but many of these proved to be too strongly held in any case, so that they delayed and diverted the Germans into yet other killing areas.

As the battle developed, the Pz.Kpfw.5 Panthers recently introduced into service began to suffer various mechanical breakdowns, while the heavily armoured Elefants – armed with the powerful 88mm gun, but with only one machine-gun for local protection – initially smashed through the Russian positions with relative ease, only to find themselves alone and isolated, so that they were then destroyed piecemeal by teams of Soviet infantrymen with a variety of anti-armour weapons and explosive charges. Incredibly, after almost a week of bitter fighting within the salient, the forward units of the two assaulting armies were still 140 miles apart, although on 11 July the attacking 1st, 2nd and 3rd SS Panzer Divisions of the Waffen-SS did at last appear to be making some progress in the area of Prokhorovka, while advancing astride the north–south rail link between Kursk and Belgorod in the vanguard of 4th Panzer Army's attack.

However, as more than 600 Pz.Kpfw.4, Pz.Kpfw.5 Panther and Pz.Kpfw.6 Tiger tanks, together with numbers of assault guns, closed up and surged forward to press their advantage on the following day, the Waffen-SS panzer divisions suddenly found themselves facing most of the T-34/76 tanks of the 5th Guards Tank Army, held in reserve until now, and with the T-34s in considerably greater numbers than the German tanks. On that day, 12 July, more than 1,500 armoured vehicles manoeuvred within the southern part of the salient,[202] while at its core some 250 German and 600 Soviet tanks became locked within a cauldron of battle which fast assumed the appearance of 'a confused, dust shrouded mass, thickened by the billowing black, oily smoke from stricken tanks and guns'.[203] Incredibly, this great armoured mêlée, later acknowledged to have been the greatest tank battle of the war, took place in an area of no more than three square miles. Indeed, the first Russian attack involved the T-34s literally driving straight into and diagonally through the flank of the German advance in a manner more reminiscent of a nineteenth-century cavalry charge than of twentieth-century warfare. All the time they engaged the panzers to deadly effect, often at less than a hundred yards' range, so that, 'The sound of armour on armour could be heard for miles around, punctuated by the bark of 76mm and 88mm guns and the explosions that followed.'[204]

The slaughter continued all day, and when night fell the scene was still illuminated by 'the sparks and swirling flame from hundred upon hundred of blazing tanks and self-propelled guns, or from the wreckage of scores of Stuka dive-bombers or Russian shturmovik [sic] tank-busting aircraft which had ranged over the battlefield, adding their own tallies of death and destruction to the holocaust below'.[205] By nightfall, 4th Panzer Army had lost 400 tanks and 10,000 men since the start of the offensive and it could advance no farther. To the north, by 12 July 9th Army had lost about 200 tanks and as many as 25,000 men.

Undoubtedly the Russians had lost much more – possibly as many as 1,800 tanks and 40,000 men in the southern part of the salient alone – but they still had sufficient reserves to be able to absorb such losses and to launch further attacks at the north of the salient, while the Germans had entirely exhausted their ability to advance any farther. Indeed, the Soviets claimed to have killed or captured as many as half a million German soldiers and to have destroyed 1,500 tanks since 5 July. Whatever the true figures might be, the losses to both sides and the sheer scale of the destruction that had resulted from the week-long battle were without doubt truly appalling. Even Hitler understood that 'Zitadelle' was no longer achievable, and he ordered that the operation be terminated (a decision that was also affected by the fact that Anglo-US forces had landed in Sicily on 10 July).

Despite the destruction inflicted upon the opposing sides – especially that sustained by the Russian forces – neither side could claim Kursk as a tactical victory. At the operational level it had signalled the end of 'Zitadelle' and the German failure to envelop the salient, but far more significantly Kursk marked the point at which the offensive initiative on the Eastern Front passed to the Russians. By early August, Army Group Centre and Army Group South had withdrawn from the Kursk area, abandoning Orel, Kharkov and Belgorod on 5 August. Then, on 7 September, the Germans began their evacuation of the Ukraine, while far to the north the Red Army recaptured Smolensk on 25 September. Everywhere the Russian ground forces (by now organized into ten army 'fronts' stretching from the Baltic to the Caucasus) were mounting co-ordinated offensives and advancing westwards against the much-weakened Wehrmacht.

So began a slow but inexorable withdrawal by the German army on the Eastern Front, a withdrawal set against the background of a series of resolute and often successful defensive operations. But as Germany's reserves and resources gradually diminished and those of the Soviet Union and the Western Allies increased, such defensive actions could never do more than temporarily delay the Soviet onslaught. Consequently, for very many of its soldiers the army's withdrawal would only end once the residue of its shattered divisions eventually reached their final defensive positions in a devastated Fatherland and, for some, amidst the rubble of a ruined Berlin two years later.

22

The Way to Armageddon, 1944–1945

SET DEEP AMID THE DARK FIR FORESTS of Rastenburg in East Prussia was the Führer's headquarters, the Wolfschanze: a complex of buildings, blockhouses and bunkers sited in a well-guarded compound. There, on 20 July 1944, a high-level planning conference had been called by Hitler for 1230 hours. The twenty-three senior military and civilian attendees (including Jodl, Keitel and their principal aides) had been joined by Hitler in the conference room of the Gästebaracke, a sizeable wooden hut with a large conference room, at the centre of which was a large table covered with situation maps. These showed the Wehrmacht's deteriorating situation all too clearly. The Allied landings in Normandy had taken place six weeks earlier. The 900-day siege of Leningrad had been raised in January, and Sevastopol was back in Russian hands in May. More than 30,000 troops had been lost at the Korsun pocket in February. The 17th Army in the Crimea had been isolated and destroyed in April and May. Odessa had fallen, and large Russian forces were already across the River Dnieper in the south and the River Bug in the west, pressing on into Romania, Poland and the rest of eastern Europe. Minsk had fallen on 3 July, allowing the Russians to strike north-westwards towards Riga and the Baltic states. Rome had fallen to the Western Allies in early June. On that July morning, it seemed almost inevitable that another difficult meeting with the increasingly temperamental Führer was in prospect.

Although not an attendee as such, another army officer was due at this particular conference, Lieutenant Colonel Claus Schenk, Graf von Stauffenberg – a 37-year-old south German who had served with distinction in a Bavarian cavalry regiment in Poland, France and North Africa before being severely wounded during an air attack in April 1943. After lengthy treatment and convalescence he had returned to duty as the chief of staff of the army's department of ordnance. Von Stauffenberg had arrived at Rastenburg shortly after 1000 to provide an up-dated report on the situation of the Home Army. But his undoubted courage and loyalty to the Fatherland did not extend to support for the Hitler regime; among the papers, files and reports in his bulging briefcase was a powerful time-bomb of British origin, and his mission that day was to kill Hitler in the hope of saving Germany from the catastrophic political policies and the sheer incompetence that by now characterized the Third Reich.

By mid-1944 von Stauffenberg was but one of a sizeable group of anti-Hitler conspirators which, as well as academics, lawyers, churchmen and politicians, also included many senior and middle-grade army officers. Even Rommel had finally indicated his support for the opposition group (but not for an assassination of Hitler) in February 1944. This clandestine group was headed by the former chief of the general staff, General Ludwig Beck, while the actual assassination plot was headed by Major General Henning von Tresckow, with von Stauffenberg taking the principal role. With Hitler dead, the group intended to negotiate a peace with the Allies based, somewhat optimistically, upon the retention by Germany of its pre-1939 borders.

Von Stauffenberg entered the conference room a little before the time he was due to give his report. He paid his respects to the Führer and placed his briefcase under the table beside Hitler. Having done so, he said that he needed to make a telephone call and left the room. In the mean-time a Colonel Brandt found the briefcase in his way and pushed it away, so that it ended up against one of the substantial table supports, which was now between the briefcase and Hitler. The OKH chief of operations, Lieu-tenant General Adolf Heussinger, was giving his report on the situation on the Eastern Front when, at 1250 precisely, the bomb detonated with a tremendous explosion that destroyed the conference table, devastated the room, blew out the tarred felt roof and threw several men straight through the building's three windows. One man died instantly, three later died of their wounds, several sustained severe injuries, and virtually all of the rest received lesser injuries. Hitler was shocked, his right arm was injured, his eardrums were damaged, and he sustained burns to his head and his right leg. But quite remarkably, given his close proximity to the explosion, the Führer was not only still alive, he was able to walk away more or less unaided from the intended scene of his demise.

The failure of the 20 July plot was a disaster for the German resistance movement and the various opposition groups, irrespective of whether or not they had known about or had been actively involved with the assassi-nation attempt. Himmler headed the post-20 July investigation and in the wake of the Rastenburg bomb about 200 alleged conspirators were arrested, tried and executed. Others (including von Stauffenberg) were summarily shot within hours of the event and so were spared the horrors and humiliations of the show trials, torture and barbaric forms of execu-tion suffered by the majority of those subsequently arrested by the

Gestapo. Several conspirators chose to commit suicide. Although Rommel had actually opposed the assassination attempt, instead advocating that Hitler be put on trial, one of the July plot conspirators had implicated him while under torture. Hitler ordered the Field Marshal, one of the army's most successful, straightforward and popular (if politically naïve) commanders to commit suicide at his home in Herrlingen bei Ulm on 14 October. The widespread purge of the officer corps in the aftermath of the July plot literally tore the heart out of the army and removed many men who might well have contributed positively to the German recovery in the post-war years. Nevertheless, in the short-term very many officers and soldiers, together with much of the German civilian population, regarded the conspirators as traitors to the Fatherland and to the officer corps; such had been the true impact of Nazism and its propaganda over the previous decade.

The bombing also provided the Nazis with an excuse and opportunity to consign many less prominent critics of Hitler and of the National Socialist regime to the concentration camps (where many were subsequently executed), while some of those military personnel considered much less culpable or to be merely an irritation were simply dismissed. One such was General Kurt Zeitzler, who was replaced as chief of the general staff by Guderian on 22 July (who immediately denounced the conspirators as having preferred to take the road of disgrace rather than 'the road of duty and honour').[206] Certainly, had von Stauffenberg been successful the whole course of the Second World War and of post-war European history would have been greatly changed in 1944, with countless lives saved on all sides.

But in the story of the German army, the July plot was especially significant, for it represented the culmination of a growing mood of dissatisfaction with Hitler and National Socialism that had existed ever since the mid-1930s. This was especially so within the army, and in 1944 many of the conspirators were former members of the general staff, together with numbers of serving officers in the headquarters of Army Group Centre, the Replacement Army, the territorial or home defence forces, and within the German military governments in Paris and Brussels. Over time, dissatisfaction had matured into opposition, then into resistance, and had finally mutated into conspiracy by March 1943, when the first of several unsuccessful (some were unlucky, others inept) assassination attempts was carried out by members of General Beck's group. Despite all that has already been said about the soldier's oath to the Führer and the German officer's commitment to honour, duty and obedience, a significant number of army officers were actively involved in the opposition to Hitler. Many of these men were senior officers, including several commanders who had already distinguished themselves fighting for the Third Reich, although the group also included lieutenants as well as generals and field marshals. Consequently, it is quite remarkable that their various attempts to kill the Führer failed so dismally. But 20 July and its immediate aftermath was a defining moment in Hitler's relationship with the army, for although he had already neutralized the OKH, the July plot served to destroy any residual trust in the army – and more particularly in its officer corps – that he might still have entertained. Remarkably, perhaps, the effects of the July plot and its aftermath upon the operational competence and fighting spirit of the army was hardly discernible, and the vigour with which Operation 'Wacht am Rhein' was prosecuted in the Ardennes just five months later provides ample evidence of this.

After 20 July, however, the overall position of the SS was significantly strengthened and this in turn meant that the Waffen-SS (already favoured by Hitler as ideologically pure, politically reliable and élite soldiers) was reinforced substantially in practical equipment, resource and manpower terms – frequently at the army's expense. Indeed, Waffen-SS units were among the best equipped and most successful in the Ardennes offensive that December. So the July plot confirmed Hitler's worst suspicions and justified his long-standing mistrust of the army. At the same time, it dramatically accelerated the climate of fear and retribution which now pervaded every part of the Third Reich and its non-SS armed forces during the final nine months of the war in Europe.

Among the other measures that were speedily implemented, Himmler was appointed commander-in-chief of the Replacement Army, an appointment which had the effect of making the SS responsible for the administration, training and discipline of all newly formed army units and formations. Even the military salute was replaced by the Nazi salute in accordance with an order issued on 23 July, while the political influence of the National Socialists' existing political organization within the army (the Nationalsozialistische Führungsoffiziere, or 'National Socialist leadership officers' – the NSFO – established in 1943) was formally strengthened. Finally, on 1 August, a new law made the relatives of soldiers responsible – and therefore punishable – for the actions and any perceived wrong-doings of their serving soldier relatives. By late-1944, none could doubt that Germany had finally become synonymous with the SS state that the Nazis had so assiduously worked to create. In this environment of fear, and with the knowledge that not even surrender could bring hope or release – as the Allies would accept nothing less than the unconditional surrender of Germany – the army now faced the coming onslaughts from east and west, together with increasing repression on the home front, with considerable apprehension. Despite this, by and large the army still maintained an unquestioning faith in Hitler's ability to snatch the final victory from what were patently the jaws of a looming and cataclysmic defeat.

Regardless of the countless brave and often suicidal battles fought, stands made and counter-attacks launched in both east and west – 'Wacht am Rhein' was a prime example of one such operation – the litany of reverses continued. In August Romania changed sides. In September Bulgaria was occupied by the Soviets. From October, the German forces in Albania and Greece withdrew. In November Soviet troops in Hungary began a siege of Budapest. By mid-January 1945, the audacious but flawed Ardennes offensive on the western front had been defeated. A major Soviet offensive was launched on 12 January, striking towards Warsaw, the River Oder and Berlin. In the west, by the end of March the Anglo-Canadian-US armies were across the Rhine in considerable strength at Remagen, at Oppenheim, and between Rees and Rheinberg. From the Rhine the Americans struck into central and southern Germany, reaching Austria and the Czech border by late April, while the Anglo-Canadian armies completed the liberation of the Netherlands, destroyed the German forces in the Ruhr, and continued their advance across north Germany towards the River Elbe. In the east, Budapest fell in mid-February, while around Lake Balaton[207] in south-west Hungary most of the remaining Waffen-SS panzer divisions were annihilated in heavy fighting, enabling the Red Army to advance into Austria – Vienna fell on 6 April – and towards Prague. Meanwhile, behind the lines the SS, the military police and 'flying courts-martial' teams ranged far and wide, sweeping up and summarily executing large numbers of deserters, 'defeatists', and officers who had ordered withdrawals against orders or who were perceived to have failed the Third Reich in some other way,[208] together with anyone suspected of 'undermining fighting morale'. During the war no fewer than 11,700 men were executed in this way, with possibly an even greater number of unrecorded executions having taken place. During the First World War, just forty-eight German soldiers had been executed for military offences.

However, Berlin was always where it would all end. The Soviet offensive to reach the city began on 16 April when almost two hundred Red Army divisions were unleashed against about fifty much-weakened German divisions. Then, on 23 April, the battle for Berlin began in earnest, as the

Red Army's 5th Shock Army, 8th Guards Army and 1st Guards Tank Army spearheaded from the east and south-east an attack which would eventually draw one and a half million Soviet troops into the onslaught against the German capital. From the north, the 47th Army, 3rd Shock Army and 2nd Guards Tank Army attacked into the suburbs; from the south 3rd Guards Tank Army and 28th Army worked their way into south-west Berlin. Some twelve miles to the south-west, 4th Guards Tank Army struck northwards towards Potsdam. The city of Berlin was defended by just 45,000 Wehrmacht and Waffen-SS troops and sixty tanks, plus about 40,000 young, old, disabled or infirm Volkssturm soldiers. A further 2,000 Waffen-SS troops of the SS-Leibstandarte regiment were also deployed specifically to defend the Chancellery and the central government area.

Two days after the beginning of the Red Army onslaught on central Berlin, on 25 April a patrol from the 69th US Infantry Division encountered a lone Soviet cavalryman near Stehla, a nondescript German village on the west bank of the Elbe, some twenty miles to the south-east of the town of Torgau. This marked the very first meeting of the Allied and Soviet ground forces (although the first officially recorded meeting of the Americans and the Russians took place on 27 April, when other soldiers of 69th US Infantry Division linked up with the 1st Ukrainian Army at Torgau on the River Elbe).

But by then Hitler and many of his immediate entourage were already closeted deep in the Führerbunker adjacent to the Chancellery and the Brandenburg Gate at the very heart of Berlin. It was there that Hitler had learned on 23 April that Göring had betrayed him, followed by Himmler (who had tried to negotiate a separate surrender to the Western Allies) shortly thereafter. He also heard that his retreat and home at the Obersalzberg in southern Bavaria had been all but obliterated by an Allied bombing raid. A few days later, on 28 April, he learned of the killing of his former Axis ally, the dictator Benito Mussolini and his mistress Clara Petacci, whose bodies had subsequently been displayed suspended by ropes in the main square of Milan. The news and details of Mussolini's demise particularly shocked Hitler.

On 29 April, with the Russian assault troops in the devastated city above almost at the gates of the Reichstag, Hitler married his mistress Eva Braun and then dictated his last will and political testament. During the afternoon of 30 April 1945, the man most responsible for the Second World War and for Germany's dark journey into the abyss put a pistol to his head and committed suicide. Eva Braun – Frau Hitler – lay dead beside the body of her new husband, having taken poison. Afterwards, both bodies were doused with petrol and burned by members of the Führerbunker staff in a shallow ditch adjacent to the main entrance to the bunker. Some of the Nazis who had been with Hitler in the bunker to the end subsequently managed to escape; several others chose to commit suicide. The Reichstag finally fell at 1300 on 2 May, although at 2250 on 30 April a group of three Red Army sergeants had already made their way to a balcony at the front of the building and there unfurled the blood-red flag which signalled the Soviet Union's victory over the forces of the Third Reich. The remaining German troops in Berlin capitulated on 2 May, having inflicted about 100,000 casualties on the attacking Soviet forces since 16 April. Many of the German prisoners-of-war in the long columns that marched eastwards out of the ruined city into captivity in the Soviet camps would never see the Fatherland again, and even those who did manage to survive and eventually return to Germany were destined to remain in Soviet captivity until the mid-1950s.

Three days later, on 5 May, the German armies in Denmark, the Netherlands and north Germany surrendered. During April alone the Western Allies took 1,650,000 prisoners, more than half of the almost 3,000,000 taken since they had landed in Normandy on 6 June 1944. On 7 May, General Alfred Jodl signed the unconditional surrender at Reims and on 9 May Field Marshal Keitel formally signed the unconditional surrender documents in Berlin with Soviet Marshal Zhukov.[209] During less than six years of war the armed forces of the Third Reich had been decimated, the Wehrmacht as a whole having lost as many as 3,500,000 men since September 1939, so that in May 1945 the powerful and much-respected army that had conquered much of western Europe so brilliantly in 1939 and 1940, and which had then fought so doggedly against the odds from late-1941 to May 1945, had literally ceased to exist.

The German army had fought its own battle of Armageddon amidst the flames and rubble of the Third Reich's capital, Berlin, and there it had finally been consumed by it. However, the seeds of its own destruction had been sown long before, by its often self-interested willingness to accept and obey the extreme and expansionist policies and actions of a Führer who had always lacked the ability to be both head of state and commander-in-chief. Hitler's perverse National Socialist ideology, his neutralization of the old general staff, and his deliberately divisive internal policies for the Wehrmacht *vis-à-vis* the SS, had gradually undermined the former. The extent of this had been such that not even the army's long-standing qualities of professional competence, technological innovation and operational flexibility, and its historical touchstones of loyalty, honour and duty, could withstand the National Socialist propaganda onslaught, together with the heady attractions and seductive lure of all that had been promised by Adolf Hitler in the tumultuous and often exciting years following his coming to power in 1933. Not least among these promises had been the prospect of new military glory and an overturning of the humiliations imposed by the Allies at Versailles in 1920. These aspirations had indeed proved to be both enticing and compelling in the political and economic chaos of Germany in the 1930s. But the desire of countless Germans (including very many German officers and soldiers) to achieve the vision of national Utopia and military dominance which had been presented to them by Hitler had subsequently led the nation and its army to the bottom of the abyss, and to total defeat at its own form of Armageddon.

PART FOUR

Resurrection and Rehabilitation

23

Cold War Warriors
1945–1990

Images and Perceptions

Sennelager military training area near Paderborn, West Germany on a bitterly cold winter's day in late January 1968, where a small group of the box-like Mark I FV 432 British armoured personnel carriers were practising tactical movement and driver training. The vehicles ploughed their way slowly across the sea of partially frozen and glutinous mud that comprised most of the Stapel training area to the north of Sennelager. The engine cooling fans screamed incessantly as they fought to prevent the vehicle's underpowered petrol engines overheating, while the long exhaust pipes running along the top left side of the carriers glowed red-hot, constantly threatening to set alight the camouflage nets and other equipment secured beside them. The heavily muffled and half-frozen commanders in their exposed cupolas atop the vehicles squinted into the biting wind and near-blinding snow flurries in a bid to direct their drivers, and so avoid them sliding off into one of the many part-frozen lakes that lay to either side of the sparsely marked track. The scene was typical of the type of mechanized infantry training that was routinely carried out by 1st British Corps during the West German winter.

Just then, from behind a hill to the north-west, beyond which lay the small town of Augustdorf and the barracks titled 'Rommel Kaserne', there emerged another and, in many ways, a contrasting martial image. Bearing down upon the British vehicles and very rapidly overhauling them was a long column of dun-coloured Leopard tanks and HS-30 (or 'Schützenpanzer SPZ 12-3') armoured personnel carriers of the Bundeswehr, all speeding south towards the training area's armoured vehicle firing ranges. A number of the angular M-113 armoured personnel carriers were at the end of the column. On the turret of each tank and the side of each armoured personnel carrier was emblazoned a large black Iron Cross, outlined in white. The perfect convoy discipline, the blue and green convoy flags displayed, the precise spacing between the vehicles, and the sheer modernity and martial might that the long lines of armour conveyed were striking.

The compact size and clean lines of the Leopards, all with their 105mm guns probing menacingly forward, seemed to exude sheer military power and their engines emitted an almost menacingly low roar, as they thundered past, their tracks showering veritable fountains of mud to their sides and rear. The vehicle commanders stood or sat low in their turrets, radio headphones clamped over their ears, and goggles covering their eyes. In 1968, these tanks were brand-new and had only been in service at Augustdorf for some twelve to eighteen months at most.

However, for an infantryman, the HS-30s were just as impressive as the tanks. These agile and low-slung fighting vehicles boasted a turret-mounted 20mm cannon and a dismountable 7.62mm machine-gun, as well as having roof hatches from which the six panzergrenadiers in the rear could fire their weapons before leaping from them into the assault, as the carrier drove right on to an enemy objective. This infantry fighting vehicle concept was so different from that of the British and US armies, with their 'battle taxi' FV 432 and M-113 armoured personnel carriers. But it was one that could very readily be identified with the German army's offensive doctrine and the Blitzkrieg concepts of a quarter of a century before. As the Bundeswehr armoured column roared past – almost dismissive of the rather dated and inordinately slow British vehicles – none of the watching British soldiers could have doubted for a moment that this vision of military power perfectly encapsulated the sort of combat capability which had by then become so necessary to counter the growing threat posed by the massed armour of the Soviet and Warsaw Pact on the Central Front in Europe.

For these British soldiers – all of whom were children of the post-1945 era, and who had been raised amid the plethora of exciting but usually sensationalized and often biased books, comics and films about the Second World War – this image of what was then the still relatively new Bundeswehr was particularly striking. Self-evidently, here was a thoroughly modern, focused, and extremely well-equipped army which had clearly recovered and bounced back most effectively from the catastrophe of 1945, and which was now all ready to counter the new threat from the east that had emerged shortly after the Second World War.[210]

However, the Bundeswehr (which in fact included the German air force (Luftwaffe), navy (Marine) and army (Heer), although hereinafter it is generally used to refer to the army unless specifically indicated otherwise) of the late-1960s was patently different in many ways from the German army of former times. Not only had it undergone a form of resurrection, it had also experienced a particularly difficult period of political soul-searching and rehabilitation as it sought to create a new army within an often anti-military society, and without the ability to build upon the historical traditions of its forebears. At the heart of its difficulties was the need for the events and actions of the German army of 1933–45 to be positively expunged from its consciousness. In the meantime, the Bundeswehr of the German Federal Republic in West Germany was but one of two post-1945 'German' armies, for beyond the Inner German Border (the 'IGB') in the German Democratic Republic of East Germany there was another but very different 'German army'. This was the Soviet-controlled Nationale Volksarmee or 'NVA'. So it was that the states of West and East Germany that eventually emerged from the débâcle of the Third Reich in 1945 each spawned a new German army, whose soldiers were destined to face one another across the IGB for the almost four decades of the Cold War, with every day of that conflict set against the very real possibility that German soldiers would be required to fight other German soldiers on the European battlefield.

The Bundeswehr

At the end of the Second World War Germany was a broken nation and its army was a broken force (the army and Waffen-SS together had sustained more than five million casualties during the war, including more than two million killed). The Allied Powers were also determined that never again would the spectre of Prussian and German militarism be able to cast its long shadow over the peace of Europe.[211] Accordingly, Germany had been divided into four sectors, occupied and controlled by the United States, Great Britain, France and the Soviet Union respectively. Events elsewhere all led to the emergence of a need for West Germany to participate actively in its own defence. These policy-shaping events included the breakdown of the Allied four-power arrangements in 1948, the Berlin airlift crisis in 1948–9, the creation of sizeable and increasingly capable paramilitary forces in East Germany, together with other developments in the Soviet Union and Eastern Europe, and the creation of the Warsaw Pact in 1955. Although the western part of Germany had (at the instigation of Chancellor Konrad Adenauer) possessed its own paramilitary internal security and border security forces, the Bundesgrenzschutz, since the end of 1950, these forces were lightly armed and limited in size to 10,000 men, so were in no sense an army, although they were well trained.

Accordingly, the United States had proposed the creation of West German military forces within NATO soon after the new organization was created in April 1949. But this was balked by the French in October 1950, when they counter-proposed that West German forces should be employed within a new European army operating in support of a 'European Defence Community' (or a 'European Defence Union' as it was termed in West Germany), a proposal that was in any case later rejected by the French assembly in August 1954. Consequently, despite many misgivings and objections from a wide range of sources both within and outside the Federal Republic of West Germany (the 'FRG'), in May 1955 it became a member of NATO. Later the same year the Bundeswehr was created as the federal state's armed forces. Within the Bundeswehr, the army (Heer) would comprise 70 per cent, the navy (Marine) 8 per cent, and the air force (Luftwaffe) 22 per cent.[212]

The international constraints imposed upon the Bundeswehr both by the former Allied Powers and by the federal government itself were based upon various agreements that had originally been negotiated or established in 1952 (when any FRG army that might be created was limited to twelve divisions) and in Paris in 1954. Aspects of these constraints were subsequently modified in 1956 to enable the development of a viable defence capability. Indeed, in accordance with the agreements concluded in 1954, the FRG had originally been excluded from altering the FRG borders or precipitating the reunification of Germany by the use of force. At the same time it had also been required not to indulge in the development or manufacture of atomic, chemical or biological weapons. Also, the revival of any organization which resembled the old German general staff had been specifically prohibited, just as it had been after the First World War.

In any event, in order to facilitate the creation of a suitable defence capability, in 1956 the Bundestag revised the constitution and basis for the development and operational role of the Bundeswehr, whose mission was based firmly if rather narrowly upon self-defence and the security of the FRG borders. Control of the Bundeswehr devolved jointly upon the executive, the Bundesrat, and the parliamentary Bundestag. To that end, the Bundeswehr could only be committed operationally after a national 'state of defence' had been agreed and declared by the Bundestag. Furthermore, other than for certain specific security tasks carried out within the FRG, the Bundeswehr's field army was entirely assigned to NATO for the defence of the Central Region and so came under the operational command of the US supreme allied commander in Europe (SACEUR).[213]

In 1955, after a decade with no national armed forces, the FRG's new ministry of defence had already been required to overcome significant presentational and political problems. Its embryo army also had to resolve a considerable number of manpower and equipment issues. In addition, with any residual nostalgia for the old Prussian and German army victories of the eighteenth and nineteenth centuries positively discouraged and the two calamitous defeats of 1918 and 1945 still within the first-hand memory of those members of the population who had survived the two world wars, the very idea of a new German army was most unpopular in many quarters. It was also of course roundly and vehemently condemned by the Soviet Union and its allies. But the traditions upon which both the FRG and the Bundeswehr were founded were far more reminiscent of the democratic-liberalism of the first half of the nineteenth century than of the nationalism and militarism of the hundred years that had followed.

With all this in mind, rigorous constitutional and legal safeguards were put in place so that the military would be unable to impose its influence upon West German society, affect the political process, or diminish the rights of the individual. Democracy and democratic principles, in the widest sense, were to pervade all aspects of military service, together with the active and total rejection of anything reminiscent of the political total-itarianism that had finally characterized the Wehrmacht. A parliamentary ombudsman was established (the 'Wehrbeauftragter des Deutschen Bundestages') and trades unions based upon the civilian model were introduced into the Bundeswehr. In parallel the civilian justice process was applied to the Bundeswehr in place of a dedicated military justice and court-martial system. Thus the concept of the German 'citizen soldier' was born. This and much more was enshrined within the provisions of the Soldier's Law of 19 March 1956, a complex and worthy piece of legisla-tion with laudable aims. Nevertheless, in order to ensure that the Bundeswehr could never emulate its Reichswehr and Wehrmacht prede-cessors, and once again become a 'state within the state', it went so far as to impose significant handicaps upon the new army during its formative years. These strictures at first diminished both its combat effectiveness and its self-esteem. Indeed, irrespective of the anti-military views of much of the post-war German population, many people were in any case firmly of the opinion that the Bundeswehr lacked any credibility, arguing that an army which rejected the time-honoured and deeply embedded German military virtues of discipline, honour and obedience could never be a truly effective military force.

None the less, the concept of compulsory military service was adopted from the outset, and the Defence Duty Law of 21 July 1956 required the new 'citizen soldiers' to serve for twelve months (later increased to eigh-teen months). The only exemptions were those who had registered as conscientious objectors and whose sincerity had been formally examined and accepted by the authorities. The right of conscientious objection to military service had been guaranteed by the constitution, and conscien-tious objectors were able to fulfil their citizen's obligations to the state by other forms of national service. Irrespective of the more altruistic political rationale behind conscription, it was inescapable that without some form of national military service the Bundeswehr could not have hoped to generate the twelve-division organization that had been set for it.

Indeed, the early problems of recruitment were many. There was the overriding need (in order to satisfy the sensitivities of the former Allied Powers just as much as those within the Bundestag) to ensure that ex-Nazis were not employed as officers and NCOs. Nevertheless, many members of the former Wehrmacht had to be engaged and the Bundeswehr undoubtedly benefited from their experience. In any event, such men were subjected to rigorous screening before their acceptance. Interestingly, despite the SS having become the 'alibi of the nation' shortly after the war, no fewer than 566 former Waffen-SS men were serving as officers in the Bundeswehr by late 1956, though this was less than one per cent of the officer corps.[214] The lack of opportunity for the new state's citizens to serve in a West German army before 1955 had already resulted in

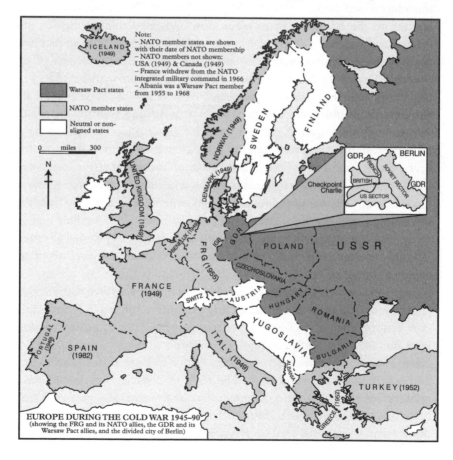

EUROPE DURING THE COLD WAR 1945–90
(showing the FRG and its NATO allies, the GDR and its Warsaw Pact allies, and the divided city of Berlin)

some very experienced former German soldiers who had served in the Wehrmacht and Waffen-SS seeking military employment elsewhere. Numbers of these men readily found a new home in the French Foreign Legion, together with new wars to fight in Indo-China and Algeria on behalf of their erstwhile and historical enemy.[215]

In the early days the new army was considerably handicapped by the training and discipline constraints placed upon an organization that was required to achieve operational readiness as soon as practicable, but with limited funding and while always having to take full account of the high level of political and human rights awareness brought to their service by many of the recruits. Indeed, the principles contained in the Basic Law (the Grundgesetz) which had been embedded at the very heart of the new West German state at the time of its birth in 1949, included a prohibition on the state engaging in wars of aggression. Carried to its natural conclusion, this prohibition meant that the primacy of the offensive which had for so long been at the heart of German military thinking should now be relegated in favour of more defensive concepts; it also laid the foundations of the fundamental principle by which the Bundeswehr would not in the future be permitted to engage in a war beyond Germany without a UN mandate to do so. At the same time, obsolete equipment – much of it American – together with shabby and ill-designed uniforms, poor discipline and low self-esteem, due to the attitude of much of the German population to the Bundeswehr, did not augur well for the future of the new force.

The early uniforms were based on a three-uniform concept, with a slate-grey 'Class A' uniform, an olive-green fatigue uniform, and a multi-coloured camouflage combat uniform. An updated version of the traditional-shaped German steel helmet was rejected, mainly for political reasons, and the ubiquitous US-pattern M1A1 two-piece combat helmet was adopted instead. Then, from September 1958, a German-designed one-piece steel helmet shaped much as the fibreglass liner of the US M1A1 was introduced, with an improved leather-lined version – the FJ 60 – being issued widely from May 1960. The camouflaged combat uniform had been abandoned by the 1960s, with an improved grey-green uniform introduced instead.[216] A small black-red-gold national flag emblem was worn on both upper arms of all variants of the combat and fatigue uniforms (shirts, jackets and cold-weather clothing). Various versions of laced and non-laced leather boots were tried and issued before a suitable calf-length, rubber-soled laced combat boot was finally adopted for all but some specialist units.

Whatever the Bundeswehr might have lacked in equipment, aesthetics, motivation or other areas, the massive military threat posed by the Soviet and (later) the Warsaw Pact forces stationed in East Germany ensured that the new army had a clearly discernible mission. This was the time-honoured obligation to which the German soldier had always been able to relate, the defence of his homeland – his Heimat.

So it was that on 2 January 1956, a typically cold and wet winter's day, some 550 new recruits for the embryo Bundeswehr arrived at the barracks in the town of Andernach on the Rhine, to form the core of the new army. Already in place was a training and support team of 200 professional officers, NCOs and soldiers, who had formed up at Andernach on 1 December 1955. Soon afterwards, the four infantry (or general-purpose) training companies (comprising a total of sixteen officers, 100 NCOs and 550 soldiers) were joined by a military band (two officers, 35 NCOs and fifteen bandsmen), an administrative and finance group (seven officers, seventeen NCOs and 70 soldiers), and a military police company (six officers, 137 NCOs and 33 soldiers). The initial manning priorities for the infantry companies, a band and a military police company had been set by the FRG ministry of defence for the Bundeswehr in a memo dated 4 October 1955.[217] This fairly unambitious prioritization serves perhaps to illustrate the considerable trepidation with which the project was at first approached. But developments proceeded apace, so that within twelve months the Bundeswehr's first 988 army personnel had quickly expanded to about 66,000, which included 9,572 former members of the Bundesgrenzschutz.[218] In parallel with the development of the army, a Luftwaffe training organization of 813 officers, NCOs and men had also been established, together with an equivalent Marine organization of 168.[219]

By 1960 there were no fewer than 270,000 soldiers serving in the Bundeswehr, and its combat potential was substantial, although its occasional crises of identity, together with what would today be called 'political correctness' and with the mismatch between its political and military imperatives, continued well into the 1970s. As the threat posed by the Soviet Union and the Warsaw Pact grew with each passing year, however, so the self-confidence and overall capability of the Bundeswehr grew also. Throughout this time its equipment was progressively updated, with many of its original US armoured vehicles and self-propelled guns and anti-aircraft artillery being replaced by a family of German-designed and built vehicles and equipment.

In the late 1960s the Leopard-A1 tank came into service, and was soon acclaimed as one of the best tanks in NATO at the time. Leopard-A3, A4 and Leopard-2 maintained that standard in the years that followed. During the 1970s the Marder infantry fighting vehicle entered service. Its firepower was potent: a 20mm cannon, two 7.62mm machine-guns and firing ports, with the later addition of a MILAN anti-tank guided-missile launcher, all in addition to its complement of seven panzergrenadiers. This remarkable infantry fighting vehicle capitalized upon the early experience gained with the HS-30 and other infantry carriers, and led the way within NATO in taking forward the doctrine for the use of armoured infantry. Leopard and Marder complemented each other, and their introduction marked the army's return (though much updated) to many of the operational principles which had been applied so successfully against the French and British in 1940 and against the Soviet Union from 1941 and in 1942.

Similarly, the Luchs eight-wheeled armoured reconnaissance vehicle was innovative in concept, as was the Gepard tracked, radar controlled, air defence gun system. The remarkable M-2 amphibious bridge or ferry, which was specifically designed to match the needs of NATO's planned operations in the Central Region, was subsequently adopted by other NATO nations as well. The joint development of weapons such as MILAN (anti-armour), Roland (anti-aircraft), HOT (anti-armour) and FH-70 (artillery) with other NATO nations was also carried out successfully. In the meantime, at the lower end of the equipment scale, the standard infantry weapon, the G-3 assault rifle, was a superb weapon which ranked as one of the best small-arms in NATO.

The Bundeswehr's visual image was also improved as its parade and combat uniforms were modernized, with unit insignia increasingly appearing on uniforms and vehicles alike. At last, some of the former *esprit de corps* of the old German army was again clearly discernible in the Bundeswehr of the 1970s and 1980s. However, the army's moves to resurrect and maintain certain of its less controversial martial traditions of earlier times always involved an element of risk. So it was that no fewer than twenty-five years after the army's creation, on 6 May 1980 a grand tattoo at the Weserstadion in Bremen scheduled to mark both the anniversary of the FRG's membership of NATO and the swearing-in of some 1,200 new recruits to the Bundeswehr – a routine ceremony usually carried out by the recruits before the assembled unit, while holding an edge of the black-red-gold national flag, and often conducted by torchlight after nightfall – was severely disrupted by large numbers of anti-war activists and anti-militarism demonstrators. No fewer than three hundred people were injured during the ensuing riot, and some Bundeswehr vehicles were set on fire in what proved to be the most violent protest that the post-1945 Bundeswehr ever experienced in connection with these traditional oath-taking ceremonies. Despite such incidents it is fair to say that by 1986 virtually all the political, manpower and technical difficulties of former times had been overcome, and that the Bundeswehr was generally at ease with itself and with the nature of the federal German state it defended, as well as being justifiably self-confident of its professional capability.

This is perhaps not surprising, given the close linkage between the state and its army. The morale, professionalism and combat readiness of the Bundeswehr had all improved in parallel with the remarkable advances in West Germany's industrial and commercial 'economic miracle' of the late 1960s and 1970s. During this period the arrangements for Germany's home defence were formalized, with a comprehensive organization of territorial commands linked directly to a peacetime Bundeswehr which by 1984 was 335,000 strong. Of these men, 181,000 were conscripts (then on 15-month engagements). The field army continued to be based on a three-corps, twelve-division organization, supported by a territorial force of some 44,200.[220] Overall control of the Bundeswehr was exerted by the Minister of Defence in peacetime and by the Chancellor in time of war, with command being exercised through the chief of staff of the federal armed forces and the service chiefs of staff in peacetime. In time of war, command functions devolved on the various military commanders, with national control only retained in respect of the territorial defence forces. The organization and composition of the Bundeswehr field army in 1986 is shown in Appendix 8.

Understandably, the federal government has always been firmly committed to the strategic concept of forward defence which had been in place since the late 1970s. Forward defence meant fighting the war as close to the IGB as possible. This concept replaced the earlier NATO strategy of massive retaliation which had been in place from the 1950s and until the late 1970s. This had called for a gradual NATO withdrawal back to the Rhine while its forces inflicted maximum damage on advancing Soviet and Warsaw Pact forces. However, it would also have meant devastating and relinquishing most of the territory of the FRG, as well as making the eventual use of nuclear weapons almost unavoidable. Clearly such a strategy was politically unsustainable in the FRG.

Operationally the Bundeswehr remained totally committed to its NATO role and was therefore entirely integrated into NATO's Central and Northern Army Groups (CENTAG and NORTHAG).[221] In NORTHAG a German corps would fight alongside Netherlands, British and Belgian corps, while in CENTAG two German corps would fight alongside corps of the US army. By 1986 the army was 495,000 strong

(671,000 including non-combatants and civilian support staff). Although it was still dependent upon conscripts (about 52 per cent of the army by the 1980s) the Bundeswehr had by then developed a sound core of regular career officers and soldiers. In time of war the Bundeswehr could have mustered some 1,200,000 personnel.[222] By the early 1980s the Bundeswehr was second only to the United States as the most powerful NATO military force in the Central Region of Europe, and many (including informed sources in the Soviet Union) rated the capability of the Bundeswehr and the professional competence of its soldiers ahead of that of the Americans.

Consequently, with its clear commitment to European defence, a constitution that still prohibited deployment beyond the NATO area, and a restored popularity (which visibly increased in direct proportion to how close one lived to the IGB) the Bundeswehr had become an indispensable part of NATO's defence plans. Its modern equipment, its generally liberal government funding, its generous terms of service, the pay and pension arrangements in place for its regular officers and soldiers, and the hard-won but finally successful blend of patriotism, service and citizenship of its personnel, were the envy of several other NATO armies.

But then the 'Peaceful Revolution' of November 1989 took place. At a stroke the world in general and West Germany in particular were turned upside down as NATO at last achieved its Cold War victory over the Soviet Union and Warsaw Pact. The Berlin Wall came tumbling down and the mission that had been the *raison d'être* of the Bundeswehr for almost thirty-five years disappeared literally overnight. On 3 October 1990 Germany – the West and the East – became one country again, and the Bundeswehr suddenly found itself having to come to terms with the need to absorb a sizeable part of the other German army, the NVA of the German Democratic Republic. This formidable fighting force had until then been characterized as one of the Bundeswehr's most implacable adversaries within the Warsaw Pact.

With the so-called 'new world order' that was proclaimed so prematurely by very many politicians throughout Western Europe in the early 1990s came an abundance of uncertainties, for despite the naïve political rhetoric of the time it had actually become a very much less secure world; and for the Bundeswehr in particular, the future now became less clear than at any time during its thirty-five-year history. A large, predominantly armoured and mechanized army, which had previously been dedicated exclusively to NATO and to the defence of the homeland against the Soviet and Warsaw Pact threat, suddenly found itself (ostensibly) with no hostile powers on any of its borders. Indeed, with German reunification, the eastern border of West Germany had instantly moved more than 300 kilometres eastwards from the former front-line position along the now defunct IGB. Clearly, the time had come for a radical reappraisal of the situation, role and structure of the Bundeswehr which would result from its assimilation of substantial parts of its former enemies of the NVA.

The Nationale Volksarmee (NVA)

Despite their declared aversion to fascism, German militarism and anything that might be construed as German rearmament – after all, some twenty-seven million Soviet soldiers and citizens had died during the recently ended 'Great Patriotic War against Fascism' – the authorities in the Russian zone from 1945 soon found it necessary to set up a locally-manned paramilitary internal security force (the Bereitschaften) to support the German communist party (masquerading as the 'Socialist Unity Party' or 'SED' from 1946). Although it relied entirely on Soviet direction and consent, the SED quickly became the controlling political power in eastern Germany. Then, when the German Democratic Republic (GDR) was established in 1949, the Bereitschaften provided the manpower base upon which a much larger paramilitary internal security and border security organization was built. It adopted the title of 'Kasernierte Volkspolizei' from 1952, a force which by then comprised some 120,000 men grouped in seven operational divisions.

Ostensibly, these organizations were the equivalent of the paramilitary forces established by the Western Allies within their own zones of occupation. But the GDR's Bereitschaften and border security units were heavily armed and equipped from the outset and, despite their 'Polizei' title, the policing content of their training was generally outweighed by its military content. The ease with which the Kasernierte Volkspolizei became the NVA after the government passed the necessary legislation to create an army for the GDR was indicative of the primarily military nature of the former force. Although its creation was presented as a response to the establishment of the Bundeswehr in West Germany, the existence of a national 'people's army' in East Germany underwrote the independence and separateness of the GDR from the FRG, as well as providing a military organization specifically designed to maintain the internal integrity of the communist state, by force of arms if necessary. As such, the East German communist leader Walter Ulbricht had at his disposal a powerful weapon, but one that was absolutely indispensable if the stability and always fragile existence of the GDR were to be maintained. In addition to the political and security roles of the NVA within the GDR, it also contributed importantly to Soviet defence objectives – both in operational and in propaganda terms – within the Warsaw Pact.

The physical appearance of the NVA soldier exemplified the ambiguities of the army to which he belonged. From head to foot the casual observer of the NVA soldier in his parade uniform might well have believed that he was simply a member of an updated Reichswehr or Wehrmacht. The design origins of the steel helmet were clearly those of 1915 and of the 1939–45 war, as well as owing something to the shape of the Soviet army helmet. The familiar 'Feldgrau' that had characterized the old imperial and Third Reich armies since 1914 was retained, together with the jackboot, cuff-titles for élite units, and many of the insignia and ceremonial trappings which (in modified form) betrayed the NVA's links with former German armies. Even the old German parade march – the 'goose-step' – continued to be used by certain NVA guard units when carrying out their ceremonial duties, such as those by the 'Felix Dzierzynski' Wacht (or 'Guard') Regiment at the Neue Wache on the Unter den Linden in East Berlin.[223] Indeed, although generally conducted on a much smaller scale, many of the ceremonial trappings and rituals of the NVA owed much to the former examples of the oath-takings, massed parades and other images of martial might, and demonstrations of loyalty to the state that were commonplace during the Nazi era. Superficially, therefore, such measures maintained the NVA's links with Germany's immediate past and thus created an illusion of national continuity both for the army and for the wider state, while in fact the fundamental changes that took place in the GDR and its army were much greater than anything with which its western comparators had to contend.

On the one hand, the influence of communism was all-pervading. The martial traditions, idealism and heroism of the liberation and revolutionary movements of the nineteenth and first half of the twentieth century were taught and emphasized constantly within the NVA during a comprehensive and interminable process of historical and political indoctrination. Wherever an individual German or Germanic group had acted in accordance with revolutionary principles or had been involved in the 'class struggle' of the workers against their oppressive masters, these instances were seized upon by the political officers and reworked or re-presented as the true German culture, and therefore as the acceptable moral and traditional basis of the NVA. Over time, the post-1945 SED government and its Soviet masters in effect modified or rewrote large parts of German history. There was much material on which to base this exercise. There were, for example, the peasant uprisings of the early sixteenth century, the Prussian–Russian accommodation negotiated by General Yorck at Tauroggen in 1812, the war of liberation in 1813, the 1848 liberal revolution, the bloody street-fighting between the heroic communist revolutionaries and the Freikorps in the industrial heartland of Germany in the early 1920s. There was also the heroism of German members of the International Brigade, suitably contrasted with the criminality of the fascist German Kondor Legion, in Spain in 1936. For the creative propagandist, the opportunities to rewrite history were almost infinite.

Some of Germany's great military reformers, such as von Scharnhorst, von Gneisenau and von Clausewitz, however, were also judged to be suitable role models, for they could be presented legitimately as theoreticians and thinkers who had sought to introduce ideas and changes that could with relative ease be presented as 'revolutionary' or innovative in nature. One particularly visible and ironic twist of history took place when the NVA-guarded Neue Wache was eventually established by the GDR government on 8 May 1960 as a 'memorial to the victims of fascism and militarism'. The immaculately Feldgrau-uniformed, helmeted and jackbooted guard detail – complete with their regimental cuff titles and 'guard regiment' cuff lace – looked remarkably similar to their forebears of the old imperial army of 1914–18, or indeed the army of 1933–45, as they mounted and dismounted the guard with a version of the goose-step that varied little from that of former times.

In practice, the development of this new historical and cultural rationale in East Germany was a masterly mix of revisionism and propaganda which progressively brain-washed much of an entire population; admittedly a population that was still traumatized by the events of 1939–45 and which had been almost entirely cut off from the outside (non-communist) world since the early 1950s. At the same time, it served very effectively to legitimize the existence and actions of the GDR's government and its armed forces, even those oppressive actions that were routinely carried out directly against its own citizens 'in the interests of the security of the state'. This then was the contrived and flawed framework of history, tradition, ideology and politics on which the government of Walter Ulbricht (and later that of Erich Honecker) relied and from which the NVA drew its heritage and its legitimacy.

Although the NVA eventually produced and introduced into service limited amounts of its own equipment and vehicles, it was almost entirely equipped with Soviet-made weaponry and armoured vehicles such as the T-54/55 (and later the T-72) tank and small-arms such as the ubiquitous

AK-47 'Kalashnikov' assault rifle and the RPG-7 grenade-launcher. Apart from some specialist units, armoured troops and paratroops, the NVA combat uniform was a 'rain-drop'-patterned camouflage suit, with multiple brown needle-shaped vertical lines printed over a grey-green base colour. Personal equipment was a mix of leather and canvas webbing, with some items made of rubberized or other synthetic materials.

In 1978 the NVA was 95,000 strong, with 1,800 battle tanks and some 850 artillery guns and rocket-launchers. This force was organized into six divisions, two of them armoured and four of mechanized infantry. In addition, the ground defence forces included 70,000 border security and police troops and 400,000 paramilitary territorial defence troops and workers' militia units. Reserves numbered 250,000, which could create at least a further two mechanized infantry divisions on mobilization. Conscription had been introduced in 1962, and in 1978 the period of obligatory military service was eighteen months. Conscientious objection was not recognized, although various forms of military service in non-combat units were permitted; though opting for such lesser forms of service would almost certainly curtail a man's subsequent civilian career. In support of the NVA were the air force (35,000 men, manning 300 aircraft grouped into six fighter regiments and two transport regiments) and a 15,000-strong navy manning two frigates.[224]

In peacetime the NVA was organized within five military districts, which broadly matched its operational organization as well as dovetailing directly into the substantial[225] Soviet forces stationed in East Germany which comprised the Group of Soviet Forces, Germany (GSFG).

NVA Military Districts in 1978

Military District	Location	Remarks
I	Strausberg, near East Berlin	Incorporating the national defence ministry.
II	Strausberg-Eggersdorf	Air defence and air force command.
III	Leipzig	Responsible for the ground defence forces in the southern GDR.
IV	Rostock-Warnemünde	Naval and coastal command.
V	Neubrandenburg	Responsible for the ground defence forces in the northern GDR.

By the mid-1980s the NVA had increased in strength to about 120,000, although it maintained its six-division structure. Its increased strength reflected not only the accelerating and changing nature of the Cold War, but also the extensive use of NVA personnel as military instructors and support teams in a number of Third World countries and conflict areas. During the 1970s they were prominent in Angola, Mozambique, Libya and Tanzania. Such deployments reflected those parts of the world in which the Soviet Union had particular interests, or in which it sought to advance the spread of communism.

Unlike its Bundeswehr equivalent, the NVA also found itself deployed on operations beyond the GDR. One such occasion was when two NVA tank divisions took part in the Soviet suppression of the Czech uprising in August 1968. On that occasion one NVA division, together with four divisions of the Soviet 1st Guards Tank Army, moved straight to the Czech border to deter any NATO intervention, while the other NVA division and four Soviet divisions of the 20th Guards Army occupied Prague. But the use of German troops to deal with the Czech uprising proved all too reminiscent of the Wehrmacht invasion of the country in 1939. This, together with the speedy disillusionment of numbers of NVA troops (especially those dispatched into Prague) who quickly discovered that, far from safeguarding Czechoslovakia against some supposed threat from abroad, their tanks had effectively crushed the seeds of a popular liberal and democratic movement, soon led to an early withdrawal of the NVA divisions back into the GDR.

Throughout the life of the GDR and its armed forces the operational roles and employment of the NVA and that of its closely allied comrades-in-arms of the border security forces were key elements for the preservation of the state and for maintaining the security threat illusions created by the communist party propagandists. All along Honecker's so-called 'Moderne Grenze', created first in Berlin (the 'Berlin Wall') in August 1961 and then rapidly extended along the full length of the IGB, the troops of the border command (officially in place to prevent a NATO incursion into the GDR) were very ready to use lethal force to stop 'criminal elements and saboteurs' from the East German population escaping into the West. The GDR's formidable border defences were manned by some 14,000 security personnel, including the border guards and the regular NVA, plus the Volkspolizei, the 'Vopos'. That the border guards were expected to shoot at would-be escapees was not in doubt, as former Unteroffizier Manfred Milde of Grenzregiment Nr. 40 explained after his own escape to West Berlin on 19 December, 1966:

> After the 'border violater' has got over the first barrier of the border, which is usually an innocent-looking fence, you are to yell at him, 'Halt! Border guard! Hands up!' If the man you're yelling at doesn't raise his hands and also doesn't

stop, you are to fire a warning shot. If he still doesn't stop, you are to aim right at him, no matter how many barriers he still has to cross. If the 'border violater' is so near to the border that yelling or firing the warning shot might give him enough time to make his escape, you are to shoot to kill right away.[226]

Between 1961 and 1989 some 258 people were killed attempting to cross the Berlin Wall. Ten more were drowned while swimming across the Teltow Canal or the River Spree, and about twenty-five border guards also lost their lives in connection with escapes or escape attempts.[227] The actual total death toll was probably somewhat higher.

However, the NVA also had well-defined strategic tasks in the event of war between NATO and the Soviet and Warsaw Pact forces. Documents and other information that have become available since 1990 indicate that in a Warsaw Pact offensive against the West the NVA would ultimately have contributed no fewer than eight divisions to the Warsaw Pact's Jutland, Coastal, Central and Luxembourg Fronts. Two more NVA divisions, supported by paramilitary units, were responsible for seizing West Berlin. Apparently non-Soviet Warsaw Pact forces were not destined to carry the battle into France, and the NVA would therefore have become responsible primarily for the military control of West Germany. This territory would by then have become the main operational and logistic area supporting the Soviet advance to the English Channel, the Baltic and the Atlantic seaboard.[228]

In the early 1970s the Soviet high command of GSFG passed responsibility for the capture of West Berlin to the GDR forces. Thereafter, the NVA had set about preparing for this prestigious task with considerable energy and its high-level planning was complemented by a series of highly secret command-post exercises and war games held annually from 1973 to 1988. The plans were reviewed and completely updated every two years. A special training facility was established at Lehnin, about twenty-five miles south-west of Berlin, where many of the urban features typically found in West Berlin were carefully reproduced and 'fought through' by units of exercising troops. At Strausberg, in Military District I, a twelve-square-metre model of West Berlin was constructed to assist the training of senior NVA commanders and planning for an attack on the western part of the city.

The NVA plans for what was designated Operation 'Centre' called for some 32,000 troops organized in two divisions (including the Soviet 6th Independent Motor Rifle Brigade from GSFG). This assault force would have available 390 tanks, 400 other armoured vehicles, 450 artillery guns and mortars, 400 anti-armour weapons and forty helicopters. The force planned to breach the defences surrounding West Berlin simultaneously in up to sixty locations. It would then launch an all-out armoured assault that would first secure the main road and rail transit point at the Kaiserdamm-brücke (at which point the main autobahn into Berlin intersected with the principal east–west highway and with the suburban S-Bahn and U-Bahn railway lines). This would have split and isolated the US, British and French garrison forces. The attackers would then have gone on to seize a number of other key-points, airfields and several 'sites of cultural heritage' – no fewer than 170 critical sites in all. Concurrently, they would have sought to destroy what it was assessed would by then be the fragmented Anglo-US-French resistance, thereby bringing about the collapse of the garrison within twenty-four hours.[229]

The plans for Operation 'Centre' remained in place and were regularly updated and practised until 1988, after which the concept underwent a major overhaul in light of a new assessment that at least 100,000 troops would in fact be required to subdue and occupy West Berlin. With the Cold War moving inexorably towards its end (although Honecker and his supporters in East Germany certainly did not accept that this was so), a more pragmatic approach of military containment was then adopted, whereby the NVA would simply besiege West Berlin and so prevent the Anglo-US-French forces from launching harassing attacks into what would by then have become the Soviet and Warsaw Pact administrative and logistic rear areas. Assuming that the Warsaw Pact offensive into Western Europe had indeed developed successfully, the western part of the city would simply be starved into submission or contained until NATO surrendered. This revised plan might have allowed lower-quality troops to conduct the siege of West Berlin, thereby releasing the two NVA divisions originally earmarked to carry out the assault on the city to join the Soviet and Warsaw Pact's main offensive into Western Europe.

Whatever the viability of Operation 'Centre' and the intended use of the NVA as part of the wider Soviet strategic plans to overrun Western Europe, it is a matter of record that throughout the Cold War the NVA was consistently assessed by NATO intelligence analysts to be militarily the most professional and politically reliable of all the Warsaw Pact armies. Throughout the 1970s and into the 1980s the manning of NVA units was maintained at 85 per cent of immediate operational readiness, with all vehicles fully loaded with their war scales of ammunition and full fuel tanks, while most East German militia and paramilitary units kept their personal weapons at their place of work. Such measures not only ensured operational readiness, they also maintained very effectively the myth of the immediacy of the threat posed to the GDR by NATO.

Despite this, the actual willingness of the NVA conscripts to fight directly against the West Germans was always debatable; although the readiness of the GDR's military and paramilitary organizations to act against their own citizens perhaps provided some indication of their probable conduct in general combat. But this proposition must be balanced by the evidence provided by the actions of the NVA soldiers in Czechoslovakia in 1968. The nagging doubt which always persisted in the minds of the Soviet high command over the reliability and enthusiasm of the NVA engaged in a war in Central Europe meant that its divisions forever remained under Soviet operational command, while throughout its life the NVA was always closely monitored and regularly constrained by the governing East German communist party and its Soviet masters.

Perhaps the allocation to the NVA of the mission to capture West Berlin was prompted by a Soviet desire to keep the best NVA troops well within the rear area (and therefore firmly under Soviet control), engaged upon a mission that would pit them primarily against US, British and French forces rather than against the Bundeswehr (which had no forces stationed in Berlin). At the same time the Soviet high command might also have decided that the NVA soldiers would be better motivated by a mission which in part involved them capturing many of the historic and cultural sites that had played such an important part in the German nation's earlier history.

In any event, whatever the NVA's motivation and probable performance might have been once committed to fight a war in Europe, the military training advisers who served in various Third World conflict areas in the 1970s and early 1980s, together with the army's redoubtable special forces units, earned an unequivocal reputation for uncompromising military professionalism which generally exceeded that of any other Warsaw Pact nation, including that of the Soviets.

On 7 October 1989 the GDR marked the fortieth anniversary of its creation with a military parade on Karl-Marx-Allee in East Berlin. The main streets were cleaned and hosed down, the official state media were in their allotted vantage points, and the colourful flags, banners and the symbols of the GDR and its political organizations were everywhere. There also were the route liners, the traffic controllers, the Vopos, the men of the ministry for state security (the MfS), and the 'Stasi', the GDR's secret policemen. As was customary, the salute was taken by Erich Honecker, who was flanked on the reviewing stand by numerous

SED officials and functionaries. The guest of honour accompanying Honecker on the stand was Mikhail Gorbachev, president of the Soviet Union. Following a typically robust speech by Honecker about the clear advantages of socialism set against the dire threats posed by the forces of international reaction, large contingents of the GDR's armed forces marched past, followed by the political and youth organizations. Massed bands preceded the troops of the Felix Dzierzynski Regiment,[230] after which came line after line of wheeled and tracked armoured vehicles. The naval contingent, workers' militias and other organizations followed on, with the various youth delegations completing the display. The young people in these last contingents dutifully waved their flags and banners in acknowledgement of their leader as they passed before the reviewing stand. The form and content of the 1989 parade virtually mirrored that which had been staged on the GDR's thirtieth anniversary in 1979.

However, as events were soon to show, the 1989 parade would in fact prove to be somewhat different from its predecessors, as it was in the margins of this event that Gorbachev warned Honecker and the principal SED leaders that the Marxist–Leninist ideology which had sustained the GDR ever since 1946 had become unsupportable in light of the new realities of the modern world. Even the Soviet Union itself was changing rapidly, and the GDR could not hope to avoid the dramatic changes that this would precipitate throughout the communist bloc. Despite Gorbachev's blunt warning, Honecker was in a state of denial. Surely the impressive display of military might they had both just witnessed was irrefutable evidence of the invulnerability and permanence of the GDR? By 1989 Honecker and very many of his supporters had come to believe in the veracity of their own propaganda.

In reality the outwardly imposing parade on 7 October 1989 exemplified the true superficiality and fragility of the GDR and of the NVA itself, a situation which had deteriorated rapidly during the second half of the decade. For on that day's parade 'some of the items of military ironware on display were actually wooden copies exact in every visual detail down to the last centimetre. The immaculately turned-out troops came from filthy, run-down barracks with only two shower heads per company and hot water available only on Fridays.'[231] Such facts were indicative of the wider malaise and economic deprivation which by then afflicted much of the civilian population of the GDR and its armed forces. So it was that the commemorative parade of 7 October proved to be the very last such parade carried out in East Berlin.

The details of the momentous and world-changing events that soon followed are beyond the scope of this work. Suffice to say that on 19 October Honecker was forced out of office then, on 24 October, soldiers of the Felix Dzierzynski Regiment were deployed on the streets of East Berlin to protect government buildings. Next, in early November Honecker's successor, Egon Krenz, declared a free travel policy between East and West Germany. This announcement was quickly followed by Günter Schabowski's declaration on 9 November that the border between the GDR and the FRG was open, with no restrictions on travel. Finally, on 10 November the Berlin Wall which had physically split the former German capital, and had stood ever since its construction in August 1961 as the definitive symbol of the Cold War and of the post-war division of Germany, became an irrelevance. So also were the hundreds of miles of the IGB that had scarred Germany for so long. The Cold War had come to its somewhat abrupt end and the NVA, the border regiments, the Vopos and the numerous internal security and paramilitary organizations which had ostensibly been established to counter the NATO threat (but which had in fact existed to ensure the continuance of a Soviet-dominated GDR) no longer had any reason to exist.

On Wednesday 3 October 1990, West and East Germany were re-unified, the GDR was consigned to history, and Germany once again became a single state. But now among the very many pressing matters remaining for the leaders of the much enlarged FRG was the uncertain future of the sizeable residue of the men and equipment of the NVA, much of which still remained in the various barracks and installations of the former East Germany.

Almost 120 years after Bismarck and Wilhelm I had proclaimed the unification of Germany and the establishment of the Second German Empire in the Hall of Mirrors at Versailles during the Franco-Prussian War, and just forty-five years after the victorious Allies had divided Germany at Yalta and Potsdam in the closing days of the Second World War, Germany was once again a single national entity,[232] and as such it once more needed a single German army for its defence. But, with the Soviet and Warsaw Pact threat now no more than a recent memory, the development of an appropriate military structure to achieve this would be no easy task, neither would the even more difficult job of identifying an appropriate role for the post-1990 Bundeswehr. Meanwhile, implicit in all of this was the considerable challenge of assimilating large parts of an army that had for four decades been ideologically and politically opposed to the FRG and all it stood for. It was also an army that possessed an enormous amount of Soviet-produced weapons and equipment, none of which was compatible with that of the Bundeswehr. These were but a few of the issues that faced the German federal government and the officers and men of the Bundeswehr as they once again set about restructuring and developing what would be in many respects a new German army – one that would be ready to meet the defence needs of the reunified nation and which would also be able to deal with the potential conflicts and very different security challenges of the twenty-first century.

24

Reunification and the Bundeswehr in the 21st Century

SUDDENLY, THE IGB WAS GONE. East Germany had ceased to exist, and much of the army of the former West German Bundeswehr's erstwhile enemy was now to be absorbed into the Bundeswehr of the newly re-united country. In relatively short order 3,000 of the NVA's officers, 8,000 of its soldiers and a whole array of former Warsaw Pact equipment were integrated into the army of their former enemies in the West.

All sorts of potential difficulties were raised by this. Those NVA officers of the rank of colonel and above were automatically debarred from membership of the new German army, as it was considered that their ideological loyalty to the former communist regime made them an unacceptable security risk. Meanwhile, once their previous non-involvement with the communist party or the GDR's secret police (the Stasi) had been ascertained, many of the more junior NVA officers were given the option of joining the Bundeswehr either on a regular contract (of two years initially) or on a probationary or trial basis. Unfortunately, a number of professionally less capable NVA officers opted for a contract from the outset, while considerably more of the better-quality NVA officers joined on the probationary terms of service so as to be able to make an informed decision as to whether they wished to continue as army officers or to employ their undoubted talents in civilian life. But with the threat from the east removed, and with Russia making substantial reductions of the Bundeswehr, a formal prerequisite for Moscow's acceptance of German reunification, it was impossible to justify the reunified Germany retaining an army of the size that it had previously maintained in West Germany during the final decade of the Cold War. When the inevitable downsizing took place, those officers on contracts were necessarily retained, at least for the duration of their contract, while those who at that stage decided to change their engagements from probationary to regular or contracted service were in many cases unable to do so, and were subsequently discharged.

In the meantime, by as early as 1995 very little of the vast stocks of Soviet and Warsaw Pact equipment that had formerly been held by the NVA remained in Bundeswehr service. Most of the larger items of weaponry, vehicles and equipment were sold or disposed of for spares, and huge quantities of weapons, ammunition and explosives were destroyed. At a more trivial level, enormous quantities of NVA uniforms, most of them brand-new and unissued, together with all sorts of insignia and medals, were deposited on to the open market soon after 1990. Even some fifteen years after the end of the GDR, the market stalls of the many militaria traders in several districts of the former East Berlin (especially about the Alexanderplatz at the very heart of the former GDR's capital) are still crammed with all sorts of colourful and often very collectable NVA badges, caps and other uniform items.

The removal of a clearly discerned threat to a nation poses something of a dilemma for its armed forces. On the one hand, the collapse of the Soviet and Warsaw Pact threat was quite patently a victory for NATO and for the Bundeswehr in particular. On the other, this turn of events had entirely removed the Bundeswehr's principal reason for its existence. Arguably, by 1989 none of the other NATO armies in the Central Region of Europe had been as well prepared, as well motivated and so well equipped to combat the communist threat from the east as had been the West German army. But by 1990 the world defence scene had changed irrevocably, and so the West German government, together with its NATO allies, set about a major review of the future role, size and shape of the Bundeswehr. In September 1990 the so-called 'Two-Plus-Four' treaty ('Treaty on the Final Settlement with Respect to Germany') was signed, which dovetailed with the provisions of the wider treaty on Conventional Forces in Europe (CFE) that was signed in November.

As its contribution to the so-called 'peace dividend', the German government pledged to reduce the peacetime strength of the Bundeswehr (air force, navy and army) to 370,000 by the end of 1994, of which overall total the army and the air force would together comprise 345,000 personnel. By early 1995 the army alone numbered about 255,000 men, of whom about 123,000 were conscripts. Then, in January 1996, the Bundeswehr's overall manpower target was further reduced to a ceiling of 340,000. Over the same period the length of compulsory conscripted service was reduced first from fifteen months to twelve, and then to ten months, with about 135,000 conscripts still in uniform towards the end of the 1990s. Up to 140,000 reserve soldiers were still liable to be called up annually for training and exercises, and the call-up of reservists in time of crisis could potentially raise the overall strength of the Bundeswehr to between 650,000 and 750,000 personnel. Subsequently, however, the period of conscripted service was further reduced to nine months, with the total number of army conscripts also dropping to as few as 80,000.[233]

As recently as the late summer of 2005 – the year in which the Bundeswehr marked its half-centenary – it was announced[234] that no fewer than 105 Bundeswehr bases were to be closed down, being no longer required. Self-evidently this decision was politically sensitive and received much media coverage, because (at a time of rising unemployment in Germany) such closures have an impact not only upon military capability but also on the local civilian economy in the sixteen states within which these bases are located.[235]

The gathering momentum of this trend is clear, and it is intended that the current overall manpower ceiling of the Bundeswehr of some 285,000 will be reduced to about 250,000 by 2010 (the so-called 'Structure 2010'), with a fully mobilized strength of not more than about 500,000. Within Structure 2010 the force mix is intended to produce, as required, some 35,000 personnel (1st Panzerdivision, Hanover) for 'intervention' missions, 70,000 for 'stabilization' missions (10th Panzerdivision, Sigmaringen, and 13th Panzergrenadierdivision, Leipzig), and about 106,000 for 'support operations'. Broadly speaking, these tasks translate respectively into forms of 'war-fighting' or 'peace enforcement', 'internal security'[236] or 'peace-keeping', and 'humanitarian' or 'peace support' operations.

The extent of the swing of the Bundeswehr's capability pendulum away from a more traditional and familiar defence capability towards one that accords more nearly with the needs generated by the economic and domestic difficulties of the twilight years of Chancellor Gerhard Schröder's Social Democratic (SPD) government is striking. Inextricably bound up with this is what might well be viewed as a large measure of political correctness and, arguably, an excessive preoccupation with the requirement for the Bundeswehr to maintain its wider political acceptability within Germany in the twenty-first century world. But while some downsizing and reorientation of the Bundeswehr's role was always inevitable post-1990, the sheer scale and speed – little more than one decade – of this process might well attract accusations of political opportunism rather than being applauded as a well-considered response to Germany's much-changed situation in a much-changed world. With the final demise of Schröder's Social Democrat administration in 2005, it remains to be seen whether Structure 2010 will be implemented as planned from 2007; although the very close nature of the new Chancellor Angela Merkel's Christian Democrat (CDU) election victory (which resulted in a coalition government with the SPD) suggests that a major revision of the Structure 2010 plan is unlikely in light of Germany's current domestic difficulties and economic priorities.

So, just a decade after its Cold War victory, the Bundeswehr has already down-sized quite dramatically, with further reductions in prospect. From a powerful war machine within which the army alone numbered almost half a million men by 1986 and which could at that time have mustered a total of no fewer than 1,200,000 soldiers, sailors and airmen on initial mobilization, it now plans for a mobilized strength of no more than 500,000 in case of war.

Accordingly, although some of these successive reductions were inevitable, it is arguable that they have already gone too far, and that they now owe as much to Germany's current economic difficulties and over-generous and extremely expensive social welfare programmes as they do to a realistic analysis of Germany's defence and security needs.

Irrespective of the restructuring and cost-cutting that has taken place since 1990, almost from the day that the Berlin Wall was breached it was always quite clear to many among its military leadership that (if the Bundeswehr was not to become yet another victim of the politically expedient, often opportunistic and in many cases precipitate policies later justified throughout much of Western Europe as the 'peace dividend') the German army would quickly need to identify a role commensurate with its changed circumstances in the post-Cold War world. And in due course it found this new role amid the plethora of UN and NATO-sponsored peacekeeping operations of the 1990s, being given added political impetus by Chancellor Schröder's aspiration to gain for Germany a seat on the UN Security Council.

Germany's military involvement in such multi-national operations also underlined the new political, financial and international confidence of the country on the world stage. While the government chose to retain its commitment to collective defence within NATO, a commitment which could involve the full range of its army units with their regular, conscripted and reservist troops, it also expressed a new readiness to participate in operations other than war. These missions were to be carried out only by regular and by volunteer soldiers (including conscripts who could volunteer for an extended period of up to twenty-three months of military service). The scope of these operations was wide-ranging: from disaster relief and humanitarian support to peace-keeping and peace enforcement by the use of armed force.[237]

Despite some resistance, the German constitution was adjusted or re-interpreted to allow units of Germany's new war machine to operate beyond its borders, which implicitly modified the exclusively defensive role that had constrained the Bundeswehr for thirty-five years.[238] Accordingly, after some hesitant beginnings during its first UN operations in Cambodia in 1992, in Africa, and during its limited involvement in the early stages of the Bosnian conflict, the Bundeswehr became committed in ever-increasing numbers to NATO operations in the former Yugoslavia and Kosovo,[239] and in Afghanistan. Consequently, as at mid-2005, there are some 2,000 German soldiers serving with the NATO peace-keeping force in Afghanistan, while a further 5,000 personnel are currently deployed in the Balkans. More UN military involvement is planned, a new UN observer mission to Sudan having been approved by the Bundestag on 22 April 2005. An overview of the full extent of the Bundeswehr's operational deployments beyond Germany from 1990 to 2005 is shown at Appendix 9. The operational trend is quite clear, and of course accords with the Structure 2010 capability and the implied future role of the Bundeswehr. But it comes in large part at the expense of the Bundeswehr's hard-won war-fighting capability.

In parallel with its reorientation towards peacekeeping (together with a plethora of humanitarian and other operational offshoots) the Bundeswehr had also realized an idea first raised by Helmut Kohl in 1987 for the creation of a Franco-German brigade. The brigade had first formed as an independent, lightly equipped, mixed-nationality mechanized formation in January 1989, and was originally intended for a conventional Cold War mission. But it was soon overtaken by events, and by the time it was finally declared operational in October 1991 the Cold War was over. For the next two years the Franco-German brigade continued to maintain its headquarters at Böblingen but with its future somewhat uncertain. It was under the overall command of the French forces in southern Germany and of the German 10th Panzer Division specifically. However, with a new emphasis upon Franco-German and wider European defence co-operation, on 1 October 1993 it was placed under command of the newly created Eurocorps, eventually serving alongside a Belgian mechanized infantry division, German and French divisions, and a Spanish mechanized infantry brigade. Although the role of the Eurocorps is defined as being the defence component of the European Union (EU) and the means of reinforcing the European contribution to NATO, it also has particular significance for the Western European Union's (WEU) defence aspirations and (despite regular rebuttals of the suggestion) as the foundation upon which a European army might one day be built.

Therefore, despite the Franco-German and EU dimensions, the Bundeswehr remains actively committed to NATO and to maintaining a powerful and modern conventional war-fighting capability. Despite its restructuring and force level reductions, the army has continued to maintain and operate within a three-corps framework; although this corps structure is now multinational, with no single or exclusively German corps currently in existence. For warfare the army could at present field up to five armoured or mechanized divisions, the core and framework of each of which also exists in peacetime. But these divisions would require numbers of mobilized reservists to bring them to their full war strength. These divisions would normally serve within the five principal multi-national NATO corps, while the German headquarters of the 2nd (German and US) Corps also has the additional contingency missions of serving as a national headquarters for a discrete German military operation mounted at higher than division-level, or as the force headquarters to command a military operation mounted by the EU. Although it maintains a most effective nuclear (or 'atomic'), biological and chemical defence capability, it holds no nuclear, biological or chemical offensive weapons.

To support such a range of war operations, the army has developed and introduced into service an enviable range of thoroughly reliable modern equipment and most potent weaponry. All of this supports directly the German army's long-standing commitment to mobile or manoeuvre warfare, to the primacy of the offensive, and to the continuance of the Auftragstaktik concept in its command and control doctrine. Well to the fore among this equipment are updated and much improved versions of the formidable Leopard 2 main battle tank, with the A5 and A6 versions now in service. These tanks have for many years been complemented by the Jaguar 2 tank destroyers armed with TOW missiles, although these ageing fighting vehicles are now being taken out of service. Information gathering and reconnaissance is still carried out by troops using the versatile and proven eight-wheeled Spahpanzer Luchs, now in its A2 version. However, the Luchs is being replaced today by the new Fennek light reconnaissance and combat vehicle, which is also wheeled rather than tracked. A Fennek variant will also provide a highly mobile combined artillery and air fire support co-ordination capability. The infantry, specifically the panzergrenadiers of the intervention division, still use the redoubtable Marder infantry fighting vehicle. But the Marder 1A3 version currently in service is significantly more capable, better protected and more user-friendly than its predecessors of the late Cold War years. Nevertheless, beginning in 2007 the Marders will be replaced by some 405 of a new wheeled infantry fighting vehicle, the Puma. Meanwhile, more than 3,000 of the ageing but still indispensable M-113G tracked armoured personnel carriers, produced in Germany since the 1970s, remain in service, now in their upgraded M-113G2 and M-113G3 versions, fulfilling numerous command, control and other specialist functions (together with the Fuchs six-wheeled amphibious vehicle).

Air defence and anti-armour capabilities continue to feature prominently in the Bundeswehr's inventory, and take forward several concepts which have clear origins in the Wehrmacht's experience of warfare during the Second World War. The Gepard 1 A1 and A2 point air defence self-propelled (on a Leopard tank chassis) gun system has been considerably updated, and a complementary Stinger anti-aircraft missile system is now to be fitted to it. Also (possibly with memories of the successful use of the old 88mm anti-aircraft gun of 1939-45 in the ground role in mind) the Gepard is now equipped with armour piercing as well as anti-aircraft ammunition. Meanwhile, the Roland 3 air defence missile system (although almost at the end of its effective life), which is mounted on the Marder chassis, and the LeFlaSys light air defence missile system equipped with Stingers and mounted on the Wiesel 2 light armoured tracked carrier, both still provide very adequate short-range air defence for static and mobile units alike. The highly mobile Wiesel carrier is also employed in several variants with a range of weapon options. These include TOW missile versions for the airborne forces, an ambulance version, and personnel carriers (which have already proved their worth on peace-keeping operations in the Balkans with IFOR, SFOR and KFOR, and elsewhere).

Finally, the artillery has continued to reflect the importance accorded to this arm by the Prussian and German armies ever since the nineteenth century. The most recently introduced artillery equipment is the Panzer-haubitze (PzH) 2000 155mm self-propelled howitzer, with several hundred of these currently in service alongside the long-serving but much-updated M-109 self-propelled howitzer. As many as 500 types of M-109 are currently in service or could be made available on mobilization (and these will eventually be superseded by the PzH 2000 by 2015). The gun systems of the artillery are complemented by multiple-launch rocket systems (MLRS), with the most recently introduced GMLRS able to deliver salvoes of twelve inertially guided rockets on to targets as far as forty miles away.

Although several of the foregoing vehicles, weaponry and equipment have limited applications in nationally based security or peace-keeping operations, the six-wheeled Fuchs amphibious armoured personnel carrier could easily be used in such roles. Although one of its specialist functions in general war is atomic, biological and chemical (ABC) defence and monitoring, it also serves as an agile, robust and reliable troop carrier, as an electronic warfare VHF jammer and direction-finder platform (the Hummel), as an ambulance vehicle, and as a mobile forward command post. A recently upgraded variant provides a high degree of armour protection and self-defence armament. Another such dual-role vehicle recently taken into service is the Dingo armoured personnel carrier, a wheeled vehicle which has been used extensively for peace-keeping, patrolling and reconnaissance missions in Macedonia, Kosovo and Afghanistan. The Dingo is also used as a mobile platform for the loud-speaker operations of the psychological units, always a key element in any information warfare campaign.

In 2006, Germany, the United Kingdom and the Netherlands are due to receive the first deliveries of a brand-new multi-role eight-wheeled armoured vehicle (the MRAV, or as it is known in Germany the Gepanz-ertes Transportkraftfahrzeug, or 'GTK') developed as a collaborative project, with subsequent orders by the Bundeswehr possibly being for as many as 2,000 vehicles. This further movement from tracks to wheels for armoured combat vehicles indicates the dilemma posed by the need to be equipped with armoured vehicles that can be used in all types and levels of conflict and which are readily transportable by air.

Today, the army is still supported by an impressive range of modern armed and transport helicopters, unmanned aerial reconnaissance vehi-cles, cargo carriers of all sorts, amphibious bridging and engineer construction equipment, and a host of state-of-the-art command, control, communications and intelligence data-processing equipment. But in the next few years a significant quantitative price is due to be paid for this qualitative excellence, as Structure 2010 begins to have an impact upon the quantities of this equipment held, and as the units and troops neces-sary to man it are steadily reduced. It is currently envisaged in the Struc-ture 2010 plan that from 2007 the fleet of Leopard tanks will reduce from 2,528 to just 350 by 2010 – with only six panzer battalions remaining in the army's order of battle. The current holding of 2,077 infantry fighting vehicles (predominantly the Marders) will reduce to 410 over the same period, while the artillery – despite its role as a key element of the Prus-sian and German armies since time immemorial – will lose 935 of its guns, leaving it with no more than 120 by 2010. Meanwhile (and arguably much less justifiable in light of the Bundeswehr's new missions), the army will more than halve its helicopter fleet, reducing it from 530 to 240 aircraft. The outline organization of the army planned under Structure 2010 and

projected to show the situation as at 2008 is at Appendix 10. The Luftwaffe is due to suffer reductions on a similar scale, and, although overall
less affected by Structure 2010, the navy (which has already seen the naval
air wing pass under command of the Luftwaffe) will reduce its submarine
fleet and replace most of its fast patrol-boat capability with a small number
of frigates.

It can certainly be argued that much of the state-of-the-art equipment
currently in service was originally conceived or designed during the Cold
War era to wreak destruction on a grand scale, or to provide a viable
defence while countering high tempo offensive operations against a
broadly comparable 'first world' enemy. In consequence (and in spite of
the swingeing cuts currently planned for implementation from 2007),
some might well posit that the cost and practical difficulties involved in
maintaining such a high level of military capability are unjustified in
today's world, where 'asymmetric' rather than conventional threats are
now considered by most security experts to be the order of the day. In light
of this, Germany's approach to its defence needs, and more immediately
to its attitude to the ongoing so-called 'war on terror', merits further
consideration.

In purely professional terms, numbers of German military personnel
might well welcome the Bundeswehr's greater involvement in what is
currently the only 'live' or all-arms war in which its 'intervention' forces
might conceivably be able to play a part – the always contentious conflict
in Iraq. But this was ruled out when Schröder's SPD government, together
with that of President Chirac in France, actively and unequivocally
distanced themselves from the Anglo-US invasion and the subsequent
military campaign in Iraq from 2003. At the same time the German
government tried to strengthen its participation in Europe-based missions
such as that in the Balkans, where Bundeswehr troops have enjoyed
considerable success. Indeed, the army's contribution to the IFOR and
SFOR psychological warfare (termed 'Operational Information' or
'OpInfo' in the Bundeswehr) campaigns in the former Yugoslavia proved
masterly, using subtlety and the German OpInfo soldiers' European
perspective, language skills and knowledge to effect real and positive
changes in the attitudes and behaviour of the indigenous population and
disparate hostile groups within Bosnia.[240]

Nevertheless, Schröder's condemnation of the Anglo-US adventure in
Iraq from 2003 was probably motivated more by his weakening political
position within Germany and his consequent desire to pursue populist
domestic policies, rather than for any more altruistic reasons. Despite this,

even if only by accident, the constraints imposed by Germany's constitution, with its consequent non-involvement in that particular conflict and its insistence upon UN approval for such action, has undoubtedly served to place it on the moral high ground. Consequently, the Bundeswehr has managed to contribute usefully to the UN and NATO approved operations in the Balkans and Afghanistan, while at the same time avoiding the political quagmire and military maelstrom that the second Iraq war has become; particularly after its doubtful legality and total lack of connection to the 11 September 2001 attacks in New York became clear for all to see. For Germany, this situation is unlikely to change in the foreseeable future, as Frau Angela Merkel, elected on 22 November 2005 to succeed Gerhard Schröder as the new Chancellor of Germany, had previously declared herself to be against involving German troops in the continuing Iraq conflict, thereby maintaining the policy line established by her predecessor.

Indeed, while claims by Prime Minister Tony Blair that the Iraq war has not increased the terrorist threat against Great Britain are patently nonsense, it is noteworthy that Germany – despite its large Turkish and wider Muslim community – has so far been spared the terrorist attacks by Islamist extremists that took place in Madrid in March 2004 and in London in July 2005. If the Bundeswehr had been actively engaged in the Iraq conflict from 2003 there is a high probability that Germany and its citizens abroad would also have been under threat from the terrorists.

None the less, such matters do inevitably pose interesting questions for the Bundeswehr and it has now arrived at a major crossroads in the course of its post-Cold War evolution. By chance, its arrival at that point coincided not only with the important and controversial German national election result of 2005, but also with the Bundeswehr's celebrations to mark the fiftieth anniversary of its official birth on 7 June 1955. Despite half a century having passed since 1955, a military musical tattoo (a 'Zapfenstreich') staged at the Reichstag by torchlight on the evening of 26 October attracted up to 1,000 protesters. Some of these people suggested that this traditional ceremony signalled a return to the days of the Imperial army and of the Wehrmacht, while – more significantly perhaps – others saw the wider celebrations as marking an expansion of the Bundeswehr's role from one that was purely defensive to one that permitted – though with important constitutional constraints and caveats – offensive operations and expeditionary warfare beyond Germany's borders. Implicit in this latter perception was an apparent unease at the retention of what is still a very potent war-fighting capability, the recent and projected reductions notwithstanding.

While these are patently minority views, it does prompt an objective consideration of whether the army should or can afford to maintain a war capability without any clearly identifiable external threat. France is clearly out of the equation, being focused primarily on its own internal security needs, and maintaining an independent nuclear capability. Despite the size of the armed forces and the existence of their nuclear weapons, the once-formidable international and strategic significance of France has weakened somewhat in recent years, in parallel with uncertainties over that country's economy, which has been accompanied by a recent upsurge of internal unrest. Politically, in the immediate wake of German reunification, the Franco-German axis has remained solid; although some divergence on strategic and foreign policy might occur in the future if Angela Merkel and the CDU are able further to strengthen their position in Germany, and President Chirac eventually relinquishes office. Significantly, Merkel's first external visit after her election as Chancellor was to Paris, thus providing a very clear indication of the continuing Franco-German diplomatic policy accord and 'business as usual'.

In the meantime, to the east, German–Polish relations remain cordial but sometimes difficult. This situation is the historical legacy of so many territorial disputes over the centuries and of the traumas of the Third Reich era, but here also an armed conflict between Poland (especially as a newly joined member of the EU and the enthusiastic host for NATO military training exercises) and Germany is inconceivable. This truism has been reinforced by the recent creation of a German-Danish-Polish Multinational Corps North-East (MNC NE) based in Stettin, Poland.

Farther east, Russia still poses a potential if generally unquantifiable military threat not only to Germany but to the West, despite dramatically improved East–West relations ever since the early 1990s. This threat now stems not from any ideological aspirations or the old Cold War desire to invade Western Europe and achieve world domination. Rather, it is a function of the inherent instability of a former superpower still awash with military hardware, including numbers of nuclear weapons, and which is itself encountering increasing levels of nationalist dissent and Islamist extremism in parts (such as Chechnya) of its vast territory. At the same time, centralized control in Russia is significantly less effective today than it was during the Cold War years, while there is also considerable discontent within its armed forces over various aspects of pay, conditions of service, equipment, and Russia's much-reduced strategic importance and military capability. Historically, heads of state and governments that have problems at home all too often resort to war as a means of distracting and uniting a disaffected populace, and what might begin as an internal war can all too easily spread and become an international conflict. It follows that Germany, never a nation well trusted by Russia and which is still actively despised by many former Soviet citizens for Operation 'Barbarossa' in 1941 and the subsequent excesses committed during the three years of Nazi occupation, is probably right to maintain a suitably robust conventional fighting capability. This is necessary to guarantee the security of Germany's eastern borders and territory, as well as to deter aggression and to influence and reassure its other east and south-east European neighbours. However, the current improbability of actually needing to go to war in this way does attract motivational problems for the leaders of the Bundeswehr. Also, the much more likely possibility that conventional German forces might need to deploy in strength beyond Germany's borders to deal with some as yet unforeseen threat or extension of NATO, EU or German national security policy, will probably continue to be a difficult argument for the politicians to support both domestically and internationally, particularly in light of Germany's twentieth-century history prior to the end of the Third Reich in 1945.

In parallel with such considerations, there is also the question of how far the Bundeswehr should – or indeed could – become involved in counter-terrorist operations. In the past these activities have traditionally been the preserve of the police and the Bundesgrenzschutz, specifically the élite anti-terrorist unit GSG-9; and counter-terrorism within Germany currently remains a matter exclusively for the German police forces.[241] Accordingly, the question here is in any case very hypothetical and is perhaps less easily answered than was the case with the conventional threat. On balance, the army has no real tradition or depth of experience of colonial or imperial policing (its operations in China and Africa at the beginning of the twentieth century apart), while its activities against partisans, resistance groups, saboteurs and suchlike within occupied territories in wartime cannot be equated to the sort of skills needed to combat terrorism in the twenty-first century.

Consequently, it would probably be both inappropriate and impracticable for the Bundeswehr as a whole to attempt to emulate the counter-terrorist capability that can be found within, say, the British or French armies as a result of their separate experiences in Malaya, Northern Ireland, Indo-China, Algeria and elsewhere during the imperial and colonial draw-down of the previous century. Nevertheless, over time many German officers and soldiers will undoubtedly acquire the necessary skills as individuals, as well as and through their service with Germany's specialist counter-terrorist units and during exchange assignments with other NATO armies; no doubt numbers of them have already done so. In general, however, it will probably be right for the army to continue to be regarded primarily as a back-up for Germany's specialist counter-terrorist units rather than being trained for and becoming directly involved in the fight against terrorism. But to deny it such direct involvement where a clear and present international threat exists might also be to deny the Bundeswehr a readily discernible role with which its young soldiers can easily identify. There is clearly a potential dilemma here – one that has no ready or simple solutions.

While some other armies might be more experienced in waging counter-terrorist campaigns, the post-1990 Bundeswehr has already established an enviable reputation for its work in peace enforcement, information warfare and humanitarian operations, and for better or worse this is a powerful indicator of the direction in which its new destiny surely lies.[242] By so doing, the Bundeswehr is in many ways tackling successfully many of the causes of terrorism instead of simply countering terrorism head-on with armed force. There is a certain irony in this, as its successes in these fields perhaps sit somewhat uneasily with the less esoteric traditions of militarism established by the German war machine during the previous three centuries. But this does serve to underline the extent to which 1939–45 was truly a watershed for German militarism as well as one of the most significant and defining moments in its history. If the Wehrmacht had not been so utterly destroyed at the end of the Third Reich, if Germany had not been divided by the Allies at the end of the war, and if the Bundeswehr had not been forced to undergo the traumatic process of seeking an entirely new identity and role during the 1950s and 1960s, who can say what direction the course of European history might have taken? Certainly the somewhat ambiguous defeat of the Kaiser's army in 1918 in practice served Germany and its army particularly ill during the two decades that followed, and was (together with the ill-judged terms set by the major Allies at Versailles in 1920) a significant contributor to the rise of Nazism and the outbreak of the Second World War.

Accordingly, it may reasonably be argued that the post-Cold War changes in the nature of the Bundeswehr are indicative of its new maturity and resonance with the security needs of the twenty-first century, rather than of any wholesale abandonment of the military professionalism and traditions established by Prussia and Germany in former times. Certainly the modern Bundeswehr remains a military force to be reckoned with, as well as a force currently untainted by what many have erroneously or mischievously characterized as the 'war against Islam' by the United States, the United Kingdom and others. As such, the German army today has it within its power to be a powerful force for good, with a potent ability to impose stability in troubled areas and to carry out peace enforcement operations underwritten by real military power. Nevertheless, it may well be that the intended force balance and full extent of the equipment reductions envisaged in Structure 2010 will in due course prove to be a step too far. Consequently, it is possible that some serious rethinking by the newly formed CDU-led coalition government on the Structure 2010 concept may yet take place. This is less likely in the short-term and such action might well be impossible until Angela Merkel and the CDU have an opportunity to gain a more decisive subsequent election victory – something that could not now happen before 2009.

Indeed, on her formal election to power in 2005, Chancellor Angela Merkel found herself at the head of a fragmented and apparently fairly fragile government, for which the implementation of each and every significant change of policy would probably prove to be a considerable challenge. Contrary to many of the early predictions, however, the new CDU/SPD coalition government has now begun to coalesce and Chancellor Merkel has already gained a domestic and international stature well beyond that which was anticipated by a host of political pundits. A survey in January 2006 found that her popularity both within Germany and beyond was already significantly greater than that which had been achieved by Schröder at any time during his chancellorship.[243]

Nevertheless, her well-justified domestic policy aspirations to reduce Germany's budget deficit, to raise tax levels such as VAT, to reduce employment protection and social benefits and to increase economic incentives for trade and industry will dominate the early years of her administration. Accordingly, it is unlikely that her government will have the time or the inclination to undertake a significant reworking of the Bundeswehr's Structure 2010 plan. For the Bundeswehr, a period of considerable uncertainty is in prospect. It now finds itself serving a coalition government that is still somewhat ill at ease with itself, and which is headed by a chancellor who must maintain Germany's cordial relations with the United States and the other NATO members while simultaneously preserving intact the long-standing Franco-German alliance and its position on many core EU policies; all this despite the often highly critical pronouncements of the French leadership on aspects of Washington's foreign, strategic and security policy.

At the same time, Merkel's declared commitment to the Bundeswehr's continued involvement in peace-keeping and humanitarian operations where appropriate – presumably those conducted under the auspices of the UN, the EU or NATO rather than unilaterally – will continue to demand the creation and maintenance of the requisite levels of military training, resources and manpower to undertake and sustain such international commitments. Necessarily, this capability would be in addition to the Bundeswehr's extant fighting potential. Indeed, in the troubled and increasingly unstable and uncertain world in which we live today, such worthy missions as those designated as 'peace-keeping', 'stabilization' and 'humanitarian' operations may not be quite enough to guarantee peace and security.

But if this is indeed so, or if Germany should be threatened with military force in the future, none should doubt that its army would once again rise to meet the ultimate challenge of war. It has carried out this historic mission ever since that time long ago when Frederick William the Great Elector declared his laudable aim for the states of Germany never again to suffer the destruction, devastation and degradation of the thirty years of chaotic conflict that had begun in 1618; to which end he set about creating one of the most formidable, professional and history-making armies that the world has ever seen.

Neither should anyone doubt that in such circumstances the citizens of the reunified Germany would once more be prepared to defend their nation, and to fight to the very utmost for their Heimat. For a true German to deny this historic obligation or to contemplate any lesser response to the call of duty would be unthinkable. It would be a betrayal of the heritage and history of the German nation, and of the remarkable army that has sought to advance and defend the interests of that nation and its people for some 350 years – a redoubtable force which today represents many of the very best traditions, national characteristics and professionalism of its illustrious forebears, and which stands ever-ready to fulfil its own historic role by defending and if necessary 'fighting for the Fatherland'.

Notes

1. See also David Stone, *Cold War Warriors: the Story of the Duke of Edinburgh's Royal Regiment (Berkshire and Wiltshire) 1959–1994.* Pen & Sword Ltd., 1998, pp. 76–114 and 222–49. In addition to serving as an infantry officer in Minden 1968–9, in West Berlin 1971–2 and Osnabrück 1978 and 1982, the author also served as a military intelligence officer with HQ 1st British Corps in Bielefeld, West Germany 1980–1, so was fairly well acquainted with various aspects of the threat posed to NATO by the Soviet and the non-Soviet Warsaw Pact forces during the early 1980s. Subsequently, he served both with and alongside Bundeswehr troops in a training appointment at Sennelager 1984–7, as a staff officer at SHAPE in Belgium 1987–9, and on NATO operations in the Balkans 1995–6. Finally, he again served in Bielefeld from 1998–2001. Since completing his military service in 2002 he has been a frequent visitor to the reunified Germany.

2. The historic significance of Arminius' victory over the Roman commander Varus is still very evident today in the form of the massive monument and statue (the figure alone is almost eighty feet high) of Arminius that was constructed in 1875. It is set high on a wooded ridgeline close to the town of Detmold (in the area of what was originally, but incorrectly, identified as the site of the battle). As such, despite all that occurred in Germany during the first half of the twentieth century, it remains in place as a proud memorial to German nationalism and to the nation's heritage. For a full account of Arminius' defeat of Varus and the successful quest to identify the true site of the battle (at Kalkriese) see *In Quest of the Lost Legions* by Major Tony Clunn (Arminius Press, 2002).

3. In some respects this was akin to Arthurian legend in England. However, whereas much of the Arthurian legend was based – albeit fairly loosely – on a number of historical facts and actual events which were blended into a consolidated legend, the historical basis of *The Nibelungen* (and later Wagner's opera version, *The Ring*) were arguably much more tentative, and the tales somewhat more fanciful. In *Parsifal*, written by Wolfram von Eschenbach in the thirteenth century, German folklore moved much closer to the Arthurian legend, with the knight Parsifal pursuing his quest to find the Holy Grail.

4. See also Mackenzie, Donald A. *Teutonic Myth & Legend.* Gresham Publ. Co., London, n.d., possibly *c.*1910.

5. A permanent exhibition of the history of the Teutonic Order is on display at the Preussen-Museum Nordrhein-Westfalen, Simeonsplatz 12, D-32427 Minden, Germany, together with comprehensive coverage of the social, economic and military rise of Brandenburg and Prussia. The assistance of this museum with aspects of the early research for this work in 1999 and 2000 is gratefully acknowledged.

6. See also Appendix 1.

7. See Bibliog. Sigel and Specht, p. 4.

8. *Ibid.*

9. The (edited) general description and specific examples of the privations and atrocities carried out between about 1634 and 1637 are drawn primarily from Wedgwood, C. V, *The Thirty Years War.* (Penguin Books Ltd., London, 1961, pp. 255–6, 291–2 and 363–6. Her work quotes more than a dozen (mainly German) texts as references for these parts of her account.

10. Wedgwood, pp. 447–8.

11. Wedgwood, p. 446. Although her text was originally written in 1938 (i.e., before the Allied defeat of Germany in 1945), she apparently saw no reason to amend her assessment either in the 1956 updated introduction to her work or in subsequent editions of her book.

12. It might be more accurate to quote a figure of 'about 30,000', as sources do vary on this matter. Sichel and von Specht (p. 5) state that the army was 26,850 strong, but Rosinski (p. 11) suggests a total strength of 31,000 men.

13. This practice eventually produced the cocked and tricorne hats worn by the soldiers of most European armies in the late- seventeenth and throughout the eighteenth century.

14. Accounts of the Swedish–Brandenburg War of 1674–9 vary as to the actual size of this force, with some quoting the Swedish expeditionary force size as about 12,000 men, others putting it at 15,000, and yet others 16,000.

15. In the European armies of the seventeenth century (and in civilian life) physicians prescribed medicines and advised on health matters, medical treatment, internal disorders and so on, but they did not carry out surgery, this activity being exclusively the preserve of the members of the Guild of Barbers! The title

'Master' indicated that Johann Dietz was a licensed and fully accredited member of his guild. The consolidated account of his life (1665–1738) was compiled by Dietz at the age of seventy, and the original text of his manuscript was eventually lodged in the Royal Library in Berlin, later being published by Dr Ernst Consentius in German c.1914 and in English (tr. Bernard Miall) in 1923. Some aspects of the capture of Ofen are drawn from pp. 48–87 of the 1923 English-language imprint of Dietz's original manuscript by George Allen & Unwin Ltd., London. In many cases Dietz's words are quoted verbatim in order to convey their original impact; in others the author has taken the liberty of editing some of the original text for greater clarity.

16 The site of the modern Hungarian city of Budapest.

17 Frederick William, The Great Elector, married twice: first (in 1646) to Luise Henriette of Nassau-Oranien who died in 1667, then (in 1668) to Sophie Dorothea of Holstein Sonderburg-Glücksburg – and had thirteen children. He died in the palace at Potsdam on 9 May 1688 and was buried in the cathedral in Berlin.

18 Interestingly, the letters 'FR' (Fridericus Rex) at the centre of the Prussian eagle helmet plates of many nineteenth-century German regiments' Pickelhaube helmets – and which remained thereon until 1918 – were in memory of Frederick I, the first King of (or 'in') Prussia. This singular honour was accorded and maintained despite Frederick I's minimal contribution to the development of the Prussian army, compared to that of his predecessor and successors.

19 Rieger (tr. Colin Hall), p. 20.

20 Laffin, Jackboot (Sutton Publ. edn), devotes much text (pp. 2–3) to the Potsdam Grenadiers, or the 'Potsdam Giants', the 'Giant Grenadiers' or the 'Big Prussian Blues'. He quotes Frederick William: 'He who sends me tall soldiers can do with me whatever he likes', and the literal consequences of this were both remarkable and bizarre. Peter the Great sent from eighty to 200 tall Muscovites to Prussia each year from 1714 until his death. Fifteen very tall Irishmen arrived (under military escort!) in Berlin via England in 1720, and throughout Europe Prussian agents bought or kidnapped suitably tall men to fill the ranks of the Potsdam Grenadiers. This élite and favoured regiment – almost entirely manned by pressed men – achieved a maximum strength of 3,030, which was the equivalent of about three ordinary regiments of the line.

21 Yet again the totals vary from source to source. Sigel and von Specht (p. 5) quote 82,000; Laffin (p. 3) suggests 89,000; Rosinski (p. 20) 80,000.

22 The 'Pour le Mérite' became Imperial Germany's highest award for bravery in combat. Its origins lay in the French knightly order of St Louis founded by Louis XIV as an award to French Catholic officers for military service to France. Subsequently his further need to make awards to non-Catholics led to the founding of the military Order of Merit. On his accession in 1740, Frederick II copied this award and adopted it for Prussia for civilian and military merit alike. His successor, Frederick III directed that the 'Pour le Mérite' should be a distinction awarded exclusively for military merit. The design of the 'Pour le Mérite Cross' (or the 'Blue Max' as it was commonly known during the First World War) was (1914–18 pattern) described as a gold-edged blue enamelled Maltese cross set upon a backing of gold German imperial eagles set between the arms of the cross. The upper arm bears the Prussian or Imperial crown, above the letter 'F', with the words 'Pour le Mérite' broken up irregularly between the side and lower arms of the cross. The cross was worn as a neck decoration, suspended on a black and white ribbon.

23 An extract from notes on New Regulations for the Prussian Infantry, originally published in London in 1757 and subsequently reproduced in an article by Lt Col J. B. R. Nicholson in Tradition magazine, vol. III, issue No. 13 (Belmont-Maitland Publishers, London, c. mid-1960s). The capitalization used within the text reflects that of the original article.

24 Quoted in Laffin, p. 11.

25 Although a simple and fairly obvious technological advance, the invention of the socket bayonet, in place of the old plug bayonet which prevented the musket being fired when it was fitted, had dramatically increased the speed with which the infantry could close on the enemy immediately after firing a volley, having fired with their bayonets already fixed. Similarly, the ability of the infantry to deter and repel cavalry was much enhanced by their ability to establish at short notice and then maintain a formidable wall of steel, whether actually firing or simply holding firm on their position.

26 Stated by Frederick himself, and quoted in Montgomery, A History of Warfare, p. 327.

27 Two hundred years later, the Allied Powers' insistence on Germany's unconditional surrender in 1945 would once again severely limit the strategic options available to the leaders of what was by then a very different sort of Germany.

28 Some accounts indicate a lesser allied strength of 30,000 French and up to 11,000 Imperial troops and the Prussians fielding between 20,000 and 22,000. Even such a reduced strength of the allied army would have

produced a 2:1 superiority against Frederick's army.

29 Count Hadik later accepted the sum of 300,000 thalers as recompense for his agreement to vacate Berlin: an occupation that he must in any case have known he could not have long maintained if and when Frederick had once more been in a position to confront him. This was not the only occasion on which the Prussian capital was directly involved or threatened during the war. Following Frederick's defeat at Kunersdorf on the River Oder on 12 August 1759, the victorious Austro-Russian army failed to exploit its clear advantage and seize Berlin, which would almost certainly have ended the war and resulted in the decisive strategic defeat that Frederick could not countenance. But the moment passed and the opportunity was lost; Prussia and its capital remained safe, and its army went on to win more victories in the succeeding years.

30 The elm tree from which Frederick directed the battle was later named the 'Fritzenbaum', literally 'Old Fritz's tree', and the tree – or more probably its supposed successors – at Lunstädt retained this historic distinction from that day forward.

31 Duffy, p. 65. Some other sources quote figures of between 3,000 and 5,000.

32 Quoted by Duffy, p. 65. Sadly, the later career of Captain Gaudi was less than he deserved in light of the service he had rendered to his monarch and the army on 5 November 1757. Apparently, he was subsequently assigned to regimental service and relative obscurity, with the inference that at Rossbach he had not shown the courage required of a Prussian officer. Perhaps Gaudi had observed just a little too closely what some might reasonably judge to have been a near-critical delay by Frederick in his response to the Franco-Imperial threat from the south?

33 The issue of Silesia and, much later, the strategic significance of Poland's western border with Germany were forever bound to the story of the rise of Prussia and the eastwards expansion of Germany. Almost two centuries later, this subject and its inter-relationship with the post-1945 future of Germany dominated many of the discussions during the Allied strategic summits of the Second World War. See David Stone, *War Summits*, pp. 250–6.

34 Quoted in Laffin, p. 25, and sundry other sources. This historic meeting at a farmhouse or hamlet on the road to Leuthen (probably a few miles to the west of the village of Borne) was the subject of a painting by Fritz Roeber.

35 Some German accounts indicate a Prussian fighting strength of not more than 34,000 men.

36 The son of Leopold of Dessau, who had been instrumental in training the army of Frederick William I, the 'Soldier King'.

37 The Butterberg Hill feature is also shown as the 'Scheuberg' in some accounts of the battle.

38 During the battle, Frederick had become directly involved in the combat when he saved an unhorsed staff officer from a group of Austrian cavalrymen, killing two of them and protecting the officer until assistance arrived.

39 Frederick's unexpected arrival at Schloss Lissa was much later portrayed in a painting by the renowned German military artist R. Knötel. Laffin, p. 29, quotes Frederick as saying to the surprised Austrians 'Good evening, gentlemen, I dare say that you did not expect me here. Can one get a night's lodging along with you?' Despite Frederick's initial courtesy, a separate German source records that the Austrian cavalry officers were made prisoners in short order!

40 Austrian losses quoted by Laffin, p. 29.

41 At Frederick's order, General Ziethen had assumed command of Bevern's beaten army on 28 November. This force had joined with Frederick's on 3 December and then played a crucial part in the battle at Leuthen, as well as providing further evidence of how speedily a defeated army could become a victorious army, given the necessary standards of discipline, morale and training.

42 Once again, the recorded strength of the Prussian army engaged in these battles varies considerably between sources. Several German sources, together with Laffin, indicate strengths of between 26,000 and 30,000, but other non-German sources state that the actual Prussian strength might have been as high as 50,000. For example, see *The Oxford Companion*, p. 323, although this particular reference entry also indicates Prussian losses of 47,000 men from a force of 50,000 at Kunersdorf, incredibly high losses which the author has not been able to verify from any other source. In any event, where it is quoted, the figure of about 50,000 might well include the additional Prussian forces that were actively involved in the campaign, but which were not engaged directly in these specific battles. Notwithstanding these anomalies, it is indisputable that Frederick achieved victories while seriously outnumbered, that he also suffered some severe reverses, and that both in victory and in defeat his army's losses were often devastating and potentially crippling.

43 See also Rosinski, pp. 30–41. This interesting account by a German author, written just prior to the Second World War, is much more critical of Frederick's divisive approach to the officering of the Prussian army than most other accounts. Consequently, it both balances Frederick's clear attributes and also shows him to have been something of an enigma, not

entirely free of human flaws, frailties and prejudices.

44 See Laffin, p. 36.

45 In fact, his strategic priority was then the destruction of the Austrians, and to take forward French ambitions in Belgium, so his reluctance to risk his troops against the Prussians at Valmy is understandable.

46 'Auerstadt' is also shown as 'Auerstedt' and 'Auerstädt' in various sources.

47 Some sources quote a Prussian strength at Auerstadt of as few as 35,000. However, the French strength is extensively recorded, together with a Prussian superiority of '2:1'. Accordingly, the figure of '60,000' Prussians is quoted here. It may well be that this total does include various Prussian reserve formations that were under Brunswick's command, but which were not directly committed to this particular combat.

48 Von Schill, by then a major, was killed during the assault on Stralsund on 31 May that year, and was subsequently proclaimed as a Prussian national hero. As such, von Schill's name was used to rally patriotic support for the uprising of 1813–14, and during the Prussian War of Liberation in 1814. For a full account of von Schill and his role in the military uprising of 1809, see also the article by T. Snorrason, *The Assault on Stralsund, 1809*, in *Tradition* magazine no. 52 (Belmont-Maitland Publ, Ltd., London, *c*.1975). In 1945, Kolberg once more gained historical prominence, when its small *ad hoc* garrison's spirited defence against the Russian onslaught from mid-March until the town's successful evacuation by sea on 18 March were master-minded and conducted by Colonel Fritz Fullriede, for which this elderly veteran officer was awarded a well-deserved Knight's Cross (a full account of this action is at Hastings, pp. 525–6).

49 The Iron Cross was first instituted on 10 March 1813. There is a certain irony in the fact that Germany's most famous military award was instituted by one of its lesser martial leaders. Under the terms of its introduction the award was to be reinstituted at the outbreak of each subsequent major conflict. Accordingly, it was revived by Bismarck during the Franco-Prussian War 1870–1, and for both World Wars. Although the detailing on the face of the medal changed for each conflict, its basic form continued to be a black cast-iron cross bordered by a milled and raised silver rim. Initially the ribbon (when worn) was black-and-white but after 1939 a black-white-red-white-black ribbon was adopted. From its inception until 1939 the medal was awarded in three classes, and as breast and neck decorations, plus a breast-star version. On 1 September 1939 it was reinstituted with a number of design changes, qualifying

requirements, and the introduction of a new grade. This was the Knight's Cross (which also had a number of sub-grades). For more details see Violet E. Buchan, *Imperial German Decorations 1914-1918*, in *Tradition* magazine, No. 62, Belmont-Maitland Publ., *c*. late 1960s) and Snyder, pp. 83 and 297.

50 The German ability to circumvent the terms of an externally imposed limitation on the national military capability was a skill in which they would once again prove themselves particularly adept more than a century later. During the years immediately prior to the Second World War, after Adolf Hitler became the German Chancellor in 1933, the manpower ceiling of 100,000 for the Reichsheer that was allowed by the 1919 Treaty of Versailles was progressively exceeded by various ingenious contrivances.

51 Laffin, p. 56. Those Prussian regiments that had surrendered or otherwise acquitted themselves poorly during the war were disbanded.

52 Some sources (e.g., Laffin, p. 71) attribute Scharnhorst's fatal wound to the 'closing stages of the battle [of Leipzig]', and not to Lützen (but see Uffindell, p. 186). However, while the two battlefields are certainly geographically close to each other, there was a six-month time interval between the two battles, and as far as the author can ascertain, Gneisenau had in any case assumed the appointment of Blücher's chief of staff well before Leipzig. Simpson (p. 46) attributes Scharnhorst's wound to 'the battle of Grossgörschen', but is quite specific that he died on 28 June 1813 – almost four months before Leipzig.

53 By the Carlsbad Decrees of August, 1819, the German states had agreed to take decisive and co-ordinated action to halt and if necessary suppress the spread of nationalist and liberal ideas and movements among the young people of Germany. Then, a few months later, the performance of the Landwehr was severely criticized by the regular officer corps following its autumn 1819 manoeuvres. Taken together, this reactionary and potentially Draconian decree and the subsequent placing of the Landwehr under the direct command of the army were so unacceptable to liberals and military reformers such as Boyen, Grolman and others that they had no course other than to resign from a government whose policies they could no longer support.

54 Forbes, *My Experiences*, vol. I, pp. 7–8.

55 The name 'uhlan' was adopted from that of the much-admired Polish light cavalry troops of former times.

56 The weapon had been invented by Nikolaus von Dreyse in 1829. This breech-loading narrow-bore rifle had a needle-type firing pin within the bolt which, when the trigger was

squeezed, was pushed forward by a spring, first of all piercing the paper cartridge case, then striking the detonating cap, thus igniting the charge that propelled the bullet. Despite a claimed rate of fire of three rounds each minute, this was frequently bettered with training and practice. Remarkably, the clear benefits of this weapon (apart from some early technical difficulties in setting up the production line for its manufacture in large numbers) were ignored by numbers of officers who still favoured the retention of the Prussian army's bronze muzzle-loading weapons. But, by the mid-1860s the Dreyse needle-gun was in general use throughout the Prussian army.

57 The battle of Langensalza took place to the south of the Harz Mountains, on 27 June 1866. The Hanoverian forces were moving south and east to link up with the Austrians when they were intercepted by Prussians. Hanover was generally credited with winning the battle that day, but its army had insufficient resources to sustain any further operations and so was forced to capitulate to the Prussians two days later. Langensalza meant the end of the old Hanoverian Army, which soon thereafter was integrated into the Prussian system and into the Army of the North German Confederation. Following Hanover's defeat, a number of its officers chose virtual exile in England and to serve (as had many of their predecessors with the King's German Legion (KGL)) in the British army rather than in a German army that would clearly thereafter be dominated by Prussia.

58 Some accounts show an Austro-Saxon strength as high as 240,000.

59 Quoted in Maguire & Herbert, p. 53.

60 Archibald Forbes, a Scotsman and the son of a clergyman, was born in 1838. After leaving Aberdeen University with many debts and no degree, he enlisted in the 1st (Royal) Dragoons in 1859, apparently making what was remarkably rapid progress to the rank of acting quartermaster sergeant by 1864, when he was discharged. Subsequently, he used a natural talent for writing, a workable knowledge of French and German, and his years of military experience to follow a career as one of the first true 'war correspondents'. His various attachments to the German armies during the Franco-Prussian War and the dispatches he produced made his fame and fortune. Forbes continued to write successfully about a number of later conflicts. In declining health, he died in 1900 and was buried in Aberdeen.

61 Forbes, vol. I, p. 19.

62 National or regional identity was shown by a comprehensive system of coloured cockades (or roundels). These were affixed to head-dress (usually under the chinstrap rivet at the side of

helmets and shakos and at the front of cloth field or barracks caps). The cockade colour combinations were (from outer edge to centre): black-white-black (Prussia), white-light blue-white (Bavaria and Schwarzburg-Sonderhausen), white-green-white (Saxony), white-red-white (Hesse), blue-red-blue (Oldenburg), blue-yellow-blue (Brunswick), green (Anhalt), black-red-black (Württemberg), yellow-red-yellow (Baden), blue-yellow-red (Mecklenburg), green-yellow-black (Saxony-Weimar), green-white-green (Saxon Herzogtümer), light-blue-white-light-blue (Schwarzburg-Rudolfstadt), yellow-red (Lippe), white-red-white (Bremen), white-red-blue (Schaumburg-Lippe), and yellow-red-black (Waldeck Reuss). The cities of Hamburg and Lübeck adopted variations of a Maltese-style cross in red on a white background. After the war of 1870–1 a national German cockade (black-white-red) was adopted by the military forces of the new German Empire and was worn by all its soldiers in addition to their state or regional cockades.

63 In addition to the scroll running across its wings and upper chest, the helmet plate's Prussian eagle usually bore the letters 'FR' or 'FWR' at its centre. Until 1918, 'FWR' was used on the eagle badge of the original twelve Prussian infantry regiments that existed before the Wars of Liberation 1813–15, and denoted Frederick William III (born 1770; ruled 1797–1840), who instigated a number of major reforms of the army during his reign. Similarly, until 1918, 'FR' was used on the eagle badges of all other infantry (and many other) units formed post-1815, to denote and commemorate the first king of Prussia, Frederick I (who was crowned 'King in Prussia', 18 January 1701).

64 Forbes, vol I, pp. 379–80.

65 Seaton, p. 33.

66 There are various theories about the origin and style of the Pickelhaube. In one case its appearance was attributed to the painter Heinrich Stilke (1803–60) who was allegedly commissioned by the King of Prussia to do this design work. Another painter, Moritz von Schwind of Bavaria, may also have contributed to the process, perhaps unwittingly, as a fresco painted by him in the Knights' Hall of the royal castle at Hohenschwangau, Bavaria, in the mid-1830s featured a helmet very similar to the Prussian design adopted in 1842. In the same timeframe, the steelworks of Wilhelm Jaeger of Elberstadt were reported to have provided the Prussian General Staff with a prototype helmet made of sheet steel for evaluation. Indeed, both metal and leather versions of the Pickelhaube were developed and used. Finally, in yet another account, the Prussian King Frederick William IV reputedly saw a prototype

NOTES

✠✠✠✠✠✠✠✠✠✠✠✠

Pickelhaube-style helmet on the desk of Tsar Nicholas I during a state visit to Russia. He so liked its design that on his return he ordered the development and production of the helmet for the Prussian army before the Russians could introduce it into theirs. Whatever the truth may be, it is a matter of record that the Pickelhaube first appeared in 1842 and, with minor improvements and modifications, its overall shape or image remained synonymous with Prussian and German militarism for some eighty years thereafter.

67 The Pickelhaube was the military head-dress on which the British army helmet, introduced into general use in 1878, was closely modelled, although the British version (which remained in general service until 1914) was slightly taller and not so angular in shape as its German counterpart.

68 Forbes, vol. I, pp. 219–20.

69 Although not employed by the Germans during the war with France, the innovative and then still largely experimental use of gas-filled balloons in support of military operations for tactical observation and communication tasks, became in later years the specific responsibility of special balloon detachments of the engineer troops.

70 The conclusion of the formal period of fighting between Germany and France was not quite the end of the story for the French, and for the population of Paris in particular, where the sense of France's humiliation by Prussia and of the nation's betrayal by the French government were both very great. By the time that peace had finally been restored within France in the spring of 1871, much of the capital was a smouldering ruin and Paris had in effect endured its third revolution and civil war; but in this one, more Parisians died than had been killed during the whole of the first French Revolution, including the Reign of Terror. Indeed, some 20,000 French citizens – almost all in Paris – were killed in a final bloodbath that set Frenchman against Frenchman during the suppression of the Paris Commune and the National Guard by the French regular army.

71 Although first written in 1961 (with the subsequent publication of other editions), the most comprehensive political and military account of all aspects of the Franco-Prussian War remains Professor Michael Howard's *The Franco-Prussian War*. However, for a more recent account of the war which deals in particular with the part played by the Prussian and German army, see David Stone's *'First Reich': Inside the German Army during the War with France 1870–71* (Brassey's, London, 2002).

72 Also shown as 'Pestel' in some accounts.

73 In most German contemporary accounts of the battle this officer is described as the '2nd Count von Gneisenau'.

74 Forbes, vol. I, pp. 51–3. Unlike that of most other armies of the day, the German high command understood the propaganda benefits that could be gained from media exposure, and positively welcomed the presence of newspaper correspondents, though this was subject to the understandable proviso 'that the military authorities should control the whole of the Press when in the field'. This policy was subsequently formalized in a general staff publication that dealt with broad aspects of the conduct of operations, the *Kriegsbrauch im Landkriege*.

75 Forbes, vol. I, pp. 55–7.

76 The French army's mitrailleuse was similar in concept to the American Gatling gun. It had twenty-five 13mm concentric barrels and could deliver five 25-round bursts of fire per minute at ranges up to 3,000 yards. Almost two hundred of the guns were in service by 1870. The near-obsessive secrecy accorded to it before 1870 constrained development of its correct tactical use, which should unquestionably have been for the close support of the infantry. Consequently, in 1870, it was generally misemployed as a form of field artillery, and so did not fulfil its true potential. Nevertheless, on the relatively few occasions when it was used correctly it usually inflicted heavy casualties on the Germans.

77 Forbes, vol. I, p. 59.

78 Ascoli, David. *A Day of Battle – Mars-la-Tour – 16 August 1870* (Harrap, London, 1987).

79 Forbes, vol. I, p. 150.

80 Ascoli, *op. cit.*

81 The third regiment of Bredow's 12th Cavalry Brigade was usually the 13th Dragoons, but they had been deployed earlier that morning to reinforce the 11th Cavalry Brigade on the German left flank, to the north of Mars-la-Tour.

82 Sigel and von Specht, pp. 38–40.

83 Contrary to Forbes's account, Ascoli indicates (p. 187) that this attack did not begin until 5 p.m.

84 In this case, the failure to carry out a proper reconnaissance before the attack meant that neither General Voigts-Rhetz nor the 19th Division's commander, General Schwarzkoppen, were aware of the presence of the ravine until the 38th Brigade's infantrymen were confronted by the obstacle.

85 Sigel and von Specht, p. 28.

86 In fact, the 20th German Division was meant to have supported the 38th Brigade's assault; but apparently the 20th Division did not receive the order to attack, with the almost inevitable outcome described.

87 Ascoli also noted the involvement in the great mêlée of the '16th Dragoons, the divisional cavalry of 20th Division'. He recorded that the '… 49 squadrons in close order – met with a

411

clash that echoed east to Vionville and north to Bruville, and grappled together under a giant cloud of dust which obscured the view not only of observers but of the combatants themselves ...' (which resulted in at least one instance during the mêlée of French dragoons mistakenly attacking their own lancers).

88 General Legrand also fell in this engagement, at the head of his squadrons of French dragoons. Meanwhile, the Oldenburg Dragoons had lost 13 officers and 104 men by the end of the mêlée.

89 Sigel and von Specht, pp. 40–2. The original version of this account shows 'du Barail' incorrectly as 'du Bareil' and 'Montaigu' incorrectly as 'Montagu'.

90 Hooper, pp. 160–1.

91 Lieutenant General Konstantin von Alvensleben was already 61 years old by 16 August 1870, and for him the battle was a personal triumph. This very competent and experienced soldier's military career had begun in 1827 and he had served with the Great General Staff from 1853, first in the rank of major and then as a lieutenant colonel. Later, he also served on the staff as a major general in 1864, during the Schleswig-Holstein campaign. His command experience included regimental command in 1861 and divisional command in 1866, when he gained a reputation for being sound of judgement and very calm under pressure. The events of 16 August were the highpoint of his career, and the successful outcome of the battle of Mars-la-Tour–Vionville, arguably against all the odds, was due primarily to his performance as a commander that day.

92 Forbes, vol. I, p. 170.

93 Although this corps was usually part of the 1st Army, the 8th German Corps had in fact been placed under the direct command of the German high command in advance of this particular battle. But von Steinmetz and von Goeben chose to ignore these arrangements, which had been so carefully contrived by von Moltke (and were an indication of the latter's well-founded reservations concerning von Steinmetz's ability as a commander).

94 The 33rd Regiment of Fusiliers, although recruited in East Prussia, had been part of the garrison of Köln when war broke out. Consequently it was included in the 8th (Rhine Provinces) Corps. The regiment's casualties at Gravelotte–St-Privat were their heaviest during the entire war and on 18 August it lost 655 men, including 183 killed, 463 wounded and nine missing. Of those killed and wounded, twenty-four were officers. A contemporary account recorded that 'The dead were buried in an open field at the exit from Gravelotte, close to the north

end of the road to St-Hubert. The officers were laid to rest without coffins, clad in full uniform ... No salute was fired [at the funeral] for fear of causing a false alarm. In any case, on 19th August, the Commander-in-Chief had ordered "No funeral volleys shall be fired during the war; the enemy's fire is the most honourable salute."' By the end of the war the 33rd Regiment, which had been 3,000 strong on mobilization, had sustained a total of 1,304 casualties, including 432 killed.

95 Brigadier Peter Young. 'The 33rd East Prussian Fusiliers in the War of 1870–71 (1966)' (extracted from an article in the *Journal of the Royal United Services Institution* (Nos 167 and 168) entitled 'Précis of the Regimental History of the 33rd East Prussian Fusiliers in the War of 1870–71', compiled by Major G. F. R. Henderson (1854–1903) of the York and Lancaster Regiment, and subsequently published in *Tradition* Magazine, Nos. 14 and 15.

96 Forbes, vol. I, pp. 181–4.

97 Forbes, *ibid.*.

98 Forbes, vol. I, p. 189. The French mistake resulted in 300 French soldiers being burned to death. Despite Bazaine's telegraph to Napoleon III on 17 August which stated that 'The wounded have been evacuated to Metz', in excess of 5,000 wounded Frenchmen, with a number of surgeons, were left behind after the battle of 16 August.

99 The 12th (Royal Saxon) Corps had been ordered to conduct a wide flanking march north-east past Jarny and then swing east towards Ste-Marie-aux-Chênes to complete the encirclement of the Army of the Rhine.

100 In fact, the attack was ordered by Prince Frederick Charles, in consultation and with the willing agreement of the commander of the Guard Corps, Prince Augustus of Württemberg. Ascoli (*op. cit.*) indicates that Prince Augustus of Württemberg was particularly keen to commence the Guard Corps attack, in order to 'steal the thunder of the Crown Prince of Saxony', whose 12th (Royal Saxon) Corps was still advancing on his left. The tactical need for the Germans to take St-Privat was not in dispute, but the Guards' somewhat unimaginative direct axes of advance across about a mile of open ground, with a lack of effective artillery support for almost the first three hours, resulted directly in the very large numbers of casualties sustained during the series of attacks. Yet again, weapons technology had advanced more quickly than had the tactics of those employing or suffering the effects of these weapons.

101 Sigel and von Specht, pp. 24–5.

102 Sigel and von Specht, p. 25. The painting by Alphonse de Neuville is *Le cimetière de Saint-*

Privat, which was first shown publicly at the Paris salon of 1881.

103 Young, *op. cit.*

104 Young, *op. cit.*

105 The collapse of elements of the German 1st Army at the Mance ravine was one notable – but arguably excusable – exception to this assessment.

106 It is a matter of record that the German soldiers' response to the sometimes less than competent actions of their commanders was certainly very different from that of the French soldiers, whose criticism of Marshal Bazaine and others of their leaders became increasingly vehement as the campaign developed, despite the inherent patriotism of the ordinary French soldier.

107 This new command arrangement led (very predictably!) just three weeks later, on 7 September, to a complaint by Frederick Charles to King William that von Steinmetz 'was deliberately withholding from him the customary civilities due to a superior officer', or in other words that he was guilty of insubordination. The removal of von Steinmetz quickly followed on 15 September, through the diplomatic device of his appointment into 'honourable retirement as Governor of Posen [Poznan]'. Thus did von Moltke, somewhat belatedly, achieve another – but this time much more personal – goal in the wake of the battle of Gravelotte–St-Privat.

108 Young, *op. cit.*

109 By Chassepot sniping, sorties, skirmishes and artillery fire, the French continued to cause casualties throughout the siege of Metz; by late September 'the 4th Regiment lost (killed and wounded) 35 officers out of a total of 60, and 1,000 men out of 3,000. The 45th Regiment, lying in its vicinity, had lost yet more of its officers. Out of 60 no fewer than 42 had fallen.' Such casualties meant rapid promotions in the field and consequently 'a large number of "Vice-feldwebels" and several sergeants had received commissions. As these were comparatively inexperienced in their new duties, they were daily receiving assiduous instructions from their seniors.' (Forbes, vol. I, p. 312).

110 *Ibid.*, p. 304.

111 *Ibid.*, p. 308.

112 *Ibid.*, p. 320.

113 *Ibid.*, p. 319.

114 *Ibid.*, pp. 347–8.

115 *Ibid.*, pp. 350–4.

116 A branch of the English ambulance service was also involved in the war, operating independently. This organization, a tentative forerunner of the British Red Cross and similar organizations, was based at and directed from its headquarters in Remilly, and was under the control of Mr. Austin Lee, described as 'a young gentleman endowed with unquestionable administrative talent and great energy'. Lee was supported by his assistant, a Captain Norman.

117 The statistics are taken from Forbes, vol. I, p. 419, who was present to witness the surrender of Metz at first-hand. It is possible that the total figure for the number of general officers captured may have been even higher. At least one source states that the total garrison may have numbered as many as 180,000 as at 28 October, although Wawro (p. 251) indicates a figure of 133,000, but he also states (p. 186) that 'the 140,000-man Army of the Rhine retreated to Metz' (after its defeat at Gravelotte–St-Privat). Accordingly, a figure of about 173,000 (which of course includes the already in-place garrison) is generally considered to be correct and is reflected in most of the French and German sources.

118 The military potential of balloons was well noted by the German high command (and by other European military observers) at the siege of Paris. After the war, units of balloon troops were speedily introduced into the German Corps of Engineers, with specialist detachments based in Berlin and Munich. Usually, these engineer troops operated hydrogen-filled captive observation balloons, the observer in the basket reporting by telephone. The planned altitude for the balloons was about 1,800 feet, and their position and height could be adjusted by the controlling troops on the ground to match the mission and changing tactical situation. The use of free-flight balloons by besieged garrisons (as by the French in Paris) or by surrounded troops was also envisaged. Interestingly, a balloon unit still existed in the modern Federal German Army (Bundeswehr) in the 1990s, with an important role in psychological (or 'Operative Information – OpInfo') operations as a means of leaflet dissemination into inaccessible or enemy territory. This concept was used successfully during almost thirty years of leaflet-distributing flights across the Inner German Border (IGB) into the former East Germany (DDR) during the Cold War.

119 Forbes, vol. II, pp. 63–4.

120 See Cassell, vol. I, pp. 218–21, *et seq.*

121 Forbes, vol. I, pp. 299–300.

122 Forbes, vol. II, pp. 243–5.

123 Extract from one of a number of unpublished letters written by Ralph von Kreusser during the Franco-Prussian War, kindly provided to the author by Mr Edward Piper. Von Kreusser's service began in 1865, as a volunteer cadet in the 2nd Bavarian Infantry Regiment. He was commissioned into the 1st Infantry Regiment in 1866 and served in a number of the battles, including Wörth,

Beaumont, Bazeilles, Sedan, Orléans, and during the siege of Paris. Subsequently, he was appointed adjutant to Prince Ludwig of Bavaria and instructor or military adviser to Prince Rupprecht of Bavaria and later (from 1890 to 1895) commanded a battalion of the 15th Infantry Regiment. He retired as a lieutenant colonel in 1900 and died at Munich on 27 January 1918.

124 Forbes, vol. II, pp. 275–6.

125 It is a moot point whether an indefinite prolongation of the siege of Paris would have resulted in its capitulation without the bombardment. Certainly starvation was rife within the less affluent and more imprudent sections of the population by mid-January. Meat had been rationed since October, and even then was generally limited to horsemeat. But as the weeks passed cats, dogs, rats and even some of the more exotic animals from the Paris Zoo found their way to the dining-tables of those who could afford them. Milk and fresh vegetables were unobtainable fairly early in the siege. Fuel shortages became widespread and critical as the winter drew on, and gas lighting throughout the city was reduced. Queues for food and fuel were seen everywhere, if buyers could afford the inflated prices! So, although Paris was not in a state of total collapse when it capitulated, it is probable that it would have eventually succumbed to starvation, no doubt with a parallel collapse of authority in the city leading to serious internal disorder. This would almost certainly have occurred within a matter of weeks of its actual surrender, but the great unknown remains of course the extent of German political will and the ability of the military to prolong the siege indefinitely without resort to bombardment. In hindsight, the bombardment of Paris was probably inevitable.

126 In the years that followed, Bismarck found himself increasingly at odds with the newly proclaimed Kaiser and his successor, because of his continued authoritarian approach to government and diplomacy. He fell increasingly into disfavour, and was finally dismissed by Kaiser William II in 1890. But for better or worse, he was undeniably the true architect of the new German Empire, having demonstrated on numerous occasions his particular talent for applying first the Prussian and then the German war machine to achieve his political objectives.

127 Forbes, vol. II, pp. 495–9.

128 Ibid., p. 500.

129 Ibid., pp. 500–3. The descriptions of the return of the Kaiser and the Prussian soldiers to Berlin in March 1871 were the last reports submitted by Forbes on his experiences with the German army during the war. He subsequently covered several other late-nineteenth century European, imperial and colonial conflicts.

130 The Rifle Type '88 weighed 8.37 pounds and was 49.01 inches long. Its range was appreciably greater than that of the needle-gun, and it had a fixed sight set at 273 yards, a drop sight set at 386 yards and a Vernier adjustable sight graduated from 490 to 2,238 yards.

131 In the early 1980s, on the direction of Lieutenant General (later Field Marshal) Sir Nigel Bagnall, the 1st British Corps in West Germany also embraced Auftragstaktik, based mainly upon studies of the German campaign in Russia 1941–4. Subsequently, the understanding, assimilation and practical adoption of Auftragstaktik both in 1st British Corps and later in the wider British army was not an easy process and took many years before it achieved widespread recognition and acceptance.

132 Lt Col. B. Granville Baker, 'Recollections of a Prussian Hussar', in The Cavalry Journal, 1927. Repr. in Tradition Magazine No. 26, pp. 17–18, Belmont-Maitland Publ. Ltd., London, c.1966.

133 Sigel & von Specht, p. 92.

134 Op. cit. p. 92.

135 Count von Baudissin, Life in a German Crack Regiment, T. Fisher Unwin, London, 1904. This first English language edition was published in October 1904, reprinted in November and further reprints in March 1908 and October 1914.

136 Granville Baker, in Tradition No. 25, p. 7, c.1967.

137 In fact, the late Frederick III had issued a timely and well-judged instruction that officers were only to wear uniform when on duty. But after his untimely death from cancer in 1888 just three months after becoming Kaiser, this order was generally ignored, as the well-established mystique and perceived prestige attaching to a German officer's military uniform perpetuated into the twentieth century.

138 Laffin, p. 114.

139 Ibid., pp. 110–12.

140 Granville Baker, in Tradition, No. 27, p. 14, c.1967.

141 See also Laffin, pp. 110-113.

142 Granville Baker, in Tradition, No. 23, pp. 6–7, c.1966.

143 Op. cit., No. 23, p. 8, c.1966.

144 Op. cit., No. 27, p.15, c.1967.

145 Details of the German forces in China 1899-1901 are drawn primarily from Bodin, p. 28.

146 See also the references to the Kriegsbrauch im Landkriege at Chapter 15 concerning the German attitude to such 'native' and 'irregular' fighters.

147 Jünger, *Copse 125*, p. vii. Ernst Jünger (1895–1998) wrote extensively and eloquently about his experiences of the war. Having enlisted in 1914, by mid-1918 he was a lieutenant commanding a company in his infantry regiment, the 73rd (Hanoverian) Regiment of Fusiliers 'Field Marshal Prince Albrecht of Prussia', on the Western Front. He was awarded the *Pour le Mérite* on 22 September 1918 for his wartime service. His books (more than sixty in total) were at the same time patriotic, objective, thoughtful and realistic – with vivid descriptions of combat, and the nature of soldiering and the German soldier. From the mid-1920s he was increasingly involved with nationalist and veterans' organizations, such as *Stahlhelm*. His works later found favour with Hitler, although Jünger always distanced himself from the Nazis and he was never a NSDAP member. In uniform once again during the Second World War, Jünger served as a captain with the army in France 1940–4. As a convinced European, Jünger was closely associated with Chancellor Kohl and President Mitterand. He died aged 102.

148 Jünger, E. *Storm of Steel* (Chatto & Windus, London, 1929), quoted by Laffin, p. 135.

149 Such killings do of course embrace a multiplicity of circumstances and situations. These could include unauthorized individuals acting in the heat of the moment, to local retributional or reprisal action, to troops carrying out such orders as a matter of deliberate policy. For some examples of the summary killing of prisoners of war by the Allies during the Second World War, see Hastings, p. 438 *et seq.*

150 Strachan, p. 51. There are some parallels here with the action of the Bavarian troops in their attack on Bazeilles on 1 September 1871 (see Stone, 'First Reich', pp. 140–1).

151 In fact, Grünert and especially Hoffman were as much the architects of the German victory at Tannenberg as von Hindenburg and von Ludendorff, although the accolades that it produced were generally and almost exclusively accorded only to the latter two men. While this was probably appropriate in respect of von Hindenburg, as the commander who ultimately took the decision to adopt the plan, in von Ludendorff's case he undoubtedly received more credit for Tannenberg than he deserved; but true to form did not seek to redress this situation.

152 Jünger, *Copse 125*, pp. 18 and 19.

153 *Ibid.*, p. 40.

154 *Ibid.*, p. 85.

155 *Ibid.*, p. 107.

156 See also Marion, R. J. and Embleton, G. A. 'Germany 1914–18, Assault Detachments (Stosstruppen)' in *Tradition* magazine, No.

25, pp. 14 and 22–3, for a full listing of the allocation of storm battalions and companies to armies as at the beginning of 1918.

157 The attrition of regular officers during the early part of the war (the regular officer corps was doubled to 45,923 by 1918, with 11,357 killed during the war (Simpson, p. 106) necessitated an increase in reserve officer numbers from about 29,000 in 1914 to just over 226,000 by 1918 (Rosinski, pp. 159–60). This meant that heavy reliance was placed on officers of whom many had received no more than six weeks of specialist officer training, and so were ill-prepared for their work. Despite the army's critical need of experienced officers, the social prejudices of former times perpetuated, so that the commissioning of the socially and intellectually acceptable Einjährigen (some 200,000 during the war) compared most unfavourably with the commissioning of some 240 NCOs (of whom ninety were in the Bavarian forces) who met the stringent criteria for personal bravery in action that such promotions required.

158 Rosinski, p. 161.

159 Subsequently, both during and after the war, von Falkenhayn was strongly criticized as the architect of the German blood bath at Verdun. But during the two years following his dismissal as chief of staff his undoubted qualities as a competent senior field commander were well in evidence. He commanded the German-Austrian-Bulgarian force which so decisively defeated Romania in December 1916. In 1917 he served in Palestine and then in White Russia in 1918.

160 Cambrai has often been over-stated as the vindication of the concept of the tank. But the British success there, notably a 4,000-yard penetration of the German front, was gained primarily by the complete surprise achieved and by the effectiveness of the artillery support, which was co-ordinated with the armoured attack. See Strachan, *The First World War*, p. 306.

161 Nevertheless, morale in parts of the German army was also weakening by 1918, when von Ludendorff himself declared that 'tens of thousands' of German soldiers had already deserted, either to neutral countries, or simply to return to their homes where their presence was (by that stage of the war) 'tolerated' by their families and by the once fervently patriotic local community. The need of a great German victory to restore the morale and confidence of the army was another important consideration underlying von Ludendorff's spring 1918 offensive.

162 Jünger, *Storm of Steel*, p. 228. Some other sources state that the artillery opened fire at 0440, but some counter-battery fire was

certainly in progress prior to 0505 to suppress British artillery seeking to engage the German troop concentrations. In any event, it is reasonable to assume that the time recorded by Jünger refers to the start of the bombardment of the British defensive positions, of which he had a clear view.

163 Jünger, *Storm of Steel*, p. 229.

164 The fire plan on 21 March 1918 owed much to the experience of a German artillery officer, Georg Brüchmuller, who had successfully used the technique to secure German victories at Riga and at Caporetto in 1917.

165 Jünger, *Storm of Steel*, p. 240.

166 *Ibid.*, p. 243.

167 By early 1918 the German medical staff in some areas had run out of cloth bandages and were using *ersatz* bandages of crêpe paper. Elsewhere, the exhaustion of the army's remaining horses, and lack of petrol had dramatically reduced the army's mobility. Allied to this, the unavailability of rubber for tyres meant that many of those motor vehicles that were still in use had been fitted with iron tyres, which quickly destroyed the roads and so further slowed movement.

168 Contrary to the somewhat optimistic general staff estimate of early 1918, no fewer than 200,000 American troops had landed in France during the few weeks after 21 March that year.

169 General Groener was an intellectually astute and politically very aware member of the general staff who was destined to carry through several historic measures that were undoubtedly for the good of Germany and its army. But, given the mood of recrimination that swept Germany in 1918 and 1919 his efforts earned him much criticism and abuse through his inevitable association with a republican government viewed by most as that which had negotiated the armistice and thus betrayed Germany in general and its soldiers in particular. Nevertheless, it was in large measure Groener's diplomacy and political manoeuvring that safeguarded the officer corps, made possible the suppression of the revolutionary movements in post-war Germany, and paved the way for development of the post-war Reichswehr from 1919.

170 Only those serving soldiers born between 1896 and 1899 (the most recent army intakes) were planned to be retained in the active army. However, increasing indiscipline and their lack of training soon led to them also being demobilized, in March 1919.

171 Rosinski, p. 170.

172 General Groener retired from the army in late 1919, having by then established the body that would determine the organization and way forward for the new army. He had refused an offer by Ebert to head the reorganized army and instead took up the cabinet-level appointment of Minister of Transport. Later, in the 1930s, he served as defence minister and provisional minister of the interior. He finally resigned from the government on 12 May 1932, having come into conflict with the NSDAP deputies over his action to ban the SA (Sturm Abteilung), also having 'become finally unacceptable to the chief officers of the Reichswehr' (Kolb, p. 118). Groener died in 1939. Despite his having been several times a cabinet minister, an appointee approved originally by von Hindenburg (although he eventually lost the latter's confidence), a chief of the general staff and a *de facto* head of the army, the Reichswehr chose to ignore his death entirely. Only one of his former friends and colleagues, Hammerstein, 'dared to attend his funeral'. (Rosinski, p. 173).

173 Rosinski, p. 175.

174 *Ibid.*, p. 177.

175 *Ibid.*, p. 180.

176 The late 1920s or early 1930s publication *Das Reichsheer und Seine Tradition* was a particularly fine example of this, being a collection of 328 full colour cards produced for insertion in a bound album with text which related the history of the army and the historical correlation between every regiment of the Kaiser's army and its predecesors and the units of the current Reichsheer. It also provided the location of every unit featured.

177 There are certainly some parallels here with the aims and objectives of General von Scharnhorst in 1808, and the problems that he then faced. However, whereas the Prussian circumstances of the time meant that von Scharnhorst was literally building the army as part of the international renaissance of the wider Prussian state, it can be argued that von Seeckt was concerned with reviving a German military capability in relative isolation, rather than as a fundamental element of the German state – which was at that time in any case a republic much despised by many in the high command and the wider Reichswehr.

178 Rosinski, pp. 185–6.

179 *Ibid.*, p. 189.

180 Sixteen Nazis and three policemen were killed when some 3,000 of Hitler's supporters confronted 100 policemen. Subsequently, Hitler was arrested and tried at Munich; he received a five-year sentence of 'fortress arrest' at Landsberg am Lech, although he only served nine months in fact. During this period of imprisonment he wrote the first part of *Mein Kampf.*

181 In 1925 von Hindenburg became President

of Germany, and a period of relative stability ensued during the next few years. With much of his work accomplished, von Seeckt's power and influence declined in the new era of political rather than military activity. In late 1926 the Minister of War, Gessler, forced his resignation after he allowed the Crown Prince of Prussia's son – a member of the politically unacceptable Hohenzollern royal family – to take part in military manoeuvres as a temporary officer. General Hans von Seeckt, architect and principal creator of the Reichswehr, died in 1936, having spent much of the ten years of his retirement actively involved in politics and in writing his memoirs, as well as, for a short time, as a military adviser to Chiang Kai-shek.

182 In the spring of 1935 Hitler effectively terminated the Soviet-German military co-operation which had been agreed at Rapallo in 1922, and which had so benefited the Reichswehr during the following decade.

183 Uniform regulation references quoted in Davis, p. 10 and Hormann (vol. II), p. 23. Simpson also states (p. 123) that 'in February 1934 ... Blomberg ordered that the Nazi Party's emblem ... was to be worn on the uniforms of all members of the armed forces.'

184 Rosinski, pp. 251–2.

185 *Ibid.*, p. 251.

186 Reichsführer-SS (RFSS) directive dated 1 December 1939, published 8 March 1940. A subsequent SS-Führerhauptamt directive dated 22 April 1941 ordered that the terms 'SS-Verfügungstruppe (SS-VT)' and 'SS-Totenkopfverbände' were obsolete and no longer to be used.

187 See also Bender and Odegard, pp. 206–78, and Davies, *Panzer Regiments.*

188 Von Blomberg and Eva Gruhn left Germany and went into voluntary exile in Capri, taking no further part in German military affairs. However, his previous work to enable Hitler's military aspirations was remembered at the end of the war, and he died in a US military prison at Nuremberg on 4 March 1946. Von Fritsch was publicly rehabilitated on 11 August 1938 and remained in Germany, fulfilling various duties; in August 1939 he assumed command of Artillery Regiment No. 12 in East Prussia immediately prior to the Polish campaign. On 22 September 1939, he was killed by machine-gun fire in open ground on the outskirts of Warsaw.

189 Simpson, p. 136.

190 See Stone, *War Summits,* pp. 5–6.

191 Rosinski, p. 267.

192 A further 174 light and 156 medium tanks were subsequently shipped to France from England for British 1st Armoured Division's vain attempt to support the short-lived French campaign around Cherbourg during June, following the Dunkirk evacuation.

193 Statistical information drawn primarily from Williams, pp. 16–17. In some cases the figures provided for the numbers of divisions finally deployed for Fall Gelb in some other sources such as Macksey, Pimlott and Simpson vary slightly.

194 Pallud, p. 189, pp. 183–92. Although the actual circumstances of the 'Malmédy Massacre' remain the subject of debate to this day, it probably occurred in the immediate wake of a confused skirmish between retreating US troops and advancing Germans. The outcome of this was a situation in which some of the US soldiers had already accepted their capture and 'prisoner-of-war status' while others had attempted to resume the fight or escape in the general confusion. There is no evidence that this was a premeditated execution of prisoners-of-war. But in the aftermath of the initial period of firing, the deliberate dispatch of the wounded survivors of the 'massacre' unquestionably transformed the incident into a war crime.

195 See Stone, *War Summits,* pp. 70–1.

196 Consideration of the politically and ideologically-inspired operations carried out by the 'special duty' detachments of the Allgemeine-SS and the Waffen-SS against the Jews and other groups have no place in this work. But as early as 1940 the combat record of the SS-Leibstandarte Adolf Hitler and the SS-Totenkopf Division had already been marred by the actions of certain of their units on the battlefield. On 27 May, SS-Hauptsturmführer Fritz Knöchlein, the commander of 3. Kompanie of SS-Infanterie-Regiment 2 of the SS-Totenkopf Division ordered the summary execution of ninety-nine British prisoners-of-war of the British Norfolk Regiment at Le Paradis, near le Cornet Malo. An SS medical company tried to conceal the massacre by burying the bodies on 29 May, but an army general staff officer observed them before the task had been completed. Knöchlein was tried by a British war crimes court after the war and executed. The SS-Totenkopf had already murdered twenty-three civilians at Pont-du-Guy near Arras on 23 May, ninety-eight more around Aubigny, and forty-five at Vandélicourt. On 28 May, near Wormhout, soldiers of the 2nd Battalion of the SS-Leibstandarte Adolf Hitler murdered most of a group of about ninety prisoners-of-war, predominantly from the Royal Warwickshire Regiment, using small-arms fire and (against those prisoners held in a barn) hand-grenades. While the SS units attracted most of such accusations, some army units also committed atrocities, and on 27 May the army's 225th Infantry Division

summarily shot eighty-six civilians after the capture of Vinkt in Belgium. Atrocious as such incidents are, it must also be said that British, French and American troops were also guilty of shooting German prisoners on a number of occasions. However, it has ever been the case that the final victors of a war are rarely brought to account for such incidents, with retribution usually visited only upon the ranks of the defeated. See also Pallud, pp. 354, 428, 440–1.

197 Acting entirely independently and against the express wishes of his Führer, Hitler's deputy Hess flew to Scotland with a view to negotiating a British alliance against the Soviet Union through the Duke of Hamilton. He was captured, imprisoned and later tried at Nuremberg, subsequently serving a life sentence in Spandau prison, West Berlin, where he died in 1987.

198 Beevor, *Stalingrad*, pp. 14–17. Hassell was later implicated in the unsuccessful assassination attempt against Hitler on 20 July 1944 and was hanged at Plötzensee prison, Berlin, on 8 September 1944.

199 As ever, the precise figures for the forces involved vary between sources, although those quoted in the main text reflect a reasonable concensus. Pimlott (pp. 65–7) quotes 600,000 vehicles, 3,580 tanks, 7,184 guns and 1,830 aircraft and a total of 120 divisions; although Simpson (p. 150) suggests a total of 145 divisions 'in the east', though a number of these were almost certainly not involved in the initial campaign. Some sources also quote an overall manpower figure of 'three million', others quote 'four million'. Beevor, in *Stalingrad*, quotes 3,050,000 German troops within the total of four million. But the best available information indicates that three million German soldiers were committed on 22 June 1941, plus up to a million other Axis and complementary military, non-army and paramilitary forces.

200 Simpson, p. 156.

201 Yet again, the relative strengths at Kursk quoted by different sources vary. These variations are generally not great, although Pimlott does suggest that as many as 5,000 tanks may have been available to the Soviets at Kursk, rather than the 3,300 to 3,600 quoted in most other sources. Pimlott's higher figure might possibly have included self-propelled guns and tank destroyers as well as tanks. In any event, it is noteworthy that the Russian forces committed at Kursk were (if expressed as percentages of the total strength and capability of the whole of the Red Army in mid-1943) no fewer than 20 per cent of its men and guns, at least 33 per cent of its tanks, and 25 per cent of its combat aircraft.

202 The total number of tanks engaged in the core tank battle between 4th Panzer Army and 5th Guards Tank Army was probably no more than 850, with the balance of up to 1,400 or 1,500 deployed in the adjacent area. Some sources imply that as many as 1,000 (Pimlott) and 1,500 (Orgill) armoured vehicles were engaged in the central part of the battle.

203 Orgill, p. 121.

204 Pimlott, p. 127.

205 Orgill, pp. 121–3.

206 Guderian subsequently served with von Runstedt and Keitel on the three-man court of honour convened by Hitler to investigate the conduct of the army officers arrested in connection with the July plot. Those who were found guilty by this court were dismissed from the army and consigned to the so-called 'People's Court' presided over by the notorious Roland Freisler for trial as civilians, which was followed in virtually every case by their execution.

207 Following the defeat at Lake Balaton, Hitler ordered that the Waffen-SS officers who had fought in that action should be stripped of their decorations – an order that was greatly resented by them and which indicates that by this stage of the war Hitler had lost faith in even his most loyal fighting units.

208 The officer who had been responsible for defending and if necessary for destroying the Rhine bridge at Remagen which US troops seized intact on 7 March 1945 was one such victim of this form of summary justice.

209 Of all the Western Allied and Soviet military commanders, Zhukov unquestionably did more than any other operational commander to bring about the final German military defeat. Most appropriately, he was the principal Soviet commander involved in the final battle for Berlin and in the formal acceptance of the German surrender in May 1945.

210 All the foregoing text is an extract from David Stone, *Sixties Subaltern*, an as yet unpublished personal account of the life and times of a British army infantry officer in the late 1960s.

211 The elimination of German militarism and eradication of the very existence of Prussia (which was still seen as the source of German militarism) were key objectives of the 'Big Three' Conferences at Yalta 4–11 February 1945 and at Potsdam 17 July–2 August 1945. See also Stone, *War Summits*, chapters 17 and 19.

212 For simplicity, the term Bundeswehr is used throughout this chapter, although in the context of this work all use of 'Bundeswehr' should be taken as referring to the army (the Heer) unless indicated otherwise.

213 While the three corps or twelve divisions of the field army ('Feldheer') were under NATO

command, the territorial forces ('Territorialheer') that was later formed remained under national command and control. The three corps-sized territorial commands ('TerrKdos') were based on Mannheim (South), Mönchengladbach (North) and Kiel (Schleswig-Holstein).

214 Simpson, p. 184.

215 See Appendix 1.

216 Not until the end of the 1980s was a camouflage combat uniform (with a pattern which closely resembled that of the former Waffen-SS), together with a new non-metal helmet (whose 'Stahlhelm' design origins were instantly recognizable), introduced into the Bundeswehr.

217 Bundesminister für Verteidigung 2830/55 n.f.d, Bonn, den 6. Oktober 1955.

218 Details of Bundesgrenschutz volunteers stated by Simpson, p. 184.

219 See *40 Jahre Bundeswehr in Andernach:Von den Anfängen 1955 bis zum Einzug der PSK 1962* (publ. by Bundeswehr (Heer) Fernmeldebataillon 950, 56626 Andernach, 1995). Although some sources show the training facility operating from 1 January, the first recruits in fact arrived the following day (a not unreasonable arrangement, given that 1 January is usually a public holiday in Germany).

220 Statistics for 1984 from Simpson, p. 185.

221 In practice, the 6th Panzergrenadierdivision was under the operational command of LANDJUT (a corps-size German/Danish formation) controlled by HQ BALTAP (Baltic approaches) in Denmark.

222 Statistics for 1986 from official Bundeswehr sources.

223 Felix Dzierzynski was Polish by birth, and was the first head of the Soviet secret police – the Cheka or OGPU – in the 1920s.

224 Wiener, pp. 24–5.

225 In 1978, there was a total of 375,000 Soviet ground troops in ten armoured divisions, ten motor rifle divisions and one artillery division stationed in the GDR. The Group of Soviet Forces, Germany (GSFG) was organized into 1st Tank Army, 2nd, 8th and 20th Guards Army, and 3rd Shock Army. It was generally understood that in time of war the six NVA divisions would have been subordinated as necessary to one or more of these Soviet armies, assuming their use beyond the GDR. The war headquarters of GSFG was based in the complex of former Wehrmacht command bunkers at Zossen-Wünsdorf near Berlin.

226 Interview recorded in Rainer Hildebrandt, *Vom '13 August' zur 'Modernen Grenze'*, Arbeitgemeinschaft 13. August e.v., 1 Berlin 33, 1969, and quoted in Stone, *Wars of the Cold War*, pp. 79–80.

227 No fewer than 2,200 border guards defected to the West during the first two years of the Berlin Wall's existence. See also Le Tissier, pp. 376–401.

228 See Miller, pp. 358–62. In fact, Miller suggests that three NVA divisions were assigned to capture West Berlin, not two. But material made available to the British military authorities in Berlin in 1994 indicate that two NVA divisions would have undertaken this task, although additional East German reserve and paramilitary forces (probably equivalent to a third division in overall strength) would have supported the two NVA assault divisions.

229 In addition to all the Anglo-US-French barracks and installations, the key-points to be seized included West Berlin's airfields, radio and television broadcasting stations, publishing houses, police stations, telephone exchanges, gas, water and electricity facilities, government and political offices (including the Reichstag), universities, banks and financial houses, communications sites and a nuclear research plant. The 'cultural sites' to be captured as a matter of priority included the national gallery, the state library, the Egyptian museum, the museum of antiquity, Schloss Bellevue, Schloss Charlottenburg and the foundation of Prussian cultural heritage. Many of the other details of Op 'CENTRE' were summarized in an article by Colonel Andrew Meek, which was published in *British Army Review* in 1994, together with an assessment of its viability.

230 Although this regiment wore NVA uniforms and is broadly considered to be a part of the NVA, it was in practice the overt military arm of the MfS or Stasi.

231 Le Tissier, p. 405.

232 But Poland retained the former German territory it had acquired to the east of the former GDR.

233 The reduction in the length of conscripted service headlined for political purposes was in practice achieved by no longer showing the leave period during conscripted service as 'active duty'. Thus the amount of time spent on duty remained more or less unchanged. Meanwhile, the new (November 2005) CDU-led government has already announced its intention to increase the number of conscripts in the future.

234 Defence information provided at dw-world.de dated 18 August 2005.

235 These closures are expected to save up to two billion Euros per year for ground rents, building maintenance and so on, some or all of which funding could undoubtedly be used to good effect elsewhere in the defence budget.

236 'Internal security' has certain connotations in Germany and other countries that extend beyond the interpretation generally understood in British military circles. A more precise interpretation of the term 'internal security' in the German defence concept would be 'national defence' or similar.

237 In fact, Bundeswehr personnel have participated in various disaster relief and aid missions beyond Germany ever since the 1960s, although these have generally been on a small scale, conducted under national control, and involved the deployment of specialist personnel such as medical and engineer troops.

238 However, 'war fighting' as it is generally understood in London and Washington remained (and is still) prohibited by the constitution; hence Berlin's continued insistence upon achieving a UN mandate as the prerequisite for any external intervention operations by the Bundeswehr.

239 Although several senior NATO appointments, including that of the deputy supreme allied commander in Europe, had been open to German officers for some time, it was in late 1999 that a German officer, General Klaus Reinhardt, was appointed to command the allied force in Kosovo. He was the first German officer since 1945 to achieve the command of troops in an active theatre of operations at that level. This appointment demonstrated and reinforced the fact that the Bundeswehr had clearly found a new post-Cold War role and identity, although some within its ranks, together with a number of German politicians and citizens, were not entirely comfortable with its new mission. Even half a century later the memories of 1933–45 had by no means faded from the German consciousness.

240 The author headed the UK military contribution to this part of the multi-national operation for six months in 1995–6, serving alongside US, French and German contingents. Of all these, and despite the considerably greater size and equipment capability of the US Psyops unit, the most effective national psyops unit at that time was almost certainly the OpInfo element provided by Germany.

241 Beyond Germany's borders, responsibility for direct action counter-terrorist operations lies with the German Special Forces Command (the KSK). This command facility was established recently, together with a new Special Operations Division as its military or 'Kommando' arm. Members of this force are known to have participated in military operations in the Balkans and are currently deployed in Afghanistan.

242 The recent establishment of the Bundeswehr's CIMIC Centre (for military/civil co-operation on operations) and the expansion of its OpInfo and Psychological Operations capabilities recognized both its recent successes and its future needs in these increasingly important and overlapping military-civil areas.

243 *The Times*, 23 January 2006.

German–English Glossary

German	English Translation or Explanation
ABC-Abwehr(bataillon)	atomic, biological and chemical defence (battalion)
Allgemeine-Kriegsschule	general (i.e. non-specialist) military school
Allgemeine-SS	general SS
Angriffsschlacht	offensive battle
Anschluss	union (of Germany and Austria in 1938)
Appel	routine (usually daily) inspection or muster parade
Aufklärung	reconnaissance
Aufmarsch	approach march immediately prior to tactical deployment
Auftragstaktik	mission-led operational concept focusing upon the wider aims and objectives rather than specifying in detail the means by which they should be achieved
Avantageur	officer candidate (19th century)
Bataillon	battalion
Bereitschaften	internal security force established in the Soviet zone of occupation in Germany in 1945
Blitzkrieg	'lightning war'
Bund	confederation of German states established in 1816
Bundesgrenzschutz	paramilitary border security police force established in West Germany post-1945
Bundesrepublik Deutschland (BRD)	Federal Republic of Germany (FRG)
Bundeswehr	armed forces established in West Germany in 1955
Chassepot	French rifle (19th century)
Chef der Heeresleitung	chief of the army high command
'Corporalschaft'	a junior non-commissioned officer (19th century)
'Correspondence Karte'	official-issue field postcard (19th century)
Czapska	a distinctive headdress worn by uhlans (lancers)
'Degenfähnrich'	an officer candidate (cadet) trained but not yet commissioned as such (19th century)
Deutsche Afrika Korps (DAK)	German Africa Corps (WW 2)
Deutsche Demokratische Republik (DDR)	German Democratic Republic (GDR)
Dreyse Zündnadelgewehr	Dreyse needle-gun (rifle) (19th century)
Einjährig-Freiwillige	one-year period of voluntary full-time military service completed in the course of obtaining a reserve officer commission
Eisenbahn	railway
Entfaltung	tactical action of moving from the line of march into an attack formation
Entwicklung	tactical action of moving from an attack formation into an assault formation

German	English Translation or Explanation
Ersatz	substitute or replacement
Ersatzheer	the Replacement Army (WW 2)
Fall (Gelb)	case or plan (Yellow)
Feldpost	field post (office)
Feldgrau	field-grey (uniform colour adopted in 1914)
Feldmutze	uniform cap worn in the field and in barracks
Feldwebel	sergeant-major (warrant officer)
Fernmelde (bataillon)	signals communication (battalion)
Flugabwehr (regiment)	air defence (regiment)
Francs-tireurs	French irregular or guerrilla forces (1870–1)
Freikorps	literally 'free corps' and variously used over time to describe local militia, irregular and other armed groups and paramilitary forces
Freistadt	free city or free town
Friseur	barber
Garde	guard (usually as part of a unit title)
Gebirgs(division)	mountain (division)
Gepard	cheetah (mobile air defence weapon system)
Götterdämmerung	twilight of the gods
Gott	God
Hakenkreuz	swastika or hooked cross
Heer	army
Heimat	homeland
IGB	Inner German Border (between the BRD and the DDR)
Instandsetzungs(bataillon)	repair and maintenance (battalion)
Jäger	literally 'hunter', but used to indicate light infantry
Jäger zu Pferde	mounted infantry
Jugend	youth
Junkers	the aristocratic and landed classes (17th and 18th centuries)
Kadetten Corps	corps of cadets
Kaiser	emperor
Kaisermanöver	large-scale annual manoeuvres overseen by the Kaiser
Kaiserschlacht	the 'Kaiser's Battle', the final German offensive in 1918
Kampfgruppe	battlegroup
Kasernierte Volkspolizei	paramilitary internal security force in the DDR from 1952
König (or Koenig)	king
Kommando	special task detachment
Kommando Spezialkräfte	Special Forces
Kompagnie	company
Kräfte	force, manoeuvre force
Kraftfahrabteilungen	motor transport unit
Krankenträger	stretcher bearer
Kriegsbrauch im Landkriege	literally, 'the rules for conducting land warfare'
Kriegsakademie	military staff training or 'war' college
Kriegsheer	field army
Kriegskommissariat	military service support organization

✠✠✠✠✠✠✠✠✠✠✠✠

German	English Translation or Explanation
Kriegsschule	military training or 'war' school
Kriegsspiel	literally 'war game', or military exercise for commanders with or without troops deployed
Kürassier (or Cuirassier)	heavy cavalryman
Landesmannschaften	The concept whereby the local regions of Germany were directly involved in the provision of their manpower for locally based and regionally-linked military units
Landespolizeigruppe	regional police group
Lehr	instruction or training
Leib	literally 'life' or 'lifeguard', but used in the military context to indicate 'bodyguard', e.g. 'Leibstandarte-SS Adolf Hitler'
Landsknecht	mercenary soldier (15th and 16th centuries)
Landsturm	secondary reserve, home guard or local defence force
Landwehr	reserve or militia force
Luchs	lynx (armoured reconnaissance vehicle)
Luftbewegliche (brigade)	air transport (brigade)
Luflandebrigade/division	airmobile or airborne brigade/division
Luftstreitkräfte	military air service (1916)
Luftwaffe	air force
Marder	pine marten (armoured personnel carrier)
Marine (or Kriegsmarine)	navy
'Mit Gott für Koenig und Vaterland'	'With God for King and Fatherland'
Mitrailleuse	French machine-gun (mid-19th century)
Musketen (battalion)	automatic rifle (battalion) (1917)
'Nach Paris!'	'Onward to Paris!' (1870)
Nationalesozialistische Deutsche Arbeiterpartei (NSDAP)	national socialist German workers party (Nazi party)
Nationalesozialistische Führungsoffiziere (NSFO)	the politically influential organization of 'national socialist leadership officers' within the army
Nationale Vereinigung	the right-wing 'national association' (1919)
Nationale Volksarmee (NVA)	the national people's army of the DDR
Offiziers-kaste	the officer class
Oberkommando der Heeres (OKH)	high command (HQ) of the army (WW 2)
Oberkommando der Wehrmacht (OKW)	high command (HQ) of the armed forces (WW 2)
Oberleutnant	first or senior lieutenant
'Ober-Ost'	strong spirit issued during influenza epidemic 1917–18
Oberstleutnant	lieutenant colonel
OpInfo	the Bundeswehr operational information organization dealing with information warfare and psychological operations
Panzer	tracked armoured vehicle, usually a tank
Panzerdivision/brigade	tank division/brigade

✠✠✠✠✠✠✠✠✠✠✠✠

German	English Translation or Explanation
Panzergrenadier-division/brigade	armoured infantry division/brigade
Panzerhaubitze (PzH)	self-propelled howitzer
Pickelhaube	traditional spike or ball-topped German military helmet (19th century to 1920s)
Pionier	pioneer or engineer
'Pour le Mérite'	the highest national military award 'for merit'
Panzerkampfwagen (Pz.Kpfw.)	tank
Reichsheer	national army (1920s and 1930s)
Reichswehr	national armed forces (1920s and 1930s)
Reichskokarde	national cockade insignia (black, white, red)
Reserveoffizierskorps	reserve officers corps
Rübezahl	mythological wood demon
Sanitätsmannschaften	medical service troops or orderlies
S-Bahn	Berlin's above-ground city rail system
Schinken	ham
Schützen	rifle troops
Schützenpanzer (SPZ)	light armoured fighting vehicle or infantry personnel carrier
Schutzstaffel (SS)	élite guard (of the NSDAP and Third Reich period)
Schütztruppen	riflemen, typically of indigenous German colonial forces
Stasi	secret state security police of the DDR
Stahlhelm	German steel helmet adopted in 1916, subsequently adopted as the name of the post-1918 veterans' association
Stosstruppen	shock troops
Sturmabteilung (SA)	storm troops, known as the 'brownshirts' (of the NSDAP and Third Reich period)
Sturmkompagnie	storm or assault company
Swastika	emblem or symbol adopted by the NSDAP in the 1920s, but already in use by various right-wing groups
Totenkopf	death's head
Traditionsträger	literally 'tradition carrier', maintaining the heritage and lineage of a former unit through the creation of a new unit
Troddel	side-arm knot (indicating unit subordination, arm of service etc)
Truppenamt	military office established to administer and exert command over the army (1919)
U-Bahn	Berlin's underground city rail system
Uhlan	lancer
Vaterland	fatherland
Vaterlandspartei	the right-wing 'patriotic party' (1919)
Vicefeldwebel	a junior warrant officer (19th century)
Volksgrenadier division	often second-rate and poorly equipped replacement divisions created on an ad hoc basis during the final years of WW 2

✠✠✠✠✠✠✠✠✠✠✠✠

German	English Translation or Explanation
Volkssturm	home guard or 'people's army' employed during the final year of WW 2
Vom Kriege	*On War* (by Clausewitz)
Wache	guard or sentry
'Wacht am Rhein'	'Watch on the Rhine'
Waffen-SS	the armed SS
Wallbüchse	large-calibre heavy sniping rifle (1870–1)
Wehrbeauftragter des Deutschen Bundestages	parliamentary ombudsman for the armed forces (Bundeswehr)
Wehrmacht	armed forces (WW 2)
Wiesel	weasel (light armoured vehicle)
Zapfenstreich	military musical tattoo or ceremonial parade
Zündnadelgewehr	needle-gun (19th century)

Select Bibliography
and Other Sources

Beevor, Antony. *Stalingrad.* Penguin Books, London, 1999
— *Berlin: the Downfall 1945.* Penguin Books, London, 2003
Bender, Roger James, and Taylor, Hugh Page. *Uniforms, Organization and History of the Waffen-SS.* R. James Bender Publ., Mountain View, Cal., USA, 1971
Bender, Roger James, and Odegard, Warren W. *Uniforms, Organization and History of the Panzertruppe.* R. James Bender Publ., San Jose, Cal., 1980
Bender, Roger James, and Petersen, George A. *Hermann Göring: from Regiment to Fallschirmpanzerkorps.* R. James Bender Publ., San Jose, 1975
Bleckwenn, Hans. *Altpreussische Uniformen 1753–1786.* Harenberg, Dortmund, 1981
Bodin, Lynn E. *The Boxer Rebellion.* Osprey Publ. Ltd., London, 1989
Carr, William. *A History of Germany 1815–1990.* Arnold (Hodder Headline Group), London, 1991
Cassell. *Cassell's History of the War between France and Germany* (vols. I & II). Cassell, Petter & Galpin, London, *c.*1880s
Chambers, Walker W., and Wilkie, John R. *A. Short History of the German Language.* Methuen, New York, USA, 1981
Cobban, Alfred. *A History of Modern France*: vol. 1, 1715–1799; vol. 2, 1799–1945. Penguin Books Ltd. London, 1963
Craig, Gordon A. *Germany 1866–1945.* Oxford University Press, Oxford, 1981
Davies, W. J. K. *Panzer Regiments: Equipment and Organization.* Almark Publ. Co. Ltd., New Malden, Surrey, 1978
Davis, Brian L. *German Army Uniforms and Insignia, 1933–1945.* Arms and Armour Press, London, 1971
Deutscher Schulverein Südmark. Deutscher Volkskalender 1939 – Deutschen Schulverein Südmark, Graz, Österreich, 1939 (including 'Die Heimat des Führers' (Linus Refer); 'Der Kurier' (Karl Springenschmid); 'Kunst und Character' (Dr. Wilhelm Huber), and other articles)
Deutsches Historisches Museum, Berlin. *Pictures and Objects from German History: A Concise Guide.* Deutsches Historisches Museum, Berlin, 1995
Duffy, Christopher (ed. Professor Cyril Falls). *Great Military Battles: Rossbach 1757.* Hamlyn, Feltham, 1969
Elford, George Robert. *Devil's Guard.* New English Library (Hodder and Stoughton), London, 1987
Falls, Cyril. *Great Military Battles: Tannenberg 1914.* Hamlyn, Feltham, 1969
Forbes, Archibald. *Memories and Studies of War and Peace.* Cassell and Co. Ltd., London, 1895
— *My Experiences of the War between France and Germany*, vols I & II. Hurst and Blackett, London, 1871
Fosten, Bryan. *Wellington's Infantry.* vol. 2. Osprey Publ. Ltd., London, 1992
Geraghty, Tony. *March or Die: France and the Foreign Legion.* Grafton Books (Collins Publ. Group), London, 1986
Guderian, General Heinz (trans. Constantine Fitzgibbon). *Panzer Leader.* Futura Publ. Ltd., London, 1979
Hanisch, Prof. Dr Ernst. *Obersalzberg: The 'Eagle's Nest' and Adolf Hitler.* Berchtesgadener Landesstiftung, Bad Reichenhall, 1998

✠ ✠ ✠ ✠ ✠ ✠ ✠ ✠ ✠ ✠ ✠

Hastings, Max. *Armageddon: The Battle for Germany 1944–45*. Pan Macmillan Ltd., London, 2004

Haus Neuerburg. *Das Reichsheer und Seine Tradition*. Haus Neuerburg, Germany, c.1936

Hinrichsen, Horst. *Radfahrschwadronen: Fahrräder in Einsatz bei der Wehrmacht 1939–1945*. Podzun-Pallas-Verlag, Wölfersheim-Berstadt/Freiburg, 1996

Hofschröer, Peter. *Prussian Line Infantry 1792–1815*. Osprey Publ. Ltd., Oxford, 2002

Hooper, George. *The Campaign of Sedan: The Downfall of the Second Empire, August–September 1870*. Wyman & Sons Ltd., London, 1906

Hormann, Jörg M. *Uniforms of the Infantry, 1919 to the Present*, vol. 2. Schiffer Publ, Penn., USA, 1989

— *Uniforms of the Panzer Troops, 1917 to the Present*, vol. 1. Schiffer, 1989

Huard, C-L. (ed. E. Cornély and L. Boulanger). *La Guerre Illustrée, 1870–1871*. E. Kapp, Paris, c.1875

Jünger, Ernst (trans. Basil Creighton). *Copse 125: A Chronicle from the Trench Warfare of 1918*. Chatto & Windus, London, 1930

— (trans. Michael Hofmann). *Storm of Steel*. Allen Lane, The Penguin Press, London, 2003

Kershaw, Ian. *The Nazi Dictatorship: Problems and Perspectives of Interpretation*. Arnold (Hodder Headline Group), London, 1993

Kolb, Eberhard (trans. P. S. Falla). *The Weimar Republic*. Routledge, London, 1995

Kube, Jan K. *Militaria: A Study of German Helmets and Uniforms, 1729–1918*. Schiffer Publ Ltd., West Chester, Penn., USA., 1990

Kurowski, Franz. *Infantry Aces: The German Combat Soldier in Combat in WW II*. Stackpole Books, Mechanicsburg, Penn., USA, 2005

Laffin, John. *Jackboot: The Story of the German Soldier*. Cassell & Co. Ltd., London, 1965; Sutton Publ. Ltd., Stroud, 2003

Le Tissier, Tony. *Berlin Then and Now*. After the Battle Publications, Plaistow Press Ltd., London, 1992

Lindner, Prof. Theodor. *Der Krieg gegen Frankreich und die Einiging Deutschlands*. Usher & Co., Berlin, 1895

Macksey, Major K. J. *Panzer Division: the Mailed Fist*. Macdonald and Co. Ltd., London, 1968

Maguire, Miller T. and Herbert, Captain William V. *Notes on the Campaign between Prussia and Austria in 1866*. Simpkin, Marshall & Co., London 1866; Helion & Co., Solihull, 2001

May, Robin. *The British Army in North America 1775–1783*. Osprey Publ., London, 1992

Meek, Colonel A. D. 'Operation Centre' in *British Army Review*, Pewsey, Wiltshire, c.1994

Mercer, Charles. *The Foreign Legion*. Four Square Books (New English Library), London, 1966

Miller, David. *The Cold War: A Military History*. Pimlico, London, 2001

Montgomery, Viscount. *A History of Warfare*. Collins, London, 1968

Niemeyer, Joachim. *Die Königlich Hannöversche Armee*. Bomann-Museum, Celle, 1989

Orgill, Douglas. *T-34: Russian Armour*. Macdonald and Co. Ltd., London, 1970

Pallud, Jean Paul. *Battle of the Bulge: Then and Now*. After The Battle Publications, Battle of Britain Prints International Ltd., London, 1984

— *Blitzkrieg in the West: Then and Now*. After The Battle Publications, London, 1991

Pimlott, Dr John. *Wehrmacht: The Illustrated History of the German Army in WW II*. Aurum Press, London, 2001

Pivka, Otto von. *Napoleon's German Allies: Bavaria*. Osprey Publ. Ltd., Oxford, 2002

Reynolds, Michael. *The Devil's Adjutant: Jochen Peiper, Panzer Leader*. Spellmount Ltd., Staplehurst, 1997

— *Sons of the Reich: II SS Panzer Corps, Normandy, Arnhem, Ardennes, Eastern Front.* Spellmount Ltd., 2002

Rieger (trans. Colin Hall). *The Electors of Brandenburg, Kings of Prussia, German Kaisers*. Berlin und Karwe/bei Neuruppin, 2003

Rosinski, Herbert. *The German Army*. Hogarth Press, London, 1939

Sajer, Guy. *The Forgotten Soldier*. Sphere Books Ltd., London, 1984

Scheibert, Horst. (ed. Bruce Culver). *Panzergrenadier Division Grossdeutschland*. Squadron/Signal Publications, Inc., Warren, Michigan, USA, 1977

Schlicht, Baron von (Count von Baudissin). *Life in a German Crack Regiment*. T. Fisher Unwin, London, 1914

Schmidt, Heinz Werner. *With Rommel in the Desert*. Panther Books Ltd., London, 1968

Seaton, Albert. *The Army of the German Empire 1870–1888*. Osprey Publ. Ltd., Reading, 1973

Seligmann, Dr Matthew, Davison, Dr John, and McDonald, John, *In the Shadow of the Swastika: Life in Germany under the Nazis, 1933–1945*. Spellmount Ltd., Staplehurst, 2003

Seuling, Major Dipl.-Päd. Joachim and others. *40 Jahre Bundeswehr in Andernach*. Fernmeldebataillon 950 (Druckereizug 951), Andernach, 1995

Sigel, Gustav A. and von Specht, Major-General. *Germany's Army and Navy*. The Werner Co., Chicago, USA, 1900; Bracken Books, London, 1989

Snyder, Prof. Louis L. *Encyclopedia of the Third Reich*. Wordsworth Edns. Ltd., Ware, Herts, 1998

Stone, David. '*First Reich*': *Inside the German Army during the War with France 1870–71*. Brassey's/Chrysalis Books plc, London, 2002

— *Wars of the Cold War: Campaigns and Conflicts 1945–1990*. Brassey's/Chrysalis, London, 2004

— *War Summits: The Meetings that Shaped World War II and the Postwar World*. Potomac Books, Inc., Dulles, Virginia, USA, 2005

Strachan, Hew. *The First World War*. Simon & Schuster UK Ltd., London, 2003

Uffindell, Andrew. *Great Generals of the Napoleonic Wars and Their Battles 1805–1815*. [Chapter VII, Blücher and Gneisenau]. Spellmount Ltd., Staplehurst, 2003

US War Department. *Handbook on German Military Forces*, TM-E 30-451 dated 15 March 1945. Washington, 1945

Vogelsang, Reinhard. *Im Zeichen des Hakenkreuzes: Bielefeld 1933–1945*. Stadtarchiv und Landesgeschichtliche Bibliothek, Bielefeld, 1986

Wawro, Geoffrey. *The Franco-Prussian War: The German Conquest of France in 1870–1871*. Cambridge University Press, Cambridge, 2003

Wiener, Friedrich. *The Armies of the Warsaw Pact Nations*. Carl Ueberreuter Publ., Vienna, 1978

Williams, John. *France: Summer 1940*. Macdonald and Co. Ltd., London, 1969

Windrow, Martin. *French Foreign Legion*. Osprey Publ. Ltd., Reading, 1971

Wooley, Charles. *Uniforms & Equipment of the Imperial German Army 1900–1918*, vol. 1. Schiffer Publ. Ltd., Atglen, Penn., USA, 1999

— *Uniforms & Equipment of the Imperial German Army 1900–1918*, vol. 2. Schiffer, 2000

Young, John Robert. *The French Foreign Legion*. Thames and Hudson Ltd., London, 1984

✠✠✠✠✠✠✠✠✠✠✠✠

The author also drew variously and to varying extents upon the assistance, exhibits and archives of the following German military institutions and museums:

Bomann Museum, Celle (Schlossplatz 7, D-29221 Celle)
Celler Garnison-Museum e.V., Celle (Hafenstrasse 4, D-29221 Celle)
Deutsches Historisches Museum, Berlin (Unter den Linden 2, D-10117 Berlin)
Kreismuseum Wewelsburg, (Burgwall 19, D-33142 Büren-Wewelsburg)
Panzermuseum Munster, (Hans-Krüger-Strasse 33, D-29633 Munster)
Preussen Museum Nordrhein-Westfalen, Minden (Simeonsplatz 12, D-32427 Minden)
Preussen Museum Nordrhein-Westfalen, Wesel (An der Zitadelle, D-46483 Wesel)
Schloss Celle (D-29221 Celle)

The Universal Soldier
from Landsknecht to Legionnaire

Mercenary soldiers – those providing their services for material reward or some other personal motive – have existed in some shape or form ever since warfare began. These men, whether termed 'free lances', mercenaries, soldiers of fortune, or indeed any of a number of somewhat less complimentary descriptions, have variously fought as individuals, as *ad hoc* bands, as well-trained units, and as national groups serving within or on behalf of other national forces. Indeed, the story of the mercenary parallels is insep-arable from the story of armed conflict through the ages. However, while very many nations have been the source of mercenaries at different times in history, prominent among these in the late thir-teenth century were the French, the Cata-lans, the Italians and the Germans, and then from about 1315 Switzerland became the state which more than any other turned the profession of mercenary into a lucrative international business.

Clearly, the German soldier serving within the national army was not and is not in any sense a mercenary. However, numbers of those who served in that army also experienced what was or might be termed 'mercenary employment' either after or in some cases prior to their service in the German army or its predecessors of the Prussian, Saxon, Bavarian and other state armies. For that reason, a brief review of four readily identifiable 'merce-nary' or 'non-national' organizations or types of military service that involved German fighting men between the thir-teenth century and the present day merits inclusion in any wider account and anal-ysis of the army that either benefited from or (much more frequently) provided an abundance of practical military experi-ence for those Germans who subse-quently followed the mercenary path.

Also, given the fairly ready acceptance of the concept of 'foreign legions' within the Waffen-SS during the Second World War, the German attitude to the merce-nary concept is perhaps both pragmatic and much less condemnatory than that of some other nations. It follows that the service of Germans as mercenaries, however broadly that term might be inter-preted, does bear upon the wider subject of German militarism and therefore of the army through which that militarism was usually expressed or demonstrated.

While many other examples from history might also deserve to be catego-rized as 'mercenary' service or German military involvement in the direct support of foreign armies (such as the support of Bavaria, Saxony, Westphalia and Kleve-Berg for Napoleon's *Grande Armée* in 1812), there are four significant examples of German fighting men being employed to fight for foreign or non-German causes. First, there were the Lands-knechts of medieval times. Then, there were the troops from Hesse-Cassel, Brunswick, and some other German states who were employed by the British army during the War of American Inde-pendence in the late eighteenth century. This was at a time when the British army had already accepted as a matter of policy that it was considerably less costly to hire numbers of German troops for a specific conflict rather than to maintain a large standing army. Next, there was the King's German Legion (the 'KGL') which provided such excellent service fighting within the British army during the Napoleonic Wars. Finally, and sometimes controversially, there has been the signifi-cant contribution made by many indi-vidual Germans to the illustrious fighting record of the French Foreign Legion from 1831 to the present day.

✠✠✠✠✠✠✠✠✠✠✠✠

The Landsknechts

The hiring of mercenaries on a contract basis by the Condottiere system emerged during the Hundred Years War, which began in 1337, when soldiers whose reputation and ability were well known had attracted other 'free lances' to join them in formed bands of men-at-arms who would hire themselves out to the various warring monarchs of the time. A network of agents developed, which served to identify and negotiate the required fees and terms of employment of these bands. Foremost among the states employing mercenaries through *Condottiere* during that century were the Italian city states, and in fourteenth-century Italy the armies of these city states were almost exclusively manned by mercenaries. There, a renegade Knight Templar, Roger de Flor, commanded a 'Great Company' of some 18,000 German, French, Catalan and Italian mercenaries who had suddenly found themselves unemployed when, in 1302, Frederick of Aragon made peace with Charles II of Naples. Yet more soldiers became unexpectedly unemployed in 1360, when the war between France and England was ended by the Treaty of Bretigny. The age of the European mercenary had well and truly arrived, and indeed throughout history the end of a major conflict has always produced a surge of would-be mercenaries from the ranks of those soldiers no longer required by their national employers.

The Swiss set the professional standard of the medieval mercenary which some other countries then sought to emulate. In 1486 the Emperor Maximilian raised a force of German pikemen and halberdiers who were titled 'Landsknechts', being modelled upon the Swiss mercenaries, armed with their eighteen-foot ash staffs tipped with a ten inch steel spike. The Landsknechts were organized into companies of about 400 men, but sometimes more and often less. Landsknecht 'regiments' usually comprised anything between ten and eighteen of these companies, while the largest grouping of Landsknechts would normally be three such regiments.[1] Maximilian's aim had been to recruit an effective but non-standing army on the cheap, by entering into separate contracts with a number of mercenary commanders. Within the empire, the Landsknecht units were organized by Count Eitel, Frederick von Zollern and George von Frundsberg. The intention was that these Landsknechts would also be imbued with the courage, ruthlessness and military code of their Swiss counterparts. Any member of the Swiss mercenary groups who showed cowardice in the face of the enemy was subject to summary execution by his comrades-in-arms. But in practice the only immediately obvious similarity between the two groups was the imperative of maximizing their financial gain. Generally, the professional performance of the Landsknechts was inferior to that of the Swiss, who in any case despised their German imitators. These feelings of animosity were enthusiastically reciprocated, so that whenever these groups met in battle on opposing sides neither ever gave quarter to the other. Finally, whereas a condition of the Landsknechts' terms of service had been that they would not fight against the emperor, many of them later responded to better offers of financial reward by doing just that!

Many Landsknechts were recruited from the Low Countries as well as from the German states. The prospective recruit would be lured by promises of adventure, conquest, gold, drink and plunder. He might be required to prove his physical fitness for Landsknecht service by jumping over a stand of three pikes or halberds before being enlisted into the company. He would also be expected to provide his own arms, armour and (if appropriate) his own horse. In addition to the more familiar pikemen who were the main arm of the Landsknecht organization, the companies also included about 100 'Doppelsöldener' (men who received double the pay of the ordinary pikemen). These men were usually most proficient fighters, armed and equipped specifically

431

for close combat with (for example) two-handed swords, helmets, suitable body armour and suchlike. They would invariably be in the van of an attack, with the task of breaking open the cohesion of the front ranks of an enemy formation so that the main body could then exploit this break. Each company also had a further twenty-five to fifty Schützen, who were armed with cross-bows and (later) the arquebus and other firearms of the period. They would provide supporting fire in addition to engaging the enemy before the pikemen of the main body closed with the opposing force.[2] Within the Landsknechts unit there might also be a group of élite troops who safeguarded the Blutfahne (or 'blood flag'), and who could be employed as necessary to restore a critical situation against the odds, or to provide a final decisive assault or sortie to ensure a victory.[3]

While the Landsknecht organization created in 1486 had more or less disappeared by the end of the following century, these redoubtable warriors had nevertheless provided the foundation for a German mercenary culture which then remained in place for almost two hundred years. Although many were thoroughly effective fighting men, who undoubtedly performed loyal and valuable service for their employers, the mercenary profession in Germany finally achieved unprecedented levels of violence, debauchery and brigandage during the horror and chaos of the Thirty Years War. Consequently, a desire to end the dependence of the state upon the use of mercenaries was one of the important factors that prompted Frederick William the Great Elector to develop a well-trained standing army for Brandenburg-Prussia during the second half of the seventeenth century, thereby ending a way of fighting European wars which had perpetuated for centuries.

The British Campaign in America
1776–1783

Soldiers from Hanover were already a familiar sight within the army of George III, having served in the Anglo-Hanoverian army in Europe during much of the Seven Years War. Then, when George III launched the campaign that was intended to subdue the rebelling colonists in Britain's North American territories in 1775, he concluded various treaty arrangements designed to provide some 32,000 German troops – predominantly those provided by Landgrave Frederick II of Hesse-Cassel – to supplement the British troops in America. The Hessians comprised four grenadier battalions, fifteen infantry regiments, two Jäger companies, and three companies of artillery. In fact, the several German contingents together comprised more than 30 per cent of the total British forces committed to deal with the rebellion, and most were actively engaged in the war from 1776. In addition to the large Hessian presence (17,000 men), there were German contingents from Brunswick (the second largest contingent with 6,000), Ansbach-Bayreuth (2,500), Waldeck (1,200), Anhalt-Zerbst (1,100) and Hesse-Hanau. Meanwhile, 2,400 Hanoverian troops relieved British troops in Gibraltar and Minorca.

The course of the war is beyond the scope of this short account, but the nature of the German soldier hired out for service with the British army from 1776 to 1783 is an interesting example of the mercenary in the eighteenth century. The conflict was by and large conducted as a relatively gentlemanly war, although the German troops had little interest in the welfare of the predominantly English colonial population or the British cause. As ever, their priority was personal material gain. New York, Long Island and the area about Trenton all experienced extensive plundering by German troops, who were not subject to the Draconian punishments regularly meted out to their British comrades-in-arms for such activities. Similarly, the Germans acquired a reputation, albeit often much exaggerated, for giving no quarter to those seeking to surrender. Nevertheless, the considerable worth of many of the German regiments on the battlefield was significant. But as the war progressed and moved towards the final British defeat, a number of these men (principally the Hessians) did desert or simply disappeared when the forces they served surrendered. Many of these men remained in America and subsequently settled into a new life there.

The fortunes of these German regiments in America varied, and a brief overview will provide a flavour of the nature and exigencies of their service. For example, the Grenadier Regiment Rall landed with the first contingent of Hessian troops at Staten Island, New York on 15 August 1776. The grenadiers distinguished themselves at Long Island, White Plains and the capture of Fort Washington, but then on 26 December at Trenton they and two other German regiments suffered defeat and captivity. The regiment lost 302 officers and men killed, wounded and captured (about half its strength), including its commander, Colonel Johann Gottlieb Rall, who was fatally wounded. The survivors of the battle were formed into a succession of composite battalion-size units, subsequently fighting in Philadelphia and at Brandywine Creek in 1777. In July 1778 a prisoner exchange produced some 500 German prisoners from the regiments Knyphausen, Lossberg and Rall which had been defeated at Trenton. This enabled what had subsequently become the composite Grenadier Regiment von Weollwarth to be brought up to strength in time to play a major part in the successful attack at Savannah on 29 December 1778. By then it had already been redesignated the Grenadier Regiment von Trumbach. The regiment was later involved in the attack on Charleston in May 1779, and the successful defence of Savannah against a combined Franco-American army in September. By the end of 1779 the regiment had been renamed yet again, when it became the Grenadier Regiment d'Angelelli, in order to reflect the name of its new commander. From May 1780 until January 1783 the regiment formed part of the Charleston garrison, being evacuated by ship via New York that month. It arrived back in Germany on 12 August 1783.

Although the troops provided by Hesse-Cassel were probably the best prepared and best equipped, two of the three Hessian artillery companies were raised specifically for the campaign and so had first of all to be trained both as artillerymen and to operate their guns in the same way as the British artillery. In contrast, the Brunswick contingent was very poorly prepared, and when it arrived at Portsmouth *en route* for America the British government had to spend some £5,000 to bring the soldiers' clothing up to the required standard. However, corruption and profiteering on the part of the military contractors meant that it was not until the regiment was in America that it finally began to receive winter clothing appropriate for campaign service. Similarly ill-prepared was the Brunswick Dragoon Regiment Prinz Ludwig Ernst, which had been appropriately equipped for mounted service and had expected to receive its horses on arrival in the American colonies, but none were provided. The regiment never did become mounted and instead served as infantry, soon exchanging its heavy riding boots for the more practical shoes and gaiters. Virtually the entire regiment was killed or captured at the battle of Bennington on 16 August 1777, where the German troops suffered a telling defeat. Indeed, it was also at Bennington that Lieutenant Colonel Breymann (who was widely known as a brutal and tyrannical commander) then commanding the reserve force comprised of the grenadier and light companies of several German regiments, was shot down by his own men after he had used his sabre to lethal effect against four of his grenadiers who were trying to flee the battlefield.

While most of the German troops were actively and often decisively engaged in the war, the small contingent from Anhalt-Zerbst (a little-known German principality about twenty miles to the south-east of Magdeburg) finally arrived in 1778, but never saw action. Perhaps this was fortuitous, as the population of Anhalt-Zerbst numbered no more than 20,000 and its prince had committed his state to provide two battalions each of 550 men. Consequently, he had to extend his recruiting efforts well beyond Anhalt-Zerbst. Having finally managed to muster the two battalions, their journey to America had been frustrated, first of all by Frederick the Great, who denied them passage through Prussian territory while at the same time seeking to purloin as many of the contingent as possible for Prussian military service. Their overland journey to the coast through seven other states enabled numerous desertions and further reduced the force to no more than 60 per cent of its intended size. Although the 600 men (no more than one battalion in reality) who sailed to America in April 1778 were later reinforced, the contingent had an uneventful war, serving in garrisons in New York and Canada until the end of the conflict.

Of all the German mercenary units recruited to serve the British Crown in America, probably those which were most in tune with the German way of life and military culture of old were the green-uniformed Jägers of the Hesse-Cassel Feld Jäger Corps. This organization had an establishment of 1,000 men, although it probably never exceeded 500 in practice. The Jäger corps was recruited from the gamekeepers, foresters and huntsmen of Hesse-Cassel, and many of the members of its five foot companies and one mounted squadron came armed with their own hunting rifles. These expert marksmen, who invariably operated in small groups or individually, were in many ways the forerunners of the British army's rifle brigade regiments of the Napoleonic Wars.[4]

Inevitably, numbers of Germans also saw service in North America as mercenaries fighting on the side of the rebels and they therefore found themselves opposing the Germans in British service from time to time. One of these men, General Friedrich Wilhelm von Steuben, had gained considerable experience in the Prussian army during the Seven Years War, and provided invaluable service to the rebel army as principal military adviser to George Washington.[5]

The King's German Legion

The origins of the King's German Legion were to be found in the Napoleonic Wars and the French occupation of Hanover in 1803. The Hanoverian army had been disbanded, but many of its officers and soldiers subsequently made their way to England, where a King's German Regiment was formed in July 1803 by Lieutenant Colonel von der Decken at Lymington in Hampshire. Recruits usually enlisted for ten years, but never less than seven. Potential recruits had to be at least five feet, three inches tall and under forty years of age. The oath of allegiance they swore was to King George, and they were subject to the British army's Articles of War.

This regiment was later expanded to form the King's German Legion. This was an all-arms organization which rendered particularly distinguished service against the French while serving under Wellington's command during the Peninsular War and the Waterloo campaign. Some 15,000 officers and soldiers served with the regiment and the Legion between 1803 and 1816, of whom about 75 per cent were Hanoverians, 17 per cent were from other German states, and the remainder were from various non-German states. A number of the latter soldiers – mainly Poles, Hungarians and Dutchmen – were admitted into the KGL from the prison hulks. The Legion's service included the campaigns in Germany from 1805 to 1806, the Baltic in 1807, the Mediterranean and Sicily from 1808 to 1811, the Peninsula from 1808 to 1814, Walcheren in 1809, Italy 1814, North Germany from 1813 to 1814, and Waterloo in 1815. With the defeat of Napoleon, the KGL was disbanded and its members returned to Germany to become part of the reconstituted Hanoverian army.[6]

French Foreign Legion

German involvement with the French Foreign Legion dates from its inception in 1831 as a volunteer force raised and designed to maintain French dominance over its North African territories, and between 1831 and 1983 more than 10,000 German nationals served in the Legion.[7] As a matter of deliberate policy, when the Legion was formed in 1831 each battalion was manned by a separate nationality, and of its first four battalions (three more were added in 1833) the 2nd and 3rd Battalions were designated as the German battalions. On 27 April 1832 the 1st (Swiss) Battalion and the two German battalions carried out their first major engagement when they successfully assaulted the well-defended township of Maison Carrée, a few miles to the east of Algiers. Thereafter, the contribution of the German legionnaire to the varying fortunes of the Legion in North Africa, the Crimea, Mexico, Indo-China, Europe and on many of France's other colonial and imperial battlefields was always significant and frequently heroic, although the actual number of Germans serving in the Legion has sometimes been overstated. Suffice it to say that their influence often exceeded their physical presence, particularly as very many Germans achieved non-commissioned officer rank.

So long as the Legion was not deployed in Europe, there was little risk of a clash of loyalties affecting German legionnaires who might be required to engage in combat against German troops. But just such a potential conflict of interests arose in 1870 when France embarked upon the Franco-Prussian War. In 1866 a survey of the Legion's nationalities had indicated that 58.3 per cent were of German origin. Thus alerted, the French government decreed that the troops of the *Armée d'Afrique* sent to fight against the German army in France in 1870 were not to include any units of the North African-based Foreign Legion.[8]

Despite this precautionary move, in the aftermath of the crushing French defeat in 1871 the loyalty of the many German non-commissioned officers then serving in the Legion was (quite unjustifiably) viewed with some suspicion. Consequently, in a bid to find scapegoats for France's military humiliation at the hands of Prussia, the government of the Third Republic directed in June 1871 that in the future only volunteers from Alsace and Lorraine would be accepted into the Legion. On 16 June 1874 the governor-general of Algeria, Marshal Chanzy, even went so far as to demand that the Legion should be suppressed on the grounds that the high number of Germans serving in the Legion threatened the security of the territory for which he was responsible. Chancy's demand was rejected, but after 1871 there had in any case been a positive effort to fill the Legion's key posts with Frenchmen, with the result that by the early 1880s French nationals were in the majority in the Legion. This situation continued until 1920.

Despite the hostility with which they had been viewed in the 1870s, German legionnaires continued to serve courageously and loyally alongside their French and other non-German comrades-in-arms at the forefront of the Legion's campaigns in North Africa, Indo-China and elsewhere during the next four decades – regularly winning the promotions and awards commensurate with their actions. In 1896–7 the records show that within a total Legion strength of about 11,000 men, there were 2,511 Germans.

Then, with the outbreak of war in 1914, the potential problem of Germans fighting Germans was raised yet again. As at 1 January 1913 Germans comprised 17.6 per cent of the Legion's manpower strength. As a result, when much of the *Armée d'Afrique* (this time including several Legion battalions) embarked to fight in Europe, two battalions remained in Morocco to hold that territory for France, being comprised almost entirely of German and Austrian legionnaires who had chosen (as was their right) not to fight against their own countrymen. In 1915 a reorganization of forces and the need to meet commitments elsewhere meant that the number of Legion battalions serving on the Western Front was reduced to three from the sixteen that had initially deployed to the French mainland.

Nevertheless, numbers of Germans continued to serve as volunteers with the

Legion on the Western Front, and of 32,000 foreigners who joined the French army between 21 August 1914 and 1 April 1915, no fewer than 1,072 were Germans. On the Western Front during the war, the number of German corporals, sergeants and warrant officers was almost 280 (8.4 per cent), whilst 102 (3.1 per cent) were from Germany's ally Austria-Hungary. In 1914 as many as 70 per cent of the NCOs of the 2nd Mounted Company of the 1st Foreign Regiment were German, as was the unit's RSM. Between 1914 and 1918 the Legion's strength increased to 42,883, with a total of 3,087 Germans serving in its ranks during this period.

Following the armistice in 1918, and even more significantly the announcement of the punitive terms of the Treaty of Versailles affecting post-war Germany, there was a steady flow of German volunteers into the Legion. The numbers of Germans recruited by the Legion during the decade immediately prior to the Second World War were:

Year	Germans	Total Legion (all nationalities)
1929	1,304	3,182
1934	375	1,013
1935	597	3,111
1939	1,171	8,146

The inter-war years saw the Legion actively involved in its traditional role of suppressing dissent and maintaining French sovereignty in France's North African territories, as well as participating in some other overseas campaigns.

Although the suspicions raised about German legionnaires in the post-1871 and pre-1914 period were undoubtedly misplaced, the growing likelihood of war in the late 1930s resurrected the issue. This time French concerns may have been better founded, as there were various reports that in anticipation of the conflict the Nazi authorities had 'made efforts to infiltrate agents into the Legion with a view to organizing mutinies among the large number of German NCOs in the event of hostilities.'[9] In response to this perceived threat the French authorities interned hundreds of German personnel on the outbreak of war. In parallel with this, the government stated its intention not to deploy the Legion to mainland Europe, while at the same time some 6,000 'duration only' volunteers were enrolled into the Legion in a bid to broaden its nationality base.

However, as the war developed, and with France divided in 1940, part of the Legion found itself fighting for the Allies with General de Gaulle's Free French forces while other units fought as members of the Vichy French forces. After the armistice of 1940 the Vichy authorities actively co-operated with the Nazis to locate and arrest those German nationals who had been identified by Berlin as opponents of the Nazi regime, and one place in which such fugitives were sure to be found was in the ranks of the Legion.

A German armistice sub-commission repeatedly sought information about these men, including those who had completed their Legion service, those who had been demobilized since the armistice, and those still serving. The Nazis demanded nominal rolls, personal details, enlistment dates, re-engagement dates, length of service, current location (if still serving, or if discharged but living in France) and so on. The result of this work became evident towards the end of 1940 when two separate groups of former legionnaires, one of forty and one of fifty men, were apprehended and handed over to the German sub-commission for repatriation. A special German Control Commission was established from 31 October 1940 to process these groups and those other German legionnaires subsequently disclosed by the Vichy authorities. However, the Legion invariably looks after its own. Accordingly, whenever an inspection visit by the German commission to the Legion's desert garrisons of French North Africa was imminent, these were often circumvented 'by sending such legionnaires as were likely to attract German attention out on long training marches ... 'Wanted' legionnaires were quietly shipped off to the 5e REI in Indo-China. The 4e REI, redesignated 4e Demi-Brigade, was filled out with men anxious to avoid German scrutiny and shipped out to Senegal.'[10]

Although some of those apprehended were no doubt categorized as 'wanted' by the Nazis and would have been dealt with accordingly once back in Germany, some 2,000 repatriated legionnaires were formed into Infantry Regiment 361, a unit of the Deutsches Afrika Korps' 90th Light Division. This regiment later fought against the British at Alamein and, according to some sources, it may also have taken part in the action at Bir Hakeim in 1942, which would have brought them into direct conflict with those Legion units which were by then fighting with the Allies. At the end of the North Africa campaign, many members of Infantry Regiment 361 were taken prisoner, when 'Nearly all wished to rejoin the Foreign Legion from which the Nazis had separated them. Although it was forbidden and they were marched off to prison camps, many re-applied to the Legion after the end of the war and were accepted.'[11]

After the Allies' victory in North Africa both the Vichy and the Free French units of the Legion came together under Allied command. But by then only those Germans who had successfully avoided detection by the Vichy authorities during the previous two years, and who were still content to fight against Germany, probably remained in their ranks (together with those German legionnaires who had been serving in the remaining far-flung overseas garrisons, such as those in Indo-China and Senegal).

True to the pattern of the mercenary profession, the end of the Second World War produced a surge of new recruits for the Legion, and its strength increased to 26,000. In the immediate post-war years France had burgeoning problems in its overseas territories, notably Indo-China

and North Africa, and it was quite happy to recruit experienced fighting men from the ranks of the defeated and now defunct Wehrmacht and Waffen-SS. Not surprisingly the United States and Britain protested at the alacrity with which France sought to recruit for the Legion within the French-occupied zone of Germany. Predictably, France took little notice, although 'French intelligence officers made sure that known war criminals were barred from the Legion'.[12]

Certainly the Legion benefited enormously from a pool of potential recruits which included many hundreds of well-trained professional soldiers who had lost their homes, their families and (in East Germany) their country. Such men gravitated quite easily back to the profession of arms. There were also hundreds of thousands of homeless, destitute and displaced persons roaming about Europe, for whom the Legion offered a chance of regaining their personal pride and of a sense of belonging once again. While the various figures quoted for the number of German nationals enlisted into the Legion during the immediate post-war period vary considerably, 'Perhaps one-half of the enlisted men, perhaps a shade more, were Germans.'[13] Within the Legion as a whole, the overall German percentage presence varied only slightly in the post-war era, being an average of 12.9 per cent in 1945 to 1960 and 12 per cent between 1975 and 1983.

A book by George Robert Elford, *Devil's Guard*, first published in the USA in 1971, purports[14] to be a first-hand account of a former Waffen-SS officer, Hans Josef Wagemueller (a pseudonym), who had been a Partisan-jäger (guerrilla hunter) in Russia and then in Czechoslovakia. In the closing days of the conflict, writes Elford, Wagemueller was an Obersturmführer in command of a Waffen-SS unit that was part of a composite motorized unit of army, Luftwaffe, Sicherheitsdienst ('security service', or 'SD'), and Waffen-SS men, operating in the mountains to the east of Liberec in Czechoslovakia. About to be overwhelmed by Soviet armoured and infantry units (notwithstanding that the end of the war was imminent) and fully aware of his fate if he were to be captured, Wagemueller and thirty-six of his Waffen-SS comrades disposed of their distinctive insignia and set off back to Germany on foot. Indeed, despite the fact that the war had just ended, the almost 300 non-SS German troops who had been fighting alongside them had already surrendered as a group and had promptly been massacred by the Soviet forces.

Eventually, after avoiding or dealing with several groups of Russian troops, and finally swimming the Elbe near Pirna – when nine of his men drowned while making the crossing – the group reached Bavaria. In a quarry near Cham they ate a last meal together then went their separate ways. Finally, having walked via Augsburg, swum the Danube, and reached Konstanz, Wagemueller crossed into Switzerland and found temporary safety with other former Waffen-SS men at a villa near Zürich. Despite local Swiss tolerance of the fugitives, increasing international pressure on the Swiss authorities meant that they had to move on. Allied-occupied Germany was no longer an option, and so quite soon Wagemueller found himself in southern France. There, he quickly appreciated that, because France had a rapidly escalating colonial war to fight in the Far East, 'they would offer an arrested SS officer a choice: join the Foreign Legion or be hanged!' Clearly, the ever-pragmatic French military authorities 'could not afford to ignore a rich well from which experienced veterans had been flowing ever since the day of the armistice' as 'they required little training and even less explanation about their coming jobs'.[15]

Consequently, he became a Foreign Legionnaire, serving briefly at the depot at Colomb-Béchar near Oran before spending five years fighting the Viet Minh in the jungles and mountains of Indo-China during the late 1940s and early 1950s. According to Elford's account, the so-called 'battalion of the damned' was comprised primarily of former members of the Waffen-SS and of other German élite military units. Its disbandment was eventually forced in 1952 in response to political pressure in the face of the ever-effective communist propaganda. By then it had existed for 'exactly 1,234 days, during which it destroyed 7,466 guerrillas by body count, 221 Viet Minh bases, supply dumps, and camps; it liberated 311 military and civilian prisoners from terrorist captivity and covered roughly 11,000 kilometres on foot'.[16] The battalion lost 515 men. Elford indicates that Wagemueller was sixty-four years old at the time when the author spent some eighteen days interviewing him.

After 1945, German legionnaires continued to serve France in Indo-China until 1954, when many Germans were to be found in the ranks of the several Legion units forming part of the ill-fated force which suffered a devastating defeat at the hands of the Viet Minh at Dien Bien Phu. Subsequently, many fought in France's particularly bitter and unsuccessful struggle to maintain its control of Algeria from 1954 to 1962, and so also suffered the ignominious political and military aftermath of that campaign.

More recently, wherever the Legion has served – Djibouti, Kolwezi, the Middle East, Chad, the Balkans, Iraq, and in numerous other little-known French garrisons and lesser-known conflicts – many other young Germans have chosen to fulfil their desire to be professional soldiers and to continue the German military tradition through their service as foreign legionnaires.

Whatever his motivation and however accurate the description of his service as a mercenary might or might not be, and however morally correct or questionable his cause and conduct, the German fighting man has always been prominent in the ranks of those who are by definition among the most professional of soldiers – the mercenaries and their many near equivalents and close comparators. Indeed, and quite apart from any normal

APPENDIX I

✠✠✠✠✠✠✠✠✠✠✠✠

service in his country's army, across the wide span of history from fifteenth-century Landsknecht to twenty-first century legionnaire, the German fighting man has demonstrated time and again that

he is imbued with the military traditions and a natural competence in military matters that so well qualify him to be regarded as one of history's 'universal soldiers'.

NOTES

1 See also the details of the Landsknecht organization in chapter 1.
2 Details and factual verification drawn from Colonel H. C. B. Rogers, OBE, *Mercenary Soldiers*, pp. 9–10 (Tradition No. 49, Belmont-Maitland Publishers, London, c.1960s) and the Oxford Companion to Military History, p. 490.
3 The significance of the Nazi 'Blutfahne', a relic of the 9 November 1923 Beer Hall Putsch in Munich, and its implied historical linkage with the Landsknecht Blutfahne of earlier times is striking.
4 Details and factual verification drawn from Walter T. Dornfest, *A German Regiment in America 1776–1783*, (Tradition No. 69, Belmont-Maitland Publishers, London, c.1960s) pp. 14–15 and May, pp. 34–9.
5 In 1778–9, von Steuben wrote *Regulations for the Order and Discipline of the Troops of the United States Army*. This important publication was based upon the Prussian Infantry Field Manual produced for the army of Frederick the Great.
6 Niemeyer, *Die Königlich Hannoversche Armee*, also Simpson, p. 49, and Fosten, pp. 24–5. Somewhat ironically, the Hanoverian army suffered a similar fate just fifty years later, on 27 June 1866. This was during the opening stages of the Austro-Prussian War at Langensalza, to the south of the Harz Mountains. The Hanoverian forces were moving south and east to link up with the Austrians when t hey were intercepted by Prussians. Hanover was generally credited with winning the battle that day, but its army had insufficient resources to sustain any further operations and so was forced to capitulate to the Prussians two days later. Langensalza resulted in the end of the Hanoverian army, which soon thereafter was integrated into the Prussian system and into the army of the North German Confederation. However, following Hanover's defeat, a number of Hanoverian officers chose virtual exile in England and to serve (as had many of their predecessors with the King's German Legion) in the British army rather than in a Prussian-dominated German army.
7 Young, pp. 205 and 208.

8 As a result of this, a 5th Foreign Regiment of volunteers was recruited in France specifically for service in the war, and formed at Tours on 22 August. It subsequently gave a good account of itself in the battles about Paris during the siege and against the Bavarians at Orléans and Coulmiers in October and November. On 6 March 1871, all these foreign volunteers were demobilized. However, a residue of French legionnaires from this unit formed as the *Régiment de Marche Étranger* and joined the French Army of Versailles just in time to take a leading role in the violent suppression of the Paris commune in May 1871.
9 Windrow, p. 28.
10 Windrow, pp. 29–30.
11 Mercer, p. 230.
12 Mercer, p. 234.
13 Mercer, p. 234.
14 George Robert Elford's *Devil's Guard* (New English Library, Hodder and Stoughton, London, 1987) is a unique and (if true) revealing account of the transition of a former Waffen-SS officer into a Foreign Legionnaire following the German defeat in 1945. Somewhat bizarrely, the book's US publishers state that 'The characters and situations in this book are entirely imaginary and bear no relation to any real person or actual happening', which belies the inferred authenticity and level of detail contained in the account. Although the extensive use of dialogue and the often very immediate descriptive material in the work indicate that the account has deliberately been written for a readership well beyond the historical market, it also contains several illuminating passages that, in some cases with a fair degree of success, seek to explore the mind of the Waffen-SS soldier and the ideology which motivated him. If anything, the Publisher's Note at the start of the book, which quite forcibly disassociates the publisher from any of the actions or points of view described in it, tends if anything to add rather than to detract from the authenticity of the account, whether in whole or in part!
15 Elford, p. 68.
16 Elford, pp. 348–9.

APPENDIX 2

The Army of Frederick the Great (in 1760)*

Infantry

Category	Battalions	Personnel
Line Infantry and Grenadiers	97 (in 48 regiments)	94,404
Garrison Infantry	40 (in 18 regiments)	48,600
Saxon Infantry	10 (in 5 regiments)	9,850
Chasseurs à pied	1	800
Freikorps	12	10,000
Total	160	163,654

Notes:
1. Line Infantry. Each line infantry regiment usually comprised three battalions, with a total of 1,970 men. Three exceptions to the rule were the Kahlden Regiment (three battalions; 2,436 men), the Gardes des Grenadier (one battalion; 879 men), and the Garde du Roi (three battalions; 2,439 men). Each battalion had six companies (including a grenadier company).
2. Fusilier Regiments. Fifteen of the 97 line infantry regiments were fusilier regiments.
3. Grenadier Battalions. Six battalions (titled Wangenheim, Lossow, Rathan, Rohr, Unruh and Benekendorf) of grenadiers were formed by concentrating the grenadier companies from the line regiments. When formed, these grenadier battalions increased the total number of battalions to 166.

Cavalry

Category	Regiments	Squadrons	Personnel
Cuirassiers	13	63	10,640
Dragoons	12	70	12,502
Hussars	10	95	14,820
Chasseurs à Cheval	1	4	600
Total	36	232	38,562

Notes:
1. Prussian doctrine for the employment of cavalry forbade the use of the carbine while mounted (other than by reconnaissance troops and flank guards), and emphasized the use of the sword alone to produce a shock effect resulting from a carefully co-ordinated and controlled mass charge.
2. To compensate for the lack of suppressive firepower available to the cavalry, horse artillery batteries were formed to accompany and support the horsemen and thus enable them to manoeuvre into a suitable position from which to launch their charge.

Artillery

Category	Companies	Battalions	Personnel
Line Artillery	12	2	1,970
Garrison Artillery	12	2	2,000
Total	24	4	3,970

---

* Information based upon the work *Etat général de toutes les troupes de sa Majesté le Roi de Prusse, sur pié en 1760*, by Jacques André Frederic, Augsburg 1760. The original French titles have been retained in these extracts.

✠✠✠✠✠✠✠✠✠✠✠✠✠✠

Note:

The artillery included numbers of howitzers or mortars which were able to fire shells on a high trajectory over walls into fortifications, defended towns and suchlike, and – much more significantly for an army conducting manoeuvre warfare – into the dead ground provided by the reverse slopes of hills and into the deep valleys, in both of which enemy reserve formations sought to conceal themselves or to move to reinforce their engaged units, or in which stocks of ammunition were held.

Supporting Services and Cadets

Category	Companies	Battalions	Personnel
Pioneers	12	2	1,970
Engineers			60
Cadets	3		300
Total			2,330

Prussian Order of Battle
June 1866

1st Army (93,000 men)
Commander	Prince Frederick Charles
Chief of Staff	Lieutenant General von Voigts-Rhetz

2nd Corps
Commander	Lieutenant General von Schmidt
3rd Division	Lieutenant General von Werder
4th Division	Lieutenant General von Hewarth

3rd Corps
Commander	None
5th Division	Lieutenant General von Tümpling
6th Division	Lieutenant General von Manstein

4th Corps
Commander	None
7th Division	Lieutenant General von Fransecky
8th Division	Lieutenant General von Horn

Cavalry Corps
Commander	Prince Albrecht
1st Cavalry Division	Major General von Alvensleben
2nd Cavalry Division	Major General Hann von Weyhern

2nd Army (115,000 men)
Commander	The Crown Prince of Prussia
Chief of Staff	Major General von Blumenthal

1st Corps (reallocated to 2nd Army from 1st Army on or about 11 June 1866)
Commander	General von Bonin
1st Division	Lieutenant General von Grossman
2nd Division	Lieutenant General von Clausewitz
Reserve Cavalry Brigade	Colonel von Bredow

5th Corps
Commander	General von Steinmetz
9th Division	Major General von Löwenfeld
10th Division	Major General von Kirchbach

6th Corps
Commander	General von Mutius
11th Division	Lieutenant General von Zastrow
12th Division	Lieutenant General von Prondzinsky

Guard Corps
Commander	Prince August of Württemberg
1st Guard Division	Lieutenant General Hiller von Gärtringen
2nd Guard Division	Lieutenant General Plonski
Reserve Cavalry Division	
Commander	Major General von Hartmann

APPENDIX 3

Army of the Elbe (46,000 men)

Commander	General Herwarth von Bittenfeld
14th Division	Lieutenant General von Münster
15th Division	Lieutenant General von Canstein
16th Division	Lieutenant General von Etzel

Reserve Corps (Berlin) (24,000 men)

Guard Landwehr Division	General von Rosenberg
Combined Landwehr Division	General von Bentheim
Landwehr Cavalry Division	Major General Count Dohna

Other Units

Division Manteuffel (Altona) (14,000 men)
Division Beyer (Wetzlar) (20,000 men)
13th Division (Minden) (14,000 men)
Detachments Stolberg and Knobelsdorf (Upper Silesia) (9,000)

Notes:

1. Information from Maguire & Herbert, *Notes on the Campaign between Prussia and Austria 1866* (London, 1897), pp. 3–6. Some other sources put the strength of the Prussian army that confronted the Austrians in mid-1866 as high as 470,000. However, this huge force level is certainly both tenuous and largely theoretical, as it could only have been achieved had the war continued well beyond its seven weeks' duration, when the Prussians could over time have drawn from the Landwehr a further 130,000 to 140,000 reserves, many of which men were untrained in June 1866.

2. The lack of permanent corps commanders for two of the 1st Army corps is noteworthy. It was indicative of the flexible style of command applied by the Prussians at division-level, where the division was regarded as being the basic tactical unit on operations, and so it could routinely be redeployed beyond its nominal corps subordination as and whenever the operational situation demanded.

APPENDIX 4

The Army of the North German
Confederation in 1870

1. Peace and War Establishments

Category	Personnel	Horses	Artillery
Peace Establishment	302,633 (including 299,704 combatants)	73,212	808
War Establishment	555,835 (12,777 officers; 543,058 men)	155,896	1,212
Depot & Garrison Troops	205,054 (6,376 officers; 198,678 men)	15,698	234
Reserves	186,220 (3,280 officers; 182,940 men)	22,545	234

Note:

Table 1 includes the troops of the 25th (Hessian) Division, but not those of the other South German states (Bavaria, Württemberg and Baden). The Landwehr reserve capability was organized into 216 battalion districts, and thereby underwrote the overall organization and capability of the army to sustain operations in the longer term by providing a significant reinforcement potential.

2. Operational and Unit Organization

Unit	Quantity	Composition	Sub-Unit Totals
Infantry Regiments	118	Each of 3 battalions	350 battalions
Rifle (Jäger) Battalions	18		
Cavalry Regiments	76	Each of 5 squadrons	380 squadrons
Field Artillery Regiments	13		163 batteries and 39 batteries of horse artillery
Hessian Field Artillery Division	1		
Siege Artillery Regiments	9		
Pioneer Battalions	13		88 companies of pioneers
Hessian Pioneer Company	1		
Military Train Battalions	13		
Hessian Military Train Division	1		

Notes:

1. The figures shown for infantry regiments include four Hessian infantry regiments, each of two battalions. An infantry battalion (comprising four companies) or a Jäger battalion was about 600 strong in peacetime, rising to over 1,000 in time of war. Thus, a regiment was 1,800 strong in peacetime and increased to 3,200 for war. By 1870, all the infantrymen were armed with the single-shot, breech-loading Dreyse needle-gun.

2. The categories 'Infantry' and 'Cavalry' include the Guard and Guard Cavalry Regiments.

3. A cavalry regiment was usually about 700 strong.

4. Artillery batteries were usually of six guns and manned by about 100 men in peacetime, rising to 170 in time of war. Horse artillery batteries supported the cavalry division. Corps artillery normally included 84 to 90 guns. Foot artillery units manned the siege artillery and were organized in companies each of about 150 men.

5. 'Pioneer' units were in fact engineer units.

6. Table 2 includes the troops of the 25th (Hessian) Division, but not those of the other South German states (Bavaria, Württemberg and Baden).

✠ ✠ ✠ ✠ ✠ ✠ ✠ ✠ ✠ ✠ ✠ ✠ ✠

3. Personnel Available to the German Field Army

Army	Infantry	Cavalry	Other Arms (including garrisons & depots)
North German Confederation	385,000	48,000	982,000
Bavaria	50,000	6,000	129,000
Württemberg	15,000	1,500	37,000
Baden	12,000	1,800	35,000
Total	462,000	57,300	1,183,000

Note:
The totals shown for the North German Confederation include the 25th (Hessian) Division.

4. Manoeuvre Forces Available to the German Field Army

Army Corps

The Guard Corps (inclusive of the Guard Cavalry Division)

1st Corps (East Prussia)	2nd Corps (Pomerania)
3rd Corps (Brandenburg)	4th Corps (Lower Saxony & Anhalt)
5th Corps (Posen & Liegnitz)	6th Corps (Silesia)
7th Corps (Westphalia)	8th Corps (Rhine Provinces)
9th Corps (Schleswig-Holstein & Hesse)	10th Corps (Hanover, Oldenburg & Brunswick)
11th Corps (Hesse-Nassau & Saxe-Weimar)	12th (Royal Saxon) Corps
1st Bavarian Corps	2nd Bavarian Corps

Separately Grouped or Independent Divisions

Baden Division (infantry)	Six cavalry divisions (1st to 6th)
Württemberg Division (infantry)	12th (Royal Saxon) Cavalry Division

Artillery
A total of 1,194 guns, of all types and from all contingents, were available to support the above formations.

Notes:
1. An army corps normally comprised two divisions (a total of 25,000 infantry) and a cavalry brigade. There were usually four infantry regiments in a division, with two to each of the division's two brigades. The Guard Corps and 12th (Royal Saxon) Corps each had an infantry strength of about 29,000 but neither of these corps had any cavalry organic to them. Some divisions routinely included a battalion of Jäger or Schützen (light infantry or 'rifles').
2. A cavalry division comprised about 3,000 men. In July 1870, several of the army corps were each supported by a 'cavalry division' and the German Army also maintained (in August 1870) a two-division cavalry reserve. Consequently, while some contemporary references show only one cavalry division in the North German Confederation Army (formed by the Guard Cavalry Division and the 12th (Royal Saxon) Cavalry Division, grouped together), other references show a further six separate cavalry divisions. In addition, there were also several cavalry units that supported specific formations and operated (on reconnaissance missions for example) outside the control of any formal higher level of cavalry organization.
3. Table 4 includes the troops of the 25th (Hessian) Division grouped with the 9th Army Corps, rather than as a separate South German division

The German Army
1880–1900

Unit or Formation	c.1880	c.1895	1900
Army corps districts	19	20	23
Infantry regiments	166	215	215
Infantry battalions	513	605	625
Jäger or Schützen battalions	21	19	19
Cavalry regiments	93	93	96
Cavalry squadrons	469	469	482
Field artillery regiments	37	43	45
Field artillery batteries	364	494	574
Foot artillery battalions	31	37	38
Pioneer battalions	19	23	26
Engineer battalions	Nil	7	11
Railway regiments	2	3	3
Railway battalions	5	7	7
Telegraph battalions	Nil	3	3
Balloon detachments	2	2	2
Military train battalions	18	21	23
Total officers	About 20,000	About 23,000	About 23,000
Total NCOs & enlisted soldiers	479,229	479,229	495,500 (estb)
Approximate war strength of the fully mobilized army	Up to 1,702,300	Up to 2,360,000	Up to 3,000,000

Notes:

1. The numbers shown at the table are derived in the main from contemporary sources showing the authorized peacetime strengths indicated. The figures for 1900 reflect precisely the manning figures approved by the German Imperial Diet on 16 March 1899. The authorized established strengths shown were implemented on 1 April 1899, apart from those for the field artillery, which were implemented on 1 October 1899.

2. For clarity, some of the numbers shown in the table have been simplified and summarized to provide a clearer indication of the changes to the size of parts of the army during the period. However, as the actual army organization evolved continuously during the three decades after the Franco-Prussian War, some of the figures shown for the two periods prior to 1900 might differ slightly from those actually in place for a specific year. Similarly, organizational anomalies such as the inclusion of engineer functions first of all within the pioneers, and then of the railway, telegraphic and balloon function within the engineers, together with the existence at various stages of depot squadrons of cavalry, of half-strength infantry battalions, as well as of a number of independent or incremental (usually non-Prussian) units, may affect slightly some of the figures shown for the two periods prior to 1900.

3. The approximate war strengths shown for the mobilized army include all trained reservists and indicate a best-case situation at a point between two and four weeks after mobilization begins. By 1913 the army strength stood at about 700,000. Then, in August 1914, it increased to 3,840,000 men in just six days, of whom 2,100,000 were in the field army.

Army Corps and District Locations in 1900

Corps	HQ Location	District
Guard Corps	Berlin	Prussia & Alsace-Lorraine
1st	Königsberg	East Prussia (designated as a 'frontier corps')
2nd	Stettin	Pomerania
3rd	Berlin	Brandenburg
4th	Magdeburg	Prussian Saxony
5th	Posen	Duchy of Posen

✠✠✠✠✠✠✠✠✠✠✠✠

Corps	HQ Location	District
6th	Breslau	Silesia
7th	Münster	Westphalia
8th	Koblenz	Rhineland
9th	Altona	Schleswig-Holstein
10th	Hanover	Hanover
11th	Kassel	Thuringia & Hesse-Nassau
12th (Royal Saxon No. 1)	Dresden	Eastern Saxony
13th (Royal Württemberg)	Stuttgart	Württemberg
14th	Karlsruhe	Baden (designated as a 'frontier corps')
15th	Strasburg	Alsace
16th	Metz	Western Lorraine
17th	Danzig	West Prussia
18th	Frankfurt-am-Main	Hesse (created 16 March 1899)
19th (Royal Saxon No. 2)	Leipzig	Western Saxony (created 16 March 1899)
1st Royal Bavarian	München	Southern Bavaria
2nd Royal Bavarian	Würzburg	Lower Franconia & Palatinate
3rd Royal Bavarian	Nuremberg	Northern Bavaria (created 16 March 1899)

Note:
By 1914 a further two army corps had been added, making a total of twenty-five. The two new corps were the 20th in South East Prussia, with its headquarters in Allenstein, and the 21st in Eastern Lorraine, with its headquarters in Saarbrücken.

APPENDIX 6
The German Army in 1914

Infantry

Prussian foot guards	5 regiments
Prussian guard grenadiers	5 regiments
Prussian guard fusiliers	1 regiment
Line grenadiers	12 regiments
Line infantry and fusiliers	182 regiments
Bavarian infantry	24 regiments
Jäger and Schützen	15 battalions
Prussian guard machine-gunners (not included within infantry regiments)	2 detachments
Line machine-gunners (not included within infantry regiments)	9 detachments
Fortress machine-gunners	15 detachments
Reserve infantry	113 regiments
Landwehr infantry	96 regiments
Ersatz infantry	86 battalions
Landwehr Ersatz infantry	21 battalions

Cavalry

Prussian heavy cavalry (Kürassiers)	10 regiments
Bavarian heavy cavalry	2 regiments
Saxon cavalry	3 regiments
Dragoons	26 regiments
Bavarian light cavalry	8 regiments
Hussars	21 regiments
Lancers (Uhlans)	23 regiments
Mounted rifle regiments (Jäger zu Pferde)	13 regiments

Artillery

Field artillery	642 batteries
Foot (heavy) artillery	400 batteries

Note:
As with most military organization tables, different sources vary on certain matters of detail. This table was compiled originally from the information at Fosten and Marrion p. 7, subsequently updated and modified by reference to Simpson, Seaton, Laffin and Rosinski, as well as by research at museums in Germany, then verified and further amended by cross-referencing to Sichel and von Specht (by far the most comprehensive English-language source, but which provides detailed information only as at 1 October 1899). On specific categories of unit, the post-1900 information provided in a number of issues of *Tradition* published during the late-1960s and the 1970s was also useful. Nevertheless, while providing a valid overview of the scale and composition of the German army on the outbreak of the war in 1914, the reader or researcher should be aware that some of the figures shown for the infantry in particular will vary slightly between different sources, depending on categorization and the 'as at' date.

APPENDIX 7
German Rearmanent (Army)
1933–1939

Date	Rearmament Activity	Remarks
30 January 1933	Nazi Party achieves power.	From the outset, it was widely understood that one of the Nazis' primary goals was to overcome or 'revise' the Versailles treaty. The army was also aware that the introduction of conscription was both a Nazi intention and also inevitable if Germany was to fulfil its newly declared destiny.
1 April 1933	Specialist support sub-units formed in addition to the Reichswehr existing organizations. These support weapons companies, communications units and suchlike had previously necessarily been found at the expense of combat troops within battalions and regiments.	For the first time since 1920, this moved the Reichswehr manpower level beyond the 100,000 that had been laid down by the Allied Powers at Versailles. The training of administrative and logistics staff and instructors was accelerated, together with increases in the numbers of these support personnel. After 1933, the existing transport battalions (Kraft-fahrtabteilungen), which had concealed the covert development of an armoured arm, provided the nucleus of the newly formed tank or panzer divisions.
From April 1933	Officer shortfall of 30,000 addressed by recalling recently retired Reichswehr officers, transferring paramilitary police officers into the army and commissioning several hundred non-commissioned officers.	At the time that the expansion was ordered, there were only 4,000 officers, of whom about 450 were medical and veterinary officers. Also, some 500 officers and a number of non-commissioned officers were subsequently reassigned to the new Luftwaffe. Meanwhile, only one war college existed, training intakes of no more than 180 officers each year.
1 April 1934	First large-scale enlistment of volunteers for one year of military service.	
1 October 1934	Policy introduced of concealing actual military strengths of the Reichswehr by titling existing and projected units with garrison names rather than regimental numbers.	
October 1934	Recall of officers who had been forced to retire in 1919.	Where appropriate these officers of the former imperial army were reinstated in their former rank. Those who were by 1934 no longer fit for active service were assigned to administrative posts, thereby releasing other officers for active duty.

Date	Rearmament Activity	Remarks
16 March 1935	Proclamation of conscription; together with a declared final target size for the army of about 600,000 men in twelve corps (or thirty-six divisions). Announcement of the formation of the Luftwaffe.	Remarkably, the international disquiet at this blatant statement of the German government's intent to reject the constraints imposed by Versailles was muted. The lack of any substantive action by the Allied Powers beyond a few *de rigueur* voices of protest meant that German rearmament could henceforth continue unconstrained and that Versailles could finally be ignored with impunity.
1 October 1935	All of the paramilitary German police units incorporated into the army.	This produced an army of about 480,000 men in ten corps (with twenty-four divisions and three panzer divisions). After the German reoccupation of the Rhineland in 1936, the Landespolizei battalions from that area were also incorporated into the army.
During 1935	Development of a Kriegsheer or 'war army' concept.	The Kriegsheer comprised the standing or peacetime Feldheer or 'field army' and a post-mobilization Ersatzheer or 'replacement army'.
24 August 1936	Period of obligatory military service increased from one year to two years.	This measure had the effect of almost doubling the overall size of the army within a few months of its introduction.
14 September 1936	Issue of new colours and standards to the Wehrmacht.	Linked to the establishment of traditions and ceremonies stemming from a National Socialist perspective rather than from the army's older military heritage. New uniforms, insignia and awards had also been introduced from 1935, many of which commemorated or recognized political events and individual achievements.
From 1936 to 1939	Elements of the panzer arm and the Luftwaffe were engaged as 'volunteers' in support of General Franco's forces during the Spanish Civil War.	During this period much of the new army equipment was used, tested and developed on operations: notably tanks, various other motor vehicles and motorcycles, aircraft, machine-guns and other small-arms, together with the basic tactics and doctrine for their employment.
1 October 1936	Last two of the original twelve corps formed (some fifteen months earlier than had originally been anticipated).	This represented the attainment of the target size for the army that had been declared on 16 March the previous year. The fully mobilized strength of the army was thirty-six divisions (including three panzer divisions, each comprising one panzer brigade of two regiments, plus one motorized infantry brigade), one mountain brigade and one cavalry brigade. There were also four reserve divisions and twenty-one Landwehr divisions. However, during the 1936 manoeuvres most battalions still had no more than two officers per company, with most platoons being led by non-commissioned officers.

Date	Rearmament Activity	Remarks
During 1936	Formation of an army parachute infantry company.	This move followed the successful formation of a parachute infantry battalion from the Landespolizeigruppe (later Regiment) 'General Göring' in January 1936. The battalion was part of the Luftwaffe from 1 October 1935 and overall command of the German parachute forces was transferred to the Luftwaffe in January 1938, when any army parachute units were also subsumed into it. The Luftwaffe had already gained control of the army's air defence artillery units in 1935.
March 1937	About 18,000 officers in post.	Still a significant shortfall set against the 30,000 required, and the need to fill staff officer posts in the new formations. This led to much cross-posting and short-touring, which was in turn disruptive and affected unit cohesion and team building.
19 October 1937	13th and 14th Corps formed.	Additional to the twelve corps originally declared in 1935.
During 1938	15th, 16th, 17th and 18th Corps formed.	Enabled by the incorporation of formed units (five divisions) from the Austrian army and of individual Austrians and Sudeten Germans for conscripted military service (after the Austrian Anschluss of March 1938 and the Munich settlement of 29 September 1938 concerning the future of the Sudetenland in Czechoslovakia).
		A continuing shortfall in officers was alleviated by declaring that all officers (including retired officers) were henceforth permanently liable for indefinite military service. This included former officers living outside Germany and over-age former officers; the latter being required to serve as instructors where appropriate. These measures increased the number of officers to about 25,000 by the end of the year.
By end 1938	Army strength reached about two million men, with 500,000 conscripts joining for two years of training annually.	This produced an army of some fifty-one divisions, which included five panzer divisions, two independent panzer brigades, four light armoured (cavalry) divisions and three mountain divisions.
	Five military academies were in place for officer training, with an output of 3,000 per year based upon a training course reduced from two years to between eleven and fourteen months.	In 1938, about 60 per cent of all boys leaving high school declared their wish to become officers. However, at a time at which the education system was stagnating in response to the ever-increasing National Socialist ideology and constraints imposed upon it, very many boys lacked the necessary academic or intellectual aptitude to enter the military academies.

Date	Rearmament Activity	Remarks
	Introduction of a four-and-a half-year enlistment for NCOs, together with increased opportunities for commissioning.	Although three NCO training schools had been established (with a two-year training course), the rapidly expanding army had suffered from the departure of many good NCOs after just two years' military service, during which the first year would usually be spent as assistant instructors and the second on specialist courses. With much more emphasis on technology, two years was too short and a mandatory four and a half years meant that the army derived a reasonable benefit from the trained NCO, as well as encouraging those who were suitable to apply for a commission. Meanwhile, the poorer quality NCOs had often stayed on for the ten years plus two years' retraining to which they were entitled, but which had not offered a full career for the more capable or ambitious NCO.
By June 1939	Fully mobilized army strength was, in theory, 103 divisions.	However, the viable strength of the field army remained at about fifty-one divisions, as the total of 103 included many divisions for which the necessary manpower remained largely untrained or part-trained as at mid-1939.
		There were still only seven panzer divisions and four fully motorized infantry divisions in the army, with the larger part of the army (some eighty-six divisions) still reliant upon horses and requisitioned ordinary motor vehicles for its mobility, for its transport tasks, and to tow its artillery. As most of the infantry had no integral transport its units were therefore still limited to moving on foot, as well as by railways where these were available. During the major manoeuvres of 1936 and 1937, observers noted that 'large units were able to accomplish marches up to forty-five miles in twenty-four hours'.

APPENDIX 8
The Bundeswehr Field Army in 1986

Formation	Subordinate Formations	Peacetime Location
1st Army Corps (Münster)		
Luftlandebrigade 27 (airmobile)		Lippstadt
1st Panzerdivision		Hanover
	Panzergrenadierbrigade 1	Hildesheim
	Panzerbrigade 2	Brunswick
	Panzerbrigade 3	Nienburg
3rd Panzerdivision		Buxtehude
	Panzergrenadierbrigade 7	Hamburg-Fischbeck
	Panzerbrigade 8	Lüneberg
	· Panzerbrigade 9	Münster/Oertze
7th Panzerdivision		Unna
	Panzergrenadierbrigade 19	Ahlen
	Panzerbrigade 20	Hemer
	Panzerbrigade 21	Augustdorf
11th Panzergrenadierdivision		Oldenburg
	Panzergrenadierbrigade 31	Oldenburg
	Panzergrenadierbrigade 32	Schwanewede
	Panzerbrigade 33	Celle
2nd Army Corps (Ulm)		
Luftlandebrigade 25 (airmobile)		Calw
4th Panzergrenadierdivision		Regensburg
	Panzergrenadierbrigade 10	Weiden
	Panzergrenadierbrigade 11	Bogen
	Panzerbrigade 12	Amberg
1st Gebirgsdivision (mountain)		Garmisch-Partenkirchen
	Panzergrenadier Brigade 22	Mittenwald
	Gebirgsjägerbrigade 23	Bad Reichenhall
	Panzerbrigade 24	Landshut
10th Panzerdivision		Sigmaringen
	Panzerbrigade 28	Dornstadt/Ulm
	Panzerbrigade 29	Sigmaringen
	Panzergrenadier Brigade 30	Ellwangen
1st Luftlandedivision (airborne)		Bruchsal
3rd Army Corps (Koblenz)		
Luftlandebrigade 26 (airmobile)		Saarlouis
2nd Panzergrenadierdivision		Kassel
	Panzergrenadierbrigade 4	Göttingen
	Panzergrenadierbrigade 5	Homburg/Efze
	Panzerbrigade 6	Hofgeismar/Kassel
5th Panzerdivision		Diez/Lahn
	Panzergrenadierbrigade 13	Wetzlar
	Panzerbrigade 14	Neustadt/Marburg
	Panzerbrigade 15	Koblenz

Formation	Subordinate Formations	Peacetime Location
12th Panzerdivision		Veitshöchheim/Würzburg
	Panzerbrigade 34	Lahnstein/Koblenz
	Panzergrenadierbrigade 35	Hammelburg
	Panzerbrigade 36	Bad Mergentheim
Land Command, Jutland		Rendsburg
6th Panzergrenadierdivision		Neumünster
	Panzergrenadierbrigade 16	Wentorf
	Panzergrenadierbrigade 17	Hamburg
	Panzerbrigade 18	Boostedt/ Neumünster

Note:

With the exception of any amplifying text shown in brackets, all of the command, formation and unit designations shown in the tables reflect those used by the Bundeswehr.

APPENDIX 9

Bundeswehr Operational Deployments
1990–2005

Note that specific dates are not shown, since several of the operations listed below are recurring or continuing commitments.

Operation or Deployment	Region	Category
Mine Clearing in the Gulf	Persian Gulf	Peace-keeping
Aid to the Kurds	Turkey, Iran & Iraq	Humanitarian
Transport support for UN weapons inspection teams	Iraq	UN observer mission
UNSCOM	Cambodia	UN observer mission
UNOSOM	Somalia	Peace-keeping
UNPROFOR	Croatia, Bosnia & Herzegovina	UN observer mission
IFOR	Bosnia & Herzegovina	Peace-keeping (NATO)
SFOR	Bosnia & Herzegovina	Peace-keeping (NATO)
EUFOR (Operation Althea)	Bosnia & Herzegovina	Peace-keeping
Kosovo air campaign	Former Republic of Yugoslavia (FRY)	Peace enforcement (NATO)
KFOR	Kosovo	Peace-keeping (NATO)
Task Force Fox (Operation Allied Harmony/Concordia)	Macedonia (FYROM)	Peace-keeping
Operation Active Endeavour	Mediterranean Sea and Kuwait	Peace-keeping
Operation Enduring Freedom	Kuwait & Persian Gulf	Peace-keeping
UNOMIG	Georgia	UN observer mission
STRATAIRMEDEVAC	Balkans & Afghanistan	Humanitarian
ISAF / PRT & PRG ISAF	Afghanistan	Peace-keeping
UNMEE	Ethiopia & Eritrea	UN observer mission
Reconstruction of Iraq	Iraq	Training mission based outside Iraq
UNMIS/AMIS	Sudan	Peace-keeping & UN observer mission
Disaster relief support	Mozambique	Humanitarian (post-flood disaster)
Operation Eagle Assist	USA	NATO air surveillance mission
INTERFET	East Timor	Humanitarian
Disaster relief support	South-East Asia	Humanitarian (post-Tsunami 2005)
Disaster relief support	Pakistan	Humanitarian (post-earthquake 2005)

Bundeswehr 'Structure 2010'

Strategic or Operational Categorization	Subordinate Formations and Units	Peacetime Location	Remarks
Army Operational Command		Koblenz	Overall command responsibility for all of the following forces
Operational Command of Operational Forces		Ulm	In practice, a corps-level command
	Fernmeldebataillon 200	Ulm	Communications support
Multinational Forces			
Multinational Corps North-East (MNC NE) (German contingent of)		Stettin, Poland	In practice, a corps-level command
	Fernmeldebataillon 610	Prenzlau	Communications support
EUROCORPS (German contingent of) German/French Brigade (German contingent of)		Strasbourg, France Müllheim	
	Infanteriebataillon 292	Donaueschingen	
	Panzerartillerie-bataillon 295	Immendingen	
	Panzerpionier-kompanie 550	Immendingen	Armoured engineer unit
	Instandsetzungs-bataillon	Müllheim	Repair and maintenance unit
1st German/Netherlands (GE/NL) Corps		Münster	
	GE/NL Signal Battalion	Eibergen, Netherlands	
	HQ Support Battalion	Münster	
National Forces			
1st Panzerdivision		Hanover	Intervention division
	Panzerbrigade 21	Augustdorf	
	Panzerlehrbrigade 9	Münster	
	Artillerieregiment 100	Mühlhausen	
	Pionierregiment 100	Minden	Engineer unit
	Flugabwehrlehr-regiment 6	Lütjenburg	Air defence unit
	Stabs/Fernmelde-regiment 1	Rotenburg/ Wümme	Command and communications unit
	Instandsetzungs-bataillon 3	Rotenburg/ Wümme	Repair and maintenance unit

Strategic or Operational Categorization	Subordinate Formations and Units	Peacetime Location	Remarks
	Aufklärungslehr-bataillon 3	Lüneburg	Reconnaissance unit
	ABC-Abwehr-bataillon 7	Höxter	Atomic, biological and chemical defence unit
10th Panzerdivision		Sigmaringen	Stabilization division
	Panzerbrigade 12	Amberg	
	Gebirgsbrigade 21	Bad Reichenhall	Mountain troops
13th Panzergrenadier-division		Leipzig	Stabilization division
	Infanteriebrigade 37	Frankenberg	
	Panzergrenadier-brigade 41	Torgelow	
Division Kräfte		Veitshöchheim	Air manoeuvre division
Heerestruppen-kommando		Bruchsal	
	ABC-Abwehr-regiment 750	Bruchsal	Atomic, biological and chemical defence unit
	Artillerielehr-regiment 345	Kusel	
	Flugabwehr-bataillon 12	Hardheim	Air defence unit
Luftbewegliche Brigade 1		Fritzlar	
	Mittleres Lufttransport regiment 15	Rheine	Army air transport unit (medium)
	Mittleres Lufttransport regiment 15	Laupheim	Army air transport unit (medium)
	Lufttransport regiment 30	Niederstetten	Army air transport unit
Division Spezielle Operationen		Stadtallendorf	
Kommando Spezialkräfte		Calw	Special forces
Luftlandebrigade 31		Oldenburg/ Seedorf	Airmobile unit
Luftlandebrigade 26		Saarlouis	Airmobile unit

Notes:
1. The above table indicates the projected peacetime locations of the Bundeswehr's army headquarters, formations and major units at or by 2008, pursuant to achieving the Structure 2010 end-state.
2. The information shown is correct as at January 2006 and is the best available from official Bundeswehr sources as at that time. However, it is possible (and almost inevitable) that some unit details or locations will be changed or modified during the subsequent implementation of the Structure 2010 plan.

Index

Numbers shown in *italic* refer to endnote numbers rather than to pages.

INDEX

✠ ✠ ✠ ✠ ✠ ✠ ✠ ✠ ✠ ✠ ✠ ✠

Liberation, 95, 100, 111; during Waterloo campaign, 100–1, 113
Bock, Field Marshal Fedor von, 350
Bolshevism, 283, 291, 344, 345; see also 'Russian Revolution (1917)'
Bonin, von, 124
Bourbaki, General, 216
Boxer campaign (1900–1): German involvement in, 229, 244–6; behaviour of German troops, 246
Boyen, General Hermann von, 106, 114–16
Brandenburg, army of (1640–88): reform and development of, 34–6; creation of officer corps, 34–5; organization of, 35, 50; uniforms, weapons and equipment of, 35–6, 44–5; at Fehrbellin (1675), 37–41; in war against France and Sweden, 36–41; in campaign against Turks in Hungary, 41–9; at siege of Ofen (1686), 44–9; living conditions on campaign, 42–4, 46–7, 49–50; medical arrangements for, 44, 50; artillery of, 44–5, 49; importance of religion to 43, 47; at end of rule of the Great Elector, 50–1
Brandenburg, General von, 164
Brauchitsch, General Walther von, 326, 335, 350–1
Bredow, General von, at Mars-la-Tour (1870), 161–2
Brest-Litovsk Conference (1917), 283
British Expeditionary Force (BEF): in 1914, 258; in 1939–40, 337, 339–41
'Brownshirts' – see 'Sturmabteilung (SA)'
Brunswick, Field Marshal Karl Wilhelm Ferdinand, Duke of, 88, 90, 93–4
Buddenbrock, General, 159–60
Bülow, General Karl von, 258
Bundesgrenzschutz, 371, 376, 402
Bundesrepublik Deutschland (BRD) – see 'Federal Republic of Germany (FRG)'
Bundeswehr (1955–90): origins and development of, 370–9; first unit at Andernach, 376; and NATO, 371–2, 376–9; command and control of, 372, 378; constitutional and political status, 372–4; organization of army, 374, 376–9, 453–4; weapons and equipment of

army, 370, 375–7; uniforms of army, 375, 377; attitudes of wider populace to, 373, 375, 377; and 'Defence Duty Law', 373; recruitment for, 374; employment of former Wehrmacht personnel and NSDAP members, 374; implications of integration of NVA from 1990, 379–80, 389–90
Bundeswehr (1990–2005): integration of former NVA personnel, 391; integration and disposal of former NVA weapons and equipment, 391–2; organization and role of, 392–6, 401–5; reduction of, 391–3, 394, 398; weapons and equipment of, 396–9; Structure 2010 plan, 393, 395, 398–9, 404, 436–7; NATO commitments beyond Germany, 394–7, 400, 405, 455; UN commitments beyond Germany, 394–5, 400, 405, 455; and Franco-German brigade, 395; and Eurocorps, EU and 'European army', 395–6, 405, 456; and 'war on terror', 399–400, 402–3; future of, 401–5
Bürde, Lieutenant, 130–1

Cannowski, Adjutant General, 38
Canrobert, Marshal, 161
Canton Regulations (1727), 57–8
Caprivi, Colonel, 158
Carlsbad Decrees (1819), 115, 55
Chanzy, General, 215, 435
Chassepot rifle, 167, 176, 183–4, 187–8, 197–8, 207, 216
Churchill, Prime Minister Winston Spencer, 345
Clausewitz, General Carl Philip Gottlieb von, 96, 99, 109; and On War, 65, 111–12, 325
Cold War (1945–90), 370–1, 375–6, 379, 389; Bundeswehr during, 369–90; NATO strategy in Central Europe during, 378–9; NVA during, 380–9; see also 'Soviet Union'
Command of Combined Arms Combat (1921), 310
conscription and compulsory military service, 55, 57, 83, 87, 106–7, 114–16, 122, 124, 317, 373, 383, 392, 394, 449–50, 233
Crémer, General, 215

Daun, Field Marshal, 77, 79
Davout, Marshal, 94

Derfflinger, Field Marshal Georg, 38
Dessau, Prince Maurice of, 79
Dietrich, SS-Oberst-Gruppenführer 'Sepp', 342
Dietz, Master Johann (and Brandenburg army), 42, 15; on campaign in Poland, 43–4; on campaign in Hungary, 44–9; at Pesth, 44; at Ofen, 44–9; witness to atrocities, 44, 48–9; illness of, 43–4, 46; return to Berlin, 49–50
Douay, General Abel, 155
Dreisen, General, 81
Dreyse needle-gun, 116, 128, 135, 160, 216, 226, 444, 56
Dumouriez, General Charles-François du Perier, 88

Ebert, Friedrich, 291–2, 295, 299, 301, 312
Elford, George Robert (author), 437–8
Enigma code, 354
Eugene, Prince of Württemberg, 79

Faidherbe, General, 216
Falkenhayn, General Erich von, 267–8, 276, 281
Favre, Jules, 193
Federal Republic of Germany (FRG), 370–2; Four-Power control of (1945), 371; in Cold War, 370–1; and Berlin, 371; and NATO, 372, 392, 394–405; attitudes to military, 373, 375, 377, 399–400; 'economic miracle' of, 378, future security threats to, 401–5
Feldgrau (uniform), 247, 305, 381
feldpost, 143, 200–1, 211–12
First World War (1914–18), 247–8; enthusiasm for, and Aufmarsch (1914), 248, 251–2, 279; battles and campaigns of: Belgium (1914), 257–8; Mons (1914), 258; France (1914), 257–9; The Marne (1914), 258; Gumbinnen (1914), 260; Tannenberg (1914), 262–6; Masurian Lakes (1914), 265; Western Front (1914–18), 267–92; German East Africa (1914–18), 268–9; Verdun (1916), 276–7; The Somme (1916), 276; Caporetto (1917), 284; Cambrai (1917), 284; Ypres (1917), 284; Ludendorff spring offensive (1918) (the 'Kaiserschlacht'), 284–91; Allied counter-offensives (1918), 290; end of, 292

459

✠✠✠✠✠✠✠✠✠✠✠✠

✠✠✠✠✠✠✠✠✠✠✠✠